Economic Reform in Latin America

Economic Reform in Latin America

— *edited by* —

Harry Costin
Hector Vanolli

The Dryden Press
Harcourt Brace College Publishers

Fort Worth Philadelphia San Diego New York Austin Orlando San Antonio
Toronto Montreal London Sydney Tokyo

Publisher: *George Provol*
Acquisitions Editor: *John Weimeister*
Product Manager: *Lisé Johnson*
Developmental Editor: *Steve Schoen*
Project Editor: *Andrea Wright*
Art Director: *Linda Wooton*
Production Manager: *Lois West*
Cover Image: *Marc Brown*

ISBN: 0-03-017987-4
Library of Congress Catalog Card Number: 97-73493

Address for orders:
The Dryden Press
6277 Sea Harbor Drive
Orlando, FL 32887-6777
1-800-782-4479

Address for editorial correspondence:
The Dryden Press
301 Commerce Street, Suite 3700
Fort Worth, TX 76102

Web site address:
http://www.hbcollege.com

Printed in the United States of America

7 8 9 0 1 2 3 4 5 6 066 9 8 7 6 5 4 3 2 1

The Dryden Press
Harcourt Brace College Publishers

Preface

By the mid-1980s, a quiet revolution began to shake the traditional foundations of Latin American economic thought. Slowly but steadily, the once undisputed popularity of state interventionism, inward-looking development, and protectionism began to erode while the values associated with free markets, liberalization, and privatization started to influence the policy dialogue. Intellectuals and institutions associated with the new vision were actively courted, and politicians who supported the implementation of economic programs based on those principles, including many of those who had previously promoted populist policies, began to gain power through free elections.

The new vision strongly questioned the traditional role of the state. To most analysts, the perceived ever-growing intervention of the state in the different areas of economic activity had become the main obstacle to efficiency and growth. The political discourse in most countries routinely began to confine the state to its most basic functions, and governments started launching ambitious programs to privatize a range of public enterprises.

By the early 1990s, the neoliberal vision had firmly taken hold throughout the hemisphere. Most countries in the region had opened their economies to international trade, deregulated financial markets, and implemented programs of economic stabilization and fiscal austerity. The growth model based on traditional premises had been not only dismantled but also blamed for the calamities of the 1980s. "So completely does the free market idea . . . dominate the current Latin American debate that opposing ideas are increasingly treated with the bemused condescension usually reserved for astrological charts and flat earth manifestos," bitterly complained an editorial in an influential alternative magazine.

However, the dominance of neoliberalism was not free of criticism. The social impact of the reforms had been called into question from the onset, even by some of the staunchest advocates of the model. To many, the problems of poverty and income distribution during the period of neoliberal predominance worsened. Additionally, social unrest, notably the Zapatista rebellion in Chiapas in southern Mexico, drastically reminded lawmakers that needed reforms should not only be economically sound in the long term but also politically sustainable in the short term. Public unrest as a reaction to economic reform policies in Venezuela and Argentina, and the Mexican crisis of 1994, fueled additional doubts about the sustainability of the reforms.

Today, many of the doubts and criticisms concerning the neoliberal model's impact on social indicators have gradually been taken into account by multilateral development institutions and policy makers. For example, the *World Bank's World Development Report 1997* strongly warns that those countries "which have concluded that the role of the state should be less prominent ought to consider how the dazzling growth of East Asia, and even the industrial revolution, were made possible by an 'effective state'—one which harnesses the energy of private business and individuals, and acts as their partner and catalyst, instead of restricting their partnership."

Critical Issues

Any analysis of economic development and reform in Latin America, particularly of the virtues and limitations of the neoliberal model, needs to address complex questions and issues, such as the following:

How different is the current reform wave, based on the neoliberal model, from prior similar strategies or efforts tested in Latin America? In other words, how new is the neoliberal model?

Contrary to common belief, Latin American countries did not always pursue import substitution industrialization, that is, policies that attempted to promote indigenous industries. Until the Great Depression of the 1930s, most Latin American economies were open and relied heavily on exports of commodities produced by large companies that were predominantly foreign owned. In other words, they were pursuing an export-led economic growth strategy, and they were benefiting from substantial inflow of foreign direct investment in export industries and infrastructure development (railroads, for example).

Can all Latin American countries pursue or benefit from the same economic development model? Do country-specific circumstances exist that would require major policy adaptations to achieve similar overall goals?

Most Latin American countries have embraced a similar set of neoliberal economic recipes, which include, among others, reduction of inflation to single digits, elimination of trade barriers, and privatization of state-owned companies. The countries of the region, however, are far from homogeneous. Although the World Bank classifies most Latin American countries as middle income, stark differences are evident across the continent. Can the needs of a country such as Bolivia, which experiences extreme rural poverty and a dismal lack of infrastructure, be compared to those of Brazil, a federation that encompasses a wide variety of states, many of which are as large as other Latin American countries and range from highly developed (such as the state of Sao Paulo) to extremely poor? If the current spectrum of reforms represents a minimum common denominator of sound policies, how can it be complemented by economic and social strategies that would address country-specific needs?

What role do equity concerns play in the current reform model? Should the main goal of the current neoliberal reform wave be economic growth or "development" more broadly defined, that is, embracing the goals of improved income distribution and better public health care and education for the disadvantaged?

All analysts agree that an increase in gross national product alone is not enough to bring about development. Equity concerns are considered to be at least as important as growth. However, when it comes to implementing strategies to bring about desired development, it has been argued that economic growth is the first step, and therefore policies need to remain focused on goals such as reduction of inflation and sustained economic growth if they are to be effective. According to this position, the implementation of neoliberal strategies generates new resources that can be redistributed to pursue increased equity goals using other national policy instruments.

Those who remain skeptical about the argument that growth is the first step to development have pointed out that economic growth does not necessarily translate into increased equity and that those in the lowest strata of society cannot wait for economic growth "down the road." Their needs are pressing and may lead to social unrest if they are not addressed in tandem with growth-promotion strategies.

The United Nations Development Project's *Human Development Index* shows that economic growth can be notably different from overall human development. For example, the 1996 UNDP *Human Development Report* (based on 1993 statistical information) ranked Argentina 30th in terms of human development, Uruguay 32nd, and Chile 33rd. However, if the economic development (per capita gross domestic product [GDP]) of these countries is taken into account, Chile ranks higher than Argentina and Uruguay ($8,900 against $8,350 and $6,550, respectively). Based on its economic development, one would expect Chile to rank higher in terms of human development. By contrast, though Uruguay's per capita GDP may be considered modest, its overall development ranks high. More striking even is the case of Costa Rica, which ranks 31st in human development with a per capita GDP of only $5,680.

Is the experience of Southeast Asian countries such as South Korea and Taiwan relevant to Latin America?

There is a widespread belief that the Southeast Asian "tigers" owe their impressive economic development over the past decades to export-led growth strategies. The Latin American proponents of outward-oriented growth strategies have also embraced this perspective. These advocates justify the comparison between the Asian and Latin American economies pointing out that the 1950 level of economic development for the Southeast Asian and Latin American countries was similar. In the post–World War II period, the "tigers" pursued export-led growth while Latin America chose import-substitution-industrialization. A few decades later the results of these two different models are self-evident. The "tigers" have boomed while Latin America strives to recover from the lost decade of the 1980s and to reintegrate with the world economy.

However, some analysts question the accuracy of identifying export-oriented growth as the main cause of Southeast Asia's economic development. They argue that other reasons, such as a strong industrial policy and heavy involvement of the state in the economy (which would be considered anathema to growth by the neoliberals), are causal factors at least as important as export-oriented growth. These critics of mainstream thinking also point to cultural and political causes (i.e., that East Asian countries benefited from a highly educated workforce and Confucianist work ethics, as well as a privileged access to the U.S. market). Therefore, according to this view, equating economic growth with export promotion may reflect a naive and misleading interpretation. Furthermore, if in fact the Asian experience were relevant to Latin America, what remains to be explored is whether the policies pursued by countries such as South Korea, Taiwan, or Singapore can be appropriately described as *neoliberal.*

About This Book

The objective of this book is to provide a general overview of the issues and problems posed by the implementation of the neoliberal model in the hemisphere. On that account, the consensus built around some of the basic premises of the new economic model, as well as concerns about the social effects of neoliberal policies, are widely reflected in the contributors' papers.

None of the contributors dispute the basic premises of the model. As Carlos Waisman states, "ideological contention turns into a debate between options within the model itself, the most powerful indication of the growing hegemony of the new economic regime." Even Paul Krugman, who provides one of the most critical views, acknowledges that the "Victorian virtue" advocated by the new model is probably "the only plausible course of action." According to the MIT economist, "it is, in fact, probably true that free markets and sound money—if not necessarily fixed exchange rates—are the best policy for developing countries to follow."

Enrique Iglesias clearly states the need to address social claims. According to the Inter-American Development Bank president, the economic reforms currently underway, which are aimed at economic efficiency, are not sufficient to ensure "a pattern of development that responds to our historic experience and our social and political life." Hence, besides supporting these reforms, "other measures related to the political situation, the social conditions and the institutional structure of the Latin American countries must also be implemented."

In light of this criticism, Iglesias sees "a trend toward agreement about certain specific points which, on the one hand, depart from the traditional view of Latin American development prevalent in the post-war era and, on the other, tend to correct the excesses of the neoliberal policies applied in the most severe phase of the adjustment period." What is at issue, states Iglesias, "is not the absolute truth of our cherished ideas about development but rather to what extent these ideas reflect the new characteristics and, therefore, the new challenges."

According to Dilmus James, this trend toward agreement is best synthesized by the neostructuralist approach. Neostructuralists, states James, "have learned a great deal from the past excesses associated with the state-led, inward-looking approach to development and from the successes of the neoliberal experience." On the one hand, they explicitly acknowledge the virtues of market mechanisms, stability, and restraint in matters affecting government expenditure, as well as the existence of government failures, among other things. On the other hand, they retain some important aspects from their structuralist background, including a "holistic methodology that weds economic analysis to political, social and cultural considerations, often within a historical context." Although neoliberal views "have partially triumphed" in this ongoing debate, neostructuralists are, in the author's estimation, quickly gaining popularity.

Organization of the Book

This book is divided in four parts. Part 1 provides a historical backdrop to help illuminate the nature and objectives of the current reform wave. Part 2 discusses the theoretical and conceptual tenets of neoliberalism as implemented in Latin America. Part 3 examines the implementation of extensive economic reform policies in some countries of the hemisphere. Finally, Part 4 focuses on economic integration and trade liberalization.

Part 1 includes papers by Victor Bulmer-Thomas and Dilmus James.

Bulmer-Thomas offers a general overview of Latin American economic development from the 1820s to the present. After independence, the author writes, the reports of contemporary writers and chroniclers predicted a bright future for the newly formed republics. "All that was needed, it was thought, were capital and skilled labor to unlock the natural resources in Latin America's vast unexploited interior and unrestricted access to the wealthy markets of western Europe." However, almost two centuries later, Latin America's bright promise of progress and abundance remains unfulfilled. "None of the twenty republics in Latin America can be classified as developed, and some remain extremely poor," Bulmer-Thomas highlights.

However, the author concludes, the lessons from Latin American economic history suggest that "nothing is predetermined about the region's current lowly status in terms of economic development in general and real income per head in particular." Although there is no magic formula to bring about development instantly, Latin America still has the potential to fulfill its old promise. "Not all the Latin American countries can expect to make the transition to developed-country status, but it would be surprising if a few did not succeed," the author predicts.

James reviews economic development theory as it influenced Latin America over the past five decades. After describing and analyzing the application of the structuralist and neoliberal policies in that period, James focuses on the work of the neostructuralists who, in his view, are "in the forefront of those attempting to reshape thinking on development theory and policy in Latin America." The way for the structuralists, states James, was facilitated by the ordeal posed by the neoliberal stabilization and adjustment process, together with a mixed record of achievements.

The debate over the virtues and limitations of the different economic models implemented by the countries of the hemisphere during the past decades, concludes James, must include "some issues on which no school of thought can claim an exemplary track record—they include sustainable growth with equity and poverty reduction, a foreign exchange regime compatible with economic stability, and establishing an economic environment conducive to technology capacity-building."

Part 2 includes papers by Enrique Iglesias, Albert Fishlow, Carlos Waisman, Isaac Cohen, John Williamson, and Paul Krugman.

Reviewing Latin American economic thinking over the past 50 years, Enrique Iglesias highlights the "considerable degree of consensus" that has been achieved in the region in recent years concerning the causes and the solutions to the economic problems experienced in the past. "No one today seriously thinks that the Latin American economies should resume looking only inward to support growth or that they should again become deeply pessimistic about foreign markets, negligently manage short-term macroeconomic policy, be complacent about overall imbalances, or advocate excessive state intervention with large public outlays," he asserts. What most economists would agree on today, Iglesias suggests, is that the raising of living standards should receive special priority. To achieve such goals, "the restoration of macroeconomic balances is essential but not sufficient, just as basing the development effort on a series of standard, preconceived notions would be inadequate."

The progress toward such a consensus, Iglesias points out, could not have been possible without the emergence of a new political consensus. The fall from power of various governments with a populist orientation, he asserts, facilitated the emergence of a "new civic philosophy," one that is "more realistic and pragmatic, less impatient and more mature, less inclined toward aggression and more willing to seek areas of agreement, more removed from extremes and more moderately oriented."

The new political consensus, however, must be sustained in the long term by the ability of the new model to address the region's pressing social conditions, Iglesias believes. Hence, the new consensus "depends largely on society's perception of the fairness of the adjustment burden and the promise that today's austerity holds for tomorrow." For that reason, the new political consensus must be constantly reinforced by an overall improvement of public services, and "an effective reflection of social communication and skillful government, which will be put to the test in such difficult and challenging circumstances."

The magnitude of the past crisis, Iglesias concludes, tends to make people forget the important lessons learned. As he sees it, these lessons constitute "Latin America's greatest asset in solving its problems or unresolved challenges." Among them, he points out, are the return of democracy to the countries of the region; the implementation of stabilization programs to deal with inflationary processes; the growing openness of Latin America to foreign trade; the reorganization of the state; the implementation of programs designed to solve the debt problem, which were oriented toward alleviating the burden of debtor countries; and "some intangible advances," such as changes of attitude toward development.

Fishlow discusses the role of the state in the economic development of Latin America. In particular, he suggests that the present vitality of the neoliberal views "come less from newfound ideological conviction in the virtues of the market than from ineffective macroeconomic policy in the 1980s." In his view, the principal problem confronted by the countries of the region is a fiscal shortfall, not "massive inefficiency resulting from misallocation of resources." In that sense, he sees the state playing a very constructive role. However, to perform that role effectively, countries in the region need "a new coalition of political support" based on reduced external finance, larger domestic savings, an expanded and competitive international market for manufactured products, and limits to the tax base, among others.

For Fishlow, the prospects for economic development in the region depend largely on the outcome of the process of state reform currently underway. The task, he asserts, is formidable and will take more time than previously anticipated. "Changing the state is much more than a matter of introducing new rules and regulations. At base, broad institutional continuity is necessary, the kind that comes about over a generation."

Waisman discusses the political dynamics associated with the economic reform process. In this framework, he sees three possible alternatives: the Chilean one ("in which privatization, deregulation and the opening-up of the economy preceded democratization"), the Venezuelan one ("in which the liberalization of the economy takes place in the context of political institutions that have been in place for several decades"), and the Argentine one ("in which economic liberalization and the consolidation of democracy take place more or less at the same time").

Although the three cases pose problems and dangers, the least favorable is the Argentine alternative because economic liberalization and the consolidation of democracy are governed by what the author calls "two opposing social logics": the logic of differentiation and the logic of mobilization. Privatization, deregulation, and the opening-up of the economy are governed by the first, whereas the consolidation of democracy is governed by the latter.

According to Waisman, these two logics have the potential for inhibiting each other and consequently for hampering or altering the liberalization of the economy, the consolidation of democracy, or both. The fact that no serious clashes have occurred between these two logics is due to the existence of "moderating factors," which inhibit political mobilization. Of those factors, the one calling for additional reform in most countries is what the author calls "institutional change" or "institutional design." Both the strengthening of civil society and the enhancement of state capacity needed for the consolidation of democracy and the success of economic transformation could be "substantially advanced by the right kind of institutional design." The author points to three main areas in which institutional change may contribute to the strengthening of civil society and the improvement of state capacity: the reform of electoral systems, the moderation of the presidentialist tradition, and the strengthening of the judiciary.

Cohen discusses Latin American nationalism in a historical context. For him, the roots of economic nationalism, which prevailed until the early 1980s, can be found in the Great Depression of the 1930s. "The abrupt plummeting of the prices of primary products, as well as the breakdown of the multilateral trading system and its replacement with Imperial Preferences and Reciprocal Trade Agreements, led Latin America in the thirties to the pursuit of deliberate import substitution and protectionism."

The polarization of the center-periphery dispute was heightened during the cold war, while there was an active search for an ideological "third way" combined with defensive economic policies throughout the region. The next dramatic shift came about with the end of the cold war and the depression of the 1980s, which brought about a trend that has been characterized as a "movement to the right" by which "in country after country, socialist and other left parties have taken the ideological road back to capitalism."

The sweeping economic reforms that have accompanied this ideological shift and have effectively dismantled the "basic components of defensive nationalism, have coincided with a return to democratic and civilian regimes, in what constitutes the incipient beginning of an opening of the exclusionary political regimes that frequently coexisted with defensive economic nationalism."

Williamson revisits his famous "Washington Consensus," a conceptual framework that he developed in 1990. In the paper included in this book, Williamson addresses the question of whether and how the passage of time and the advent of the Clinton administration have modified the original set of policies and to what extent those policies have been implemented in the countries of the region.

According to his evaluation, Clinton policies did not affect the vast range of support enjoyed by the reforms summarized in the Washington Consensus. The changes since 1989 concern "not the abandonment of anything that was then accepted but rather additions to the list." The possible components to be added to the original list of Washington's policy prescriptions are poverty reduction, birth control, and social expenditure. Williamson concludes that the Washington Consensus should become, like democracy and human rights, "a part of the basic core of ideas that we hold in common and do not need to debate endlessly."

Paul Krugman's article adds a strong cautionary note to the debate over the prospects of recent economic reforms. The Mexican crisis of 1994, he asserts, made evident the drastic limitations of the new economic model to bring about quick growth and prosperity to the region. In his view, the crisis of the Mexican peso was "neither a temporary setback nor a purely Mexican affair" but "an accident waiting to happen" because the astonishing initial success of the new economic model was based not on sound accomplishments but on "excessively optimistic expectations."

In this atmosphere of excessive optimism, he points out, the benefits of some of the basic policies associated with free market economics were clearly overstated. In particular, he points to the allegedly huge gains from low inflation and free market policies. An objective analysis of the likely effects of the economic reforms undertaken in developing countries in recent years, concludes Krugman, "did not and does not seem to justify wild enthusiasm." Although the application of free market policies is "almost surely" a good initiative, "the idea that they will generate a growth takeoff represents a hope rather than a well-founded expectation."

Because the 1990–1995 euphoria about the prospects of developing countries was clearly unrealistic, Krugman concludes, "the Mexican crisis is likely to be the trigger that sets the process in reverse." That is to say that the rest of the decade "will probably be a downward cycle of deflating expectations." And "because reforms will no longer be instantly rewarded by the capital markets, it will be far more difficult to sell such reforms politically. Thus the common assumption that free trade and free market policies will quickly spread around the world is surely wrong."

Part 3 contains papers by Miguel A. Kigel and Julio Nogues, Felipe Larraín and Jeffrey Sachs, Valdir Ramalho, Felipe Larraín and Raúl Labán, and Miguel Urrutia.

Kigel and Nogues analyze the Argentine "convertibility plan" adopted by the Menem government in 1991 to stop inflation. In the authors' view, the plan is not only the most comprehensive effort to stabilize and reform the Argentine economy but the most successful one in the last half century. Since its inception, Kigel and Nogues assert, inflation has fallen to acceptable international levels, and the economy has grown at an average rate of 7 percent per year.

Although the plan was severely challenged in 1994 by the so-called Tequila effect, the authors contend that the economy is once again experiencing an expansionary phase while inflation remains under control. "The structural reforms implemented since 1989 and deepened with the convertibility plan in 1991 continue to bear fruit and indicators show that the economy has entered a new era where exports and investment will be the engines of growth, where openness, monetary and fiscal discipline will be the guiding principles, and where a rise in domestic savings will slowly but surely finance an increasing capacity of the economy to create productive employment opportunities."

Larraín and Sachs discuss Bolivia's economic reforms between 1985 and 1992, including the implementation of the program known as New Economic Policy, or as Supreme Decree 21060. The authors claim that the Bolivian reform package represents one of the most successful economic adjustment programs implemented in the post-war era. Its success, they claim, has subsequently influenced the design of similar programs in Eastern Europe and the former Soviet Union.

In a short period of time, Larraín and Sachs assert, hyperinflation was eliminated and economic growth was restored after years of dismal economic performance. These remarkable changes were accomplished in spite of a dramatic series of adverse external shocks, such as the collapse of world tin prices, a disadvantageous renegotiation of its natural gas contract with Argentina, and the drop of coca paste world prices, costing the economy approximately $600 million annually (which represents 10 percent of the country's gross national product). Larraín and Sachs' paper is based on a report commissioned by the Bolivian government to analyze policy options. Consequently, the authors outline a number of tasks that the government should accomplish to facilitate economic growth and to lower poverty levels.

In his paper, Ramalho analyzes the stabilization program known as "Plano Real," implemented in Brazil in July 1994. The author asserts that the Plano Real plan is perhaps "the most successful program in the country's history." The dramatic drop in inflation that followed the plan's implementation, the author says, was achieved with higher growth rather than with a production slowdown, a phenomenon that "may be surprising to some, considering the usual association in the macroeconomic literature between inflation reduction and production slowdown."

In order to put the Plano Real plan in context, Ramalho reviews previous Brazilian efforts, such as President Collor's economic plan to stop inflation and to stabilize the economy. The author contends that Collor's stabilization plan was "an awkward combination of another price freeze with what was intended to provoke a major monetary contraction, the seizing of most financial assets held by families and firms."

Larraín and Labán discuss the issue of continuity and change in the Chilean policy regime. The analysis refers to some of the main challenges facing the country's economy into the mid-1990s. According to the authors, despite major progress, a significant sector of the Chilean population still lives below the poverty line. "Consolidating a strong and stable path of economic growth is an essential component in the defeat of poverty and underdevelopment," the authors believe. In their opinion, consistent economic growth in the order of 7 percent annually is an attainable economic goal for Chile to pursue into the next decade.

The Chilean economy, the authors assert, has changed dramatically since the mid-1970s. "From the very high levels of protection and pervasive state intervention, it has been transformed into an economy integrated to world markets, where the engine of growth is the private sector," the authors highlight. However, the transformation of the Chilean economy faced severe challenges. Two major depressions (in 1975 and 1982–1983) and a complex political transition from a military regime to a democratic system tested the Chilean resolve to consolidate the economic reforms. To some, the authors note, the opposition's victory in the presidential elections of December 1989 presented a serious threat to the existing economic model. However, those fears proved to be wrong. In Larraín and Labán's view, the advent of democracy deepened and legitimized Chile's economic reforms.

Urrutia, writing from the perspective of the early 1990s, discusses the reforms implemented in the 1989–1991 period by the Gaviria administration to liberalize the Colombian economy. Colombia's case, the author asserts, is unique because it did not result in response to any of the circumstances that commonly precede economic liberalization. "As so often is the case, liberalization in Colombian trade, foreign exchange, and capital control liberalization does not fit the standard Latin American pattern," Urrutia contends. The Colombian liberalization process, he asserts, "did not take place as a reaction to an economic or foreign exchange crisis, nor at the start of an administration, when its popularity would be at its highest." It should be noted that, unfortunately, Colombia has recently experienced a revival of drug-related violence, which has destabilized the process of economic development.

Part 4 includes papers by Sebastian Edwards, Roberto Lavagna, and Miguel Rodriguez-Mendoza.

Edwards evaluates the recent process of trade reform in the Latin American countries. According to the author, the opening of Latin American economies to the rest of the world is perhaps "the most impressive achievement of the reform programs, and effectively ended more than four decades of import-substitution policies that encouraged what turned out to be a largely inefficient industrial sector."

After reviewing recent trade liberalization reforms in the region and the existing regional trading blocs, including the MERCOSUR, the Andean Group, the Central American Common Market, and the North American Free Trade Agreement (NAFTA), the author discusses the prospects for global trade liberalization. Although Latin America embarked on "one of the most substantial unilateral trade reforms in modern economic history," Edwards asserts, there is serious concern among the region's political leaders about the lack of reciprocity from the industrialized countries. "While the Latin American nations greatly opened up their trade sector to foreign competition, most industrial nations continued to follow protectionist practices." However, the resolutions adopted during the General Agreement on Tariffs and Trade's (GATT's) Uruguay Round in 1993 provide "some hope" that multilateralism will lead to a more open world trade system in the future.

Lavagna examines the role of regional agreements as instruments "for both trade discrimination and promotion of freer trade." Taking the example of Argentina and its relationship with MERCOSUR and NAFTA, the author examines the problems and dilemmas facing the Southern Cone countries given the "oversupply" of regional agreements. According to Lavagna, "the proponents of freer trade must think not only about deepening regional agreements but also about permanently enlarging and inter-relating them." In this framework, the author considers critical both the sequence and the timing of that process. He analyzes both "the static and dynamic effects to consider the problems of sequence and timing for Argentina and Brazil in choosing between deepening MERCOSUR or switching to a large agreement with NAFTA."

In the case of Argentina, the author concludes, strengthening and deepening the accord with MERCOSUR are "valuable, both in terms of the static analysis of trade creation and trade diversion and its dynamic effects." Analyzing the opportunities developed in recent years for less restricted trade, the author sides with those who think that "liberalization is only possible because these regional agreements supply a methodology for opening economies without making countries face unbearable social and economic costs due to a sudden restructuring of production."

Rodriguez-Mendoza discusses some of the difficulties the Andean Group currently faces in strengthening its integration mechanisms. In the author's view, the Andean Group experience illustrates, among other things, how liberal trade policies adopted by most countries of the region in the 1980s have influenced the old Latin American integration mechanisms.

The transformation of the Andean Group in the 1990s, the author asserts, has been noteworthy. From an "entity on the brink of collapse" in the 1980s, it quickly overcame its difficulties and succeeded in achieving important integration goals in a short period of time. At the core of this remarkable transformation, Rodriguez-Mendoza says, lie the economic reforms undertaken by country members since the mid-1980s, particularly the trade liberalization measures.

However, the author warns, in spite of its accomplishments, the Andean Group faces important and numerous difficulties that may prevent it from further advancing the integration process, including the fact that the group has not yet consolidated itself as a customs union. "The time has come for the Andean presidents to be directly involved again in the subregional integration process. Much of what the Andean Group has achieved during the last five years is a direct result of decisions taken at the presidential level at the beginning of the decade. To lead the Andean Group out of its present difficulties, political guidance would be helpful," he concludes.

Concluding Remarks

Today, the debate concerning the best model to bring about sustained economic growth and social equity to Latin America is far from over. Following the great hopes generated by the alleged opportunities for sustained growth provided by the neoliberal model and the bitter frustration following the Tequila effect of 1994, the accumulated experience of the first half of the decade is largely mixed.

According to the Economic Commission for Latin America and the Caribbean (ECLAC), economic growth in the region during the 1990s has been "modest," "unstable," and "too slow to bring about an improvement in the employment situation or wages." Economic growth fell from a high of 5.3 percent in 1994 to 0.3 percent in 1995 and then climbed back to 3.4 percent in 1996, averaging 3.1 percent in the 1991–1996 period. Additionally, "most of the employment created during the 1990s has been in the informal sector, while average labor productivity has stagnated." Quoting data from the International Labor Organization (ILO), ECLAC points out that of every 100 new jobs created between 1990 and 1995, 84 were in the informal sector where 56 percent of all the region's employed workers were occupied. According to ECLAC, "these figures help to explain why real wage levels are below those of 1980, despite almost generalized increases in the 1990s." Simultaneously, unemployment continued to rise, reaching 8 percent in 1996.

On the other side, and as Iglesias, Waisman, and other contributors to this book have pointed out, Latin America today is a different place than in previous decades, and political rhetoric has largely been replaced by more pragmatic policy analysis. Further, the concept of partnerships has emerged as a powerful counterweight to cutthroat competition in an era of globalization. These partnerships have taken the form of new or revitalized economic cooperation among countries, increased cooperation between the public and private sectors, and increased respect and confidence in grassroots organizations, Nongovernmental Organizations, and small businesses as they become critical actors for bringing about economic development and increased social equity.

Contents

PREFACE v

PART 1 Historical Framework 1

Reading 1 Latin American Economic Development: An Overview 3
Victor Bulmer-Thomas

Reading 2 Economic Development Theory and Policy in Latin America: The Second World War to the Present 42
Dilmus D. James

PART 2: The New Economic Model 57

Reading 3 From Adjustment Policies to Structural Reforms 59
Enrique Iglesias

Reading 4 The Latin American State 74
Albert Fishlow

Reading 5 The Political Dynamics of Economic Reform in Latin America 87
Carlos H. Waisman

Reading 6 The New Latin American and Caribbean Nationalism and Economic Reform 97
Isaac Cohen

Reading 7 Latin American Reform: A View from Washington 106
John Williamson

Reading 8 1995 and Beyond: The Era of Deflated Expectations (Dutch Tulips and Emerging Markets) 112
Paul Krugman

PART 3: Case Studies 123

Reading 9 Restoring Growth and Price Stability in Argentina: Do Policies Make Miracles? 125
Miguel A. Kiguel and Julio J. Nogués

Reading 10 Bolivia 1985–1992: Reforms, Results, and Challenges 145
Felipe Larraín B. and Jeffrey D. Sachs

Reading 11 "Plano Real": The End of Hyperinflation in Brazil 169
Valdir Ramalho

Reading 12 From the Military to Democracy: Two Decades of Chilean Economic Policies 193
Felipe Larraín B. and Raúl Labán M.

Reading 13 Economic Reform in Colombia 217
Miguel Urrutia

PART 4: Economic Reform and Integration **243**

Reading 14 The Opening of Latin America 245
Sebastian Edwards

Reading 15 Opening a Medium-Size Economy: A Case of Regional Agreements—Argentina and MERCOSUR 297
Roberto Lavagna

Reading 16 The Andean Group's Integration Strategy 317
Miguel Rodríguez-Mendoza

APPENDIX 335

Electronic Research on Economic Reform in Latin America 337
Kate Randall Haley

CREDITS 343

INDEX 345

PART 1

Historical Framework

READING 1

Latin American Economic Development: An Overview

VICTOR BULMER-THOMAS
University of London

The expression "Latin America," apparently coined in 1856 by the Colombian José María Torres Caicedo,[1] at first had little more than geographical significance—it referred to all those independent countries south of the Río Grande in which a language derived from Latin (Spanish, Portuguese, French) was predominantly spoken. In this original meaning, the only characteristics common to the countries of Latin America were their location in the Western Hemisphere and the origins of their language. In many respects the differences between the countries were considered to be as important—if not more so—as what they shared.

These differences—whether of size, population, race, natural resources, climate, or level of development—are still very important, but it has also become clear that the republics are held together by much more than geography and language. The shared colonial experience, as divisions above all of the Spanish or Portuguese empires, was crucial in shaping the economic and political destinies of the new republics after independence. The pattern of development in the nineteenth century, based on the export of natural resources to the industrialized countries, reinforced this sense of a shared past.

Thus there is real meaning to the phrase "Latin America," and the factors in common are stronger than those that bind the countries of Africa or Asia or Europe. Furthermore, the membership of the Latin American club has been fairly stable since independence, with relatively few additions or subtractions as a result of border changes, secession, or annexation; indeed, the boundaries of Latin American states, although often the source of interstate conflict and still not entirely settled,[2] have changed much less in the last 150 years than have frontiers in Europe, Africa, and Asia.

[1]See Bushnell and Macaulay (1988), 3.

[2]The main border disputes (including maritime boundaries) still outstanding are the following: Guatemala and Belize; Colombia and Venezuela; Venezuela and Guyana; Ecuador and Peru. The long-standing territorial dispute between Argentina and the United Kingdom over the Falkland/Malvinas islands also remains unresolved.

The countries of Latin America are the ten republics of South America (excluding the three Guianas), the six republics of Central America (including Panama but excluding Belize), Mexico, Cuba, the Dominican Republic, and Haiti—a grand total of twenty. Spanish is the main language in eighteen republics, whereas Portuguese is predominant in Brazil and French-derived *kréyol* in Haiti. Indian languages are still spoken by large pockets of the population in Mexico, Guatemala, Ecuador, Peru, Bolivia, and Paraguay; and English is the first language of numerous minorities throughout the region. Japanese can be heard on the streets of São Paulo, Brazil, where at least one million inhabitants are of Japanese descent, and there are important colonies of Chinese origin in many republics.

Puerto Rico, a Spanish colony until 1898, was annexed by and remains a commonwealth associated with the United States.[3] Although clearly part of Latin America in the nineteenth century, Puerto Rico is often excluded from the definition in the twentieth century—a decision which many find harsh but which has been justified by its very different pattern of development as a result of its special relationship with the United States. By contrast, Panama was not listed as a Latin American country in the nineteenth century because it was still part of Colombia. Its secession in 1902, aided and abetted by President Theodore Roosevelt, led to independence. It is therefore included in the list of twentieth-century Latin American republics.[4]

The majority of Latin American countries won independence from their European rulers in the 1820s.[5] Contemporary accounts by Latin Americans and foreigners were filled with glowing reports of the prospects that could be achieved once Spain and Portugal were deprived of their commercial and other monopolies in the region. Standards of living were low, but not much lower than in North America, probably on a par with much of central Europe and perhaps higher than the newly discovered countries in the antipodes. All that was needed, it was thought, were capital and skilled labor to unlock the natural resources in Latin America's vast unexploited interior and unrestricted access to the wealthy markets of western Europe.

Nearly two centuries later, that dream has not been fulfilled. None of the twenty republics in Latin America can be classified as developed, and some remain extremely poor. Pockets of wealth can be found in all republics, but these cannot conceal the deprivation and hardship suffered by the region's poorest inhabitants. Although Latin America is not among the poorest regions in the world, it has now been overtaken by parts of Asia that almost certainly had much lower standards of living throughout the nineteenth century.[6] Latin America's achievements in the fields of literature, art, music, and popular culture rightly

---

[3]On Puerto Rican history and its peculiar constitutional status, see Carr (1984). Its people's preference for commonwealth status was reconfirmed by a referendum in November 1993.

[4]For the secession of Panama from Colombia and its creation as an independent republic, see Lafeber (1978).

[5]The exceptions are as follows: Haiti won its independence from France in 1804, Uruguay was created in 1828 as a buffer state between Argentina and Brazil, the Dominican Republic secured independence from Haiti in 1844, Cuba won its independence from Spain in 1898, and the special case of Panama has already been mentioned (see note 4).

[6]Examples are South Korea and Taiwan. By 1990 even Malaysia had overtaken almost all Latin American republics in terms of dollar income per head (see World Bank, 1992, Table 1).

win admiration around the world, but this is only partial compensation for failure to bridge the enormous gap between the levels of economic development in the region and in the developed countries.

Economic development is usually measured by a series of indicators, of which the most commonly used are gross domestic product (GDP) and gross national product (GNP) per person.[7] Other indicators are life expectancy at birth, calorie consumption per head, infant mortality, telephones per thousand people, and so on. Almost irrespective of the choice of indicators, Latin America comes out midway between the developed countries (DCs) of North America and Western Europe and the poorest countries of sub-Saharan Africa and South Asia (see Table 1.1). The World Bank classifies all the Latin American republics as "middle-income" except Haiti, Honduras and Nicaragua which are classified as "low-income"; but this cannot disguise the fact that in 1990 GNP per head in the region was only one-tenth the level found in the DCs.[8]

Lack of economic success has not meant stagnation. On the contrary, change has been rapid in Latin America, and this is nowhere more apparent than in the rate of urbanization. Population expansion has been centered on cities, in part as a result of international

TABLE 1.1

Comparative Development Indicators for Latin America, circa 1990

REGION OR COUNTRY	GNP PER HEAD (IN U.S. $)	LIFE EXPECTANCY (IN YEARS)	INFANT MORTALITY RATE[a]	DAILY CALORIE SUPPLY (PER HEAD)
Developing Countries	800	63	65	2,468
South Asia	320	58	95	2,116
Sub-Saharan Africa	340	51	107	2,011
Latin America[b]	1,950	67	50	2,724
Developed Countries[c]	19,090	76	8	3,417
United Kingdom	14,610	76	9	3,252
United States	20,910	76	10	3,666
Switzerland	29,880	78	7	3,547

[a]Number of children dying under one year old per thousand live births.

[b]Latin America defined in source to include main English-speaking Caribbean countries and to exclude Cuba.

[c]Defined as all members of the Organization for Economic Cooperation and Development (OECD).

Source: World Bank (1991b).

[7]GDP refers to the net output generated by factors of production irrespective of whether they are resident. GNP adjusts the GDP figure for net factor income paid abroad. The difference can be important in a number of Latin American republics as a result, for example, of the presence of foreign-owned companies.

[8]International GNP comparisons are very dependent on the choice of the exchange rate. Other comparisons (based, for example, on purchasing power parities) suggest a smaller gap, though the difference still remains considerable. See World Bank (1993).

MAP 1
Latin America, circa 1826

migration in the nineteenth century and rural–urban migration in the twentieth century. Thus, as Table 1.2 makes clear, Latin America is now predominantly urban, with more than 70 percent of its inhabitants living in towns or cities. Because the average rate of urbanization for all middle-income countries is only 58 percent and that for all DCs is 77 percent, this has led to the charge that Latin America is "prematurely mature." Indeed, the spectacular growth of the informal sector in Latin American cities is evidence of the difficulty many new entrants to the urban labor market have in finding secure, productive jobs.[9]

[9]Numerous definitions of the informal sector exist, but it is easiest to think of it as employing all those workers not absorbed by medium- or large-scale firms in the private and public sectors. By that definition the urban informal sector accounts for more than 50 percent of the labor force in many Latin American cities. See, for example, Portes (1989).

MAP 2

Latin America, circa 1990

Latin America includes some of the largest urban areas in the world; Mexico City (18 million) and São Paulo (16 million) have all the problems of pollution associated with large conurbations in industrial countries. What is striking about Latin American urbanization, however, is the problem of primacy; that is, the disproportionately rapid growth of the principal city in each republic. Except in Brazil, Venezuela, and El Salvador, the proportion of the urban population living in the main conurbation is far above the world average. Thus the capital city is usually the leading industrial, commercial, financial, and cultural, as well as the administrative, center.[10]

[10]The main exception is in Brazil, where the capital was moved from Rio de Janeiro to the newly created Brasília in the 1950s. The new capital, though an important city in its own right, is still overshadowed by Rio de Janeiro and São Paulo in almost all areas of private enterprise.

TABLE 1.2
Demographic Indicators

			Population Growth (% per year)		
COUNTRY	1990 POPULATION (IN THOUSANDS)	URBANIZATION[a]	1961–70	1970–80	1980–90
Argentina	32,322	86.3	1.4	1.7	1.4
Bolivia	7,171	51.2	2.4	2.6	2.5
Brazil	149,042	78.9	2.8	2.4	2.1
Chile	13,173	85.9	2.3	1.6	1.7
Colombia	32,300	70.0	3.0	2.2	2.0
Costa Rica	3,035	47.1	3.4	2.8	2.9
Cuba	10,610	67.0	2.0	1.3	0.9
Dominican Republic	7,170	60.4	3.2	2.6	2.3
Ecuador	10,547	56.0	3.2	3.0	2.6
El Salvador	5,172	44.4	3.4	2.3	1.3
Guatemala	9,197	39.4	2.8	2.8	2.9
Haiti	6,486	28.3	2.0	1.7	1.9
Honduras	5,138	43.7	3.1	3.4	3.4
Mexico	81,250	72.6	3.3	2.9	2.3
Nicaragua	3,676	59.8	3.2	3.1	2.8
Panama	2,418	53.4	3.0	2.8	2.1
Paraguay	4,277	47.5	2.9	3.0	3.1
Peru	21,550	70.2	2.9	2.7	2.2
Uruguay	3,094	85.5	1.0	0.4	0.6
Venezuela	19,321	90.5	3.5	3.5	2.5
Latin America	426,949	71.5[b]	2.8[b]	2.4[b]	2.1[b]

[a]Defined as percentage of population living in urban areas. The population classified as urban follows national definitions. See Wilkie (1985), Table 657.

[b]Latin America defined in source to include main English-speaking Caribbean countries and to exclude Cuba.

Sources: IDB (1990) (1992) (1993) for all countries except Cuba; for Cuba, Wilkie (1993).

The rate of population growth, as Table 1.2 makes clear, has begun to slow down. The demographic transition, under which birth rates start to fall in line with the earlier fall in death rates, is well under way, and some countries—notably Argentina, Chile, Cuba, and Uruguay—have already achieved very modest rates of population growth. Brazil and Mexico, the two most populous countries, have had high rates of population growth, however, until quite recently. Their share of the Latin American total—54 percent in 1990—can be expected to stabilize now that birth rates are falling.

In most less-developed countries (LDCs) a rapid rate of urbanization is consistent with an increasing rural population. Rural–urban migration is important, but the small size of the urban areas means that they cannot absorb all the increase in the rural population. The expanding populations must still find new work opportunities in rural areas. In many

Latin American countries, however, urbanization has been pushed to the point where rural–urban migration leads to a fall in the rural population—not just in its rate of growth. Uruguay, for example, has seen a 40 percent decline in its rural population since 1960, and only 14 percent of its labor force was classified as agricultural in 1990.

By contrast, Latin America's population in the 1820s—not much larger in total than Mexico City's is today—was overwhelmingly rural, with the labor force concentrated in agriculture and mining. The natural resources produced by these sectors provided the link with the rest of the world, and international flows of labor and capital were concerned directly or indirectly with increasing the exportable surplus. Some of the commodities for which Latin America is still famous, such as sugar, were already in place by the time of independence; many others, such as coffee, joined the list in the nineteenth century.

The importance of these primary commodities has been declining, but they still accounted for two-thirds of all exports at the end of the 1980s (see Table 1.3). Furthermore, many of the nontraditional manufactured exports from Latin America—such as textiles, leather products, and furniture—are based on natural resources. Thus it is fair to say that

TABLE 1.3

Primary Commodity Exports as Proportions of Total Exports

COUNTRY	FIRST PRODUCT (1985–87)	PERCENTAGE	SECOND PRODUCT (1985–87)	PERCENTAGE	ALL PRIMARY PRODUCTS (1989)
Argentina	Maize	8.0	Beef	6.7	68
Bolivia	Natural gas	54.2	Tin	20.5	95
Brazil	Coffee	8.5	Iron ore	5.2	40
Chile	Copper	42.9	Grapes	4.6	90
Colombia	Coffee	49.0	Oil	12.6	75
Costa Rica	Coffee	31.9	Bananas	20.4	70
Cuba	Sugar	75.5	Citrus	2.2	86
Dominican Republic	Sugar	22.2	Ferronickel	16.0	74[a]
Ecuador	Oil	49.0	Bananas	10.6	97
El Salvador	Coffee	68.1	Cotton	1.9	80
Guatemala	Coffee	40.4	Cotton	3.5	83
Haiti	Coffee	23.9	Sugar	0.2	27[a]
Honduras	Bananas	32.8	Coffee	31.3	88
Mexico	Oil	43.6	Coffee	3.5	55
Nicaragua	Coffee	43.0	Cotton	22.2	97
Panama	Bananas	22.4	Shrimp	18.5	80
Paraguay	Cotton	32.4	Soybeans	29.1	92
Peru	Copper	16.4	Fishmeal	6.8	81
Uruguay	Wool	19.1	Beef	14.0	61
Venezuela	Oil	79.1	Aluminum	4.2	92
Latin America	Oil	20.0	Coffee	7.0	66

[a]Data are for 1988.

Sources: IDB (1988); CEPAL (1988); International Monetary Fund (1990); World Bank (1991b).

primary commodities still provide the main link with the rest of the world. This statement is even more accurate if we include illegal drugs, such as cocaine and marijuana, in the export list. Although these narcotics have a street value far in excess of what Latin America receives, an estimated U.S. $6 billion (approximately 5 percent of exports in 1990) still return to Latin America through a variety of channels.[11]

The exploitation of natural resources in Latin America, as in so many parts of the world, has been carried out with scant respect for the environment. The forest cover has been depleted, rivers and lakes have been polluted, and dangerous chemicals have entered the food chain. Local awareness of these problems has been slowly increasing, but Latin America faces the additional problem that the Amazon Basin—shared by Brazil, Colombia, Ecuador, Peru, Venezuela, and the Guianas—houses the world's largest and most important reserves of tropical rain forests. Their destruction is widely believed to be a major contributor to global warming and to the greenhouse effect, so Latin America finds itself under pressure from the outside world to adopt environmental standards considered appropriate by richer countries.[12]

The problem of environmental damage, however, is not limited to natural resources. Rapid urbanization in the larger republics has been accompanied by impressive industrial growth. Chemical plants, steel mills, cement factories, and automobile assembly lines have proliferated throughout the region as governments have adopted policies that favor industrialization. This process, which began toward the end of the nineteenth century in the major countries of the region, accelerated after 1930 as the Great Depression and the Second World War provided a stimulus for firms that were able to replace manufactured imports with local products. By 1955 the contribution of manufacturing to real GDP had overtaken agriculture,[13] and by 1990 its contribution had reached 24.5 percent, compared with 10.3 percent for agriculture and 4.0 percent for mining (see Table 1.4).

Industrial growth has been rapid for much of the twentieth century, but it has not been notably efficient. Shielded by tariffs and other barriers to imports, industrial firms (including multinational companies, or MNCs) have exploited the domestic market with high-priced, low-quality goods. Most firms were therefore unable to compete internationally, so foreign loans still had to be serviced with earnings from primary products. The rapid accumulation of external debts in the 1970s, in the wake of the two oil crises, left Latin America dangerously exposed, and primary product exports were unable to provide sufficient earnings to service external debts in the 1980s. As a result awareness of the need to make industry internationally competitive has grown, and firms have come under pressure from all sides to cut costs and improve quality.

The extraction of natural resources in Latin America, and related investments in such social infrastructure as railways, attracted foreign capital. The principal investor in the nineteenth century, Great Britain, had been replaced in most countries by the United States before 1930. Subsequently, the state steadily increased its participation in economic activity, taking over public utilities, railways, and natural resources that had previously been controlled by foreigners. However, foreign capital remained important in a number of primary

[11]Estimates of the value of narcotics exports from Latin America differ enormously. For a survey of the industry, see Bagley (1988).

[12]For a good study of the environmental issues raised by the Amazon Basin, see Barbier (1989), Chapter 6. See also Hurrell (1991) and Goodman and Hall (1991).

[13]At 1970 prices and net factor cost. See CEPAL (1978), Table 5.

TABLE 1.4

Sectoral Contribution to GDP in 1990 (1988 prices, in percentages)

COUNTRY	AGRICULTURE	MINING	MANUFACTURING	COUNTRY SHARES OF TOTAL MANUFACTURING
Argentina	14.0	4.2	22.0	8.6
Bolivia	26.6	11.6	14.0	0.4
Brazil	9.1	1.9	26.7	40.2
Chile	6.8	8.6	20.5	3.1
Colombia	17.4	6.6	21.6	4.6
Costa Rica	18.3	—[a]	20.1	0.5
Cuba[b]	16.0	—[a]	32.2	5.1
Dominican Republic	15.6	3.7	17.0	0.4
Ecuador	14.9	8.9	20.8	1.3
El Salvador	14.3	0.2	17.7	0.4
Guatemala	25.8	0.2	15.0	0.6
Haiti	32.6	0.1	14.4	0.1
Honduras	20.2	1.4	13.5	0.2
Mexico	8.1	3.1	28.1	23.3
Nicaragua	31.7	0.6	15.9	0.1
Panama	10.9	0.1	8.2	0.2
Paraguay	29.9	0.5	16.7	0.5
Peru	8.6	2.4	28.0	3.7
Uruguay	13.6	—[a]	27.4	1.1
Venezuela	6.5	13.3	19.6	5.8
Latin America[c]	10.3	4.0	24.5	100

[a]Mining included in manufacturing.

[b]The Cuban data are unofficial estimates for 1981. See Brundenius and Zimbalist (1989), p. 43.

[c]Latin America defined in source to include main English-speaking Caribbean countries and to exclude Cuba.

Source: IDB (1992).

commodities, particularly non-oil minerals, and became attracted by the new opportunities in industry after the Second World War.

State participation in the economy, now increasingly questioned, failed to reverse the sharp inequality in income distribution found in most Latin American republics. This inequality, at first a product of the unequal distribution of land inherited from colonial times, has been reinforced by industrial and financial concentration in the twentieth century, giving Latin America one of the worst income distributions in the world. Indeed, as Table 1.5 makes clear, it is common to find the top 20 percent of households receiving more than 50 percent of total household income, whereas the bottom 20 percent in many cases receive less than 3 percent.

The differences within countries are mirrored to a lesser extent in the differences between countries. In 1991, for example, GNP per head (see Table 1.6) varied from

TABLE 1.5

Income Distribution: Percentage Share of Household Income

COUNTRY	YEAR	BOTTOM 20%	TOP 20%	TOP 10%
Argentina[a]	1989	4.1	52.6	35.9
Bolivia[b]	1989	3.5	57.5	41.2
Brazil	1989	2.1	67.5	51.3
Chile	1989	3.7	62.9	48.9
Colombia	1988	4.0	53.0	37.1
Costa Rica	1989	4.0	50.8	34.1
Cuba	1986	11.3	n/a	20.1
Dominican Republic	1989	4.2	55.6	39.6
Ecuador[b]	1987	5.4	50.5	34.6
El Salvador[b]	1990	4.5	50.0	33.6
Guatemala	1989	2.1	63.0	46.6
Honduras	1989	2.7	63.5	47.9
Mexico	1984	4.1	55.9	39.5
Panama	1989	2.0	59.8	42.1
Paraguay[c]	1990	5.9	46.1	29.5
Peru[d]	1985	4.9	51.4	35.4
Uruguay[b]	1989	5.4	48.3	32.6
Venezuela	1989	4.8	49.5	33.2
Sweden	1981	8.0	36.9	20.8
United States	1985	4.7	41.9	25.0

Note: Data are ranked by income per head unless otherwise stated.

[a]Greater Buenos Aires only.

[b]Urban areas only.

[c]Capital city only.

[d]Data refer to expenditure per head.

Sources: CEPAL (1986); Brundenius and Zimbalist (1989); Wilkie (1990); World Bank (1991b, 1993); Psacharopoulos (1993).

around \$3,000 in the richest countries (Argentina, Brazil, Mexico, Uruguay, Venezuela) to \$370 in the poorest (Haiti). This implies that the average Mexican is eight times richer than the average Haitian and that the average U.S. citizen (see Table 1.1) is ten times richer than the average Latin American. Thus an economic history of Latin America must explain not only the failure of Latin America as a whole to achieve the status of a developed region, but also the differences in standards of living between individual countries within Latin America.

Most theories of economic development have tended to emphasize one side of the explanation at the expense of the other. Racial theories, for example,[14] now largely discredited,

[14]See, for example, Bryce (1912), Chapter 13.

TABLE 1.6
GNP per Head (in U.S. dollars)

COUNTRY	1980	RANK	1991	RANK
Argentina	1,970	7	2,790	4
Bolivia	490	19	650	16
Brazil	2,070	6	2,940	2
Chile	2,100	5	2,160	6
Colombia	1,180	12	1,260	10
Costa Rica	1,960	8	1,850	8
Cuba[a]	2,325	3	—[a]	
Dominican Republic	1,080	14	940	14
Ecuador	1,260	11	1,000	13
El Salvador	750	16	1,080	11
Guatemala	1,120	13	930	15
Haiti	250	20	370	19
Honduras	640	18	580	17
Mexico	2,320	4	3,030	1
Nicaragua	690	17	460	18
Panama	1,630	9	2,130	7
Paraguay	1,340	10	1,270	9
Peru	990	15	1,070	12
Uruguay	2,800	2	2,840	3
Venezuela	4,070	1	2,730	5
Latin America[b]	1,920		2,390	

[a]The official Cuban data do not refer to GNP or GDP. The estimate (GDP per head) for 1980 is from Brundenius and Zimbalist (1989).

[b]Latin America defined in source to include main English-speaking Caribbean countries and to exclude Cuba.

Sources: World Bank (1991c, 1993).

were used to explain the lowly position in terms of real income per head of Bolivia (with its predominantly Indian population) and Haiti (where the population is mainly of African origin) but could not explain the failure of countries with largely European populations, such as Costa Rica and Uruguay, to achieve DC status. Racial theories were also hopelessly inadequate at accounting for the transformation of countries from success stories to failures (e.g., Argentina) or vice versa (e.g., Venezuela).[15]

Some theories of economic development for Latin America have put considerable stress on the institutional and structural features of the region.[16] For example, the land-tenure

[15]Argentina was overtaken in terms of real GDP per head (1970 prices) by Venezuela in 1956 (see CEPAL [1978], Table 2). Argentina had been the major success story in Latin America in the half century before the 1920s; Venezuela had been one of the worst failures.

[16]See, for example, Griffin (1969) and Frank (1969).

system, which was inherited from the Iberian Peninsula, was seen as an obstacle to development; and the legal and administrative apparatus, which was inherited from the colonial powers, was seen as a barrier to private entrepreneurship and efficient decision making in the public sector. The superficial attractions of these theories should not be allowed to obscure their many deficiencies, however. The institutional and structural landscape inherited from the colonial period was not homogeneous and has changed significantly over time.

On the other hand, dependency theory, which emphasized the dichotomy between the "center" (the advanced countries) and the "periphery" (Latin America) and the unequal relations of exchange between the two regions, seemed at first to be a plausible explanation of the relative failure of Latin America to achieve the high standard of living found in the developed countries, but it was unable to offer much guidance as to why some Latin American countries performed so much better than others.[17] Furthermore, dependency theory was also unable to account for the transformation of a country such as Argentina from success to failure in a relatively short period of time.

Dependency theory is part of a long tradition of theoretical work that has seen the primary obstacle to Latin American economic development in the unequal relations with foreign powers. An abundance of circumstantial evidence illustrates the arrogant attitude toward Latin America on the part of a number of European powers (notably Great Britain and France) in the nineteenth century and of the United States in the twentieth century. It is impossible, however, to sustain the thesis that a negative relationship exists between the closeness of ties to a foreign power and the rate of economic development. Poor and backward countries (e.g., Bolivia) have never received the amount of attention that relatively rich countries have (e.g., Argentina, which, until as late as the 1940s, was often described as being an informal member of the British Empire).[18]

Orthodox theories have fared no better. Numerous theories of export-led growth have argued that countries with the highest levels of integration into the world economy would achieve the highest rates of economic growth and ultimately achieve DC status.[19] Yet some of the poorest Latin American republics, such as Honduras, have been among the most open economies in the world, whereas the transformation of Brazil from one of the poorest countries in Latin America in the 1920s to one of the richest by the 1970s was achieved against a background of delinking from the world economy for much of that period.

An extreme version of orthodoxy, neo-liberalism, has been much in vogue in recent years. It argues that Latin America was crippled by state intervention, which has distorted relative prices, prevented the emergence of a dynamic private sector, and forced many individuals into informal—often illegal—activities.[20] Critics were quick to point out the ahistorical nature of this argument, for state intervention in Latin America—as in many other regions of the world—had been in large part a response to market failure in an unregulated

[17]The classic statement of dependency theory in the Latin American context is Cardoso and Faletto (1979).

[18]On contrasting views of informal empire and the Argentine situation, see Thompson (1992) and Hopkins (1994).

[19]See, for example, Little, Scitovsky, and Scott (1970), Krueger (1978), and Balassa (1982). For an empirical test of the relationship between export and GDP growth, see Feder (1983).

[20]See, for example, De Soto (1987).

and "liberal" environment. Indeed, the half century before 1930, which was dominated in Latin America by liberal ideology, was marked by the modest role of the state and by the importance of private foreign investment. Even if state intervention was not always the appropriate response to market failure, it did not follow that the absence of state intervention would necessarily lead to a more efficient allocation of resources.

No single theory will explain both the intermediate position occupied by Latin America on the scale of world income per head and the differences that have emerged among Latin American countries over time. Yet a theoretical framework is essential if economic history is to be more than mere description. Three basic ideas can account for the position of the region as a whole and of individual countries within the region: the commodity lottery, the mechanics of export-led growth, and the economic-policy environment.

Latin America's integration into the world economy took place through exports of primary products. As we have seen, this remains the single most important link with the rest of the world. Primary products are not homogeneous, however, and the phrase "commodity lottery" is intended to draw attention to the differences among commodities. Some products (e.g., cattle), lend themselves naturally to forward linkages through further processing before export, whereas others (e.g., bananas), offer little prospect. Commodities with forward linkages can act as a stimulus to industry and urbanization—the clearest example is meat in Argentina in the nineteenth century—but commodities also differ in terms of their demand for inputs (backward linkages). Commodities that are extracted from the ground using labor only (e.g., guano[21]) provide no stimulus to industries that supply inputs, whereas other commodities (e.g., nitrates), demand a range of inputs, including machinery, before they can be exploited profitably.

Commodities also differ in terms of their demand characteristics. Some, such as meat, have enjoyed and still enjoy relatively high income elasticities of demand, so that a 5 percent increase in real-world income brings an increase in demand for the commodity of more than 5 percent. Others, such as coffee, have seen income elasticities decline over time, as the commodity in question has moved from being a luxury good to being an article of basic consumption. Some commodities (e.g., gold) have no close synthetic substitute, whereas others (e.g., cotton) face competition from synthetic fibers, so that the price elasticity of demand is high. In some products (e.g., cocaine), Latin America has a monopoly of world supply; in others (e.g., sugar), international competition is fierce.

The geographical and geological diversity of Latin America meant that each republic had only a limited choice of commodities to export. Chile, a temperate country, could export wheat but not coffee; it has huge deposits of copper but little oil. The commodity lottery dictated that Chile would be integrated into the world economy on the basis of products that were very different from those of, say, Colombia, where the tropical climate and mountainous terrain make coffee production particularly appropriate. Inevitably, these differences among countries in terms of their commodity specialization carried with them important implications for long-run growth.

Commodity specialization led to rising labor productivity in the export sector, bringing with it the prospect of export-led growth. The mechanics of export-led growth, however, are crucial. A well-oiled machine can transfer productivity gains in the export sector to the

---

[21]Guano, a natural fertilizer formed by bird droppings, was found in abundance off the coast of Peru and began to be exploited commercially in the nineteenth century.

rest of the economy, raising living standards and real income per head; a faulty machine will leave productivity gains concentrated in the export sector, often to be exploited by foreign companies rather than by domestic factors of production. The capitalist surplus made possible by export specialization is thus no guarantee of capital accumulation.

Three mechanisms are particularly important in the export-led growth machine: capital (including innovation and the transfer of technology), labor, and the state. Where these mechanisms fail to function efficiently, it is possible to have growth in the export sector and stagnation or even decline in the nonexport economy. The result will be rising exports per head and an increase in the share of real GDP accounted for by exports but no guarantee of rapidly rising living standards. Eventually, of course, as exports increase the rate of growth of real GDP must coincide with the rate of growth of exports, but by then export specialization will have reached the point at which the economy is extremely vulnerable to adverse conditions in world markets, and recession induced by cycles in world trade can be deep and long lasting. By contrast, where the three mechanisms function efficiently, the nonexport economy will expand along with the export sector. Exports per head will rise, but the share of exports in real GDP may actually fall, and living standards will certainly increase. The dynamism of the nonexport economy then shields it from adverse external shocks, so that recession induced by cycles in world trade tends to be short-lived.

The first mechanism, capital, involves the transfer of part of the capitalist surplus in the export sector to productive investment in the nonexport economy. This transfer is by no means automatic. It is less likely to occur, for example, where the surplus accrues to foreign investors, where there are few financial intermediaries, and where the domestic market is small. It is more likely to occur where the surplus accrues to local factors of production, where financial intermediation is widespread, and where the domestic market is large and expanding.

The size of the domestic market is a function not only of population but also of purchasing power. Where labor—the second mechanism—in the export sector is paid in kind, the domestic market is artificially restricted. A labor force based on slavery, for example, like that in Brazil or Cuba until the late 1880s, is a poor stimulus for transferring productivity gains in the export sector to the nonexport economy. By contrast, a skilled labor force based on wage labor represents not only an important concentration of purchasing power for sellers in the nonexport economy but also a potential source of future entrepreneurs who are able to take their skills and knowledge to other branches of the economy.

The third mechanism involves the state. The expansion of the export sector permits an expansion of imports, and taxes on foreign trade in the first stages of development are invariably the most important source of government revenue. The size of the revenue and the manner in which it is spent are crucial determinants of the success or failure of export-led growth. Where the resources are small and are used primarily to reinforce the export sector, the nonexport sector may remain undynamic; where the resources are substantial and are used to encourage the nonexport economy, both sectors can expand rapidly. The balance is delicate, however, because an excessive tax burden on the export sector can lead to its stagnation.

The commodity lottery and the mechanics of export-led growth have been important determinants of success or failure in Latin America's economic development since independence, but so has the economic-policy environment. Inconsistent economic policies or policies that are applied inconsistently have done considerable damage to both the export sector and the nonexport sector. Consistent economic policies, based on a broad consensus and backed up by political stability, on the other hand, have created an appropriate environment for transferring productivity gains from the export sector to the nonexport economy. As the Latin American economies have become more complex, the economic-policy environment has become more important—to the point that in some republics it is the principal determinant of success or failure.

For most of the first century after independence, all republics in Latin America followed a policy of export-led growth based on primary-product exports. Where the combination of the commodity lottery, the mechanics of export-led growth, and the economic-policy environment were favorable, the results could be impressive. Argentina, for example, which benefited from the commodity lottery and where the mechanics of export-led growth functioned smoothly, was among the twelve richest countries in the world in the 1920s in terms of real income per head, despite numerous deficiencies in economic policy. Where all three elements were unfavorable, as in Haiti and Bolivia, however, the results were bitterly disappointing.

In the half-century after the 1929 depression a number of countries—mainly the larger republics—turned away from export-led growth toward inward-looking development based on import-substituting industrialization (ISI). In these countries the export sector ceased to be dynamic and the commodity lottery lost its relevance, although primary-product exports remained the main source of foreign-exchange earnings. The new dynamic sector was ISI, and the problem became how to transfer the productivity gains in the ISI sector to the rest of the economy. The need for factor and product markets to function smoothly, therefore, still applied in this new situation, and the economic-policy environment became more important than ever, with mistakes being more costly.[22]

At the end of the 1960s a number of countries began to turn away from inward-looking development toward a new type of integration into the world economy, one based on nontraditional exports, including manufactures. This process gathered pace in the 1980s, and by the beginning of the 1990s a new era of export-led growth was under way throughout Latin America. Much is expected of this new model, but the lessons of the past need to be remembered. The economic-policy environment remains crucial: The global nature of the world economy now means that domestic factors of production are increasingly aware of opportunities outside the region, so policy errors are punished by capital flight and by the drain of skilled labor from Latin America. The mechanics of export-led growth have become more complicated and the transfer and diffusion of technology much more crucial, but the basic problem of transferring productivity gains in the export sector to the nonexport economy remains. The commodity lottery is no longer so important, but the choice of nontraditional exports can still have an important bearing on success or failure in economic development.

The lessons from Latin America's economic history suggest that nothing is predetermined about the region's current lowly status in terms of economic development in general and real income per head in particular. The alchemy of success is no easier to achieve today than it was at the time of independence, however. There is no magic wand to wave, and international competition is fiercer than ever. Not all the Latin American republics can expect

[22]With barriers to international trade driving a wedge between domestic and international prices, domestic economic policy became a key determinant of the allocation of resources and the rate of economic growth.

to make the transition to DC status in the next century, but it would be surprising if a few did not succeed.[23] Even so, the lessons from the past—the failures as well as the successes—must be learned if all the grandchildren of today's Latin Americans are to be assured of a decent standard of living.

Bibliography

Abente, D. (1989). "Foreign Capital, Economic Elites and the State in Paraguay during the Liberal Republic (1870–1936)," *Journal of Latin American Studies* 21 (1): 61–88.

Acevedo, E. (1902). *Historia económica de la República de Uruguay.* 2 vols. Montevideo: El Siglo Ilustrado.

Adams, F. (1914). *Conquest of the Tropics.* New York: Doubleday.

Albala Bertrand, J. M. (1993). "Evolution of Aggregate Welfare and Development Indicators in Latin America and the OECD, 1950–85." In Abel, C., and Lewis, C. M. (eds.), *Welfare, Poverty and Development in Latin America.* Basingstoke, Eng.: Macmillan / St. Antony's College.

Alberro, J. L. (1987). "La dinámica de los precios relativos en un ambiente inflacionario," *Estudios Económicos,* Número Extraordinario (October): 267–304.

Albert, B. (1988). *South America and the First World War: The Impact of the War on Brazil, Argentina, Peru and Chile.* Cambridge University Press.

Alhadeff, P. (1986). "The Economic Formulae of the 1930s; a Reassessment." In Di Tella, G., and Platt, D. C. M. (eds.), *The Political Economy of Argentina, 1880–1946.* Basingstoke, Eng.: Macmillan / St. Antony's College.

Alienes, J. (1950). *Características fundamentales de la economía cubana.* Havana: Banco Nacional de Cuba.

Amadeo, E., et al. (1990). *Inflación y estabilización en América Latina: nuevos modelos estructuralistas.* Bogotá: Tercer Mundo Editores.

Andere, E. (1992). "Regímenes antidumping de México y Estados Unidos: Consideraciones para la negociación del tratado de libre comercio." In Andere, E., and Kessel, G. (eds.), *México y el tratado trilateral de libre comercio.* Mexico, D. F.: McGraw-Hill.

Anna, T. (1985). "The Independence of Mexico and Central America." In Bethell, L. (ed.), *The Cambridge History of Latin America, Vol. III: From Independence to c. 1870.* Cambridge University Press.

Arndt, H. W. (1985). "The Origins of Structuralism," *World Development* 13 (2): 151–9.

Arriaga, E. (1968). *New Life Tables for Latin American Populations in the Nineteenth and Twentieth Centuries.* Berkeley: University of California.

Arrieta, C., et al. (1991). *El narcotráfico en Colombia.* Bogotá: Tercer Mundo Editores.

Ascher, W. (1984). *Scheming for the Poor: The Politics of Redistribution in Latin America.* Cambridge, Mass.: Harvard University Press.

Bacha, E. (1977). "Issues and Evidence in Recent Brazilian Economic Growth," *World Development* 5 (1–2): 47–67.

Baer, W. (1969). *The Development of the Brazilian Steel Industry.* Nashville, Tenn.: Vanderbilt University Press.

(1983). *The Brazilian Economy: Growth and Development.* New York: Praeger.

Baer, W., and Birch, M. H. (1984). "Expansion of the Economic Frontier: Paraguayan Growth in the 1970s," *World Development* 12 (8): 783–98.

Bagley, B. (1988). "US Foreign Policy and the War on Drugs: Analysis of a Policy Failure," *Journal of Interamerican Studies and World Affairs* 30 (2–3): 189–212.

[23] Mexico has even been accepted as a member of the Organization for Economic Cooperation and Development (OECD), the club to which all DCs belong, but this has more to do with the politics of North American free trade than with Mexico's true economic standing.

Note: The editors of this book have preserved the entire list of references because of its added value as an excellent source list.

Bairoch, P., and Etemard, B. (1985). *Commodity Structure of Third World Exports.* Geneva: Libraire Droz.

Bairoch, P., and Lévy-Leboyer, M. (eds.) (1981). *Disparities in Economic Development since the Industrial Revolution.* Basingstoke, Eng.: Macmillan.

Bairoch, P., and Toutain, J. (1991). *World Energy Production.* Geneva: Libraire Droz.

Bakewell, P. (1984). "Mining in Colonial Spanish America." In Bethell, L. (ed.), *The Cambridge History of Latin America: Vol. II: Colonial Latin America.* Cambridge University Press.

Balassa, B. (1982). *Development Strategies in Semi-Industrial Economies.* Baltimore: Johns Hopkins University Press.

Balassa, B., et al. (1986). *Towards Renewed Economic Growth in Latin America: Summary, Overview and Recommendations.* Washington, D.C.: Institute for International Economics.

Balasubramanyam, V. (1988). "Export Processing Zones in Developing Countries: Theory and Empirical Evidence." In Greenaway, D. (ed.), *Economic Development and International Trade.* Basingstoke, Eng.: Macmillan.

Ballesteros, M., and Davis, T. E. (1963). "The Growth of Output and Employment in Basic Sectors of the Chilean Economy, 1908–1957," *Economic Development and Cultural Change* 11: 152–76.

Banco de Guatemala (1989). *Banca Central,* No. 1. Guatemala City: Banco de Guatemala.

Banco de la República (1990). *El Banco de la República: Antecedentes, evolución y estructura.* Bogotá: Banco de la República.

Banuri, T. (1991). *Economic Liberalization: No Panacea. The Experiences of Latin America and Asia.* Oxford: Clarendon Press.

Barbier, E. B. (1989). *Economics, Natural-Resource Scarcity and Development.* London: Earthscan Publications Ltd.

Barraclough, S. (ed.) (1973). *Agrarian Structure in Latin America.* Lexington, Mass.: Heath.

Batou, J. (1990). *One Hundred Years of Resistance to Underdevelopment.* Geneva: Libraire Droz.

(1991). *Between Development and Underdevelopment.* Geneva: Libraire Droz.

Bauer, A. (1986). "Rural Spanish America, 1870–1930." In Bethell, L. (ed.), *The Cambridge History of Latin America, Vol. IV: c. 1870–1930.* Cambridge University Press.

Bauer Paíz, A. (1956). *Cómo opera el capital yanqui en Centroamérica (el caso de Guatemala).* Mexico, D. F.: Editorial Ibero-Mexicana.

Bazant, J. (1985). "Mexico from Independence to 1867." In Bethell, L. (ed.), *The Cambridge History of Latin America, Vol. III: From Independence to c. 1870.* Cambridge University Press.

Beckerman, P. (1989). "Austerity, External Debt, and Capital Formation in Peru." In Handelman, H., and Baer, W. (eds.), *Paying the Costs of Austerity in Latin America.* Boulder, Colo.: Westview.

Benoit, P. (1954). *1804–1954: cent cinquante ans de commerce exterieur d'Haiti.* Port-au-Prince: Institut Haitien de Statistique.

Berend, I. T. (1982). *The European Periphery & Industrialization: 1780–1914.* Cambridge University Press.

Bergad, L. (1983). *Coffee and the Growth of Agrarian Capitalism in Nineteenth Century Puerto Rico.* Princeton, N.J.: Princeton University Press.

Bergquist, C. (1978). *Coffee and Conflict in Colombia, 1886–1910.* Durham, N.C.: Duke University Press.

Bergsman, J. (1970). *Brazil: Industrialization and Trade Policies.* London: Oxford University Press.

Berry, A. (1983). "A Descriptive History of Colombian Industrial Development in the Twentieth Century." In Berry, A. (ed.), *Essays on Industrialization in Colombia.* Tempe: Center for Latin American Studies, Arizona State University.

(1987). "The Limited Role of Rural Small-Scale Manufacturing for Late-Comers: Some Hypotheses on the Colombian Experience," *Journal of Latin American Studies* 19 (2): 279–94.

Berry, A., and Cline, W. (1979). *Agrarian Structure and Productivity in Developing Countries.* Baltimore: Johns Hopkins University Press.

Bethell, L. (1970). *The Abolition of the Brazilian Slave Trade.* Cambridge University Press.

(1985). "The Independence of Brazil." In Bethell, L. (ed.), *The Cambridge History of Latin America, Vol. III: From Independence to c. 1870.* Cambridge University Press.

Bethell L. (ed.) (1991). *The Cambridge History of Latin America, Vol. VIII: Latin America since 1930: Spanish South America.* Cambridge University Press.

Bethell, L., and Roxborough, I. (1988). "Latin America between the Second World War and the Cold War: Some Reflections on the 1945–8 Conjuncture," *Journal of Latin American Studies* 20 (1): 167–89.

(1992). *Latin America between the Second World War and the Cold War, 1944–1948.* Cambridge University Press.

Blakemore, H. (1974). *British Nitrates and Chilean Politics, 1886–1896: North v Balmaceda.* London: Athlone Press.

(1986). "Chile from the War of the Pacific to the World Depression, 1880–1930." In Bethell, L. (ed.), *The Cambridge History of Latin America, Vol. V: c. 1870 to 1930.* Cambridge University Press.

Blaug, H. (1976). *Economic Theory in Retrospect,* 3d ed. Cambridge University Press.

Blomström, M. (1990). *Transnational Corporations and Manufacturing Exports from Developing Countries.* New York: United Nations.

Blomström, M., and Meller, P. (eds.) (1991). *Diverging Paths: Comparing a Century of Scandinavian and Latin American Economic Development.* Washington, D.C.: Inter-American Development Bank.

Bocco, A. M. (1987). *Auge petrolero, modernización y subdesarrollo: El Ecuador de los años setenta.* Quito: Corporación Editora Nacional.

Bogart, E. L. (1908). *The Economic History of the United States.* London: Longmans.

Boloña, C. (1981). "Tariff Policies in Peru, 1880–1980." D.Phil. dissertation, Oxford University.

Bonilla, H. (1985). "Peru and Bolivia from Independence to the War of the Pacific." In Bethell, L. (ed.), *The Cambridge History of Latin America, Vol. III: From Independence to c. 1870.* Cambridge University Press.

Booth, J. A. (1982). *The End and the Beginning—The Nicaraguan Revolution.* Boulder, Colo.: Westview.

Bourgade, E. de (1892). *Paraguay: The Land and the People. National Wealth and Commercial Capabilities.* London: George Philip.

Brading, D. (1978). *Haciendas and Ranchos in the Mexican Bajío: León 1700–1860.* Cambridge University Press.

Broadberry, S. N. (1986). *The British Economy between the Wars: A Macroeconomic Survey.* Oxford: Basil Blackwell.

Brockett, C. D. (1988). *Land, Power and Poverty: Agrarian Transformation and Political Conflict in Central America.* Boston: Unwin Hyman.

Brogan, C. (1984). *The Retreat from Oil Nationalism in Ecuador, 1976–1983.* London: Institute of Latin American Studies.

Brothers, D. S., and Solís, M. L. (1966). *Mexican Financial Development.* Austin: University of Texas Press.

Brown, J. (1979). *A Socio-Economic History of Argentina, 1776–1860.* Cambridge University Press.

Browning, D. (1971). *El Salvador: Landscape and Society.* Oxford: Oxford University Press.

Brundenius, C. (1984). *Revolutionary Cuba: The Challenge of Economic Growth with Equity.* Boulder, Colo.: Westview.

Brundenius, C., and Zimbalist, A. (1989). *The Cuban Economy: Measurement and Analysis of Socialist Performance.* Baltimore: Johns Hopkins University Press.

Bruno, M., Fischer, S., Helpman, E., and Liviatan, N. (eds.) (1991). *Lessons of Economic Stabilization and Its Aftermath.* Cambridge, Mass.: MIT Press.

Bruton, H. (1989). "Import Substitution." In Chenery, H., and Srinivasan, T. N. (eds.), *Handbook of Development Economics,* Vol. 2. Amsterdam: North-Holland.

Bryce, J. (1912). *South America: Observations and Impressions.* London: Macmillan.

Buiter, W. (1983). "Measurement of the Public Sector Deficit and the Implications for Policy Evaluation and Design," *IMF Staff Papers* 30 (2). Washington, D.C.

Bulmer-Thomas, I. (1965). *The Growth of the British Party System.* 2 vols. London: Baker.

Bulmer-Thomas, V. (1987). *The Political Economy of Central America since 1920.* Cambridge University Press.

(1988). *Studies in the Economics of Central America.* Basingstoke, Eng.: Macmillan; New York: St. Martin's.

(1990a). "Honduras since 1930." In Bethell, L. (ed.), *The Cambridge History of Latin America, Vol. VII: Latin America since 1930: Mexico, Central America and the Caribbean.* Cambridge University Press.

(1990b). "Nicaragua since 1930." In Bethell, L. (ed.), *The Cambridge History of Latin America, Vol. VII: Latin America since 1930: Mexico, Central America and the Caribbean*. Cambridge University Press.

Bulmer-Thomas, V., et al. (1992). *Central American Integration: Report for the Commission of the European Community*. Miami: University of Miami.

Bureau de Publicidad de la América Latina (1916–1917). *El 'Libro Azul' de Panamá*. Panama City: Bureau de Publicidad de la América Latina.

Bureau of the American Republics (1892a). *Handbook of Bolivia*. Washington, D.C.: Government Printing Office.

(1892b). *Handbook of Costa Rica*. Washington, D.C.: Government Printing Office.

(1892c). *Handbook of Ecuador*. Washington, D.C.: Government Printing Office.

(1892d). *Handbook of Haiti*. Washington, D.C.: Government Printing Office.

(1892e). *Handbook of Nicaragua*. Washington, D.C.: Government Printing Office.

(1892f). *Handbook of Paraguay*. Washington, D.C.: Government Printing Office.

(1892g). *Handbook of the Argentine Republic*. Washington, D.C.: Government Printing Office.

(1892h). *Handbook of Venezuela*. Washington, D.C.: Government Printing Office.

(1904). *Honduras: Geographical Sketch, Natural Resources, Laws, Economic Conditions, Actual Development, Prospects of Future Growth*. Washington, D.C.: Government Printing Office.

Burns, E. B. (1980). *The Poverty of Progress: Latin America in the Nineteenth Century*. Berkeley: University of California Press.

(1991). *Patriarch and Folk: The Emergence of Nicaragua 1798–1858*. Cambridge, Mass.: Harvard University Press.

Bushnell, D. (1970). *The Santander Regime in Gran Colombia*. Westport, Conn.: Greenwood.

Bushnell, D., and Macaulay, N. (1988). *The Emergence of Latin America in the Nineteenth Century*. New York: Oxford University Press.

Cantarero, L. A. (1949). "The Economic Development of Nicaragua, 1920–1947." Ph.D. dissertation, University of Iowa.

Cárdenas, E. (1984). "The Great Depression and Industrialization: The Case of Mexico." In Thorp, R. (ed.), *Latin America in the 1930s: The Role of the Periphery in World Crisis*. Oxford: Macmillan / St. Antony's College.

Cárdenas, E., and Manns, C. (1989). "Inflación y estabilización monetaria en México durante la revolución," *El Trimestre Económico* 56 (221): 57–79.

Cardoso, E. (1981). "Food Supply and Inflation," *Journal of Development Economics* 8 (3): 269–84.

(1991). "From Inertia to Megainflation: Brazil in the 1980s." In Bruno, M., Fischer, S., Helpman, E., and Liviatan, N. (eds.), *Lessons of Economic Stabilization and Its Aftermath*. Cambridge, Mass.: MIT Press.

Cardoso, E., and Helwege, A. (1992). *Latin America's Economy: Diversity, Trends and Conflicts*. Cambridge, Mass.: MIT Press.

Cardoso, F. H., and Brignoli, H. (1979a). *Historia económica de América Latina. Vol. 1: Sistemas agrarios e historia colonial*. Barcelona: Editorial Crítica.

(1979b). *Historia económica de América Latina. Vol. 2: Economías de exportación y desarrollo capitalista*. Barcelona: Editorial Crítica.

Cardoso, F. H., and Faletto, E. (1979). *Dependency and Development in Latin America*. Berkeley: University of California Press.

Cariaga, J. L. (1990). "Three Policy Experiments—Bolivia." In Williamson, J. (ed.), *Latin American Adjustment: How Much Has Happened?* Washington, D.C.: Institute for International Economics.

Carnoy, M. (1972). *Industrialization in a Latin American Common Market*. Washington, D.C.: Brookings Institution.

Carr, R. (1984). *Puerto Rico: A Colonial Experiment*. New York: New York University Press.

Carroll, H. (1975). *Report on the Island of Porto Rico*. New York: Arno Press.

Catão, L. (1991), "The International Transmission of Long Cycles between 'Core' and 'Periphery' Economies: A Case Study of Brazil and Mexico, c. 1870–1940." D.Phil. dissertation, Cambridge University.

Centro Español de Estudios de América Latina (CEDEAL) (1991). *Situación latinoamericana: Informes de coyuntura económica, política y social.* Vol. 1, no. 6. Madrid: Fundación CEDEAL.

CEPAL (1959). *El desarrollo económico de la Argentina,* 3 vols. Santiago, Chile: United Nations.

(1976). *América Latina: Relación de precios del intercambio.* Cuadernos Estadísticos de la Cepal. Santiago, Chile: United Nations.

(1978). *Series históricas del crecimiento de América Latina.* Cuadernos Estadísticos de la Cepal. Santiago, Chile: United Nations.

(1986). *La distribución personal del ingreso en el Gran Buenos Aires en el período 1974–1983,* Documento de Trabajo No. 23. Buenos Aires: CEPAL.

(1988). *Preliminary Overview of the Latin American Economy 1988.* Notas Sobre la Economía y el Desarrollo. Santiago, Chile: United Nations.

(1991). *Preliminary Overview of the Latin American and Caribbean Economy 1991.* Notas Sobre la Economía y el Desarrollo. Santiago, Chile: United Nations.

(1992). *Preliminary Overview of the Latin American and Caribbean Economy 1992.* Notas Sobre la Economía y el Desarrollo. Santiago, Chile: United Nations.

(1993). *Preliminary Overview of the Latin American and Caribbean Economy 1993.* Notas Sobre la Economía y el Desarrollo. Santiago, Chile: United Nations.

Cerdas Cruz, R. (1990). "Costa Rica since 1930." In Bethell, L. (ed.), *The Cambridge History of Latin America, Vol. VII: Latin America since 1930: Mexico, Central America and the Caribbean.* Cambridge University Press.

Chalmers, H. (1944). "Inter-American Trade Policy." In Harris, S. E. (ed.), *Economic Problems of Latin America.* New York: McGraw-Hill.

Chalmin, P. G. (1984). "The Important Trends in Sugar Diplomacy before 1914." In Albert, B., and Graves, A. (eds.), *Crisis and Change in the International Sugar Economy 1860–1914.* Norwich, Eng.: ISC Press.

Chenery, H. (1960). "Patterns of Industrial Growth," *American Economic Review* 50 (3): 624–54.

Chowning, M. (1990). "The Management of Church Wealth in Michoacán, Mexico, 1810–1856: Economic Motivations and Political Implications," *Journal of Latin American Studies* 22 (3): 459–96.

Clark, V., et al. (1975). *Porto Rico and Its Problems.* New York: Arno Press.

Clark, W. (1911). *Cotton Goods in Latin America, Part II.* US Dept of Commerce and Labor, Washington, D.C.: Government Printing Office.

Cline, W. R. (1978). "Benefits and Costs of Economic Integration in Central America." In Cline, W. R., and Delgado, E. (eds.), *Economic Integration in Central America.* Washington, D.C.: Brookings Institution.

Coatsworth, J. (1978). "Obstacles to Economic Growth in Nineteenth Century Mexico," *American Historical Review* 83 (1): 80–100.

(1981). *Growth against Development—The Economic Impact of Railroads in Porfirian Mexico.* Dekalb: Northern Illinois University Press.

Colburn, F. D. (1990). *Managing the Commanding Heights: Nicaragua's State Enterprises.* Berkeley: University of California Press.

Collier, S. (1986). *The Life, Music and Times of Carlos Gardel.* Pittsburgh, Pa.: University of Pittsburgh Press.

Conaghan, C., and Espinal, R. (1990). "Unlikely Transition to Uncertain Regimes? Democracy without Compromise in the Dominican Republic and Ecuador," *Journal of Latin American Studies* 22 (3): 553–74.

Connell-Smith, G. (1966). *The Inter-American System.* London: Oxford University Press.

Conniff, M. L. (1985). *Black Labor on a White Canal: Panama, 1904–1981.* Pittsburgh, Pa.: University of Pittsburgh Press.

Consejo Monetario Centroamericano (1991). *Boletín Estadístico 1991.* San José, Costa Rica: Consejo Monetario Centroamericano.

Corden, W. M. (1971). *The Theory of Protection.* Oxford: Clarendon Press.

Cortés Conde, R. (1985). "The Export Economy of Argentina, 1880–1920." In Cortés Conde, R., and Hunt, S. J. (eds.), *The Latin American Economies: Growth and the Export Sector, 1880–1930*. New York: Holmes & Meier.

(1986). "The Growth of the Argentine Economy c. 1870–1914." In Bethell, L. (ed.), *The Cambridge History of Latin America, Vol. V: c. 1870–1930*. Cambridge University Press.

Council of Foreign Bondholders (1931). *Annual Report*. London: Council of Foreign Bondholders.

Cowell, F. A. (1977). *Measuring Inequality*. Oxford: Philip Allan.

Cuddington, J. T., and Urzúa, C. M. (1989). "Trends and Cycles in the Net Barter Terms of Trade: A New Approach," *Economic Journal* 99 (396): 426–42.

Cukierman, A. (1988). "The End of High Israeli Inflation: An Experiment in Heterodox Stabilization." In Bruno, M., et al. (eds.), *Inflation Stabilization: The Experience of Israel, Argentina, Brazil, Bolivia and Mexico*. Cambridge, Mass.: MIT Press.

Cumberland, W. W. (1928). *Nicaragua: An Economic and Financial Survey*. Washington, D.C.: Government Printing Office.

Dalton, L. (1916). *Venezuela*. London: T. Fisher Unwin.

Dawson, F. G. (1990). *The First Latin American Debt Crisis: The City of London and the 1822–25 Loan Bubble*. New Haven, Conn.: Yale University Press.

Dean, W. (1969). *The Industrialization of São Paulo, 1880–1945*. Austin: University of Texas Press.

(1987). *Brazil and the Struggle for Rubber: A Study of Environmental History*. Cambridge University Press.

Deas, M. (1982). "The Fiscal Problems of Nineteenth-Century Colombia," *Journal of Latin American Studies* 14 (2): 287–328.

(1985). "Venezuela, Colombia and Ecuador: The First Half-Century of Independence." In Bethell, L. (ed.), *The Cambridge History of Latin America, Vol. III: From Independence to c. 1870*. Cambridge University Press.

(1986). "Colombia, Ecuador and Venezuela, c. 1880–1930." In Bethell, L. (ed.), *The Cambridge History of Latin America, Vol. V: c. 1870–1930*. Cambridge University Press.

Deas, M. (ed.) (1991). *Latin America in Perspective*. Boston: Houghton Mifflin.

De Franco, M., and Godoy, R. (1992). "The Economic Consequences of Cocaine Production in Bolivia: Historical, Local and Macroeconomic Perspectives," *Journal of Latin American Studies* 24 (2): 375–406.

de Janvry, A. (1990). *The Agrarian Question and Reformism in Latin America*. Baltimore: Johns Hopkins University Press.

Dell, S. (1966). *A Latin American Common Market?* London: Oxford University Press.

Denny, H. (1929). *Dollars for Bullets: The Story of American Rule in Nicaragua*. New York: Dial Press.

De Soto, H. (1987). *El otro sendero: La revolución informal*. Buenos Aires: Editorial Sudamericana.

de Vries, M. G. (1986). *The IMF in a Changing World*. Washington, D.C.: International Monetary Fund.

de Vylder, S. (1976). *Allende's Chile*. Cambridge University Press.

Diakosavvos, D., and Scandizzo, P. (1991). "Trends in the Terms of Trade of Primary Commodities, 1900–1982: The Controversy and Its Origins," *Economic Development and Cultural Change* 39 (2): 231–64.

Dias Carneiro, D. (1987). "Long-Run Adjustment, the Debt Crisis and the Changing Role of Stabilisation Policies in the Recent Brazilian Experience." In Thorp, R., and Whitehead, L. (eds.), *Latin American Debt and the Adjustment Crisis*. Basingstoke, Eng.: Macmillan / St. Antony's College.

Díaz-Alejandro, C. F. (1965). *Exchange Rate Devaluation in a Semi-Industrialized Country: The Experience of Argentina, 1955–1961*. Cambridge, Mass.: MIT Press.

(1970). *Essays on the Economic History of the Argentine Republic*. New Haven, Conn.: Yale University Press.

(1976). *Colombia (Foreign Trade Regimes and Economic Development)*. New York: National Bureau of Economic Research.

(1981). "Southern Cone Stabilization Plans." In Cline, W. R., and Weintraub, S. (eds.), *Economic Stabilization in Developing Countries*. Washington, D.C.: Brookings Institution.

(1984a). "Latin America in the 1930s." In Thorp, R. (ed.), *Latin America in the 1930s: The Role of the Periphery in World Crisis*. Basingstoke, Eng.: Macmillan / St. Antony's College.

(1984b). "Latin American Debt: I Don't Think We Are in Kansas Anymore," *Brookings Papers on Economic Activity*, 2.

Diederich, B. (1982). *Somoza and the Legacy of US Involvement in Central America*. London: Junction Books.

Dietz, J. L. (1986). *Economic History of Puerto Rico: Institutional Change and Capitalist Development*. Princeton, N.J.: Princeton University Press.

Dirección General de Estadística (México) (1933). *Censo industrial*. México, D.F.: Dirección General de Estadística.

Dirección General de Estadística y Censos (Costa Rica) (1930). *Anuario estadístico 1929*. San José: Dirección General de Estadística y Censos.

(1974). *Censo agropecuario*. San José: Dirección General de Estadística y Censos.

Domínguez, J. (1989). *To Make a World Safe for Revolution: Cuba's Foreign Policy*. Cambridge, Mass.: Harvard University Press.

Dore, E. (1988). *The Peruvian Mining Industry: Growth, Stagnation and Crisis*. Boulder, Colo.: Westview.

Downes, R. (1992). "Autos over Rails: How US Business Supplanted the British in Brazil, 1910–28," *Journal of Latin American Studies* 24 (3): 551–83.

Drake, P. W. (1989). *The Money Doctor in the Andes: The Kemmerer Missions, 1923–1933*. Durham, N.C.: Duke University Press.

Duncan, K., et al. (1977). *Land and Labour in Latin America: Essays on the Development of Agrarian Capitalism in the Nineteenth and Twentieth Centuries*. Cambridge University Press.

Dunkerley, J. (1982). *The Long War: Dictatorship and Revolution in El Salvador*. London: Junction Books.

(1984). *Rebellion in the Veins: Political Struggle in Bolivia 1952–1982*. London: Verso.

Eakin, M. (1989). *British Enterprise in Brazil: The St. John d'el Rey Mining Company and the Morro Velho Gold Mine, 1830–1960*. Durham, N.C.: Duke University Press.

Echeverri Gent, E. (1992). "Forgotten Workers: British West Indians and the Early Days of the Banana Industry in Costa Rica and Honduras," *Journal of Latin American Studies* 24 (2): 275–308.

ECLA (1949). *Economic Survey of Latin America, 1948*. New York: United Nations.

(1951). *Economic Survey of Latin America, 1949*. New York: United Nations.

(1956). *Study of Inter-American Trade*. New York: United Nations.

(1959). *Inter-American Trade: Current Problems*. New York: United Nations.

(1963). *Towards a Dynamic Development Policy for Latin America*. New York: United Nations.

(1965). *External Financing in Latin America*. New York: United Nations.

(1970). *Development Problems in Latin America*. Austin: University of Texas Press.

(1971). *Income Distribution in Latin America*. New York: United Nations.

ECLAC (1988). *ECLAC 40 Years (1948–1988)*. Santiago, Chile: United Nations.

(1989). *Anuario estadístico de América Latina y el Caribe,* 1988. Santiago, Chile: United Nations.

(1992). *Anuario estadístico de América Latina y el Caribe,* 1991. Santiago, Chile: United Nations.

Edel, M. (1969). *Food Supply and Inflation in Latin America*. New York: Praeger.

Eder, G. J. (1968). *Inflation and Development in Latin America: A Case History of Inflation and Stabilization in Bolivia*. Ann Arbor: University of Michigan.

Eder, P. (1912). *Colombia*. London: T. Fisher Unwin.

Edwards, S. (1984). "Coffee, Money and Inflation in Colombia," *World Development* 12 (11/12): 1107–17.

(1989). "Exchange Controls, Devaluations and Real Exchange Rates: The Latin American Experience," *Economic Development and Cultural Change* 37 (3): 457–94.

Edwards, S., and Cox Edwards, A. (1987). *Monetarism and Liberalization: The Chilean Experiment*. Chicago: University of Chicago Press.

Eichengreen, B., and Portes, R. (1988). *Settling Defaults in the Era of Bond Finance*. Birkbeck College, Discussion Paper in Economics, 1988/8.

El-Agraa, A. M. (1988). "The Theory of Economic Integration." In El-Agraa, A. M. (ed.), *International Economic Integration*. Basingstoke, Eng.: Macmillan.

El-Agraa, A. M., and Hojman, D. (1988). "The Andean Pact." In El-Agraa, A. M. (ed.), *International Economic Integration.* Basingstoke, Eng.: Macmillan.

Elías, V. (1992). *Sources of Growth: A Study of Seven Latin American Economies.* San Francisco: International Center for Economic Growth.

Enock, R. (1919). *Mexico.* London: T. Fisher Unwin.

Escudé, C. (1990). "US Political Destabilisation and Economic Boycott of Argentina during the 1940s." In Di Tella, G., and Watt, C. (eds.), *Argentina between the Great Powers, 1939–46.* Pittsburgh, Pa.: University of Pittsburgh Press.

Evans, P. (1979). *Dependent Development: The Alliance of Multinational, State and Local Capital in Brazil.* Princeton, N.J.: Princeton University Press.

Ewell, J. (1991). "Venezuela since 1930." In Bethell, L. (ed.), *The Cambridge History of Latin America, Vol. VIII: 1930 to the Present.* Cambridge University Press.

Fajnzylber, F. (1990). *Unavoidable Industrial Restructuring in Latin America.* Durham, N.C.: Duke University Press.

Farrands, C. (1982). "The Political Economy of the Multifibre Arrangement." In Stevens, C. (ed.), *EEC and the Third World: A Survey, Vol. II: Hunger in the World.* London: Hodder and Stoughton / ODI / Institute of Development Studies.

Fass, S. M. (1990). *Political Economy in Haiti: The Drama of Survival.* New Brunswick, N.J.: Transaction Publishers.

Feder, G. (1983). "On Exports and Economic Growth," *Journal of Development Economics* 12 (1/2): 59–73.

Fei, J., Ranis, G., and Kuo, S. (1979). *Growth with Equity: The Taiwan Case.* New York: Oxford University Press.

Feinberg, R. E. (1990). "How to Reverse the Defunding of Latin America by the Multilateral Lending Agencies." In Felix, D. (ed.), *Debt and Transfiguration? Prospects for Latin America's Economic Revival.* Armonk, N.Y.: M. E. Sharpe, Inc.

Felix, D., and Caskey, J. P. (1990). "The Road to Default: An Assessment of Debt Crisis Management in Latin America." In Felix, D. (ed.), *Debt and Transfiguration? Prospects for Latin America's Economic Revival.* Armonk, N.Y.: M. E. Sharpe, Inc.

Ferns, H. S. (1960). *Britain and Argentina in the Nineteenth Century.* Oxford: Clarendon Press.

Ferns, H. (1992). "The Baring Crisis Revisited," *Journal of Latin American Studies* 24 (2): 241–73.

Fetter, F. (1931). *Monetary Inflation in Chile.* Princeton, N.J.: Princeton University Press.

Ffrench-Davis, R. (1988). "The Foreign Debt Crisis and Adjustment in Chile: 1976–86." In Griffith-Jones, S. (ed.), *Managing World Debt.* New York: Harvester Wheatsheaf.

(1990). "Debt and Growth in Chile: Trends and Prospects." In Felix, D. (ed.), *Debt and Transfiguration? Prospects for Latin America's Economic Revival.* Armonk, N.Y.: M. E. Sharpe, Inc.

Ffrench-Davis, R., Muñoz, O., and Palma, J. G. (1994). "The Latin American Economies, 1950–1990." In Bethell, L. (ed.), *The Cambridge History of Latin America, Vol. VI: Latin America since 1930: Economy, Society and Politics,* Part 1. Cambridge University Press.

Fields, G. S. (1980). *Poverty, Inequality and Development.* Cambridge University Press.

Finch, M. H. J. (1981). *A Political Economy of Uruguay since 1870.* Basingstoke, Eng.: Macmillan.

(1988). "The Latin American Free Trade Association." In El-Agraa, A. M. (ed.), *International Economic Integration.* Basingstoke, Eng.: Macmillan.

Fischel, A. (1991). "Politics and Education in Costa Rica." Ph.D. dissertation, University of Southampton.

Fisher, J. (1985). *Commercial Relations between Spain and Spanish America in the Era of Free Trade, 1778–1796.* Liverpool: Centre for Latin American Studies, University of Liverpool.

Fishlow, A. (1972). "Origins and Consequences of Import Substitution in Brazil." In Di Marco, L. (ed.), *International Economics and Development.* New York: Academic Press.

(1973). "Some Reflections on Post-1964 Brazilian Economic Policy." In Stepan, A. (ed.), *Authoritarian Brazil: Origins, Policies, and Future.* New Haven, Conn.: Yale University Press.

(1991). "Some Reflections on Comparative Latin American Economic Performance and Policy." In Banuri, T. (ed.), *Economic Liberalization: No Panacea. The Experiences of Latin America and Asia.* Oxford: Clarendon Press.

Fitzgerald, E. V. K. (1976). *The State and Economic Development: Peru Since 1968.* Cambridge University Press.

Fitzgerald, H. (1992). *ECLA and the Formation of Latin American Economic Doctrine in the 1940s.* Working Paper Series, No. 106. The Hague: Institute of Social Studies.

Floyd, R. H., Gray, C., and Short, R. (1984). *Public Enterprise in Mixed Economies: Some Macroeconomic Aspects.* Washington, D.C.: International Monetary Fund.

Fodor, J. (1986). "The Origin of Argentina's Sterling Balances, 1939–43." In Di Tella, G., and Platt, D. C. M. (eds.), *The Political Economy of Argentina, 1880–1946.* Basingstoke, Eng.: Macmillan / St. Antony's College.

Fodor, J., and O'Connell, A. (1973). "La Argentina y la economía atlántica en la primera mitad del siglo XX," *Desarrollo Económico* 13 (49): 1–67.

Foner, P. S. (1963). *A History of Cuba and Its Relations with the United States, Vol. II: 1845–1895.* New York: International Publishers.

Ford, A. G. (1962). *The Gold Standard, 1880–1914: Britain v Argentina.* Oxford: Oxford University Press.

Fortín, C., and Anglade, C. (1985). *The State and Capital Accumulation in Latin America, Vol. I: Brazil, Chile, Mexico.* Pittsburgh, Pa.: University of Pittsburgh Press.

Foxley, A. (1983). *Latin American Experiments in Neo-Conservative Economics.* Berkeley: University of California Press.

Frank, A. G. (1969). *Capitalism and Underdevelopment in Latin America.* New York: Monthly Review Press.

Fritsch, W. (1988). *External Constraints on Economic Policy in Brazil, 1889–1930.* Basingstoke, Eng.: Macmillan.

Funkhouser, E. (1992). "Migration from Nicaragua: Some Recent Evidence," *World Development* 20 (8): 1209–18.

Furtado, C. (1963). *The Economic Growth of Brazil.* Berkeley: University of California Press.

(1976). *Economic Development of Latin America: A Survey from Colonial Times to the Cuban Revolution,* 2d ed. Cambridge University Press.

Gallo, E. (1986). "Argentina: Society and Politics, 1880–1916." In Bethell, L. (ed.), *The Cambridge History of Latin America, Vol. V: c. 1870 to 1930.* Cambridge University Press.

García, R. (1989). *Incipient Industrialization in an "Underdeveloped Country." The Case of Chile, 1845–1879.* Stockholm: Institute of Latin American Studies.

Gerchunoff, P. (1989). "Peronist Economic Policies, 1946–55." In Di Tella, G., and Dornbusch, R. (eds.), *The Political Economy of Argentina, 1946–83.* Basingstoke, Eng.: Macmillan.

Gilbert, A. J. (ed.) (1982). *Urbanization in Contemporary Latin America.* Chichester, Eng.: John Wiley.

Gleijeses, P. (1991). *Shattered Hope: The Guatemalan Revolution and the United States, 1944–1954.* Princeton, N.J.: Princeton University Press.

(1992). "The Limits of Sympathy: The United States and the Independence of Spanish America," *Journal of Latin American Studies* 24 (3): 481–505.

Gold, J. (1988). "Mexico and the Development of the Practice of the International Monetary Fund," *World Development* 16 (10): 1127–42.

Gonzales, M. J. (1989). "Chinese Plantation Workers and Social Conflict in Peru in the Late Nineteenth Century," *Journal of Latin American Studies* 21 (3): 385–424.

Goodman, D., and Hall, A. (eds.) (1991). *The Future of Amazonia: Destruction or Sustainable Development?* London: Macmillan.

Gootenberg, P. (1989). *Between Silver and Guano: Commercial Policy and the State in Post-Independence Peru.* Princeton, N.J.: Princeton University Press.

(1991). "North–South: Trade Policy, Regionalism and *Caudillismo* in Post-Independence Peru," *Journal of Latin American Studies* 23 (2): 273–308.

Gravil, R. (1970). "State Intervention in Argentina's Export Trade between the Wars," *Journal of Latin American Studies* 2 (2): 147–66.

Greenhill, R. (1977a). "The Brazilian Coffee Trade." In Platt, D. C. M. (ed.), *Business Imperialism, 1840–1930: An Inquiry Based on British Experience in Latin America.* Oxford: Clarendon Press.

(1977b). "Merchants and Latin American Trades: An Introduction." In Platt, D. C. M. (ed.), *Business Imperialism, 1840–1930: An Inquiry Based on British Experience in Latin America.* Oxford: Clarendon Press.

(1977c). "The Nitrate and Iodine Trades, 1880–1914." In Platt, D. C. M. (ed.), *Business Imperialism, 1840–1930: An Inquiry Based on British Experience in Latin America.* Oxford: Clarendon Press.

(1977d). "Shipping, 1850–1914." In Platt, D. C. M. (ed.), *Business Imperialism, 1840–1930: An Inquiry Based on British Experience in Latin America.* Oxford: Clarendon Press.

Greenhill, R., and Crossley, C. (1977). "The River Plate Beef Trade." In Platt, D. C. M. (ed.), *Business Imperialism, 1840–1930: An Inquiry Based on British Experience in Latin America.* Oxford: Oxford University Press.

Grieb, K. J. (1979). *Guatemalan Caudillo: The Regime of Jorge Ubico, Guatemala—1931 to 1944.* Athens: Ohio University Press.

Griffin, K. (1969). *Under-Development in Spanish America.* London: George Allen and Unwin Ltd.

Griffith-Jones, S. (1984). *International Finance and Latin America.* London: Croom Helm.

Griffith-Jones, S., Marcel, M., and Palma, G. (1987). *Third World Debt and British Banks: A Policy for Labour.* London: Fabian Society.

Grindle, M. (1986). *State and Countryside Development Policy and Agrarian Politics in Latin America.* Baltimore: Johns Hopkins University Press.

Grosse, R. (1989). *Multinationals in Latin America.* London: Routledge.

Ground, R. L. (1988). "The Genesis of Import Substitution in Latin America," *CEPAL Review*, No. 36: 179–203.

Grunwald, J., and Musgrove, P. (1970). *Natural Resources in Latin American Development.* Baltimore: Johns Hopkins University Press.

Guadagni, A. A. (1989). "Economic Policy during Illia's Period in Office." In Di Tella, G., and Dornbusch, R. (eds.), *The Political Economy of Argentina, 1946–83.* Basingstoke, Eng.: Macmillan.

Gudmundson, L. (1986). *Costa Rica before Coffee: Society and Economy on the Eve of the Export Boom.* Baton Rouge: Louisiana State University Press.

Guerra Borges, A. (1981). *Compendio de geografía económica y humana de Guatemala.* Guatemala City: Universidad de San Carlos.

Gupta, B. (1989). "Import Substitution of Capital Goods: The Case of Brazil 1929–1979." D.Phil. dissertation, University of Oxford.

Haber, S. (1989). *Industry and Underdevelopment: The Industrialisation of Mexico, 1890–1940.* Stanford, Calif.: Stanford University Press.

(1992). "Assessing the Obstacles to Industrialization: The Mexican Economy, 1830–1940," *Journal of Latin American Studies* 24 (1): 1–32.

Haddad, C. (1974). "Growth of Brazilian Real Output, 1900–47." Ph.D. dissertation, University of Chicago.

Hale, C. A. (1986). "Political and Social Ideas in Latin America, 1870–1930." In Bethell, L. (ed.), *The Cambridge History of Latin America, Vol. IV: c. 1870 to 1930.* Cambridge University Press.

Halperín Donghi, T. (1985). "Economy and Society in Post-Independence Spanish America." In Bethell, L. (ed.), *The Cambridge History of Latin America, Vol. III: From Independence to c. 1870.* Cambridge University Press.

Handelman, H., and Baer, W. (eds.) (1989). *Paying the Costs of Austerity in Latin America.* Boulder, Colo.: Westview.

Hanson, S. (1938). *Argentine Meat and the British Market.* Stanford, Calif.: Stanford University Press.
Harpelle, R. N. (1993). "The Social and Political Integration of West Indians in Costa Rica: 1930–50," *Journal of Latin American Studies* 25 (2): 103–20.
Harris, S. (1944). "Price Stabilization Programs in Latin America." In Harris, S. (ed.), *Economic Problems of Latin America.* New York: McGraw-Hill.
Harrod, R. S. (1951). *The Life of John Maynard Keynes.* London: Macmillan.
Haslip, J. (1971). *The Crown of Mexico: Maximilian and His Empress Carlota.* New York: Holt, Rinehart and Winston.
Heath, D., Erasmus, C., and Buechler, H. (1989). *Land Reform and Social Revolution in Bolivia.* New York: Praeger.
Herrera Canales, I. (1977). *El comercio exterior de México, 1821–1875.* Mexico, D.F.: Colegio de México.
Hewitt de Alcantara, C. (1976). *Modernizing Mexican Agriculture.* Geneva: UNRISD.
Hillman, J. (1988). "Bolivia and the International Tin Cartel, 1931–1941," *Journal of Latin American Studies* 20 (1): 83–110.
(1990). "Bolivia and British Tin Policy, 1939–1945," *Journal of Latin American Studies* 22 (2): 289–315.
Hirschman, A. O. (1963). *Journeys towards Progress: Studies of Economic Policy Making in Latin America.* New York: Twentieth Century Fund.
(1981). *Essays in Trespassing.* Cambridge University Press.
Hoetink, H. (1986). "The Dominican Republic, c. 1870–1930." In Bethell, L. (ed.), *The Cambridge History of Latin America, Vol. V: c. 1870 to 1930.* Cambridge University Press.
Holloway, T. (1980). *Immigrants on the Land: Coffee and Society in São Paulo, 1886–1934.* Chapel Hill: University of North Carolina Press.
Hood, M. (1975). *Gunboat Diplomacy 1895–1905: Great Power Pressure in Venezuela.* London: George Allen & Unwin.
Hopkins, A. G. (1994). "Informal Empire in Argentina: An Alternative View," *Journal of Latin American Studies* 26 (2).
Horn, P. V., and Bice, H. E. (1949). *Latin American Trade and Economics.* New York: Prentice-Hall.
Horsefield, J. K. (1969). *The International Monetary Fund 1945–1965. Vol. 1: Chronicle.* Washington, D.C.: International Monetary Fund.
Hughlett, L. J. (ed.) (1946). *Industrialization of Latin America.* New York: McGraw-Hill.
Humphreys, R. A. (1946). *The Evolution of Modern Latin America.* Oxford: Clarendon Press.
(1961). *The Diplomatic History of British Honduras.* Oxford: Oxford University Press.
(1981). *Latin America and the Second World War 1939–1942.* London: Athlone Press.
(1982). *Latin America and the Second World War 1942–1945.* London: Athlone Press.
Hunt, S. (1973). *Prices and Quantum Estimates of Peruvian Exports, 1830–1962.* Woodrow Wilson School Research Program in Economic Development, Discussion Paper No. 31. Princeton, N.J.: Princeton University.
(1985). "Growth and Guano in 19th Century Peru." In Cortés Conde, R., and Hunt, S. (eds.), *The Latin American Economies: Growth and the Export Sector, 1880–1930.* New York: Holmes and Meier.
Hurrell, A. (1991). "The Politics of Amazonian Deforestation," *Journal of Latin American Studies* 23 (1): 197–215.
Imlah, A. (1958). *Economic Elements of the Pax Britannica.* Cambridge University Press.
Instituto Brasileiro de Geografia e Estatística (IBGE) (1987). *Estatísticas históricas do Brasil.* Rio de Janeiro: IBGE.
Instituto de Relaciones Europeo-Latinoamericanas (IRELA) (1992). *Prospects for the Processes of Sub-Regional Integration in Central and South America.* Madrid: IRELA.
Inter-American Development Bank (IDB) (1981). *Economic and Social Progress in Latin America, 1980–81 Report.* Washington, D.C.: IDB.
(1982). *Economic and Social Progress in Latin America: The External Sector, 1982 Report.* Washington, D.C.: IDB.
(1983). *Economic and Social Progress in Latin America: The External Sector, 1983 Report.* Washington, D.C.: IDB.

(1984a). *Economic and Social Progress in Latin America: The External Sector, 1984 Report.* Washington, D.C.: IDB.

(1984b). *External Debt and Economic Development in Latin America: Background and Prospects.* Washington, D.C.: IDB.

(1986). *Economic and Social Progress in Latin America 1986 Report.* Washington, D.C.: IDB.

(1988). *Economic and Social Progress in Latin America 1988 Report.* Washington, D.C.: IDB.

(1989). *Economic and Social Progress in Latin America 1989 Report.* Washington, D.C.: IDB.

(1990). *Economic and Social Progress in Latin America 1990 Report.* Washington, D.C.: IDB.

(1991). *Economic and Social Progress in Latin America 1991 Report.* Washington, D.C.: IDB.

(1992). *Economic and Social Progress in Latin America 1992 Report.* Washington, D.C.: IDB.

(1993). *Economic and Social Progress in Latin America 1993 Report.* Washington, D.C.: IDB.

International Monetary Fund (1986a). *Government Finance Statistics Yearbook 1986.* Washington, D.C.: International Monetary Fund.

(1986b). *Yearbook of Balance of Payments Statistics 1986.* Washington, D.C.: International Monetary Fund.

(1987). *Yearbook of International Financial Statistics 1987.* Washington, D.C.: International Monetary Fund.

(1990). *Yearbook of International Financial Statistics 1990.* Washington, D.C.: International Monetary Fund.

James, E. W. (1945). "A Quarter Century of Road-Building in the Americas," *Bulletin of the Pan American Union* 79 (1): 609–18.

Jenkins, R. (1984). *Transnational Corporations and Industrial Transformation in Latin America.* Basingstoke, Eng.: Macmillan.

(1987). *Transnational Corporations and the Latin American Automobile Industry.* Basingstoke, Eng.: Macmillan.

Jones, C. (1977a). "Commercial Banks and Mortgage Companies." In Platt, D. C. M. (ed.), *Business Imperialism, 1840–1930: An Inquiry Based on British Experience in Latin America.* Oxford: Clarendon Press.

(1977b). "Insurance Companies." In Platt, D. C. M. (ed.), *Business Imperialism, 1840–1930: An Inquiry Based on British Experience in Latin America.* Oxford: Clarendon Press.

Jones, C. L. (1940). *Guatemala Past and Present.* Minneapolis: University of Minnesota Press.

Jorgensen, E., and Sachs, J. (1989). "Default and Renegotiation of Latin American Foreign Bonds in the Interwar Period." In Eichengreen, B., and Lindert, P. (eds.), *The International Debt Crisis in Historical Perspective.* Cambridge, Mass.: MIT Press.

Joseph, E. (1982). *Revolution from Without: Yucatán, Mexico and the United States, 1880–1924.* Cambridge University Press.

Joslin, D. (1963). *A Century of Banking in Latin America.* London: Oxford University Press.

Kahil, R. (1973). *Inflation and Economic Development in Brazil 1946–1963.* Oxford: Clarendon Press.

Kahler, M. (1990). "Orthodoxy and Its Alternatives: Explaining Approaches to Stabilization and Adjustment." In Nelson, J. M. (ed.), *Economic Crisis and Policy Choice: The Politics of Adjustment in the Third World.* Princeton, N.J.: Princeton University Press.

Karlsson, W. (1975). *Manufacturing in Venezuela: Studies on Development and Location.* Stockholm: Latinamerika-institutet i Stockholm.

Karnes, T. L. (1978). *Tropical Enterprise: Standard Fruit and Steamship Company in Latin America.* Baton Rouge: Louisiana State University Press.

Katz, F. (1981). *The Secret War in Mexico: Europe, the United States and the Mexican Revolution.* Chicago: University of Chicago Press.

Katz, J. M. (1987). *Technology Generation in Latin American Manufacturing Industries.* Basingstoke, Eng.: Macmillan.

Kaufman, E. (1988). *Crisis in Allende's Chile: New Perspectives.* New York: Praeger.

Kay, C. (1989). *Latin American Theories of Development and Underdevelopment.* London: Routledge.

Kelly, M., et al. (1988). *Issues and Developments in International Trade Policy.* Washington, D.C.: International Monetary Fund.

Kepner, C. (1936). *Social Aspects of the Banana Industry.* New York: Columbia University Press.

Kepner, C., and Soothill, J. (1935). *The Banana Empire: A Case Study in Economic Imperialism.* New York: Vanguard Press.

Kindleberger, C. (1987). *The World in Depression*. London: Penguin.

Kirsch, H. W. (1977). *Industrial Development in a Traditional Society: The Conflict of Entrepreneurship and Modernization in Chile*. Gainesville: University Presses of Florida.

Klarén, P. F. (1986). "The Origins of Modern Peru, 1880–1930." In Bethell, L. (ed.), *The Cambridge History of Latin America. Vol. V: c. 1870 to 1930*. Cambridge University Press.

Klein, H. S. (1982). *Bolivia: The Evolution of a Multi-Ethnic Society*. New York: Oxford University Press.

(1992). *Bolivia: The Evolution of a Multi-Ethnic Society*, 2d ed. New York: Oxford University Press.

Knape, J. (1987). "British Foreign Policy in the Caribbean Basin 1938–1945: Oil, Nationalism and Relations with the United States," *Journal of Latin American Studies* 19 (2): 279–94.

Knight, A. (1986a). *The Mexican Revolution: Vol. I: Porfirians, Liberals and Peasants*. Lincoln: University of Nebraska Press.

(1986b). *The Mexican Revolution: Vol. II: Counter-revolution and Reconstruction*. Lincoln: University of Nebraska Press.

(1990). "Mexico, c. 1930–46." In Bethell, L. (ed.), *The Cambridge History of Latin America, Vol. VII: Latin America since 1930: Mexico, Central America and the Caribbean*. Cambridge University Press.

Knight, F. (1990). *The Caribbean: The Genesis of a Fragmented Nationalism*, 2d ed. Oxford: Oxford University Press.

Kock-Petersen, S. A. (1946). "The Cement Industry." In Hughlett, L. J. (ed.), *Industrialization of Latin America*. New York: McGraw-Hill.

Koebel, W. H. (n.d.). *Central America*. New York: Scribner.

(1911). *Uruguay*. London: T. Fisher Unwin.

(1919). *Paraguay*. London: T. Fisher Unwin.

Korol, J. C., and Sábato, H. (1990). "Incomplete Industrialization: An Argentine Obsession," *Latin American Research Review* 25 (1): 7–30.

Kravis, I. B., Heston, A. W., and Summers, R. (1978). "Real GDP Per Capita for More Than One Hundred Countries," *Economic Journal* 88 (349): 215–42.

Krehm, W. (1984). *Democracies and Tyrannies of the Caribbean*. Westport, Conn.: Lawrence Hill.

Krueger, A. (1978). *Liberalization Attempts and Consequences*. New York: National Bureau of Economic Research.

Kuczynski, P. (1988). *Latin American Debt*. Baltimore: Johns Hopkins University Press.

Kuznets, S. (1965). *Modern Economic Growth*. New Haven, Conn.: Yale University Press.

Lafeber, W. (1978). *The Panama Canal: The Crisis in Historical Perspective*. New York: Oxford University Press.

Langley, L. (1968). *The Cuban Policy of the United States: A Brief History*. New York: Wiley.

Langley, L. D. (1983). *The Banana Wars: An Inner History of American Empire 1900–1934*. Lexington: University Press of Kentucky.

Larraín, F., and Selowsky, H. (1991). *The Public Sector and the Latin American Crisis*. San Francisco: ICS Press.

Latham, A. J. H. (1987). *The International Economy and the Undeveloped World 1856–1914*. London: Croom Helm.

Latin America Bureau (LAB) (1987). *The Great Tin Crash, Bolivia and the World Tin Market*. London: LAB.

Latin Finance (1992). *Privatization in Latin America*. Coral Gables, Fla.: Latin American Financial Publications, Inc.

League of Nations (1925). *Statistical Yearbook*. Geneva: League of Nations.

(1926). *Statistical Yearbook*. Geneva: League of Nations.

(1927). *Statistical Yearbook*. Geneva: League of Nations.

(1928). *Statistical Yearbook*. Geneva: League of Nations.

(1930). *International Yearbook of Agricultural Statistics, 1929/30*. Geneva: League of Nations.

(1931). *Statistical Yearbook*. Geneva: League of Nations.

(1933). *International Yearbook of Agricultural Statistics, 1932/3*. Geneva: League of Nations.

(1938). *Public Finance*. Geneva: League of Nations.

(1945). *Statistical Yearbook, 1942/4*. Geneva: League of Nations.

Leff, N. H. (1968). *The Brazilian Capital Goods Industry 1929–1964.* Cambridge, Mass.: Harvard University Press.

(1982a). *Underdevelopment and Development in Brazil, Vol. I: Economic Structure and Change, 1822–1947.* London: George Allen & Unwin.

(1982b). *Underdevelopment and Development in Brazil, Vol. II: Reassessing the Obstacles to Economic Development.* London: George Allen & Unwin.

León Gómez, A. (1978). *El escándalo del ferrocarril. Ensayo histórico.* Tegucigalpa: Imprenta Soto.

Levi, D. (1987). *The Prados of São Paulo: An Elite Family and Social Change, 1840–1930.* Athens: University of Georgia Press.

Levin, J. (1960). *The Export Economies: Their Pattern of Development in Historical Perspective.* Cambridge, Mass.: Harvard University Press.

Levine, V. (1914). *South American Handbooks: Colombia.* London: Pitman.

Lewis, A. (1978). *Growth and Fluctuations, 1870–1913.* London: Allen & Unwin.

Lewis, C. (1986). "Industry in Latin America before 1930." In Bethell, L. (ed.), *The Cambridge History of Latin America, Vol. IV: c. 1870 to 1930.* Cambridge University Press.

Lewis, C. (1983). *British Railways in Argentina 1857–1914.* London: Institute of Latin American Studies.

Lewis, P. H. (1990). *The Crisis of Argentine Capitalism.* Chapel Hill: University of North Carolina Press.

(1991). "Paraguay since 1930." In Bethell, L. (ed.), *The Cambridge History of Latin America, Vol. VIII: Latin America since 1930: Spanish South America.* Cambridge University Press.

Lewis, W. A. (1989). "The Roots of Development Theory." In Chenery, H., and Srinivasan, T. N. (eds.), *Handbook of Development Economics.* Amsterdam: North-Holland.

Libby, D. C. (1991). "Proto-Industrialization in a Slave Society: The Case of Minas Gerais," *Journal of Latin American Studies* 23 (1): 1–35.

Lieuwen, E. (1965). *Venezuela.* London: Oxford University Press.

(1985). "The Politics of Energy in Venezuela." In Wirth, J. D. (ed.), *Latin American Oil Companies and the Politics of Energy.* Lincoln: University of Nebraska Press.

Lin, C. (1988). "East Asia and Latin America as Contrasting Models," *Economic Development and Cultural Change* 36 (3): S153–S197.

Lindo-Fuentes, H. (1990). *Weak Foundations: The Economy of El Salvador in the Nineteenth Century, 1821–1898.* Berkeley: University of California Press.

Linke, L. (1962). *Ecuador: Country of Contrasts.* London: Oxford University Press.

Little, I., Scitovsky, T., and Scott, M. (1970). *Industry and Trade in Some Developing Countries: A Comparative Study.* London: Oxford University Press.

Lockhart, J., and Schwartz, S. B. (1983). *Early Latin America: A History of Colonial Spanish America and Brazil.* Cambridge University Press.

Lomnitz, L., and Pérez-Lizaur, M. (1987). *A Mexican Elite Family 1820–1980.* Princeton, N.J.: Princeton University Press.

Looney, R. E. (1985). *Economic Policymaking in Mexico: Factors Underlying the 1982 Crisis.* Durham, N.C.: Duke University Press.

Love, J. (1994). "Economic Ideas and Ideologies in Latin America since 1930." In Bethell, L. (ed.), *The Cambridge History of Latin America, Vol. VI: Latin America since 1930: Economy, Society and Politics,* Part 1. Cambridge University Press.

Lundahl, M. (1979). *Peasants and Poverty: A Study of Haiti.* London: Croom Helm.

(1992). *Politics or Markets? Essays on Haitian Underdevelopment.* London: Routledge.

Lynch, J. (1985a). "The Origins of Spanish American Independence." In Bethell, L. (ed.), *The Cambridge History of Latin America, Vol. III: From Independence to c. 1870.* Cambridge University Press.

(1985b). "The River Plate Republics from Independence to the Paraguayan War." In Bethell, L. (ed.), *The Cambridge History of Latin America, Vol. III: From Independence to c. 1870.* Cambridge University Press.

Macario, S. (1964). "Protectionism and Industrialization in Latin America," *Economic Bulletin for Latin America* 9 (1): 62–101.

Macbean, A., and Nguyen, T. (1987). "International Commodity Agreements: Shadow and Substance," *World Development* 15 (5): 575–90.

McBeth, J. S. (1983). *Juan Vicente Gómez and the Oil Companies in Venezuela, 1908–1935.* Cambridge University Press.

McClintock, M. (1985). *The American Connection, Vol. II, State Terror and Popular Resistance in Guatemala.* London: Zed Books.

McCloskey, D., and Zecker, J. (1981). "How the Gold Standard Worked, 1880–1913." In McCloskey, D. (ed.), *Enterprise and Trade in Victorian Britain.* London: Allen & Unwin.

McCreery, D. (1983). *Development and the State in Reforma Guatemala 1871–1885.* Athens: Center for International Studies, Ohio University.

MacDonald, C. A. (1990). "The Braden Campaign and Anglo-American Relations in Argentina, 1945–6." In Di Tella, G., and Watt, C. (eds.), *Argentina between the Great Powers, 1939–46.* Pittsburgh, Pa.: University of Pittsburgh Press.

McDowall, D. (1988). *The Light: Brazilian Traction, Light and Power Company 1899–1945.* Toronto: University of Toronto Press.

McGreevey, W. P. (1971). *An Economic History of Colombia, 1845–1930.* Cambridge University Press.

(1985). "The Transition to Economic Growth in Colombia." In Cortés Conde, R., and Hunt, S. (eds.), *The Latin American Economies: Growth and the Export Sector, 1880–1930.* New York: Holmes and Meier.

Machinea, J. L., and Fanelli, J. M. (1988). "Stopping Hyperinflation: The Case of the Austral Plan in Argentina, 1985–87." In Bruno, M., et al. (eds.), *Inflation Stabilization: The Experiences of Israel, Argentina, Brazil, Bolivia and Mexico.* Cambridge, Mass.: MIT Press.

McKinnon, R. I. (1973). *Money and Capital in Economic Development.* Washington, D.C.: Brookings Institution.

McLure, C., et al. (1990). *The Taxation of Income from Business and Capital in Colombia.* Durham, N.C.: Duke University Press.

Maddison, A. (1985). *Two Crises: Latin America and Asia, 1929–38 and 1973–83.* Paris: Organization for Economic Cooperation and Development.

(1991). "Economic and Social Conditions in Latin America, 1913–1950." In Urrutia, M. (ed.), *Long Term Trends in Latin American Economic Development.* Washington, D.C.: Inter-American Development Bank.

Maizels, A. (1963). *Industrial Growth and World Trade.* Cambridge University Press.

(1970). *Growth and Trade: An Abridged Version of Industrial Growth and World Trade.* Cambridge University Press.

(1992). *Commodities in Crisis.* Oxford: Clarendon Press.

Major, J. (1990). "The Panama Canal Zone, 1904–79." In Bethell, L. (ed.), *The Cambridge History of Latin America, Vol. VII: Latin America since 1930: Mexico, Central America and the Caribbean.* Cambridge University Press.

Mamalakis, M., and Reynolds, C. W. (1965). *Essays on the Chilean Economy.* Homewood, Ill.: Irwin.

Manchester, A. (1933). *British Preeminence in Brazil, Its Rise and Decline: A Study in European Expansion.* Chapel Hill: University of North Carolina Press.

Marcel, M. (1989). "Privatización y finanzas públicas: El caso de Chile, 1985–88," *Colección Estudios CIEPLAN* 26 (June): 5–30.

Marichal, C. (1989). *A Century of Debt Crises in Latin America: From Independence to the Great Depression.* Princeton, N.J.: Princeton University Press.

Marshall, O. (1991). *European Immigration and Ethnicity in Latin America: A Bibliography.* London: Institute of Latin American Studies.

Mathieson, J. A. (1988). "Problems and Prospects of Export Diversification: Case Studies–Dominican Republic." In Paus, E. (ed.), *Struggle against Dependence: Nontraditional Export Growth in Central America and the Caribbean.* Boulder, Colo.: Westview.

May, S., and Plaza, G. (1958). *The United Fruit Company in Latin America*. Washington, D.C.: National Planning Association.

Maynard, G. (1989). "Argentina: Macroeconomic Policy, 1966–73." In Di Tella, G., and Dornbusch, R. (eds.), *The Political Economy of Argentina, 1946–83*. Basingstoke, Eng.: Macmillan / St. Antony's College.

Mecham, J. L. (1961). *The United States and Inter-American Security, 1889–1960*. Austin: University of Texas Press.

Meier, G. M. (1984). *Pioneers in Development*. New York: Oxford University Press / World Bank.

(1987). *Pioneers in Development (Second Series)*. New York: Oxford University Press / World Bank.

Mendels, F. (1972). "Proto-industrialization: The First Phase of the Industrialization Process," *Journal of Economic History* 32 (2): 241–61.

Menjívar, R. (1980). *Acumulación originaria y desarrollo del capitalismo en El Salvador*. San José, Costa Rica: EDUCA.

Mesa-Lago, C. (1978). *Social Security in Latin America: Pressure Groups, Stratification and Inequality*. Pittsburgh, Pa.: University of Pittsburgh Press.

(1981). *The Economy of Socialist Cuba: A Two-Decade Appraisal*. Albuquerque: University of New Mexico Press.

(1991). *Social Security and Prospects for Equity in Latin America*. Washington, D.C.: World Bank.

Meyer, M. C., and Sherman, W. L. (1979). *The Course of Mexican History*. New York: Oxford University Press.

Miller, S. (1990). "Mexican Junkers and Capitalist Haciendas, 1810–1910: The Arable Estate and the Transition to Capitalism between the Insurgency and the Revolution," *Journal of Latin American Studies* 22 (2): 229–63.

Millot, J., Silva, C., and Silva, L. (1973). *El desarrollo industrial del Uruguay de la crisis de 1929 a la postguerra*. Montevideo: Instituto de Economía, Universidad de la República.

Mills, G. J. (n.d.). *South American Handbooks: Argentina*. London: Pitman.

(1914). *South American Handbooks: Chile*. London: Pitman.

Mitchell, B. (1980). *European Historical Statistics*. London: Macmillan.

(1983). *International Historical Statistics: Australasia and Americas*. London: Macmillan.

(1988). *British Historical Statistics*, 2d ed. London: Macmillan.

(1993). *International Historical Statistics. The Americas 1750–1988*. Basingstoke, Eng.: Macmillan.

Modiano, E. M. (1988). "The Cruzado First Attempt: The Brazilian Stabilization Program of February 1986." In Bruno, M., et al. (eds.), *Inflation Stabilization: The Experiences of Israel, Argentina, Brazil, Bolivia and Mexico*. Cambridge, Mass.: MIT Press.

Molina, F. (1851). *Bosquejo de la República de Costa Rica*. New York: S. W. Benedict.

Molina Chocano, G. (1982). *Estado liberal y desarrollo capitalista en Honduras*. Tegucigalpa: Universidad Nacional de Honduras.

Morales, J. A. (1988). "Inflation Stabilization in Bolivia." In Bruno, M., et al. (eds.), *Inflation Stabilization: The Experiences of Israel, Argentina, Brazil, Bolivia and Mexico*. Cambridge, Mass.: MIT Press.

Morawetz, D. (1981). *Why the Emporer's New Clothes Are Not Made in Colombia: A Case Study in Latin American and East Asian Manufactured Exports*. New York: Oxford University Press.

Moreno Fraginals, M. (1986). "Plantation Economies and Societies in the Spanish Caribbean, 1860–1930." In Bethell, L. (ed.), *The Cambridge History of Latin America, Vol. IV: c. 1870–1930*. Cambridge University Press.

Moya Pons, F. (1985). "Haiti and Santo Domingo: 1790–c. 1870." In Bethell, L. (ed.), *The Cambridge History of Latin America, Vol. III: From Independence to c. 1870*. Cambridge University Press.

(1990a). "The Dominican Republic since 1930." In Bethell, L. (ed.), *The Cambridge History of Latin America, Vol. VII: Latin America since 1930: Central America and the Caribbean*. Cambridge University Press.

(1990b). "Import-Substitution Industrialization Policies in the Dominican Republic, 1925–61," *Hispanic American Historical Review* 70 (4): 539–77.

Mulhall, M. G., and Mulhall, E. T. (1885). *Handbooks of the River Plate*. London: Trubner & Co.

Munro, D. (1964). *Intervention and Dollar Diplomacy in the Caribbean 1900–1921.* Princeton, N.J.: Princeton University Press.

Nickson, A. (1989). "The Overthrow of the Stroessner Regime: Re-establishing the Status Quo," *Bulletin of Latin American Research* 8 (2): 185–209.

Ocampo, J. A. (1984). *Colombia y la economía mundial 1830–1910.* Bogotá: FEDESAROLLO.

(1984b). "The Colombian Economy in the 1930s." In Thorp, R. (ed.), *Latin America in the 1930s: The Role of the Periphery in World Crisis.* Basingstoke, Eng.: Macmillan / St. Antony's College.

(1987). "Crisis and Economic Policy in Colombia, 1980–5." In Thorp, R., and Whitehead, L. (eds.), *Latin American Debt and the Adjustment Crisis.* Basingstoke, Eng.: Macmillan / St. Antony's College.

(1990). "Import Controls, Prices and Economic Activity in Colombia," *Journal of Development Economics* 32 (2): 369–87.

(1991). "The Transition from Primary Exports to Industrial Development in Colombia." In Blömstrom, M., and Meller, P. (eds.), *Diverging Paths: Comparing a Century of Scandinavian and Latin American Economic Development.* Washington, D.C.: Inter-American Development Bank.

Ocampo, J. A., and Montenegro, S. (1984). *Crisis mundial, protección e industrialización: Ensayos de historia económica colombiana.* Bogotá: Fondo Editorial CEREC.

O'Connell, A. (1984). "Argentina into the Depression: Problems of an Open Economy." In Thorp, R. (ed.), *Latin America in the 1930s: The Role of the Periphery in World Crisis.* Basingstoke, Eng.: Macmillan / St. Antony's College.

Oddone, J. A. (1986). "The Formation of Modern Uruguay, c. 1870–1930." In Bethell, L. (ed.), *The Cambridge History of Latin America, Vol. V: c. 1860–1930.* Cambridge University Press.

Ohkawa, K., and Rosovsky, R. (1973). *Japanese Economic Growth: Trend Acceleration in the Twentieth Century.* Stanford, Calif.: Stanford University Press.

Oribe Stemmer, J. E. (1989). "Freight Rates in the Trade between Europe and South America, 1840–1914." *Journal of Latin American Studies* 21 (1): 23–59.

Ortega, L. (1990). "El proceso de industrialización en Chile, 1850–1970." Paper presented at the 10th World Congress of Economic History. Leuven.

Ortiz, G. (1991). "Mexico beyond the Debt Crisis: Toward Sustainable Growth with Price Stability." In Bruno, M., Fischer, S., Helpman, E., and Liviatan, N. (eds.), *Lessons of Economic Stabilization and Its Aftermath.* Cambridge, Mass.: MIT Press.

Palma, G. (1979). "Growth and Structure of Chilean Manufacturing Industry from 1830 to 1935." Ph.D. dissertation, Cambridge University.

(1984). "From an Export-Led to an Import-Substituting Economy: Chile 1914–39." In Thorp, R. (ed.), *Latin America in the 1930s: The Role of the Periphery in World Crisis.* Basingstoke, Eng.: Macmillan / St. Antony's College.

Pan-American Union (1952). *The Foreign Trade of Latin America Since 1913.* Washington, D.C.: Pan-American Union.

Parkin, V. (1991). *Chronic Inflation in an Industrialising Economy: The Brazilian Experience.* Cambridge University Press.

Pastor, M. (1991). "Bolivia: Hyperinflation, Stabilisation and Beyond," *Journal of Development Studies* 27 (2): 211–37.

Paus, E. (1988). *Struggle against Dependence: Nontraditional Export Growth in Central America and the Caribbean.* Boulder, Colo.: Westview.

(1989). "Direct Foreign Investment and Economic Development in Latin America: Perspectives for the Future," *Journal of Latin American Studies* 21 (2): 221–39.

Pederson, L. (1966). *The Mining Industry of the Norte Chico, Chile.* Evanston, Ill.: Northwestern University.

Peek, P., and Standing, G. (1982). *State Policies and Migration: Studies in Latin America and the Caribbean.* London: Croom Helm.

Peláez, C. (1972). *Historia de industrialização brasileira.* Rio de Janeiro: APEC.

Peña, F. (1992). "The MERCOSUR and Its Prospects: An Option for Competitive Insertion in the World Economy." In Instituto de Relaciones Europeo-Latinoamericanas (IRELA), *Prospects for the Processes of Sub-Regional Integration in Central and South America.* Madrid: IRELA.

Peñaloza Cordero, L. (1983). *Nueva historia económica de Bolivia de la independencia a los albores de la guerra del Pacífico.* La Paz: Editorial Los Amigos del Libro.

Pérez-López, J. (1974). "An Index of Cuban Industrial Output, 1950–58." Ph.D. dissertation, State University of New York at Albany.

Pérez-López, J. F. (1991). "Bringing the Cuban Economy into Focus: Conceptual and Empirical Challenges," *Latin American Research Review* 26 (3): 7–53.

Perloff, H. S. (1950). *Puerto Rico's Economic Future: A Study in Planned Development.* Chicago: University of Chicago Press.

Petrecolla, A. (1989). "Unbalanced Development, 1958–62." In Di Tella, G., and Dornbusch, R. (eds.), *The Political Economy of Argentina, 1946–83.* Basingstoke, Eng.: Macmillan / St. Antony's College.

Phelps, D. M. (1936). *Migration of Industry to South America.* New York: McGraw-Hill.

Philip, G. (1982). *Oil and Politics in Latin America: Nationalist Movements and State Companies,* Cambridge University Press.

Pinder, J. (1991). *European Community: The Building of a Union.* Oxford: Oxford University Press.

Platt, D. C. M. (1971). "Problems in the Interpretation of Foreign Trade Statistics before 1914," *Journal of Latin American Studies* 3 (2): 119–30.

(1972). *Latin America and British Trade 1806–1914.* London: Adam & Charles Black.

Platt, D. C. M. (ed.) (1977). *Business Imperialism, 1840–1930: An Inquiry Based on British Experience in Latin America.* Oxford: Clarendon Press.

Portes, A., Castells, M., and Benton, L. (eds.) (1989). *The Informal Economy: Studies in Advanced and Less Developed Countries.* Baltimore: Johns Hopkins University Press.

Potash, R. (1969). *The Army and Politics in Argentina, 1928–45: Yrigoyen to Perón.* Stanford, Calif.: Stanford University Press.

(1980). *The Army and Politics in Argentina, 1945–62: Perón to Frondizi.* Stanford, Calif.: Stanford University Press.

Potash, R. A. (1983). *The Mexican Government and Industrial Development in the Early Republic: The Banco de Avío.* Amherst, Mass.: Stanford.

Powell, A. (1991). "Commodity and Developing Country Terms of Trade: What Does the Long Run Show?" *Economic Journal* 101 (409): 1485–96.

Prado, L. (1991). "Commercial Capital, Domestic Market and Manufacturing in Imperial Brazil: The Failure of Brazilian Economic Development in the XIXth Century." Ph.D. dissertation, University of London.

Programa Regional de Empleo para América Latina y el Caribe (PREALC) (1990). *Ventas Informales. Relaciones con el sector moderno.* Santiago, Chile: PREALC.

Psacharopoulos, G., et al. (1993). *Poverty and Income Distribution in Latin America: The Story of the 1980s.* Washington, D.C.: World Bank.

Rabe, S. (1988). *Eisenhower and Latin America: The Foreign Policy of Anticommunism.* Chapel Hill: University of North Carolina Press.

Ramos, J. (1986). *Neoconservative Economics in the Southern Cone of Latin America, 1973–1983.* Baltimore: Johns Hopkins University Press.

Ramos Mattei, A. (1984). "The Growth of the Puerto Rican Sugar Industry under North American Domination: 1899–1910." In Albert, B., and Graves, A. (eds.), *Crisis and Change in the International Sugar Economy 1860–1914.* Norwich, Eng.: ISC Press.

Ramsett, D. (1969). *Regional Industrial Development in Central America: A Case Study of the Integration Industries Scheme.* New York: Praeger.

Randall, L. (1977). *A Comparative Economic History of Latin America, 1500–1914. Vol. I: Mexico.* New York: Institute of Latin American Studies, Columbia University.

(1987). *The Political Economy of Venezuelan Oil.* New York: Praeger.

Rangel, D. (1970). *Capital y desarrollo: El rey petróleo.* 2 vols. Caracas: Universidad Central de Venezuela.

Ranis, G. (1981). "Challenges and Opportunities Posed by Asia's Superexporters: Implications for Manufactured Exports from Latin America." In Baer, W., and Gillis, M. (eds.), *Export Diversification and the New Protectionism: The Experiences of Latin America.* Champaign: Bureau of Economic and Business Research, University of Illinois.

Ranis, G., and Orrock, L. (1985). "Latin American and East Asian NICs: Development Strategies Compared." In Durán, E. (ed.), *Latin America and the World Recession.* Cambridge University Press / Royal Institute of International Affairs.

Reed, N. (1964). *The Caste War of Yucatán.* Stanford, Calif.: Stanford University Press.

Regalsky, A. M. (1989). "Foreign Capital, Local Interests and Railway Development in Argentina: French Investments in Railways, 1900–1914," *Journal of Latin American Studies* 21 (3): 425–52.

Remmer, K. (1986). "The Politics of Economic Stabilisation: IMF Standby Programs in Latin America, 1954–84," *Comparative Politics* 19 (6): 1–24.

Reynolds, C. W. (1965). "Development Problems of an Export Economy: The Case of Chile and Copper." In Mamalakis, M., and Reynolds, C. W., *Essays on the Chilean Economy.* Homewood, Ill.: Irwin.

Rippy, J. F. (1945). *Historical Evolution of Hispanic America.* New York: Appleton-Century-Crofts, Inc.

(1959). *British Investments in Latin America 1822–1949: A Case Study in the Operations of Private Enterprise in Retarded Regions.* Minneapolis: University of Minnesota Press.

Rock, D. (1986). "Argentina in 1914: The Pampas, the Interior, Buenos Aires." In Bethell, L. (ed.), *The Cambridge History of Latin America, Vol. V:c. 1870 to 1930.* Cambridge University Press.

(1987). *Argentina 1516–1987: From Spanish Colonization to Alfonsín.* Berkeley: University of California Press.

(1991). "Argentina, 1930–46." In Bethell, L. (ed.), *The Cambridge History of Latin America, Vol. VIII: Latin America since 1930: Spanish South America.* Cambridge University Press.

Rockland, H. A. (1970). *Sarmiento's Travels in the United States in 1847.* Princeton, N.J.: Princeton University Press.

Roddick, J. (1988). *The Dance of the Millions: Latin America and the Debt Crisis.* London: Latin America Bureau.

Rodríguez, L. (1985). *The Search for Public Policy: Regional Politics and Public Finance in Ecuador, 1830–1940.* Berkeley: University of California Press.

Rodríguez, M. (1991). "Public Sector Behavior in Venezuela." In Larraín, F., and Selowsky, M. (eds.), *The Public Sector and the Latin American Crisis.* San Francisco: ICS Press.

Roemer, M. (1970). *Fishing for Growth: Export-Led Development in Peru, 1950–1967.* Cambridge, Mass.: Harvard University Press.

Roett, R., and Sacks, R. S. (1991). *Paraguay: The Personalist Legacy.* Boulder, Colo.: Westview.

Ros, J. (1987). "Mexico from the Oil Boom to the Debt Crisis: An Analysis of Policy Responses to External Shocks, 1978–85." In Thorp, R., and Whitehead, L. (eds.), *Latin American Debt and the Adjustment Crisis.* Basingstoke, Eng.: Macmillan / St. Antony's College.

Rosenberg, M. (1983). *Las luchas por el seguro social en Costa Rica.* San José: Editorial Costa Rica.

Rosenzweig Hernández, F. (1989). *El desarrollo económico de México 1800–1910.* Toluca, Mex.: El Colegio Mexiquense / Instituto Tecnológico Autónomo de México.

Rowe, J. (1965). *Primary Commodities in International Trade.* Cambridge University Press.

Saborio, S. (1992). *The Premise and the Promise: Free Trade in the Americas.* Washington, D.C.: Overseas Development Council.

Sachs, J. (1985). "External Debt and Macroeconomic Performance in Latin American and East Asian NICs," *Brookings Papers* 2.

Sachs, J. D. (1989). *Development Country Debt and the World Economy.* Chicago: University of Chicago Press.

Sahota, G. S. (1990). *Poverty Theory and Policy: A Study of Panama.* Baltimore: Johns Hopkins University Press.

St. John, S. (1888). *Hayti or the Black Republic.* London: Smith Elder.

Salazar-Carrillo, J. (1982). *The Structure of Wages in Latin American Manufacturing Industries.* Miami: Florida International University.

Salvucci, R. J. (1987). *Textiles and Capitalism in Mexico: An Economic History of the Obrajes, 1539–1840.* Princeton, N.J.: Princeton University Press.

Samper, M. (1990). *Generations of Settlers: Rural Households and Markets on the Costa Rican Frontier, 1850–1935.* Boulder, Colo.: Westview.

Sánchez-Albórnoz, N. (1977). *La población de América Latina desde los tiempos precolombianos al año 2000.* Madrid: Alianza Universidad.

(1986). "The Population of Latin America, 1850–1930." In Bethell, L. (ed.), *The Cambridge History of Latin America, Vol. IV: c. 1870–1930.* Cambridge University Press.

Sanderson, S. (1981). *The Transformation of Mexican Agriculture: International Structure and the Politics of Rural Change.* Princeton, N.J.: Princeton University Press.

Sandilands, R. (1990). *The Life and Political Economy of Lauchlin Currie: New Dealer, Presidential Adviser and Development Economist.* Durham, N.C.: Duke University Press.

Scammell, W. M. (1980). *The International Economy since 1945.* Basingstoke, Eng.: Macmillan.

Schneider, J. (1981). "Terms of Trade Between France and Latin America, 1826–1856: Causes of Increasing Economic Disparities?" In Bairoch, P., and Lévy-Leboyer, M. (eds.), *Disparities in Economic Development since the Industrial Revolution.* Basingstoke, Eng.: Macmillan.

Schneider, R. M. (1991). *Order and Progress: A Political History of Brazil.* Boulder, Colo.: Westview.

Schoonover, T. D. (1991). *The United States in Central America, 1860–1911: Episodes of Social Imperialism and Imperial Rivalry in the World System.* Durham, N.C.: Duke University Press.

Selowsky, M. (1979). *Who Benefits from Government Expenditure? A Case Study of Colombia.* New York: Oxford University Press / World Bank.

Serrano, M. (1992). *Common Security in Latin America: The 1967 Treaty of Tlatelolco.* London: Institute of Latin American Studies.

Shaw, E. S. (1973). *Financial Deepening in Economic Development.* New York: Oxford University Press.

Sheahan, J. (1987). *Patterns of Development in Latin America: Poverty, Repression, and Economic Strategy.* Princeton, N.J.: Princeton University Press.

Short, R. P. (1984). "The Role of Public Enterprise; An International Statistical Comparison." In Floyd, R. H., Gray, C., and Short, R., *Public Enterprise in Mixed Economies: Some Macroeconomic Aspects.* Washington, D.C.: International Monetary Fund.

Singer, M. (1969). *Growth, Equality and the Mexican Experience.* Austin: University of Texas Press.

Sjaastad, L. A. (1989). "Argentine Economic Policy, 1976–81." In Di Tella, G., and Dornbusch, R. (eds.), *The Political Economy of Argentina, 1946–83.* Basingstoke, Eng.: Macmillan / St. Antony's College.

Sklair, L. (1989). *Assembling for Development: The Maquila Industry in Mexico and the United States.* Boston: Unwin Hyman.

Smith, P. (1969). *Politics and Beef in Argentina's Patterns of Conflict and Change.* New York: Columbia University Press.

Smith, R. (1972). *The United States and Revolutionary Nationalism in Mexico, 1916–32.* Chicago: University of Chicago Press.

Smith, R. F. (1986). "Latin America, the United States and the European Powers, 1830–1930." In Bethell, L. (ed.), *The Cambridge History of Latin America, Vol. IV: c. 1870 to 1930.* Cambridge University Press.

Solís, L. (1983). *La realidad económica mexicana: Retrovisión y perspectivas.* Mexico, D.F.: Siglo Veintiuno.

Solomou, S. (1990). *Phases of Economic Growth 1850–1973: Kondratieff Waves and Kuznets Swings.* Cambridge University Press.

The South American Handbook, 1924. London: South American Publications.

Spender, J. (1930). *Westman Pearson, First Viscount Cowdray.* London: Cassell.

Spraos, J. (1983). *Inequalising Trade?* Oxford: Clarendon Press.

Squier, E. G. (1856). *Notes on Central America.* London: Samper Low.

Staley, E. (1944). *World Economic Development.* Montreal: International Labour Office.

Stallings, B. (1987). *Banker to the Third World: US Portfolio Investment in Latin America 1900–1986.* Berkeley: University of California Press.

Stein, S. (1957). *The Brazilian Cotton Manufacture.* Cambridge, Mass.: Harvard University Press.

Stewart, W. (1964). *Keith and Costa Rica: The Biography of Minor Cooper Keith, American Entrepreneur.* Albuquerque: University of New Mexico Press.

Strachan, H. W. (1976). *Family and Other Business Groups in Economic Development: The Case of Nicaragua.* New York: Praeger.
Stubbs, J. (1985). *Tobacco on the Periphery: A Case Study in Cuban Labour History, 1860–1958.* Cambridge University Press.
Sunkel. O. (1982). *Un siglo de historia económica de Chile, 1830–1930: Dos ensayos y una bibliografía.* Madrid: Ediciones Cultura Hispánica.
Sunkel, O., and Cariola, C. (1985). "The Growth of the Nitrates Industry and Socio-economic Change in Chile, 1880–1930." In Cortés Conde, R., and Hunt, S. (eds.), *The Latin American Economies: Growth and the Export Sector, 1880–1930.* New York: Holmes and Meier.
Swerling, B. (1949). *International Control of Sugar, 1918–1941.* Stanford, Calif.: Stanford University Press.
Syrquin, M. (1988). "Patterns of Structural Change." In Chenery, H., and Srinivasan, T. (eds.), *Handbook of Development Economics,* vol. 1. Amsterdam: North-Holland.
Taylor, C. C. (1948). *Rural Life in Argentina.* Baton Rouge: Louisiana State University Press.
Ten Kate, A., and Wallace, R. B. (1980). *Protection and Economic Development in Mexico.* Westmead, Eng.: Gower.
Thiesenhusen, W. C. (1989). *Searching for Agrarian Reform in Latin America.* Boston: Unwin Hyman.
Thomas, H. (1971). *Cuba or the Pursuit of Freedom.* London: Eyre & Spottiswoode.
Thomas, J. (1992). *Informal Economic Activity.* New York and London: Harvester Wheatsheaf.
Thomas, V. (1985). *Linking Macroeconomic and Agricultural Policies for Adjustment with Growth: the Colombian Experience.* Baltimore: Johns Hopkins University Press.
Thompson, A. (1992). "Informal Empire? An Exploration in the History of Anglo-Argentine Relations, 1810–1914," *Journal of Latin American Studies* 24 (2): 419–36.
Thomson, G. (1985). "Protectionism and Industrialization in Mexico, 1821–1854." In Abel, C., and Lewis, C., *Latin America: Economic Imperialism and the State.* London: Athlone Press.
(1989). *Puebla de los Angeles: Industry and Society in a Mexican City, 1700–1850.* Boulder, Colo.: Westview.
Thorp, R. (1967). "Inflation and Orthodox Economic Policy in Peru," *Bulletin of the Oxford University Institute of Economics and Statistics* 29 (3): 185–210.
(1971). "Inflation and the Financing of Economic Development." In Griffin, K. (ed.), *Financing Development in Latin America.* Basingstoke, Eng.: Macmillan.
(1986). "Latin America and the International Economy from the First World War to the World Depression." In Bethell, L. (ed.), *The Cambridge History of Latin America, Vol. IV: c. 1870 to 1930.* Cambridge University Press.
(1991). *Economic Management and Economic Development in Peru and Colombia.* London: Macmillan.
(1992). "A Reappraisal of the Origins of Import Substituting, Industrialisation, 1930–50," *Journal of Latin American Studies* 24 (Quincentenery Suppl.): 181–98.
(1994). "The Latin American Economies, 1939–c. 1950." In Bethell, L. (ed.), *The Cambridge History of Latin America, Vol. VI: Latin America since 1930: Economy, Society and Politics,* Part I. Cambridge University Press.
Thorp, R. (ed.) (1984). *Latin America in the 1930s: The Role of the Periphery in World Crisis.* Basingstoke, Eng.: Macmillan / St. Antony's College.
Thorp, R., and Bertram, G. (1978). *Peru 1890–1977: Growth and Policy in an Open Economy.* Basingstoke, Eng.: Macmillan.
Thorp, R., and Whitehead, L. (eds.) (1979). *Inflation and Stabilisation in Latin America.* Basingstoke, Eng.: Macmillan / St. Antony's College.
(1987). *Latin American Debt and the Adjustment Crisis.* Basingstoke, Eng.: Macmillan / St. Antony's College.
Thoumi, F. E. (1989). *Las exportaciones intrarregionales y la integración latinoamericana y del Caribe en perspectiva.* Washington, D.C.: Banco Interamericano de Desarrollo.
Torre, J. C., and Riz, L. de (1991). "Argentina since 1946." In Bethell, L. (ed.), *The Cambridge History of Latin America, Vol. VIII: Latin America since 1930: Spanish South America.* Cambridge University Press.

Travis, C. (1990). *A Guide to Latin American and Caribbean Census Material: A Bibliography and Union List.* London: British Library / Standing Conference of National and University Libraries / Institute of Latin American Studies.

Trebat, T. (1983). *Brazil's State-Owned Enterprises, A Case Study of the State as Entrepreneur.* Cambridge University Press.

Tregarthen, G. (1897). *The Story of the Nations: Australia.* London: T. Fisher Unwin.

Triffin, R. (1944). "Central Banking and Monetary Management in Latin America." In Harris, J. (ed.), *Economic Problems of Latin America.* New York: McGraw-Hill.

Truslow, F. A. (1951). *Report on Cuba.* Baltimore: Johns Hopkins University Press.

Tulchin, J. (1971). *The Aftermath of War: World War I and US Policy toward Latin America.* New York: New York University Press.

Tyler, W. (1976). *Manufactured Export Expansion and Industrialization in Brazil.* Tubingen: Mohr.

(1983). "The Anti-Export Bias in Commercial Policies and Export Performance: Some Evidence from Recent Brazilian Experience." *Weltwirtschaftliches Archiv* 119 (1): 97–107.

United Nations (1986). *World Comparisons of Purchasing Power and Real Product for 1980.* New York: United Nations.

Urrutia, M. (1985). *Winners and Losers in Colombia's Economic Growth of the 1970s.* New York: Oxford University Press / World Bank.

Urrutia, M., and Arrubla, M. (eds.) (1970). *Compendio de estadísticas históricas de Colombia.* Bogotá: University Nacional de Colombia.

Vaitsos, C. (1974). *Intercountry Income Distribution and Transnational Enterprises.* Oxford: Oxford University Press.

(1978). "Crisis in Regional Economic Cooperation (Integration) among Developing Countries: A Survey," *World Development* 6 (6): 719–70.

Van Dormael, A. (1978). *Bretton Woods: Birth of a Monetary System.* London: Macmillan.

Vedovato, C. (1986). *Politics, Foreign Trade and Economic Development: A Study of the Dominican Republic.* London: Croom Helm.

Véliz, C. (1961). *Historia de la marina mercante de Chile.* Santiago: Ediciones de la Universidad de Chile.

Vernon, R. (1981). "State-owned Enterprises in Latin American Exports." In Baer, W., and Gillis, M. (eds.), *Export Diversification and the New Protectionism.* Cambridge, Mass.: National Bureau of Economic Research.

Versiani, F. (1979). *Industrial Investment in an "Export" Economy: The Brazilian Experience before 1914.* London: Institute of Latin American Studies.

(1984). "Before the Depression: Brazilian Industry in the 1920s." In Thorp, R. (ed.), *Latin America in the 1930s: The Role of the Periphery in World Crisis.* Basingstoke, Eng.: Macmillan / St. Antony's College.

Villela, A., and Suzigan, W. (1977). *Política do governo e crescimento da economia brasileira.* Rio de Janeiro: IPEA/INPES.

Viotti da Costa, E. (1986). "Brazil: The Age of Reform, 1870–1889." In Bethell, L. (ed.), *The Cambridge History of Latin America, Vol. V: c. 1870 to 1930.* Cambridge University Press.

Vivian, E. (1914). *South American Handbooks: Peru.* London: Pitman.

Wachter, S. (1976). *Latin American Inflation: The Structuralist-Monetarist Debate.* Lexington, Mass.: Lexington Books.

Wadsworth, F. (1982). "La deforestación, muerte del Canal de Panamá." In Heckadon Moreno, S., and McKay, A. (eds.), *Colonización y destrucción de bosques en Panamá.* Panama City: Asociación Panemeña de Antropología.

Walle, P. (1914). *Bolivia. Its People and Its Resources. Its Railways, Mines and Rubber-Forests.* London: T. Fisher Unwin Ltd.

Wallich, H. (1944). "Fiscal Policy and the Budget." In Harris, S. (ed.), *Economic Problems of Latin America.* New York: McGraw-Hill.

(1950). *Monetary Problems of an Export Economy.* Cambridge, Mass.: Harvard University Press.

Watkins, V. (1967). *Taxes and Tax Harmonization in Central America*. Cambridge, Mass.: Harvard University Press.

Webster, C. K. (ed.) (1938). *Britain and the Independence of Latin America, 1812–1830*. 2 vols. Oxford: Oxford University Press.

Weeks, J. (1985). *The Economies of Central America*. New York: Holmes and Meier.

Weeks. J., and Zimbalist, A. (1991). *Panama at the Crossroads: Economic Development and Political Change in the Twentieth Century*. Berkeley: University of California Press.

Welch, J. H. (1993). "The New Face of Latin America: Financial Flows, Markets and Institutions in the 1990s," *Journal of Latin American Studies* 25 (1): 1–24.

Wells, J. (1979). "Brazil and the Post-1973 Crisis in the International Economy." In Thorp, R., and Whitehead, L. (eds.), *Inflation and Stabilisation in Latin America*. Basingstoke, Eng.: Macmillan.

(1987). *Empleo en América Latina: Una búsqueda de opciones*. Santiago, Chile: PREALC.

Weston, A. (1982). "Who Is More Preferred? An Analysis of the New Generalised System of Preferences." In Stevens, C. (ed.), *EEC and the Third World: A Survey*, vol. 2. London: Overseas Development Institute.

White, A. (1973). *El Salvador*. London: Ernest Benn Ltd.

Whitehead, L. (1987). "The Adjustment Process in Chile: A Comparative Perspective." In Thorp, R., and Whitehead, L. (eds.), *Latin American Debt and the Adjustment Crisis*. Basingstoke, Eng.: Macmillan / St. Antony's College.

(1991). "Bolivia since 1958." In Bethell, L. (ed.), *The Cambridge History of Latin America, Vol. VIII: Latin America since 1930: Spanish South America*. Cambridge University Press.

(1994). "State Organization in Latin America since 1930." In Bethell, L. (ed.), *The Cambridge History of Latin America, Vol. VI: Latin America since 1930: Economy, Society and Politics*, Part 2. Cambridge University Press.

Wickizer, C. (1943). *The World Coffee Economy with Special Reference to Control Schemes*. Stanford, Calif.: Stanford University Press.

Wilcox, M., and Rines, G. (1917). *Encyclopaedia of Latin America*. New York: Encyclopaedia Amazona Corporation.

Wilkie, J. W. (1974). *Statistics and National Policy*, supplement 3. Los Angeles: University of California.

(1985). *Statistical Abstract of Latin America*, 23. Los Angeles: University of California.

(1990). *Statistical Abstract of Latin America*, 28. Los Angeles: University of California.

(1993). *Statistical Abstract of Latin America*, 31, Part 1. Los Angeles: University of California.

Williams, G. (1991). *The Welsh in Patagonia: The State and the Ethnic Community*. Cardiff: University of Wales Press.

Williams, J. (1920). *Argentine International Trade under Inconvertible Paper Money, 1880–1900*. Cambridge, Mass.: Harvard University Press.

Williams, R. E. (1986). *Export Agriculture and the Crisis in Central America*. Chapel Hill: University of North Carolina Press.

Williams, R. W. (1916). *Anglo-American Isthmian Diplomacy, 1815–1915*. London: Oxford University Press.

Williamson, J. W. (1990). *Latin American Adjustment: How Much Has Happened?* Washington, D.C.: Institute for International Economics.

Winters, L. A. (1990). "The Road to Uruguay," *Economic Journal* 100 (403): 1288–1303.

Woodward, R. L. (1985). "Central America from Independence to c. 1870." In Bethell, L. (ed.), *The Cambridge History of Latin America, Vol. III: From Independence to c. 1870*. Cambridge University Press.

World Bank (1950). *The Basis of a Development Program for Colombia*. Baltimore: Johns Hopkins University.

(1980). *World Tables*, 2d ed. Washington, D.C.: International Bank for Reconstruction and Development / World Bank / Oxford University Press.

(1983). *World Tables*, 3d ed. Washington, D.C.: International Bank for Reconstruction and Development / World Bank / Oxford University Press.

(1984). *World Development Report 1984*. Washington, D.C.: International Bank for Reconstruction and Development / World Bank / Oxford University Press.

(1986). *World Development Report 1986*. Washington, D.C.: International Bank for Reconstruction and Development / World Bank / Oxford University Press.

(1987). *World Development Report 1987*. Washington, D.C.: International Bank for Reconstruction and Development / World Bank / Oxford University Press.

(1989). *World Development Report 1989*. Washington, D.C.: International Bank for Reconstruction and Development / World Bank / Oxford University Press.

(1990). *World Development Report 1990*. Washington, D.C.: International Bank for Reconstruction and Development / World Bank / Oxford University Press.

(1991a). *Social Indicators of Development 1990*. Washington, D.C.: World Bank.

(1991b). *World Development Report 1991*. Washington, D.C.: International Bank for Reconstruction and Development / World Bank / Oxford University Press.

(1991c). *World Tables 1991*. Washington, D.C.: International Bank for Reconstruction and Development / World Bank / Oxford University Press.

(1992). *World Development Report 1992*. Washington, D.C.: World Bank.

(1993). *World Development Report 1993*. Washington, D.C.: International Bank for Reconstruction and Development / World Bank / Oxford University Press.

Wythe, G. (1945). *Industry in Latin America*. New York: Columbia University Press.

Yotopoulos, P. A. (1989). "The (Rip)Tide of Privatization: Lessons from Chile," *World Development* 17 (5): 683–702.

Young, D. (1966). *Member for Mexico: A Biography of Weetman Pearson, First Viscount Cowdray*. London: Cassell.

Young, J. P. (1925). *Central American Currency and Finance*. Princeton, N.J.: Princeton University Press.

Zimbalist, A. (1992). "Teetering on the Brink: Cuba's Current Economic and Political Crisis," *Journal of Latin American Studies* 24 (2): 407–18.

Zuvekas, C., and Luzuriaga, C. (1983). *Income Distribution and Poverty in Rural Ecuador 1950–1979*. Tempe: Center for Latin American Studies, Arizona State University.

READING 2

Economic Development Theory and Policy in Latin America: The Second World War to the Present

DILMUS D. JAMES
University of Texas—El Paso

In attempting to describe how economic development theory has influenced Latin America over the past five decades, space constraints dictate that the scope be confined to the main streams of thought in that area and to those ideas that have exercised considerable impact on policy formulation and implementation in the region. Many tributaries, even important ones, receive little or no attention,[1] and the interaction of economic theory with political and sociological development theories must await a lengthier treatment. The following three sections focus on structuralism, neoliberalism, and neostructuralism, respectively, and the chapter concludes with a brief speculation on some future elements that may be incorporated into economic development theory and policy in Latin America.

I. STRUCTURALISM

The field of economic development was in its formative stage after World War II, a period that was extremely conducive to state-led development strategies. The "visible hand" of state participation in economic affairs was clearly evident. There was the impressive economic performance period of "accidental-Keynesianism" (Peterson and Estenson 1992, 784) in the United States during the war and the Cold War aftermath. Gradually Keynesian policies became purposeful and dominant in many developed countries. The rapid growth of the USSR during the 1950s and 1960s also affected development thinking, as did the remarkable economic recovery of war-torn Europe. In addition, it was not lost on students of eco-

[1]The chief casualties are Marxist development theory and the dependency school of thought, which was heavily influenced by Marxist economics. Although extremely popular in Latin American universities during the 1960s and 1970s, the effect of these perspectives on Latin American development policy was either episodic—albeit extremely important episodes occurred—or indirect.

nomic development that Latin America had experienced spurts of industrial growth when sporadic balance of payments crises, the depression of the 1930s, or the two world wars forced the region to rely on its own resources.[2]

Leading development economists during the post–World War II era, such as Albert Hirschman, Gunnar Myrdal, Hla Myint, Ragnar Nurkse, Raul Prebisch, Rosenstein-Rodan, and Hans Singer, while holding diverse views, posed arguments that supported some form of state planning in Third World nations. Even models that called for patiently building up preconditions (Walter Rostow) or capital accumulation to dry up a large pool of surplus labor (Arthur Lewis) tempted planners to try to nudge the process along by state-activated measures.[3] Economic development texts emphasized the presence of externalities, discontinuities, and disequilibria in developing economies, and policy instruments focused on choice of production technique, investment criteria, sectoral sequencing (balanced versus unbalanced growth), and overall programming and planning methods. Economic planning was a major component of development literature.[4]

Such were the broad outlines of general economics and, more specifically, development economics during the 1950s and 1960s. By far, however, the most important figure in our story is Raul Prebisch, who along with Hans Singer (1950, working independently) saw the long-term decline in the terms of trade of raw commodity exporting countries as a cornerstone for policies needed for the economic development of Latin America and other developing regions.[5] Prebisch believed that he had established a convincing empirical foundation for demonstrating a secular decline in the terms of trade for raw commodity exports vis à vis manufactured imports and he explained the phenomenon by pointing to (1) a competitive market for raw commodities, as opposed to an oligopolistic one for manufactured goods, (2) protectionist policies by mature industrial (or "center") economies targeting raw-commodity intensive products, (3) taxes by wealthier countries biased against the same types of products, and (4) low-income elasticities for these products. Prebisch was optimistic about increases in productivity in Latin America's raw commodity sector, but the decreased unit costs, due to the conditions just cited, meant that importing countries, mainly developed nations, would reap the benefits in the form of lower commodity prices.

In addition to the belief that the secular terms of trade were declining, Prebisch and his followers, many of whom were associated with the United Nations Economic Commission for Latin America (ECLA),[6] stressed the supply-side bottlenecks such as (1) agricultural production, (2) the provision of infrastructure, (3) the availability of foreign exchange, and (4) tax revenue (inelastic with respect to changes in income). Because these problems were

---

[2]For more on how such events affected Latin America during the 1930s, see the collection of essays in Thorp (1984); for more on the 1940s, see Diaz-Alejandro (1984).

[3]A review of the early ideas of these economists, except Rostow, can be found in Higgins (1959). Higgins's second edition (1968) contains a critique of Rostow's stages of economic development thesis.

[4]Meier (1995, 556) mentioned the following as being general introductions to development planning: Dobb (1960), W. Arthur Lewis (1966), Jan Tinberegen (1967), Griffin and Enos (1971), and Michael P. Todaro (1971).

[5]See Prebisch (1949, 1959) for what are perhaps the best presentations of his terms of trade arguments.

[6]The organization is now the Economic Commission for Latin America and the Caribbean with the English acronym, ECLAC.

seen to be rooted in the prevailing structure of economic, social, political, and cultural forces, all heavily conditioned by historical experience in the region, the term *structuralism* was applied to the body of thought associated with the Prebisch/ECLA school.[7]

Structuralists championed several measures by which developing (or "periphery") countries could extricate themselves from their backward situation. Among the domestic measures were, according to Foxley, "(1) land reform, (2) the reorientation of public development programs toward small producers, (3) increasing expenditures in housing, health, and education, and (4) generous wage policies" (1983, 13–14). Among policies directed toward external economic relations, Prebisch, as director of the United Nations Conference on Trade and Development (UNCTAD), pushed for regional integration of developing countries and global schemes for stabilizing raw commodity prices.

By far, however, the most central policy instrument was import-substitution-industrialization (ISI). As the term implies, the objective was to encourage domestic production of industrial products heretofore imported. A whole range of measures were employed, including tariff protection, quotas, import licenses, easier access to credit, subsidized interest rates, tax rebates, preferential government purchases, subsidized utility rates, and skewed provision of infrastructure, all targeting the industrial sector. In addition, domestic currencies were often overvalued, which encouraged the importation of capital goods and other productive inputs in order to stimulate import substitution in consumer products. Price controls on basic agricultural products were frequently employed, which had the effect of skewing the internal terms of trade further in favor of the industrial sector. The development model that emerged was state led and inward looking.

The ISI model showed impressive results in terms of economic growth. During the ISI period, roughly from 1950 to 1975, economic growth in real terms exceeded 6 percent. Fairly early on, however, shortcomings began surfacing. The conscious channeling of resources to industrial pursuits, combined with an overvalued domestic currency, had palpable negative impacts on the agricultural sector, especially on agricultural exports and other traditional export products. Initially, entrepreneurs expanded the production of goods for which technology and skill-level requirements were fairly simple and for which a large proportion of inputs were obtainable domestically. As these products were exhausted, industrialization edged progressively toward products requiring more sophisticated skills and material inputs, which meant (1) a wider difference between domestic and international prices and (2) a greater reliance on imported inputs. The protected "hothouse" economic environment is often cited as a cause for poor gains in efficiency—the wide protective umbrella not only dampened incentives but protected legions of losers as well as bona fide infant industry candidates. Furthermore, protected losers furnished downstream inputs to potential winners, thus retarding the efficiency of the entire industrial system.

By emphasizing one of the most capital-intensive sectors, the creation of productive job opportunities lagged and income distribution remained heavily biased toward the upper strata of society. Indeed, despite a very impressive rate of growth for two-and-a-half decades, surplus labor in the region was reduced only marginally and the inegalitarian pattern of income distribution was altered even less. Inflation in most Latin American nations was inordinately high by international comparison, and balance of payments difficulties

[7]Illustrative of the sizable literature on structuralism are Baer (1962), Furtado (1964), Baer (1972), Rodriguez (1980), Gurrieri (1982), Arndt (1985), Hodara (1987), and Kay (1989).

were prevalent. Political chinks in the system arose when ISI began to move into the production of capital goods, which disturbed those already unfavorably disposed to the ISI model. This move also did not sit well with industrialists concentrating on consumer goods who were importing capital goods and technology from abroad.[8]

ISI, even in its early days, did not escape criticism. In the 1960s, Prebisch and the ECLA had misgivings as to the excessive bias against industrial exports that ISI implementation exhibited.[9] From the very beginning, orthodox economists had been critical of ISI on the general proposition that state interventions resulted in market distortions and moved away from Ricardian-based specialization along the lines of comparative advantage. Two disputes were especially spirited: the root causes of inflation in Latin America and the behavior of the terms of trade of raw-commodity exporting countries over the long term. As to inflation, the structuralists emphasized the role of supply-side deficiencies whereas the more traditional, neoclassical economists stressed excessive government spending and growth in the quantity of money. The controversy over terms of trade continues to this day with definitional, statistical, and conceptual disagreements involved.[10]

II. NEOLIBERALISM

The 1970s and 1980s witnessed a sea of changes in economic theory, development economics, and Latin American economic policy. Many of the theoretical underpinnings of the "new classical economics," as the body of thought is often called, were in place in the late 1960s—cornerstones included monetarism, the concept of a "natural" rate of unemployment, and a synthesis between macro and micro economics in which the former could be explained largely by the precepts of the latter. Later "rational expectations" were added to the arsenal. The new classical economics represents a sophisticated resurrection of earlier classical economics in the neoclassical tradition that built on many of the analytical devices (but with different interpretations) that had been generated by Keynesian analysis. The Latin American strain of this school of economics is ordinarily labeled "neoliberalism."[11]

The scene was set by a constellation of historical events. There was major dissatisfaction with Keynesian economics due to prolonged high rates of unemployment in most of Western Europe and "stagflation" in the United States. Supply-side shocks in the 1970s drew attention to the unbalanced preoccupation with aggregate demand by Keynesian economists. The inefficiencies that were becoming evident in centrally planned economies supported a more market-driven economic model, a perception bolstered by the then current interpretation that the East Asian "superexporters" had attained success by eschewing

---

[8]On this point, see Bastos (1995).

[9]See Kay (1989, Chapter 2) and literature cited therein.

[10]Baer (1967) has a good early survey of the inflation argument; for a more recent summary see Kay (1989, Chapter 2). Bath and James (1976) review the early criticisms of the declining terms of trade thesis; for a more recent review of the controversy, see Diakosavvas and Scandizzo (1991).

[11]There is plenty of room for confusion since the term *neoconservative* was in vogue in Latin America and some have used *monetarism* and *neomonetarism*. It appears, however, that *neoliberalism* has become the designation of choice.

state intervention and relying heavily on unfettered market signals. Conservative governments came to power in the United States, United Kingdom, and other nations; a proliferation of think-tank institutions was spawned to further market-oriented economic policies,[12] and the influence of the International Monetary Fund and World Bank, institutions that became the main repositories of new classical economists, began to rise.[13]

The economics of the neoclassical counter-revolution tends to be ahistorical and to abstract from particular cultural and social conditions, tendencies that support a conviction that the "scientific," value-free aspects of economic analysis, has universal application. The behavioral aspects posited by neoclassical microeconomists loom large in the scheme of things and the private, profit-seeking firm is the primary unit of analysis. Rational behavior is posited, as well as smooth, continuous functional relations that eliminate problems for marginal substitution. Dynamic macroeconomic analysis is typically based on reductionist assumptions derived from microeconomic foundations and is frequently achieved through the employment of comparative statistics. Neoclassical methodology relies heavily on abstract mathematical models pointing the way to a single equilibrium that optimizes a given economic variable (efficiency, profit, consumer utility, welfare, and so on).[14] Economic growth is seen as a spontaneous by-product of establishing the proper incentives at the microlevel.[15]

To a large extent economic development as a subdiscipline of economics, in both academe and in practice, was reduced to getting prices right through market forces. As Gerald Meier described the new configurations of development economics:

> Criticisms came to be directed at a widening range of governmental activities—at a disequilibrium system and a set of trade, fiscal, financial, industrial and wage policies that were seen to be contradictory and self-defeating. The plea to "get prices right" became more generally to "get policies right." And for guidance to the right policies, "good economics" was needed. Neoclassical economics was to be the safeguard against policy-induced distortions and nonmarket failures. (Meier 1987, 8)

Some went further and referred to the "decline of development economics"—those such as Albert Hirschman (1981) lamented the deterioration, whereas others, like Deepak Lal, celebrated it: "The demise of development economics is likely to be conducive to the health of both the economics and economies of developing countries" (1983, 109).[16]

---

[12]Killick (1989) contains an extensive list of conservative think tanks.

[13]Concomitantly, the United Nations Industrial Development Organization (UNIDO), International Labour Organization (ILO), and United Nations Conference on Trade and Development (UNCTAD), traditionally more sensitive to special problems in Third World nations, have been losing influence in the world's political arena (Todaro 1989).

[14]Robert Lucas, one of the pillars of rational expectations theory and the recipient of the 1995 Nobel Prize for economics, has maintained that "progress in economic thinking means getting better and better abstract, analogue models, not better verbal observations about the real world" (Lucas 1981, 276). Methodological lines between the neoliberals and structuralists could not be more clearly drawn.

[15]Presumably, the same view is held regarding the accumulation of technological capacity, although little is said explicitly on this matter.

[16]The observation by Lal is cited by Toye (1987, 71).

Two studies were particularly influential: Little et al. (1970), which was highly critical of ISI, and Balassa and Associates (1971), which predicted the success of the outward-oriented economies, Hong Kong, Singapore, South Korea, and Taiwan. Other neoclassical economists such as P. T. Bauer, Jagdish Bhagwati, Gottfried Habeler, Arnold C. Harberger, Anne Krueger, and Theodore W. Schultz were influencing the development of economic thinking and policy formulation.[17]

On the Latin American scene during the 1970s, one can cite (1) the shortcomings of the ISI already mentioned; (2) extreme maladjustments in government deficits, external debt burdens, rates of inflation and balance of payments; (3) the leverage gained by international financial institutions as providers of capital funds for stabilization and adjustment programs, (4) the rise to power of political leadership, including military-authoritarian regimes, that was receptive to neoliberal policies; (5) the festering of an adversarial and mutually untrusting relationship between the business and public sectors, and (6) the emergence of an influential cadre of Latin American economists that had been trained in the new classical economics.[18]

Government interventions have been criticized for being too rigid and inflexible, thwarting individual effort related to productive activity, encouraging unproductive rent-seeking activity, incurring excessive administrative or enforcement costs, and leading to a predatory state invested with powerful and privileged groups.[19] Market failures, especially after netting out the likely costs of correcting government interventions, are ordinarily viewed as trivial or tolerable and, as a corollary, externalities, whether beneficial or detrimental, are equally minimized. Considerable attention was focused on the credibility of policies in the eyes of economic agents acting on their expectations—usually this called for rapid, "shock-treatment" implementation of policy measures and repeated assurances that authorities would stay the course.

Neoliberal thought is especially rich regarding the benefits of insertion into the competitive global economy. The realization of scale and scope economies, enhanced efficiency from exposure to international competition, broadened and more intensive technical learning linkages, the attraction of foreign capital, and increased savings from the more efficient allocation of resources are among the advantages often cited.[20]

Neoclassical-based policy packages,[21] on an ad hoc and sporadic basis, were not unknown in Latin America during the 1950s and early 1960s, as illustrated by Chile

---

[17]For the development of Bauer's ideas, see the relevant chapter in Meier and Seers (1984); chapters on Habeler, Harberger, and Schultz are in Meier (1987).

[18]The neoliberals, designated "Chicago School," or "Chicago Boys," after the Milton Friedman-inspired students and faculty at the University of Chicago, were nowhere more evident than in Chile. See the list of Chilean economists in positions of power that were exposed to Chicago School economics provided by Silva (1991). It should be noted that Silva includes one "Chicago Girl," an adviser to the ministry of labor. A book-length treatment is available in Valdes (1995), which is reviewed at length by Barber (1995).

[19]Nicholas Stern (1989) gives a good synopsis of some problems associated with state intervention. For more on rent-seeking behavior, see Krueger (1974); for more on the concept of the predatory state, see Lal (1984).

[20]Krueger (1980) provides a good example of this line of thought.

[21]The term then in vogue was *monetarism*.

(1956–1958), Argentina (1959–1962), Bolivia (1956), Peru (1959), and Uruguay (1959–1962) (Foxley 1983). But beginning with the Southern Cone countries in the mid-1970s, and in many other Latin American nations in the aftermath of the debt crisis of the early 1980s, a much more systematic, thorough, and durable brand of neoclassically oriented policies, generally known as neoliberalism, was implemented.

Neoliberal policies track closely with International Monetary Fund and World Bank conditions for receiving loans for stabilization and adjustment during economic crises.[22] Although the IMF has tended to stress short-term stabilization measures and the World Bank has concentrated on longer-term adjustment,[23] there is considerable overlap between the two. As a package, bearing in mind that individual applications varied, the policy instruments typically encompass the suppression of demand, especially public expenditures; monetary and credit restraint; controls on wages; privatization of state enterprises, the instigation of user fees for some public services; deregulation of the domestic economy, including the financial sector; elimination of broadly applied subsidies;[24] import liberalization; and exchange rate realignment.

Stewart (1995) cites World Bank–designated categories of the intensity of adjustment based on the number and duration of adjustment loans by the IMF and World Bank during the 1980s. Intensively adjusting countries were Bolivia, Brazil, Chile, Colombia, Costa Rica, Jamaica, and Mexico, whereas other adjusters were Argentina, Ecuador, Guyana, Honduras, Panama, and Uruguay. In terms of the impact of stabilization and adjustment on economic growth, the World Bank often uses the phrase "getting across the desert," which Acuna and Smith (1994) depict as a four-stage process with (1) a sharp drop in output as "painful measures" are implemented in response to a crisis,[25] (2) a further decline as monetary stability is achieved, (3) a turning of the corner based on a more intensive use of idle capacity, and (4) a healthier growth trajectory due to renewed investment. The neoliberal record looks reasonably good with respect to growth. After stagnant or negative GDP performance in the early 1980s, adjusting countries, with the exception of Argentina, achieved positive growth for the decade of 1980–1990 and all, except Jamaica, had higher growth rates for 1990–1994 compared to the previous decade. Furthermore, two-thirds of the adjusting countries had higher growth rates for the 1990–1994 period than Latin America as a whole (IDB 1995).

Like structuralists, neoliberals are not a monolithic group and internal disputes abound. Although they cannot be pursued in any detail here, two are particularly lively. The first dispute revolves around the question, what sequence and at what pace should liberalization of the (1) domestic market (especially financial markets), (2) external trade, and (3) foreign capital flows be implemented. As Bruno remarked, "Theory tells us virtually nothing about optimal transition paths from a distorted system to one that is more liberalized. Unfortunately, this is the most important problem for any successful reform" (1987, 867). Simultaneous freeing of domestic and foreign financial markets, Bruno continued, has been "particularly disastrous." Illustratively, Lal (1987) suggests a reduction of deficit spending along with liberalization of the domestic financial system, followed by exchange rate reform,

[22]Stabilization refers primarily to reducing inflation, whereas adjustment refers mainly to curing external disequilibria (Ramos 1993).

[23]See Stewart (1995).

[24]Those retained were targeted to specific social groups.

[25]Acuna and Smith (1994) use the term *economic performance* instead of *output*.

along with an announcement of a phased program for reducing distortions in commodity markets, and, finally, the implementation of the phased commodity adjustment. Permutations on Lal's sequence are not difficult to find.[26] The majority position seems to be that at high rates of inflation (say, above 25 percent annually) liberalization programs should await successful stabilization.[27]

The other controversy concerns what foreign exchange regime should be adopted during stabilization, adjustment, and beyond. There is far less agreement on this matter. Fixed exchange rates were preferred in neoliberal programs in the 1970s as an anchor against inflation and a device to impose fiscal and monetary discipline on the state. This gave way to a crawling peg system that has been common for much of the 1980s and early 1990s. Some, including a number of economists within the IMF, are now arguing that the crawling peg, as implemented, coupled with large capital inflows, has led to overvalued domestic currencies and eroded competitive positions. The earlier anchor of a fixed exchange regime seems to be gaining neoliberal support.[28] It should be noted that in both of these conflicts the credibility of political leaders is a central issue—the avoidance of frequent, capricious policy reversals is seen as absolutely essential.

III. NEOSTRUCTURALISM

Perhaps a pendulum-like swing in development economics is to be expected when any school of economics sits in a predominant position for an extended period of time, but the somewhat-worn pendulum metaphor is inordinately mechanical. It conceals the weaknesses of the starker strains of neoliberalism and the extensive intellectual undertakings of heterodox economists. Heterodoxy fed on revisionist work on the East Asian miracle that revealed state intervention far greater than earlier perceptions had admitted.[29] Also, the initiation of market-oriented policies in Eastern Europe has been anything but an unqualified success. In addition, revisionist work on ISI has questioned whether the model was flawed per se or whether wrong-headed macroeconomic mismanagement was to blame.[30]

The lengthy and costly ordeal of neoliberal-guided stabilization and adjustment, along with a spotty record of achievements, paved the way for the neostructuralists who are at the forefront of the attempt to reshape thinking on development theory and policy in Latin America.[31] Neostructuralists have learned a great deal from the past excesses associated with

[26]For a thorough treatment, see Edwards (1992).

[27]See the literature cited by Meier (1995, 500).

[28]For literature on the IMF debate on the appropriate foreign exchange policy, see Edwards (1994, 46).

[29]A voluminous and growing literature can be found on the role of a proactive state in east Asian success stories. One often-cited example on Korea is Amsden (1989).

[30]See Pazos (1985/1986), who claims that as late as the early 1970s domestic and external disequilibria were not out of control in Latin America as a whole.

[31]Representative neostructuralist literature includes Bitar (1988), Ffrench-Davis (1988), Rosales (1988), Sunkel and Zuleta (1990), and the collection of essays in Mellor (1991). An outstanding compilation of neostructuralist thought is found in Sunkel (1993).

a state-led, inward-looking approach to development and from the successes of the neoliberal experiences. Few doubt that the market mechanism is a powerful instrument for allocating resources, one that must not be taken lightly in any policy formulation. Similarly, few quarrel with the virtues of stability and restraint in matters affecting government expenditure, the price level, and the balance of payments, all of which were treated somewhat cavalierly during the ISI era.[32] A corollary is that many agree that when economic destabilizations do occur due to economic or financial mismanagement or internal or external shocks, timely macroeconomic stabilization and adjustment policies are in order. Neostructuralists also agree that the direction and pace of economic activity depend on expectations (of future prices, wages, exchange rates, interest rates, and so on) which, in turn, rest on the credibility of economic policies, although they disagree with neoliberals as to how credibility can be established and maintained.

Although not often explicitly stated, one gets the impression that neostructuralists clearly see the disadvantages of a confrontational relationship between the state and the private sector. They do not eschew interventions to alter or supplement operations of the market, but neostructuralists are acutely aware of the existence of government failures. Finally, there is general concurrence that an outward-oriented economic stance is the proper one. All of these positions represent complete or partial concessions to neoliberal tenets. Perhaps it also bears mentioning that over the past decade or so, both neoliberals (as exemplified by the World Bank) and neostructuralists have become acutely cognizant that the development of human resources is crucial to the development process.[33]

On the other hand, neostructuralists retain some important facets from their structuralist roots, including a holistic methodology that weds economic analysis to political, social, and cultural considerations, often within a historical context. One important example is their belief that inflation, aside from depending on purely monetary matters, is rooted in social and political conditions (history counts) centering on demands made by powerful groups or classes. Ramirez (1993) cites Hirschman, who, with characteristic insight, saw inflation as "a remarkable invention that permits a society to exist in a situation that is intermediate between the extremes of social harmony and civil war" (Hirschman 1981, 201). Temporary, "fade-away" price controls and incomes policies are essential components of neostructural recommendations, not for keeping the lid on inflation as long as possible but to allow wages, prices, interest rates, and foreign exchange rates to gradually adjust to an economic environment characterized by greater reduced excess demand and intensified exposure to domestic and international competitive forces.

Another example is the concern that elevated levels of poverty and further skewing of income and wealth due to neoliberal stabilization and adjustment efforts will weaken social and political cohesion and undermine the goal of achieving long-term, sustainable development.[34] The generally poor record of neoliberal policies in poverty reduction has

---

[32]As Ramos has put it, "Because experience demonstrates that the cost of restoring economic equilibria can be quite high—normally higher than the potential benefit from risking equilibria—a central objective of steady state macroeconomic policy should be to avoid such excesses" (1993, 118).

[33]See Ramos (1994) for an outstanding exposition of the neostructuralist position on human resource development.

[34]Acuna and Smith discussed and analyzed some variations on the theme of economic performance and social stability.

both humanitarian and substantive implications. On the whole, poverty increased during the period of stabilization and adjustment during the 1980s, but some countries, for example, Chile and Colombia, fared better than most—not because they let demand compression chips fall as they may, but due to their judicious and conscious antipoverty programs.[35] Relatedly, the poor showing on closing, or even maintaining, disparities in income distribution has been noted (Altimer 1994, Stewart 1995).

Although the specifics differ somewhat, stress is placed on market failures in the form of externalities or discontinuities that echo the old structural bottlenecks. As Ramos and Sunkel expressed it:

> The market needs as its complement the active and dynamic support of the state to provide not simply its classical functions (public goods, macroeconomic balances, equity) but also—vigorously to: (1) promote or stimulate missing markets (long-term capital markets and futures markets in foreign exchange); (2) strengthen incomplete markets (the market for technology); (3) eliminate or correct structural distortions (the heterogeneity of the production structure, the concentration of property, the segmentation of capital and labor markets); and (4) eradicate or compensate the most significant market imperfections arising from economies of scale, externalities, and learning (arising from technology or trade), among others. (1993, 7)

Furthermore, neostructuralists are convinced that stabilization and adjustment, when necessary, can result in much less short- and intermediate-term damage by implementing selective measures (1) to facilitate resource switching from the nontrade sector to the production of exports and import-competing goods and services, (2) to ameliorate the decline in domestic investment and imports of capital goods and other productive inputs, and (3) to dampen the decline in tax revenue. Regarding the expenditure-switching efforts, the neoliberal reduction of demand and letting the "chips fall where they may" was counterproductive in that reductions in output fell inordinately on the nontradable sector, when the pressing need was to curtail the domestic consumption of tradable goods and services. The result was a loss of about two-and-one-half dollars in domestic production in order to save one dollar in foreign exchange (Ramos 1993). Selective measures are taken to decrease domestic consumption of tradables and encourage exports. The issue of expenditure-switching also broaches the time horizon for implementation, the neostructuralist position being that since it takes time for resources to be enticed from the nontradable sector, shock treatment will be inefficient.[36] Regarding compression of capital formation, in effect, the reduction of demand needed to restore equilibria in domestic and external economic arenas just about equaled the reduction in capital formation in Latin America. Consumption-reducing measures, directed at both nationally produced items and imports, could ameliorate the damage done to long-term growth.[37]

---

[35]For a comprehensive assessment of poverty and adjustment, see Stewart (1995).

[36]In the first two years of adjustment, construction (nontradables) fell by 30 percent, but production of tradables also dropped by more than 10 percent. A better approach, according to the neostructuralists, would be to release resources from the nontradable sector at a pace consonant with the ability of the tradable sector to employ them productively (Ramos 1993).

[37]The same argument is made for maintaining investment in human capital.

In addition, although not wedded to the idea of a big state, neostructuralists are keen to ensure that it has a crucial role to play, if for no other reason than to carry out the traditional functions of government. In addition there is a degree of optimism about the ability of government institutions to evolve, adapt, improve, and learn.[38] In the opinion of Salazar-Xirinachs:

> Neostructuralism emphasizes the great variety of intermediaries that exist between the individual or the state (cooperatives, associations of producers, tradespeople, labor unions), which form a rich and varied network with substantial power over economic decisions and the feasibility of economic policy. (1993, 382)

IV. Concluding Thoughts

One certainty is that disputations between neoliberals and neostructuralists will continue. Were the attempts to stabilize prices and exchange rates with Argentina's Austral Plan and Brazil's Cruzado Plan doomed because of the inclusion of heterodox elements in both schemes, or was it simply a matter of the inability or unwillingness to control government spending? Was neoliberal restructuring in Chile less costly in the post-1982 phase than it was during the 1974–1981 period because of a more gradualist stance with respect to trade and financial liberalization (Paus 1994)? Or, for that matter, to what extent does Chile's growth every year for over a decade rest on neoliberal foundations and how much is owed to robust copper prices and patient sectoral-oriented policies by state agencies in the fruit and forestry industries that have spearheaded the growth in nontraditional exports (Paus 1994)? How potent was a de facto incomes policy in Mexico in lowering inflation rates to below 10 percent in 1994?[39] Can the Mexican peso crisis of December 1994 be laid at the feet of the neoliberal model, or was it due to macro-mismanagement in relying on short-term portfolio capital to finance long-term development, horrendously poor banking practices and surveillance, and political shocks such as rebellion in Chiapas and the assassination of the leading presidential candidate? Did Chile avoid a similar financial meltdown because of establishing penalties on premature withdrawal of short-term portfolio capital? The list of controversies, of course, could be extended considerably, but the point is that a wholesome, potentially productive debate has been launched and is likely to dominate theory, as it pertains to Latin American development, in the immediate future.

The theoretical quest must also include some issues on which no school of thought can claim an exemplary track record. They include sustainable growth with equity and poverty reduction, a foreign exchange regime compatible with economic stability, and establishing an economic environment conducive to technology capacity building.

Neoliberalist views have partially triumphed as demonstrated by the differences between the old structuralist and neostructuralist views mentioned earlier. Yet, in my

[38]For more on the role of the state from a neostructuralist vantage, see Gerchunoff and Torres (1992) and Salazar-Xirinachs (1993).

[39]The Economic Solidarity Pact began in Mexico in 1987; it was renamed the Pact for Stability and Growth in 1988. As Ramirez has observed, "It amounted to an income policy" (1993, 1022).

own estimation, neostructuralists are in an ascendant position,[40] and I look for the movement to derive strength and enrichment from other heterodox schools of economics. Much can be gained from an interaction between neostructuralists and institutionalist economists. I refer not to the new institutionalists, *a la* Oliver Williamson, but to the old institutionalists who draw inspiration from John Commons and Thorstein Veblen, as outlined by Osvaldo Sunkel (1989). Perhaps a more promising interaction is with neo-Schumpeterian economists, especially the phalanx of this school that concentrates on the dynamic interaction of technology and trade.[41] Neostructuralists already share some views with post-Keynesians, especially regarding the desirability of an incomes policy, but almost inevitably, in the wake of the financial turmoil in Mexico and close calls in Argentina and Chile, neostructuralists will seriously examine the strand of post-Keynesian economics inspired by Hyman Minsky (1986), who makes the case that market-grounded financial markets are inherently unstable.[42]

REFERENCES

Acuna, Carlos H., and William C. Smith. "The Political Economy of Structural Adjustment: The Logic of Support and Opposition to Neoliberal Reform." In *Latin American Political Economy in the Age of Neoliberal Reform*, edited by William C. Smith, Carlos H. Acuna, and Eduardo A. Gamarra, 17–66. New Brunswick, NJ: Transaction Publishers, 1994.

Altimer, Oscar. "Income Distribution and Poverty Through Crisis and Adjustment." In Bird and Hewledge, 265–302.

Amsden, Alice H. *Asia's Next Giant: South Korea and Late Industrialization*. New York: Oxford University Press, 1989.

Arndt, H. W. "The Origins of Structuralism." *World Development* 13, no. 2 (February 1985): 151–59.

Balassa, Bela, and Associates. *The Structure of Protection in Developing Countries*. Baltimore: Johns Hopkins Press, 1971.

Barber, William J. "Chile con Carne: A Review Essay." *Journal of Economic Literature* 33, no. 4 (December 1995): 1941–49.

Baer, Werner. "The Economics of Prebisch and ECLA." *Economic Development and Cultural Change* 10, no. 2, Part II (January 1962): 169–82.

Baer, Werner. "The Inflation Controversy in Latin America: A Survey." *Latin American Research Review* 2, no. 2 (spring 1967): 3–25.

Baer, Werner. "Import Substitution and Industrialization in Latin America: Experiences and Interpretations." *Latin American Research Review* 7, no. 1 (spring 1972): 95–122.

Bastos, Maria Ines. "State Autonomy and Capacity for S&T Policy Design and Implementation in Brazil," in *Politics of Technology in Latin America*, edited by Maria Ines Bastos and Charles Cooper, 68–108. London and New York: Routledge, 1995.

Bath, C. Richard, and Dilmus D. James. "Dependency Analysis of Latin America: Some Criticisms, Some Suggestions." *Latin American Research Review* 11, no. 3 (1974): 3–54.

Bird, Graham, and Ann Hewledge. *Latin America's Future*. London: Academic Press, 1994.

Bitar, Sergio. "Neo-Conservatism versus Neo-Structuralism in Latin America." *CEPAL Review*, no. 34 (April 1988): 45–62.

---

[40]Indeed, Bitar (1988) considers neostructuralism to already be the mainstream economic thinking in Latin America.

[41]Dosi et al. (1988) is the best source for neo-Schumpeterian economics in general; Dosi et al. (1990) lays out the technology and trade connections.

[42]For a post-Keynesian analysis of the current Mexican peso crisis, see Grabel (1996).

Diakosavvas, Dimitris, and Pasquale L. Scandizzo. "Trends in the Terms of Trade of Primary Products, 1900–1982: The Controversy and Its Origin." *Economic Development and Cultural Change* 39, no. 2 (January 1991): 231–64.
Diaz-Alejandro, Carlos. "The 1940s in Latin America." In *Economic Structure and Performance: Essays in Honor of Hollis B. Chenery*, edited by Moshe Syrquin, Lance Taylor, and Larry E. Westphal, 341–62. Orlando, FL: Academic Press, 1984.
Dobb, Maurice. *An Essay on Economic Growth and Planning*. New York: Monthly Review Press, 1960.
Dosi, Giovanni, Christopher Freeman, Richard Nelson, Gerald Silverberg, and Luo Soete, eds. *Technical Change and Economic Theory*. London: Pinter, 1988.
Dosi, Giovanni, Keith Pavitt, and Luo Soete. *The Economics of Technical Change and International Trade*. London: Pinter, 1990.
Edwards, Sebastian. *The Sequencing of Structural Adjustment and Liberalization*. San Francisco: ICS Press, 1992.
Edwards, Sebastian. "Trade Liberalization Reforms in Latin America: Recent Experiences, Policy Issues, and Future Prospects." In *Latin America's Future*, edited by Graham Bird and Ann Hewledge, 11–50. London: Academic Press, 1994.
Feinstein, Osvaldo Nestor. "Neostructuralismo y Paragigmas de Politica Economica." *Trimestre Economico* 51, no. 210 (enero/marzo 1984): 99–130.
Ffrench-Davis, Ricardo. "An Outline of a Neo-Structuralist Approach." *CEPAL Review*, no. 34 (April 1988): 37–44.
Foxley, Alejandro. *Latin American Experiments in Neo-Conservative Economics*. Berkeley: University of California Press, 1983.
Furtado, Celso. *Development and Underdevelopment: A Structural View of the Problems of Developed and Underdeveloped Countries*. Berkeley, CA: University of California Press, 1964.
Gerchunoff, Pablo, and Juan Carlos Torres. "What Role for the State in Latin America?" In *Towards a New Strategy for Latin America: Pathways from Hirschman's Thought*, edited by Simon Teitel, 259–80. Washington: Inter-American Development Bank, 1992.
Grabel, Ilene. "Stock Markets, Rentier Interest, and the Current Mexican Crisis." *Journal of Economic Issues* 30, no. 2 (June 1996): 443–49.
Griffith, K., and John Enos. *Planning Development*. Reading, MA: Addison-Wesley, 1971.
Gurrieri, A., ed. *La Obra de Prebisch en la CEPAL*. Mexico, DF: Fondo de Cultura Economica, 1982.
Higgins, Benjamin. *Economic Development: Principles, Problems and Policies*. New York: W. W. Norton, 1959.
Higgins, Benjamin. *Economic Development: Principles, Problems and Policies*. 2nd ed. New York: W. W. Norton, 1968.
Hirschman, Albert O. *Essays in Trespassing: Economics to Politics and Beyond*. Cambridge: Cambridge University Press, 1981.
Hodara, Joseph. *Prebisch y la CEPAL: Sustancia, Trayectoria y Contexto Institucional*. Mexico, DF: El Colegio de Mexico, 1987.
Inter-American Development Bank. *Economic and Social Progress in Latin America, 1995 Report*. Washington: IDB, 1995.
Kay, Cristobal. *Latin American Theories of Underdevelopment*. London and New York: Routledge, 1989.
Killick, Tony. *A Reaction Too Far: Economic Theory and the Role of the State in Developing Countries*. London: Overseas Development Institute, 1990.
Krueger, Anne O. "Trade Policy as an Input to Development." *American Economic Review* 70, no. 2 (May 1980): 288–92.
Krueger, Anne O. "The Political Economy of Rent-Seeking." *American Economic Review* 64, no. 3 (June 1974): 291–303.
Lal, Deepak. *The Poverty of "Development Economics."* London: Institute of Economic Affairs, 1983.
Lal, Deepak. *The Political Economy of the Predatory State*. Development Research Department Discussion Paper 105. Washington: World Bank, 1984.
Lal, Deepak. "The Political Economy of Economic Liberalization." *World Bank Economic Review* 1, no. 2 (January 1987): 273–99.

Lewis, W. Arthur. *Development Planning: The Essentials of Economic Policy*. London: G. Allen, 1966.

Little, Ian, Tibor Scitovsky, and Maurice Scott. *Industry and Trade in Some Developing Countries: A Comparative Study*. New York: Oxford University Press, 1970.

Lucas, Robert E. *Studies in Business Cycle Theory*. Cambridge, MA: MIT Press, 1981.

Meier, Gerald M. *Pioneers in Development, Second Series*. New York: Oxford University Press, 1987.

Meier, Gerald M. *Leading Issues in Economic Development*. 6th ed. New York: Oxford University Press, 1995.

Meier, Gerald M., and Dudley Seers, eds. *Pioneers in Development*. New York: Oxford University Press, 1984.

Mellor, Patricio, ed. *The Latin American Development Debate: Neostructuralism, Neomonetarism and Adjustment Processes*. Boulder, CO: Westview, 1991.

Pazos, Filepe. "Have Import Substitution Policies Either Precipitated or Aggravated the Debt Crisis?" *Journal of Interamerican Studies and World Affairs* 27, no. 4 (winter 1985/1986): 55–73.

Peterson, Wallace C., and Paul S. Estenson. *Income, Employment, and Economic Growth*. 7th ed. New York: W. W. Norton, 1992.

Prebisch, Raul. "El Desarrollo Economico de la America Latina y Algunos de sus Problemas," mimeographed. Santiago: Economic Commission for Latin America, 1949. Appeared in English in *Economic Bulletin for Latin America* 7, no. 1 (February 1962): 1–22.

Prebisch, Raul. "Commercial Policy in the Underdeveloped Countries." *American Economic Review* 49, no. 2 (May 1959): 251–73.

Ramirez, Miguel D. "Stabilization and Adjustment in Latin America." *Journal of Economic Issues* 27, no. 4 (December 1993): 1015–40.

Ramos, Joseph R. "Macroequilibria and Development." In Sunkel, 83–123.

Ramos, Joseph R. "Employment, Human Resources and Systemic Competitiveness." In *The New Paradigm of Systemic Competitiveness: Toward More Integrated Policies in Latin America*, edited by Colin I. Bradford, Jr., 249–69. Paris: Organization for Economic Co-operation and Development, 1994.

Ramos, Joseph R., and Osvaldo Sunkel. "Toward a Neostructuralist Synthesis." In *Development from Within: Towards a Neostructuralist Approach for Latin America*, edited by Osvaldo Sunkel, 5–19. Boulder, CO: Lynne Rienner, 1993.

Rodriguez, Octavio. *La Teoria del Subdesarrollo de CEPAL*. Mexico, DF: Siglo XXI Editores, 1980.

Rosales, Osvaldo. "An Assessment of the Structuralist Paradigm for Latin American Development and the Prospects for Its Renovation." *CEPAL Review*, no. 34 (April 1988): 19–36.

Rostow, Walter W. *Stages of Economic Growth: A Non-Communist Manifesto*. New York: Cambridge University Press, 1960.

Salazar-Xirinachs, Jose Manuel. "The Role of the State and the Market in Economic Development." In Sunkel, 361–95.

Silva, Patricio. "Technocrats and Politics in Chile." *Journal of Latin American Studies* 23, no. 2 (May 1991): 385–410.

Singer, Hans. "The Distribution of Gains Between Investing and Borrowing Countries." *American Economic Review* 40 (May 1950): 470–85.

Stern, Nicholas. "The Economics of Development: A Survey." *Economic Journal* 99, no. 397 (September 1989): 577–85.

Stewart, Frances. *Adjustment and Poverty: Options and Choices*. London and New York: Routledge, 1995.

Sunkel, Osvaldo. "Structuralism, Dependency and Institutionalism: An Exploration of Common Ground and Disparities." *Journal of Economic Issues* 23, no. 2 (June 1989): 519–33.

Sunkel, Osvaldo, and Gustavo Zuleta. "Neo-Structuralism versus Neo-Liberalism in the 1990s." *CEPAL Review*, no. 42 (December 1990): 35–51.

Sunkel, Osvaldo, ed. *Development from Within: Towards a Neostructuralist Approach for Latin America*. Boulder, CO: Lynne Rienner, 1993.

Thorp, Rosemary. *Latin America in the 1930s: The Role of the Periphery in World Crisis*. New York: St. Martin's Press, 1984.

Tinbergen, Jan. *Development Planning*. London: Weidenfield and Nicholson, 1967.
Todaro, Michael P. *Development Planning: Models and Methods*. Nairobi: Oxford University Press, 1971.
Todaro, Michael P. *Economic Development in the Third World*. 4th ed. New York: Longman, 1988.
Toye, John. *Dilemmas of Development: Reflections on the Counter-Revolution in Development Theory and Policy*. Oxford: Basil Blackwell, 1987.
Valdes, Juan Gabriel. *Pinochet's Economics*. Cambridge: University of Cambridge Press, 1985.

Part 2

The New Economic Model

Reading 3

From Adjustment Policies to Structural Reforms

Enrique Iglesias
Inter-American Development Bank

Twenty years after the Prebisch Report, the world is radically changed. Contributing to this change are the three decades of unprecedented prosperity that began in the postwar years, during which time the industrialized countries experienced an average annual growth rate of 5 percent and their production quadrupled, while world trade grew 50 percent more rapidly and multiplied six times. The accelerated growth of trade, the exporting of U.S. technology and capital to countries whose economies were destroyed by the war, and the expansion of transnational companies made possible by this process gave rise to an increasingly interdependent and integrated world economy.

The most important changes, however, were qualitative. A century dominated by the same industries, technologies and energy sources (oil and petrochemicals, steel and the internal combustion engine, transportation and durable goods), and controlled by the same countries and primary sectors, has come to an end as we enter a new world in which other countries, sectors, products and technologies are interacting. A new technological paradigm holds, based on information, microelectronics and knowledge in general, while the world economy for the first time is not so narrowly dependent on labor and natural resources. The traditional relationship between production and finances is also changing—so much so that the value of international capital movements is fifteen times greater than the value of world trade. All of this has profoundly changed productive structures, the configuration of the work force, social preferences, demand, the composition of the gross domestic product, the way in which companies operate, and the role of services therein, with particular emphasis on information and communications. Latin America could not be left out of this process of change.

Partly because of these changes, but even more as a result of endogenous causes, Latin America has also changed. A brief summary of some of the concepts mentioned above regarding this transformation will be helpful. Between 1950 and 1980, the region's gross domestic product grew at an average annual rate of 5.5 percent, which was higher than the rate attained by other developing areas and slightly above the growth rate of the industrialized countries. This growth was accompanied by a relatively intense process of investment, and productive and technological change. The region's industrial capacity was expanded and diversified, making it possible to satisfy with domestic production almost all the demand for consumer goods and a growing percentage of capital goods. The steady advances in infrastructure development greatly facilitated the integration and sectoral interdependence of the Latin American economies, which, after the crisis, was to become a very important consideration in their restructuring or reform.

The 1973 oil crisis and the successive recessions the world economy was then enduring hit the region hard. Nevertheless, the rebirth of the international capital markets, made possible by the antirecession policies of the industrial nations and the deposits of petrodollars in private banks, allowed the countries of the region to avoid the impact of the crisis for several years by utilizing foreign credit. In doing so, the Latin American countries merely took advantage of the opportunities provided by the prevailing extraordinary climate of international financial permissiveness to mitigate the effects of the crisis, without realizing that they were compromising their future. It could be said, then, that the seventies represented the true turning point on the road to development sought by the Latin American countries in the postwar period, and that with the erosion of the discipline of development, they prepared the way for the lost decade.

In the early 1980s, the sudden rise in interest rates, the drying up of foreign capital flows and the long-term decline in the terms of trade thrust the region into the worst crisis the world had seen since the Great Depression of the thirties. The rest of the decade was dominated by a succession of more or less unilateral or coordinated strategies aimed at managing the debt problem, and by the implementation of a series of adjustment policies designed to curb imports, expand exports and obtain the foreign resources the economies needed to satisfy their limited import requirements and to service the debt.

After the long process of transformation and development in Latin America during the postwar period, and the external debt crisis and sacrifices necessitated by the adjustment policies of the 1980s, the Latin American countries, using various approaches, began to intensively apply measures responding for the most part to domestic needs, but also taking external considerations into account. These measures departed from the traditional view of Latin American development and were aimed at overcoming the inherent limitations of the adjustment policies that had been followed until then.

Most leaders and experts as well as the public believed that these measures were based primarily on the perceptions of the economic authorities of the developed countries and the multilateral financial organizations, which had a large presence in Latin America. With the passage of time, responses to the debt crisis evolved from the implementation of monetary adjustment policies to the introduction of more expansive structural reforms; from measures aimed solely at ensuring service of the debt to greater concern for economic growth and reduction of the debt; from a preponderant emphasis on the financial position of the creditor banks to more concern for the recovery of the debtor countries; from coordinated management of the debt problem, primarily by the creditor banks, to other methods that assigned a significant role first to the IMF and later to the World Bank; from the relative exclusion of the monetary authorities of the creditor countries to their greater involvement in the solution of the problem; and from strategies that included only the parties directly involved in the problem—creditors and debtors—to an array of market solutions.

In these responses, it is difficult to separate the influence of the creditor countries, primarily the United States, from the initiatives of the Latin American countries. Consequently, the origin of this series of reforms is not entirely clear. Although at one time an attempt was made to label them the "Washington Consensus," it is not wholly accurate, not only because these reforms were generally the result of very specific national needs and initiatives but also because the Latin American countries, as already mentioned, began to experiment with liberalization and openness as far back as the 1960s.

In any case, these responses were not formulated unilaterally by U.S. banking institutions or the international financial organizations, but were rather a combination—in arguable proportions—of their recommendations and the economic modernization and trade liberalization initiatives undertaken at various stages by the Latin American countries themselves. Moreover, this was not a generally accepted name but rather a handy label applied to this particular set of prescriptions by an institution and one of its writers.[1] It was really just a useful means of easily identifying the series of measures proposed to the Latin American countries in recent years. It would seem more appropriate to conclude that these measures were being developed in response to the gradual emergence of a Latin American political and economic consensus.

Another interesting aspect of this consensus, apart from its institutional origins, is its conceptual history. The new strategy implicit in this series of measures owed its existence partly to the obsolescence of the development model the Latin American countries had followed in the postwar era, partly to the weariness of the industrialized countries with respect to foreign aid—which was a major component of the conventional model mentioned above—and partly to a general loss of interest in development theory.

There is another reason why, in academic circles, development theory was ignored and had seemingly become irrelevant, especially in the North, but also among Latin American economists whose responsibility was to help formulate economic policies aimed at alleviating the crisis in the short term. Basically, the Washington Consensus was more than a set of new ideas and recommendations; it represented the return of the strong influence that "mainstream economics" had always exerted in our countries over and above the alternatives proposed by Latin American development theory.

In recent years a considerable degree of consensus has been achieved in Latin America concerning the origins of and solutions to the crisis it experienced in the eighties, a consensus that emerged from the lessons the Latin American countries learned at so high a cost.

Above all, the causes and the nature of the crisis are more clear today. Unlike the period immediately following the crisis, today there is a clearer understanding of its most fundamental aspects: the role of both external and internal factors in igniting the crisis; whether it was a short- or long-term phenomenon; whether it was basically a financial problem or should be viewed primarily as an economic growth issue; the nature of the measures implemented to deal with it; and the need to replace recessionary adjustment policies and to institute structural reforms geared more toward renewed economic growth. It is also clear that these reforms should not focus solely on the recovery of macroeconomic balances, an essential but not exclusive condition for development, but should go further and include policies aimed at vigorously promoting development. Naturally, unanimity is more difficult to achieve when the objective is to advance from a series of general recommendations, which could apparently be implemented uniformly, to the adaptation of each recommendation to the specific needs of each country. Growth policies are more in need of such adaptation than are policies related to overall balances. For the reasons given, it is also difficult to agree on the pace, sequence and amount of time required to implement such reforms.

---

[1]The Institute for International Economics and one of its most distinguished researchers, John Williamson.

It follows, then, that the countries themselves are better qualified to make the necessary adjustments than are the multilateral organizations.

This modest but significant progress toward a Latin American economic consensus would not have been possible without a new political consensus. The same is certainly true of the inward-oriented development policies followed by the countries of the region in the postwar period. The emergence of this new political consensus coincided with the fall from power—for the most diverse reasons—of various governments with a populist or ideological political orientation, characterized by confrontation and conflict, and by poor discipline or extremism. As they were replaced, a new civic philosophy evolved, one that was more realistic and pragmatic, less impatient and more mature, less inclined toward aggression and more willing to seek areas of agreement, more removed from extremes and more moderately oriented. Less political impatience and a renewed emphasis on moderation, stability and consensus made it easier for the leaders to effect reforms that would have been impossible in a different political context. Therefore, just as our economic leaders have realized that our development strategies must be modernized, so must our political leaders accept these new truths.

A dynamic political consensus is taking shape in many countries concerning the requirements and aims of economic reform, sustained in the long term by the ability of the new model to respond to the region's extraordinary social conditions.

Economic reforms are legitimized politically by their effectiveness in the social sphere. In the difficult adjustment period, however, this consensus depends largely on society's perception of the fairness of the adjustment burden and the promise that today's austerity holds for tomorrow. Consequently, the consensus must be reinforced by the provision of high-quality public services, an effective reflection of social communication and skillful government, which will be put to the test in such difficult and challenging circumstances.

What Is Structural Reform?

The growing perception of how best to deal with the debt crisis was based on fiscal austerity, the liberalization of domestic markets and the opening of the economy. To achieve these objectives, a series of structural reforms was proposed. These reforms differed substantially from the principles of the structuralist view: import substitution, orientation toward the domestic market, various forms of tariff, fiscal or exchange rate protection (or discrimination), redistributive programs subsidized by the government, State intervention and planning, and excessive public expenditures. The new economic policy objectives depended fundamentally on the free operation of the markets. In this connection, the term "structural reforms" began to be used to refer to a set of measures aimed at liberalizing domestic markets, privatizing State enterprises and certain social services, and opening the economies to international trade and private capital inflows.

At a conference on the subject in 1989, John Williamson listed ten areas in which the structural reforms were concentrated. The country studies presented in this conference tried to give an idea of the extent to which national viewpoints on these subjects coincided with what the publisher of Williamson's book called the "Washington Consensus."

These studies focused on several groupings, including Bolivia, Chile and Peru, considered as three experiments in policies; Brazil, Mexico and Argentina, the largest debtors of the region; Colombia and Venezuela; and the Caribbean and Central American countries.

The principal common denominators were fiscal discipline, control of public expenditures, improvement of the tax system, deregulation of the financial system, management of the exchange rates, trade liberalization, promotion of direct foreign investment, privatization of public enterprises, deregulation and protection of property rights.*

It would be both difficult and premature to attempt an evaluation of the results of structural reform in Latin America. First, because such reforms were initiated only a very few years ago. Second, because not all of the countries have undertaken them. Third, because the pace, emphasis and results of the reforms vary. Nevertheless, for the time being, a number of questions need to be answered.

The first question could be elucidation of the degree of consensus among the financial institutions in Washington concerning specific solutions to the problems of given countries. Many Latin American economic experts assert, whether explicitly or implicitly, that what is needed to restructure their economies and revitalize growth, especially from a political viewpoint, is a national consensus rather than one imported from abroad. In fact, many Latin American governments instituted these reforms in response to their own needs and past experiences. On the one hand, as mentioned above, the countries of the region began to repudiate the import substitution strategy about twenty years ago, on the basis of both conceptual considerations and the evaluation of their results. On the other hand, in these same circles, there is an obvious trend toward forms of economic thinking more inclined toward internal deregulation of the economies, their opening to the exterior and the promotion of exports. The Washington community, meanwhile, is no longer interested solely in promoting adjustment policies aimed at stabilizing and normalizing the balance of payments position, but is also proposing reforms designed to create a climate more favorable to economic growth, the pursuit of equity, the revaluation of development theory and even the State's role in this process.

In this connection, Washington's agenda is expanding to include such vital concerns as social equity, protection of the environment, the fight against drug trafficking, defending human rights and promoting democracy. It would be contradictory, then, if the economic reforms proposed to the Latin American countries made it difficult to achieve goals such as those mentioned above.

THE NEW ECONOMIC DEBATE

I have already noted how concern about economic growth—or development— which was so strong among the classical economists, was eclipsed in this century, a situation that continued until the end of the Second World War. This conflict marked the demise of colonialism and the entrance of the world's least developed regions onto the international stage. Some economists of the period began observing that the economies of the underdeveloped countries had characteristics very different from those of the more advanced countries. The most striking of these difference stemmed from their close economic, political and cultural ties to some of the developed countries, to which they exported the raw materials they specialized in and from which they imported manufactures, capital goods, technology, invest-

*Editor's Note: The ten areas of policy reform suggested by John Williamson as defining the "Washington Consensus" are discussed in Reading 7.

ments, institutions, ideas and the values upon which their development processes were based. The fledgling industries of the least developed countries were characterized by extreme structural heterogeneity and were divided into sectors of different size, productivity and capacity to absorb the work force, with very few linkages between them.

With the exception of export activities and the urban sector, there were practically no markets for goods and services since most of the economic activity and the majority of the active population were concentrated in very backward rural endeavors. There were very few modern capitalist enterprises; most were involved in the export sector and relied on foreign capital, with few venturing into the manufacturing sector. The physical infrastructure was very precarious and was designed primarily to serve the export sectors and urban areas, while social services—health and education—were also limited to the cities. There were not many banking institutions and the ones that did exist were weak and predominantly foreign; due to the imbalance and lack of intersectoral integration of the underdeveloped economies, there were almost no financial markets. As already mentioned, because of these same characteristics, the commodity and factor markets were very far from functioning smoothly. The State was institutionally weak and politically uninvolved, barely concerned about development problems, and had virtually no presence in rural areas. The scholarly Latin Americans who began to write in the postwar period, such as Raúl Prebisch and the economists who participated in his work and ideas— Celso Furtado, Victor Urquidi and many others—along with social analysts of the stature of José Medina Echavarría, made extremely important contributions to the analysis of the social and economic structures of their countries.

The difficulties they had in explaining the functioning of these economies from the viewpoint of neoclassical thinking, whether marginalist or Keynesian, with its emphasis on markets and the price system as the determinants of short-term economic performance, led them to seek an interpretation of the structure of the Latin American economies founded on their historical evolution and a careful study of the various national realities.

These analyses led to the structuralist view of the development process referred to above. As is well known, this name was conferred in a dispute between these analysts and traditional economists about the causes and possible remedies of inflation, an endemic problem in the Latin American economies, which the traditionalists tried to explain and to attack from a purely monetary perspective, ignoring the structural origins of the process. Other Latin American analysts believed that the markets and the price system were unable to function properly in these economies because of a series of structural distortions or bottlenecks, which included, first, a kind of productive specialization and a form of commercial integration with the large industrial centers that caused the terms of trade to evolve consistently in a manner contrary to the interests of these countries, forcing them to transfer to such centers a large part of the surplus generated by their productive activities; the lack of international or domestic financial markets, which further restricted the investment capabilities of these countries, thus reinforcing the limitations created by the poor purchasing power of their exports; the predominance of a vulnerable, disjointed and extremely diverse economic structure, which tended to concentrate technical advances and income and was incapable of productively absorbing the increase in the labor force; and the need for various forms of State intervention to correct these distortions, given the market's inability to do so.

The structuralists departed from the traditional view, which held that development was powered by capital accumulation and the creation of full employment guided by the market, in three basic areas.

For them, and from a macroeconomic point of view, the main component of the accumulation process was not domestic savings but foreign resources, which, because of the form of international economic integration of these countries and the trend toward the deterioration of their terms of trade, would always be insufficient to enable them to import the goods needed for their development. The reallocation of resources to the import sector was not a solution due to the inelasticity of demand caused by the price of such goods and the buyers' incomes. Therefore, it was not possible to count on obtaining the resources needed to import industrial goods through foreign trade, and it was preferable to develop a domestic manufacturing sector to replace such imports. Moreover, it was believed that the manufacturing sector was the standard bearer of technical progress, which could be disseminated from that sector to the rest of the economy. Naturally, under the existing circumstances, this process could not move forward in an environment of heavy competition without a reasonable degree of protection. The objective of the commercial policy of these countries was not to correct their balance of payments but to restructure relative prices in favor of the industrial sector—to the detriment of agriculture—by means of monetary, tariff or fiscal measures of a preferential nature.

Second, at the microeconomic level, structuralism pointed out the flaws and the lack of continuity in the Latin American economies. One major problem was the slow progress of agriculture, attributed primarily to the prevalence of outmoded landholding systems. The lack of intersectoral integration of the productive system and, consequently, of positive forward and backward linkages between the various productive activities was also criticized. This lack of integration also lowered the incentive to invest and to organize true capital markets in these countries. The shortcomings of the physical and social infrastructure and the geographic imbalances of the economic activities constituted additional barriers to the normal functioning of the markets.

The macro and microeconomic conditions mentioned above pointed to the need for a strong presence of the State in the economy to overcome them, an outlook which differed from that of the neoclassicists who, in this regard, remained faithful to Adam Smith and the other founders of economic thought. It was believed that development was a consequence of the implementation of effective public policies and not a natural evolution of market forces or of free competition. The State's action was supposed to correct the deficiencies in the market through planning, as well as contributing directly to capital formation through expansion of the infrastructure, the financing of large industrial projects and the operation of public enterprises.

The structuralist view was translated into policy proposals. The orientation toward the domestic market and the replacement of imports were the key components of these policies. There was great distrust of the foreign market and of primary exports. Import substitution seemed much more appropriate than the traditional strategy, which was oriented toward foreign markets and benefited the agricultural sector. Nevertheless, as already pointed out, the new strategy soon encountered limitations, failed to overcome the external financial vulnerability of the Latin American economies, created sectoral imbalances, and unleashed inflationary and fiscal pressures.

After a time, criticism of structuralism, which had started at the very outset, began to intensify. In the 1960s, structuralist programs benefited from injections of capital from the Alliance for Progress, but the latter's influence soon waned, further exposing the weaknesses of this strategy. Because of its reformist approach, its redistributive content and its State-oriented character, structuralism and its strategies were opposed from the beginning by conservatives, who favored more traditional policies and the reduction of the size and role of the State. Structuralist strategies also drew attacks from radical political groups, who wanted more sweeping, revolutionary measures and who expressed their views through the dependency theory. But it was the conservative critics who finally gained the upper hand and imposed their views. In the mid-1960s, in both Brazil and Argentina, the civilian governments were replaced by military regimes committed to more traditional economic policies and ending inflation. Circumstances again challenged the structuralist school when the oil crisis erupted in 1973–1974 and it became necessary to implement adjustment policies conditioned by a process of heavy foreign borrowing, made possible by conditions in the international financial markets in the midst of an unstable, recessionary world economic environment. The crisis in 1982 caused by servicing the external debt again made it necessary to try new policies.

The obsolescence of the import substitution model and the subsequent debt crisis made it impractical to continue as before. To become integrated in the world economy, the Latin American countries had to reestablish macroeconomic stability and productive competitiveness. They had to ensure fiscal equilibria, correct exchange rates, positive interest rates that would not subsidize capital-intensive import substitution industries, real wages determined by international competition, and substantially curtailed State intervention. The experience of the Southeast Asian countries in the preceding twenty years was especially relevant to this development strategy.

Thus, the stabilization and adjustment policies the countries of the region had to implement to deal with the crisis were generating experiences of a different nature, which the structuralist camp began to analyze critically. The perceptions of the realities of the region, together with the lessons learned from the collapse of the planned economy system and the experience of the economies of Southeast Asia, began to be analyzed in light of the structuralist view of the Latin American economy.

There is a marked revisionism in Latin American thought concerning not only the past but also certain basic perspectives of the original Latin American consensus. These revisionist tendencies hold that the basic limitations of Latin American development, identified by the structuralist school, are still present; namely, the existence of an inadequate pattern of external integration, the predominance of a disparate productive structure, and the persistence of inequitable income distribution. Other structural aspects remain that affect the functioning of the Latin American economies more than the rules of the market. These included the type of foreign trade the countries specialize in, the degree of market concentration, the intensity and orientation of forward and backward productive linkages, control of the means of production by various sectors (e.g. the State, the private sector and transnational capital), the landholding system, the pattern of income distribution, the functioning of the financial markets and the degree of incorporation of advanced technology, together with sociological and political factors related to the level of labor organization, the class structure and the political system.[2]

Nevertheless, more than the predominance of the neoclassicist or the neostructuralist view, what stands out in the economic thinking of Latin America and in the economic policies of the respective governments is a trend toward agreement about certain specific points which, on the one hand, depart from the traditional view of Latin American development prevalent in the postwar era and, on the other, tend to correct the excesses of the neoliberal policies applied in the most severe phase of the adjustment period.

---

[2]See O. Sunkel, *El desarrollo desde dentro: un enfoque neoestructuralista para América Latina,* Mexico, Fondo de Cultura Económica, 1992.

Included among these points are, first, concern about the size and the effects of the transfer of resources abroad to service the debt. On the one hand, this massive transfer of resources threatens stabilization, which is one of the main objectives of these policies, and on the other, occurs at the expense of the resources available for investment, thus jeopardizing the development process in both the short and the long term.

Second, this incipient merger of ideas gives new importance to—and views from a new perspective—the old problem of inflation, in contrast to the relatively superficial responses of the monetarist school and the complacency regarding this phenomenon exhibited by the old structuralists. The new consensus not only assigns the highest priority to stabilization but also recognizes the fact that inflation is caused by incompatible pressures on the factors of production and can be corrected only insofar as a firm income policy is formulated, which could include specific ways of controlling prices and/or wages and, in general, explicitly negotiated social compacts that tend to alleviate these pressures.

Third, there is also agreement on a more pressing concern having to do with the distribution of income and the need to attack the problem of extreme poverty using the scarce resources available, within the context of clearer consensual policy decisions, more imaginative solutions and more sharply focused programs.

Fourth, the emerging view unanimously stresses the importance of trade liberalization and the entry of the Latin American economies in the international arena. This transformation requires a more active, more selective and better-oriented integration by endogenous forces and institutions to allay the undesirable effects of trade liberalization on our economies and to enable them to create dynamic advantages through conscious support for the most promising activities and integration in the appropriate markets.

Finally, there is also a more consensual and less ideological view of the State's role, which is in need of major reform, although the orientation and extent of such a reform are still not clear. In this regard, it seems to be generally agreed that the market must be supported by selective action on the part of the State, which, in addition to its usual functions (having to do with maintaining macroeconomic balances, social equity and the provision of public services), includes the promotion or stimulation of missing markets (such as long-term capital markets), the strengthening of incomplete markets (such as the technological market), the correction of structural distortions (such as the disparateness of the productive structure), the concentration of ownership and income or the fragmentation of the capital and labor markets, and the elimination or overcoming of limitations to growth caused by insufficient returns to scale, learning processes or externalities.

In any case, it appears that no one today seriously thinks that the Latin American economies should resume looking only inward to support growth or that they should again become deeply pessimistic about foreign markets, negligently manage short-term macroeconomic policy, be complacent about overall imbalances, or advocate excessive State intervention with large public outlays.

THE QUIET TRANSFORMATION OF LATIN AMERICA

In fact, as is true of every major crisis, all was not lost in this process. Just as the recovery of the world economy was made possible by the destruction caused by the war, so can the Latin American economies by revitalized after the havoc caused by indebtedness and the adjustment process, which can be considered the "moral equivalents of war." What did we gain in the lost decade? The magnitude of the crisis and its painful costs tend to make us forget that we also learned important lessons and even made some progress as a result of a kind of quiet revolution. As I see it, these lessons constitute Latin America's greatest asset in solving its problems or unresolved challenges. Of these, I would like to point out the following:

To begin with, I should mention a benefit of great importance: the return of democracy to most of our countries. This fact cannot be undervalued because of setbacks in the economic order. The advances in the restoration of democratic institutions, the practice of political consensus or agreement and the defense of human rights constitute an attainment of historic importance, especially since it occurred in the restrictive environment of the crisis. In light of the recent past, the restitution of democracy conveys three important messages: first, the humanist tradition and social maturity of the Latin American countries ultimately demonstrated that the establishment of exceptional regimes is not the only possible response in periods of transition and unrest; second, in many cases, the notion that stability and economic growth can be achieved by only authoritarian systems of government was also disproved; and, third, it has become much clearer that economic, technological and social modernization can only be effected rapidly and enduringly in a climate of respect for freedoms, social participation and the integration of all sectors. But perhaps the most outstanding characteristic of the new Latin American political climate is the tendency to seek consensus and agreement, which is, moreover, in keeping with the current style of world politics.[3]

On this plane, the first achievement has been the establishment of stabilization programs to deal with inflationary processes that, in many cases, bordered on hyperinflation. The region can now point to some of the most notable cases of combating runaway inflation, such as the experiences of Bolivia, Costa Rica and Chile, and, more recently, Ecuador, Mexico and Venezuela. The drop in inflation rates in recent years is a clear demonstration of the positive results of the current policies. Argentina, Peru and Nicaragua provide further evidence of this trend. Debt reduction programs, because of their significant impact on fiscal accounts, have played an important role in the success of these policies.

Along with stabilization programs, nearly all of the countries have initiated strict fiscal adjustment programs. Latin America now recognizes that the subject of fiscal deficits is at the center of the major macroeconomic disequilibria it has experienced in the past and that unless it is addressed decisively and courageously, it will be extremely difficult to establish a minimum degree of stability upon which sound, self-sustaining development processes can be based. The region as a whole is now moving toward greater macroeconomic balance, which is not always easy and, moreover, has high political and social costs. The change is a clear manifestation of the determination to combat one of the factors that contributes most to perpetuating injustice in Latin American societies today: the prevalence of high inflation rates. The people of Latin America now understand very clearly that the most damaging tax on the lower classes is high inflation, and, therefore, that the social cost of implementing stabilization programs is far less than the persistent costs that have fallen on these social groups in recent years as a result of inflationary disequilibria. Hence, we have witnessed the political courage and even the unprecedented degree of social tolerance that have supported many of these programs in the recent experience of Latin America.

A third aspect of this quiet transformation is the growing openness of Latin America to foreign trade. It is now acknowledged that in an increasingly interdependent world char-

[3]See D. J. Dionne, Jr., *Why Americans Hate Politics*, New York, Simon and Schuster, 1991.

acterized by the emergence of a global economy, if vigorous economic development is to be achieved, there is no alternative to ever more competitive participation in the international economy. This concept has been absorbed and assimilated by the people of Latin America and is now a generally-held conviction. There is no economic development in isolation and, consequently, the countries must become in tune with the world economy by increasing their international competitiveness. To achieve this position, unprecedented trade liberalization, tariff reduction and export promotion programs have been launched throughout Latin America. The lowering of the levels of protection in Latin America places it on par with the economies of the industrialized countries; in some cases, this change was achieved with a rapidity and a thoroughness unknown in international experience. All of this points to the acceleration of a process leading to the creation of economies that are much more competitive than they were in the past. Nevertheless, the persistence of recessionary trends in the world economy and the danger that the current protectionist trends will continue to pose, raise doubts about how these efforts will be received by the international community. This uncertainty reveals a potential lack of symmetry between its response and the efforts that the Latin American countries have made to open their economies.

A fourth area of this transformation process in which advances have been made is the reorganization of the State and the objective of greater efficiency in the performance of its functions, as well as the growing trend toward the limitation of such functions to a smaller number of centralized activities. The kind of involvement it had in the past in innumerable economic activities is now being ruled out. This tendency has led to an intensification throughout Latin America of the search for greater efficiency in the public sector in general, especially public enterprises, and to the initiation of a series of privatization processes and other decentralization efforts by the State. State reform is now not only an important element in terms of deepening the democratization process at all levels but also an essential condition for increasing the economic efficiency of our countries. As explained below, modernization of the State is a key component of the productive reorganization and the international integration of our countries.[4]

These mainstays of the adjustment policies and structural reforms were accompanied by programs designed to solve the debt problem, which, once the initial concern about protecting the creditor bank's position was allayed, were oriented toward alleviating the burden on the debtor countries. This shift occurred under the Brady Plan and, more recently, the Enterprise for the Americas Initiative, which allowed some of these countries to turn away from their deep concern about external indebtedness that prevailed in the eighties. As mentioned above, this change does not mean that the subject is no longer important or that it is not still a serious concern for some countries.

There have also been some intangible advances, which represent additional lessons learned from the crisis. Those of us who have worked in Latin America for many years know that progress which is not reflected in the statistics has been made in the region. In many cases, this progress has consisted of changes in attitude, in the forms of social, governmental or business organization, or in the lessons that the development experience has provided in recent decades. The first of these lessons is the one apparently learned by most of our

---

[4]See R. Wade, *Governing the Market, Economic Theory and the Role of Government,* Princeton University Press, 1990, and F. Larrain and M. Selowski, *The Public Sector and the Latin American Crisis,* San Francisco, ICS Press, 1991.

political leaders, who are now more wary of populist options and who are committed to more prudent policies aimed at maintaining overall balances. Beyond these circles, the region's economic leaders generally understand the necessity of making the adjustment and more efficiently utilizing economic resources, both human and capital, thereby increasing the competitiveness of their countries. We have also learned that runaway inflation is socially costly and difficult, which reinforces the objective of achieving economic stability as a condition for making the adjustment and subsequently instituting policies aimed at economic growth in a stable environment. Similarly, we have learned that without adjustment, social problems can become insoluble and more devastating. But we have also learned that there is a limit to how much society will tolerate and that adjustment programs must therefore be accompanied by emergency social compensation measures and a clear vision of a different future for disadvantaged social groups.

Another lesson concerns the need to give priority to market mechanisms when State intervention in economic processes becomes excessive, as it did in recent decades; this change involves a gradual process of market deregulation, which will promote efficiency in the use of resources by both the public and the private sectors. A complementary lesson indicates that State reform is necessary in Latin America to eliminate its chronic deficits, increase its efficiency and advance the privatization of public enterprises and the decentralization of State functions; this type of reform does not imply, however, that the State will disappear or be weakened. We are also beginning to understand that the pressing social needs that have been accumulating in the region must be attended to gradually, that the modernization of our economies and the revitalization of growth are essential conditions for attending to these needs, and that even now it is possible to begin doing so by reorienting and sharpening the focus of social spending. Another lesson is that the expansion and diversification of exports and, consequently, the liberalization of foreign trade and the opening of the economies constitute a key factor for managing the debt problem and furthering the economic transition.

The results of this quiet transformation of Latin America are already appearing on several levels:

a) The growth rate has improved. The Bank's most recent reports indicate that in 1991 the GDP of the region as a whole had grown approximately 3 percent, in contrast to a decrease of nearly 1 percent in 1990;
b) Inflation has abated in most countries, although it is still high in others, which, consequently, are in the initial stages of the process. According to ECLAC, inflation indexes, which had hovered around 1,200 percent in 1989 and 1990, dropped to 300 percent per annum in 1991 and show promising signs for the future; and
c) Capital is again flowing to the region. The repatriation of Latin American capital has been remarkably energized, strong incentives have been created for foreign investments and the securities markets in most of the countries have been revitalized. According to the latest report of the OECD, in 1991 the region experienced a positive transfer of resources for the first time since 1983. As indicated above, between 1983 and 1990, negative transfers abroad were around $20 billion a year. In 1991 this transfer turned positive, representing a resource flow of approximately $15 billion.

All of these numbers are important indicators of the early results of the quiet revolution mentioned above.

TOWARD A LATIN AMERICAN ECONOMIC CONSENSUS

There are undoubtedly wide areas of agreement between the world's major financial centers and Latin America about how to reignite the development process at this stage, including certain principal points and basic objectives as well as numerous policies and specific measures. Nevertheless, there are also differences in emphasis and, in many instances, differences of perception.

It is only natural, after so many years of making adjustments and struggling to achieve stability, that the renewal of development and the raising of living standards should be given special priority. To achieve these objectives, the restoration of macroeconomic balances is essential but not sufficient, just as basing the development effort on a series of standard, preconceived notions would be inadequate.

Latin America needs, above all, to make an enormous internal effort focused not only on development but also on the quality of such development, in order to solve the problems of equity and to address the problems of poverty.

To achieve these goals, with all the uncertainties, surprises, successes and failures of any such process, the region must analyze its own vision and its own internal discipline before resolutely undertaking the fascinating task of economic and social development.

It is toward this objective that the quiet transformation in Latin America is moving, in harmony with similar changes taking place throughout the world. Nevertheless, some questions that are worth reconsidering remain. In Latin America, have we discovered a definitive formula that will put an end to economic stagnation and allow us to look forward to a future of sustained development? To what extent will our economic reforms be sufficient to ensure positive results in this direction?

Regarding the first question, both economic history and developmental experience prove that there are no magic formulas or absolute models for orienting these processes. One of the factors that has most compromised the political and economic growth of the Latin American countries is the tendency to attribute a kind of ideological intangibility to policies that seem appropriate at a given moment. Any policy is, by definition, a response to a given set of circumstances. Only the adherents of historic materialism or the most extreme liberalism could have thought themselves capable of predicting or putting an end to history. History changes constantly and unceasingly, creating different experiences and giving rise to various stages and situations that require appropriate responses. Consequently, I do not believe that there is any one, absolute formula for addressing the problems of Latin America and the world.

Regarding the effectiveness of the proposed measures, I would venture to say that the economic reforms currently underway, which are the fruit of recent years' experience, are a necessary component which, in and of themselves, are not sufficient to ensure a pattern of development that responds to our historic experience and our social and political life. Hence, in addition to supporting these reforms, which are aimed at economic efficiency, other measures related to the political situation, the social conditions and the institutional structure of the Latin American countries must also be implemented. This path will not be easy and, therefore, a number of concerns about Latin America's future remain.

If some of the major concerns from the Latin American perspective were to be singled out, mention would have to be made, first of all, of the need to recognize the differences that exist between the economies of the region in terms of their size, productive structure, form of external integration and socio-political systems. These differences explain the various reactions to similar reforms occurring in the countries of the region. Liberalism postulated that rational calculation and freedom of choice are essential characteristics of the economic agents operating in markets free of any distortion. Structuralism made an important contribution to economic analysis by hypothesizing that the behavior of such agents is determined by a set of behavioral principles imposed by the historical, socio-economic and institutional contexts in which they operate. The greater or lesser degree of resistance the structural reforms have encountered in the various countries in which they have been introduced, and the greatly differing results produced by each of them, are largely explained by these differences. Hence, we see the danger of making too many generalizations.

Another concern is the pace and sequencing of these reforms in light of each individual case. The industrialized countries' own experience indicates that reforms cannot always be implemented quickly; they must proceed in stages. Marcelo Selowsky has proposed a plan for this process; the first stage would focus on curbing inflation and reducing fiscal deficits; the second on establishing a system of incentives and reforming the public sector, including efforts to increase competitiveness through deregulation; and the third stage would seek to revitalize growth by increasing the level of investment.

An additional concern relates to what has been said about maintaining macroeconomic balances as a necessary but insufficient condition for promoting development. The essential elements in this regard are a thorough industrial reorganization and true economic competitiveness. There is no guarantee that economic stability will automatically lead to the necessary reforms. Such reforms require a vision and a conscious effort. This effort must not be oriented preferentially to the domestic market, as it was in the early stages of Latin American development, but rather to international markets, taking into account the changes that have occurred in this regard both within and outside the region. The State must be modernized in order to meet this challenge. The lack of confidence in the market that prevailed in the early decades of the Latin American experience must be overcome in order to assign a preponderant role to business and the private sector, duly integrated in a full network of connections between their labor base, the educational system, the technological infrastructure, the financial system, the public and private institutional apparatus and the international markets.

There is also concern about the danger of neglecting pressing social problems, especially extreme poverty, unemployment, social security systems and, above all, the education of the young. The quality of education and the development of the human resources needed to effect the essential productive transformations must be a cause for concern in our countries.

Finally, I would like to emphasize Latin America's concern with foreign relations. I am not going to insist here on the need for improvements in the international economic environment and in cooperative programs for development, because I plan to do so later, but they are essential conditions for supporting the economic reforms currently underway in Latin America. I would like to stress the need for Latin America to open its markets to the world and, in so doing, to cultivate its special historic relationship with the United States and Europe, as well as with Asia and other developing countries. Greater political and economic ties with the rest of the world will have the positive effect of "anchoring" our development strategies, as occurred with the countries that more recently joined the European Community, and achieved greater stability because of their association with major economic and world political centers. Latin America's development options are to be found not in isolation but rather in its integration with the rest of the world.

I would like to add to these concerns three comments, which may help to clear up some of the confusion we sometimes feel in this transitional stage.

First, what is at issue in the current discussion of Latin America's alternatives are not conflicting economic theories or development models but rather an up-to-date reading of the new political and economic circumstances our countries are facing vis-à-vis an interpretation based on diagnoses of past situations. What is at issue, in other words, is not the absolute truth of our cherished ideas about development but rather to what extent these ideas reflect the new characteristics and, therefore, the new challenges.

Second, although as always in the history of Latin American development there is now a discrepancy between the ideas and interests of the industrialized countries and our own, what stands out is not the difference of opinion but the growing margin of consensus that could be identified both within the region and between it and the international community if the region were to complete its "productive transformation with equity" and reinforce its processes of integration to negotiate with the industrialized world from more mature positions based on shared interests.

Third, an interpretation of the new circumstances implies adapting many of the basic development objectives pursued in the postwar era to these same circumstances. Thus, what at one time might have been accomplished through industrialization must now be achieved through the productive transformation of Latin America by means of a comprehensive modernization process in which protection must be reconciled with the objectives of greater international competitiveness. Interdependence with the international economy must be managed on the basis of profits derived from competitive integration within Latin America and between the region and the rest of the world, thereby developing comparative advantages. The State's action is still essential, but it must support rather than stifle the action of the private agents. This role implies more selective and efficient State involvement, including the establishment of rules favoring market forces, the strengthening of its regulatory capacity, the acceptance of its primary responsibility for social policies and the search for sustainable environmental development.

In fact, longstanding Latin American development objectives, as yet unfulfilled, must be adapted to the new conditions. And to identify them, new institutions are needed. Perhaps the most important message conveyed by this latter comment is that the greatest task confronting the countries of the region is that of effecting a thorough institutional overhaul, encompassing not only a reform of the State and greater interaction between it and the market, but also the strengthening of agents such as civil corporations, small businesses and the informal sector, regional and local communities, and the participation of women and young people in development, primarily through educational reform. Nearly twenty years ago Paul Streeten stressed the importance of the administrative skills "that determine the ability to change production structures through public policies as well as the time needed to do so" and added that "the political structure and the interests and loyalties of the governing groups determine what actions are possible and in which cases sociological and political restrictions apply."[5]

[5]P. Streeten, "Comments," in H. Hughes, ed., *Prospects for Partnership: Industrialization and Trade Policies in the 1970s*, Baltimore, Johns Hopkins University Press, 1973.

READING 4

The Latin American State

ALBERT FISHLOW
Council on Foreign Relations

The role of the state in Latin American economic development is undergoing fundamental reconsideration. Even while political scientists have been bringing the state back in, economists have been busy trying to take it out (Evans, Rueschmeyer and Skocpol, 1985). Reduced government intervention has seemingly been the winning side. Earlier presumptions about the clear benefits of public guidance no longer orient development strategy in most countries in the region. Instead, there is new vitality to the claims for the advantages of market liberalization and privatization of state enterprise. An apparent new consensus regarding a diminished role for the state in Latin America has emerged, reinforced by the rising liberal tendencies in industrialized countries and the precipitate rejection of central planning in the socialist bloc.

This debate is central to development economics as a field, so much so that Deepak Lal (1985, p. 53) identifies its demise with this new recognition of the importance of "policy induced, and thus far from inevitable, distortions created by irrational dirigisme." But this reconsideration takes on a special significance in Latin America for two reasons. First, the model of state-led industrialization through import substitution is identified with the region. Raul Prebisch and the Economic Commission for Latin America (1950) were the most prominent advocates of this new, post-World War II development strategy, and it still is esteemed by many Latin Americans. Second, countries of the region . . . experienced a sharp break with past growth trends in the 1980s, experiencing a cumulative average decline in per capita income of some 10 percent during the decade. There is strong impetus for a new approach.

This essay focuses on the reasons underlying the new commitment to reduced state participation. In particular, I suggest that the impetus comes less from newfound ideological conviction in the virtues of the market than from ineffective macroeconomic policy in the 1980s. The principal problem confronted by the countries of the region is a fiscal shortfall, not massive inefficiency resulting from misallocation of resources. Latin America is not Eastern Europe, where reform translates into elimination of the monopoly of state ownership and the structure of central command. Latin American countries have adhered to market capitalism, but without experiencing its magical effects in recent years. It is the contest between the micro- and macroeconomic explanations that illuminates why surface agreement on a reduced state role conceals a continuing divergence of views within the region.

VISIBLE AND INVISIBLE HANDS

At least through the early 1970s, development economics largely defined itself as a subfield by its emphasis upon market imperfections and the potential for Pareto-improving government intervention. Attention was especially directed to how government could seek out dynamic externalities and exploit large divergences between private and social rates of return to investment. The belief was that private markets would lead to inferior solutions if left to themselves. After all, historical reliance on markets had not closed the development gap.

The World Bank (1988, p. 49) has labeled such a perspective as the "public interest" view. One can separate out several components. First, there is a problem of providing public goods and infrastructure, where market response leads to inadequate supply or natural monopoly. Second, there are other market failures owing to externalities, imperfect information, and so on. Third, there is a need for state policy to determine appropriate levels of capital accumulation, since future generations are not well represented in private preferences. Finally, and not least, the concentration of private power and wealth constitutes a reason for state correction in the name of social justice and equality. This adds up to an active and positive role for the state through direct production of goods and services, management of revenues and expenditures and regulation of private activity.

In the specific context of Latin America, the theory of industrialization through import substitution enshrined almost all these principles. A pillar of the approach was the belief that static market signals overestimated the returns to primary exports because of potential deterioration of the terms of trade. Prebisch's emphasis upon an inevitably negative trend rang true scant years after the decline in commodity prices during the Great Depression. On the domestic side of the market, private rates of return underestimated the advantages of investment in industry, by neglecting the savings from avoiding costly imports, the benefits of technological and labor skill externalities and the consequences of coordinated production decisions. Individual consumption decisions, especially given the large disparities in income distribution, did not add up to an appropriate savings rate. The policy obligation of government was not only to offer the appropriate shadow prices through trade restrictions and credit and tax subsidies, but also to undertake complementary investment in infrastructure and strategic sectors and increase overall capital accumulation.

For some larger Latin American countries, principally Brazil and Mexico, import substitution policies were compatible with accelerated industrialization and high rates of aggregate growth. From 1953 to 1973, Brazil and Mexico increased their share of regional income from 43 to 54 percent, reflecting their relatively higher rates of growth. For other countries, the results were deficient. The share of regional income going to Argentina and Chile declined from 27 to 19 percent (ECLA, 1978).

But even where a strategy of import substitution worked, it was at the expense of growing disequilibrium in three critical dimensions. First, policy-induced exchange rate overvaluation discriminated against exports, especially non-traditional ones, making the balance of payments and access to essential imports more precarious. Second, an increase in government expenditures was not matched by increased tax revenues, thus giving rise to larger deficits financed primarily by accelerating inflation. Third, the emphasis upon industrialization frequently occurred at the expense of inadequate agricultural development that left significant pockets of rural poverty and hampered development of an ample internal market.

An import substitution strategy was deliberately unbalanced, and hence not permanently viable even where initially favorable. Successful implementation required timely adaptations to stimulate exports, enhance revenues and sustain increases in agricultural productivity. Few countries were so adroit. The first post-1945 development crisis in the region occurred in the early 1960s, as evidenced by an aggravating balance of payments problem and rising inflationary pressures afflicting many countries.

The external constraint and fiscal deficits motivated new efforts to increase inflows of public resources. Through the creation of the Inter-American Development Bank and establishment of the Alliance for Progress, assistance was provided to finance structural reforms. These were still much oriented to the domestic economy and in the spirit of public intervention. Indeed, planning was enshrined as a national requirement, and because of its political origins, the Alliance emphasized land reform and greater income equality.

Only by the mid-1960s, under continuing strains and sometimes under military aegis, did there begin to be wider acceptance of the importance of market signals and the opportunities for greater expansion of exports. Import substitution thus was not a monolithic or unchanging doctrine. By the time that a professional literature critical of the import substitution style of Latin American state intervention began to appear in the late 1960s and 1970s,[1] reality (and local criticism) had already made itself felt.

For Latin America as a whole, economic growth accelerated from 5.2 percent per year in the decade 1953–63 to 6.4 percent in 1963–73; the proportional increase in per capita performance was a much more dramatic 50 percent. The more successful countries were able to sustain a large public presence while also giving greater scope to market signals and the opportunities afforded by continuing expansion of international markets. Export performance, and access to imports, emerged as the most significant determinants of country growth rates during this period (Cardoso and Fishlow, 1989, p. 14).

Even the oil shock could be withstood, but at the expense of increased external indebtedness and deterioration of domestic policy in the more difficult external environment. Regional growth slowed after 1973, but was still higher than the results in other areas. The true precariousness of the Latin American situation only became apparent when the second oil shock coincided with an abrupt rise in real interest rates and OECD recession. Countries had chosen their new style of adjustment via debt rather than blindly following the original import substitution and interventionist model, and the choice was a bad one. Asymmetric integration into the world economy through financial flows instead of exports took a heavy toll. When voluntary capital inflows virtually ceased after 1982, the only immediate possibility was drastic reduction in imports and income. The rest of the decade has been characterized by large resource transfers, accompanied in most countries by high real interest rates, large deficits financed by internal debt, accelerating inflation and economic stagnation (Fishlow, 1986, 1988).

This Great Depression of the 1980s, made more pointed by Asian success, has directed attention to structural deficiency. External agencies, on which almost all countries came to rely, conditioned their money on a greater commitment to liberalization. Plans to assist with the debt burden, whether proposed by Baker or Brady, required evidence of

[1]Among the critical literature, Little, Scitovsky, and Scott (1970) was first. But note that back in 1964, ECLA's *Economic Bulletin for Latin America* carried two articles critical of excessive protectionism and recognizing the end of the import substitution model.

emphasis on the private sector. At the same time, more open politics and a regular electoral calendar in most Latin American countries have assured mounting domestic debate and pressure to redefine the role of the state.

The outcome has been new emphasis upon the virtues of the invisible hand. That commitment has been given greater force by two theoretical amendments to the standard Pareto efficiency argument. First, the rent-seeking literature has emphasized the additional distortion created by "directly unproductive profit-seeking" activity in response to opportunities afforded by government intervention (Bhagwati, 1982; Krueger, 1974). Second, there has been a special emphasis upon outward orientation as the key source of successful economic development. A corollary proposition is also frequently implicitly or explicitly added: liberalized domestic markets as well as freer imports are necessary to guarantee the competitiveness required for export growth.[2]

Despite their prominence, neither of these new criticisms of state intervention is decisive. They do not rule out the existence of externalities and imperfections that justified policy activism in the first place. The focus on rent-seeking correctly highlights the importance of how intervention is implemented, but in many cases only costs of response are reckoned, to the exclusion of positive benefits from public action. Even those costs are often assumed without regard to institutional mechanisms like auctions and performance-related allocation of subsidies that can do much to reduce the deadweight burden. The rent-seeking model posits a static competitive Eden as the counterfactual alternative rather than the reality of powerful private interests and inadequate price signals.

If anything, modern economic theory has reinforced a more skeptical view of laissez-faire. Incomplete markets, imperfect information, strategic interactions, principal-agent problems, transactions costs, and bounded rationality take up a large part of the microeconomic literature. Stiglitz (1988) sees this new theory as the unifying element in tackling development issues. Economies of scale, external economies, and path dependence are now at the heart of the new growth economics (Arthur, 1988; Shleifer, 1989).

The appeal of outward orientation is its empirical basis. The calculations of effective protection and the oft-replicated statistical linkage between export performance and economic growth lend support to the critique of dirigiste policy. Two cautionary notes are in order about these findings. The data do not speak with a single voice with regard to the virtues of outward orientation; and the contribution of liberalization to successful export growth remains a contentious one.

High effective protection levels frequently exaggerate actual productive inefficiency; tariff reforms are not followed by massive failures and significant reallocation of resources. Multiple cross-section studies demonstrating a favorable impact of exports on aggregate performance are not fully satisfying in three ways (Fishlow, 1989). First, causality remains an issue. Improved productivity yields greater international competitiveness as well as the other way around. A majority of countries fail a Sims-Granger causality criterion. Second, the source of improved performance may be excessively attributed to exports by the production function framework utilized; there is strong evidence that access to imports is equally or more important. That means that exports partially count for their earnings of foreign exchange, not their allocative benefits. Third, the favorable impact of export growth will

[2]For a summary of the arguments concerning outward orientation, and more extensive references, see Krueger (1985) and Balassa (1989).

be mediated by its form; export-led industrialization is different from specialization in exports that are resource-based.

This is not an argument against fully exploiting international market opportunities. Latin American countries have no doubt exaggerated the benefits of a focus on the internal market. But that does not make an export emphasis the appropriate universal alternative. Export growth of 10 to 15 percent a year may not be feasible. Rather than such an ambitious export-led process of development, the objective for many countries should be an export-adequate strategy where diversifying exports regularly keep up with product growth and earn needed foreign exchange. Unlike the econometric inferences of an elasticity of output growth to export growth of .3, computable general equilibrium models show a much smaller effect of an order of .1 (Chenery, Robinson and Syrquin, 1986, pp. 321–22). Less is at stake.

But a still more critical question is the relationship between market signals and successful export penetration. Overvalued exchange rates are prejudicial. But simply getting them right, without other complementary policies that encourage investment and technological change, may not be enough. The response to the exchange rate depends not only on entrepreneurial capacity but the flexibility of the productive structure. The objective is not to get prices right in isolation, but to follow consistent policies long enough for productive transformation to occur. Liberalization of the financial system and trade may be the consequence of successful industrialization rather than the cause of competitive efficiency.

In sum, no one has yet shown that the failure of government intervention *necessarily* outweighs market failure. On the contrary, effective state action is widely regarded as an underlying feature of successful outward-oriented Asian economic performance. Korea and Taiwan did not succeed in exports because of simple liberalization, but rather as a result of a conscious and state-directed development strategy. In Latin America as well, before this last dismal decade, the steady record of Brazilian and Mexican economic growth was associated with technocratic policy design and implementation.

Even if there has been implementation failure in Latin America, that is an argument for correcting it, not for pursuing a second-best policy of laissez-faire in the presence of externalities that can be exploited to accelerate economic development. Paradoxically, the very array of powerful private interests celebrated by the rent-seeking and related literature requires a strong state to manage successful reform. In the absence of state capacity, concentrated market and political power and other imperfections may make laissez-faire an *n*th-best choice.

From Satisfactory Performance to Stagflation: The Deficit as Cause

The argument in favor of an altered state role in Latin America has to come from the side of macroeconomic failure, not a debilitating sectoral misallocation. Despite a greater public presence in many countries in the 1970s, evidence suggests that there had already been more, not less, attention to market signals and international competitiveness. Despite the eloquence of Hernando de Soto (1989) in chronicling a stifling Peruvian mercantilism, the earlier tide of structuralism has been in retreat. In most of the region, rent-seeking was arguably less prevalent in the 1970s than it had been in the 1950s and 1960s, and export performance improved during the decade. Even in the dismal 1980s, according to the Inter-American Development Bank (1989, p. 4), "[E]xport activity has grown much more rapidly than the rest of the economy. . . . [It] increased by 32.3 percent between 1980 and 1987, while the rest of the economy did so by only 7.4 percent."

Rather, the real villain of the piece is fiscal inadequacy.[3] This has made it more difficult for Latin American countries to adjust effectively to the less favorable external economic environment of the 1980s. The rise in world interest rates and an initially high external debt reflected itself in increased public expenditures. For the region, external debt service rose from about 3 percent of GNP in 1977–78 to as much as 8 percent in 1984, before falling to around 6 percent in the late 1980s (World Bank, 1984, 1989). Because much of the debt was public or publicly guaranteed, it helped to elevate interest costs to significant fractions of public expenditures: for large debtors the amounts were a fifth and more. Those countries that successfully managed the export surpluses required to effect the payment thus faced an internal transfer problem: how was the indebted public sector to acquire the foreign exchange?

The stylized answer is through increased domestic finance of an increased deficit. Despite some reduction in non-interest governmental expenditure, principally for investment, no full compensation occurred. Hence countries faced larger deficits and at the same time less access to foreign finance; that is what made it such a crisis. In aggregate, Latin American government deficits (after some correction for the inflation component of interest payments) rose from 4 percent of national product in 1980 to levels of 7 to 8 percent in the period 1981–87 (ECLA, 1989). Longer-term comparable data are available for Brazil, where government deficits (excluding the central bank component) rose from approximate balance in the early 1970s to 5 percent and more in the early 1980s.

The options for financing this deficit were either increases in real internal debt or a tax on financial intermediation: the inflation tax on base money plus indirect effects through reserve requirements and credit controls. For many countries, in the absence of a developed capital market, the only resort was accelerated inflation; for others, principally Brazil and Mexico, increased domestic debt figured prominently. Neither was a viable solution. As private agents protected themselves against the inflation tax, higher rates of inflation were required, possibly extending well beyond the point of maximum revenue collection. As internal debt put pressure on domestic interest rates, not only was private investment crowded out, but interest payments themselves grew at faster rates than revenues. In the end, the financeable deficit compatible with stable inflation tended to decrease even while the actual deficit increased. Tax collections were eroded by accelerating inflation, directly through the Tanzi-Olivera effect[4] and indirectly by the increased incentives for evasion to compensate for reductions in wealth. Indexing assured that past inflation rates reproduced themselves.

Under these conditions, the deterioration in economic performance in Latin America is no great puzzle. Investment declined on the supply side, and demand was stifled to try

---

[3]For recent treatment of, and extensive other references to the fiscal problem, see Reisen and von Trotensburg (1988) and Easterly (1989). There is a considerable difficulty in assembling the comparable comprehensive data on the consolidated public sector needed for analysis.

[4]The consequence of inflation in eroding real tax collections through sheer delay in receipt was given prominence, and empirical justification, in Tanzi (1977). The independent and earlier discovery by Julio Olivera, an Argentine economist, is usually given recognition by those steeped in the Latin American tradition.

to dampen inflation. Uncertainty was fed by the considerable variability in real magnitudes as inflation levels climbed. Public policy floundered between efforts to stabilize through fixing exchange rates and public sector prices, and price liberalization to reduce subsidies and public enterprise deficits.

By 1985, inflation necessarily became a principal preoccupation in several countries as it exceeded all previous bounds. The array of special circumstances elicited a heterodox response, the first of a series whose most recent manifestation was Brazil's March 1990 program. These plans, in their varying form in different countries, have much to say about the critical fiscal problem and the role of the Latin American state.

The Argentine Plan Austral and the Brazilian Plano Cruzado were the first, launched in 1985 and 1986, respectively. They started from a theory of inertial inflation. Both ended indexing arrangements that institutionalized adjustment to past inflation; wages were set to nominal levels corresponding to their real average over a previous period. Both promised more rigorous monetary and fiscal policy. Both anchored prices to a newly devalued and more realistic exchange rate. Both introduced new monetary units and froze prices and wages to create instantaneous disinflation. Both were launched in an overt political fashion by civilian presidents and gained initial widespread support.

After initial successes, both soon unravelled, as price and wage controls eroded and repressed inflation became overt. Despite a series of new partial programs in the same spirit, inflation soared. In Argentina it was necessary to advance the inauguration of a new president in 1989 as speculation defeated all attempts to stabilize; and in Brazil, inflation exceeded 70 percent a month in early 1990 in the last months of the lame-duck government.

By contrast, the Bolivian stabilization plan put in place in 1985 and the Mexican effort initiated in 1987 have thus far been more successful and enduring. The former, under conditions of hyperinflation and dollarization, relied on massive devaluation and a subsequently fixed exchange rate to anchor price stability. The latter was structured around a negotiated incomes policy to restrain inflation to lower levels of price and wage increase with the exchange rate again serving as anchor. In both, import liberalization was also pursued to provide an external check on domestic prices.

What especially characterizes both of these successful stabilization programs are much greater underlying fiscal discipline and restraint on demand than in Argentina or Brazil. In Bolivia, there were significant dismissals in state enterprises (in COMIBOL, the state mining company, from 30,000 to 7000) and a reduction in public sector real wages. Revenues from increased taxes on petroleum rose sharply in the short term, while more wide-ranging reform has proceeded more slowly. In Mexico, in 1987 the primary surplus (exclusive of interest payments) was already close to 5 percent of gross product; in both 1988 and 1989 the surplus continued to increase (CIEMEX-WEFA, 1990).

Rational expectations theory has been a misleading guide in its implication that inflation can be stopped at modest costs, something all too appealing to Latin American ears. There has been too much attention to changing expectations and establishing the credibility of fixed exchange rates and monetary restraint and too little to the need to remedy the underlying fiscal imbalance. The future orientation of the theory works best when there is a memory of earlier stability to which to return. In Latin America, the gold standard was itself less the rule than the exception; postwar inflation at high rates erased any residual memory.

Previous experiments with international monetarism in Chile and Argentina at the end of the 1970s foundered out of misplaced faith in an exchange rate anchor and the automaticity of adaptive international flows. The later heterodoxy in Argentina and Brazil,

Macroeconomic equilibrium, once achieved, will not by itself guarantee economic development. The length of the crisis has intensified uncertainty and rewarded private sector caution. Restarting and sustaining economic growth is where the public sector has a central and critical role. First, increased public investment is essential to larger private investment; deteriorating infrastructure and lack of adequate public services have reduced private returns. Increased spending also sends the important signal that the fiscal emergency is over. Second, there is need for larger social expenditures for the improvement of education and health as well as expanded programs targeted to the poor. Evidence suggests significant increases in inequality and poverty as a counterpart of the stagnation and accelerating inflation of the 1980s. Political stability requires more than rhetorical recognition of this fact. Third, the public sector must become a better regulator and subsidizer, even as it divests some of its productive activities and liberalizes trade. Natural monopolies in private hands will have to be overseen; financial activity cannot be left unattended; priority private investment will have to be encouraged. Industrial policy in developing countries starts from knowing what has gone before; it does not have to be, and especially for the smaller countries should not be, synonymous with an emphasis on the internal market.

In short, there is still a very constructive role for the state, based upon theory and practice. To perform that role effectively requires a new coalition of political support that is founded on both new and old realities: much reduced external finance and need for larger domestic saving, especially of the public sector itself; an expanded, but more competitive, international market in manufactured products, based upon diffusion of technology and imports of capital goods; limits to the domestic tax base; and unacceptably high income inequality throughout the region. Political transformation is very much a component of redesign of the state; democratization is only a beginning.

Populism, with its primary focus on inequality and its predisposition to a very activist and inward looking state, is not the principal constraint to such transformation in most of Latin America.[5] Raging inflation has weakened its appeal. Opposition to effective policies has not come from mass organization; the poor do not speak with a single, or very loud, voice. Labor unions are divided and less powerful than in the 1960s. Real wages have undergone significant decline in almost all countries.

The blocking forces have been others. One has been the absence of an effective structure of political parties. Another has been a private sector interested more in guaranteed benefits than risk taking, and comfortable with a state presence that provided transfers and assured order without threat from below. Technocrats were able to satisfy those demands so long as they had abundant resources; as those diminished, so did the quality of their policies.

The technocrats have been blamed for the failure, while the private sector has emerged in some eyes as the future savior. The conversion to a narrow market-oriented view risks discarding a three-decade process of increasing sophistication of Latin American public administration. Bureaucrats do not only wear black hats. Some have contributed to imaginative policies and defended the national interest against powerful private rent seekers. The

[5]See Sachs (1989) and Dornbusch and Edwards (1990). Both papers come perilously close to identifying macroeconomic failure with populism tautologically. Nominal wage demands obviously reinforce inflation and impede stabilization. What is needed, however, is careful analysis of the special force of wage demands and their channels of pressure under populist regimes rather than others; and a careful look at whether wages were the decisive causal factor in provoking initial macroeconomic disequilibrium.

heart of the matter is not simply taking the state out, but bringing the private sector, and civil society, back in more positively.

The challenge to the countries of the region is formidable. There are no simple blueprints. The Asian developmental state cannot be copied. That brand of corporatism where authority was more centralized, resources readily available to the state and pressures from income inequality less salient proved much more functional than the Latin American style of catering to all. The prospects for economic development in the region during the decade ahead and beyond hinge upon the outcome of the process of redesign of the state that is now under way. The longer it takes to bring this process to successful fruition, the more the accumulated forces of economic erosion of the last decade make success difficult to achieve.

A Few Final Thoughts

This essay was originally written some seven years ago. Yet it remains quite relevant today, in the midst of a Mexico recovering from crisis in 1994, an Argentina feeling pressure from the resignation of Finance Minister Domingo Cavallo, and a Brazil with need to reduce definitively its fiscal deficit. What is clear is that changing from past policies is not a matter of switching from night to day, even if there is broad commitment and support. To succeed in gaining credibility for the new strategy of low inflation, increased weight for foreign exports, lesser reliance on foreign debt, etc. requires continuity in commitment.

Conversion to popular election has occurred virtually everywhere in the hemisphere. What it has interestingly revealed is the public's willingness to afford governments ample chance to create the foundation of an effective state. Whether one refers to Argentina, Peru, or the maintenance of Christian Democratic power in Chile, one sees much greater continuity than had existed previously; and now even the President of Brazil, Fernando Henrique Cardoso, has committed himself to constitutional change to permit re-election. Such a tendency is not a measure of the weakness of popular choice, but rather the recognition that immediacy is not the answer to fundamental problems that continue in the region.

And, in addition, one sees the growth of regionalism as a positive aid to the process. This is not the regionalism of the past, when a Latin American Free Trade Area was sought as a mechanism solely to protect domestic industrial interests, but rather a means of expanding market size and efficiency. Already one sees a NAFTA, inclusive of Mexico. Mercosur now not only has its original four members—Argentina, Brazil, Paraguay and Uruguay—but two associates—Bolivia and Chile—that seem likely to increase by the end of 1996 to three with the addition of Venezuela. This is not import substitution writ large, but rather an important new impulse to productivity, dynamic comparative advantage and competition. The 1994 Treaty of Miami has unfurled a process that is now taking new directions, not entirely dependent upon the United States.

Still, what remains clear is that these changes all over the continent will take more time and effort than I had initially anticipated. Changing the state is much more than a matter of introducing new rules and regulations. At base, broad institutional continuity is necessary, the kind that comes about over a generation. It is perhaps no accident that Chile should have shown such signs of rapid advance in the last decade. The circumstances of military intervention required a successor state capable of keeping some of the good as well as seeking to eliminate the bad features of the Pinochet years.

What now remains to be seen is whether other countries are able to meet the challenges of conversion. In addition to all the factors initially mentioned, one additional one requires emphasis. That is the importance of domestic savings. The current levels found in the region are those of the early 1960s. That is not good enough. To be able to grow satisfactorily requires savings rates some five percentage points greater, at a minimum 25 percent of GDP. Foreign inflows can help, but only partially. The Mexican experience makes clear the dangers of excessive dependence on capital imports. Something of the order of 3 percent of GDP begins to approach the maximum.

Reliance on high internal rates of interest as a means of encouraging personal savings is subject to doubt. Recent research suggests a small positive effect for positive rates of an order of 3 percent annually, but they are far different from the actual high rates required to combat inflationary expectations. Note as well that a strategy of continuing high interest rates implies worsening of the income distribution. It is the well off that have assets.

The savings problem in the region should be seen more as a public than a private option. Here is where borrowing from the East Asian experience is legitimate. Latin American countries require surpluses, not merely as a way of assuring price stability, but also to finance needed capital accumulation. Getting governments and publics to think this way will not be easy. One must opt for ample public collection of resources with private allocation of some part. This is exactly the opposite model of what occurred in the past when governments made state investments without needed public savings.

This challenge is heightened because the income distribution cannot simply be left on its own. It is too serious and widespread a problem, and an ultimate challenge to the capacity of states to devise effective policies. Latin America has impressively taken on the inflation problem and made much progress. Now it must show equal effort in the savings and distribution dimensions for a real and enduring change to be possible.

REFERENCES

Arthur, Brian, "Self-Reinforcing Mechanisms in Economics." In Anderson, P., K. Arrow, and D. Pines, eds., *The Economy as an Evolving Complex System.* Redwood City: Addison-Wesley, 1988, 9–31.

Balassa, Bela, "Outward Orientation." In Chenery, Hollis, and T. N. Srinivasan, eds., *Handbook of Development Economics,* vol. 2. Amsterdam: North-Holland, 1989, 1645–1689.

Bhagwati, Jagdish, "Directly Unproductive Profit-Seeking Activities," *Journal of Political Economy,* 1982, 902, 988–1002.

Cardoso, Eliana, and Albert Fishlow, "Latin American Economic Development: 1950–1980," NBER Working Paper No. 3161, 1989.

Chenery, Hollis, S. Robinson, and M. Syrquin, *Industrialization and Growth: A Comparative Study.* Oxford: Oxford University Press, 1986.

CIEMEX-WEFA, *Mexican Economic Outlook,* March 1990.

DeSoto, Hernando, *The Other Path.* New York: Harper and Row, 1989.

Dornbusch, Rudiger, and S. Edwards, "Economic Crises and the Macroeconomics of Populism in Latin America," *Journal of Development Economics,* 1990, forthcoming.

Easterly, William, "Fiscal Adjustment and Deficit Financing During the Debt Crisis." In Hussain, I., and I. Diwan, eds., *Dealing with the Debt Crisis.* Washington, D.C.: The World Bank, 1989, 91–113.

Economic Commission for Latin America, *The Economic Development of Latin America and Its Principal Problems.* New York: United Nations, 1950.

Economic Commission for Latin America, *Economic Bulletin for Latin America,* 1964.

Economic Commission for Latin America, *Series Históricas del Crecimiento de América Latina,* Santiago, 1978.

Economic Commission for Latin America, *América Latina: La Política Fiscal en los Años Ochenta,* Serie Política Fiscal, 2, Santiago, 1989.

Evans, Peter, D. Rueschmeyer, and T. Skocpol, eds., *Bringing the State Back In.* Cambridge: Cambridge University Press, 1985.

Fishlow, Albert, "Latin American Adjustment to the Oil Shocks of 1973 and 1979." In Hartlyn, J., and S. Morley, eds., *Latin American Political Economy.* Boulder: Westview, 1986, 54–84.

Fishlow, Albert, "From Crisis to Problem: Latin American Debt 1982–87." In Wesson, R., ed., *Coping with the Latin American Debt.* New York: Praeger, 1988, 7–18.

Fishlow, Albert, "Latin American Export Strategy in the 1990s," mimeo, Inter-American Development Bank, 1989.

Inter-American Development Bank, *Economic and Social Progress in Latin America,* 1989.

Krueger, Anne, "The Political Economy of the Rent-Seeking Society," *American Economic Review,* June 1974, *64,* 291–303.

Krueger, Anne, "Import Substitution versus Export Promotion," *Finance and Development,* 1985, *22,* 20–23.

Lal, Deepak, *The Poverty of Development.* Cambridge: Harvard University Press, 1985.

Little, Ian, Tibor Scitovsky, and Maurice Scott, *Industry and Trade in Some Developing Countries: A Comparative Study.* Oxford: Oxford University Press, 1970.

Reisen, Helmut, and Axel von Trotensburg, *Developing Country Debt: The Budgetary and Transfer Problem.* Paris: OECD, 1988.

Sachs, Jeffrey, "Social Conflict and Populist Policies in Latin America," NBER Working Paper No. 2987, 1989.

Shleifer, Andre, "Externalities as an Engine of Growth," mimeo, University of Chicago, 1989.

Stiglitz, Joseph, "Economic Organization, Information, and Development." In Chenery, Hollis, and T. N. Srinivasan, eds., *Handbook of Development Economics,* vol. 1. Amsterdam: North-Holland, 1988, 39–71.

Tanzi, Vito, "Inflation, Lags in Collection and the Real Value of Tax Revenue," *IMF Staff Papers,* 1977, 24, 154–167.

World Bank, *World Debt Tables, 1983–84.* Washington D. C.: The World Bank, 1984.

World Bank, *World Bank Development Report, 1988.* New York: Oxford University Press, 1988.

World Bank, *World Debt Tables, 1989–90.* Washington D.C.: The World Bank, 1990.

READING 5

The Political Dynamics of Economic Reform in Latin America

CARLOS H. WAISMAN
University of California, San Diego

For the past two decades, Latin America (as well as Eastern Europe, the other semi-industrialized periphery in the world system) has been undergoing two simultaneous transformations: from a semiclosed to an open economy and from an authoritarian to a liberal democratic polity. The pervasive nature of these transitions is indicated by the fact that they have been independent of the level of development and of political regime. Most countries in the region, from relatively underdeveloped Bolivia and Paraguay to relatively industrialized Brazil and Argentina, have moved from military rule to liberal democracy in the past decade. As for economic liberalization, it took place in authoritarian Argentina and in democratic Argentina, both under radical and Peronist administrations; in authoritarian Chile and in democratic Chile; in state-corporatist Mexico, in social-democratic Venezuela, and in social-Christian Venezuela. Like the depressions of the 1870s or the 1930s, this appears to be a critical juncture, a reshaping of domestic economic and political institutions, which is part and parcel of the reorganization of the world system. The following comments focus on the political dynamics associated with the economic transformation.

THE EXTERNAL ENVIRONMENT

Economic liberalization was the result of a constellation of internal and external determinants. In most cases, the former seem to be central, but in any case exogenous factors constituted a powerful set of incentives and constraints pushing countries toward the liberalization road. These external causes can be conveniently classified as economic, political, and cultural.

[1]On the institutional and ideological contexts of the debt crisis of the 1980s, see David Felix, ed., *Debt and Transfiguration: Prospects for Latin America's Economic Revival* (Armonk, NY: M. E. Sharpe, 1990); Miles Kahler, ed., *The Politics of International Debt* (Ithaca, NY: Cornell University Press, 1986);

The debt crisis of the 1980s was, for many Latin American countries, the central economic constraint.[1] This crisis forced highly indebted countries to increase and diversify exports, which presupposed a higher rate of investment, and to reduce government spending. These objectives could have been sought with variable mixes of industrial policy ("picking the winners") and trade liberalization, but the policies of creditors and international lending agencies produced strong incentives for privatization, deregulation, and the opening-up of the economy. Saying that the debt crisis in the 1980s was both a powerful constraint and a substantial incentive for economic liberalization does not mean, of course, that the relationship between crisis and reform was necessary or sufficient. In fact, liberalization began in the 1960s and 1970s as a consequence of perceived export opportunities, of export-oriented foreign investment, or of deliberate attempts by governments to overcome stagnating tendencies in the economy. The difference is that what was a developmental option in previous decades is now an imperious necessity.

As for political factors, the end of the cold war not only facilitated political liberalization, which is more or less obvious, but it also paved the way for large-scale economic reform, especially in democratic settings. The collapse of communism led to the organizational and ideological disarmament of the radical left, and this rendered armed subversion less likely. Second, and most important, under the new international conditions the fear, be it realistic or paranoid, of externally induced revolution either weakened or disappeared. This fear, often unrealistic, was not only a central determinant of the exclusionary policies carried out by local elites and a reason for American and European support for authoritarian regimes but also a constraint on elite behavior. During the cold war, important segments of the state and political elites in many countries espoused the view that populist and protectionist economic policies were an antidote to communism, and many believed that the drastic social consequences of the dismantling of autarkic capitalism would be a breeding ground for revolution.[2]

Finally, since the early 1980s the international demonstration effects received by the segments of Latin American societies most open to outside influences (economic and political elites, middle classes, and the intelligentsia) have favored both economic and political liberalization. The economic success of capitalist economies and the crisis in the socialist ones, as well as the "bourgeois revolutions" in Eastern Europe, have conferred an aura of empirical validity to two propositions: first, that capitalism and liberal democracy are both efficacious (whereas socialism as both an economic and a political formula is not) and, second, that a capitalist economy and a democratic polity presuppose each other. I will return to this issue later.

Joan Nelson, ed., *Economic Crisis and Policy Choice: The Politics of Adjustment in the Third World* (Princeton, NJ: Princeton University Press, 1990); Barbara Stallings and Robert R. Kaufman, eds., *Debt and Democracy in Latin America* (Boulder, CO: Westview Press, 1989); United Nations, Economic Commission for Latin America and the Caribbean (ECLAC), *Debt, Adjustment, and Renegotiation in Latin America: Orthodox and Alternative Approaches* (Boulder, CO: Lynne Rienner, 1986); Robert G. Wesson, ed., *Coping with the Latin American Debt* (New York: Praeger, 1988); and Miguel S. Wionczek, *La crisis de la deuda externa en America Latina* (Mexico: Fondo de Cultura Economica, 1987).

[2]See my argument in relation to Argentina in Carlos H. Waisman, *Reversal of Development in Argentina: Postwar Counterrevolutionary Policies and Their Structural Consequences* (Princeton, NJ: Princeton University Press, 1987).

THE REVOLUTION FROM ABOVE

These external factors interacted with endogenous determinants. The most important of these was the realization by state and political elites (as well as by economic and intellectual ones) that autarkic capitalism had run its course and caused, in many countries, stagnation or retrogression in the economy and instability and illegitimacy in the polity. It was simply no longer viable as an institutional model.

Autarkic capitalism was carried to its extreme in the countries of the Southern Cone: Argentina, Chile, and Uruguay.[3] The long-term effects of radical import-substituting industrialization could only be stagnation, or at least stagnating tendencies, because industrialization was based on the transfer of resources from the internationally competitive export sector to a manufacturing sector shielded from the world by extraordinarily high levels of protection, both tariff and nontariff (outright prohibitions to import included). Advanced autarkic industrialization led to a situation in which most of the capital and labor in the society was committed to this captive domestic market. The outcome of this massive misallocation of resources could only be, in the long run, stagnation and even retrogression.

This pattern of development had complex consequences for the social structure. Industrialization led to the expansion of industrial capitalists, labor, and modern commercial, bureaucratic, and professional middle classes, to the extent that the occupational structures of the countries with the most urban and industrialized labor forces, such as those in the Southern Cone, looked very much like those of Western Europe. However, this "modernity" was superficial. For autarkic capitalism was a variety of neomercantilism: Behind this facade lay a state that controlled and regulated not only the economy but many areas of social and cultural life as well. State corporatism and populist and authoritarian regimes were political manifestations of this peculiar type of interrelationship between state and society.

In the inception of autarkic capitalism, the state had subordinated much of society to its control. Over time, modernization produced strong social forces, but a perverse dynamics set in. The economy weakened and declined, but capital kept growing and concentrating. Hothouse capitalists increased their ability, sometimes in alliance with rent-seeking unions, to appropriate and institutionalize prebends of different kinds: not only protection (sometimes absolute), but also cheap credits from government banks, subsidized inputs, guaranteed demand, government contracts, export subsidies, and so on. Gradually, the neomercantilist state was penetrated by distributional coalitions and rent-seeking social forces.[4]

Instability and illegitimacy were the long-term outcome of autarkic industrialization, because this pattern of growth eventually produced an explosive combination: a stagnated economy and a society made up of highly mobilized and organized social forces, labor and the intelligentsia in particular. Stagnation led to the mobilization of large segments of the lower classes and the intelligentsia. In some countries, such as those of the Southern Cone in the 1960s and 1970s, truly revolutionary situations, in the Leninist sense of the

---

[3]See my discussion in Carlos H. Waisman, "Capitalism, the Market, and Democracy," in *Re-examining Democracy: Essays in Honor of Seymour Martin Lipset,* ed. Larry Diamond and Gary Marks (Beverly Hills, CA: Sage, 1992).

[4]See the discussion in Waisman, "Capitalism, the Market, and Democracy."

term, appeared. Eventually they triggered, or justified, the establishment of authoritarian regimes.

The demise of autarkic capitalism was the result, as was the case with communism, of a revolution from above.[5] In both situations it was the elites who dismantled the existing regimes, after having reached the conclusion that the stagnation and illegitimacy experienced by their societies were the consequence of existing institutions and that there was no solution to the economic and political crises within these institutions. In some cases, such as in Argentina and Chile, this realization took place when radical import substitution had approached its limits and produced not only stagnation but a revolutionary regime in Chile and guerrillas and food riots in Argentina. In other cases, such as in Brazil, the switch is taking place before these consequences appear, largely as a consequence of the demonstration effects of other Latin American countries.[6]

The Contradictory Logics of Economic and Political Transformation

There are three possible sequences between economic and political liberalization.[7] To give them Latin American names, they would be the Chilean pattern, in which privatization, deregulation, and the opening-up of the economy precede democratization; the Venezuelan one, in which the liberalization of the economy takes place in the context of political institutions that have been in place for several decades; and finally the Argentine sequence, in which economic liberalization and the consolidation of democracy take place more or less at the same time. Many countries in Latin America, including of course Argentina and Brazil, fit this latter pattern, as do all Central/Eastern European nations. The three sequences are fraught with dangers, but the third is the least favorable. The reason is that economic liberalization and the consolidation of democracy are governed by what I call two opposing social logics.

Privatization, deregulation, and the opening-up of the economy are governed by the logic of differentiation. Their first impact on the society is the increase of social differentiation in both the vertical and the horizontal senses: Polarization between rich and poor

---

[5]For an application of this argument to the case of Argentina, see Carlos H. Waisman, "Argentina's Revolution from Above," in *The New Argentine Democracy: The Search for a Successful Formula,* ed. Edward C. Epstein (New York: Praeger, 1992).

[6]See Juarez B. Lopes, "Obstacles to Economic Reform: Brazil, 1986–1991," in *Institutional Design in New Democracies,* ed. Arend Lijphart and Carlos H. Waisman (Boulder, CO: Westview Press, 1996).

[7]The following discussion is based on Arend Lijphart and Carlos H. Waisman, eds., *Institutional Design in New Democracies,* chap. 1. I also examined the issue in Carlos H. Waisman, "La decada del 90 vs. el periodo de entreguerra: el mundo actual y las perspectivas del radicalismo de derecha," in *El Genocidio Ante la Historia y la Naturaleza Humana,* ed. Carlos Escude and Beatriz Gurevich (Buenos Aires: GEL, 1994). For analyses of the interaction between economic and political liberalization, see also Stephan Haggard and Robert R. Kaufman, *The Political Economy of Democratic Transitions* (Princeton, NJ: Princeton University Press, 1995); Luis C. Bresser Pereira, Jose M. Maravall, and Adam Przeworski, *Economic Reforms in New Democracies: A Social-Democratic Approach* (New York: Cambridge University Press, 1993); and Adam Przeworski, *Democracy and the Market: Political and Economic Reforms in Eastern Europe and Latin America* (New York: Cambridge University Press, 1991).

as a whole intensifies, and so does polarization between "winners" and "losers" within each social class and also between sectors of the economy and regions of the country. Upward mobility intensifies, and so does downward mobility. Markets for luxury goods expand, and so do markets for informal labor. The most competitive sectors, or those shielded from foreign competition (for example, some services) expand, while the least competitive branches of the economy (or those most dependent on the consumption of strata negatively affected by economic liberalization) contract. Regions that house the expanding sectors are likely to thrive, while those that specialize in activities that now appear nonviable will turn into rust belts or their agrarian equivalents.

On the other hand, the consolidation of democracy is governed by the logic of mobilization. The political context of a new democracy renders the mobilization of those affected by economic liberalization more likely, due to the lowering of the costs of political action in relation to what was the case in the predemocratic period. Moreover, new democracies create incentives for political entrepreneurship, for under the new political conditions political and labor activists must secure and organize social and political bases. Economic liberalization presents them with an inventory of grievances that easily translates into a political agenda. Thus, both from below and from above, institutional factors are conducive to the articulation of movements of resistance to economic liberalization.

These two logics have the potential for inhibiting each other and, consequently, for blocking or derailing economic liberalization, the consolidation of democracy, or both. This is why the third pattern listed previously is less favorable than either of the other two: In the first case (the Chilean sequence), the political consequences of the social dislocation produced by economic liberalization are contained by an authoritarian regime; in the second case (the Venezuelan pattern), the social order facing dislocation can draw, at least for some time, from the capital of legitimacy accumulated by democratic institutions over several decades.

Yet economic liberalization and the consolidation of democracy are occurring simultaneously in many Latin American countries (as well as in most of Central/Eastern Europe), and so far no serious blockage or derailing has occurred as a consequence of the interaction between these processes. (This is also true for other parts of the world undergoing radical economic liberalization: the breakup of Yugoslavia and the consequent civil war among several of its constituent republics were caused by underlying ethnic cleavages.) In many countries, there is an impressive consensus, involving state and economic elites and even labor and some of the parties in the left and center that had supported state socialism or economic nationalism in the past.

The reason that, so far, the two opposing logics just discussed have not clashed lies in the operation of three "cushions," or moderating factors, which inhibit political mobilization. These can be classified as structural, institutional, and cognitive-ideological. The first and third factors operate in a spontaneous manner, whereas the second entails deliberate social action.

STRUCTURAL INHIBITORS

The structural cushion consists simply in the fact that economic liberalization itself weakens and destroys the power bases of the coalitions supporting the old regime (rent-seeking entrepreneurs and unions, and in some cases managers and workers in the public sector) and in general of those hurt by trade liberalization, privatization, and deregulation. On the one hand, these processes of economic transformation generate insecurity and economic deprivation, and thus discontent. On the other, impoverishment and marginalization also reduce social groups' capacity for organization and mobilization in defense of their interests.

The capacity for organization and mobilization is a function of the intensity of the threat to group interests and of the degree of marginalization of those affected by the transformation. Whenever workers, the middle classes, and business sectors are subject to threats that are not very intense, they are usually able to deploy the power resources under their control (numbers, organization, social capital, wealth) in order to protect their interests. On the other hand, when the threat is very intense, two inhibiting factors are at work. First, and for all groups, the energy and attention of most members are focused on sheer survival, and on the search for individual exit options. Second, and for the working class in particular, a large labor reserve is formed, and this is the most effective deterrent of labor mobilization.

Finally, after individuals have been expelled from the middle or the working classes, their capacity for continued collective action is very limited for two reasons. The first is structural: the weakening or dissolution of social ties among the individuals in question and with the class or stratum of origin. The second is psychological: the intense demoralization that is the usual correlate of recent marginalization. Groups in this condition are likely to display political passivity, punctuated by sudden, short-lived, and (in the case of the lower classes) frequently violent explosions of political activity.

Business elites, both private and public, must choose between recycling into competitive capitalists or dropping out from the elites. This group is usually differentiated, and its most entrepreneurial elements—and/or those endowed with large amounts of economic and social capital—usually join, or become, the elite in the open economy. Labor is also polarized by these factors. Workers in the competitive sectors of the economy, or in sectors insulated from foreign competition (for example, those producing nontradeable goods), are likely to join the train of economic conversion and engage in bargaining-oriented unionism. Sectors weakened by deindustrialization, by the increase of unemployment, and in general by the growth of poverty, on the other hand, are likely to develop confrontational forms of political action, but in the end their impact is likely to be modest due to the factors discussed earlier. In many countries, the weakening of labor actually began before economic liberalization, for impoverishment and the growth of the labor reserve were manifestations of the crisis of the old regime itself.

Institutional Change

In the second place, the clash between the two opposing logics discussed earlier has been inhibited by institutional change. The design or redesign of some of the basic economic and political institutions is in many cases a necessary component and in general an important contributing factor to successful transitions. This is a commonsense proposition as far as economic institutions are concerned, but the importance of changes in political frameworks is equally important.

With respect to the economic transition, new or reformulated institutional mechanisms are obviously a central aspect of liberalization itself (the strengthening of capital markets through the privatization of pensions, the deregulation of labor markets, and so on) and a necessary complement for the control of its differentiating effects (the establishment of a safety net for the poorest strata, programs for the retraining of labor, and so on). These mechanisms both convert citizens into stakeholders of the new economic regime (for example, the privatization of pensions) and alleviate some of its most extreme negative consequences. Unfortunately, policies focused on the mitigation of differentiation have not been pursued as extensively as the situation in most countries would warrant.

As for institutional design in the political sphere, the reestablishment of competitive politics, even if democracy in many countries is limited, inefficient, and riddled with corruption, has had a legitimizing effect, not only on political institutions but also on economic policies and institutions. The intense process of constitutional and legal reform in many Latin American countries since the return to democracy has also contributed to the legitimation of the new economic and political regime. The continuation of the process of political design is of crucial importance not only for the consolidation of democracy but also for the success of the economic transformation. I will return to this topic at the end of the paper.

THE NEW CONSENSUS

Finally, cognitive-ideological factors have both external and internal sources. As argued earlier, economic nationalists as well as leftists have been affected by the collapse of communism (and also by the apparent success of the Thatcher-Reagan economic policies) and by a process of political learning triggered by the experience of the economic and political consequences of the old regime. The cumulative effect of these cognitive processes has been not only the abandonment of autarkic capitalism but also the acceptance of the liberal model, either under the form of active support or because of ideological surrender produced by the exhaustion of alternatives.

To understand the consequences of the de-legitimation of alternative institutional formulae (autarkic capitalism, socialism), it is useful to conceive of legitimacy in terms of codes: The legitimacy of a given institutional model is to a large degree a function of the legitimacy of its manifest or latent alternatives. Autarkic capitalism and socialism have failed, and therefore only open-market capitalism remains as an apparently efficacious formula, even to nationalist and leftist politicians and intellectuals. Ideological contention turns into a debate between options within the model itself, the most powerful indication of the growing hegemony of the new economic regime.

Given this quasi-consensus, the negative consequences of the economic transformation are not conceptualized by large segments of economic, political, and intellectual elites as necessary or permanent attributes of the emerging institutional model but to a large extent are viewed as the product of the failure of autarkic capitalism. And the new course is not perceived as a leap in the dark but as a transition whose undesirable side effects are in any case the inevitable and temporary costs of the only process that can ensure in the long run affluence and even a higher measure of equality of opportunity in the society. The most significant leftist and radical arguments, on the other hand, focus on the espousal of social democracy in opposition to the most radical forms of the market economy, sometimes a strawman called "Darwinian" or "savage" capitalism. In most countries, ideological supporters of the old regime are vanishing from the political mainstream.

The Need for Political Design

As noted earlier, the structural and cognitive "cushions" are largely exogenous to the policies of economic transformation, whereas institutional design is the result of deliberate governmental action. This is an area in which further reform is pertinent in most Latin American countries. Both the strengthening of civil society and the enhancement of state capacity, two necessary conditions not only for the consolidation of democracy but also for the success of the economic transformation, could be substantially advanced by the right kind of institutional design.

The typical situation in the countries that are undergoing the double transformation is that the state is shrinking while its effectiveness remains questionable in many areas. At the same time, the corporatist apparatus that was characteristic of autarkic capitalism is being dismantled. Civil society has been weakened by the authoritarian experience and by the increased social differentiation that follows economic liberalization. The consensus supporting the new course could erode unless the new model is institutionalized, something that cannot happen without a more effective state and a stronger civil society.

This is an inflection point in the relationship between state and society, a conjuncture that could be conceptualized as both a danger and an opportunity. The danger resides in the fact that in these conditions the structural, institutional, and cognitive cushions discussed earlier could gradually lose their effectiveness. The social dislocation produced by economic liberalization would either increase the atomization of the society, and lead to mass anomie, or facilitate "praetorian" mobilization. The first outcome would entail a deterioration of the already modest quality of the new democracies (and contribute to their transformation into "delegative" ones), whereas the second would lead to disturbances ("social explosions," such as those that occurred in Argentina and Venezuela in the early 1990s). In both cases the legitimacy of the policies of economic transformation would fall precipitously. This danger is exacerbated by the political institutions that centralize too much power in the presidency, allow for fragmented parliaments and narrow-based party systems, and fall short in the administration of justice. But because this situation involves a restructuring of institutions, it also represents an opportunity for design oriented toward strengthening civil society.

The consequences of the economic transformation on civil society are complex. On the one hand, this transformation produces the social dislocation discussed earlier; on the other hand, it also solidifies autonomous associations in some areas of social life (vertically and horizontally, among the class segments and regions that are the "winners" in the process of economic differentiation), and it decreases the penetration of the society by the state. These processes may contribute to the generation of a system of bargaining and peaceful conflict resolution among interest groups, that is, to the enhancement of societal self-regulation. This is what the nebulous formula "a strong civil society," so popular among students of transitions, actually means: the existence of strong networks of autonomous associations that represent interests as well as values, and that limit the power of the state because of their ability to manage social processes through interaction within institutional channels.[8] The reform of the state may be conducive to such an outcome.

---

[8]On the links behind the correlation between civil society and democracy, see the discussion in Ernest Gellner, *Conditions of Liberty: Civil Society and Its Rivals* (London: Hamish Hamilton, 1994). See also John

As for the strengthening of state capacity, it should be clear that an open-market economy and an efficient democracy presuppose a state not only smaller but also stronger than the one that existed under autarkic capitalism. It would be smaller not only in the sense that it would encompass a more limited proportion of the labor force or produce a more modest share of the gross domestic product (GDP) but also because its ability to regulate the society and control its organizations would be drastically reduced. But it would also be stronger vis-à-vis the society, for it would have enhanced capabilities—in comparison, again, with the autarkic capitalist state—to extract resources from the society through taxation, to administer justice, and to manage defense, health, education, and social security in a more effective manner.

Institutional change may contribute to the invigoration of civil society and the enlargement of state capacity in three main areas. The first is electoral reform, and more specifically the switch in electoral procedures, al least for the election of one of the houses of Congress, or for most of the congressional seats, from proportional representation to majoritarian systems. This change would have two beneficial consequences for the legitimacy of both the state and its policies, economic ones included. First, it would weaken political machines and thus generate more direct ties between citizens and members of Congress. Second, and most important, in electoral procedures it would foster the formation of broad-based parties, less ideological and more oriented toward consensus than the ones generated by proportional representation.[9]

The second area in which institutional change may invigorate society is in the relationship between the executive and the legislative powers. The legitimation of new democracies, as well as that of economic policies carried out by democratic governments in question, would be enhanced by a moderation of the very strong presidentialist tradition in many Latin American countries where some presidents look very much like elected monarchs (consider Mexico and, to a lesser extent, Argentina).[10] Not only does this situation foster authoritarian temptations by the holders of the executive, but it is also conducive to blockage in cases in which strong presidents face congresses controlled by opposition parties not oriented to bargaining and compromise. And proportional representation, which prevails in

A. Hall, ed., *Civil Society: Theory, History, Comparison* (Cambridge: Polity Press, 1995). For empirical analyses, see Victor M. Perez-Diaz, *The Return of Civil Society: The Emergence of Democratic Spain* (Cambridge: Harvard University Press, 1993); and Robert D. Putnam, *Making Democracy Work: Civic Traditions in Modern Italy* (Princeton, NJ: Princeton University Press, 1993).

[9]On the question of the political effects of electoral regimes, see Arend Lijphart and Bernard Grofman, eds., *Choosing an Electoral System: Issues and Alternatives* (New York: Praeger, 1984); Lijphart and Grofman, *Electoral Laws and Their Political Consequences* (New York: Agathon Press, 1986); Robert A. Newland, *Comparative Electoral Systems* (London: McDougall Fund, 1982); and Andrew Reeve and Alan Ware, *Electoral Systems: A Comparative and Theoretical Introduction* (New York: Routledge, 1992).

[10]For the debate on presidentialism versus parliamentarism, see Juan J. Linz, "The Perils of Presidentialism," *Journal of Democracy* 1, no. 1 (winter 1990): 51–69; Juan J. Linz and Arturo Valenzuela, eds., *The Failure of Presidential Democracy* (Baltimore, MD: Johns Hopkins University Press, 1994); Scott Mainwaring, "Presidentialism in Latin America," *Latin American Research Review* 25, no. 1 (1990): 157–79; Carlos S. Nino, "Hyperpresidentialism as the Main Target of Constitutional Reform in Argentina," in Lijphart and Waisman, *Institutional Design in New Democracies*; and Matthew S. Shugart and John M. Carey, *Presidents and Assemblies: Constitutional Design and Electoral Dynamics* (New York: Cambridge University Press, 1992).

Latin America, is more likely than majoritarian systems to produce parties with these characteristics.[11] The solution would not necessarily be the establishment of parliamentary regimes, whose legitimacy in most of Latin America would be hard to establish, but the establishment of mixed forms, such as versions of French-style semipresidentialism. The recent constitutional reform in Argentina is a first step in that direction.

Finally, the strengthening of the judiciary is an imperative need in most countries in the region. This process should have three dimensions: improvement of the efficacy of judicial institutions, greater independence from the executive, and more power of judicial review. In this connection, the experience of the constitutional courts in some new democracies in Central Europe should be of interest to the students of Latin America.[12]

[11]The argument has been made by Juan Linz, "The Perils of Presidentialism." Also see the literature cited earlier on this subject.

[12]See the articles in the special issue of the *East European Constitutional Review* 2 (1993), vol. 2.

READING 6

The New Latin American and Caribbean Nationalism and Economic Reform*

ISAAC COHEN
Economic Commission for Latin America and the Caribbean

INTRODUCTION

This paper examines how the present turn toward a more positive form of nationalism in Latin America and the Caribbean supports the process of economic reform, which started in the region as a result of the depression of the 1980s. These and other developments will be examined as they apply to the contemporary trend toward economic reform in the Latin American and Caribbean context.

The discussion begins with a brief description of the origins of "defensive nationalism" and of the search for a "third way," which prevailed in Latin America and the Caribbean during the years of the cold war.

Second is an attempt to show how the limits of defensive nationalism became manifest as a result of the depression of the 1980s, "the lost decade" for the development of Latin America and the Caribbean. This section also highlights how the slump of the 1980s revealed some of the most striking social and economic shortcomings of defensive nationalism, and it describes how the search for a "third way" has unraveled.

Third, the paper illustrates the rise of a new nationalism in the Western Hemisphere by focusing on some of its positive manifestations, which are more congruent with present circumstances. Also, the primacy of economics, which prevails in inter-American relations, is described by focusing on the displacement of security objectives from the top of the agenda.

To conclude, the external and internal factors that can support or contradict these trends reveal that the region is presently at a decisive juncture, which may lead either to the strengthening of this new, more positive, form of nationalism in a prosperous and democratic hemisphere or, alternatively, to the return of depression and dictatorship.

*Published by permission of the author. Originally published in The Annuals (Vol. 526) March 1993.

THE ROOTS OF DEFENSIVE NATIONALISM

In the scars left by the Great Depression of the 1930s can be found the roots of the defensive form of economic nationalism that prevailed in Latin America and the Caribbean until the beginning of the 1980s. The abrupt plummeting of the prices of primary products, as well as the breakdown of the multilateral trading system and its replacement with Imperial Preferences and Reciprocal Trade Agreements, led Latin America in the 1930s to the pursuit of deliberate import substitution and protectionism.[1] These two were the basic components of the main line of defense against a disappointing international economic system that failed, because it demonstrated it could not be relied upon to sustain the aspirations to welfare and development that were becoming generalized throughout the world.

The war effort, with the imposition of price controls and captive markets, to secure the supply of strategic raw materials confirmed these trends toward protectionism, which prevailed everywhere, in developed as well as in developing economies.

Additionally, the almost generalized acceptance of Keynesian economics consecrated full employment as the basic goal of economic policy, which in its turn became one of the essential elements of the dominant paradigm of what later would be known as development economics. In Albert Hirschman's terms:

> Development economics took advantage of the unprecedented discredit orthodox economics had fallen into as a result of the depression of the thirties and of the equally unprecedented success of an attack on orthodoxy from within the economics "establishment" . . . the Keynesian Revolution of the thirties, which became the "new economics" and almost a new orthodoxy in the forties and fifties.[2]

The conclusion of the hostilities led to the attempt to create a universal, multilateral trading system, based on the most favored nation principle, institutionalized in the General Agreement on Tariffs and Trade (GATT). This also marked the beginning of a divergence of perspectives, which would endure throughout the cold war.

Keynes himself supported some "popular and populist heresies," which contributed to this split. Among them, the "horror of horrors," which holds that the "mercantilist" imposition of import duties and export subsidies "*can* improve the trade balance and domestic employment."[3] This divergence pitted what was characterized originally as "the center against the periphery," or what later became the "North-South" confrontation, to which Latin American economic thought made a decisive contribution.

---

[1]The movement toward import substitution was not uniform. There were several latecomers such as the Central American countries. See ECLAC, *A Collection of Documents on the Economic Relations Between the United States and Central America, 1906–1956* (Santiago, Chile: ECLAC, 1991), U.N. Sales No. E.91.II.G.4, 176–204.

[2]"The Rise and Decline of Development Economics," in *Essays in Trespassing* (New York: Cambridge University Press, 1981), 1–24.

[3]Albert O. Hirschman, "How the Keynesian Revolution Was Exported from the United States, and Other Comments," in *The Political Power of Economic Ideas: Keynesianism Across Nations*, ed. Peter A. Hall (Princeton, NJ: Princeton University Press, 1989), 349.

The experience of Raúl Prebisch, a young Argentinean economist, as a central banker and a trade negotiator during the Great Depression, illustrates the impact these events had in the outlook of Latin American economic decision makers.[4] After the war, as executive head of the newly created United Nations Economic Commission for Latin America (ECLA) Prebisch led the effort to generate a body of economic thought adapted to the new post-war world and to the peculiar circumstances of Latin America. With the intensification of the cold war, development planning and industrialization became part of the instrumental reforms envisaged in the Alliance for Progress for the accomplishment of the overwhelming security objective of halting communist penetration in the hemisphere.

By the mid-1960s, Raúl Prebisch moved out of the hemisphere to head the United Nations Conference on Trade and Development (UNCTAD) in what became an attempt to universalize the tenets of defensive nationalism to the rest of the developing world.[5] The creation of UNCTAD institutionalized, it is tempting to say ritualized, the North-South confrontation, which coexisted uneasily with the central East-West confrontation throughout the cold war. The end of the cold war has revealed how intertwined the North-South confrontation was with the East-West contradiction, or at least how the end of the cold war has affected the terms of the North-South confrontation.

THE SEARCH FOR A "THIRD WAY"

Even before the onset of the cold war, with very few exceptions found among the extremes of the political spectrum, there was an intense search for a "third way," particularly among several indigenous, Latin American political movements.[6] Consequently, during the cold war years, instead of the most radical alternative of turning toward what was known as the socialist camp, the most common expressions of Latin American and Caribbean nationalism were the defensive economic policies practiced throughout the region, as well as the search for a third way between capitalism and socialism. The fate of these two, sometimes

[4]An intellectual biography of Raúl Prebisch has not been published yet. Edgard Dosman and David Pollock are presently working on it in Canada. They recently presented an article based on their extensive research, "Raúl Prebisch, 1901–1971: The Continuing Quest," to a seminar sponsored by the Inter-American Development Bank on "Latin American Economic Thought: Past, Present and Future," held in Washington, D.C., on November 14–15, 1991. See also the comments on the Dosman-Pollock paper presented by Hans Singer at the same seminar. In his comments, Singer describes how he was "struck by some of the similarities between Keynes and Prebisch," 43. Both essays are reproduced in *The Legacy of Raúl Prebisch*, ed. Enrique Iglesias (Washington: Inter-American Development Bank, 1994), 11–48.

[5]This time the "manifesto" was *Towards a New Trade Policy for Development*. See UNCTAD, *The History of UNCTAD 1964–1984* (New York: United Nations, 1985), U.N. Sales No. E.85.II.D.6, 8–10.

[6]In effect, "Keynesianism, with its revaluation of the proper roles of the state, the world of business, and the intellectuals (economists in particular), supplied an attractive 'third way' that could compete with the various fascist and Marxist creeds of the time." Hirschman, "How the Keynesian Revolution Was Exported," 350.

mutually supportive options illustrates some of the consequences that the end of the cold war is having on Latin American and Caribbean nationalism.

When the United States made the confrontation with the Soviet Union the cornerstone of its foreign policy, the defensive form of nationalism that had flourished in Latin America and the Caribbean, as a consequence of the depression and the war, became subordinated to what were considered higher security objectives. One of the main limits confronted by this defensive form of nationalism was external, in the sense that it could go only as far as it would not imperil the overriding security objective of defeating communism.[7] During the cold war years, these security concerns dominated the agenda of inter-American relations and furnished the standard to measure the acceptability and legitimacy of the policies applied throughout the hemisphere. By contrast, in Latin America and the Caribbean, the mirror image corresponding to the primacy of anticommunism and security as criteria of legitimacy expressed itself in terms of trying to gain some distance from these security concerns. Remember the saying, "poor Mexico, so far from God and so close to the United States."

Standards of radicalism were set according to the degree to which they criticized or opposed the United States to the point that nationalism in Latin America and the Caribbean almost became synonymous with overt or covert opposition to the United States. First Cuba, then Nicaragua, epitomized the radical option of switching camps. However, the most common stance strived to remain somewhere in the middle, searching for a proverbial "third way" between capitalism and socialism. This attempt at equidistance was practiced with different degrees of intensity, among others, by the Peruvian *Alianza Popular Revolucionaria Americana* (APRA), the Peronists in Argentina, and the *Partido Revolucionario Institucional* (PRI) in Mexico, as well as by several other parties of a social democratic persuasion. The assertiveness with which security concerns were placed above any other consideration transformed practically any form of Latin American or Caribbean self-affirmation into overt or covert opposition to the United States, because any attempt at self-assertion was perceived as of potential benefit to the adversary.

The Limits of Defensive Nationalism

It is common today to blame defensive nationalism for almost all the shortcomings of Latin American and Caribbean development, particularly for the profound depression that swept the region during the 1980s. However, this judgment is only passed with the benefit of hindsight.

For one thing, it is difficult to argue that these policies were as negative as they are depicted today, because they were applied in a context of sustained expansion. During those years, by stark contrast with what came afterward, the economies of Latin America and the Caribbean experienced an impressive average annual rate of gross domestic product

---

[7]In Latin America, this limit became evident very early in the form of the covert operation that in 1954, at a very low cost to the United States, overthrew the moderately nationalist and communist-supported Arbenz regime in Guatemala. What for many years will remain the definitive work on this episode has appeared recently, Piero Gleijeses, *Shattered Hope: The United States and the Guatemalan Revolution 1944–1954* (Princeton, NJ: Princeton University Press, 1991).

(GDP) of 5 percent. What happened was that the turnaround, in the favorable circumstances that supported these inward-looking policies, arrived quite suddenly. Now, it is accepted that the drying-up of the sources of international private and official finance as well as the abrupt fall in commodity prices were in effect indicating the end of an expanding trading system and of the relatively easy access to financial resources.

However, it took a while before it became generally accepted that the option of defensive economic nationalism had been exhausted. What followed, after the collapse of the favorable circumstances that sustained it, was the spectacle offered by some decision makers who were struggling desperately to continue applying the same policies, as if nothing had changed. Among other consequences, this led to some spectacular cases of hyperinflation not seen before in the region.

Sooner or later, this impressive turnaround led to the search for new forms of insertion in the international economy. The response has taken the form of adopting more open trade regimes, which has led to the diversification of the export sector, as well as to the opening of these economies, by means of the unilateral dismantling of tariff and nontariff barriers.

However, it is perhaps within its internal limits where the most decisive shortcomings of defensive nationalism can be found. More precisely, these shortcomings are found in the inability to incorporate the majority of the population to the benefits generated by three decades of sustained economic expansion. The persistence throughout the region, with very few exceptions, of a regional average of almost 40 percent of all households living under the poverty line represents the most blatant shortcoming of the defensive form of nationalism practiced during those years.[8] This nationalism, in effect, left out sizable portions of the nation. What these levels of poverty reveal is that defensive nationalism was far from being inclusive. Almost everywhere in the region it resulted in the protection of exclusive privileges enjoyed by very restricted numbers of rent-seeking elites, which, allied to co-opted fractions of the middle classes, often resulted in the emergence of exclusionary political regimes.[9]

THE DEMISE OF THE "THIRD WAY"

In contrast to the rather abrupt unraveling of defensive economic nationalism, which started in the beginning of the 1980s with the onset of the debt crisis, the demise of the search for a third way took a bit longer, almost another decade. It finally came, along with

[8]ECLAC, "Magnitud de la pobreza en América Latina en los años ochenta," *Estudios e Informes de la CEPAL* (no. 81), U.N. Sales Number S.91.II.G.10, Santiago de Chile, August 1991; *La equidad en el panorama social de América Latina durante los años ochenta* (LC/G.1686), Santiago de Chile, October 31, 1991; *Panorama social de América Latina* (LC/G. 1688), Santiago de Chile, October 31, 1991.

[9]In those years, one hypothesis even proposed that there was "an inherent association between advanced industrialization and bureaucratic authoritarianism in Latin America." See David Collier's introduction to the fascinating debate generated by this proposal, contained in the collection of papers reproduced in *The New Authoritarianism in Latin America*, ed. David Collier (Princeton: Princeton University Press, 1979), 7.

the fall of the Berlin Wall and of the Soviet Union, and took everybody by surprise in 1989.

As Seymour M. Lipset has found, "equally important if less dramatic shifts have been occurring in the noncommunist parties of the left. Although less noteworthy, since they do not involve revolutionary economic and political changes, they are as significant ideologically."[10] In his review of how "the revolutions of 1989" have affected "the social democratic world," Lipset characterizes the trend as "a movement to the right," by which "in country after country, socialist and other left parties have taken the ideological road back to capitalism," with Latin America and the Caribbean offering no exception.[11]

As part of this worldwide inventory of the fate of social democratic parties, Lipset describes the Peronist rejection of the concept of the state as the motor of the economy, the Democratic Labor Party of Brazil's acceptance of the minimal state, Acción Democrática and the Movement Toward Socialism in Venezuela's support for privatization, the promise by the Christian Democrats in Chile to maintain the basic features of the open economy, and the Partido Revolucionario Institucional in Mexico attacking the tradition of a big paternalistic government. Similar stories are found in Bolivia, Costa Rica, and Peru, as well as in the Caribbean, with the significant examples of Prime Minister Michael Manley in Jamaica and Juan Bosch in the Dominican Republic.

The Roots of the New Nationalism

How do we account for these profound changes, and what do they mean for Latin American and Caribbean nationalism?

One of the primary sources of the impressive changes taking place was the experience brought on by the depression of the 1980s, perhaps because this profound contraction, which lingered throughout the last decade, came after almost 30 years of sustained economic expansion.[12] As a result of what was the most severe economic downturn of the past 50 years—amidst immense resource transfers out of the region, falling commodity prices, and increased levels of poverty—the Latin American and Caribbean economies have undergone a spectacular adjustment.

This transformation has been portrayed by highlighting, almost exclusively, some of its most painful consequences. However, as time goes by and as the indicators reveal the begin-

[10]Seymour Martin Lipset, "No Third Way: A Comparative Perspective on the Left," in *The Crisis of Leninism and the Decline of the Left: The Revolutions of 1989*, ed. Daniel Chirot (Seattle: University of Washington Press, 1991), 183–232.

[11]*Ibid.*, p. 183. Also, in Ralf Dahrendorf's terms, "Communism has collapsed, social democracy is exhausted." *Reflections on the Revolution in Europe* (New York: Random House, 1990), 77.

[12]These three decades have been characterized by Albert O. Hirschman as *"les trente glorieuses"* in Latin America. However, he also found that the "fairly general human trait" of a "reluctance to celebrate or even acknowledge progress while it unfolds before our eyes" has been "particularly marked" in Latin America. With the consequence that there prevailed "a conspiracy of silence about the good news as long as it was still coming." See Hirschman's "The Political Economy of Latin American Development: Seven Exercises in Retrospection," *Latin American Research Review* 22, no. 3 (1987): 8.

ning of an incipient economic reactivation,[13] several positive consequences are beginning to emerge.[14]

First and foremost, some of the most persuasive evidence of this transformation appears more prominently in the external economic relations of the region. As a result of the profound reforms in their trade regimes, almost all the Latin American and Caribbean economies, with different degrees of intensity and speed, have undertaken the unilateral dismantling of tariff and nontariff barriers.[15] These economies have started the 1990s with trade regimes that are more open than those that existed at the beginning of the 1980s. The significance of these reforms, carried out unilaterally in the middle of a deep economic slump, should not be missed.

Equally significant transformations can be found in the structure of the region's foreign trade, particularly in the composition of exports. As a consequence of the sustained fall in the prices of traditional products, with very few exceptions Latin American and Caribbean exports have undergone a major diversification, so much so that in 1990 more than half were nontraditional (by contrast, in 1980 these represented only one-fourth of total exports).

On the side of imports, the most prominent feature in the 1980s was their drastic curtailment, of almost 40 percent, in order to generate the surplus necessary to service the external debt. This was also the result of the steep fall in the prices of traditional exports as well as of the scarcity of foreign exchange that plagued the region throughout the 1980s.

With the incipient economic reactivation initiated in the 1990s, imports are beginning to recover, supported by the decisive measures of unilateral liberalization already mentioned as well as by the positive transfer of resources generated by the inflows of private capital. In some cases, these flows consist of the return of both flight capital and private foreign investment.

At the same time, these sweeping economic reforms to dismantle some of the basic components of defensive nationalism have coincided with a return to democratic and civilian regimes in what constitutes the incipient beginning of an opening of the exclusionary political regimes that frequently coexisted with defensive economic nationalism.

THE PRIMACY OF ECONOMICS

Several factors indicate that there is more than a mere coincidence between these mutually reinforcing trends toward the adoption of profound economic reforms aimed at opening these economies and the opening of political regimes.

First of all, the diversification of the export sectors has contributed to some degree of diversification of the economic elites, with new groups emerging around the successful penetration of external markets by nontraditional exports. "Several success stories of

[13]ECLAC, *Preliminary Overview of the Latin American and Caribbean Economy 1991* (LC/G.1696), Santiago de Chile, December 18, 1991.

[14]Pedro Aspe, Andrés Bianchi, and Domingo Cavallo, *Sea Changes in Latin America* (Washington: Group of Thirty, 1992).

[15]ECLAC, *Latin American and Caribbean Trade and Investment Relations with the United States in the Eighties* (LC.WAS/12), September 23, 1991.

export diversification can be mentioned, such as frozen concentrated orange juice from Brazil, Chilean fruit, Colombian cut flowers and textiles, or Guatemalan new agricultural exports."[16] The fact that today these nontraditional products represent more than half of all exports has punctured the tidiness and cohesiveness of the economic elites, because the newcomers are more interested in penetrating foreign markets than in enjoying the exclusive benefits of closed internal markets.

Furthermore, with the absence of security concerns in the hemisphere, economic issues have moved to the top of the agenda.[17] By contrast, other highly controversial matters have been displaced from the agenda, in some cases because they have been successfully addressed through mutual understanding. One of the best examples of this new consensus on security issues can be found in the production of nuclear weapons, recently renounced as a result of the agreement between the governments of Brazil and Argentina.[18] Thus, the accomplishment of the long-sought-after objective of making Latin America a nuclear-free zone constitutes one of the most significant events to have taken place since the end of the cold war.

This displacement of security concerns by economic objectives from the top of the agenda, such as those generated by the emergence of more competitive and more open economies, is based on the perception that external economic relations, even asymmetrical interdependence, no longer fatally and exclusively leads to zero-sum outcomes.[19] Perhaps the most poignant example of this radical change of perspective can be found in the participation of Mexico in the negotiations with the United States and Canada for the creation of a North American Free Trade Area (NAFTA).[20] The same can be inferred from the positive Latin American and Caribbean response generated by the proposal of extending the free-trade area to the rest of the hemisphere, from Alaska to Patagonia.

---

[16]Limitations of space make it impossible to describe in detail some of these "success stories." Several studies that describe them are available. See ECLAC, *La cadena de distribución y la competitividad de las exportaciones latinoamericanas: La exportación de jugo de naranja concentrado y congelado de Brasil* (LC/R.844), December 29, 1989; *La fruta de Chile* (LC/G.1639), July 31, 1990; *Cadenas agroexportadoras en Chile: transformación productiva e integración social* (LC/L.637), July 24, 1991; *Las exportaciones de manzanas y peras del Alto Valle del Río Negro, Argentina* (LC/G. 1683), December 24, 1991; *Análisis de cadenas agroexportadoras en Guatemala: transformación productiva y diversificación comercial* (LC/R.1112), December 30, 1991; *Las exportaciones de confecciones de textiles de Colombia* (LC/L.676), January 15, 1992.

[17]Isaac Cohen, "Economic Questions," in *The United States and Latin America: Redefining U.S. Purposes in the Post-Cold War Era*, ed. G. Pope Atkins (Austin: Lyndon B. Johnson School of Public Affairs, The University of Texas, 1992).

[18]See *Foz de Iguazú Declaration on the Joint Nuclear Policy of Argentina and Brazil, Signed on November 28, 1990*, circulated as an official document in the Permanent Council of the Organization of American States (OAS), (CP/INF.3071/90 corr 1), January 3, 1991. Also see Eugene Robinson, "S. America Steps Back From Atomic Brink," *The Washington Post*, 26 January 1992.

[19]See Luiz Carlos Bresser Pereira, "Brasil: integración latinoamericana o americana?" *América Latina/Internacional* (Argentina) 8, no. 30 (October/December 1991): 460–65. Also see Luiz Carlos Bresser Pereira and Vera Thorstensen, "From MERCOSUR to American Integration," in *Trade Liberalization in the Western Hemisphere* (Washington: Inter-American Development Bank [IDB] and Economic Commission for Latin America and the Caribbean [ECLAC], 1995), 413–35.

[20]A brief but illustrative statement about this turn toward a more positive form of nationalism in Mexico is by David Ibarra, "Cambio y Nacionalismo," *Comercio Exterior* (Mexico) (January 1992): 81–82.

The days seem to be gone when the guiding principle of Latin American and Caribbean foreign policies rested on the distance these countries could exhibit from the United States. The relations between the United States and Latin America and the Caribbean today are beginning to resemble the relations that prevail between the United States and Canada, where security matters have been displaced from the agenda by the search for positive outcomes and mutual gain in the economic sphere. Latin American and Caribbean nationalism has become more positive, less defensive, and more outward-looking, in the sense that now the interest lies in finding mutually beneficial outcomes in increased levels of economic interdependence.

THE HEMISPHERE AT A CROSSROADS

The question is, what internal and external challenges must be met in order to sustain these positive trends? Internally, the region must address the existence of a majority of households trying to survive under the poverty line. Neither a nation nor a democracy can be said to have taken hold until these vast populations have access to the benefits of freedom and growth. This is the central message that ECLAC presented to the member governments during its session, held in Santiago, Chile, on April 8–15, 1992.[21] Externally, the unilateral opening experienced by the economies of Latin America and the Caribbean must not remain unrequited. The new and more positive form of nationalism that prevails in the region must not be rejected. The emergence of a free-trade area in the Western Hemisphere, as set in the agenda of the Enterprise of the Americas Initiative (EAI), is crucial for strengthening pluralism so as to support new exporters and new entrepreneurs as well as to attain the levels of prosperity required to overcome poverty.

In these circumstances, the countries of Latin America and the Caribbean presently find themselves at an unprecedented and challenging crossroads. One path can lead to a prosperous hemisphere in which democracy and open societies prevail. The other path can lead to "bending the twig,"[22] through a slide back into depression and dictatorship.

[21]ECLAC, *Changing Production Patterns and Social Equity: An Integrated Approach* (LC/G.1701), Santiago de Chile, 6 February 1992.

[22]According to Isaiah Berlin, a wounded aspiration for self-determination may transform itself into nationalist aggression, as is illustrated in Berlin's brilliant metaphor, "like a bent twig, forced down so severely that when released, it lashes back with fury." Nathan Gardels, "Two Concepts of Nationalism: An Interview with Isaiah Berlin," *The New York Review of Books* 21 (November 1991): 19–23; also see Isaiah Berlin, "The Bent Twig: On the Rise of Nationalism," in *The Crooked Timber of Humanity* (New York: Knopf, 1991), 238–61. Originally published in 1972.

READING 7

Latin American Reform: A View from Washington*

JOHN WILLIAMSON
World Bank

Despite my 1989 attempt to distill a consensus about the policy advice being directed at Latin America from Washington,[1] it is not really true that Washington holds monolithic views about anything very much except perhaps the desirability of democracy and human rights. Certainly it was never true that there were monolithic preferences across the whole range of economic policy. What I did argue was that views had coalesced within the policy community sufficiently to allow one to identify a nontrivial lowest common denominator, which I labeled the "Washington Consensus."[2]

In this paper I start by describing the Washington Consensus as I first laid it out. I then go on to discuss whether and how the passage of time and the advent of the Clinton administration have modified what can command a consensus in Washington and then sketch the extent to which those policies have been implemented in Latin America. The paper concludes with reflections provoked by some recent Brazilian polemics.

THE WASHINGTON CONSENSUS

I laid out ten specific policy prescriptions as commanding a consensus in Washington. These may be summarized as follows:

---

*Outline of remarks at the seminar on "*O Brasil e o Novo Cenário Mundial*" at UERJ on 9-11 August 1994.

[1]John Williamson, ed., *Latin American Adjustment: How Much Has Happened?* (Washington: Institute for International Economics, 1990), chap. 2.

[2]I was criticized by some of my Latin friends afterward for naming it as I did because this suggested that Latin Americans who embraced it were having economic correctness imposed on them by Washington. In fact, my view is that the Washington Consensus is the outcome of worldwide intellectual trends to which Latin America contributed (primarily through the work of Hernando de Soto) and that had their most dramatic manifestation in Eastern Europe rather than the Western Hemisphere. This suggests that it would have been preferable to adopt Richard Feinberg's alternative term, the "universal convergence," but my name has stuck and it is now too late to change it.

- *Fiscal discipline.* Budget deficits, properly measured to include provincial governments, state enterprises, and the central bank, should be small enough to be financed without recourse to the inflation tax. This typically implies a primary surplus (that is, before adding debt service to expenditure) of several percent of gross domestic product (GDP) and an operational deficit (that is, the deficit disregarding that part of the interest bill that simply compensates for inflation) of no more than about 2 percent of GDP.
- *Public expenditure priorities.* Expenditures should be redirected from politically sensitive areas that typically receive more resources than their economic return can justify—such as administration, defense, indiscriminate subsidies, and white elephants—to neglected fields with high economic returns and the potential to improve income distribution, such as primary health and education and infrastructure.
- *Tax reform.* When broadening the tax base and cutting marginal tax rates, the aim is to sharpen incentives and improve horizontal equity without lowering realized progressivity. Improved tax administration (including subjecting interest income on assets held abroad—"flight capital"—to taxation) is an important aspect of broadening the base in the Latin context.
- *Financial liberalization.* The ultimate objective is market-determined interest rates, but experience has shown that, under conditions of a chronic lack of confidence, market-determined rates can be so high as to threaten the financial solvency of productive enterprises and government. Under that circumstance a sensible interim objective is the abolition of preferential interest rates for privileged borrowers and the achievement of a moderately positive real interest rate.
- *Exchange rates.* Countries need a unified (at least for trade transactions) exchange rate set at a level sufficiently competitive to induce a rapid growth in nontraditional exports and managed so as to assure exporters that this competitiveness will be maintained in the future.
- *Trade liberalization.* Quantitative trade restrictions should be rapidly replaced by tariffs, and these should be progressively reduced until a uniform low tariff in the range of 10 percent (or at most around 20 percent) is achieved. There is, however, some disagreement about the speed with which tariffs should be reduced (with recommendations falling in a band between three and ten years), and about whether it is advisable to slow down the process of liberalization when macroeconomic conditions are adverse (recession and payments deficit).
- *Foreign direct investment.* Barriers impeding the entry of foreign firms should be abolished; foreign and domestic firms should be allowed to compete on equal terms.
- *Privatization.* State enterprises should be privatized.
- *Deregulation.* Governments should abolish regulations that impede the entry of new firms or restrict competition and ensure that all regulations are justified by such criteria as safety, environmental protection, or prudential supervision of financial institutions.
- *Property rights.* The legal system should provide secure property rights without excessive costs and make these available to the informal sector.

AN UPDATING

To what extent would "Washington" (meaning essentially the U.S. government and the international financial institutions) still endorse this agenda, and are there additional policy issues on which consensus has since coalesced?

It is in my view wrong to interpret the advent of the Clinton administration as marking any general weakening of support for the range of reforms summarized in the Washington Consensus. There were of course changes of emphasis: for example, somewhat less hypocrisy was involved in the support for fiscal discipline on the part of others, and somewhat more in the call for other countries to liberalize their trade policies. There was surely more enthusiasm for increasing public expenditure on basic education and health, and less concern to achieve fiscal discipline by cutting public expenditure rather than by increasing taxes. But by and large I would judge there is about as much support for the program as a whole as there was before, which is hardly surprising inasmuch as I had drawn up the list on the basis of the lowest common denominator of what could command a consensus and the Clinton appointees were not a bunch of Washington outsiders in the way that the original Reagan appointees were.

Similarly, the advocacy of what were termed "market-friendly policies" by the 1991 *World Development Report* marked an attempt to give a more positive emphasis to the role of the state implied in my list by the remarks on public expenditure priorities rather than any rejection of what I intended the Washington Consensus to comprise. Other changes in view regarding the role of the state, such as greater sympathy for industrial policy on the part of the Clinton administration than its predecessor, relate to topics that I had deliberately excluded from my list because I did not believe they commanded a consensus.

The important changes since late 1989 in what commands a consensus in Washington concern not the abandonment of anything that was then accepted but rather additions to the list. Until the end of the 1970s it was generally taken for granted that policy should be concerned not just with the level and growth of income but also that income distribution mattered (with a more egalitarian distribution being presumptively better). That view was self-consciously rejected by the first Reagan administration, but concern with the social dimension of economic policy subsequently reemerged gradually. In 1989, in the course of discussing my paper "What Washington Means by Policy Reform," Stanley Fischer offered an alternative summary of the policy consensus that he agreed had emerged, which he summarized as a sound macroeconomic framework, an efficient and smaller government, an efficient and expanding private sector, and poverty-reduction policies. On the latter, he wrote:

> Emphasis on poverty reduction has increased in recent years and will continue to do so. The concern with poverty reduction goes beyond the belief that economic growth will reduce poverty, to the view that specific policies, such as targeted food subsidies as well as the medical and educational programs to which Williamson refers, can reduce the number of poor people in a given country and should be used for that purpose.

I was delighted that Fischer felt that the World Bank had got back to the point where such a view could be expressed by its chief economist, but I nonetheless doubted whether his inclusion of poverty reduction in the wider consensus was justified at that time.

However, his prediction that the issue would become increasingly salient proved to be correct. The World Bank devoted the 1990 issue of its *World Development Report* to poverty. The Inter-American Development Bank held a major conference on Social Reform and Poverty in early 1993 and now devotes a large portion of its lending program to socially oriented projects. Concern with the social dimension was fully reinstated with the advent of the Clinton administration. Both the Agency for International Development (AID) and the World Bank now explicitly include "sustainable development" among their priorities.

Can this concern be summarized by any propositions comparable to the preceding ten in terms of their scope and the breadth of the consensus that they can command? Two possible candidates stand out:

- *Birth control.* Universal access to birth control should be provided at the earliest possible date.
- *Social expenditure.* Public expenditure priorities should include social expenditures with a high payoff in terms of assisting the most disadvantaged and improving income distribution, such as targeted welfare payments and the provision of piped water and low-cost, self-help housing.[3]

I doubt that one could go further by claiming a consensus in favor of more progressive taxation or land reform. These strike me as among the many important topics on which differences of view persist among those who think of themselves as part of the broad middle ground that takes mainstream middlebrow economics seriously.

POLICY REFORM IN LATIN AMERICA

The primary purpose of my 1990 study cited in footnote 1 was to assess how much progress had been made in Latin America in introducing the several policy reforms that I listed. To that end we convened a conference where experts from each of the principal Latin American countries gave an authoritative account of how reform had been progressing in their country. I have no similar body of work on which to draw in presenting the following assessment. Nevertheless, I hope it is of some interest to relate my impressions of what has been happening in the seven principal countries during the intervening years.

The record is one of substantial but still uneven progress. Argentina, Chile, Colombia, Mexico, and more recently Peru have all gone a long way toward stabilizing, liberalizing, and opening their economies. Brazil has also done more than it was credited with: At least prior to the Plano Real the persistence of chronic inflation swamped everything else in the minds of most foreign observers, so the country got little credit for the very real opening initiated by the Collor government. Venezuela is today the sad example of a country that, after a brief fling with a vigorous liberalization that was never endorsed by public opinion, turned back to the policies of the past and found itself rapidly overwhelmed by a crisis.

Progress is also uneven if we look at the subject headings. Fiscal discipline has come a long way almost everywhere: Even Argentina has begun running surpluses, and more recently Brazil put its accounts in order before launching the Plano Real (although we wait from one week to the next fearing news of some populist giveaway that will destroy the hope that

[3]This goes further than the second entry in the earlier list in endorsing social expenditures with a high equity payoff even if they cannot be rationalized by a presumption of an increased rate of growth. It retains the basic view that equity concerns should be addressed through fiscal measures, primarily the composition of public expenditures, rather than through directed or subsidized credit, trade policy, or populist macroeconomics.

Brazil is about to join Argentina and Germany as a country whose past inflation excesses have inoculated it against future inflation).

Reordering public expenditure priorities was the heading under which I judged there to have been the least progress up to 1990, and I am not sure the situation has changed much since. It is certainly true that Brazil desperately needs some action on this front: The latest *Human Development Report* reveals that only 20 percent of children complete primary education in Brazil, compared with an average in all developing countries of 71 percent (and 57 percent even in sub-Saharan Africa) and figures near 100 percent in the successful East Asian countries. It is not surprising that Brazil has the second most unequal income distribution in the world with a statistic like that.

Liberalization of trade and foreign direct investment (FDI) has also been general (until the recent Venezuelan retrogression) and remarkably profound.

Exchange rate policy reveals an important divergence between countries. Argentina and Mexico are using a fixed or semifixed exchange rate as a nominal anchor, and in consequence are suffering significantly overvalued currencies. Chile and Colombia (and, until the [temporary?] freeze involved in introduction of the real, Brazil) have instead used a crawling peg dedicated in large measure to maintaining an adequate level of competitiveness. Peru has floated, and, given the pressure from excessive capital inflows, also suffers from overvaluation. The way I phrased the Washington Consensus on this point, as favoring a competitive exchange rate, implies that one should declare that Chile and Colombia (and presumably Brazil) are in compliance, and I would argue that this is the main reason that their growth rates look so much more healthy than that of Mexico.[4] I have to confess, however, that on reflection I am not quite sure that I was an accurate reporter of the state of Washington opinion on this issue. The International Monetary Fund (IMF) had a lot of adherents of the nominal anchor theology that has again got Mexico into trouble, and the U.S. government tends to be populated by gung-ho floaters, so it is not clear that there is a consensus for making the preservation of competitiveness the priority task for exchange rate policy. I wish it were otherwise.

Privatization has been pursued rather generally, though with more urgency in Argentina and Chile than in Brazil and Venezuela. Property titling has been undertaken primarily in Peru.

I do not have the impression that a lot has yet been done to address the sort of social agenda that I earlier argued could now be added to the original Washington Consensus. It is not only Brazil that scores badly for the percentage of children completing primary education: Available figures for the other large Latin American countries are Chile, 77 percent; Mexico, 72 percent; Colombia, 56 percent; and Venezuela, 48 percent.

Neoliberalism and All That

I think I first heard the Washington Consensus described as a neoliberal program by Luiz Carlos Bresser Pereira at a conference in 1992. I was not very clear what neoliberalism was,

[4]Argentina has enjoyed strong growth since 1990, and Peru had a good year in 1993, but one still has to worry that these experiences may be more a bounce back from previous disasters (similar to that enjoyed by Venezuela in 1990–1992) rather than the beginning of a trend.

so I asked him for a definition. He gave me a very clear reply: He conceived it as consisting of monetarism, public choice theory, Austrian economics, and new classical macroeconomics. I responded that, with the possible exception of Austrian economics, this was pretty much a list of the ways in which conservative economists had tried to dress up their political prejudices as positive economics. (That is doubtless an exaggeration, but it contains an element of truth.)

Would a neoliberal economist in that sense subscribe to the Washington Consensus as I defined it? Yes, or at least I hope so, if we are speaking of the original 1989 version. The list was supposed to represent the lowest common denominator of what was accepted as desirable in Washington, and since that was the first year of the Bush administration there were still a lot of pretty conservative people in influential positions around town. But I argued before that this lowest common denominator was also subscribed to by the Clinton appointees, whom no one could reasonably accuse of being "neoliberals" in the sense that Bresser defined the term for me. In fact, as Bresser expressed it on another occasion, my version of the Washington Consensus is more a summary of the basic policy recommendations subscribed to by all mainstream economists.

I say "my version of the Washington Consensus" because in another debate Bresser told me that the mere fact that I had invented the term gave me no prerogative in defining what it means. The concept has, he asserted, taken on a life of its own. Perhaps he is right, and if Brazilian political scientists choose to use it as a political swear word, their usage is as good as mine. I hope, however, that I can still ask that they take as much trouble to define what they mean by the term as I have done.

Does Fernando Henrique Cardoso subscribe to the Washington Consensus (in my sense of the term)? I very much hope so, as I hope Lula subscribes to it, for if the next president of Brazil tries to defy the Washington Consensus, then Brazil will follow Venezuela on the road to ruin. But since Cardoso has warned us that his academic writings are not a good guide to his current views, and he has not divulged to me what those views are, I am in no position to give an assurance that he is as enlightened as I hope he now is.

Is Cardoso's program summarized by the Washington Consensus? Clearly not. He orchestrated the Plano Real, and the only feature of that plan that is contained in the Washington Consensus is the need to start with fiscal discipline. There is no hint of the idea of using an indexed unit of account as the basis for a new money, or the formulae for conversion at the mean from the old to the new money. These were distinctively Brazilian ideas that were spawned by and for the Brazilian context and that would be incomprehensible to most Washington proponents of the Washington Consensus. They were a complement to rather than a constituent of the Washington Consensus.

And that is exactly as it should be. The Washington Consensus should become like democracy and human rights, a part of the basic core of ideas that we hold in common and do not need to debate endlessly, so that we can go forward constructively to address the vast range of issues where specific national initiatives are needed and where national intellectual and political leadership is therefore going to be indispensable to progress. If I were a Brazilian, I know where I would next want to see the same imagination and determination applied as was exhibited in the design of the Plano Real. I would want to know how quickly the proportion of the population completing primary education could be quintupled. The Washington Consensus would not help me find an answer; but defying it would ensure that no answer was found.

READING 8

1995 and Beyond: The Era of Deflated Expectations (Dutch Tulips and Emerging Markets)

PAUL KRUGMAN
Massachusetts Institute of Technology

ANOTHER BUBBLE BURSTS

During the first half of the 1990s, both economic and political events in developing countries defied all expectations. Nations that most thought would not regain access to world financial markets for a generation abruptly became favorites of private investors, who plied them with capital inflows on a scale not seen since before World War I. Governments that had spent half a century pursuing statist, protectionist policies suddenly got free market religion. It was, it seemed to many observers, the dawn of a new golden age for global capitalism.

To some extent the simultaneous reversals in government policies and investor sentiment were the result of external factors. Low interest rates in the advanced countries encouraged investors to look again at opportunities in the Third World; the fall of communism not only helped to discredit statist policies everywhere but reassured investors that their assets in the developing world were unlikely to be seized by leftist governments. Still, probably the most important factor in the new look of developing countries was a sea change in the intellectual zeitgeist: the almost universal acceptance, by governments and markets alike, of a new view about what it takes to develop.

This new view has come to be widely known as the "Washington consensus," a phrase coined by John Williamson of the Institute for International Economics. By "Washington" Williamson meant not only the U.S. government, but all those institutions and networks of opinion leaders centered in the world's de facto capital—the International Monetary Fund, World Bank, think tanks, politically sophisticated investment bankers, and worldly finance ministers, all those who meet each other in Washington and collectively define the conventional wisdom of the moment.

Williamson's original definition of the Washington consensus involved ten different aspects of economic policy. One may, however, roughly summarize this consensus, at least as it influenced the beliefs of markets and governments, more simply. It is the belief that

Victorian virtue in economic policy—free markets and sound money—is the key to economic development. Liberalize trade, privatize state enterprises, balance the budget, peg the exchange rate, and one will have laid the foundations for an economic takeoff; find a country that has done these things, and there one may confidently expect to realize high returns on investments.

To many people the rise of the Washington consensus seemed to mark a fundamental turning point in world economic affairs. Now that the dead hand of the state was being lifted from Third World economies, now that investors were becoming aware of the huge possibilities for profit in these economies, the world was set for a prolonged period of rapid growth in hitherto poor countries and massive capital flows from North to South. The question was not whether optimistic expectations about growth in the big emerging markets would be fulfilled; it was whether advanced countries would be able to cope with the new competition and take advantage of the opportunities this growth now offered.[1]

And then came the Mexican crisis. The country that was widely regarded as a model for the new regime—a once-protectionist nation that had not only greatly lowered its trade barriers but actually signed a free trade pact with the United States, whose economic policy was run by articulate American-trained technocrats, and which had emerged from seven lean years of debt crisis to attract capital inflows on a scale unimaginable a few years earlier—was once again appealing for emergency loans. But what is the meaning of Mexico's tailspin? Is it merely the product of specific Mexican blunders and political events, or does it signal the unsoundness of the whole emerging market boom of the previous five years?

Many claim that Mexico's problems carry few wider implications. On one side, they argue that a currency crisis says more about short-term monetary management than about long-run development prospects. And to some extent they are clearly right. Currency crises are so similar to one another that they are a favorite topic for economic theorists, who lovingly detail the unchanging logic by which the collision between domestic goals and an unsustainable exchange rate generates a sudden, massive speculative attack. The December 1994 attack on the peso looked a lot like the September 1992 attack on the pound sterling, which looked quite similar to the 1973 and 1971 attacks on the dollar and the 1969 run on gold. So perhaps one should not draw broad conclusions from the fact that a developing country has managed to make the same mistakes that nearly every advanced country has made at some time in the past.

On the other side, defenders of the Washington consensus point to the many uniquely Mexican aspects of the current crisis. Certainly the combination of peasant uprisings, mysterious assassinations, and bizarre fraternal intrigue has no close counterpart anywhere else in the world.

And yet Mexico's crisis is neither a temporary setback nor a purely Mexican affair. Something like that crisis was an accident waiting to happen because the stunning initial success of the Washington consensus was based not on solid achievements, but on excessively optimistic expectations. The point is not that the policy recommendations that

[1]The strategy of promoting U.S. exports and investment in emerging markets remains central to the Clinton administration's economic strategy. In a March 1995 speech, Undersecretary of Commerce Jeffrey Garten declared that "our exports and jobs are dependent on gaining a larger market share in the big emerging markets. No U.S. firm will be a world-class company without substantial involvement in the big emerging markets."

Williamson outlined are wrong, but that their efficacy—their ability to turn Argentina into Taiwan overnight—was greatly oversold. Indeed, the five-year reign of the Washington consensus may usefully be thought of as a sort of speculative bubble—one that involved not only the usual economic process by which excessive market optimism can be a temporarily self-fulfilling prophecy, but a more subtle political process through which the common beliefs of policy-makers and investors proved mutually reinforcing. Unfortunately, any such self-reinforcing process unfortunately must eventually be faced with a reality check, and if the reality is not as good as the myth, the bubble bursts. For all its special features, the Mexican crisis marks the beginning of the deflation of the Washington consensus. That deflation ensures that the second half of the 1990s will be a far more problematic period for global capitalism than the first.

The Real Payoff to Reform

Economists have, of course, long preached the virtues of free markets. The economic case for free trade in particular, while not completely watertight, is far stronger than most people imagine. The logic that says that tariffs and import quotas almost always reduce real income is deep and has survived a century and a half of often vitriolic criticism nearly intact. And experience teaches that governments that imagine or pretend that their interventionist strategies are a sophisticated improvement on free trade nearly always turn out, on closer examination, to be engaged in largely irrational policies—or worse, in policies that are rational only in the sense that they benefit key interest groups at the expense of everyone else.

Yet there is a dirty little secret in international trade analysis. The measurable costs of protectionist policies—the reductions in real income that can be attributed to tariffs and import quotas—are not all that large. The costs of protection, according to the textbook models, come from the misallocation of resources: protectionist economies deploy their capital and labor in industries in which they are relatively inefficient, instead of concentrating on those industries in which they are relatively efficient, exporting those products in exchange for the rest. These costs are very real, but when you try to add them up, they are usually smaller than the rhetoric of free trade would suggest. For example, most estimates of the cost of protection in the United States put it well under one percent of GDP. Even that cost is largely due to the United States' preference for policies, like its sugar import quota, that generate high profits for those foreign suppliers granted access to the U.S. market. Highly protected economies, like most developing countries before the rise of the Washington consensus, suffer more. Still, conventional estimates of the costs of protection have rarely exceeded five percent of GDP. That is, the standard estimates suggest that a highly protectionist developing country, by moving to completely free trade, would get a one-time economic boost equal to the growth China achieves every five or six months.

Admittedly, many economists argue that the adverse effects of protection are larger, and thus the growth boost from trade liberalization is greater, than such conventional estimates suggest. Roughly speaking, they have suggested three mechanisms. First, protection reduces competition in the domestic market. The monopoly power that is created for domestic firms that no longer face foreign competition may be reflected either in slack management or, if a small number of firms are trying to secure monopoly positions, in wasteful duplication. Second, protectionist policies—and other policies like interest rate controls—create profits that accrue to whoever is influential enough to receive the appropriate government licenses.

In a well-known paper, Anne Krueger, who later became the chief economist at the World Bank, argued that in many developing countries, the resources squandered in pursuit of these profits represent a larger net cost to the economy than the distortion that protectionism causes in the industrial mix.[2] Finally, many people have argued that protectionism discourages innovation and the introduction of new products, thereby having sustained effects on growth that a static estimate misses. The important point about these arguments for large gains from trade liberalization, however, is that they are all fairly speculative; one cannot say as a matter of principle that these effects of protection discourage growth. It is an empirical question.

And the empirical evidence for huge gains from free market policies is, at best, fuzzy. There have been a number of attempts to measure the benefits of free trade by comparing countries. An influential 1987 study by the World Bank classified 41 developing countries as "closed" (protectionist) or "open" and concluded that openness was associated with substantially stronger growth. But such studies have often been critiqued for using subjective criteria in deciding which countries have freer trade; the decision to class South Korea as "open," for example, has raised many doubts. A survey by UCLA's Sebastian Edwards concluded that studies which purport to show that countries with liberal trade regimes systematically grow more rapidly than those with closed markets "have been plagued by empirical and conceptual shortcomings [that have] resulted, in many cases, in unconvincing results whose fragility has been exposed by subsequent work."[3]

There are surely additional gains to reforming economies from domestic liberalization, privatization, and so on. These gains have not been as thoroughly studied as those from trade liberalization. They are, however, conceptually very similar, and there is no reason to expect them to be dramatically larger or to change the picture of real but limited gains from reform.

All this does not mean that trade liberalization is not a good idea. It almost certainly is. Nor does it necessarily mean that the modest conventional estimates of the gains from such liberalization tell the whole story. But it does mean that the widespread belief that moving to free trade and free markets will produce a dramatic acceleration in a developing country's growth represents a leap of faith, rather than a conclusion based on hard evidence.

What about the other half of the Washington consensus, the belief in the importance of sound money? Here the case is even weaker.

If standard estimates of the costs of protection are lower than you might expect, such estimates of the cost of inflation—defined as the overall reduction in real income—are so low that they are embarrassing. Of course very high inflation rates—the triple- or quadruple-digit inflations that have, unfortunately, been all too common in Latin American history—seriously disrupt the functioning of a market economy. But it is very difficult to pin down any large gains from a reduction in the inflation rate from, say, 20 percent to 2 percent.

Moreover, the methods used to achieve disinflation in developing countries—above all, the use of a pegged exchange rate as a way to build credibility—have serious costs. A country with an inflationary history that tries to end inflation by establishing a fixed exchange

---

[2]Anne Krueger, "The Political Economy of the Rent-Seeking Society," *American Economic Review*, June 1974.

[3]Sebastian Edwards, "Openness, Trade Liberalization, and Growth in Developing Countries," *Journal of Economic Literature*, September 1993.

rate almost always finds that the momentum of inflation continues for a considerable time, throwing domestic costs and prices out of line with the rest of the world. Thus an exchange rate that initially seemed reasonable usually seems considerably overvalued by the time inflation finally subsides. Furthermore, an exchange rate that is tolerable when introduced may become difficult to sustain when world market conditions change, such as the price of oil, the value of the dollar, and interest rates. Textbook international economics treats the decision about whether to fix a country's exchange rate as a difficult tradeoff, which even countries committed to low inflation often end up resolving on the side of exchange rate flexibility.

Nonetheless, during the first half of the 1990s a number of developing countries adopted rigid exchange rate targets. (The most extreme case was Argentina, which established a supposedly permanent one-for-one exchange rate between the peso and the U.S. dollar). In large part this was a move designed to restore credibility after the uncontrolled inflation of the 1980s. Nonetheless, both governments and markets seem to have convinced themselves that the painful tradeoff traditionally involved in such a commitment no longer applied.

The Dismal Cycle

In sum, then, a cool-headed analysis of the likely effects of the economic reforms undertaken in developing countries in recent years did not and does not seem to justify wild enthusiasm. Trade liberalization and other moves to free up markets are almost surely good things, but the idea that they will generate a growth takeoff represents a hope rather than a well-founded expectation. Bringing down inflation is also a good thing, but doing so by fixing the exchange rate brings a mixture of benefits and costs, with the arguments against as strong as the arguments for. And yet the behavior of both governments and markets during the last five years does not suggest that they took any such measured view. On the contrary, governments eagerly adopted Washington consensus reform economies. Why?

Everyone is familiar with the way that a speculative bubble can develop in a financial market. Investors, for whatever reason, come to take a more favorable view of the prospects for some traded asset—Deutsche marks, Japanese stocks, shares in the South Sea Company, tulip futures. This leads to a rise in the asset's price. If investors then interpret this gain as a trend rather than a one-time event, they become still more anxious to buy the asset, leading to a further rise, and so on. In principle, long-sighted investors are supposed to prevent such speculative bubbles by selling assets that have become overpriced or buying them when they have become obviously cheap. Sometimes, however, markets lose sight of the long run, especially when the long run is complex or obscure. Thus speculative bubbles in soybean futures tend to be limited by the common knowledge that a lot more soybeans will be grown if the price gets very high. But the chain of events that must eventually end a speculative bubble in, say, the mark—an overvalued mark reduces German exports, leading to a weak German economy, so the Bundesbank reduces interest rates, making it unattractive to hold mark-denominated assets—is often too long and abstract to seem compelling to investors when the herd is running.

It seems fairly clear that some of the enthusiasm for investing in developing countries in the first half of the 1990s was a classic speculative bubble. A modest recovery in economic prospects from the dismal 1980s led to large capital gains for those few investors who had been willing to put money into Third World stock markets. Their success led other investors to jump in, driving prices up still further. And by 1993 or so "emerging market funds" were being advertised on television and the pages of popular magazines.

At the same time that this self-reinforcing process was under way in the financial markets, a different kind of self-reinforcing process, sociological rather than economic, was taking place in the world of affairs—the endless rounds of meetings, speeches, and exchanges of communiqués that occupy much of the time of economic opinion leaders. Such interlocking social groupings tend at any given time to converge on a conventional wisdom, about economics among many other things. People believe certain stories because everyone important tells them, and people tell those stories because everyone important believes them. Indeed, when a conventional wisdom is at its fullest strength, one's agreement with that conventional wisdom becomes almost a litmus test of one's suitability to be taken seriously.

Anyone who tried, two or three years ago, to express even mild skepticism about the prospects for developing countries knows how difficult it was to make any impression on either business or political leaders. Views contrary to the immense optimism of the time were treated not so much with hostility as bemusement. How could anyone be so silly as to say these gloomy things?[4]

While both a speculative bubble in the financial markets and the standard process whereby influential people rally around a conventional wisdom surely played a role in the astonishing rise of the Washington consensus, there was, however, an additional, distinctive self-reinforcing process that arguably played an even greater role. This was a political economy cycle, in which governments were persuaded to adopt Washington consensus policies because markets so spectacularly rewarded them, and in which markets were willing to supply so much capital because they thought they saw an unstoppable move toward policy reform.

One must begin with a key insight of Dani Rodrik of Columbia University. Rodrik pointed out that economists and international organizations like the World Bank had been arguing for a long time in favor of freer trade in developing countries.[5] The intellectual case for protectionism to promote industrialization, while popular in the 1950s, has been pretty much moribund since the late 1960s. Nonetheless, the stake of established interest groups in the existing system blocked any major move to free trade. When limited liberalization was attempted, it usually ended up being abandoned a few years later. Why did this suddenly change?

One seemingly obvious answer is the Third World debt crisis of the 1980s, which made the previous system untenable. But economic crises, especially when they involve the balance of payments, traditionally lead to more protectionism, not less. Why was this case different?

---

[4]Academic economists with expertise in the macroeconomics of developing countries were issuing clear warnings about excessive euphoria, which Wall Street simply shrugged off, as early as the beginning of 1993. See, in particular, Rudiger Dornbusch, *Stabilization, Debt, and Reform: Policy Analysis for Developing Countries*, Englewood Cliffs: Prentice Hall, 1993, and "Mexico: Stabilization, Reform and No Growth," *Brookings Papers on Economic Activity*, No. 1, 1994. I gave a speech warning of a peso crisis in Mexico City on March 25, 1993.

[5]Dani Rodrik, "The Rush to Free Trade in the Developing World: Why So Late? Why Now? Will It Last?" in *Voting for Reform: The Politics of Adjustment in New Democracies*, ed. Stephan Haggard and Steven B. Webb, New York: Oxford, 1994.

Rodrik's answer was that in the 1990s, advocates of free trade in developing countries were able to link free trade to financial and macroeconomic benefits. If trade liberalization is presented as a detailed microeconomic policy, the industries that stand to lose will be well-informed and vociferous in their opposition, while those who stand to gain will be diffuse and ineffective. What reformers in a number of countries were able to do, however, was to present trade liberalization as part of a package that was presumed to yield large gains to the country as a whole. That is, it was not presented as, "Let's open up imports in these 20 industries, and there will be efficiency gains"; that kind of argument does not work very well in ordinary times. Instead it was, "We have to follow the strategy that everyone serious knows works: free markets—including free trade—and sound money, leading to rapid economic growth."

Calling a set of economic measures a package does not mean that they need in fact be undertaken together. One can bring inflation down without liberalizing trade, and vice versa. But voters do not usually engage in hypothetical line-item vetoes, asking which elements of an economic program are essential and which can be dropped. If a program of economic stabilization-cum-liberalization seems to work, the political process is easily persuaded that all of the package is essential.

And the point was that such packages did work, and in fact initially did so astonishingly well—but not necessarily because of their fundamental economic merits. Rather, the immediate payoff to Washington consensus reforms was in the sudden improvement in investor confidence.

Mexico is particularly noteworthy. Mexico began a major program of trade liberalization in the late 1980s, with no obvious immediate results in terms of faster economic growth. The turning point came when the country negotiated a debt reduction package, which went into effect in 1990. The debt reduction was intelligently handled, but everyone involved realized that it was fairly small, not nearly enough to make much direct difference to Mexico's growth prospects.

And yet what followed the debt reduction was a transformation of the economic picture. With stunning speed, Mexico's problems seemed to melt away. Real interest rates were 30 to 40 percent before the debt deal, with the payments on internal debt a major source of fiscal pressure; they fell between 5 and 10 percent almost immediately. Mexico had been shut out of international financial markets since 1982; soon after the debt deal, capital inflows resumed on an ever-growing scale. And growth resumed in the long-stagnant economy.

Why did a seemingly modest debt reduction spark such a major change in the economic environment? International investors saw the debt deal as part of a package of reforms that they believed would work. Debt reduction went along with free markets and sound money, free markets and sound money mean prosperity, and so capital flowed into a country that was following the right path.

In the 1990s, advocates of the Washington consensus have not had to make abstruse arguments about the benefits of better resource allocation nor plead with the public to accept short-term pain in the interest of long-run gain. Instead, because the financial market offered an immediate, generous advance on the presumed payoff from free trade and sound money, it was easy to make a case for doing the right thing and brush aside all the usual political objections.

So much for one side of the political-economic cycle. The other side involved the willingness of financial markets to provide lavish rewards for economic reform. In part, of course, the markets believed that such policies would pay off in the long run. But most of the developing countries that suddenly became investor favorites in the 1990s had long histories of disappointed expectations, not just the debt crisis of the 1980s, but track records of abandoned economic reforms reaching back for decades. Why should investors have been so confident that this time the reforms would really stick? Presumably, this time reforms were taking place so extensively, and in so many countries, that investors found it easy to believe that it was a completely new world, that runaway inflation, populist economic policies, exchange controls, and so on were vanishing from the global scene.

But I have just argued, following Rodrik, that the unprecedented depth and breadth of policy reform was largely due to the perception that such reforms brought macroeconomic and financial recovery—a perception driven by the way that financial markets rewarded the reforms! So once again something of a circular logic was at work.

During the first half of the 1990s, a set of mutually reinforcing beliefs and expectations created a mood of euphoria about the prospects for the developing world. Markets poured money into developing countries, encouraged both by the capital gains they had already seen and by the belief that a wave of reform was unstoppable. Governments engaged in unprecedented liberalization, encouraged both by the self-reinforcing conventional wisdom and the undeniable fact that reformers received instant gratification from enthusiastic investors. It was a very happy picture. Why couldn't it continue?

THE REALITY CHECK

From a mere trickle during the 1980s, private capital flows to developing countries soared to about $130 billion in 1993. Relatively little of this money went to those East Asian countries that had already achieved rapid economic growth during the 1980s. Less than 10 percent of the total, for example, went to China, and the four Asian tigers—Singapore, Hong Kong, South Korea, and Taiwan—were all net exporters of capital. Instead, the bulk of the money went to countries that had done poorly in previous years, but whose new commitment to Washington consensus policies was believed to ensure a dramatic turnaround: Latin American countries, plus a few others such as the Philippines and Hungary. How well were these economies doing?

In one respect, the performance of the main recipients of massive capital inflows did represent a break with the past. The new insistence on sound money had, indeed, led to impressive reductions in inflation rates. Between 1987 and 1991, Mexico's inflation rate had averaged 49 percent; in 1994, it was less than 7 percent. In Argentina the contrast was even more spectacular, from an average inflation rate of 609 percent in 1987–91 to a rate of less than 4 percent last year.

That was the good news. Unfortunately, there was also a substantial amount of disappointing news, on three main fronts. First, while hard currency policies brought down inflation, they did so only gradually. As a result, costs and prices got far out of line with those in the rest of the world. Mexico, for example, allowed the peso to fall only 13 percent between 1990 and the first quarter of 1994, but consumer prices in Mexico nonetheless rose 63 percent over that period, compared with a rise of only 12 percent in the United States. Thus Mexico's real exchange rate—the ratio of Mexican prices in dollars to prices in the United States—rose 28 percent, pricing many Mexican goods out of U.S. markets and fueling an import boom. Argentina's drastic policy, which sought to end a history of extreme inflation by pegging the value of the peso permanently at one dollar, predictably left the country's prices even farther out of line. Between 1990 and early 1991 the Argentine real exchange rate rose 68 percent.

Second, in spite of huge inflows of foreign capital, the real growth in the recipient economies was generally disappointing. Mexico was the biggest disappointment: although capital flows into Mexico reached more than $30 billion in 1993, the country's rate of growth over the 1990–94 period averaged only 2.5 percent, less than population growth. Other countries did better: Argentina, for example, grew at an annual average rate of more than 6 percent after the stabilization of the peso. But even optimists admitted that this growth had much to do with the extremely depressed state of the economy before the reforms. When an economy has been as thoroughly mismanaged as Argentina's was during the 1980s, a return to political and monetary stability can easily produce a large one-shot rise in output. Across Latin America as a whole, real growth in the period 1990–94 averaged only 3.1 percent per year.

Finally, the benefits of growth, which was in any case barely positive in per capita terms, were also very unevenly distributed. Developing country statistics on both unemployment and income distribution are fairly unreliable, but there is not much question that even as Latin American stock markets were booming, unemployment was rising, and the poor were getting poorer.

In sum, the real economic performance of countries that had recently adopted Washington consensus policies, as opposed to the financial returns they were delivering to international investors or the reception their policies received on the conference circuit, was distinctly disappointing. Whatever the conventional wisdom might have said, the underlying basis for the conviction of both investors and governments that these countries were on the right track was becoming increasingly fragile.

Some kind of crisis of confidence was thus inevitable. It could have come in several different ways. For example, there might have been a purely financial crisis: a loss of confidence in emerging markets as investments, leading to capital flight and only then to a loss of political confidence. Or there could have been an essentially intellectual crisis: the growing evidence that the new policies were not delivering in the way or at the speed that conventional wisdom had expected might have led to soul-searching among the policy elite. But given the way that the Washington consensus had originally come to flourish, it should not be surprising that the crisis, when it came, involved the interaction of economics and politics.

Consider the essentials of the Mexican situation as it began to unravel in 1994—the factors that would surely have provoked a crisis even without the uprisings and assassinations. Despite the popularity of the country among foreign investors, growth had slowed in 1993 to a virtual crawl, creating a considerable rise in unemployment. This growth slowdown was in a direct sense due to the rise in Mexico's real exchange rate after 1990, which discouraged any rapid growth in exports and caused growing demand to be spent primarily on imports rather than domestic goods. More fundamentally, the free market policies had not, a least so far, generated the kind of explosion of productivity, new industries, and exports that reformers hoped for.

Given these economic realities, the Mexican government was faced with a dilemma. If it wanted to get even modest growth going again, it would need to do something to make its industries more cost-competitive—that is, devalue the peso. But to do so, given the emphasis that the government had placed on sound money, would be very damaging to its credibility. In the event, the approach of the presidential election seems to have led the

Mexicans neither to devalue nor to accept slow growth, but rather to reflate the economy by loosening up government spending. The result was a loss of credibility even worse than that which would have been produced by an early devaluation. And then the usual logic of currency crisis came into play: because investors thought, with some reason, that the currency might be devalued, they became unwilling to hold peso assets unless offered very high interest rates; and the necessity of paying these high rates, together with the depressing effect of high rates on the economy, increased the pressure on the government to abandon the fixed exchange rate—which made investors even less willing to hold pesos, in a rapid downward spiral familiar to scores of former finance ministers around the world.

The point is that while the details could not have been predicted, something like the Mexican crisis was bound to happen. Without the Chiapas uprising or the assassination of presidential candidate Luis Donaldo Colosio, Mexico might not have hit the wall in December 1994, but it probably would not have gone unscathed through 1995. An early, controlled devaluation might have done less damage than the display of confusion that actually took place, but it would still have done considerable harm to the government's credibility. And even if Mexico had somehow avoided getting into trouble, the disparity between the glittering prizes promised by the Washington consensus and the fairly dreary reality was bound to produce a revolution of falling expectations somewhere along the line.

AN AGE OF DEFLATED EXPECTATIONS?

Because the 1990–95 euphoria about developing countries was so overdrawn, the Mexican crisis is likely to be the trigger that sets the process in reverse. That is, the rest of the decade will probably be a downward cycle of deflating expectations. Markets will no longer pour vast amounts of capital into countries whose leaders espouse free markets and sound money on the assumption that such policies will necessarily produce vigorous growth; they will want to see hard evidence of such growth. This new reluctance will surely be directly self-reinforcing, in that it means that the huge capital gains in emerging market equities will not continue. It will also, more or less directly, lead to a further slowing of growth in those countries, comprising much of Latin America and several outside nations, whose hesitant recovery from the 1980s was driven largely by infusions of foreign capital.

Because reforms will no longer be instantly rewarded by the capital markets, it will be far more difficult to sell such reforms politically. Thus the common assumption that free trade and free market policies will quickly spread around the world is surely wrong. Indeed, there will doubtless be some backsliding, as the perceived failure of Washington consensus policies leads to various attempts either to restore the good old days or to emulate what are perceived as alternative models. Many developing country politicians will surely claim that truly successful development efforts have been based not on free markets and sound money but on clever planning and rationed foreign exchange. At the moment, most developing country governments are still reluctant even to hint at a return to interventionist and nationalist policies because they fear that such hints will be swiftly punished by capital flight. But sooner or later some of them will rediscover the attractions of capital controls. As has happened so many times in the past, some countries will in desperation impose regulations to discourage capital flight. They will discover that while such regulations do raise the cost of doing business, that cost seems minor compared with their newfound ability to contain temporary speculative attacks without imposing punitive interest rates.

And these two trends will surely reinforce each other. As it becomes clear to the markets that reform need not always advance, they will become increasingly reluctant to offer advances on reform. As it becomes clear that such rewards are not available even to the most virtuous of reformers, the willingness to suffer economic pain to placate the markets will erode all the more.

But will the conventional wisdom represented by the Washington consensus be so easily displaced? Before the Mexican crisis, when some warned that the rhetoric about a golden age for global capitalism was excessive, the reply was often that there was no alternative. Communism is dead. The old protectionist development strategies in South Asia and Latin America were unambiguous failures. Even if Victorian virtue does not yield the easy rewards some may have expected, it is still the only plausible course of action left. And such arguments have a point. It is, in fact, probably true that free markets and sound money—if not necessarily fixed exchange rates—are the best policy for developing countries to follow.

But it seems strangely unimaginative to assume that because there are no other popular paradigms for policy currently in circulation, nobody will be able to come up with a rationale for policies that are very much at odds with the Washington consensus. Indeed, there are already audible rumblings about emulating a supposed Asian model. Developing countries should try, some people say, to be like Japan (as they imagine it) rather than America. The intellectual basis for such ideas is far weaker than that for the Washington consensus, but to suppose that bad ideas never flourish is to ignore the lesson of history.

Part 3

Case Studies

READING 9

Restoring Growth and Price Stability in Argentina: Do Policies Make Miracles?

MIGUEL A. KIGUEL AND JULIO J. NOGUÉS
Under Secretary of Finance of Argentina
Executive Director at the Board of the World Bank Group

INTRODUCTION

The implementation of the convertibility plan that started in 1991 marked a major turning point in the economic performance of Argentina. After more than two decades of low growth in which gross domestic product (GDP) per capita stagnated and rising rates of inflation culminated in a hyperinflation episode, the economy is now enjoying—for the first time in recent history—a period of price stability and growth. Since the implementation of the convertibility plan, GDP has grown on average at a rate slightly above 5 percent per year, while the rate of inflation fell to international levels.

In this paper we will examine the nature and causes of this dramatic change. We begin by offering the reader a brief historical overview of inflation, fiscal deficits, and stabilization attempts as they have affected Argentina. Next we argue that the combination of a major stabilization program—which was based on a significant and sustainable fiscal adjustment, a fixed exchange rate, and monetary discipline—and far-reaching structural reforms—including, among others, privatizations, tax reform, deregulation, and trade liberalization—was the key to this success. These substantial changes in policies amounted to a change of regime of the type that has been needed historically to stop hyperinflations. In the last section we stress some of the most significant benefits of the convertibility plan.

The success of the program was challenged in 1995 by the Mexican devaluation that occurred in 1994, the so-called Tequila effect (discussed later). As a consequence, the economy suffered a significant capital outflow, which led to a 50 percent reduction in the price of some government bonds and a sharp loss in banking deposits. In contrast to previous episodes, this time the policy was to stick to sound fiscal, monetary, and exchange rate policies and to deepen the structural reforms that have resulted in an economic turnaround. After a temporary drop in output and an important increase in the unemployment rate, Argentina's economy is now returning to the rates of growth shown during the early years of the program, while inflation remains under control.

BRIEF HISTORICAL OVERVIEW

Argentina's long tradition of high inflation goes back to the 1940s. The rates of inflation slowly increased over the years, rising from average annual rates of around 20 percent in the 1950s and 1960s to 170 percent in the second half of the 1970s, finally peaking with the hyperinflation of 1989–1990, when the annual rate reached 4,923 percent (Table 1).

The origin of inflation was closely linked to the large fiscal deficits. This trend started toward the end of the 1940s during the first Peronist government, when the deficits increased significantly and the rate of inflation started to get out of control. Unfortunately, over the years fiscal discipline was never recovered; in fact, budget deficits became chronic and larger with predictable effects on inflation. This effect is clearly illustrated in Figure 1, which shows the close relationship between the fiscal deficits and inflation during these decades.

The rise in inflation and in budget deficits was accompanied by a reduction in the rate of growth. After growing at relatively good rates in the 1960s, Argentina entered a period of stagnation and economic decline that lasted for the next two decades. As the average monthly rate of inflation reached 16.8 percent in the 1980s, the economy contracted at an annual average rate of 0.8 percent per year. This means that GDP per capita fell by more than 15 percent during this period.

But the large budget deficits and the high rates of inflation were not the sole causes of the poor growth performance. Other policies were probably as important. A large number of public enterprises were managed on political, rather than on economic criteria. The resulting losses compounded the fiscal problems, but poor management meant that the economy did not receive the quality and quantity of services that these enterprises were supposed to deliver. By the end of the 1980s, power outages were a common phenomenon, telephones were a precious and scarce good with each connection costing thousands of dollars, and, more generally, the country's infrastructure had seriously deteriorated. In addition, export taxes discouraged the generation of foreign exchange, while high-tariff and nontariff barriers were used to protect a highly inefficient domestic industry. To make matters worse, a large number of regulations in the goods and labor markets had detrimental effects on growth.

TABLE 1
Growth and Inflation

	INFLATION[1]	GROWTH[2]
1951–1960	2.12	1.22
1961–1970	1.70	4.44
1971–1980	7.02	1.21
1981–1990	16.85	–0.81
1991–1995	1.57	5.26

[1]Average of monthly changes

[2]Average of annual changes

FIGURE 1
Inflation and Fiscal Deficit

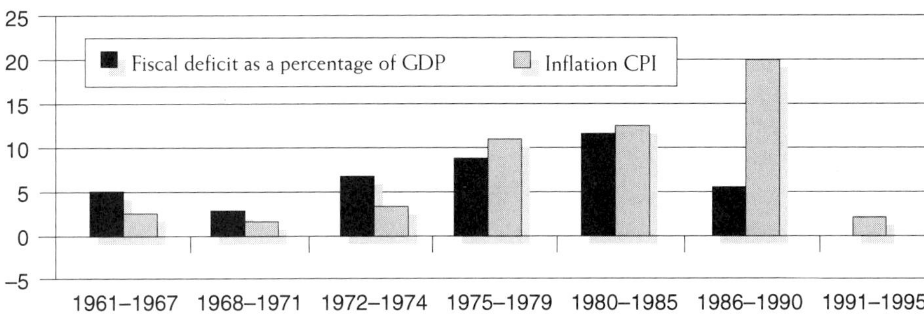

FIGURE 2
Argentine Stabilization Plans

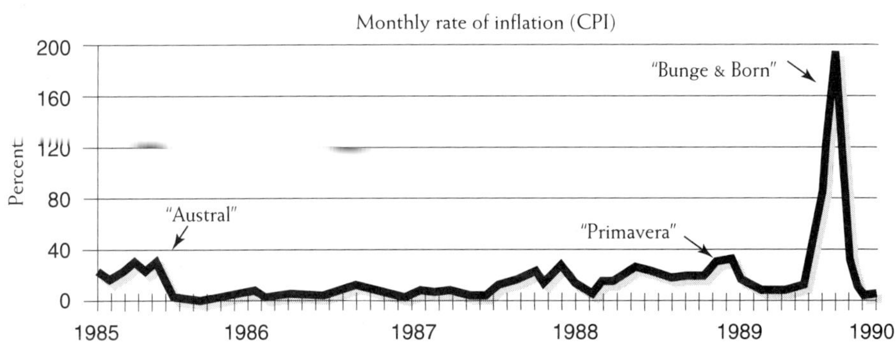

The 1980s were a particularly bad decade in terms of inflation. Not only did the rate increase, but the inflationary process became much more unstable (Figure 2). This instability developed in part as a result of stop-and-go policies toward inflation, in which most stabilization attempts were based on a large dose of income policies that did not address the underlying causes of inflation in an appropriate way.

The 1985 Austral plan represented a break with previous stabilization efforts as it was the first serious and comprehensive stabilization program in many years. It was a heterodox program, as it combined orthodox elements—namely, a reduction in the budget deficit and a fixed exchange rate—with the heterodox component—wage and price controls. The initial success was later reversed when money to finance deficits started to be printed once again, and inflation picked up momentum.

Of course, failed stabilization attempts would not have resulted in hyperinflation if the economy was not already experiencing high inflation. Likewise, high inflation could have been avoided by the adoption of policies to bring it down at an earlier stage. It was the combination of high inflation and the induced nominal instability caused by unsound stabilization strategies that created the conditions for inflation to explode.

The first inflationary outburst, which started in February 1989, was stopped by the Bunge & Born program implemented by the incoming President Menem administration in July 1989. As with previous programs, it combined a quick-and-easy fiscal adjustment with a fixed exchange rate accompanied by a dose of income policies. And, as was true with previous programs, it was short lived; by December inflation was on the rise once again and the economy was suffering its second hyperinflation outburst, this one lasting until March. At that time, Minister Erman González launched an orthodox stabilization program that brought inflation down to monthly rates of about 10 percent. But this effort did not bring about price stability, and toward the end of the year inflation was once again on the rise.

The hyperinflation in Argentina was a very costly and traumatic episode, with negative effects on growth, investment, consumption, and the overall quality of life. Previous inflationary episodes were manageable, as economic agents had developed mechanisms to live with inflation (such as indexation, more extensive use of the dollar as a unit of account and means of payments, and so on). But these mechanisms became ineffective during the hyperinflation because of the fast speed of price adjustments and the large variability in relative prices. Many firms were unable to quote prices given the uncertainty about replacement costs, and customers were unhappy as they could not purchase the merchandise available in the stores.

The costs of the hyperinflation were dramatic: output fell by 6.2 percent in 1989, consumption by 4.1 percent, and imports by 18 percent, while investment collapsed as it declined by 24.4 percent. There was also a sharp de-monetization of the economy as M3 reached just 5 percent of GDP. The economy became much more dollarized as agents were searching for a stable currency to effect their transactions. The run out of Austral denominated assets and into dollars led to sharp real depreciation.[1] All these elements made the situation unsustainable.

The economy was in need of a major change in regime in order to restore growth. But such changes were hard to implement, especially in a democracy, because although the policy regime was certainly harmful for growth, some important and powerful groups had benefited from this regime. These groups included the suppliers of public enterprises, the speculators who had inside information about devaluations and important changes in inflation rates, and those who had the power to lobby for special privileges. A change of regime requires a significant popular demand for change. In Argentina, hyperinflation was the catalyst for change.

THE CONVERTIBILITY PLAN

The convertibility plan was a response to this demand for price stability and is undoubtedly the most ambitious and comprehensive program to stop inflation in Argentina. It is

[1]The Austral was the Argentine currency at the time of the hyperinflation. It was introduced in 1985 as part of the so-called Austral stabilization plan.

a unique program based on three pillars: (1) a bold exchange rate monetary policy, (2) significant fiscal adjustment, and (3) far-reaching structural reforms. The objective was to bring inflation down to international levels and restore growth in a sustainable way.

Exchange Rate Policy and the Monetary Regime

A central part of the program was the adoption of a fixed exchange rate within the framework of a quasi-currency board. The new exchange rate policy was adopted by law and supported by Congress, which clearly shows that the program enjoyed broad-based support. The convertibility law set the exchange rate at one peso per U.S. dollar and established that any change in the exchange rate had be to approved by Congress.

The crucial element of this law was that it required the monetary base to be fully backed by international reserves.[2] This meant that the Central Bank could not directly finance the treasury, as it had done in the past. It could finance the treasury only indirectly, through the purchase of government bonds, but even in this case it was severely limited because the stock of government bonds could not increase more than 10 percent in one year. Last, but not least, the Central Bank became independent when its president and board members were appointed for a six-year term with the approval of the Senate.

This strong commitment to the exchange rate policy and the limitations on the ability of the Central Bank to print unbacked money were a direct response to failed policies of the past. Most of the stabilization programs of the second half of the 1980s included a fixed exchange rate. In addition, the famous *Tablita*, the exchange rate–based stabilization program under Minister Martínez de Hoz in the late 1970s and early 1980s, had left sour memories about this stabilization strategy. In the absence of a commitment of the type included in the convertibility law, it would have been extremely difficult to generate credibility in the program.

In practice the monetary regime that prevailed under the convertibility law meant that the changes in the money supply required a counterpart in changes in international reserves. This meant that the Central Bank had lost its ability to run monetary policy, as it had in the past, and had became a quasi-currency board that expanded the money supply when it gained reserves (that is, there was an excess supply of foreign currency) and contracted it when there was an excess demand for foreign currency (see Figure 3 showing monetary base and reserves). The Central Bank retained some traditional functions such as setting reserve requirements, which it used during the banking crisis that followed the Mexican devaluation.

Fiscal Policy

A deep fiscal adjustment was the second key pillar of the convertibility plan. Of course, this adjustment was necessary as the treasury lost its access to Central Bank financing. Nevertheless, it is now apparent that there was a clear understanding of the importance of the elimination of the fiscal deficit in order to guarantee stability and reverse inflationary expectations.

---

[2]The law established that dollar-denominated government bonds valued at market prices could be used to back up to one-third of the monetary base. The law emphasized the need for these bonds to be liquid, as a way of ensuring that the Central Bank could easily sell them to obtain U.S. dollars.

FIGURE 3
Monetary Liabilities and International Reserves (in billions of dollars)

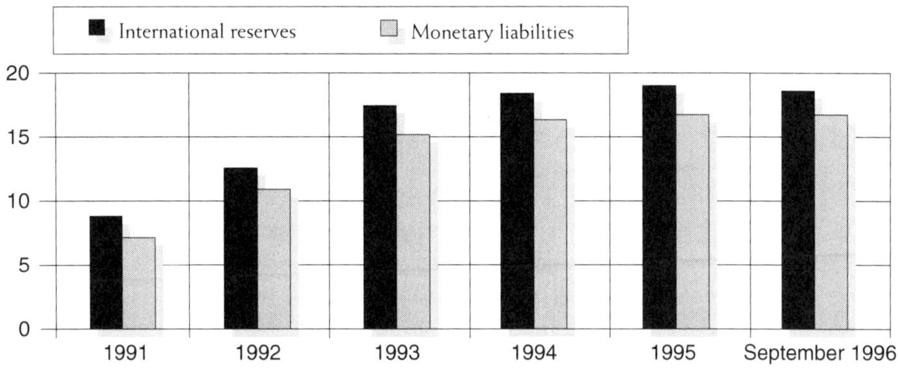

FIGURE 4
Overall Balance (cash basis excluding privatizations)

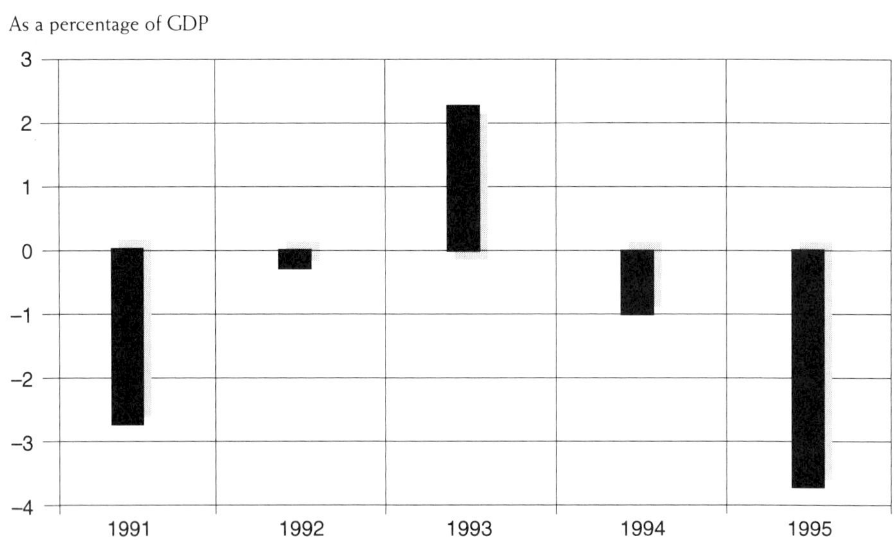

For the first time in decades the government ran surpluses or very small budget deficits. As shown in Figure 4, the government ran primary fiscal surpluses since 1991, and the fiscal balance showed surpluses during most years of the convertibility plan. These fiscal results are in contrast with the large deficits (in excess of 6 percent of GDP) observed in the 1980s.

Much of the improvement in the fiscal accounts was achieved through an increase in tax collections. As shown in Figure 5, tax revenues rose continuously, increasing by 78 percent in nominal terms during this period. It is important to highlight that the rise in rev-

FIGURE 5
Tax Collection (including Social Security taxes, in billions of dollars)

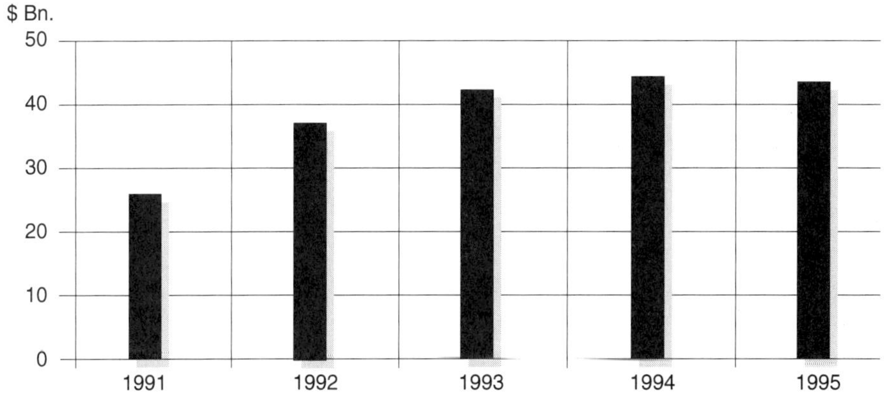

enues was achieved while the government was reducing or eliminating many of the most distortionary taxes, such as those on exports, bank debits, and at least 20 others. Through an improvement in tax administration, the government managed to obtain most of its revenues essentially from five taxes: income tax, value added tax (VAT), trade taxes (which are mainly import tariffs), personal wealth, and Social Security taxes.

The privatization of public-sector enterprises was central to the fiscal adjustment. This helped in two ways. First, the revenues from privatization helped to consolidate the fiscal situation and to finance some of the more needed reforms such as severance payments for laid-off workers and the cancellation of old debts to suppliers and pensioners. Second, because most of these firms were money losers, the privatization reduced government transfers.

In addition, some measures were taken to improve government solvency and hence ensure the sustainability of the fiscal situation. Among them, there was a major reform of the pension system with the creation of private pension funds as a way to reduce future liabilities. This was done in 1993 when the *Sistema Integrado de Jubilaciones y Pensiones* (Integrated System of Retirement and Pension Funds) was created. The new legislation maintained the pay-as-you-go system and at the same time created a private pension option managed by the *Administradoras de Fondos de Jubilaciones y Pensiones* (AFJP) (Administration of Retirement and Pension Funds), which was fully funded and based the retirement pension on the individual's contributions. The new legislation has been successful; as of late 1995 affiliation to the AFJP numbered around five million workers. The value of the assets that they are managing has been increasing steadily, reaching $4.5 billion in 1996. In addition, the government has set limits through the budgetary process to the losses of the social security system and to other contingent liabilities, such as those resulting from lost trials. All these reforms have helped to contain the budget deficit and to make it more predictable.

STRUCTURAL REFORMS

The third pillar of the program was an ambitious agenda of structural reforms that not only attempted to consolidate the stabilization process but also to shift the growth strategy from the inward-oriented policies that had been followed for decades to a set of policies that were based on (1) an open trade policy; (2) a deregulation of the economy, including rules for investment, elimination of marketing boards, rules governing commerce, and so on; (3) a dramatic shift in the role of government from a producer of goods and services to a regulator of the new private utilities; and (4) major reforms in the financial sector. Structural reforms have been far reaching and have affected most sectors of the economy. In what follows we will concentrate on those that are most important for the economy.

Trade Policy

The Argentine economy had traditionally followed protectionist policies by taxing agricultural exports while protecting import-completing industries. Because of these policies, exports remained undiversified and represented a small share of GDP. Although the liberalization process had timidly started during the Alfonsín administration eliminating the most drastic restrictions, the economy still remained heavily protected and traditional exports were discouraged. At the end of the Alfonsín administration there were foreign trade barriers of all sorts. Some of these restrictions were lifted during the first years of the Menem administration, but the trade liberalization process was finally deepened during the years of the convertibility plan. For instance, nontariff barriers (NTBs) that covered around 32 percent of domestic production in 1988 are essentially nonexistent today. Likewise, whereas in 1988 the average all-inclusive tariff was 39 percent, by 1994 it had declined to 18 percent.

The participation in the Mercosur trade agreement, of which Argentina is the second largest partner, has also implied an additional movement toward trade liberalization. After a relatively short transition period, a common external tariff (CET) and free intraregional trade for a majority of tariff lines were implemented in January 1995. Although some goods remain on exception lists and rules of origin are also stringent, we may conclude safely that the Mercosur agreement has implied trade liberalization over and above what was achieved through unilateral measures and those agreed in the Uruguay Round.

Finally, Argentina also participated actively in the Uruguay Round. Three examples suffice. First, at the Uruguay Round, Argentina bound the maximum tariff rate at 35 percent. Second, as an efficient agricultural exporter, the country was a member of the Cairns Group where it endorsed wholeheartedly the reduction of barriers to agricultural trade. Finally, this active trade participation also prompted the adoption of important international rules such as those governing antidumping and countervailing duties.

In summary, since 1989 Argentina has implemented a major trade liberalization program with third countries and more deeply with its Mercosur partners. As a consequence, trade flows have accelerated, and this in turn has been a major cause in increasing competitive pressures and productivity levels.

Deregulation

The trade liberalization process was accompanied by the deregulation of the domestic markets. An important measure in these areas was the elimination of the marketing boards for cereals, sugar, tobacco, and wine, among others, which were vestiges of the interventionist policies of the 1930s. Another important policy was the deregulation of ports, which limited the power of an important labor union and allowed ports to operate 24 hours a day.

Investment regulations have also been significantly liberalized. First, the government eliminated all controls on foreign investment flows. Second, the country now embraces a number of investment principles including national treatment and the free transfer of capital and profits. Third, the preceding policies and principles have made it possible for Argentina to sign bilateral investment treaties with practically all capital-exporting countries. Fourth, Argentina no longer requires the resolution of investment disputes by domestic courts. In fact, it is now a member of the International Center for the Settlement of Investment Disputes (ICSID), to whom it is willing to discharge the resolution of these disputes.

These measures, introduced to an environment in which many other important liberalization and deregulation policies were being implemented simultaneously, have attracted significant investment flows.

Privatizations

The privatization of public sector enterprises has been a central component of the structural reforms. These measures were important not only because of their effects on the budget and the improvement on efficiency, but also because they sent a strong signal about reversal of the model where the state had a leading role in providing services, as well as in the infrastructure, and in heavy industry. In addition, it was a break from the policies initiated in the 1930s and 1940s that gave the state a more prominent role regarding the regulation of private-sector activities or the nationalization of public utilities and other industries.

As of early 1996, practically everything that used to be owned by the national government and that could be privatized has already been privatized. Some of the few remaining assets of the national government—including some stocks in privatized enterprises, a few banks, and some power-generating units like the Yacyretá dam—are likely to be privatized in the near future.

Privatization has reached not only huge conglomerates producing tradable goods such as steel, petroleum, and petrochemicals but also natural monopolies producing goods such as water, gas, electric power, railroads, and telecommunications. Obviously, to protect consumers from the potential abuses of privatized natural monopolies, regulation was required; therefore, regulatory bodies in many areas—including water, gas, and energy—have been created. After very few start-up problems, these agencies are now complying efficiently with their mandates of securing the supply of services and impeding monopolistic practices. Together with these new policies, a significant amount of legislation has been implemented to eliminate an important number of unproductive regulations (see Pablo Rojo, "Desregulación de la Economía Argentina," *Novedades Económicas*, August 1992).

The philosophy underlying these reforms is that the state should not intervene in areas for which competitive markets ensure supply and an efficient allocation of resources. Even when competitive markets cannot do the job, as in the case of natural monopolies, the government will not engage in productive activities as long as it can be sure that the private sector, in conjunction with efficient regulation, can come close to replicating the outcome of competitive markets.

Financial Sector Reform

A central part of the program has been the strengthening of the financial sector. The objective is to create a competitive and solvent financial system that can allocate credit efficiently, remains solvent, will not become a source of quasi-fiscal deficit.

To enhance competitiveness, the Central Bank eliminated all barriers to entry (except those necessary for prudential reasons) and liberalized lending and deposit interest rates. Banks are free to choose the best borrowers and to charge them the appropriate interest rate. Foreign banks are treated in the same way as domestic banks and do not face any restrictions to opening subsidiaries or branches.

In addition, the role of public banks has been reduced. The National Development Bank (*Banco Nacional de Desarrollo*) was closed, and many provincial banks have been privatized. By the end of 1995, more than half of the provinces had either privatized or had advanced the privatization process for their banks.

The Central Bank adopted a set of prudential regulations to ensure the solvency and liquidity of the financial system. These regulations frequently follow the international standards determined by the Basel Accords of the Bank of International Settlements, but in most cases they are more stringent because of the higher risks that banks face in an economy subject to volatile capital flows. For instance, minimum capital requirements are set at 11.5 percent of assets at risk, much higher than the 8 percent recommended by Basel. In addition, the Central Bank also sets tight standards for the provisioning of loans, for the role of external auditors, and for credits to related enterprises.

Finally, the Central Bank also sets high reserve requirements, as a prudential regulation, to compensate for the limitations that the convertibility law imposes on it to act as lender of last resort. In contrast to other countries where the reserve requirements are imposed as a way to finance the government, in Argentina they are used as a reserve of liquidity to finance a possible loss in deposits. The banks will have access to those reserves in case they are needed because the Central Bank holds the international reserves to back them.

THE INITIAL OUTCOMES OF THE CONVERTIBILITY PLAN

The convertibility plan has resulted in an extremely successful stabilization program. Inflation fell quickly from an annual rate of 171 percent in 1991 to 10 percent in 1993 and 0 percent in 1995. No stabilization program in Argentina, or in any other Latin American country, in the last few decades has managed to reduce inflation so rapidly. For instance, the program used in Chile, which was started in the mid–1970s when inflation hovered around 500 percent per year, took more than a decade to stabilize the annual rate of inflation to around 20 percent. Even today, after two decades of sustained sound macroeconomic policies, inflation remains slightly above international levels. Likewise, the successful 1985 Israeli plan reduced the annual rate of inflation to approximately 20 percent, and it took around a decade to bring it down to rates in the range of 10 percent per year.

One reason for the rapid reduction of inflation in Argentina is that this program enjoyed much more credibility than previous stabilization attempts. This can be clearly noticed in the fast reduction of the differential between interest rates for the peso and U.S. dollar during the plan. It is useful to compare the evolution of this differential during the convertibility plan and during the exchange rate–based stabilization launched by Martínez de Hoz in the late 1970s. This plan included an announcement about the path of the exchange rate, but whereas in the convertibility plan the exchange rate is fixed, in the *Tablita* it was based on a pre-announced sliding peg with decreasing rates of devaluation. As Figure 6 (top and bot-

FIGURE 6
Interest Rate Differentials Argentine versus International (top) 1979–1980, (bottom) 1991–1994

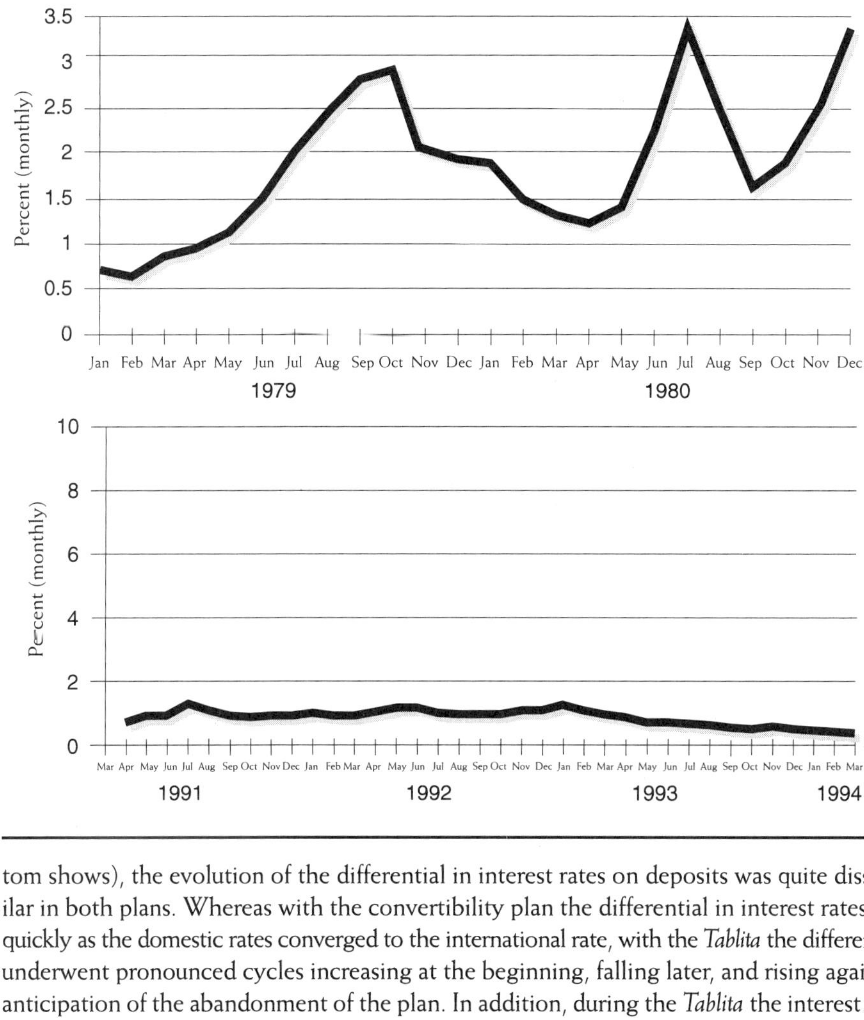

tom shows), the evolution of the differential in interest rates on deposits was quite dissimilar in both plans. Whereas with the convertibility plan the differential in interest rates fell quickly as the domestic rates converged to the international rate, with the *Tablita* the differential underwent pronounced cycles increasing at the beginning, falling later, and rising again in anticipation of the abandonment of the plan. In addition, during the *Tablita* the interest rate differential always exceeded 1.5 percent per month, thus staying well above international levels; with the convertibility plan, however, this differential fell as low as 1 percent per year.

The decline in inflation led to a rapid remonetization of the economy. During the hyperinflation of 1989–1990 the economy experienced a dramatic demonetization as the cost of holding Austral-denominated assets became extremely high.[3] As a result of this process, M1 fell to just 3 percent of GDP, while the broader monetary aggregate collapsed to just 5 percent of GDP compared with 18 percent of GDP in the mid–1980s. This reduction in the monetary aggregates was reversed during the convertibility plan, as economic

[3]The Austral was the currency in use when the convertibility plan was launched.

FIGURE 7
Levels of Deposits in the Bimonetary System (in millions)

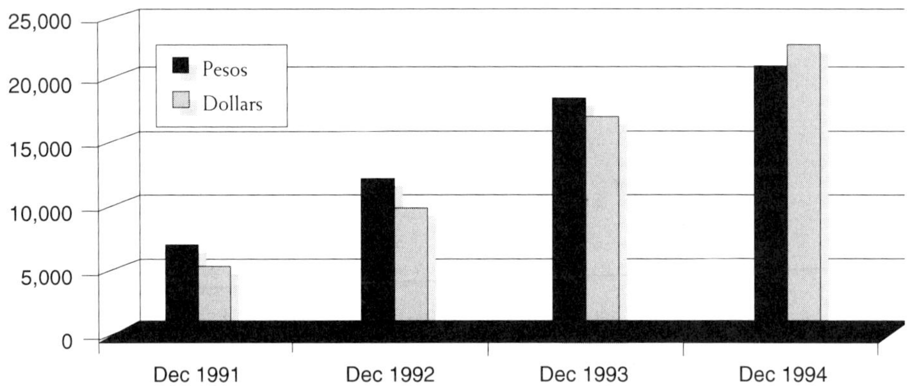

agents recovered their confidence in the peso (the new currency created during the convertibility plan), which started being used in most transactions.

By 1994 the economy recovered the monetization levels of the mid–1980s as M3 reached 17 percent of GDP. A distinctive feature of this process was the growth of U.S. dollar–denominated deposits (or Argendollars). These deposits existed since the mid–1980s, but before 1991 they represented a very small share of overall deposits. These deposits have been important since 1991, in part because the economy had become much more dollarized during the hyperinflation. As Figure 7 shows, the Argendollars grew very rapidly between 1991 and 1994, when they reached around 50 percent of total deposits. The fastest growth was observed in time deposits, where the dollar segment represents around 70 percent of the total, whereas peso deposits still make up the bulk of checking accounts, as most transactions still take place in pesos.

The increase in domestic credit is related to the growth in deposits. The Argentine financial system has had high reserve requirements in the 1990s, implying a relatively low multiplier of the monetary base. As of 1994, reserve requirements were 43 percent for checking and saving accounts and 3 percent for time deposits 90 days or shorter. In practice this meant that on average the credit multiplier was approximately 1.5; in other words, it was relatively low. These high reserve requirements that were initially designed as a prudential measure to improve banks' solvency and liquidity in practice reduced credit growth and helped to sterilize part of the monetization generated by the large capital inflows that took place during this period.

The expansion in monetary aggregates was accompanied by a significant increase in output. Between 1991 and 1994 the Argentine economy experienced strong and sustained growth. As Table 2 and Figure 8 illustrate, GDP grew an average of 7 percent per year during this period. Investment was one of the driving forces underlying this strong performance as it increased from 14 percent of GDP in 1990 to 19.9 percent of GDP in 1994. Consumption also expanded during this period but went through a cycle: it increased strongly in 1991–1992 but grew at a lower rate in 1993 and 1994. This cycle in

TABLE 2

Argentina and Chile: Growth Performance and Aggregate Coefficients of Investment Trade and Savings: 1981–1995

	Rates of Growth				Aggregate Investment Coefficient		Aggregate Trade Coefficient		Aggregate National Savings Coefficient	
	GDP		Per Capita GDP							
Year	Argentina	Chile	Argentina	Chile	Argentina	Chile	Argentina	Chile	Argentina	Chile
1981	–5.7	n/a	–7.3	n/a	22.7	n/a	19.4	n/a	20.7	n/a
1982	–3.1	n/a	–4.7	n/a	21.8	n/a	15.3	n/a	24.8	n/a
1983	3.7	n/a	2.2	n/a	20.9	n/a	14.5	n/a	24.6	n/a
1984	–1.2	n/a	–2.8	n/a	20.0	13.7	14.7	58.6	23.4	2.4
1985	–3.7	7.1	–5.2	5.9	17.6	17.2	15.7	53.4	24.9	7.8
1986	7.3	5.6	5.8	3.9	17.5	18.9	14.5	55.1	18.7	11.5
1987	2.6	6.6	1.1	4.9	19.6	22.3	14.7	58.1	18.1	17.3
1988	–1.9	7.3	–3.3	5.6	18.6	22.8	15.6	60.7	22.9	22.3
1989	–6.2	9.9	–7.6	8.2	15.5	25.6	16.0	66.5	24.3	23.7
1990	0.1	3.3	–1.3	1.6	14.0	26.3	18.0	68.6	24.3	24.2
1991	8.9	7.3	7.6	5.6	14.6	24.5	18.9	70.1	17.0	24.1
1992	8.7	11.0	7.4	10.2	16.7	26.8	22.4	14.8	12.8	24.8
1993	6.0	6.3	4.8	4.0	18.2	28.8	22.9	76.0	14.1	23.9
1994	7.4	4.2	6.2	2.7	19.9	26.8	25.2	77.6	14.6	26.4
1995	–4.4	8.5	–5.6	7.0	17.5	27.4	27.5	83.8	16.1	27.6
Simple Average										
1981–1985	–2.0	7.1	–3.5	5.9	20.6	15.4	15.9	56.0	23.7	6.1
1986–1990	0.4	6.5	–1.1	4.8	17.0	23.1	15.7	61.8	21.7	19.8
1991–1995	5.3	7.5	4.1	5.9	17.4	26.3	23.3	76.5	18.9	25.1

Sources: Argentina: Ministry of Economy; Chile: Central Bank of Chile.
n/a: Not available.

FIGURE 8
GDP Growth Rate

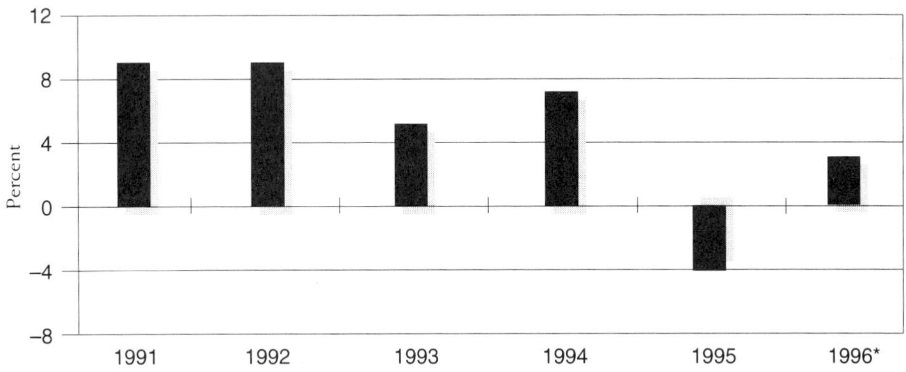

*Projected

FIGURE 9
Trade Flows (in billions of dollars)

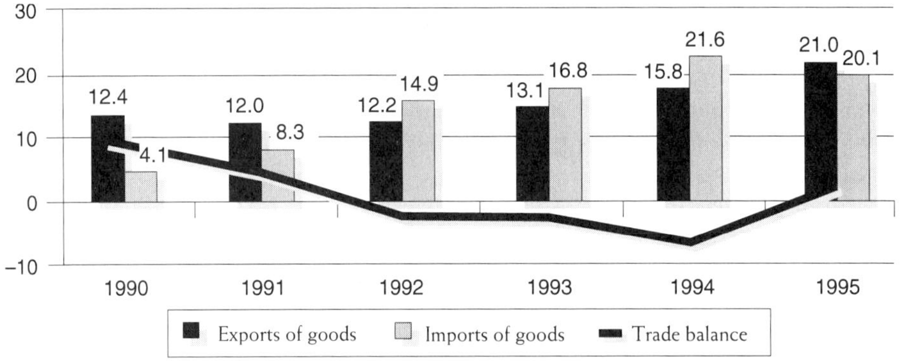

consumption, starting with a boom that recedes at a later stage, is typical of exchange rate–based stabilizations.[4]

On the external side, Figure 9 shows that between 1991 and 1993 there was a strong growth in imports financed by capital inflows, whereas the growth in exports began slowly but picked up later on. Overall, as Figure 10 shows, the rate of growth of foreign trade has been very high. In part as a result of the behavior of imports, the current account shifted from a surplus of 1.3 percent of GDP in 1990 to a deficit of 1.5 percent of GDP in 1992. The impressive growth in imports, which more than doubled between 1990

[4]Kiguel and Liviatan (1991) present the stylized facts of the consumption boom in exchange rate–based stabilizations, and Calvo and Végh (1990) discuss in some detail the underlying reasons for the existence of this cycle.

FIGURE 10
Growth Rate of the Value of Foreign Trade

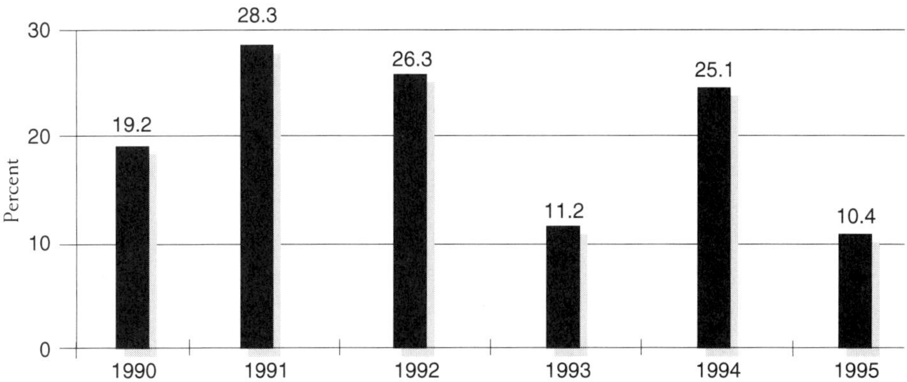

and 1992, can be explained by the drastic trade liberalization described earlier and the increase in consumption typical of exchange rate–based stabilizations. As said, the country had no difficulties financing these deficits as capital inflows increased significantly during this period. This increase resulted from exogenous and endogenous factors. Among the former were the reduction in U.S. interest rates and the improved perception in the region abroad, especially following the structural reforms in Mexico during the 1980s. Among the latter were the impressive structural changes in Argentina and the privatization of the public enterprises that increased investment dramatically.

In contrast to previous stabilization programs, the deterioration in the current account did not reach unsustainable levels. By 1994, when the deficit reached its peak, it represented only 3.5 percent of GDP, well below the deficit of 14 percent of GDP that Chile experienced before the foreign exchange crisis of 1983 and much lower than the 8 percent deficit of GDP that Mexico was having prior to the devaluation in December 1994. Besides, given the large capital inflows, Argentina had no difficulties financing those deficits, and there were no signs of overvaluation, as exports were growing at a reasonable pace in 1994.

In summary, Argentina underwent an enviable period during the first four years of the convertibility plan, with high rates of GDP growth and investment, increasing domestic savings, a drastic reduction in inflation and interest rates, capital inflows, and increases in imports and exports. In addition, the incidence of poverty fell dramatically as the proportion of people living below the poverty line declined from 38.2 percent in 1990 to 17.6 percent in 1994. On the whole, this represented one of the most prosperous periods in Argentina's economic history. But the program faced a severe test as a result of the Mexican devaluation that occurred in December 1994, the subject of the next section.

CONVERTIBILITY DURING THE TEQUILA EFFECT

The Mexican devaluation that began on December 20, 1994, brought a large external shock to Argentina and a great challenge to the convertibility plan. There was an important turnaround in capital flows, especially those of a short-term nature. This meant that the economy needed a strong adjustment to the current account of the balance of payments, which had to be effected without a devaluation in order to maintain the fixed exchange rate and convertibility.

But the largest challenge by far confronted the financial system, which faced an 18 percent drop in deposits in just three months (Figure 11). There are few precedents for shocks of this magnitude. During the Great Depression in the United States, for instance, deposits fell by around 35 percent, but the reduction was spread over a period of four years. Argentina faced half the reduction of deposits in 10 percent of the time.

In addition, the banking crisis in Argentina was particularly difficult to manage because the convertibility law and the Central Bank's charter imposed severe limits on its capacity to act as lender of last resort. In contrast to the policies employed in other countries, Argentina's Central Bank can only assist banks facing liquidity problems when it holds excess international reserves. The Central Bank of Argentina had a stock of excess reserves of around 2 billion dollars prior to the crisis, which set the margin that could be used for assisting banks. Finally, the financial system was more vulnerable to runs because it lacked deposit insurance.

The run on banks had severe effects on the banking sector. The lack of a lender of last resort and the absence of a deposit insurance scheme created uncertainty among depositors who rushed to cash their deposits among the perceived weakest banks. This situation generated great distress among many banks and forced the merger of several of them. It also triggered the failure of around 12 financial institutions that were in weak conditions prior to the crisis. Finally, the crisis induced the privatization of many provincial banks, which became liquidity strapped.

Despite the seriousness of the banking crisis and the restrictions on assisting banks during this period, the challenge was successfully overcome. The assistance of the Central Bank through liquidity rediscounts (which could be effected up to the amount of its excess reserves), repose, and reductions in reserve requirements provided enough liquidity to offset three-quarters of the outflow of deposits. The balance was financed through foreign borrowing and reductions in domestic credit.

FIGURE 11
Impact of the Tequila Effect on the Financial System (in billions of dollars)

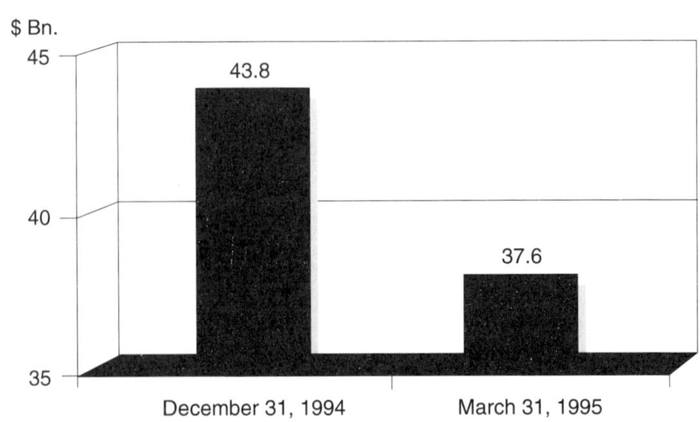

The overall cost to depositors and taxpayers was small compared with other episodes. Depositors lost less than 1 percent of the deposits in the banking system, whereas the fiscal cost of the crisis has been estimated at less than half of 1 percent of GDP. This last figure is surprisingly small, because the cost of banking sector crises are typically between 4 percent and 8 percent of GDP and have been as high as 20 percent of GDP (such as in Chile in the early 1980s).

The reversal of the banking and foreign exchange crises was achieved through a major fiscal adjustment announced in mid-March 1995 within the framework of an IMF package accompanied by a substantial amount of external financing from the multilateral organizations. In addition, domestic and foreign investors supported this package through the subscription of a patriotic bond that provided 2 billion dollars of additional financing. The overall package amounted to more than 12 billion dollars (4 percent of GDP), which included 4.5 billion dollars that would be generated through a reduction in the fiscal deficit. In addition, the government used 4.5 billion dollars to create two fiduciary funds, one for the public and another for the private sector banks, whose main objective was to privatize public (mainly provincial) banks and to restructure and recapitalize private ones. These measures were supplemented by the creation of a private deposit insurance corporation.

One important factor to note is that in spite of the seriousness of the crisis, the convertibility plan was maintained. In fact, this episode showed that the strict rules imposed by the convertibility plan were effective. Argentina withstood a large shock without any change in the monetary or exchange rate regimes or in the basic incentive system (such as changes in import tariffs, quotas, or export taxes) as had been the case with previous stabilization programs. This marked a clear break with the past, because this was the first banking–foreign exchange crisis that did not finish in a devaluation, a widespread bailout of depositors and banks, or widespread foreign exchange controls.

Although the rules were successful in containing the costs of the banking crisis, the replies from the Mexican devaluation did have important real costs. Domestic interest rates skyrocketed, there was a severe recession as GDP fell by 4.4 percent in 1995, domestic credit contracted, and investment fell. Nevertheless, there were some bright spots within this overall negative picture as exports increased more than 32 percent and the economy ended with a trade balance surplus.

The Recovery after the Tequila Effect

The Argentine economy recovered relatively quickly from the impact of the Tequila effect. The recovery in the financial markets was particularly impressive as confidence was restored. Deposits went back to the pre-Tequila levels (45 billion dollars) by the end of 1995 and grew an additional 10 percent in the first half of 1996 surpassing the 50 billion dollars mark. In addition, most of the growth occurred in the peso segment and as a result, the share of peso deposits went back to around 52 percent. The large rise in deposits was accompanied by a sharp reduction in interest rates in both pesos and dollars, which by mid–1996 had returned to international levels.

The return of private capital flows was a second indication of greater confidence in the program. International reserves grew rapidly in the second half of the year and reached an all-time record of more than 17 billion dollars in mid–1996 (Figure 12). Private corporations

FIGURE 12
Interest Rates

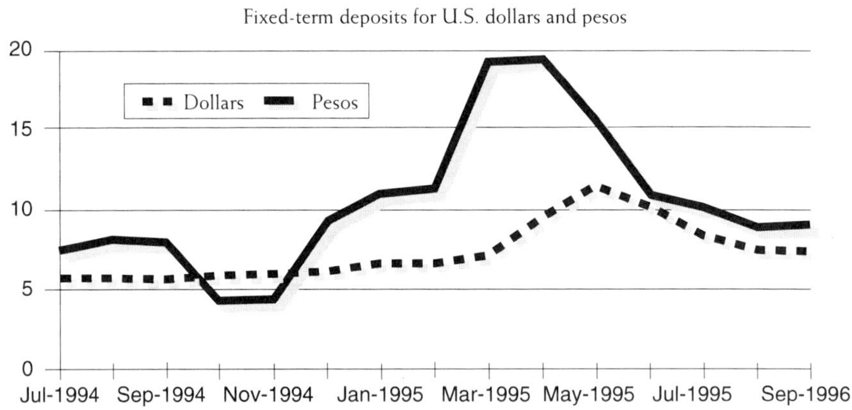

and the government regained the same the degree of access to the international credit markets that they enjoyed in 1994.

The improvement in financial aggregates had positive effects on the real economy. GDP, which fell throughout 1995, started a slow but steady recovery in 1996, and by the second quarter of 1996 there were clear indications that the economy was experiencing widespread recovery. Preliminary estimates indicate that GDP growth is now close to 3 percent, and industrial production is growing at a faster pace. Imports are also recovering after a reduction in 1995, and the most recent estimates indicate that they will reach an all-time record. Export growth continues to be healthy, and exports are now being helped by an improvement in the terms of trade.

Unemployment is the only indicator displaying worrisome signs (see Figure 13). In April 1995, while the economy was still suffering the full impact of the Tequila effect, unemployment reached 18 percent and since then it has fallen by 1 percentage point. These high rates of unemployment reflect cyclical as well as structural factors. There is no question that the recession of 1995 was the main reason for the increase in the rate of unemployment, from 12 percent in October 1994 to 18 percent in May 1995. Unemployment has also been pushed upward by a significant increase in the aggregate productivity of the economy (more than 5 percent per annum during 1990–1994) and by an increase in the labor force participation rate, from around 39 percent in 1990 to more than 41 percent in 1995. In addition, the large number of regulations in the labor markets and the high costs of firing workers are also important deterrents for employment creation. Thus, even as the economy enters its new expansionary phase, the rate of unemployment might not fall if the government does not succeed in a major deregulation of the labor market.

All in all, almost every indicator shows that Argentina is leaving behind the ripples of the Tequila effect and is now returning to a path of sustained growth. Convertibility was strengthened by the Tequila effect, as it showed that it is sufficiently resilient to withstand a large external shock without any changes in the basic rules. Equally important is the understanding among policy makers that it is critical to achieve adjustment without resorting to

FIGURE 13
Rise in Unemployment in 1995

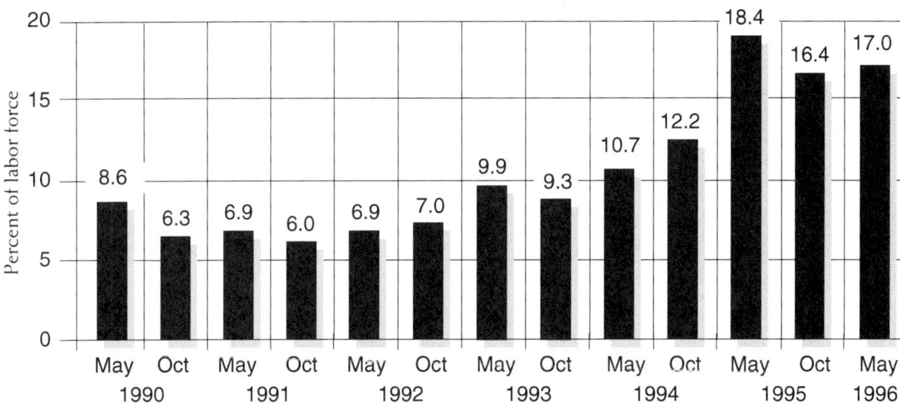

the easy but very damaging rules of the past, such as foreign exchange and import controls and devaluations that sooner or later always end with higher fiscal deficits and inflation.

CONCLUDING REMARKS

The convertibility plan has gone a full cycle since its inception. The first phase was difficult to implement but rich in rewards. The plan was the most comprehensive effort to stabilize and reform the Argentine economy, and it has certainly been the most successful program in the last half-century. Inflation fell very quickly to international levels, the economy grew at an average rate of around 7 percent per year, and this expansion was accompanied by a rapid increase in investment, international trade, and domestic savings. Bank deposits increased sharply, interest rates fell, and the country recovered its access to private international capital markets.

This initial success was challenged by a major external shock in late 1994, the Mexican devaluation, which sent its ripples throughout Latin America. Argentina was hit particularly hard by this shock, and the convertibility plan confronted a very serious threat. Large capital outflows and a sharp drop in bank deposits put the program at the verge of a balance of payments cum banking crisis. This was accompanied by a collapse in bond prices and a sharp increase in interest rates all indicating that the financial markets were betting against the sustainability of the plan. Nevertheless, the government's decision to maintain its adherence to the exchange-rate rule and to deepen the fiscal adjustment with the support of the international multilateral organizations proved the right course of action. Argentina passed the severe test and by the middle of 1995 financial markets started to stabilize, bond and stock prices rebounded, and the first signs of economic recovery started to show up.

The economy is once again enjoying an expansionary phase with price stability and declining interest rates. The structural reforms implemented since 1989 and deepened with the convertibility plan in 1991 continue to bear fruit and indicators show that the economy has entered a new era in which exports and investment will be the engines of growth; openness and monetary and fiscal discipline will be the guiding principles; and a rise in domestic savings will slowly but surely finance an increasing share of domestic investment. If these policies can be strengthened with a streamlining of government expenditures (particularly in the provinces) and a deregulation of the labor markets, the virtuous cycle of growth with prize stability and the economy's increasing capacity to create productive employment opportunities will be reinforced.

READING 10

Bolivia 1985–1992: Reforms, Results, and Challenges*

FELIPE LARRAÍN B. AND JEFFREY D. SACHS
Harvard University Harvard University

INTRODUCTION

Bolivia's defeat of hyperinflation in the mid-1980s, and its subsequent economic reforms, represent one of the most successful economic adjustment programs of the postwar era. In a short period of time, hyperinflation was decisively eliminated, and economic growth was restored after years of plummeting output.

These accomplishments were carried out despite a series of adverse external shocks that sharply reduced Bolivia's export earnings and national income. In part because of these shocks, and in part because of Bolivia's chronically low levels of national saving and investment, economic growth since stabilization has been modest and so far too small to make a major dent in the country's extreme poverty and generally low standard of living.

One key to generating higher growth will be to increase national saving and investment rates. Several areas of financial and state enterprise reform—including pension reform and capitalization of the public enterprises—are key parts of a growth strategy. More attention must be paid to raising rural productivity, both to enhance economic growth and to address Bolivia's deep crisis of extreme rural poverty. This will require a multifaceted effort on agriculture R&D and improved provision of health and education services in the countryside.

*This paper is partly based on a report written in 1993, commissioned by the government of Bolivia, to review the main macroeconomic trends in the Bolivian economy since 1985 and to analyze policy options for the administration of President Sánchez de Losada. We are grateful to Presidents Victor Paz Estenssoro, Jaime Paz Zamora, Gonzalo Sánchez de Losada, Hugo Banzer for support of our work in Bolivia since 1985, and other members of the Bolivian government for support in preparing this report. We especially thank UDAPE for use of its facilities and outstanding studies. We are also grateful to Corporacion Andina de Fomento (CAF) for financing this project. The views expressed herein, however, are strictly our own and do not necessarily represent those of the government of Bolivia, the CAF, or any other institution.

This paper analyzes Bolivia's economic reforms since 1985, their results, and some of the main challenges ahead. It is organized as follows. The next section offers a brief description of the Bolivian hyperinflation and the economic reform program introduced in 1985 to stabilize the economy and restore economic growth. In the section titled "The New Economic Policy," we describe Bolivia's economic performance during the administration of President Victor Paz Estenssoro (1985–1989), and we stress the effects of the reform program and the external shocks that hit Bolivia during those years. "The Reemergence of Growth" describes the consolidation of reforms during the administration of President Jaime Paz Zamora (1989–1993) and the return to sustained economic growth. In "The Limitations of Economic Adjustment during the 1985–1992 Period," we outline some of the main macroeconomic tasks facing the Bolivian economy: increased economic growth and amelioration of the extreme poverty still prevalent in rural Bolivia. The last section, "An Agenda for the Future," studies some of the main needs to accomplish higher growth and poverty alleviation in terms of investment, saving, rural development, and social services.

Background

On August 6, 1993, with the inauguration of President Gonzalo Sánchez de Losada, Bolivia celebrated its fourth consecutive democratic transfer of power in 11 years. This is a remarkable and satisfying accomplishment for a country that had previously been known worldwide for coups, revolution, and dictatorship. When democracy was reestablished in 1982, after 16 years of military rule punctuated by brief, failed democratic governments, the circumstances for establishing a stable democracy were far from auspicious.

President Hernan Siles Suazo took office in 1982 in the midst of an extreme debt crisis. He left office one year early, in 1985, after failing to control a severe macroeconomic crisis that eventually exploded into full hyperinflation. The bold economic reforms that have been carried out since 1985 deserve much of the credit for reestablishing a working economy and laying the groundwork for a vigorous democracy. In turn, healthy democratic life is making possible the continuation and strengthening of economic reforms.

The economic chaos of the first half of the 1980s had been preceded by a period of relatively rapid economic growth under the military regime of General Hugo Banzer. During the 1971–1978 period, GDP growth averaged 5.4 percent per year. Part of that economic achievement was illusory, however, because it was built on a rapid accumulation of foreign debt. Even the real successes were reversed by the remarkable period of political instability that followed the Banzer era. As we see in Figure 1, gross domestic product (GDP) growth ended in 1978 and was followed by a precipitous collapse. Per capita income fell by 30 percent between 1978 and 1985.

No fewer than 11 heads of state held office during the 1979–1982 period, including the internationally notorious regime of General Luis Garcia Meza, who was personally implicated in cocaine trafficking. The Garcia Meza regime pushed Bolivia into utter economic collapse, as international creditors withdrew from the country, fomenting an acute balance-of-payments crisis. President Hernan Siles Suazo restored democratic government in 1982, but proved to be ineffectual in facing the rapidly deteriorating economic situation. His government made enormous financial concessions to powerful trade unions within his political coalition and was unable to organize a sustained program of macroeconomic stabilization. The result was a burgeoning inflation and a rapidly collapsing real economy.

FIGURE 1

Gross Domestic Product, 1961–1992 (in millions of 1988 U.S. dollars)

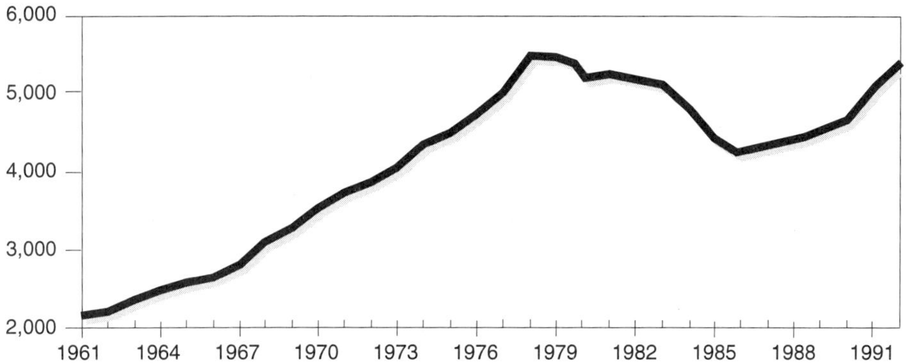

Source: International Monetary Fund, International Financial Statistics, various issues.

In 1984 Bolivia became the first country in world history to reach hyperinflation during peacetime (see Figures 2 and 3).[1] The government of President Siles Suazo tried repeatedly to halt the spiraling inflation, and he in fact launched six stabilization attempts between November 1982 and February 1985. These attempts were defeated by internal inconsistencies, weakness of the government in the face of trade union demands, and political opposition in the Bolivian Congress. With the situation out of control, President Siles Suazo called for emergency elections and stepped down one year early.

The 1985 elections brought President Victor Paz Estenssoro to his fourth term as president (1952–1956, 1960–1964, 1964, and 1985–1989). After less than one month in office, President Paz Estenssoro unveiled a remarkably bold and wide-ranging economic program, the New Economic Policy (or NEP, also known as Supreme Decree 21060), that was to change completely the face of the country. President Paz Estenssoro soon won the backing in Congress of the Acción Democrática Nacionalista (ADN), led by General Hugo Banzer, and the NEP was carried out on the basis of a quasi-coalition government between Paz Estenssoro's Movimiento Nacionalista Revolucionario (MNR) and the ADN. The NEP succeeded in stabilizing the economy and setting the basis for renewed economic growth. The turnaround is notably evident in Figures 1, 2, and 3. As we shall stress, this renewed growth came in the face of deeply adverse international shocks. As Gonzalo Sánchez de Losada said in 1985, the NEP was designed to "reinvent Bolivia," and it has done so economically as well as politically.

Four years later, during the 1989 elections, all the major candidates promised to maintain the economic direction of the NEP. As in 1985, the 1989 election produced no clear

[1]Until the Bolivian hyperinflation, all historical cases had been in the context of war, civil war, or revolution. Sadly, Bolivia's peacetime hyperinflation was subsequently followed by several other examples, including those experienced in Argentina, Brazil, Peru, Poland, Russia, and pre–civil war Yugoslavia. For a history of hyperinflation, see Sachs and Larrain (1993, chap. 23).

FIGURE 2
Inflation, 1961–1992 (annual average)

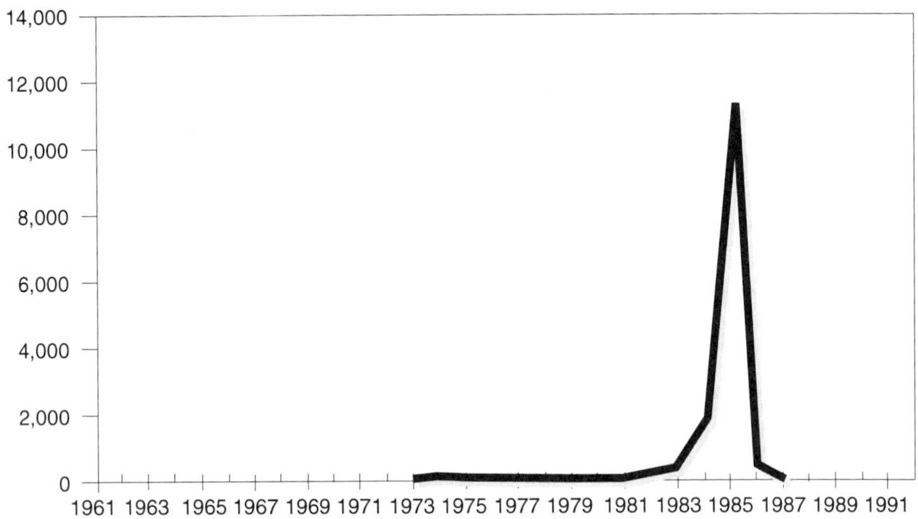

Source: International Monetary Fund, International Financial Statistics, various issues.

FIGURE 3
Inflation, 1961–1992 (annual average)

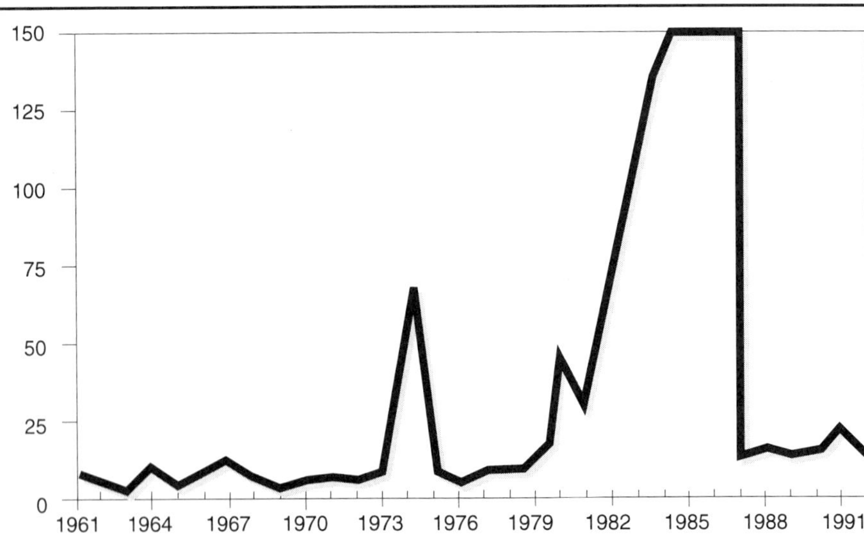

Source: International Monetary Fund, International Financial Statistics, various issues.

winner, requiring that the president be selected by the newly elected Congress. President Jaime Paz Zamora, leading the left-of-center Movimiento de Izquierda Revolucionario (MIR), came to power on the basis of a coalition with ADN. This government maintained the thrust of the economic policies and was able to continue the reduction of Bolivia's inflation to one of the lowest levels in Latin America. Economic growth increased as well, ranging from 3 percent to 3.5 percent per year in 1992 and 1993. The 1993 elections produced a wide plurality in favor of Gonzalo Sánchez de Losada, the architect of the 1985 economic reform, who was elected president by the Bolivian Congress for the 1993–1997 period.

THE NEW ECONOMIC POLICY

The government of President Paz Estenssoro was quick to implement comprehensive economic reforms in August 1985. Although the most urgent goal of the program was to stop the hyperinflation, the policy package went far beyond macroeconomic stabilization measures, because it addressed a remarkable range of structural issues as well. It can be said that the Bolivian program was the most comprehensive case of economic shock therapy that had yet been undertaken in the postwar world economy. Its success has subsequently helped to influence similar programs in Eastern Europe and the former Soviet Union.

For at least three reasons, the NEP went beyond strict stabilization measures to include issues such as trade liberalization and massive price decontrol. First, it was clear to the new government that Bolivia needed deep structural changes in the economy, particularly in the promotion of new industries to replace the faltering traditional tin mines. Second, the government simply lacked the capacity to administer the intricate set of regulations and controls on trade, prices, and interest rates that were then on the books. These regulations were not only unenforced but had given rise to substantial corruption. Third, some of the structural reforms supported the stabilization effort. Trade liberalization, for example, implied that competition from abroad would discipline domestic enterprises after prices were decontrolled.

The main steps in Supreme Decree 21060 were the unification and stabilization of the exchange rate; major fiscal consolidation, centering on a sharp rise of public-sector prices (especially those that were energy related), a cutback in subsidies and public investment, and a comprehensive tax reform (implemented in 1986); trade liberalization, including an immediate reduction of tariffs to a nearly uniform rate of around 20 percent and the elimination of most nontariff barriers; decontrol of private-sector wages and most prices; and liberalization of labor-market activity, including the rights to hire and fire workers. The New Economic Policy also made explicit the government's intention to restore creditworthiness with the international community, particularly with the multilateral financial institutions.

The program was characterized by speed as well as comprehensiveness. The decontrol of prices, the reduction of the deficit through higher energy prices, and the liberalization of trade were virtually immediate. The exchange rate was unified by eliminating the artificial exchange rate (which was only 5 percent of the black market rate on the eve of reforms!) and allowing the rate to be set in an auction market (though one with heavy government participation in the purchase and sale of foreign exchange).[2] All capital controls were eliminated as well. The exchange rate was thereby unified at the former black market rate, and it quickly stabilized thereafter as a result of the implementation of fiscal and monetary austerity. Because price setting had been substantially dollarized during the hyperinflation, it was possible to stop domestic price increases merely by ending the depreciation of the currency. Therefore, the hyperinflation was ended within days of the implementation of Supreme Decree 21060. The stabilization was threatened briefly in early 1986 when the exchange rate started to depreciate because of over-expansionary policies, but the government was able to restore overall macroeconomic control and thereby sustain the hard-won fight against hyperinflation.

Tax reform was another important part of the program, though it was one that could be implemented only in the intermediate run. The Congress did not pass the tax reform legislation until nearly one year after the start of the NEP because the legislation was subject to long Congressional and public debate, and then there were administrative lags in implementing the new measures. The main goal of the tax reform was to broaden the tax base and to implement more efficient taxes. To this purpose, the tax legislation created a new value-added tax, new patrimony taxes, and a uniform 10 percent income tax.

The Terms of Trade Collapse

The world economy could not have provided a more adverse blow to Bolivia's initial reforms than the October 1985 collapse of world tin prices. Only two months after the start of the NEP, the international tin cartel, which had been artificially sustaining world tin prices by purchasing tin for inventory, went bankrupt. The accumulated tin stockpiles had by that point accumulated to nearly one year's worldwide consumption. The price of tin immediately plummeted by around 60 percent, from $5.60 per pound to $2.60 per pound. The London Metal Exchange even ceased quoting trade in tin. At the time, tin was Bolivia's second most important legal export (third if the unrecorded trade in coca paste is included), contributing some $150 million per year to export earnings, or 25 percent of total recorded exports. The export decline not only represented a sharp loss of national income, but constituted a deep fiscal shock and a social crisis as well. In 1985, the state Bolivian tin company, COMIBOL, employed 30,000 workers, almost all of whom would be made redundant by the collapse in world prices.

This shock was soon followed by another, almost as severe from a fiscal point of view. Bolivia's main recorded export in 1985 was natural gas, which it sells almost exclusively to Argentina. After the fall in world energy prices in 1986, Bolivia had to renegotiate its natural gas contract with Argentina, at a loss of around $100 million in annual export earnings. Moreover, Argentina was suffering a fiscal crisis nearly as acute as Bolivia's, and it proved unable or unwilling to continue timely payments for its natural gas imports. As a result, Bolivia not only lost the contractual earnings but suffered extended periods of arrearages from Argentina, rising to an accumulated arrearage of around $325 million by 1989.

[2]Although the auction market (the "bolsin") was managed, the gap between the official rate (set in the bolsin) and the black market rate (set in the street) was insignificant, as there were virtually no restrictions on participation in the bolsin, and the rate set there was always a market-clearing rate.

Ironically, Bolivia not only suffered deep losses from its main legal exports but also from its unrecorded coca trade. It appears that world prices for coca paste fell sharply in the mid-1980s, perhaps related to the surge of production in Peru and Amazonian Brazil. Moreover, the government reinforced its interdiction efforts against narcotics traffickers and even launched joint military operations with the United States in 1987. These shocks probably cut from $100 million to $300 million from Bolivia's estimated $600 million annual exports of coca leaf and coca paste.

The conjunction of these external shocks was an unexpected and deep blow to the reform process. In total, they probably cost Bolivia around $600 million per year, or 10 percent of gross national product (GNP), if account is taken of Argentina's nonpayments for energy as well as the loss in unrecorded coca earnings. As shown in Figure 4, Bolivia's terms of trade (export prices divided by import prices) declined by around 70 percent between 1980 and 1992! This magnitude of loss in national income due to external shocks is virtually unprecedented in a period of one decade, and it is perhaps four times larger in relation to the economy than the shock suffered by the United States in the 1970s from the rise in world oil prices.

The external shocks vastly complicated the reforms in several ways: the loss of fiscal revenue (particularly from tin and gas); the need for a major reduction of employment in COMIBOL, with all of the attendant social and political consequences; the squeeze on real incomes, almost universally (and mistakenly) attributed both inside and outside the country to economic reforms rather than to the international events; and the urgency of establishing alternative bases for growth in the economy after the losses in the main export sectors.

FIGURE 4
Terms of Trade (1980 = 100)

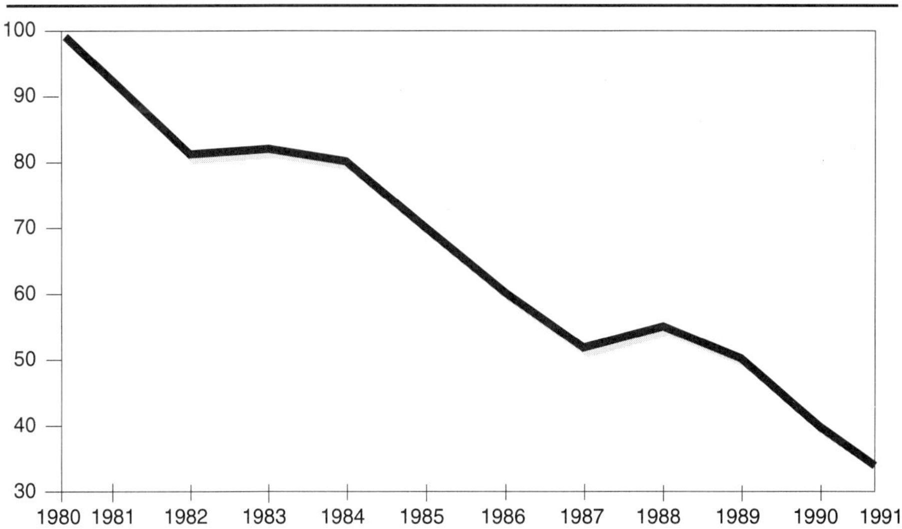

Source: Unidad de Análisis de Políticas Económicas (UDAPE), La Paz, Bolivia.

SUCCESSFUL STABILIZATION: 1985–1989

We have noted the remarkable speed of the initial stabilization. After the huge initial depreciation of the official exchange rate (from 67,000 pesos/dollar to 1.1 million pesos/dollar), the tenfold increase in gasoline prices, and the elimination of most price controls, at the start of September 1989, it took just a little over one week for hyperinflation to end. Prices increased by almost 40 percent in the first week of the program and then dropped by 4.6 percent the following week. Inflation was kept under control during the following 12 months, except for a brief outburst in the last weeks of 1985 and the start of 1986 as the result of an excessive increase in the money supply. Higher public-sector prices, particularly in energy, and other gains in tax collection made possible by the slowdown of inflation allowed fiscal revenues to increase by nearly 10 percent of GDP in the first year of the program, thus providing the underlying basis for continued stability.

Stabilization also brought a remonetization of the economy, and a revival of the banking sector. One measure of monetization, the ratio of M2 to GDP, fell to 8.8 percent in 1986 and then recovered to 15 percent by 1989 (see Figure 5). Much of the increase in high-powered money in the economy after 1985 came from an inflow of capital (probably Bolivian money holdings that had gone offshore during the high-inflation period) in the context of a pegged exchange rate. The Central Bank of Bolivia bought foreign exchange reserves and thereby increased the peso money supply. Gross foreign exchange reserves rose from \$60 million in August 1985 to around \$150 million by the end of 1985 and almost \$400 million by 1989.

FIGURE 5
Financial Deepening (M2/GDP)

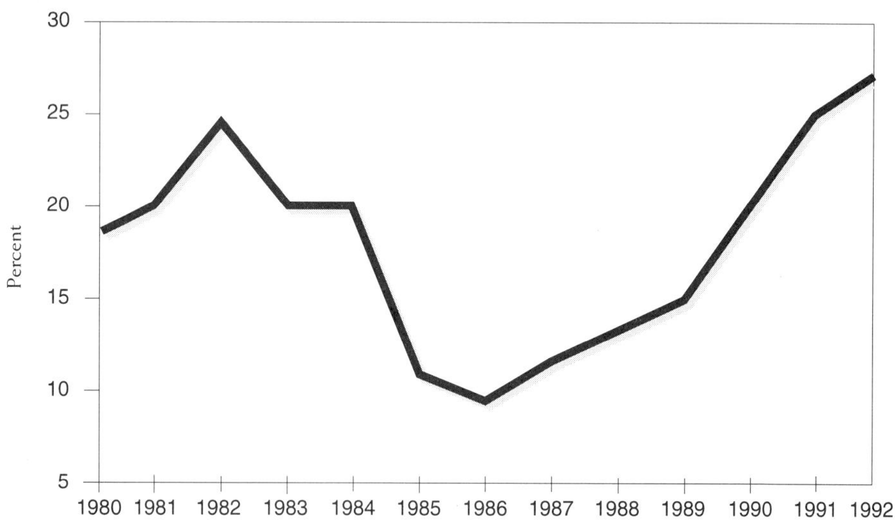

Source: Unidad de Análisis de Políticas Económicas (UDAPE), La Paz, Bolivia. International Monetary Fund, International Financial Statistics, various issues.

It has often been claimed that Bolivia's stabilization was highly contractionary, contributing to a fall in output and a rise in unemployment. This argument is not convincing, however, when Bolivia's poststabilization experience is compared to the previous trends in the economy and when one considers the external shocks that hit Bolivia in 1985 and after. We already saw in Figure 1 that per capita income fell sharply every year between 1979 and 1985, the start of the NEP. In October 1985, Bolivia was hit by the collapse of tin prices. In 1986, GDP fell again, by 2.5 percent, which was a relatively mild recession in the face of the strong stabilization and the huge external shocks. In 1987, GDP began to rise for the first time in six years. During the 1988–1992 period, per capita GDP rose every year. Thus, the NEP marks the beginning of economic recovery, not the onset of recession.

Even the argument that the fiscal contraction in 1985 reduced aggregate demand is tenuous. Rather the inflation tax, which was running at about 12 percent per year, was replaced by explicit taxes (mainly on energy products) of a like amount. Stabilization therefore amounted to a shift of taxes rather than a net rise of taxes. Moreover, the reestablishment of creditworthiness with the international financial institutions led to substantial inflows of official finance (as well as a partial cancellation of preexisting debts), and these inflows supported a rise in domestic investment spending.

Unemployment did rise, however, in the first years of the reform, but this unemployment was, to a substantial extent, the result of the closure of most of COMIBOL's tin operations. Total employment in COMIBOL dropped by around five-sixths, from 30,000 to 5,000 employees. The unemployment rate rose significantly, as shown in Figure 6, and only began to decline in 1989. To offset some of the economic hardship on the lower income groups, the government established the Emergency Social Fund (ESF), an internationally

FIGURE 6
Unemployment

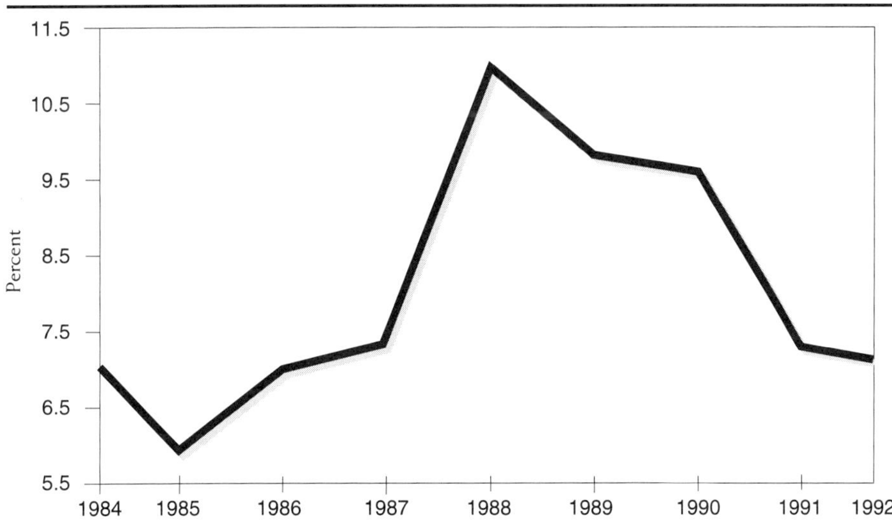

Source: Economic Commission of Latin America and the Caribbean (ECLAC) "Balance Preliminar de la Economia de America Latina y el Caribe," various issues.

funded program to promote employment through small-scale infrastructure projects. Nongovernmental organizations (NGOs) throughout the country ran many of the ESF projects at the local level. The ESF is widely and rightly regarded as a major success in terms of social policy, temporary employment creation, and small-scale infrastructure development. Several other countries in Latin America have studied Bolivia's ESF to model their own social efforts. During the Paz Zamora administration, the ESF was converted into the Social Investment Fund, which continues operating today.

During this period, Bolivia was also able to reach a comprehensive settlement for reduction of its external debts. Bolivia became the first country in the world to sign a debt-reduction agreement with its commercial bank creditors, two years before the Brady Plan was unveiled (indeed, elements of Bolivia's pioneering debt agreement were incorporated into the Brady Plan). The basic agreement allowed Bolivia to use donor-country funds to buy back much of its debt at 11 cents on the dollar. By the end of the Paz Estenssoro administration, approximately two-thirds of the commercial bank debt had been written off in this manner.[3] This process was completed during the Paz Zamora administration, with the final repurchases made at around 16 cents per dollar. As described later, the Paz Zamora government also achieved agreements with official creditors for significant cuts in the official debt.

By combining strong domestic reforms with tough international negotiations, always in a cooperative setting, Bolivia was able to reduce its foreign debt and acquire new official financing at the same time. This contrasted sharply with Peru's experience during the Garcia presidency, when Peru's confrontational suspension of debt servicing was not backed up by suitable internal reforms. Peru, like Bolivia, did not service its debts, but it also obtained no formal settlement for debt reduction and was basically cut off from new official funds. Thus, although both Bolivia and Peru were in arrears to the banks throughout the second half of the 1980s, Bolivia was able to achieve a net positive resource transfer (new loans in excess of debt servicing), whereas Peru continued to experience a negative net resource transfer.[4]

The Reemergence of Growth: 1989–1993

The first three years under the NEP succeeded in ending high inflation and stopping the continuous decline of the real economy. These accomplishments were carried out in the context of highly adverse international shocks. Although growth resumed in 1987 and 1988, it remained low. The achievement of the next administration was to build on these early and tentative successes in order to increase the nation's growth rate.

The Consolidation of Stability and Economic Growth

The 1989 elections brought to power President Jaime Paz Zamora in a coalition with General Banzer's Acción Democrática Nacionalista (ADN). As promised during the campaign, the

[3]For a detailed analysis of Bolivia's negotiation with commercial banks, see Sachs (1990).

[4]A comparison of Peru's and Bolivia's experience with external debt is carried out in Larrain and Sachs (1991).

basic economic policies of the previous administration were maintained. During the Paz Zamora administration, the country was able to reduce inflation to just 13 percent in 1992 and to around 10 percent in 1993. At the same time, economic growth edged upward from 1.5 percent per year during the 1986–1989 period to a rate of 4 percent per year during the 1990–1992 period, representing a per capita growth rate of around 1.7 percent per year (population growth is estimated at 2.3 percent per year).

Bolivia's experience, along with international comparative evidence, strongly suggests that political stability supports economic growth, in part by improving the quality and quantity of investment spending. In Bolivia, domestic fixed capital formation (including both public- and private-sector investments) increased from a low of less than 10 percent of GDP in 1983 to around 16 percent of GDP in 1992. Even more remarkable has been the recovery of Bolivia's private investment, which rose from $95 million (in U.S. dollars) in 1988 (2 percent of GDP) to $420 million in 1992 (7.5 percent of GDP). Private investment thereby increased from 20 percent to 44 percent of total investment.

Bolivia's growth prospects were further strengthened during the Paz Zamora administration by new reductions in the country's external debt burden through the partial cancellation of official indebtedness. The first step was the cancellation of long-term debts to Argentina in 1989, matched by the elimination of Argentina's short-term debts to Bolivia. By the end of 1989, Bolivia had reached a similar agreement with Brazil, leading to the cancellation of around $330 million owed to Brazil. President Bush's Enterprise for the Americas initiative led to the elimination of more than $370 million of debt owed to the United States. In 1991 Bolivia became the first country in Latin America to obtain Toronto terms in its negotiations with the Paris Club. These terms, previously reserved for the lower-income countries of sub-Saharan Africa, allowed Bolivia to reduce another $89 million of foreign debt.

GROWTH IN NONTRADITIONAL EXPORTS

During the 1985–1992 period, Bolivia had to confront an enormous terms of trade decline and had to, in effect, reinvent itself as an exporting nation. Tin disappeared as the leading export sector. Natural gas exports also declined sharply, partly because of falling energy prices in world markets (reflected in Bolivia's contract prices on sales to Argentina) and partly because of Argentina's announced intention to substitute its own energy resources for its previous imports from Bolivia. As we have mentioned, the country's terms of trade have collapsed by almost 70 percent since 1980, among the greatest declines in the world. As a result, Bolivia's total exports almost halved, from more than $1 billion in 1980 to just $570 million in 1987. However, exports recovered to $830 million in 1992. In spite of this recovery, dollar exports are still $200 million below the level reached in 1980.

Looking at the aggregate numbers, the export picture is quite bleak. Nonetheless, the picture is more encouraging if we look at a decomposition of export earnings by sector (nontraditional versus traditional and public versus private). The drop in export earnings is concentrated in traditional exports of the public sector. Since 1985, Bolivia has experienced major growth in nontraditional exports. They have increased from a mere $35 million in 1985 to $220 million in 1992 ($50 million higher than in 1980), as shown in Figure 7. At the same time, traditional exports declined from $867 million in 1980 to $638 million in 1985 and $610 million in 1992 (although they have risen from their lows of $460 million in 1987). Private-sector exports soared from $86 million in 1984 to $564 million in 1992,

FIGURE 7
Traditional and Nontraditional Exports (in millions of U.S. dollars)

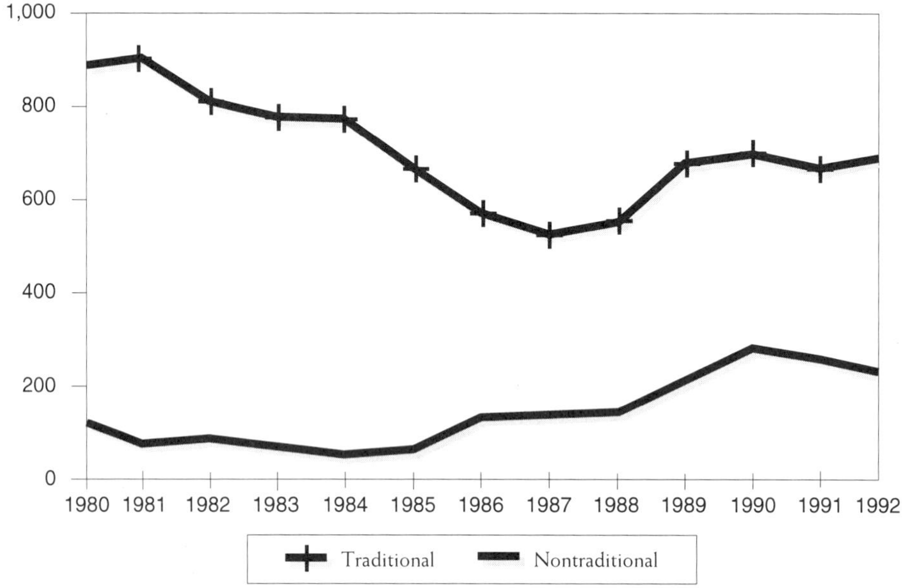

Source: Unidad de Análisis de Políticas Económicas (UDAPE), La Paz, Bolivia.

as shown in Figure 8. Public-sector exports, on the other hand, dropped consistently throughout the period, from \$760 million in 1982 to \$570 million in 1985 and to \$266 million in 1992. It is the private, nontraditional exports that will hold the key for much of Bolivia's future growth.

What are the causes of this spectacular rise in private exports? Clearly, the depreciation of the real exchange rate by more than 50 percent between 1984 and 1986, and its relative stability thereafter, is one important reason. Another is the restoration of private investment, much of which has been concentrated in new export projects, with particularly significant increases in soybean exports. Later on, we will discuss further policy steps that might be taken to broaden and deepen the growth of nontraditional exports.

Recovery of the Financial Sector

The financial sector has experienced significant changes since 1985. Interest rates and the investment decisions of commercial banks have been liberalized. State banks, such as the Agricultural Bank (Banco Agricola) have been closed. The regulatory environment has been strengthened with the creation of a superintendency of banks.

Financial liberalization and a stable macroeconomic environment have been instrumental in the continued growth of the financial sector. After increasing from less than 9 percent of GDP in 1986 to around 15 percent in 1989, M2 climbed to 23 percent of GDP in 1992

FIGURE 8

Public and Private Exports (in millions of U.S. dollars)

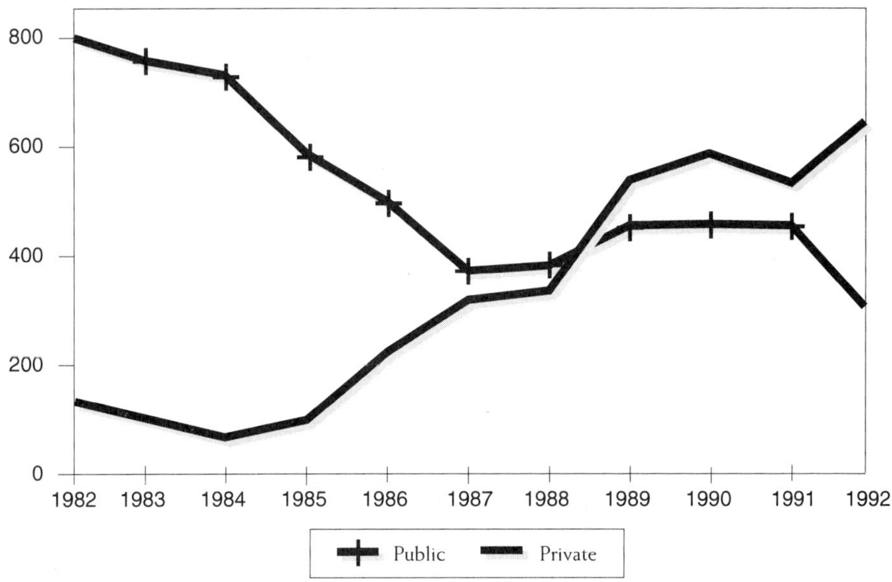

Source: Unidad de Análisis de Políticas Económicas (UDAPE), La Paz, Bolivia.

(see Figure 5). Consequently, the loan portfolios of the commercial banks have increased at an average rate of 40 percent annually since 1985, from a low of less than $50 million in 1985 to almost $1.4 billion in 1992.

PUBLIC SECTOR RESTRUCTURING

The restructuring of the state sector began with the fiscal reforms of the NEP and the substantial scaling down of Corporación Minera de Bolivia (COMIBOL). The Paz Zamora government continued this restructuring. In a key effort to improve the efficiency of government action, the law on State Administration and Financial Control (SAFCO) was enacted in July 1990. This law established enhanced mechanisms of administration and oversight of all public institutions, and it requires detailed statements on the use of resources by all public-sector entities.

A law on privatization passed in April 1992, allowing for the privatization of all state enterprises except for COMIBOL and the state oil company, Yacimientos Petrolíferos Fiscales de Bolivia (YPFB). The law also established that natural monopolies require the enactment of regulatory procedures prior to privatization. By the middle of 1993, however, there had been few sales of large enterprises, and some of the sales of smaller enterprises had generated enormous controversy.

The Limitations of Economic Adjustment during the 1985–1992 Period

By the end of the Paz Zamora administration, and despite major economic achievements between 1985 and 1993, Bolivia still had many profound economic challenges to overcome. Although overall economic growth has been positive since 1987, the growth has been modest in a country that has one of the highest levels of poverty in Latin America. The slow rise in per capita income since 1987 implies a very modest rise in living standards and only a tiny dent in poverty. The adverse external circumstances certainly account for some of the lack of growth. We have noted that external shocks probably reduced Bolivian real income by around 10 percent. Nonetheless, Bolivia will have to undertake further efforts if it is to raise its modest growth rates to more satisfactory levels.

In addition to a harsh international environment for traditional exports, Bolivia's slow growth is due to very low levels of saving and investment, as well as the population's low average levels of educational attainment. Even after years of recovery from the extremely low levels of investment in the first half of the 1980s, Bolivia's investment rates as a percent of GDP are among the lowest in Latin America and less than half the rates of the fast-growing countries of East Asia. The situation is even more dramatic with respect to domestic savings rates, as Table 1 shows. Much of Bolivia's investments are actually financed from abroad, via foreign loans from official institutions. Domestic savings accounts for only one-half to two-thirds of investment, and savings as a percent of GDP is between one-third and one-half of Latin American saving rates and around one-fourth of the savings rates of East Asia. This is not only a matter of Bolivia's poverty, because other very poor countries in Asia, such as China, save a much higher proportion of national income.

Table 1

Investment and Saving (as a percentage of GDP, 1991)

	Gross Domestic Investment	Gross Domestic Savings
Bolivia	15	9
Argentina	12	15
Brazil	20	30
Chile	19	24
Mexico	23	20
Peru	16	13
Hong Kong	29	32
Korea	39	36
Malaysia	36	30
Singapore	37	47
Thailand	39	32

Sources: Bolivia: Instituto Nacional de Estadísticas; other countries: the World Bank, *World Development Report*, 1993.

Bolivia continues to be plagued not only by slow growth but also by extreme poverty and dismal social conditions in the countryside. Recent estimates suggest that about 80 percent of the country's population lives in poverty, with about 55 percent of urban households in poverty and nearly 90 percent of households in the agricultural highlands in poverty.[5]

Because the highest levels of poverty are concentrated in the rural areas, poverty is closely related to traditional agriculture (as distinct from commercial agriculture in the eastern lowlands). Peasant agriculture is characterized by very small land plots, serious ecological erosion, unclear property rights (such as the lack of land title enabling the mortgaging of land), and traditional technologies that have not increased productivity in recent years. Although productivity has risen in many modern sectors of the economy, traditional agricultural sectors have shown no productivity growth for the past two decades.[6] Peasant agriculture continues to account for about 85 percent to 90 percent of the total cultivated area for potatoes, maize, soybeans, and wheat and for about 75 percent of the total output of these products.[7]

Other social indicators also give evidence of the extreme poverty in Bolivia. As Table 2 shows, life expectancy at birth in Bolivia is just 60 years, much lower than the average for lower-middle-income countries (68 years), the appropriate reference group for Bolivia. Child mortality (under age 5) in Bolivia is a staggering 125 per thousand, three times the rate of lower-middle-income countries and worse than several countries in sub-Saharan Africa. Infant mortality (under age 1) is 83 per thousand, twice the rate of lower-middle-income countries. Malnutrition is prevalent among 18 percent of children under age 5. The adult illiteracy rate is 23 percent. As Table 2 shows, most of these indicators have improved over the last 20 years, but Bolivia remains at or near the bottom of Latin America with regard to all of the social indicators.

AN AGENDA FOR THE FUTURE

The most important overall goal for Bolivia is an acceleration of economic growth from the levels of about 4 percent per year achieved in the past few years. Only a higher growth rate—on the order of 6 percent annually as in the low-income countries of Asia and as in Chile since the mid-1980s—promises to lift Bolivia from extreme poverty and into the mainstream of Latin American economies. Chile's economic growth followed nearly a decade of economic liberalization and stabilization, starting in the mid-1970s. It took time for these reforms to lay the basis for renewed private-sector investment and sustained increases in export earnings. Like Chile, Bolivia has been setting the groundwork for renewed growth. Now it must put together the necessary ingredients for the coming years.

SOURCES OF GROWTH IN BOLIVIA

We can gain perspective on Bolivia's growth prospects by examining economic growth in an international setting. Why do some countries grow rapidly and other countries grow

[5]The World Bank (1990) and Pereira and Velasco (1993).

[6]The World Bank (1992).

[7]Godoy, de Franco, and Echeverría (1993).

TABLE 2

Social Indicators

	Health								Education					
	Life Expectancy at Birth		Child Mortality Rate (per 1,000 live births)		Crude Death Rate (per 1,000 pop.)		Births Attended by Health Staff (as a percentage)	Prevalence of Malnutrition (for children under 5 years)	Adult Illiteracy (as a percentage)	Primary Net Enrollment (as a percentage)		Primary Pupil/ Teacher Ratio	
	1960	1990	1960	1991	1960	1991	1985	1990	1990	1975	1990	1970	1990
Bolivia	43	60	251	125	19	10	36	18	23	73	82	27	25
Argentina	67	72	73	26	9	9	—	—	5	96	—	19	19
Brazil	52	66	179	69	10	7	73	13	19	71	88	28	23
Chile	55	73	155	20	10	6	97	2	7	94	86	50	29
Mexico	56	70	148	38	10	5	—	14	13	—	98	46	31
Peru	45	65	233	73	14	8	55	13	15	—	95	35	28
Korea	53	72	133	10	9	6	65	—	4	99	100	57	36
Hong Kong	64	78	53	7	5	6	—	7	—	92	—	33	—
Singapore	65	74	48	8	5	5	100	9	—	100	100	30	26
Malaysia	56	71	106	20	10	5	82	24	22	—	—	31	20
Lower middle income	—	68	87	42	12	8	—	—	26	—	87	33	25

Source: The World Bank, *World Development Report,* 1993.

slowly? Of course, economists are far from providing a complete answer to this question, but in recent years many studies have shed light on the basic determinants of growth. In several studies, Professor Robert Barro of Harvard University has been able to identify many of the key determinants of economic growth. He has used a cross-section statistical analysis in which a country's economic growth rate over an extended period of time is related to structural characteristics of the country, such as its level of income at the start of the period and the extent of education of the labor force.

The main explanatory variables in the Barro studies[8] are as follows:

- *The initial level of income in the country.* Poorer countries tend to grow faster than richer countries, all other things equal (in part because they are able to import the more advanced technologies and capital from the richer countries).
- *The educational attainment of the labor force.* A more educated labor force raises the growth rate of the economy.
- *The ratio of government consumption expenditure to GNP.* A higher share of government consumption expenditure tends to reduce the growth rate of the economy.
- *The number of revolutions, coups, and political assassinations during the observation period.* Political instability tends to lower the growth rate.
- *The relative price of capital goods in the economy.* A high price of capital goods tends to reduce the growth rate of the economy.
- *The share of investment in GDP.* A high rate of investment tends to raise the growth rate of the economy.

According to these studies, Bolivia grew on average at a rate of 0.8 percent per capita per year during the 1960–1985 period, compared with an overall average growth rate among the sample of 110 countries of 2.2 percent per capita annually. What accounts for this slower growth? According to Barro's statistical analysis, Bolivia should have grown faster than average because it was a poorer country, other things being equal. But other things were not equal. Bolivia grew more slowly than average because of a below-average educational attainment, a higher-than-average level of government consumption in GDP, a much higher degree of political instability, a relatively high price of investment goods, and a lower-than-average rate of overall investment.

Interestingly, the statistical analysis (not reported here in detail) suggests that Bolivia's political instability alone reduced its growth rate relative to the average by 1.5 percent per year, the largest single negative effect on Bolivia's growth. The poor education attainment probably slowed growth by another 0.5 percent per year compared with the average country, the low investment rate by 0.4 percent per year, and the high relative price of investment goods by 1.5 percent per year compared with the average country in the sample.

The precise values must be taken with a grain of salt. The cross-country equation for 110 countries does not precisely explain the growth rates in these countries, and so it cannot explain precisely why Bolivia has long grown less rapidly than the average country. Nonetheless, the statistical results are highly suggestive. They indicate that to grow faster, Bolivia should first and foremost maintain its hard-won political stability. The return to stable democratic rule after 1985 has probably contributed to a marked increase

[8] One of these studies is Barro (1991).

in Bolivia's growth after the mid-1980s. Bolivia must also invest more, and raise the educational attainment of the labor force, to spur its overall growth rate. We now turn to determining a more precise estimate of how much investment should rise.

Investment Needs for Higher Growth

We have already stressed that a high rate of investment is necessary to sustain an increased rate of growth in the next few years. For decades, Bolivia has had a chronically low rate of capital formation, and this has been reflected in Bolivia's chronically low rate of growth. Although investment has recovered from the very low rates of the mid-1980s, gross fixed capital formation (fixed investment) has hovered around 15 percent of GDP since 1988, as Table 3 shows. During this same period, output has grown at an annual average rate of 3.5 percent.

A brief examination of various countries that have experienced high growth in the 1980s shows that their investment efforts have been substantially higher than Bolivia's. Hong Kong, Korea, Malaysia, Singapore, and Thailand have had average GDP growth rates of between 6 percent and 9 percent during the past decade. As Table 1 showed, such growth rates are based on investment rates of around 30 percent or more.

The Asian economies have also displayed high efficiency in the allocation of investment, as measured by the incremental capital output ratio (ICOR). The ICOR is measured as the ratio of the net investment rate to the growth rate of the economy. Net investment is measured as gross investment minus depreciation. In principle, the ICOR measures how much investment would have to be raised, as a percent of GDP, for each 1 percentage point increment in the overall GDP growth rate. For example, if a country invests 30 percent of GDP and has a depreciation rate of 10 percent of GDP, then the net investment rate is 20 percent of GDP. If the economy is growing at 8 percent, its ICOR would be 2.5

TABLE 3
Saving, Investment, and Growth (percentage of GDP and rates of growth)

	1988	1989	1990	1991	1992	Average 1988–1992
Growth of GDP	2.7	2.8	4.1	4.6	3.4	3.5
Gross capital formation	17.6	13.1	10.2	17.2	21.2	15.9
Gross fixed capital formation	16.0	15.0	14.4	15.3	15.6	15.2
Inventory accumulation (% GDP)	1.6	−2.0	−4.2	2.0	5.6	0.6
Total saving	17.6	13.1	10.2	17.2	21.2	15.9
Public	0.9	1.9	2.8	3.7	3.2	2.5
Current income	28.2	27.7	29.5	30.6	30.6	29.3
Tax revenues	8.2	7.6	7.9	8.1	10.1	8.4
Nontax revenues	20.0	20.1	21.6	22.5	20.5	20.9
Current costs	27.3	25.8	26.7	26.9	27.5	26.8
External	4.9	4.8	−1.1	4.5	9.4	4.5
Private	11.8	6.4	8.5	9.0	8.7	8.9

Source: Cuentas Nacionales, 1988–1992, Instituto Nacional de Estadísticas, La Paz, Bolivia.

TABLE 4

Incremental Capital Output Ratio (Bolivia and selected Asian countries)

	1971–1988	1971–1975	1976–1980	1981–1988
Korea	2.2	3.2	2.0	2.3
Malaysia	2.3	1.9	1.8	2.9
Singapore	3.2	2.7	2.6	3.9
Thailand	2.0	2.1	1.9	2.0
				1961–1981
Bolivia				2.8

Sources: Asia: Larrain and Vergara (1993). Bolivia: Author's calculations from International Monetary Fund, International Financial Statistics.

(=20/8). In principle, to raise the growth rate to 9 percent per year would require fixed investment of another 2.5 percent of GDP. Gross investment would have to rise to 32.5 percent of GDP, and net investment to 22.5 percent of GDP. The lower the ICOR, the more efficient presumably is investment. Of course, the ICOR is not a perfect measure, and it tends to display wide fluctuations from year to year. Over a period of a few years, however, it can give a fairly accurate sense of investment needs to achieve particular rates of growth.

Table 4 shows the average ICORs of the newly industrialized countries of East Asia between 1971 and 1988. According to the ICOR indicator, the most efficient economies in this group are Korea and Thailand, which had ICORs of 2.2 and 2, respectively. Bolivia's ICOR for the 1961–1981 period was 2.8, implying that the country needed 2.8 points of net fixed investment to support an additional 1 percentage point of GDP growth. The problem with Bolivia seems to lie more with the very low investment rate rather than a high ICOR (that is, high levels of investment needed to support a modest increase in growth). For Bolivia to grow more rapidly, it will be necessary to increase significantly the rate of fixed investment from the current level of about 15 percent of GDP.

A simple exercise on investment requirements for growth in Bolivia would go as follows. Assume a depreciation of the capital stock in the order of 7 percent of GDP per year and an ICOR of 2.8, which corresponds to the average efficiency of investment during the 1961–1981 period. To grow consistently at a rate of around 6 percent per year, Bolivia will therefore need to increase its rate of fixed capital formation to around 24 percent of GDP.[9] Inventory accumulation might add another 1 percent of GDP to investment, so that total capital formation could reach 25 percent of GDP. The fixed investment rate of 24 percent of GDP likely cannot be achieved in a couple of years, given the current rate of just 15 percent of GDP.

We strongly believe that an investment rate of around 24 percent of GDP is plausible in the medium term, given Bolivia's investment opportunities in the gas pipeline to Brazil and in other key sectors of the economy. The capitalization scheme of the new government of President Sánchez de Losada is designed in part to attract several percent of GDP in new

[9]The warranted investment rate is equal to the rate of depreciation (assumed to be 7 percent of GDP per year) plus the growth rate (6 percent) multiplied by the ICOR. Thus, the warranted investment rate is 23.8 percent of GDP = 7 percent + 6 percent × 2.8. For 6.5 percent growth, fixed investment should be 25.2 percent of GDP.

investments by encouraging the recapitalization of the major economic sectors that remain under state ownership, including the oil and gas sector (YPFB), railways, electricity generation and distribution (ENDE), telecommunications, smelters, and the national airline.

The gas pipeline project by itself promises to provide a major macroeconomic boost. Investment requirements for the project until the year 2000 are estimated to be around $1.6 billion, with annual investments on the order of $156 million, or 2.5 percent of 1992 GDP. A recent study by Unidad de Análisis de Políticas Económicas (UDAPE) (1993) suggests that the project would raise GDP growth by approximately 1 percent per year during the 1993–2000 period. This is roughly consistent with our estimate of an ICOR of 2.8, because the project will contribute—on average—nearly 2.5 percent of GDP in new investments for several years. By the end of the decade, the project would also contribute as much as 5 percent of GDP in increased government revenues and $230 million per year in increased export earnings.

The Insufficiency of Saving

One important constraint on Bolivia's investment rate is the low rate of domestic saving in Bolivia. The country already relies to a remarkable extent on foreign savings, particularly in the form of concessional credits from the international financial institutions. In 1992, as we noted in Table 3, foreign savings amounted to more than 9 percent of GDP, though this was far higher than the average for the 1988–1992 period. It would be most unwise to count on an increase in foreign savings to, say, 15 percent of GDP or more in order to raise the domestic fixed investment rate to the targeted level of 24 percent of GDP. Such a large amount of foreign direct investment is unlikely. If it were achieved mainly through foreign borrowing, it would likely saddle the country with enormous foreign debts. Without an increased domestic savings effort, foreign investors will almost surely limit their own risks in the Bolivian economy.

Domestic saving has been chronically low in Bolivia, even lower than domestic investment, which historically has been bolstered by foreign savings. Bolivia's low savings rate is evident whether one compares Bolivia with industrialized economies or with other middle-income countries as we saw in Table 1. The gap between Bolivia's very low savings rate and its somewhat higher investment rate is measured by the current account deficit, which has been—on average—around 5 percent of GDP per year since the start of economic reforms in 1985.

These current account deficits, and the accumulated foreign indebtedness that they represent, have so far been manageable for two reasons. First, Bolivia has benefitted enormously from a substantial cancellation of pre-1985 indebtedness. Second, the new borrowing has generally been on highly concessional terms. In essence, most of the counterpart of the measured current account deficits are foreign grants rather than foreign debt.[10] Nonetheless,

[10]From a technical point of view, Bolivia's GNP is higher than recorded, because part of each concessional loan is in fact a transfer of income to Bolivia. The concessional portion of each loan should be added to GDP to arrive at GNP. Because of accounting conventions, however, the concessional loan is counted *entirely* as a loan rather than as a transfer. Proper economic accounting would show a somewhat higher national savings rate (because the transfer is used to support investment rather than consumption). Nonetheless, it is important to raise savings out of Bolivia's own domestic income, because the concessional financing will very likely be cut back in the future, and then Bolivia will have to save out of its own resources.

the concessional financing has its limits. Bolivia will reach limits on its ability to attract new concessional credits and will in fact have to start repaying some of the borrowing undertaken in the mid-1980s. Moreover, the major aid benefactor, the United States, is clearly cutting back on its overall international financial assistance.

For these reasons, it is urgent for Bolivia to spur domestic savings. Bolivia's national savings should rise significantly, from the current level of slightly more than 10 percent of GDP by more than 50 percent in order to finance the overall rise in capital formation to 25 percent of GDP. Although such an increase would be historically unprecedented, it would still represent an average rate of saving by international standards.

What can be done to boost Bolivia's savings rate? Although international evidence is not conclusive on this point, our belief is that capital market reform offers the best way to encourage new saving in Bolivia. In particular, we believe that the reform of the state pension system, as stated in President Sánchez de Losada's program, could play a key role in encouraging household saving, even in the traditional sectors of the economy that have not heretofore participated in the formal financial system. Of course, other factors conducive to a high savings rate include overall macroeconomic stability, modest rates of taxation on savings, and a microeconomic environment fostering the profitability of private-sector investment (clear property rights, efficient enforcement of contracts, openness of the economy).

RAISING RURAL PRODUCTIVITY AND IMPROVING SOCIAL SERVICES

The reform period has made vivid the division between the "two Bolivias": the urban sector, which has begun to take advantage of macroeconomic stability to increase investment and growth, and the peasant rural sector, which has remained stagnant in the face of the huge changes of recent years. Agricultural productivity in traditional highlands farming has remained basically unchanged for the past two decades.[11] It is very likely that the rural poor have fallen farther behind the modern sector during this period, and they may very well have lost ground in absolute terms, though comprehensive data are not available to make definitive judgments.

It is a harsh truth that Bolivian governments in recent years have done little to address the deep crisis of rural poverty. The crisis is clearly multifaceted: adult illiteracy, inadequate primary and secondary education, poor rural health including tragically high infant mortality and morbidity, stagnant technology, and ecosystems in crisis. Much of the work of the next administration will simply be to launch a strategy to address these problems; there will not be full solutions for decades.

We can only sketch some of the dimensions of an adequate strategy for this sector of the economy. We would point first to the very low level of rural productivity in traditional farming, particularly for basic staples such as wheat, potatoes, soybeans, and maize. Part of the reason for low productivity is the virtual absence of basic agricultural research and development in Bolivia.[12] What little R&D is performed tends to be devoted to commercial crops (such as soybeans in the lowlands) as opposed to the traditional staples. Table 5 shows the remarkably low level of R&D expenditures as a percentage of agricultural GDP.

[11]See the World Bank (1992).

[12]See Godoy et al. (1993).

TABLE 5

Expenditures on Agricultural Research in Selected Countries in Latin America and the Caribbean (as a percentage of agricultural GDP)

COUNTRY	YEAR*	RESEARCH EXPENDITURE AS A PERCENTAGE OF AGRICULTURAL GDP
Brazil	1981	0.847
Venezuela	1983	0.843
Paraguay	1983	0.636
Mexico	1982	0.442
Colombia	1986	0.437
Uruguay	1986	0.381
Ecuador	1986	0.317
Dominican Republic	1983	0.241
Argentina	1985	0.219
Costa Rica	1984	0.137
Bolivia	1983	0.096

*Year for which latest information is available.

Source: Godoy et al. (1993).

Bolivia's R&D effort is by far the lowest of the countries shown in the table. The recent creation of the National Council for Agricultural Research and Extension (CNIEA) is a very good step in the right direction. Now it is important that the council has adequate funding and political backing.

Another factor in low rural productivity is the absence of an adequate rural financial system that could help to finance small-scale improvements in infrastructure and farm technology. Part of the reason for the absence of adequate financial markets is the absence of clear property rights over much of the landholdings in the highlands. Without clear title, it is difficult to support a system of land mortgaging that should be part of an effective scheme of rural finance. Moreover, the absence of title might directly discourage land improvements by individual households because of fear that they will not be able to appropriate the returns to the investments.

Low rural productivity is also intimately connected with inadequate rural education and health. These problems have been widely discussed in Bolivia and were featured in the 1993 presidential campaign. The proposal to return greater control over social services to the local communities is a promising direction for change, but it is also clear that overall funding levels for rural health and education are chronically inadequate.

In the first place, Bolivia's overall government expenditures on health and education are shockingly small when compared with other countries in the region. In 1991, government spending on health accounted for a mere 0.6 percent of GDP, and spending on education accounted for 3.5 percent of GDP. In Costa Rica, by contrast, health spending was 8.3 percent of GDP, and education spending was 5 percent of GDP. This situation clearly requires an increased level of public expenditures. It makes little sense for the Bolivian military to absorb nearly one-third of the total budget when social needs are so urgent. Part of increased social spending can come from a reallocation of the overall budget; part can be financed by foreign assistance; another part, however, will have to be financed from higher government tax collections.

There is also scope for increasing the efficiency of social spending. For example, Bolivia devotes an enormous proportion of its education expenditures to higher education, which is still provided virtually free of charge, while leaving rural primary and secondary education without resources. All international studies on this topic in recent years concur that much higher social returns could be achieved by redirecting the education budget toward the lower levels of education, while requiring that university students pay part costs of their education. Moreover, education spending shows evidence of waste and fraud, with phantom (nonexistent) teachers absorbing a significant share of the payroll.

The same misallocation of resources is evident in health spending. A large proportion of the budget is devoted to high-technology tertiary facilities, while primary health clinics are devoid of the most basic supplies.[13] Fraud and abuse also drain the efficiency of government health spending. Other poor countries have been able to make great strides in reducing infant mortality and morbidity through well-administered national programs of mother-and-infant care and community health facilities. Such programs, as exemplified by the Community Health Program in Caera, Brazil, should be emulated in Bolivia. UNICEF and the World Bank should be called on for conceptual support, program design, and assistance in mobilizing international financing.

CONCLUSION

The main challenge for Bolivia in the coming years is to raise its overall rate of economic growth to 6 percent per year or more rather than the prevailing annual rate of 3.5 percent to 4 percent. Since 1985, growth has been positive but modest, in part because of external shocks and in part because of Bolivia's chronically low levels of national savings and investment.

Generating higher growth will not be easy. It will require simultaneous advances on several fronts, some of which have been outlined in this paper. One key will be to increase national savings and investment rates. Several areas of financial reform—including pension reform and capitalization of the state enterprises—are key parts of a growth strategy. Also more attention must be paid to improving rural productivity, both to enhance economic growth and to address Bolivia's deep crisis of extreme rural poverty. This will require a multifaceted effort to intensify agriculture R&D and to improve the provision of health and education services in the countryside.

On the macroeconomic front, the social agenda and the growth agenda will require continuity of careful management. Bolivia has been heavily reliant on foreign concessional loans, both to fund investment and to help finance the budget. The country must think ahead to the time when the international community will start to cut back on this financing. In preparation Bolivia can therefore begin to replace the existing foreign financing with funds it gains from cuts in wasteful expenditure combined with larger tax collections. Higher tax revenues should come from broadening the base of existing taxes and improving tax administration.

[13]As documented in Walsh (1993).

These changes will be needed to cover increases in social expenditures and important infrastructure investments. In addition to continued fiscal prudence, Bolivia needs to continue its cautiously restrictive monetary policies of recent years.

Overall, the tasks are immense and interrelated. But given the appropriate policies, and the political will to back them, Bolivia can look ahead to a much brighter economic future.

BIBLIOGRAPHY

Alesina, A. 1989. Politics and business cycles in the industrial democracies. *Economic Policy* (April).

Barro, R. 1991. Economic growth in a cross-section of countries. *Quarterly Journal of Economics* 106 (2).

Diamond, P., and S. Valdés. 1993. Social security reforms. Paper presented at the Conference on the Chilean Economy: Policy Lessons and Challenges. The Brookings Institution, Washington, D.C., April 22–23, 1993.

Edwards, S. 1992. Politica cambiaria en Bolivia: Avances recientes y perspectivas. *Análisis Económico*, UDAPE (June).

Godoy, R., M. de Franco, and R. Echeverría. 1993. A brief history of agricultural research in Bolivia: Potatoes, maize, soybeans and wheat compared. Mimeo, Harvard Institute for International Development (May).

Larraín, F., and J. Sachs. 1991. Peru's international financial relations. In *Stabilization and growth in Peru*, edited by C. Paredes and J. Sachs. Washington: The Brookings Institution.

Larraín, F., and R. Vergara. 1993. Private investment and macroeconomic adjustment: The case of East Asia (with R. Vergara). In *From adjustment to sustainable growth: The role of capital formation*, edited by L. Serven and A. Solimano. Washington: The World Bank, forthcoming.

Morales, J. A., and J. Sachs. 1990. Bolivia's economic crisis. In *Developing country debt and economic performance*, edited by J. Sachs. Chicago: University of Chicago Press.

Paredes, R. 1993. Mercado y legislación laboral en Bolivia. *Análisis Económico*, Unidad de Análisis de Políticas Económicas (UDAPE) (July 1993).

Pereira, R., and T. Velasco. 1993. Estimación de la pobreza urbana en Bolivia. Working Paper no. 02-93. Unidad de Análisis de Políticas Sociales, February.

Sachs, J. 1990. Comprehensive debt reduction: The Bolivian example. *Brookings Papers on Economic Activity*, no. 1.

Sachs, J., and F. Larraín. 1993. *Macroeconomics in the global economy*. Prentice Hall.

Unidad de Análisis de Políticas Económicas (UDAPE). 1992. Impacto macroeconómico de la venta de gas natural al Brasil. Mimeo, La Paz, November.

Unidad de Análisis de Políticas Económicas (UDAPE). 1993. La reforma de la seguridad social: Impacto fiscal y financiero. Mimeo, La Paz, June.

Vickers, J., and G. Yarrow. 1991. Economic perspectives on privatization. *Journal of Economic Perspectives* (spring).

Walsh, J. 1993. Managing health sector reform in Bolivia. Mimeo, Harvard University, July.

The World Bank. 1990. *Bolivia: Poverty report*. Washington: The World Bank, June.

The World Bank. 1992. *Bolivia: Agricultural sector review*. Washington: The World Bank, April.

The World Bank. 1993. *World development report*. Oxford: Oxford University Press.

READING 11

"Plano Real": The End of Hyperinflation in Brazil*

VALDIR RAMALHO
Universidade Santa Úrsula, Rio de Janeiro

On July 1, 1994, the name of Brazil's monetary unit was changed to *real* (plural *reais*); thus began the crucial stage of a stabilization program that has been called "Plano Real" since that time. It is perhaps the most successful program in the country's history, for inflation quickly jumped downward, the effect on output was expansionary, and the lower pace of price increases proved long lasting. This experience raises many interesting issues of macroeconomic policy and monetary theory, but only a few can be dealt with in this paper. It is my purpose here to expose the key aspects of the stabilization program from its start to the end of 1995, and at the same time to address some of those issues from a perspective that differs from the one prevailing among Brazilian economists. Specifically, I disagree on the roles of wage tightening and of disindexation (that is, prohibition of indexing clauses) in the fight against inflation, although lack of space prevents me from defending my views in detail.

The paper is organized as follows: Section 1 deals with the context of economic liberalization in which the program was born. Section 2 points out topics of macroeconomic interest whose discussion influenced the conception of the Plano Real. Section 3 provides a brief report of the inflationary process in Brazil, as well as of the circumstances under which the program was conceived. The Plano Real is described in section 4, while section 5 reviews the major developments after the critical stage of the program was reached. Section 6 addresses issues of major importance for appraising the program. An epilogue (section 7) provides a brief review of the course of the stabilization program during 1995.

*Arno Meyer carefully read earlier drafts, providing detailed suggestions and stimulating comments. Additional suggestions to the final version were made by Manoel Jorge Fajardo Villela de Andrade. Except for the author, no person or institution has any responsibility for the views expressed in the text.

1. The Context of Economic Liberalization

In the 1990s the sociopolitical climate in Brazil has become distinctly less favorable to economic interventionism and more receptive to international trade and capital, in contrast to the two previous decades. Because all speculations about the factors and persons that contributed to this change still await an adequate support through empirical research and further discussion, I shall avoid the difficult task of theorizing on the mechanisms behind such a remarkable alteration in views. Instead, I will sketch the recent history of this political turn. For the sake of conciseness, I will resort to the political categories of left and right, although these notions are crude and vague (we all know that what is deemed left-wing becomes right-wing, or vice versa, only a few years later or a few thousand miles away).

Let us start with a brief outline of 1989, the last year of José Sarney's presidency. In economic terms, this was one of the most frightening years Brazilians had in many decades. The accumulated damages of disastrous macroeconomic policies pursued by two successive governments (Figueiredo and Sarney)—particularly a desperate attempt by Sarney's minister of finance Mailson da Nōbrega to impose a third price freeze in the beginning of that year (the so-called Summer Plan)—led the country to hyperinflation. Because the executive decree-laws establishing those freezes always included measures dismantling indexation mechanisms, the protection provided by indexation was often lowest precisely during the huge jumps in prices that accompanied the breakdown of price freezes. Consequently, the acceleration of inflation proved most harmful in the aftermath of such freezes, and the one of 1989 was the worst experienced in Brazil's history. At that point, it seemed to many that the final collapse of the monetary system would come in a matter of weeks.

Taking advantage of the fact that the year would end with presidential elections, the people showed their anger at the polls: the declared preferences in the first months of the year went for the left-wing candidates Lula da Silva (of the Partidos dos Trabalhadores [PT] party) and Leonel Brizola (of the Partido Trabalhista Democratico [PDT] party), while the Partido de Movimento Democratico Brasileiro (PMDB) (the party in power and representing the political center of the spectrum) amassed very few intentions of votes. Because many still remembered the calamitous performance of the last military government (of President General Figueiredo), the right had no prestige, and thus the left seemed the public's only hope.

But, to everybody's surprise, the people's opinion was altered by a political adventurer, Fernando Collor, one of the few politicians to have noticed two facts and their usefulness in a campaign. He had seen, first, that the idea of public deficits as the cause of inflation had spread among the people and, second, that the press confusedly associated the problem of deficits with the distinct issue of high salaries paid to some high-ranking public officials (sarcastically called "maharajahs" in the press). Collor had been the governor in a small and politically uninfluential state, but in spite of this he had succeeded in creating a national image of "hunter of maharajahs" by refusing to pay some government employees in his state. In 1989 Collor decided to pose as an outsider (although he had previously supported the military regime) and to stand as candidate for president against the experienced Lula da Silva and Brizola. During the course of his presidential campaign. Collor exploited that image and pictured himself as an energetic man capable of ending the hyperinflation. Also, in a bolder move, he charged Sarney's government with incompetence and corruption. Resorting to some additional mean tricks (including—ironically, as we will see—

the accusation that his major opponent Lula da Silva planned, if elected, to seize the people's financial assets), Collor defeated his opponents and took office in March 1990.

Being the only politically viable option for the right and for the business community, Collor obtained their votes, but neither the president himself nor his economic team were acquainted with the doctrine preached, or with the recipes put forward, by the preceptors of economic liberalism. As a result, Collor's stabilization program promulgated in March 1990 was an awkward combination of another price freeze with what was intended to provoke a major monetary contraction, a seizure of most financial assets held by families and firms. The program designed by Collor's minister of finance, the inexperienced Zélia Cardoso, pleased practically no position in the political spectrum, for the left did not trust what it deemed a neoliberal government resorting to a wild monetarist policy, while intermediate positions and the right vaguely feared that the extensive infringement of property rights imbued in the program would become a precedent.

Moreover, the program showed obvious signs of failure in a few weeks. To retain the interest of the Brazilian society in his administration, Collor resorted to a rhetoric of "modernization" of the country, a vague notion confusedly associated with reduction of the public sector as well as of trade barriers with the rest of the world. In practice, a few measures of deregulation were more than offset by strong and discretionary interference with the same or other markets. As to the cuts in public expenditure, they affected far more what were, technically speaking, public goods than goods that could be replaced by private production. But it is fair to concede that the lowering of import tariffs, at first implemented merely as an attempt to save the anti-inflationary plan by means of foreign competition, ended up in a long-term commitment of the Brazilian government to a schedule of general reduction in tariffs. Also, the goals of privatization and of increased exposure of the country to global markets immediately gained political support.

In the beginning of 1991, Collor promulgated one more price freeze (the fifth Brazil bore since 1986), which resulted in yet another failure. Afterward, the antipathy of the public opinion to the traditionally harsh and wildly arbitrary "economic packages" became vehement. This created receptivity in the public opinion to the idea that economic policies should respect legal rights and private contracts. As a reaction to this, Collor replaced Zélia Cardoso with Marcílio Moreira in the ministry of finance, a move which the president admitted as a change to a "soft" line. Moreira was well known and trusted by both business and political communities, and he began at once the first of many attempts to convince the Brazilian society that henceforth contracts would not be broken, nor would legal rights be infringed by measures of economic policy taken in Collor's administration.

Public opinion, however, remained skeptical about those promises and deeply suspicious of Collor's intentions in general. Not surprisingly, this distrust impaired his subsequent moves. One of major importance was his attempt to reform the constitution, recently promulgated in 1988, as a way to strengthen his involvement with the seemingly neoliberal mood of the new times. The constitution had created a series of economic benefits that the country's limited resources and particularly the public sector in financial jeopardy were unable to provide. The solution, in the view of the right, would have to be a drastic rewriting of that document. However, fearing that Collor might take advantage of the constitutional reforms to increase his range of authoritarian action, several political forces abstained from supporting his attempts. Nonetheless, after he left office, these reforms became a major goal of the following administrations, with the wide support of public opinion.

Collor's immediate successor, President Itamar Franco, felt constrained by the new trend of opinion to embrace the goals of privatization, reform of the state, and reduction of barriers to international trade, although he was a nationalist and an interventionist by personal conviction. Indeed, Franco hesitated to take action in the first months of his administration, although political columnists doubted that he would do as promised. But his minister of finance, Fernando Henrique Cardoso, a respected left-wing figure, convinced the president that the right course was to take those goals seriously. Cardoso also reasserted the promises of his predecessor Moreira not to violate contracts or legal rights by new economic measures. This brought Cardoso a second victory, as he won the confidence of the middle class and of the business community, with the result that economic uncertainty was considerably reduced.

Of course, the extent to which so-called neoliberalism has influenced the federal administrations in the 1990s has been the subject of political controversy. During Franco's government, economic advisers and analysts in the financial markets often complained that privatization was being conducted too slowly, and they kept saying the same after Fernando Henrique Cardoso became president in January 1995. Cardoso described himself as a social-democrat, and in fact his party (the PSDB) at least nominally subscribes to social democracy. On the other hand, an alliance with the PFL, a powerful and moderately right-wing party was crucial to his election.

Be that as it may, the deepest opening of Brazilian markets to foreign goods in decades took place in the second semester of 1994, in a move to provide an external basis to the Plano Real. Also, the reform of the public sector constitutes the major item in the political program of Cardoso's government, an item that is supposed to consolidate the stabilization obtained through the Plano Real. In comparative terms, Franco's and Cardoso's macroeconomic policies have been among the least interventionist in three decades.

2. Doctrinal Issues Related to the Creation of the Program

The ideas that shaped the Plano Real evolved from debates on three issues: (1) indexation, (2) introduction of a second medium of exchange, and (3) exchange rate–based stabilization programs. Let us take a brief look at them in this order.

2.1. A well-known feature of Brazilian economy is a very high degree of indexation. Ironically, since the 1980s both the economic policies and the economists' opinions have been strongly influenced by a young group that opposes indexation. Subscribing to a view of inflation that many dub "inertialism," members of that group blame inflation's permanence on indexation, rather than on the budget deficits and the unbounded monetary expansion Brazil has had since the early 1970s. They assert that inflation exists mainly because price rises of each period are passed on to prices of the following period through indexation. From this perspective, supply shocks explain changes in the inflation rate, while policies affecting aggregate demand through fiscal or monetary actions have only negligible impact on the speed of price rises.

Inertialism was the theoretical basis for several price freezes adopted in Brazil since the Cruzado Plan in 1986, including one (the Collor Plan, in 1990) in which the freeze was combined with a blocking of the people's access to most monetary and financial assets for

24 months, on average. But the successive collapses of those freezes led the inertialists to place greater emphasis on policies affecting aggregate demand. They began to stress what at first had been only vaguely expressed: that adjustment of the public budget is a necessary condition for keeping inflation low and that after disindexation fiscal and monetary policies should be tightened in order to guarantee price stability. Of course, indexation remained the major culprit for inflation, and disindexation the basic prescription. The central question then became how to promote disindexation given that, as the inertialists acknowledged now, price freezes would not work. Two ways for carrying out that task were extensively discussed: the introduction of a "parallel" medium of exchange in the economy and the tying of the domestic to a foreign money.

It should be noted, however, that the Plano Real was designed by some inertialists who held a less radical position on indexation (André Lara Resende and Pérsio Arida, later joined by Edmar Bacha and Gustavo Franco); they conceded, although in a roundabout way and only to some extent, that indexation is of assistance in a stabilization program. While still thinking that indexation should be abolished immediately after inflation fell to nearly zero, they insisted that indexation should be stimulated and propagated as a precondition for a successful stabilization.

2.2. The history of economic thought describes many proposals for eradicating inflation by introducing a parallel or secondary medium of exchange in an economy whose chief or original money has been deteriorating in value (this is one of the many senses in which the highly ambiguous phrase "monetary reform" has been used). In the early 1980s similar suggestions were analyzed by Axel Leijonhufvud, among others. Drawing on this literature, some of the less radical inertialists adapted a similar proposal for the Brazilian economy (for a brief exposition and an analysis, see Simonsen 1984, a paper that immediately adhered to the plan of a parallel money and influenced many Brazilian economists). Much later, the Plano Real developed from such a proposal (its main features, and even the name for the monetary unit, were suggested by Francisco Lopes, 1989, when he finally accepted Resende's and Arida's views).

Of course, history also shows that many projects of a parallel money ended up in no substantive creation of a new money (that is, the country was never provided with an alternative money in any genuinely economic sense). In those cases each of the economies involved remained with only one domestic money from before to after the monetary reform, although superficial (noneconomic) features of this money were changed—such as names, numerical scales, or designs of bank notes and coins. This was the case of the Plano Real.

2.3. In early 1991, Argentina eliminated an acute inflation by establishing convertibility of her currency into U.S. dollars (the so-called Cavallo Plan). The swift success of this device made a very good impression among Brazilian economists, with the result that, henceforth, almost all discussions on fighting inflation in Brazil analyzed options of tying the domestic money to a stable foreign money. Resende, one of the future designers of the Plano Real, even abandoned his former suggestion of a parallel money and proposed a currency board for Brazil. There was so much interest in a program similar to the Cavallo Plan that nobody discarded the possibility that the government might adopt it, and this possibility continued to influence analyses and policy proposals even during the several stages in which the Plano Real took shape.

As a consequence, the prevailing expectation among both businesspersons and their economic advisers was that the Plano Real would include some form of dollarization—at the least, that the government would fix the exchange rate to the dollar. This expectation seemed confirmed when the government revealed that it would alter the numerical scale of the domestic money and that it would tailor the new scale to an exchange rate of one unit to one U.S. dollar. As was well known, the major result of a fixed exchange rate would be that prices of imported goods would become constant in terms of the national money, so that domestic producers of similar goods would also have to stabilize their prices. To everybody's surprise, however, the government made no effort to fix the market exchange rate from July 1994 on, in the weeks following the Brazilian money's change of name to real, and instead allowed an appreciation of the real in both nominal and real terms. Thus, in fact, no tying of the domestic money to a foreign money took place, although, in order to preclude prices from moving up quickly, the Plano Real did resort to the external sector, and even more strongly than many expected (more on this later).

3. From Hyperinflation to a New Anti-inflationary Program

Except for intervals of price repression, Brazil's inflation regularly intensified and became acute along the course of 25 years. Starting at about 20 percent per year in the early 1970s, the rate of change in the price level for the 12 months ending in December reached 95.2 percent in 1981, 235.1 percent in 1985, 415.8 percent in 1987, and 1,782.9 percent in 1989 (as shown by the Indice Geral de Precos Disponibilidade Interna [IGP-DI], a price index encompassing both retail and wholesale prices). After a few months of a hyperinflation (in Cagan's sense) from late 1989 to early 1990, the velocity of change in prices was temporarily brought below the hyperinflationary benchmark by the Collor Plan (March 1990), but it soon accelerated toward hyperinflation again. In early 1991 another price freeze (Collor Plan II) was imposed and also failed, but a subsequent, clumsy attempt at tightening fiscal and monetary policy succeeded in maintaining the monthly rates of change in the several price indexes fluctuating between 20 percent and 25 percent from late 1991 to late 1992. However, a slow acceleration resumed in 1993 and drove those rates to nearly 30 percent per month in May or June (depending on the specific index chosen), 35 percent in September or October, 45 percent near March of 1994, and about 50 percent in June 1994.

Despite such dramatic and frequent increases in the price level, the social, political, and economic environment was considerably orderly most of the time; thus, the ruptures popularly associated with classical hyperinflations were almost absent. The reason for this contrast is Brazil's long experience with indexation, especially its financial sector's legacy of keenly adapting to chronic and acute inflation.

By providing the economic agents with means to preserve the real value of their savings and even of their transaction balances, Brazilian economy dispelled the greatest fears that hyperinflation usually stirs up in the people and, as a result, lessened the destructive forces that arise from monetary disintegration. Of course, these forces were not entirely extinguished, particularly because the indexing of wages, salaries, rents, and long-term contracts remained rather defective. Most deficiencies ensued from the fact that the government sabotaged indexation or at least prevented the improvement of its procedures, assenting to the opinion of many economists who did not favor indexation.

In late 1992, Itamar Franco replaced Fernando Collor as president of the republic. After changing his ministers of finance and of planning several times in the first months of his administration, President Franco nominated Fernando Henrique Cardoso as minister of finance in May 1993. In contrast to those preceding him, Cardoso remained in office all the time he felt necessary to supervise the design of a complete stabilization program and to commit the government to its implementation.

Throughout the second half of 1993, Fernando Henrique Cardoso's economic team sketched the major lines of the Plano Real and made them public, although decisions about many crucial details were postponed. In early June the initial version of the program (named "Plano de Ação Imediata" or "PAI") was promulgated and some measures were enacted; but only later, in the December version, was the chief device of the URV (a unit of account with constant purchasing power, discussed later) mentioned for the first time. The program's major lines were as follows:

1. Adjustments would be made in the public sector budget in order to guarantee that the behavior of the government should not be inflationary from that time on, especially from the day inflation should be brought down.
2. Whatever might be the economic measures that would constitute the stabilization program, they would not include either price freezes, government-imposed breaches of private contracts, or seizures of assets held by families or firms (after the fact, we know that some breaches did take place, but they were far less extensive and less grave than those of previous stabilization programs).
3. Unlike the Cruzado Plan, the Collor Plan, and other price freezes, the program would be gradual. The option was not for an array of measures abruptly promulgated together on a given day, but rather for a sequence of stages—that is, for several steps taken along an extended period.
4. The economic team acknowledged that it had not yet made crucial decisions on the exact ingredients for the program, but it promised that any proposal of measures would be divulged in advance and openly discussed with formal or informal representatives of institutions and of the several sectors of society.

Other than these guidelines, the only clue to the future shape of the program was that inflation would be eliminated by means of disindexation; but throughout most of 1993, prior to the announcement of the chief device of the URV, no economist could say what that meant precisely.

In early April 1994 Fernando Henrique Cardoso quit his post of minister of finance in order to become the administration's candidate for the presidency (formally, the candidate of the PSDB, the main party in power). This fact placed another constraint on the Plano Real: the distribution in time of the several measures, and thus the program's expected successes, were predicted to strengthen Cardoso's chances of winning the election. One could reason, based on the experience of past "heterodox" stabilization programs in Brazil, that the Plano Real might decrease inflation for a very short time (such as two to four months) and engender a boom in economic activity, even if it failed later. So, the program's major stage (starting on what is later called "the critical day") was expected to begin a few months before the presidential elections in October.

However, the connection between Cardoso's candidacy and the program was made reciprocal. His followers espoused the position that his campaign must produce clear prospects of victory at all times, or the people's confidence in the plan might wane. The alleged reason was that the victory of a different candidate would probably result in a change of the economic team, with the effect that the program would not be implemented. Moreover, Cardoso's opponent was Lula da Silva, nominated by the left-wing party PT. Because of this, many businesspersons bet on the success of the program in order to help Cardoso defeat Lula. To sum up, President Itamar Franco and his candidate Cardoso gambled by tying to a party dispute what should be above the interests of all parties, an anti-inflationary program; they did win.

4. The Ingredients of the Program

Let us now turn our attention to the major stages and components of the Plano Real.

Because this stabilization program was built step by step, whenever some measures were being debated, others had already been promulgated, and still others had not even been considered. As a consequence, the program had various names at different times (such as "PAI," "Plano FHC," and "Plano URV"). What was regarded as the first stage consisted of some actions taken to improve the budget condition of the federal government. The most important was a constitutional amendment ("Fundo Social de Emergência" or FSE), which freed certain revenues from constitutional ties to expenses, raised rates of the income tax on individuals in some brackets, and increased some taxes on banks. Untied expenses were somewhat reduced, but the major effect was that untied revenues could go up without a parallel increase in expenditure. Announced in December 1993, the FSE was approved by the Congress in February 1994. By the way, FSE means "Social Fund for an Emergency," but this name has nothing to do with the actual nature of the device, and it was chosen merely to generate a favorable political impact.

How far the fiscal measures taken at the time were responsible for an improvement in the public accounts is controversial, due to the difficulty of interpreting the complex statistics on the Brazilian public sector (on the FSE, see Afonso and Carvalho 1994). The numbers do show a public deficit reduction; but since they are expressed in real terms, in percentage of the gross domestic product (GDP), or both, they tend to mislead the user by reflecting cyclical and irregular movements in the economy rather than tight or loose policies.

The operational deficit measured at current prices fell from 2.0 percent of GDP in 1992 to 1.4 percent in 1993 and to a superavit of 2.0 percent in 1994; when measured at prices of the last month in each period, the operational deficit fell from 2.3 percent of the GDP in 1992 to 1.5 percent in 1993 and to a superavit of 1.7 percent in 1994. As to the primary surplus at current prices, it increased from 1.6 percent of GDP in 1992 to 2.3 percent in 1993 and to 5.1 percent in 1994. Measured at prices of the last month in each period, the primary surplus increased from 2.3 percent of GDP in 1992 to 2.6 percent in 1993 and to 5.2 percent in 1994 (for all these numbers, see Banco Central 1996, 144–45). Most of the improvement in the statistics for 1994 may be a mirage resulting from the immense fall of the average inflation rate from 1993 to 1994 as well as the large increase in economic activity (the GDP had fallen 0.8 percent in 1992, but it went up 4.2 percent in 1993 and 5.8 percent in 1994).

The official assessment in late 1993 and early 1994 was that the budget adjustment achieved through the FSE would suit the needs of the stabilization program in the months ahead, though it was admittedly a temporary adjustment; consolidating the program would require a profound reorganization of the public sector. For this, it was assumed, the government would need constitutional amendments; so the major task of the new federal administration that would take office in early 1995 should be to persuade the Congress to promulgate those amendments.

The second stage of the program consisted in the creation of the URV ("unidade real de valor," meaning "unit of real value"), an officially sponsored unit of account with constant purchasing power and based on an average of some major price indexes calculated in Brazil. Every day the Central Bank of Brazil set a quotation for the URV in terms of domestic money, reflecting on a daily basis an estimate of the monthly inflation (as measured previously). In other words, the URV was a new price index to be employed in procedures of indexation sanctioned by the government. From then on, in contrast to several past administrations, the government encouraged and disseminated the use of indexation rather than resisting society's adherence to it. The only proviso was that freedom to index contracts and prices was conceded gradually, according to a specific schedule.

The decree-law creating the URV (MP 434, issued by the executive in February 1994) established that wage rates should be the first economic values to be indexed to the URV. Beginning with those corresponding to March, nominal wages were paid in domestic money according to their values in URV axnd the quotation for the URV on payday. It is important to know that the decree-law went beyond mere indexation, promulgating a new wage policy. It ordered that the moment wage rates were expressed and recontracted in URV they should be established as the average of the purchasing power of monthly wage rates in the four months from November 1993 to February 1994 (this length of time was chosen because the previous wages policy established the monetary correction of wages every four months).

The government's imposition of past average real wage rates is an instance of what is known in Brazil as "tight wages policies." The key characteristic of these policies is that they attempt either to perpetuate real wage losses brought about by inflation or to guarantee that nominal wages be constrained to rise slower than inflation. During the military regime those aims were achieved by the sheer prohibition of real wages increases, coupled with the repression of strikes and labor unions. Since civilians returned to power in 1985, all that tight wages policies can do is increase transactions costs for workers to preserve real wages by denying them automatic support of the law for this preservation (so that, tacitly, the support of the law goes to employers, putting workers' inaction on the side of real wages declining).

That the Plano Real included a tight wages policy is understandable, for one tenet of inertialism is that increases in the real wage rate (beyond productivity's rise in the particular year) result in higher inflation. More precisely, lower real wages brought about by inflation should be accepted as inevitable, as reflecting a relentless path of the economy toward equilibrium of the inflationary process. In their own best interests, workers should not attempt to regain their previous peak of real wages.

Somewhat arbitrarily, the average—rather than the peak, the trough, or any intermediate real wage rate—is considered by inertialists as the "natural" level, the one that keeps economic balance (as well as the one that official wage policies should impose). Besides, that average is calculated over an interval of time whose extension seems to depend solely on the discernment of the policy makers. And in spite of the fact that the average is proclaimed the "natural" or "feasible" level, wage policies are designed in a way that allows future inflation to erode, rather than preserve, that average real wage rate. The Plano Real wage policy, however, astutely incorporated a characteristic that made it look different from previous tight wage policies in that by design the deterioration would not start immediately, but only several months later. Few workers noticed that, in fact, the fall of the real wage rate would start on the critical day (that is, on the day that the money's name changed), because the process of disindexation would also start on that day, in spite of a high probability that inflation would remain well above zero.

Because of that characteristic, union leaders who saw the new wage policy as another round of wage tightening did not succeed in bringing the workers to strike against it. The policy was well received by workers, because for them it seemed a pleasant change in the government's attitude. They saw that from then on nominal wages would rise accompanying inflation, whereas up to then all federal administrations had opposed every attempt by workers to obtain either monthly adjustments of nominal wages or adjustments exactly proportional to the observed inflation rates. What workers did not take into account was that some months later, after the critical day, nominal wages should become fixed in contracts, even though nothing guaranteed that inflation would have disappeared.

After the indexing of wage contracts had been accomplished, the government allowed other nonfinancial contracts to be redenominated in URV (such as rents, tuitions, and health insurance plans). This was followed by permission to quote ordinary or spot prices (that is, those unbounded by contracts) in URV. Subsequently, banks began to make loans and to accept deposits in URV, while the government also issued some securities in the new unit of account; as a result, stores and other firms could more easily match their revenues and costs in URV with either investment or borrowing of working capital in the same unit of account.

Attention should be called to the fact that demand deposits (checking accounts, which earn no interest) and most kinds of interest-bearing deposits were not redenominated in URV. Thus, any balances held in demand deposits kept deteriorating in purchasing power. As to remunerated deposits, they simply continued to preserve the principal's real value in the way they did before (that is, without the guarantee of an indexation clause), because the respective nominal interest rates fluctuated monthly or daily and usually exceeded inflation rates.

So, the second stage of the program brought very little change to the financial system for two reasons. First, by 1993 and 1994 the sector had already imbedded in its operations considerable protection against inflation. Second, it was widely thought that meddling through that system was tantamount to risking unexpected and jeopardous reactions by depositors and investors, especially because the traumatic experience of the Collor Plan had been recent.

Let us now consider how the device of a unit of account (the URV) was thought to assist in the elimination of indexation and, at the same time, to provoke a drastic drop in inflation. In the past, successive authorities had condemned indexation and often tinkered with its procedures in order to reduce its effectiveness. Although those administrations were not successful in eradicating the people's habit of seeking compensation and protection against inflation, they had made indexing procedures more defective or had even forced economic agents to substitute unsystematic and frequent changes of nominal values for the previous regular tying to price indexes. The defects had produced significant losses and arbitrary redistributions of income because the official assaults on indexation coincided with the worst phases of the inflationary process.

Under those circumstances, the move by Itamar Franco's government to sponsor a reconstruction of indexation procedures through the URV was well received by the economic agents, for the existing forms of protection against inflation needed improvement. Thus, as desired by the economic team, the use of URV to redenominate contracts and to quote prices was quickly disseminated, at least among the best informed businesspersons in major cities and towns.

On the inertialist view, once the dissemination was complete, all prices would become approximately constant in URV and would continue to climb up uniformly in terms of the domestic money (following the nominal devaluation of the URV, which in its turn reflected daily estimates of the price indexes on which it was based); this would allow the authorities, on any day they chose, to bring down inflation almost to zero simply by ceasing to devalue the URV in nominal terms (that is, they could fix a nominal price for the URV). According to inertialism, a similar mechanism had ended classical hyperinflations, except that in Brazil a deliberately designed unit of account would fulfill the role that foreign money had played in those hyperinflations.

The third stage of the program would start the day the ratio of monetary units for one unit of URV would be fixed (what I call here "the critical day"; the press and the government called it "the day of the monetary reform" or "the day of the creation of the 'real' "). To fix a nominal value for the URV would interrupt the working of indexation, as prices and contracts indexed to the URV would suddenly cease rising in terms of the domestic money.

But the economic team wanted to eliminate indexation itself (at least for terms shorter than one year). Thus, they included in the decree-law creating the URV a clause prohibiting the indexation of contracts by means of any indicator different from the URV (thereby putting indexation clauses completely within the province of state control). Therefore, after the critical day, there should remain no legally allowed device by which economic values established in private contracts could grow according to any price index or to the exchange rate.

The third stage of the program was the most crucial one, for neither empirical evidence nor theoretical reasons were strong enough to assure anyone that the mechanism would work; one could sensibly fear that the desired, large drop in inflation might not materialize, or that it might take place only to be reversed a few months later. After the fact, we know that the mechanism of the critical day worked admirably well. However, it did not function as put forth by inertialism, because prices were not climbing up uniformly in the weeks and days just preceding the critical day. It worked because expectations of inflation for the period immediately after that day went down drastically. Thus, one question that might be raised pertains far more to social psychology than to macroeconomics; it is whether the manner in which the economic team decorated the mechanism awakened a sort of collective illusion or wishful thinking that helped to extinguish expectations of high inflation.

Therefore, to fully appreciate the impact of the critical day, it is perhaps convenient to know that the government and the economic team adorned the event with rituals and rhetoric; persistent official claims of a "new" and "strong" money to come in the months ahead were accompanied by photos of the designs for the new notes and by other news on the process of preparing the change (including the printing of notes abroad). According to one of the exaggerated claims put forth by the economic team, the real was merely another name for the URV, a money with constant purchasing power. But these were sharply different things. The URV was just a unit of account, never a medium of exchange, whereas the real was a medium of exchange. The URV was designed to have constant purchasing power (as approximately as possible), whereas the real as a unit of account was a purely nominal unit, with no protection against price level increases. What they had in common was merely the transitory exchange rate of one to one on a special day, July 1, 1994 (the critical day).

What the economic team called a "monetary reform" never created another domestic money in any substantial economic sense. There was only one government-issued domestic money all the time—that is, there existed only one kind of obligation in the form of nominal purchasing power immediately transferable and non-interest-bearing, issued by the same bank of issue, the Central Bank of Brazil. Whatever the day one takes, be it before, on, or after the critical day, the real and the cruzeiro real were merely different ways of expressing the same balances of funds Brazilians would have on that day anyway, regardless of the so-called monetary reform (in the same way that one person would have the same weight on any particular day, whether expressed in kilograms or in pounds).

What the Plano Real did in fact on the critical day was to change the name and the numerals that denoted the amounts of funds to be paid or received in the one domestic medium of exchange. Also, in the following weeks, notes and coins were replaced by others of a different design. Admittedly, despite the fact that the so-called monetary reform by itself represented no economic event, it may be that the spectacle of those changes favorably impressed the people.

5. The Critical Day and After: Stabilization Begins

Let us briefly review what was done on the critical day.

1. The nominal value established for the URV on June 30, 1994, was 2,750 cruzeiros reais; as planned, this value was maintained for July 1 and thereafter. This amounted to an extinction of the URV in the economic sense (for, economically, it was defined as having a nominal exchange rate tied to a price index). Since legally contracts remained expressed in something called URV, the move by the government imposed on them an important economic modification, taking away their protection against inflation.
2. The name of the domestic money was altered from "cruzeiro real" to "real."
3. The whole scale of price measuring was divided by 2,750; that is, instead of establishing the ratio of one real to one cruzeiro real, or perhaps of one real to one thousand cruzeiros reais, the government chose the ratio of one real to 2,750 cruzeiros reais.
4. Official declarations insisted that a new, "strong" money was being created, as strong as the U.S. dollar (or even stronger—contrary to all predictions of an official exchange rate of one real to one dollar beginning on July 1, the Central Bank allowed this rate to fall regularly from that time on).
5. As indicated already, on the same day the Central Bank began to put into circulation notes and coins of all denominations with entirely different designs (but old notes, now representing fixed numbers of reais, circulated for several weeks more).

The period of the stabilization program starting on the critical day proved remarkably successful. As shown by the consumer price index constructed by FIPE (the IPC-FIPE), inflation plummeted from 50.75 percent per month in June to 6.95 percent in July and 1.95 percent in August. A different assessment may be based on the hypotheses that, on the one hand, June's high rate may be ascribed to an acceleration engendered by the program itself and, on the other hand, inflation rates of July and August included delayed effects of that acceleration, for both rates were based on the July index number, which contains prices set in June. Therefore, one may choose to compare April's rate, 46.22 percent, with September's, 0.82 percent, or with October's, 3.17 percent.

In fact, inflation has remained low and has shown no lasting acceleration for 18 months, in marked contrast to the several programs that had instituted price freezes. For instance, the price index IPC-FIPE rose 1.48 percent in October 1995, 1.17 percent in November, and 1.21 percent in December; the accumulated increase was 11.84 percent from December 1994 to June 1995 and 32.31 percent in the 12 months since June 1994, 10.13 percent from June 1995 to December, and 23.10 percent in the 12 months ending December 1995. Leaving out periods of price repression, the early 1970s were the last time Brazilians experienced monthly inflation at similarly low rates.

Another remarkable feature of the program is that the drop in inflation was both preceded and accompanied by monetary expansion at a pace that largely exceeded the benchmark of the typical rate of output increase in Brazil. Let us compare the monetary base and the means of payments (M1), both as averages of daily balances, with their respective amounts 12 months before (for following data, see July 1995; and Banco Central 1995, 58–60. Nominal values were reexpressed by the URV rate of July 30, 1994). The monetary base grew 996.0 percent in December 1992, 2,143.1 percent in December 1993, and 4,264.2 percent in June 1994 (the peak was 8,268.0 percent in August 1994). M1 grew 972.0 percent in December 1992. 2,050.4 percent in December 1993, and 4,182.0 percent in June 1994 (the peak was 7,061.4 in July 1994).

As to the period just before and after the critical day, let us compare amounts in each month with the month before. The monetary base increased 44.1 percent in May 1994, 52.2 percent in June, 122.1 percent in July, 39.6 percent in August, and 23.8 percent in September. M1 increased 37.3 percent in May 1994, 55.2 percent in June, 105.1 percent in July, and 19.5 percent in August. The monetary base went from R$2,924 million in June 1994 to R$17,285 in December, while M1 rose from R$4,977 in June 1994 to R$20,874 in December.

Of course, along with the drop in inflation, expected inflation also declined. As a result, the demand for real money balances shifted upward. This shift was foreseen by the economic team, which, in a deliberate attempt to meet the additional demand, chose to enlarge rather than cut off monetary expansion. But since no one knew the extent of the change in the demand for money (and no one could know it under conditions of a sudden and drastic drop in inflation; for more on this see Ramalho 1993), a policy of raising the money stock in the dark risked flooding the economy with cash. A possible abundance of liquidity might accommodate and even stimulate a reversal of expectations.

To avoid a possible misunderstanding, one should mention that the final decisions made in the elaboration of the program expressed concern with the money supply. Just a few weeks before the critical day, official documents and declarations announced the intention of limiting the amount of money to be issued after that day, as well as of backing the supply of domestic money with a combination of international reserves and public-sector assets. The intention was confirmed in the decree-law that ruled the money's change of name. Some members of the economic team even wanted autonomy for the central bank (this, however, was too much neoliberalism for President Itamar Franco to swallow—he vetoed the idea with vigor).

These concerns notwithstanding, the backing contemplated in the decree-law performs no economic function, for it exists in name only—economic agents are not allowed to exchange domestic money for its backing or vice versa. In fact, the idea is so out of date and so unfamiliar to present generations of Brazilian people that it has left no perceptible impression on public opinion. Not even professional circles in financial and business areas devoted much attention to it. As a result, it made no impact on expectations, and one or two months after the critical day the government itself stopped mentioning it.

The limits on the path of the money supply from July 1994 on consisted of targets for both the aggregate balances of means of payment (M1) and the monetary base in the end of the following quarters. But those targets were loosely established and hedged with several escape clauses. To start with, each target could be surpassed up to 20 percent, by itself a high rate of expansion. Besides, though the amounts were freely and arbitrarily chosen by the economic team, the decree-law laid down that the ministers of finance and planning were allowed to meet and decide to change them in any amount as soon as these authorities found necessary.

In practice, when the monetary expansion threatened to surpass the targets, the authorities opted for redefining the quantities subject to the limits in a way that made them lower (for example, one redefinition was from end-of-the month amounts to average amounts in the quarter). Notwithstanding this, the targets were not fulfilled. The final move by the government was to reinterpret failure as success: the increase in the money stock above the targets proved that the people trusted the domestic money, and hence, that the program was working very well.

Although monetary policy in the sense of stocks of money and of the monetary base was not contractionary, interest rates in real terms were deliberately maintained very high, as they had been in the first semester of 1994 (in fact they have been so for quite a number of years). For instance, securities issued by the federal government have often paid more than 20 percent per year in real terms. The monthly real rate of interest on those securities (calculated using price index IPC-R) was 1.34 percent on average between October and December of 1994, 1.66 percent in January 1995, 2.23 percent in February, and 2.89 percent in March (1995, 26). In adopting such a policy, the economic team and the Central Bank shared the prevalent view among Brazilian economists that very high interest rates were necessary to lead holders of funds to keep the funds invested in the financial system rather than spend them.

Those who cast doubt on the anti-inflationary effect of high interest rates notice that, in the end, most of the funds invested finance government debt and expenditures. Be that as it may, Brazil's very high inflation rate, its several episodes of acceleration, as well as its cyclical bursts of economic growth have seemed insusceptible to the policy of high interest rates. In addition, a large and considerably old literature in monetary economics has insisted that high interest rates and the relative scarcity of money are not the same thing and that often the two phenomena do not even have the same effects; in other words, high interest rates should not be identified with anti-inflationary policy.

Monetary expansion would have proceeded at even higher rates if the government had not taken the preventive measure of imposing reserve requirements of 100 percent on the increase in demand deposits from the critical day on. This measure precluded a rise in the money multiplier. The reason is that the public's redistribution of financial wealth from shares in securities mutual funds (remunerated deposits) to demand deposits predictably caused most of the increase in the latter. It turns out that shares in mutual funds managed by banks (which provide automatic transfer of balances to demand deposits) were backed by government securities rather than loans to the private sector and thus functioned approximately like deposits backed by 100 percent reserves. In contrast, the reserve requirements on demand deposits were about 40 percent. Therefore, such a redistribution would strongly increase the lending power of the banking system by releasing reserves.

In implementing another of the economic team's decisions, which prevented still higher monetary expansion, the Central Bank stopped purchasing foreign exchange. This was important because, as it had also been foreseen, both the success of the program and the high level of domestic interest rates stimulated abundant capital inflows. To discourage those inflows, the government chose to tax them; but this measure proved insufficient.

The Central Bank's exit from the exchange market made the buying exchange rate in nominal terms fall 3.2 percent on June 30, 1994, and 5.2 percent on July 1 to 0.90 reais per dollar. That rate subsequently fell to 0.882 reais on August 24 and to its trough of 0.831 on November 11; it still was 0.844 on December 30, 1994, and did not change much until February 1995 (see Banco Central 1995). On an average daily basis, the price for the U.S. dollar was R$0.931 in July 1994 and fell month by month to R$0.842 in November and still was R$0.898 in May 1995 (see FGV July 1995). Such a fall took everybody by surprise, because the government had maintained the value of one URV equal to the price of the dollar in the first semester, and this policy was judged by many as appropriate to preserve the balance between internal and external sectors.

In addition to being dramatic, the drop in inflation was achieved with higher growth rather than with a slowdown in economic activity. Brazilian real GDP grew 5.8 percent in 1994; compared to an equal period of the preceding year, real GDP grew 3.7 percent in the initial six months of 1994, but increased 7.6 percent in the last six months (9.2 percent in the last quarter of the year). In a similar comparison, the growth of industrial production was 7.0 percent in 1994—3.8 percent in the first six months and 9.9 percent in the last six months (12.8 percent in the fourth quarter; see IEI-UFRJ 1995, 47).

This phenomenon may be surprising to some, considering the usual association in the macroeconomic literature between inflation reduction and production slowdown; but it is what one would expect to find if a fall of inflation expectations were accompanied by larger increases in monetary balances.

The very conception of stabilization programs the economic team entertained was that a recession would be unnecessary and ineffective and thus should be neither promoted nor allowed to develop. But the sudden boom in sales in nearly all branches of commerce, as well as the first data showing intense growth in economic activity, alarmed those economists. The feverish climate evoked the one experienced during the year of the Cruzado Plan (1986), a program that suffered a disastrous collapse following a boom; this similarity helped those economists to judge that the path of growth in late 1994 was unsustainable as well as threatening to the stability of prices.

Thus, actions were taken in October 1994 to curb consumer and retail trade financing, as well as to increase legal reserve requirements on bank liabilities; but they seemed to produce no cooling impact, so that similar measures had to be repeated several times until economic growth finally abated in the second quarter of 1995.

Somewhat in contrast to the climate of optimism and growth, the economy endured a banking crisis in the fourth quarter of 1994. It should be said that the experience of several price freezes had taught the Brazilian banking system how to adapt to an environment of low inflation and low nominal interest rates. But, of course, to be acquainted with a difficulty does not remove it. The end of inflation, as is well known, drastically reduces the demand for banking services related to bank liabilities, for depositors diminish the turnover of their funds.

The problems of Brazil's financial system became more serious in the months following the critical day because banks were impeded from increasing asset-related services to borrowers. Since the critical day, the Central Bank of Brazil had imposed marginal reserve requirements of nearly 100 percent on demand deposits, making banks far less able to expand loans than they had expected when they made plans for the times of low inflation. The result was the failure of several small banks. Government-owned banks also had their troubles, and in December the Central Bank took over the management of two important banks belonging to state governments.

From December on, the economic team had another reason to worry about the quick pace of economic growth in Brazil: the balance of payments. In late 1994 the trade surplus fell quickly and turned into a deficit.

Although exports rose from U.S.$3,216 million per month in 1993 to U.S.$3,742 million per month in the second semester of 1994 (with a peak of U.S.$4,282 in August), imports grew from U.S.$2,123 million per month in 1993 to U.S.$2,760 million in August 1994, U.S.$3,198 million in October, U.S.$4,198 in November, and U.S.$4,611 in December. In the first quarter of 1995, imports remained high (between U.S.$3,284 in January and U.S.$4,895 in May). The trade balance fell from an average surplus of U.S.$1,093 million per month in 1993 to a surplus of U.S.$644 million in October 1994, a deficit of U.S.$492 million in November and a peak deficit of U.S.$1,095 million in February 1995 (for all these data, see the Instituto de Estudos do Sector Publico [IESP] 1995, 29).

As a summary by IEI-UFRJ shows (1995, 10), accumulated values in a 12-month period were as follows. Exports went from U.S.$40,294 million in June 1994 to U.S.$43,558 million in December 1994 and U.S.$44,414 million in March 1995; imports grew from U.S.$27,379 million in June 1994 to U.S.$33,168 million in December and U.S.$39,184 million in March 1995. The trade balance fell from U.S.$12,915 million in June 1994 to U.S.$10,390 million in December and U.S.$5,230 million in March 1995. Compared to an equal period in 1993, imports accumulated in the period from January to September of 1994 grew 13.98 percent, whereas imports accumulated in the period from October to December 1994 grew 73.66 percent (IE-UFRJ 1995, 11).

The jump in imports was due not only to the increase in GDP but also to the fact that the government had reduced tariffs and barriers considerably, in addition to allowing the exchange rate to appreciate. Measured by the effective exchange rate (that is, one encompassing a basket of currencies), the appreciation attained a peak of 23 percent in February 1995 (FGV June 1995, 24). From June 1994 to May 1995, the effective exchange rate showed an appreciation of 16 percent, whereas the exchange rate in terms of reais per U.S. dollar appreciated 21.5 percent (IPEA, 1995).

On the whole, higher imports resulted from a deliberate choice of economic policy, with the aim of constraining price increases internally. It was expected that inward capital flows would cover the current account deficits, not only because liquidity was abundant abroad and domestic interest rates would be high, but also because the end of inflation as well as the election of President Fernando Henrique Cardoso (given his program of economic reforms) would make Brazil particularly attractive to foreign investment. Moreover, the Central Bank had nearly U.S.$40 billion of international reserves to cover any momentary deficiency of foreign financing.

The Mexican crisis of December changed the prospects of large inflows of foreign capital. The economic team then opted for a different target for the trade balance, that of eliminating the deficit. Hence, in the first months of 1995, the government reversed several previous decisions concerning tariffs and barriers to trade; a dramatic illustration is provided by the tariff on automobile imports, which was unexpectedly raised from 20 percent to 32 percent in February and then again was raised unexpectedly to 70 percent in April (tariffs on electronic products also went up to 70 percent). In addition, the government intensified restrictive measures on bank credit and began to raise the nominal exchange rate two to three times per month (but the rate of devaluation remained below the rate of inflation, and the frequency was later reduced to between zero and two times per month).

6. Topics for an Assessment of the Program

The experience of the Plano Real provides another good opportunity for economists to learn. They want to achieve a better understanding of monetary and macroeconomic mechanisms and, above all, confronting the claims of the inertialists, they need to ascertain whether safer and more reliable policies have really been devised. Many and broad issues might be discussed, but this would go beyond the scope of this paper. More modestly, by proposing and answering four questions, I explore a few topics that require closer attention.

Was Sufficient Attention Paid to Fundamentals?

The economic team certainly stressed the need for fiscal and monetary policies to be contractionary (or more vaguely, to be "consistent with" lower inflation). And one may grant that an effort was made to prevent additional increases in noninterest fiscal expenditure in 1993 and in 1994. In spite of this, the fact is that the policies preceding, accompanying, and immediately following the critical day were hardly contractionary enough to sustain by themselves such an ambitious drop in inflation. No major measure of expenditure cuts or of increases in tax rates was undertaken (the FSE certainly was not such a measure).

Let me begin by the public accounts. The government insisted that the public deficit was sufficiently small in 1994 (in the rhetoric for lay persons at least, that it was "balanced"), though it frankly conceded that this was achieved in a temporary and precarious way. At the outset, I may concede, at least for the sake of argument, that the public accounts as measured by our official indicators were nearly balanced. But I hasten to call attention to the fact that the public deficit has been reduced for years in Brazil with no apparent effects on the trend of inflation.

There are several reasons for this lack of effects. First, as the literature in public finance shows, though it has been oddly forgotten in the literature of stabilization programs since the 1980s, lower fiscal deficits by themselves do not indicate less expansion of aggregate demand. The only systematic assistance deficit reduction provides in fighting inflation is either directly, by lowering monetary expansion, or indirectly, by limiting the growth of a public debt that jeopardizes monetary control. Perhaps the fiscal efforts of the last ten years in Brazil have succeeded in maintaining public-sector indebtedness within feasible bounds, but they failed to show results in terms of either decelerating monetary expansion or lowering real interest rates.

Second, the official indicators of public deficits in Brazil, constructed as variants of those sponsored by the International Monetary Fund (IMF), conceal the effects of some government operations on aggregate demand and monetary expansion. Their coverage is insufficient, for they do not include the financial public sector, by means of which the government undertakes nonfiscal operations and expenses; these, nevertheless, end up affecting either the money stock, the public debt, or the level of interest rates. Public accounts fail to reflect the fact that several banks belonging to federal and state governments have notoriously been in financial straits for years.

Public deficits are calculated in real or inflation-adjusted terms rather than in nominal terms; because of this, a drop in their numbers is wholly compatible with their impact on the money supply being expansionary. Also, they are calculated on a net indebtedness basis rather than on a gross one, and thus their reduction is consistent with the perpetuation of high interest rates (the rates usually mentioned are the ones in the funds markets where the government borrows, whereas the impact of government's lending, affecting credit flows with lower or subsidized rates, is not taken into account by interest rate statistics). For all of these reasons, one should not expect that the fiscal effort by Franco's administration, whatever its extent, should show up in lower rates of inflation.

In addition, some facts indicate that if one attempts to think in terms of an overall public deficit (that is, including nonfiscal operations and focusing on changes in gross liabilities), the public-sector adjustment executed before the critical day may have left much to be desired. First, during the initial 18 months after the critical day, the Central Bank has maintained very high interest rates in real terms, rates far above the historical average rate of growth of the Brazilian economy. Second, since the critical day it imposed high reserve requirements on demand deposits, certificates of deposit, and other bank liabilities, and even on bank lending. In the light of facts like these, one may reason that if the public-sector demand for loans had been sufficiently reduced, the Central Bank would have been able to combine low monetary growth with lower or falling real interest rates. Because this combination proved unfeasible, one may conclude that the state of the public finances is not so healthy as it should be after such an abrupt fall in inflation.

By the way, recent official statistics of the whole public sector show that the operational surplus of 2.0 percent of the GDP in 1994 turned to a deficit of 3.0 percent in the period from January to October 1995 and the primary surplus fell from 5.1 percent of GDP in 1994 to 1.5 percent in the period from January to October 1995 (these data are based on deficit flows at current prices; Banco Central, 1996): measured in terms of flows at prices of the last month in the period, the operational surplus of 1.7 percent of the GDP in 1994 turned to a deficit of 2. 9 percent in the period from January to October 1995, and the primary surplus fell from 5.2 percent of GDP in 1994 to 1.6 percent in the period from January to October 1995. My assessment of these numbers is that the deterioration of the public accounts in 1995 was not as strong as the statistics show, because the improvement in 1994 was not as large as everybody thought. The large numbers for the surplus in 1994 reflect more the dramatic drop of the inflation rate and the rapid growth of economic activity than the deliberate attempts to tighten fiscal policy.

Briefly, I pass now to monetary policy. As I said before, real interest rates were high in 1994 and in 1995, but it is doubtful that this has had any anti-inflationary impact. As to monetary expansion, as discussed earlier, it proceeded at high and increasing rates for many months before the critical day. Even after the critical day, throughout the rest of 1994, money grew at high rates. Hence, in this period, monetary policy could not bring about or sustain a fall in inflation either.

IS THE SUCCESS OF THE PROGRAM EVIDENCE FOR DISINDEXATION AS A MAJOR DEVICE OF A STABILIZATION PROGRAM?

Because the alleged basis of the program is disindexation, it might seem so, especially if one accepts that fiscal and monetary policy did not play any significant role in contracting demand during the first six months. More than that, one might feel tempted to say, as inertialists of ten years ago would have, that inflation's drop was due solely to disindexation.

I distinguish two issues in need of explanation: the sudden drop of inflation from the critical day to a few days later and the maintenance of a low rate of inflation for months afterward. On closer examination of the events arising from the program, one sees that a plain, noninertialist explanation can be easily advanced. First, the device of the critical day succeeded because most economic agents believed in the plan and accordingly reduced their expectations of inflation. The plan was announced and thoroughly explained to the Brazilian society, so that most businesspersons knew what would happen. Business consultants and economists in the press and in financial markets uniformly predicted that the rate of inflation would fall to near 3 percent per month. The climate of public opinion, both lay and professional, was favorable to the plan. All that amounted to a call for firms to establish their prices in URV under the expectation that they would not need to increase them after the critical day, particularly considering that from then on wages, the exchange rate, prices of tradables, and rates of public utilities would remain constant.

It is interesting to note that inertialists have no distinctive hypotheses about financial markets (in fact, they are practically never mentioned), for a crucial difference between the inertialist and the conventional interpretations concerns the behavior of the financial markets. One may grant, for the sake of argument, that prices of goods are established nearly entirely on the basis of past inflation, as the inertialists say; but financial markets, in contrast, look at the future.

As a consequence, if financial investors had believed that inflation would be high after the critical day, they should have driven nominal interest rates up accordingly, they have abandoned the domestic money in favor of foreign exchange, or both. But they did not do so, neither immediately nor days and weeks after the critical day. Hence, this shows that their inflation expectations fell drastically. By the way, this same reasoning explains the initial success of the Cruzado Plan in 1996.

The economic team certainly deserves praise for good discernment when it chose the procedure of a unit of account in order to consciously imitate the ending of classical hyperinflations (in the sense of obtaining a dramatic drop in inflation in a matter of days). But acknowledging this does not bind one to the interpretation that such a result should be attributed to disindexation rather than to a dramatic fall in inflation expectations (it should be recalled that disindexation properly understood is freeing economic agents from contracts linked to past price increases; it leaves agents able to establish any level of prices they think proper in the present). Moreover, the success of the Plano Real from the URV stage to the critical day may be appraised as evidence that indexation helps the fight against inflation, for it was indexation to the URV, rather than any disindexation, which then played the key role.

Second, as to inflation's evolution after the critical day, one should distinguish wage tightening from proper disindexation; for neither does the initial imposition of a lower real wage rate (at the time wages are recontracted as equal to a past average) imply prohibition of indexing clauses, nor does this prohibition imply an initial imposition of a reduced wage rate. Admittedly, delaying the adjustment of fees and rates charged by utilities and by the public sector, as well as tightening wage rates, engenders a lower inflation rate than otherwise would be observed. Even so, as experience has shown, the probability is high that this effect should be obtained at the expense of a higher rate somewhere in the future after the needed adjustments are fully made. If one attributed the success of the program to those delays and to wage tightening, one would have to face the difficult task of explaining why this should have worked now when it never had been worked out before.

It is not clear that proper disindexation (that is, abstracting from those delayed price adjustments) has played any significant role in shifting inflation's path downward after the critical day. One can support this statement with the very tenet of inertialism that disindexation supposedly sets prices free to go down by noting that it also makes them more ready to move upward. Besides, inertialism puts forward a hypothesis about how prices are formed whenever indexation prevails, but no hypothesis has clearly explained what happens when indexation no longer exists.

To fill this gap, consider the following. It is very unlikely that economic agents simply ignore inflation (which would result in overlooking the evolution of production costs, as well as devaluations of the working capital), especially after having lived for so long with high rates of price rises. Either agents look at present inflation, or they estimate future inflation.

In the first alternative, as well as in the second alternative if agents do not expect future inflation to decline, the rate of inflation incorporated in prices is the same as the present one; the consequence is that the economy shows resistance to the fall of inflation by a mechanism very similar to the one attributed to indexation. Hence, disindexation does not lead to declining inflation rates in this case. Of course, it does when the estimates of future inflation foresee a deceleration of prices; but, on the other hand, if agents predict lower inflation in the future, they establish prices taking this into account even in the presence of indexation—many prices are not bound by contracts, and contracts can be reformed (especially because contracts have short duration when inflation is high, or has been high until recently).

Therefore, it is doubtful that disindexation brings about falling inflation rates. A contrary opinion seems to be based on the view that indexation locks everybody and every price into unalterable contracts of long duration, which impede agents from acting according to their own estimates of the course of the economy; but intelligent inertialists would hardly espouse this view so clearly conflicting with facts.

Why Did High Inflation Not Reappear?

One can hardly explain the first 12 months after the critical day in a typical monetarist way. For monetary expansion was very high (well above official targets) in the first six months. One may add that no discernible fiscal tightening occurred in the period either. Moreover taking into account conditions of strong demand expansion such as those experienced by Brazilian economy in the second half of 1994, some might have predicted that the fall in inflationary expectations would be reverted in a few months. But Brazilian inflation has remained low for more than 12 months, and given that disindexation is not a good explanation for this fact, what explains it?

The explanation is that the Plano Real is mainly an exchange rate–based (or better, a foreign sector–based) approach to price stabilization. This consists of decelerating or stopping the nominal devaluation of the exchange rate, while reducing tariffs and dismantling barriers to the entry of goods and financial capital from abroad (see Barletta, Blejer, and Landau 1984; Végh 1992).

The prediction previously mentioned would have been sensible for a closed-economy stabilization program, when aggregate supply, determined solely by domestic capacity, is unable to catch up with demand. In contrast, the flood of imports by Brazilian economy throughout the second half of 1994 tended to increasingly satisfy the expanded demand. Besides, since the very beginning of 1994, the government had made it clear that it would quickly open the economy to foreign goods. As a result, businesspersons were alerted and prepared to expect fierce competition from abroad. Also, one must not forget the important fact that foreign goods entered with constant prices, for the exchange rate was not allowed to rise. Also, they were made far less expensive than Brazilian goods by the strong exchange rate appreciation in real terms.

The impact of trade liberalization was impressive, considering that, in terms of the share of foreign trade in gross national product (GNP), Brazil still remained a basically closed economy. That impact may be gauged by the difference between the price increases of tradables and of nontradables after stabilization took place. In the period ending June 1995, the 12 months of stabilization, the price index IPC-FIPE rose 32.31 percent; in contrast rents went up 209.99 percent, personal services climbed 112.03 percent, and tuitions rose 53.99 percent.

Experience has shown that the external-sector approach to price stabilization is effective in reducing or ending inflation, at least until balance of payments problems become acute. Because this approach is usually chosen as an alternative to deliberately restraining aggregate demand, its adoption decreases inflation in spite of an expansionary environment. Therefore, at least in an initial stage, one has the best of both worlds: low or nonexistent inflation without recession.

Moreover, the pressure on inflation from trade liberalization with appreciating real exchange rate was helped in Brazil by two factors that, by themselves, would not sustain a reduction in inflation: in the first months after the critical day several key prices of nontradables were kept practically constant in nominal terms. They were (1) utility rates and prices of public services by discretionary decision of the federal government and (2) wages of employees and salaries of public servants, as well as of a large area of the private sector, by imposition of the new wages policy. Of course, this kind of help is only temporary, for sooner or later all prices have to be fully readjusted in a way that compensates for the inflation that remains.

IS DISINDEXATION A WAY TO FIGHT INFLATION WITHOUT RECESSION?

The answer seems to be no, considering that disindexation was not a major mechanism by which inflation fell abruptly, nor by which price rises remained low. The success of the Plano Real in combining inflation reduction with output expansion is due to the foreign-sector approach, which has long been known to allow that combination.

However, one should note that such an approach seems to postpone the stabilization crisis rather than simply to avoid it. Two kinds of events may trigger a belated stabilization crisis: a balance of payments worsening and domestic boom threatening to refuel inflation. First, because the inflow of foreign capital is not endless, and because deterioration of the current account may attain a level that the economic agents take as a signal of a future exchange-rate devaluation, sooner or later the overall balance of payments deteriorates as well. A recession occurs, either as soon as prolonged foreign competition (often subsidized by an overvalued exchange rate) forces many domestic producers of tradables out of business or after capital outflows in the wake of a balance of payments crisis reduce the supply of money and credit to domestic firms. This is what happened to Argentina under the economic policy of Martinez de Hoz in the second half of the 1970s, as well as under the Cavallo Plan in 1995.

Second, if aggregate demand is so high and economic activity so feverish that increasing imports proves unable to meet the thirst for goods, pressure on domestic prices may rise quickly. To prevent this pressure and to keep inflation low, the government may resort to traditional tight credit and monetary policies. This is what happened to Brazil in 1995 (more on this in the next section).

It is beyond the scope of this paper to provide a general analysis of the foreign sector–based approach to stabilization. Still, it is useful to remark that this approach is not suitable to just any economy suffering inflation, only to those countries that either have sufficiently high international reserves or expect to receive substantial capital inflows. But it turns out that when excess demand feeds inflation, the balance of payments also tends to deteriorate. Consequently, if a country has imbalances in its external sector, it may have to suffer still higher inflation, or lower output growth, or high real interest rates in order to prepare the external conditions that allow the application of the foreign sector–based approach to stabilization. It is by exploring a good situation in the external sector that this approach avoids a stabilization crisis at the time inflation falls.

The traditional way to fight inflation results in slower economic growth first and in declines of inflation later. The stabilization crisis is a threat to the maintenance of political support needed to carry on the program. As regards the foreign sector–based approach, a stabilization crisis takes place later, usually after the program has destabilized the balance of payments, which then needs to be adjusted one more time. Thus, similarly, the crisis may weaken political support to avoid a sudden resurgence of rising inflation. So, both options face political dangers, although the timing differs.

7. Epilogue: A Brief Review of 1995

As mentioned earlier, the economy went into an unprecedented boom in the second semester of 1994. Assessing this as hazardous to the continuity of the stabilization process, the economic authorities attempted to dampen demand by increasing bank reserve requirements and by imposing obstacles to consumer and retail trade financing. However, the feverish climate of economic activity resisted all restraining attempts until still stronger measures were taken in the first quarter of 1995.

Following a brief hesitation after the Mexican crisis, the authorities decided to intensify a new policy of tight credit and money in February 1995 and again in April. As a consequence of these and previous measures, both M1 and the monetary base fell nearly every month from January 1995 on. The accumulated fall until May attained 16.4 percent for the monetary base and 17.9 percent for M1. In November the monetary base still showed an accumulated decline of 3.0 percent, while M1 showed an accumulated decline of 1.9 percent (Banco Central 1996, 71–73). This was one of the largest contractions of monetary aggregates in 50 years. The result was that the Brazilian economy suffered a major break in economic growth. As early as in the second quarter of 1995, GDP declined 3.90 percent and industrial production fell 7.51 percent compared to the first quarter.

The Mexican events and their sequels were interpreted as a sign that the stabilization program should not count unguardedly on capital inflows and that a balance of payments crisis was more than a remote possibility. But the new option for smaller imports made it also indispensable to reduce the exchange rate appreciation; and both, in their turn, required precluding an environment of high aggregate demand, not only to render feasible a contraction in the use of foreign resources but also to dispel a possible return to rising inflation.

Brazil's international reserves had first fallen from U.S.$40,131 in June 1994 to U.S.$36,471 million in December 1994 as a result of the large increase in imports due to the liberalization. They subsequently declined to U.S.$29,918 million in May 1995 because of the Mexican crisis. After May they began to grow again to attain U.S.$49,797 million in November (Banco Central 1996, 171). The restoration of capital inflows signaled the end of the international consequences of the Mexican events on Brazilian economy; and it represented a great victory for those on the economic team who insisted on the preservation of the external basis for the Plano Real. The troublesome consequences were avoided without recourse to a big devaluation of the exchange rate, and the Brazilian economy has remained more open to foreign goods than it has been in decades, in spite of several protectionist moves by the government in the wake of the crisis.

The fall in economic activity continued in the second semester; and meanwhile the visible reduction of aggregate demand helped considerably the process of disinflation. For one thing, strong labor unions renewed contracts with employers by asking for the preservation of jobs rather than wage raises. Second, the government readjusted upward some utility rates and prices of public goods, but no lasting increase in the monthly rate of inflation resulted.

However, a wave of personal and business bankruptcies, followed by a renewal of bank failures, took place from the second quarter of 1995 on. Thereafter, some bank runs occurred, inducing the Central Bank to create special credit lines for those institutions in an attempt to preserve confidence in their soundness. Finally, impressed by the unexpected and huge consequences of their tight policy on the financial system, the Brazilian authorities decided to loosen credit again (and this they did slowly, measure by measure, throughout the second semester of 1995). Later in December, data for retail sales indicated that the recession was over.

Economists inside and outside government made practically the same diagnosis of the stabilization process when they issued their predictions for 1996. The public deficit is still too large for a consolidation of this process, particularly for a resumption of a vigorous economic growth (allowing private demand to increase would make it compete with a high public demand). Preliminary official statistics (covering only the period from January to October 1995) show that the operational surplus, measured at current prices, changed from 2.0 percent of the GDP in 1994 to a deficit of 3.0 percent in 1995; when measured at prices of the last month in each period, the operational surplus changed from 1.7 percent of the GDP in 1994 to a deficit of 2.9 percent in 1995.

The primary surplus at current prices decreased from 5.1 percent of the GDP in 1994 to 1.5 percent in 1995. Measured at prices of the last month in each period, the primary surplus decreased from 5.2 percent of the GDP in 1994 to 1.6 percent in 1995 (for all these numbers, see Banco Central 1996, 144–45). As I said earlier, these statistics are not a very good representation of the public sector's impact on aggregate demand; they particularly exaggerate the recent deterioration of the public accounts. Be that as it may, a significant part of the efforts to cut the deficit hinges on constitutional reforms rendering legal those actions needed for redesigning the public sector. The laws of these reforms, which were originally planned to be enacted in 1995, are still the object of congressional debates (for other views on the Plano Real, see Bacha 1995; Franco 1995; Instituto de Pesquisa Economica Aplicada [IPEA] 1995; Sachs and Zini 1994).

REFERENCES

Afonso, José Roberto, and Luiz Gonzaga de Carvalho. 1994. A tentativa de Ajuste fiscal através do fundo Social de Emergência. *Boletin Conjuntural Trimestral IPEA* (37 October): 33–38.

Bacha, Edmar. 1995. Plano Real: Uma avaliação preliminar. *Revista do BNDES* 2 (3 June): 3–26.

Banco Central. 1995. *Boletim do Banco Central do Brasil* 31 (9 September). Suplemento Estatistico.

Banco Central. 1996. *Boletim do Banco Central do Brasil* 32 (1 January).

Barletta, N., M. Blejer, and L. Landau, eds., 1984. *Economic liberalization and stabilization policies in Argentina, Chile, and Uruguay*. Washington: The World Bank.

FGV. 1995. *Conjuntura econômica*, several issues. Rio de Janeiro: Fundação Getulio Vargas.

Franco, Gustavo. 1995. *O Plano Real e outros ensaios*. Rio de Janeiro: Francisco Alves.

IEI-UFRJ. 1995. *Boletim de Conjuntura IEI-UFRJ* 15 (1 April). Rio de Janeiro: IEI—Universidade Federal do Rio de Janeiro.

IESP. 1995. *Indicadores IESP* 4 (41 June). São Paulo: Fundap/IESP.

IPEA. 1995. O primeiro año do Plano Real. *Carta de Conjuntura IPEA* (57 June). Rio de Janeiro: IPEA.

Lopes, Francisco. 1989. Moeda real. Chap. 8 (77–90) in *O desafio da hiperinflação*, edited by Lopes, Francisco. Rio de Janeiro: Editora Campus.

Ramalho, Valdir. 1993. Elementos para uma Avaliação de confiscos monetários. *Revista Brasileira de Economia* 47 (4 October/December): 533–64.

Sachs, Jeffrey, and Álvaro Zini Jr. 1994. Brazilian inflation and the "Plano Real." *Anais ANPEC*, Vol. 1. Florianópolis: XXII Encontro Nacional de Economia, December.

Simonsen, Mario. 1984. Desindexação e reforma monetária. *Conjuntura Econômica* 38 (11 November): 101–5.

Végh, Carlos, 1992. Stopping high inflation. *IMF Staff Papers* 39 (3 September): 626–95.

READING 12

From the Military to Democracy: Two Decades of Chilean Economic Policies*

FELIPE LARRAÍN B. AND RAÚL LABÁN M.
Harvard University — Universidad Catolica de Chile

INTRODUCTION

The Chilean economy has changed dramatically since the mid-1970s. From very high levels of protection and pervasive state intervention, it has been transformed into an economy integrated to world markets, in which the engine of economic growth is the private sector. The process, however, has not been smooth. Two major depressions—in 1975 and in 1982–1983—tested Chile's resolve in continuing free-market reforms, but the process endured. Political transition from the military regime to democracy was also an important test for the economic model. To some, the opposition's victory in the presidential elections of December 1989 posed grave threats to the economy. These fears proved to be wrong. During the 1990s Chile's economic model has been deepened and legitimized in democracy. Growth has continued unabated.

This paper studies the policies pursued by the government of President Patricio Aylwin, which took office in March 1990 and left office in March 1994, setting the stage for the succeeding administration of President Eduardo Frei Ruiz-Tagle. As background, it analyzes the economic policies of the preceding military regime (1973–1990). A main theme of this paper is the issue of continuity and change in economic policy. The analysis also touches on some of the main challenges facing the Chilean economy into the mid-1990s. Despite major progress, a significant fraction of the Chilean population still lives below the poverty line. Consolidating a strong and stable path of economic growth—on the order of 7 percent per year—is an essential component in the defeat of poverty and underdevelopment. This is attainable for Chile over the next decade.

*This paper draws on Labán and Larraín (1995).

THE ECONOMIC LEGACY OF THE MILITARY REGIME, 1973–1990

In this section, we briefly review the main economic developments and reforms implemented during the military regime (1973–1990) and describe the economic conditions under which Chile returned to democracy after 16 years of authoritarian rule.

ECONOMIC POLICY IN THE AUTHORITARIAN ERA[1]

Chile's Dramatic Economic Changes of the 1970s

From the outset of the military regime in late 1973, the Chilean economy underwent major economic and institutional reforms aimed at fulfilling three objectives: stabilization, privatization, and liberalization. The first two objectives were to be achieved immediately, whereas liberalization was supposed to occur more gradually.

Stabilization was based initially on the elimination of the imbalances in the goods markets—induced by an excess of government intervention during the previous administration—and in the public sector. By the end of 1974 and during 1975, the efforts concentrated mainly on correcting the balance-of-payments deficit provoked by the collapse in the world price of copper, Chile's main export, and the trebling of oil prices. Finally, efforts were made to control inflation. The exchange rate was fixed in June 1979, to provide a nominal anchor for the economy. Inflation, however, did not converge to international levels, mainly due to widespread indexation in labor markets and a faster growth in aggregate spending than output. The result was a major currency appreciation and a sharp drop in the competitiveness of the tradable sector.

A first round of privatization (1974–1978) was centered on the divestiture of most of the real assets that had been transferred to the state during the Unidad Popular Government (1970–1973). By 1980, the public sector controlled only 43 firms (including a commercial bank), compared to the more than 500 firms under state control during President Allende's administration. Privatization was part of a comprehensive attempt to restructure the public sector.

The role of market forces was advanced through liberalization. Most controlled prices were freed in late 1973, followed by a sweeping deregulation of the domestic financial market and the beginning of extensive trade liberalization. Capital flows were also liberalized by the end of the decade, and especially during the early 1980s.

In 1979, a major labor reform established collective bargaining at the firm level, relaxed barriers for dismissals, and restricted strikes. This reform reduced the negotiating power of workers vis-à-vis employers, compared to the pre-1973 legislation, and was strongly opposed by unions.

By the early 1980s, Chile had undergone a deep process of economic restructuring, dramatically changing the relative roles of the private and public sectors and increasing the role played by markets in the allocation of productive resources. In Chile at that time, domestic interest rates and prices (with the exception of public wages and the exchange rate) were market-determined, the exchange rate system was unified, a uniform 10 percent import tar-

[1]This section draws on Larraín (1991a, 1991b). For a detailed analysis of economic developments during this period, see also Edwards and Cox-Edwards (1987) and Meller (1990).

iff (with the exception of vehicles), and was the only trade barrier/the capital market was relatively liberalized.

As Table 1 shows, the economy experienced wide fluctuations during the 1974–1981 period. A very large contraction took place during 1975, when gross domestic product (GDP) declined more than 13 percent and unemployment surged to 16.4 percent of the

TABLE 1

Selected Macroeconomic Indicators in Chile, 1970–1994

YEARS	GDP GROWTH[a] (%)	INFLATION[b] (%)	UNEMPLOYMENT[c] (%)	REAL WAGES[d] (% CHANGE)
1970–1973	1.1	218.1	4.4	–8.5
1974–1979	2.3	177.6	16.6	6.3
1974–1989	3.1	79.9	17.3	3.0
1980–1989	3.6	21.4	17.7	1.1
1985–1989	6.6	20.4	13.0	1.1
1990–1994	6.4	46.0	6.7	3.9
1974	1.0	369.2	9.2	–13.3
1975	–13.2	343.3	16.4	–2.7
1976	3.2	197.9	19.9	10.8
1977	8.2	84.2	18.6	21.5
1978	7.8	37.2	17.9	14.3
1979	7.1	33.5	17.7	10.9
1980	7.7	35.1	15.7	8.7
1981	6.7	19.7	15.6	8.9
1982	–13.4	9.9	26.4	–0.2
1983	–3.5	27.2	30.4	–10.6
1984	6.0	19.9	24.4	0.1
1985	3.5	30.7	21.4	–4.3
1986	5.6	19.5	16.0	2.1
1987	6.6	19.9	12.2	–0.2
1988	7.3	14.7	9.0	6.5
1989	9.9	21.4	6.3	1.9
1990	3.3	27.3	6.0	1.8
1991	7.3	18.7	6.5	4.9
1992	11.0	12.7	6.7	4.5
1993	6.3	12.2	6.5	3.3
1994	4.2	8.9	7.8	4.8

[a] Central Bank of Chile. Monthly and quarterly reports.

[b] December to December; 1970–1978: Cortázar and Marshall (CIEPLAN: Corporación de Investigaciones Económicas para Latinoamérica); 1979–1994: Central Bank of Chile.

[c] 1970–1979: ODEPLAN (National Planning Office); 1980–1994: Instituto Nacional de Estadísticas (INE). Includes emergency unemployment programs (PEM and POJH).

[d] 1970–1973: industrial sector; 1974–1994: aggregate index; Instituto Nacional de Estadísticas (INE).

labor force. This was partially attributable to the terms of trade loss resulting from rising oil prices and falling copper prices, partially to a sharp decline in domestic demand stemming from restrictive fiscal and monetary policies, and partially to exchange rate devaluation, which reduced real wages by 15.6 percent during the 1974–1975 period.

It is difficult to identify how much of the reduction in real wages and the employment losses was due to macroeconomic policies implemented at that time and how much was due to other shocks. But privatization of state enterprises with overemployment and trade liberalization may be expected to induce a short-run increase in unemployment.

In 1976–1977, the economy recovered from the 1975 depression and then experienced four years of growth at an average rate of 7.5 percent. The recovery gave way to a boom in 1980–1981, spurred by a major shift in expectations, from a realistic assessment of Chile's prospects to an illusion of sustained, high growth. Unemployment, however, remained very high during the complete period.

The opening of the capital account and the abundance of foreign credit in the late 1970s and early 1980s provided the financing necessary for an unsustainable expansion in private expenditures at the time of the boom. By late 1981, Chile had accumulated a stock of foreign debt approaching U.S.$16 billion. The economy was particularly vulnerable to an increase in interest rates, because almost 60 percent of the debt was contracted at variable rates. These rates were primarily tied to the London Inter-bank Offered Rate (LIBOR), which in 1981 shot up to 16.5 percent at the same time that terms of trade declined by 6 percent. The worst would come in the following year.

From Crisis to Growth through Adjustment (1982–1989)

In 1982–1983, Chile experienced its worst economic crisis since the 1930s as real output collapsed by 16.4 percent. This major depression was partly a result of several external shocks: the drying up of voluntary external financing, the deterioration of 23 percent in the terms of trade since 1980, and the major increase in foreign interest rates. But the impact of external developments was exacerbated by several domestic policy mishandlings: the fixed exchange rate policy coupled with mandatory indexation of wages at 100 percent of past inflation; the sweeping opening of the capital account at the time of the boom; the radical liberalization of domestic financial markets without the provision of proper regulations and controls; and the belief in the "automatic adjustment" mechanism, by which policy makers expected the market to produce a quick adjustment to the new recessionary conditions without interference by the authorities.

Authorities initially responded to the crisis with a contractionary policy during the 1982–1983 period aimed at closing the income-expenditure gap. Output dropped during both years, real wages declined by almost 11 percent, and the unemployment rate reached more than 30 percent of the labor force in 1983. In addition, the exchange rate policy was erratic, as shown by the implementation of five different exchange rate regimes after the abandonment of the fixed exchange rate policy in June 1982. The external disequilibrium was reduced in 1983, but the economy continued to be depressed. This is not surprising, since most of the adjustment to Chile's external crisis initially occurred through import reduction induced by an aggregate expenditure contraction, while substitution effects in demand and exports showed little response. In 1983, imports were less than 50 percent of their 1981 level.

Aiming to ameliorate the high costs of the adjustment, the government pursued an expansionary policy during most of 1984, which helped to achieve a recovery in output but proved to be unsustainable. The current account deficit almost doubled, surpassing U.S.$2 billion, more than 10 percent of GDP. In September of that year, the exchange rate was devalued and tariffs were raised in order to induce a switch in expenditure toward domestic goods.

At the beginning of 1985, a new macroeconomic policy was implemented. Its aim was to promote a recovery of output and employment through the export-oriented structural adjustment of the economy. Policy actions centered on three fronts: the promotion of non-copper exports, the enhancement of domestic saving and investment, and the strengthening of the corporate and financial sectors.

The heavy burden of a foreign debt in excess of GDP required a vigorous effort to promote exports. At the same time, the need to diversify exports beyond copper had been recognized, and a process of export diversification had been under way since the mid-1970s. To strengthen this effort, the authorities relied on several policies: a series of devaluations first restored the loss in international competitiveness suffered during the fixed exchange rate period (1979–1982) and then stabilized the real exchange rate at a competitive level. Import tariffs were reduced from 35 percent to 15 percent in three steps. Various fiscal and administrative measures were effected, including a simplified import-duty rebate on minor exports and an acceleration of existing tax refunds for exporters. Although these measures were primarily oriented toward exports, they also provided an incentive for efficient import substitution stemming from the high level of the real exchange rate.

During 1985–1989 the volume of exports of goods and services expanded at an average annual rate of 11.3 percent, and Chile became one of the most open countries in the hemisphere: in 1989 exports of goods and services accounted for 32 percent of GDP, compared to 25 percent in 1980 (see Table 2 and Figure 1).

TABLE 2

Evolution of Imports, Exports, and the Real Exchange Rate, 1980–1994

	Imports[a]		Exports[b]		
Year	Percent of Real GDP	Annual Rate of Change	Percent of Real GDP	Annual Rate of Change	Real Exchange Rate[b] (1986=100)
1980	39.9	0	25.0	0	60.9
1981	42.4	13.3	21.3	–9.0	52.9
1982	32.3	–34.0	25.7	4.5	59.0
1983	27.6	–17.7	26.7	0.1	70.8
1984	29.1	12.0	25.7	2.2	74.0
1985	25.5	–9.5	27.9	12.4	90.9
1986	26.0	7.9	29.1	10.1	100.0
1987	29.0	18.6	29.1	6.7	104.3
1988	30.4	12.8	30.3	11.6	111.2
1989	34.5	24.5	32.0	16.1	108.6
1990	34.6	3.6	34.0	9.7	112.8
1991	35.0	8.5	35.1	10.7	106.5
1992	39.0	23.5	35.9	13.5	97.6
1993	40.8	11.2	35.2	4.2	96.9
1994	41.1	5.1	36.5	8.2	94.3

[a]Imports and exports of goods and services in 1986 pesos, National Accounts, Central Bank of Chile.

[b]Effective real exchange rate, Central Bank of Chile.

FIGURE 1
Exports and the Real Exchange Rate, 1980–1994

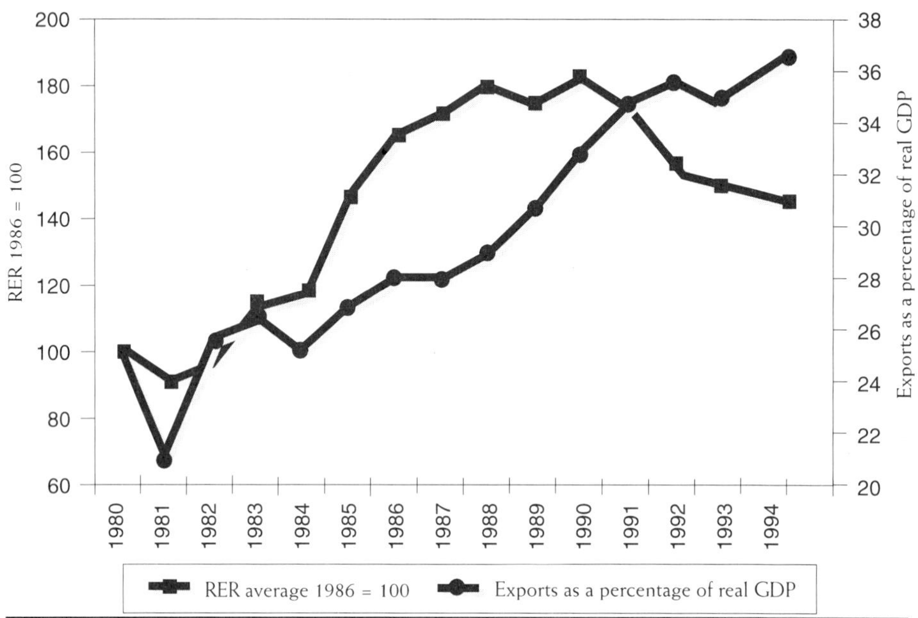

Source: Central Bank of Chile, monthly and quarterly reports.

National savings reached a remarkable low of 1.6 percent of GDP in 1982. As foreign saving became severely limited, it was imperative to improve the domestic effort in order to finance higher levels of investment. The restoration of broad macroeconomic stability was essential to increase saving. However, specific policies were also pursued. The tax reform of December 1984 promoted corporate saving through a radical reduction in the tax rate affecting retained earnings. Attempting to encourage household saving, the reform also allowed a reduction of 20 percent of certain qualified investments from the tax base.

Public revenues were hurt by the depressed economic activity, the social security reform of mid-1981 (which required increased public contributions to the state Social Security system), the 1984 tax reform (which significantly reduced direct taxation), and the reduction in import tariffs by 20 percent. In view of weakened public finances, the government implemented a series of measures. Wage adjustments in the public sector were set systematically below inflation, and Social Security disbursements ceased to be adjusted automatically to lagged inflation. Several other categories and capital expenditures were also curtailed.

During 1982–1983, nonfinancial corporations had become very weak—some outright insolvent—as a consequence of extremely high real interest rates, the effects of currency devaluation on dollar-denominated debt, and the economic depression. These factors, coupled with faulty banking practices in a permissive regulatory environment, set the stage for a major crisis in the financial sector, requiring regulators to assume control of several troubled financial institutions including the two largest private commercial banks.

In the short run, the government reacted to the crisis with a substantial aid package for banks and local debtors. This package included a preferential exchange rate for dollar debts, at times 40 percent below the official rate; credit lines at below-market rates for the financial sector; and the Central Bank's purchase of bad loans from the banking system with a repurchase agreement, which also involved a subsidy. The various programs were phased out by the end of 1986, but their cost was substantial for the public sector. The total value of subsidies for financial rehabilitation was estimated at approximately U.S.$6 billion, or about 35 percent of 1986 GDP. In an attempt to avoid the mistakes of the earlier financial liberalization, bank regulation was strengthened, and the regulatory powers of the Superintendency of Banks and Financial Institutions were enhanced. By mid-1985, the authorities started a major recapitalization program for private banks.

During the second half of the 1980s, a second round of privatization was carried out. A total of 46 firms—a number of financial institutions that were intervened in by the government to keep them from bankruptcy after the economic and financial crisis—were sold to the private sector for slightly more than U.S.$3 billion. This process was relatively rapid, considering the large number of firms and the volume of the assets sold.

Macroeconomic performance significantly improved after 1984. In 1985, the economy started a sustained recovery, accompanied by a steady improvement in the external accounts. These results came from a combination of internal and external factors. Internally, the structural adjustment program was accompanied by macroeconomic stability, which enabled response to the new policies. The fiscal deficit declined from 4.5 percent of GDP in 1984 to about balance in 1989. On the external front, the decline of world interest rates during a good part of the program and the improvement of the terms of trade in 1986–1989 certainly helped the current account and economic growth.

The structural adjustment program was quite successful in the promotion of noncopper exports and the efficient substitution of imports. The combination of a competitive real exchange rate, low and flat tariffs, and specific fiscal incentives produced a strong response from nontraditional exports. At the same time, the generalized economic recovery strengthened substantially both the financial and nonfinancial sectors.

INCOME DISTRIBUTION, POVERTY, AND THE MILITARY REGIME'S ECONOMIC POLICY

The record in terms of income distribution during the authoritarian period points toward a deterioration, both during the restructuring process of the 1970s and through most of the structural adjustment period of the 1980s. This is not surprising, given the two sharp depressions that Chile experienced in this period and the painful adjustments that followed. In each case, real wages declined significantly and unemployment increased to unprecedented levels. Additionally, some of the economic measures adopted during these periods had a regressive bias. It has been shown that the income of the poor is very accurately explained by the unemployment rate and the wage index. On the whole, wages in Chile declined more than per capita output, and unemployment was quite high on average.[2] It is likely, then, that income distribution worsened.

Several measures confirm this trend in income distribution. The Gini coefficient increased from around 0.50 in 1970 to more than 0.54 during 1982–1984. The share in national income of the highest quintile increased steadily from 55.8 percent in 1970 to 59.5 percent in 1982–1984, while the income share of the poorest two quintiles declined from

[2]The average rate of unemployment increased from 6.5 percent in the 1960s to 17.3 percent during the 1974–1989 period.

TABLE 3
Income Distribution, Real Wages, and Unemployment: Selected Years, 1970–1994

Years	Share of Income[a] Lowest 40%	Middle 40%	Highest 20%	Real Wage Index[b] (1970=100)	Unemployment Rate[c] (%)
1970	11.5	32.7	55.8	100.0	5.7
1979–1981	11.1	31.3	57.6	93.8	16.5
1982–1984[d]	10.0	30.5	59.5	94.7	27.4
1989	12.6	27.9	59.5	97.6	6.3
1990	13.3	28.7	58.0	99.4	6.0
1991	14.7	30.6	54.7	104.3	6.5
1992	13.2	30.8	56.3	109.0	6.7
1993	—	—	—	112.6	6.5
1994	12.5	30.5	56.9	117.9	7.8

Source: INE: Instituto Nacional de Estadísticas. Monthly report.

[a]MIDEPLAN, Encuestas CASEN, various years.

[b]Central Bank of Chile. Monthly report.

[c]Cortázar and Marshall (1980).

[d]The share of income of different groups corresponds to 1982–1983.

11.5 percent in 1970 to 10 percent in 1982–1984. The worst point of income distribution happened, then, at the height of the depression (see Table 3).[3] In 1989, however, the share of the bottom 40 percent had climbed back to 12.6 percent, while the top 20 percent had retained its 59.5 percent share, suggesting a recovery of income distribution in the second half of the 1980s.

A number of social expenditure items were severely affected by the adjustment to the economic and financial crisis, especially in the first half of the 1980s. Thus, the per capita health, housing, and education budgets declined by more than 20 percent during the adjustment to the crisis of the 1980s.

The economic crisis and the policies directed to close the income-expenditure gap pushed the unemployment rate to over 30 percent in 1983—including emergency employment programs (PEM [*programa de empleo mínimo,* minimum employment program] and POJH [*programa de ocupación para obreros jefes de hogar,* employment program for heads of family]). Unemployment remained over 20 percent for four years (1982–1985), real wages declined by 15 percent, and the minimum wage dropped by 40 percent in real terms during the 1981–1985 period.

Revenues of the public health system were also hurt with the privatization of middle- and high-income health care. When the option to switch to the private health institutions was given, 8 percent of the affiliates did so and carried with them 40 percent of the revenues of the public entity. Although the reform certainly increased the quality of ser-

---

[3]For a more detailed discussion on the distributive impact of the adjustment program carried out in the 1980s in the Chilean economy, see Larrain (1991b) and Meller (1991).

vice for those who switched, the lower-income groups, which did not switch, suffered from the decline in resources of the state system.

The military regime implemented several correct principles in the social sectors, such as targeting to the lower income groups and decentralization and competition in the provision of social services. Programs such as the free distribution of milk and attention to pregnant women influenced the sharp reduction in the country's infant mortality rate.[4] Nonetheless, this effort was not sufficient. A high proportion of Chileans—estimated at around 45 percent by Torche (1987)—were living below the poverty level in the mid-1980s. Although poverty in Chile is not a new problem, this high proportion was, to a significant extent, the result of the 1982–1983 depression and the adjustment pattern that followed. The economic recovery and the resumption of growth in 1986–1988 improved this situation, but it takes decades of economic expansion to break the circle of poverty.

The Legacy of the Military Regime

It is widely recognized that the first democratically elected government after 16 years of military rule in Chile inherited, in general terms, a very successful economy. This stands as a major contrast to other experiences of transition in the region.

At the end of the military government, the Chilean economy had been successful in completing its stabilization and structural adjustment. The country was a leader in the implementation of a number of economic reforms—trade and Social Security reforms and privatization, among others. The last half decade of the military regime was also the subperiod with better economic performance. During 1985–1989, real GDP expanded at an average rate of 6.6 percent, inflation averaged 19.8 percent, the volume of exports expanded at an average annual rate of 11.3 percent, and the government was able to achieve a fiscal surplus of 1.7 percent of GDP in 1989.

Nevertheless, as discussed, the adjustment process carried out during this period resulted in significant costs. Available information is robust in pointing to a deterioration of income during this period and to a high share of the population living in poverty when the transition to democracy was initiated.

By the end of the military regime, poverty had also become a very significant concern in public opinion. According to a September 1988 poll conducted by a prestigious private academic institution, Centro de Estudios Públicos, (CEP), poverty and low income levels were the principal reasons behind the vote for the "no" option in the plebiscite of October 1988, which cleared the way for competitive presidential elections in December 1989.

Macroeconomic Management after the Return to Democracy (1990–1994)

President Patricio Aylwin entered office in March 1990 as head of a center-left coalition known as Concertación. The new administration started from a strong position on the economic front and maintained the economic model inherited from the previous regime. This produced the climate of stability in economic policy and institutions necessary for strong private investment and sustained growth.

[4]For a thorough—and favorable—analysis of social policies during the military government, see Castañeda (1990).

Democratic legitimization of the free-market economic model adopted by the military regime was crucial. To this end the government had to quickly gain the support for policy continuity from organized labor and from those who were hit worst during the prolonged adjustment period of the 1980s. Among the latter were those earning the minimum wage, which at the beginning of 1990 was 35 percent lower than its 1980 real value; those receiving family allowances, not adjusted since 1985, whose purchasing power in 1990 was a third of that in 1980; the average worker, whose 1989 real wage was 1.6 percent lower than the average for 1980–1981; those receiving public-sector pensions, which declined 10 percent in real terms from 1985 to early 1990; recipients of the subsidy for extremely poor families, which declined 50 percent in real terms between 1981 and 1989; and beneficiaries of social spending, which went down 20 percent in per capita terms since 1985. Clearly, the adjustment of the economy from the deep depression of 1982–1983 had not been painless, but at the beginning of 1990 the economy was in a solid position to improve the well-being of the population.

The Aylwin administration was able to reach a climate of consensus in the conduct of economic policy, which was central at the beginning of this transitional government to shape the reforms that were implemented and to design the development strategy that was to be followed. This strategy was built on four widely accepted principles. First, the market was to play the leading role in the allocation of resources. Second, macroeconomic stability was crucial to ensure sustainable growth. Third, social spending in health, housing, pensions, and education needed to be increased. Lastly, it was recognized that external markets provide the best opportunities for small economies, and thus the government would try to maintain a competitive real exchange rate and make efforts to deepen the integration of the Chilean economy to the international markets in goods, services, and capital.

Managing Social Demands

The new democratic government faced several potential pressures from different groups of the population. An attempt to give in to all demands would have only produced short-term benefits at the cost of sacrificing macroeconomic stability and future growth. One need only witness the problems of Argentina, Brazil, and Peru in reconciling the different claims that arose with the restoration of democracy.

A broad agreement existed between the government and the opposition in that the only way to allow a larger fraction of the population to benefit permanently from modernization, and to defeat poverty, was through sustained growth. But waiting for growth alone to eliminate poverty would have taken too long to be a viable solution. And growth would not necessarily come with improved income distribution in its earlier stages, as Simon Kuznets has shown. If a large fraction of the population has to wait too long to share in the benefits of modernization, this process may be difficult to sustain in a democracy. If perceived in this way by investors, despite attractive fundamentals, this would limit the supply response to investment incentives until at least some of the uncertainty about the sustainability of pro-investment policies is resolved.[5]

---

[5]"Pessimistic" expectations may be self-fulfilling. The wait-and-see strategy deprives the economy of much needed investment, thus retarding growth and eroding the political support for policy continuity. Ultimately, this may bring about the reversal of pro-investment policies initially feared (Labán and Wolf, 1993).

Given the irreversible nature of fixed investment, stability and credibility in economic institutions and a solid basis of support for policy continuity may be more important to stimulate private investment than tax incentives and "high" ex-ante rates of return. Put in other words, if there is a high degree of uncertainty in the economic/political environment, tax breaks and ex-ante rates of return will have to be very attractive to have a significant impact on the accumulation of physical capital (Dornbusch 1990; Pindyck 1991). An important cost associated with political and economic instability is, then, its depressive impact on productive investment, and thus on economic growth.

The new administration avoided the conflict between macroeconomic stability and increased resources devoted to the lower-income groups by changing the composition of government spending toward social spending, whose share in the government budget increased by 3.4 percent of GDP between 1988–1989 and 1990–1991,[6] and by implementing a tax reform that would contribute additional resources for social spending.

In addition, the government sent to Congress in 1990 a labor reform, partly intended to balance negotiating power between employees and employers, and raised the minimum wage, the family allowance, and the subsidy for low-income families during 1990–1992. These adjustments were set in national agreements among the government, the major representatives of organized labor (Central Unitaria de Trabajadores, CUT), and of entrepreneurs (Confederación de la Producción y el Comercio, CPC), which allowed for a 21.9 percent rise in the real minimum wage between March 1990 and March 1992. In April 1991, the government, CPC, and CUT agreed that, after this first stage of recovery, further real increases in the minimum wage should be related to gains in labor productivity and that future expected inflation (as opposed to past inflation) should be used as the criterion for normal adjustments.

The minimum wage has a coverage of about 12 percent of the labor force, but its adjustment serves as a signal of inflationary expectations for the rest of the economy. Thus, the use of future expected inflation to set the minimum wage, which has been the criterion used since the 1992 negotiations, has served as a contribution to breaking indexation to past inflation (widely used in labor and financial contracts) and therefore inflationary inertia.

Some room for wage improvement existed at the onset of the democratic government, but it was necessary to be cautious in this area. Several important reasons suggested restraint from wage increases beyond productivity improvements. First, unemployment was significantly reduced during the 1988–1989 period, and the economy hit productive capacity constraints; the required increase in investment put a strict limit on real wage adjustments beyond productivity improvements. Second, real wages increased by an accumulated 8.5 percent in 1988–1989, a clear indication of a tightening labor market, which through its own workings would further increase wages as long as the economic expansion continued. Third, there were doubts about the impact that the labor and tax reforms would have on the private sector and thus on the capacity of the economy to create enough productive employment. Some economists predicted that the combined effect of the rigidities that the labor reform would introduce and the reduction of incentives for firms to invest that would be implied by the tax reform would reduce the capacity of the economy to create productive employment, resulting in a higher "equilibrium" level of unemployment. Judging from the

[6]Some significant inflexibilities were built into the budget, such as the impossibility—by law—of reducing defense spending in real terms.

FIGURE 2
Real Wage Index (year 1 = 100)

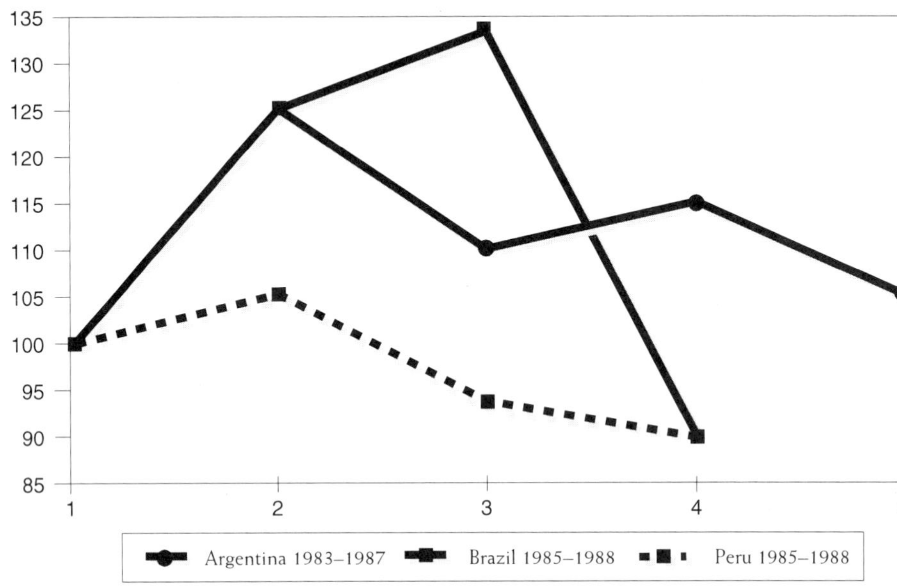

Source: Larrain 1991a.

economic performance in the 1990–1994 period, however, these concerns proved to be overly pessimistic.

The experience of other countries in Latin America helped Chile in this respect. Aggressive wage adjustments above productivity gains have proved short-lived and have quickly resulted in sharp wage contractions, as Figure 2 shows for Argentina, Brazil, and Peru in the 1980s. In the first two cases, the rise lasted for just one year and then gave way to an enormous contraction that soon left workers with lower real wages than before the start of the expansion. In Peru, wages increased for two years and then suffered a major setback that left them substantially below their initial level in 1985. Thus it is in the collective interest of workers to avoid this pattern.[7]

Real wages increased on average by 3.7 percent annually during President Aylwin's administration, and the minimum wage increased by more than double that. At the end of 1993 the unemployment rate was below 5 percent, almost 2 percentage points below that attained in 1989. At the same time, public social spending rose by almost 50 percent. As

[7]Dornbusch (1989) has argued that an artificial rise in real wages makes labor gain at the expense of capital. This has a negative impact on capital formation and may even induce capital flight. Thus the initial increase in real wages is partially dampened by a decline in the capital stock, so that the level of real wages that can be sustained in equilibrium may be lower than when this process started. For an analysis of the populist cycle, see Dornbusch and Edwards (1991) and Sachs (1990).

agreed with CUT and CPC, the government also implemented other measures to raise the income of poor families, such as increases in family allowances and subsidies to low-income families. It also made a 10.6 percent real adjustment in the minimum pension that was committed but not fulfilled in 1985 and increased wages to public-sector teachers and health workers.

Higher wages and lower unemployment reduced poverty but produced no significant improvement in income distribution, and those below the poverty line still accounted for about 30 percent of the population in 1993. Both of these remain crucial areas for improvement for Chile going into the second half of the 1990s.

Cooperation with the government from organized labor, entrepreneurial associations, and the main opposition party[8] has been crucial in the preservation of macroeconomic stability and in the implementation of a social plan directed to integrate permanently lower-income groups into the development process.

MONETARY POLICY MAKING WITH HIGHLY MOBILE CAPITAL

The new authorities thought that Chile could not sustain the high rates of GDP expansion it had experienced in 1988 (7.3 percent) and especially in 1989 (9.9 percent). They also considered the cumulative rates of expansion of private money (85 percent) and of domestic expenditure (23 percent) during 1988–1989 to be unsustainable. This rapid expansion of aggregate demand had induced an increase in imports of 35 percent in value terms during 1989. In their view, the country was running the serious risk of an inflationary outburst.[9] The annualized rate of inflation reached 30 percent in the last quarter of 1989 and showed an upward trend. Nonetheless, the monthly indicator of economic activity (IMACEC)—a widely watched index in the country—showed that the economy was decelerating since the third quarter of 1989 (see Table 4).

In early 1990, the newly independent Central Bank engineered a sharp monetary contraction aimed at reducing aggregate expenditure, thus moderating the rise of imports and helping to control inflation. Ex-ante real interest rates on ten-year Central Bank bonds were raised from less than 7 percent in the last quarter of 1989 to 9.7 percent at the beginning of 1990. At the same time, the monetary authorities announced that the adjustment would be transitory, which signaled the prospect of substantial capital gains once interest rates declined to normal levels. Enthusiasm to acquire Central Bank bonds was immense, and its stock of bonds increased by 80 percent between December 1989 and December 1990. Attracted by high interest rates on long-term public bonds, many funds invested in shorter-term assets were shifted to longer-term ones, and annual short-term real rates surged, from 6 percent at the beginning of 1989 to 13.3 percent in March 1990. This was their highest level since 1981.

International capital mobility vastly complicated the adjustment.[10] Spreads between local interest rates and international rates increased sharply, and short-term speculative capital

[8]Renovación Nacional backed both the tax reform and the labor reform, as discussed later.

[9]According to estimates by Marfán (1992), any excess productive capacity generated during the prolonged adjustment process of the 1980s had been exhausted by 1989.

[10]On capital mobility in Chile, see Labán and Larraín (1993).

TABLE 4

Macroeconomic Quarterly Data for Chile, 1989–1994 (as a percentage)

QUARTER	GDP GROWTH[a]	INFLATION[b]	REAL WAGES[c]
1989			
I	9.0	12.9	4.1
II	13.4	14.7	0.9
III	9.7	18.7	–0.4
IV	7.6	21.3	3.1
1990			
I	8.6	23.4	1.5
II	2.8	24.6	1.7
III	0.0	26.6	–0.7
IV	1.5	29.0	5.0
1991			
I	2.2	24.1	7.2
II	6.0	23.7	4.1
III	8.9	22.0	6.6
IV	12.3	18.1	2.6
1992			
I	11.3	18.7	3.2
II	9.4	15.9	5.8
III	14.0	14.2	4.4
IV	9.7	13.4	3.9
1993			
I	7.7	12.4	3.9
II	7.8	13.0	2.4
III	5.9	12.9	2.5
IV	3.7	12.6	4.2
1994			
I	3.8	14.3	4.2
II	4.7	12.7	4.4
III	4.0	11.3	5.2
IV	4.6	8.7	5.2

Source: Central Bank of Chile.

[a]Percentage change respect to same period of year before.

[b]Average 12-month rate of growth.

[c]Quarterly average.

flew massively to Chile. As a result, during the first half of 1990 the nominal exchange rate went from the upper limit of its 10 percent fluctuation to the bottom of the band and remained there for the rest of the year. Moreover, the monetary authority had to purchase dollars in order to defend the floor of the band. As a result of this intervention in the foreign exchange market, the Central Bank ended up accumulating U.S.$2.4 billion in reserves during 1990. To control the consequent rise in the monetary base, the bank sterilized the effects of foreign exchange operations by selling more of its own bonds, preventing in this way a faster decline in interest rates. But because foreign exchange reserves earned international interest rates, while Central Bank bonds paid a much higher peso rate, the Central Bank's balance sheet deteriorated.

The adjustment was costly in terms of output—GDP growth in 1990 was only 3.3 percent—but it served the monetary authority as genuine proof that it was willing to pay a cost to fight what was regarded as an overheated economy and thus to preserve macroeconomic equilibrium. Its contractionary effects, however, were milder on other variables and were soon reversed. The unemployment rate went from an average 6.2 percent during 1990–1991 to less than 5 percent in 1992; real wages increased an accumulated 6.8 percent during 1990–1991 and then rose by 4.5 percent and 3.3 percent in 1993. A significant increase in social spending and other government programs directed to lower-income groups also helped to mitigate the costs of the adjustment.

FISCAL POLICY

Fiscal policy during the first Concertación government was highly responsible. The public sector spent no more than its income, generating a consolidated surplus. Real government spending, however, increased at rates higher than GDP on average for the period, helped by booming revenues.

Fiscal revenue increased significantly during 1990–1993, due to the tax reform of 1990, a strong expansion of economic activity and imports, a relatively high price for copper, and a reduction in tax evasion. In addition to low international interest rates, this has allowed the government to increase its social spending while generating enough savings to finance its investment and have a surplus. The latter has been consistently between 1.5 and 2.5 percent of GDP.

The increase in social spending has been accompanied by a higher savings effort by the government. Nonfinancial public-sector saving, which was on average 5.3 percent of GDP in the 1980s, rose to over 7 percent of GDP in the early 1990s. At the same time, private saving increased sharply, to levels around 15 percent of GDP in the early 1990s, which is more than double its average of 7 percent of GDP in the 1980s (see Table 5).

The public sector's contribution to national saving has been partially dampened by an operational deficit at the Central Bank, which averaged 2.7 percent of GDP during the 1983–1989 period. Originally, this resulted from the government's intervention to avoid massive bankruptcies during the crisis of the early 1980s. After declining year by year since 1986, this quasi-fiscal deficit has hovered between 1.5 and 2.5 percent of GDP in the early 1990s, as the Central Bank suffered important operational losses to defend its nominal exchange rate policy and prevent a faster appreciation of the real exchange rate.

The first Concertación government contributed to a reduction in this quasi-fiscal deficit by making extraordinary prepayments to the Central Bank. This allowed the government to support the public sector surplus in a politically viable way, by increasing expenditure through prepayments, because given the social needs of the population, it is politically costly for the government to show a high nonfinancial public sector surplus.

The strength of Chile's public finances is in sharp contrast to the situation of other economies, both in the developed and developing world. Countries with different degrees of development and diverse economic policies, and with governments of different political

TABLE 5

Saving and Investment in the Chilean Economy, 1980–1994 (as a percentage of nominal GDP)

		Savings				
Year	Investment	Foreign	National	NFPS[a]	Central Bank	Private
1980–1989	16.9	7.0	9.9	5.3	2.4	7.0
1990	20.2	2.8	17.4	7.5	–2.1	12.0
1991	18.8	–0.2	19.0	6.6	–1.3	13.6
1992	22.7	1.6	21.1			
1993	25.6	4.6	21.0			
1994	24.3	1.2	23.1			

Source: Central Bank of Chile, Ministry of Finance.
[a]NFPS = nonfinancial public sector (includes Banco del Estado, the only commercial bank owned by the Chilean government).

orientation, are fighting to reduce public deficits. In many cases, they have to reduce significantly social spending and public investment, placing a high welfare cost on those with lower income and negatively affecting long-term growth prospects.

Macroeconomic Performance

Higher interest rates in 1990 had significant real effects in the economy. GDP growth decelerated from 9.9 percent in 1989 to 3.3 percent in 1990, while inflation increased from 21.4 percent to 27.3 percent. The latter was greatly influenced by the effects of the Gulf War, which were quickly passed through to consumers. After high inflation rates in September and October (between 3 percent and 5 percent per month), inflation slowed down in the last two months of 1990 and declined to 18.7 percent in 1991. By 1993, inflation was down to 12.2 percent and declined to single-digit rates (8.9 percent) in 1994 (Table 1).

The rate of fixed capital formation declined from 20 percent of GDP in 1990 to 18.2 percent in 1991 and then rebounded steadily to 25 percent of GDP in 1993.[11] The drop of investment in 1991 was quite moderate; in our view, it responded mostly to the monetary contraction of 1990, while the tax and labor reforms—implemented also in 1990—had little to do with it. Unemployment, after having dropped consistently in the second half of the 1980s from its heights of almost 30 percent in 1982, reached an average of 6.4 percent during 1990–1993 and then increased to 7.8 percent during the 1994 monetary adjustment. At the same time, real wages increased by 3.6 percent on annual average during 1990–1993.

National saving increased steadily, from 17.4 percent of GDP in 1990 to 21 percent in 1993. At these levels, the local savings effort financed, on average, more than 90 percent of domestic investment, compared to less than 50 percent in the 1980s. This helped to reduce the vulnerability of the Chilean economy to external shocks, which traditionally have accounted for a large fraction of the fluctuation that has characterized the country's growth process.

[11]The rate of capital formation in 1993 was the highest recorded in Chilean history.

The external accounts have been very strong too. The balance of payments showed a consistent surplus throughout 1990–1993. The typical pattern has been a large capital account surplus due to important inflows of medium- and long-term capital in the form of credits and direct foreign investment and—to a lesser extent—a short-term capital inflow attracted by an interest rate differential that more than compensated for devaluation expectations and other sources of risk, coupled with a current account deficit. (The exception was 1991, when the current account had a small surplus.) Exports continued to grow fast, and by 1993 they accounted for about 35 percent of real GDP. Foreign exchange reserves surpassed U.S.$10 billion in 1993, equivalent to almost twelve months of imports.

ECONOMIC AND SOCIAL REFORMS

This section deals with the main economic and social reforms carried out after the return to democracy during the Aylwin administration. The focus here is on the tax and labor reforms and on Chile's trade integration to the outside world.

THE TAX REFORM PACKAGE OF 1990

The program of the Concertación government contemplated a tax reform that could increase available resources for social programs in education, health, housing, and nutrition. The government understood that running a fiscal deficit to finance these programs would endanger macroeconomic stability. This could result in increased inflation that disproportionately hurts the poor, who receive an important part of their income in nominal terms and have far less access to inflation-proof assets. Higher inflation could also threaten national saving and investment and, in this way, the prospects for future growth and social welfare.

A large majority of the country shared the objective of helping the less well off. Among those, however, a minority considered that increasing taxes was not the appropriate way to attain this goal. An agreement between the government and the main opposition party, Renovación Nacional (RN), enabled the legislative approval of the tax reform law.

The tax package included, among other measures, a change in *corporate taxation*, whose tax base went from only distributed earnings to total earnings, as was the case until 1988. Its rate was increased from 10 percent to 15 percent for the 1991–1993 period. This increase in corporate taxation was said to be transitory in the tax reform project sent to Congress by the executive as a result of a previous negotiation with RN.

Personal income taxes[12] were raised by narrowing the income tax brackets but without touching tax rates—the highest marginal rate continues to be 50 percent—and the *value added tax* (VAT) was increased from 16 percent to 18 percent (VAT had been 20 percent during most of the military regime and was reduced to 16 percent only in 1988). Both of these tax increases were permanent in the government project; as a result of the negotiation in Congress, they were raised transitorily until 1994.

Additionally, the corporate tax base for "large" agricultural, transportation, and mining companies was changed from presumed income to effective income, leaving small companies in these activities the option of choosing between both tax bases.

[12]The so-called "global complementario" tax, whose base adds up personal income from all sources.

It is estimated that the tax reform package raised fiscal revenue by some U.S.$800 million annually, or almost 2.8 percent of 1991 GDP, and the government was committed to spend all these extra resources in social programs.

Critics argued that the tax reform would reduce investment, but evidence in this respect does not support their claim. A drop in investment from 20.2 percent of GDP in 1990 to 18.8 percent in 1991 can be mostly attributed to a lagged response to the contractionary monetary policy of 1990. As mentioned, investment recovered to reach record levels in 1993 and 1994 (25 percent of GDP on average).

Small- and medium-sized companies, however, may have been hurt by the increased cost of using retained earnings to finance investment brought by the tax reform, because of their restricted access to financial markets. To offset part of this effect, the reform allowed firms to discount up to 2 percent of the value of *new* productive investment from their corporate tax base as a way to stimulate investment independently of its financing. Its low rate (2 percent) and a maximum deduction of about U.S.$16,000 in 1990, however, made the effect of this incentive quite marginal.

There are also good arguments for a positive effect of the tax reform on investment. First of all, the rate increase was quite moderate and still left Chile as one of the countries with the lowest rate of corporate taxation. Second, the government made a commitment not to pursue further tax increases during its tenure after this reform was approved. Third, increased spending in health, education, and nutrition may be a form of investment and may mean improved capital over the medium to long term. Finally, an increase in social spending, if used efficiently, would allow a larger proportion of Chileans to feel the benefits of the economic model, thereby increasing the popular support for policy continuity, which is expected to have a positive impact on private investment.

Other critics argued that an increase in the VAT would raise inflation and thus would have a regressive social impact. The reform, however, did not have a significant effect on inflation. True, the VAT has a proportionately greater effect on lower-income families who consume a higher share of their income, but to evaluate the impact of a higher VAT on the poor, one needs to take into account also the share of higher spending—which this tax increase allowed—transferred to these families.

Before the agreed reduction of the different tax rates increased in 1990, an important debate arose between the government and the opposition concerning the convenience of maintaining the current tax rates. The government was in favor of maintaining the tax reform, arguing that it was not possible to sustain the pattern of public spending already committed (a large part of which is permanent) and at the same time reduce the tax rates in 1994 without generating a fiscal deficit. The opposition was in favor of reducing the tax rates on the grounds that the expansion in economic activity over the past couple of years allows for a reduction in tax rates while maintaining the social spending effort and without generating a significant fiscal deficit. In the end, the tax increases became permanent, which is not a surprising result.

Reforms to the Labor Legislation

By the end of 1990, a broad agreement was reached about the need to introduce changes in the labor legislation. The government had two major goals with this reform. On the one hand, it aimed to balance negotiating power between employers and employees, which the authorities considered to be biased in favor of employers. On the other hand, the government wanted to legitimize the labor legislation.

As mentioned earlier, the labor reform implemented in 1979 was largely opposed by workers. Their main criticisms were that it (1) repressed unions,[13] (2) restricted collective bargaining, (3) biased the relative bargaining power against workers,[14] and (4) allowed for arbitrary dismissal—workers could be dismissed without expression of cause and without appeal—and for a low severance payment.

The reform that was finally approved by Congress represented an intermediate position between the old law and the original project of the executive, as the government had to negotiate it with the main opposition party. This negotiation induced moderation in the reform.

The labor reform eliminated the right of employers to fire workers with no expression of cause but allowed a general cause of "needs of the company." Severance payments remained at one month of salary per year of work in the company, but the maximum was increased from five to eleven months[15] (there was no maximum in the original reform project) and workers could appeal in court. In case firing was declared unjustified by the courts, the severance payment had to be raised by 20 percent. Additionally, severance payments in case of firing from the seventh year on can now be substituted (by agreement of the parties) for an all-event payment; that is, severance can be paid if the worker is fired or if he or she quits.

The other reforms to the labor law applied to collective bargaining and unionization. Groups of nonunionized workers were allowed to participate in collective bargaining, and negotiations started to be allowed at the industry level only by common agreement between employers and employees. Before the reform, negotiations were allowed only at the firm level. The reform also eliminated the prohibition to form union associations, extended the objectives of union organizations, gave more protection to labor unions, and increased the financing of union activities. On the other hand, the new legislation went back to allowing unlimited strikes, thus eliminating the 60-day maximum.

Critics said that the labor reform would increase strike activity, push up real wages beyond productivity, and maybe raise unemployment. The evidence, however, points the other way. Days lost to strikes declined since the reform, and the unemployment rate declined to less than 5 percent in 1993, the lowest in more than two decades. Also, real wage adjustments in collective bargaining processes have declined from 4.5 percent in 1990 to between 2 percent and 3 percent in 1991–1993 and to less than 2 percent in 1994 (Table 6).

TRADE POLICY AND INTEGRATION TO THE WORLD ECONOMY[16]

Since the mid-1970s, Chile has pursued a strategy of global trade liberalization, aiming to integrate the country into the world economy without making any distinctions among

[13] During the 1980s, the unionization rate in Chile was only 11 percent, compared to 18 percent during 1965–1970 and 29 percent during 1971–1973.

[14] This law established that strikes should have a maximum duration of 60 days. If the strike was not over after 60 days, the contracts of striking workers were automatically terminated, losing them not only their jobs but also their severance payments.

[15] The idea was to give dismissed workers enough income to subsist during the average unemployment period (eight months at the time); this was important because Chile lacked an unemployment insurance program.

[16] For further details on this topic, see Larraín and Assael (1992).

TABLE 6

Initial Real Wage Adjustments Agreed to in Collective Bargaining (as a percentage)

PERIOD	LABOR UNIONS	GROUPS	TOTAL
1990			
January–March	6.1	4.9	6.0
April–June	3.7	3.7	3.7
July–September	4.6	2.1	4.1
October–December	3.5	2.9	3.4
1991			
January–March	3.2	2.5	3.1
April–June	3.0	4.7	3.5
July–September	1.4	0.8	1.3
October–December	1.6	0.8	1.5
1992			
January–March	2.9	1.7	2.7
April–June	2.0	2.9	2.1
July–September	2.6	3.4	2.7
October–December	3.0	2.1	2.9
1993			
January–March	3.0	2.3	2.8
April–June	2.7	3.9	3.0
July–September	1.9	2.4	2.0
October–December	1.7	0.3	1.5
1994			
January–March	1.9	1.1	1.8
April–June	1.7	0.6	1.5
July–September	1.6	1.8	1.7
October–December	1.9	1.4	1.9

Source: Annual Report to Congress delivered by the president of the Central Bank of Chile, various years.

countries or regions. This strategy has been immensely successful. Chile's trade has been greatly diversified, both in terms of the composition of exports and in terms of trading partners. In the early 1990s, Asia and Europe accounted each for about 30 percent of total Chilean exports, while Latin America and North America accounted for between 16 percent and 18 percent. Copper, which accounted for almost 80 percent of Chile's exports in the early 1970s, was down to less than 40 percent of total exports, in spite of increased production from new private mines. Overall, exports had increased dramatically. From about 15 percent of GDP in 1965, they had risen to around 35 percent of real GDP for 1990–1994, a ratio similar to that of South Korea. And the export sector became the main engine of economic growth in the country.

In spite of the success of unilateral integration, the country started to pursue free trade agreements (FTAs) with several countries of the continent. FTAs were signed first with

Mexico (which established a gradual decline in bilateral tariffs to 0 percent in 1996 and an elimination of all nontariff barriers), then with Colombia and Venezuela. The government soon set its sights on an FTA with the United States or on integration to the North American Free Trade Agreement (NAFTA), although by the end of the Aylwin administration negotiations had not yet started.

Chile did not abandon the goal of global trade integration. In fact, the country's flat import tariff was unilaterally cut from 15 percent to 11 percent in June 1991, and no significant nontariff barriers applied. But the trade strategy shifted emphasis toward bilateral agreements, provided that they do not result in increased barriers with the outside world.[17]

There were several reasons for the emphasis on FTAs. First, it responded to a worldwide phenomenon, the prospect of large trading blocks in Europe (and maybe in Asia) and to the U.S. Initiative for the Americas. Although it might not be optimal for a country like Chile to sign FTAs if other countries were not following this strategy, it may be optimal to do so if the world is moving toward the formation of FTAs (Krugman 1991). Second, although global free trade was recognized as the first best, there was growing frustration with slow progress in the General Agreement on Tariffs and Trade (GATT) multilateral negotiations, particularly in the Uruguay Round. Third, if Chile intended to liberalize trade anyway, bilateral agreements were a way to obtain something in return, especially when starting from low tariff levels and no nontariff barriers. Nonetheless, on our view, FTAs must be understood as a complement to, not a substitute for, global trade integration.

To deepen its integration in the world economy, Chile needed to gain increased market access, especially in large, developed countries. FTAs may cooperate in this task. The net welfare implications of bilateralism are ambiguous and mainly depend on the characteristics of the integration partners and on the international context in which the FTA is carried out. The different costs and benefits of this type of strategy should be taken into account when choosing trading partners. A recent empirical evaluation of an FTA with the United States (Coeymans and Larraín 1995) shows important gains to Chile of such an agreement, especially on the investment front.

At the end of the Aylwin administration, Chile was evaluating an important number of FTAs with Latin American countries and the United States, but the country lacked a well-specified trade strategy vis-à-vis FTAs. This led to arbitrariness in the evaluation of such agreements and to increased uncertainty on the relative profitability of different productive activities, which could have a detrimental effect on investment and growth.

CONCLUSIONS: CONTINUITY, CHANGE, AND FUTURE CHALLENGES FOR THE CHILEAN ECONOMY

Chile's economic performance since the mid-1980's has been outstanding. By the end of the first Concertación government in March 1994, the country had undergone one decade of uninterrupted growth of an annual average of almost around 7 percent, inflation was on the way to single-digit rates, and the external position of the country was extremely solid. These achievements occurred during a transition from military rule to democracy,

[17]This was a complicated aspect of the Mercado Común del Sur (MERCOSUR), a customs union (not an FTA) that by the end of the Aylwin administration had not yet agreed on its common external tariff.

in an international environment of very low growth and relatively depressed international trade.

Several reasons account for this success. The strong initial position of the economy at the end of the 1980s, with macroeconomic stability and a completed structural transformation, was no doubt a crucial asset. Another major factor was a broad political consensus on economic matters. Of course, good initial conditions and broad consensus are necessary but not sufficient. Highly responsible conduct by the economic authorities also deserves important credit.

In the end, there was more continuity than change in the economic policies applied during the first Concertación government. This is not meant as a criticism. It was sensible to preserve most of the economic policies of the previous regime, while significantly improving the social effort, thus legitimizing the free market economic model. Therefore, we regard the tax and labor reforms as important, positive, and moderate policy changes.

Despite a very healthy economic outlook, there were substantial challenges ahead for the country going into the mid-1990s. At the level of macroeconomic policies, Chile experienced difficulties in managing domestic stabilization policy in a context of large capital mobility and low international interest rates—inconsistent with internal equilibrium. This resulted in increased investment spending, deterioration of the trade balance, appreciation of the local currency and the stock market, accumulation of external reserves in order to prevent further currency appreciation, and a need for sterilization to avoid the inflationary impact of massive purchases of foreign reserves by the Central Bank. Reserve accumulation and sterilization led to important losses at the Central Bank and the requirement of maintaining high interest rates, which attract more capital.

Relatively high real interest rates in Chile (as compared to world rates) were necessary to keep aggregate demand in check so that the widely shared objective of reducing inflation to single-digit rates may be achieved by the mid-1990s. A more ambitious goal of achieving world inflation rates looks feasible only in the medium term, that is, closer to the end of the century.

At a more structural level, Chile faces two overriding and closely linked challenges: consolidating a strong and stable economic growth path, and the elimination of poverty, a condition that still affected around 30 percent of the Chilean population in 1994. Succeeding in the latter goal will take time even with the best policies. But it clearly requires the preservation of strong economic growth, because eliminating poverty will be impossible in a stagnant or slowly growing economy.

Sustaining high rates of growth (in the order of 7 percent) requires an effort in maintaining the fast pace of productivity gains and probably increasing Chile's investment rates from 25 percent of GDP. Higher investment can count on foreign saving, but up to a limit. Foreign saving of up to 3 percent to 4 percent of GDP per year is sustainable in an economy such as Chile. Thus, higher investment would require additional domestic saving. The country's national savings rate of 22 percent of GDP—on average—in 1993–1994 shows a healthy improvement over traditional savings rates in Chile, but still needed to increase in order to support investment rates exceeding 25 percent of GDP on a sustainable basis.

Another challenge for the country was to deepen its integration into the world economy in the trade of goods, services, and capital. To this end, the country unilaterally reduced import tariffs from 15 percent to 11 percent in 1991, incorporated the country in a number of free trade agreements, and was studying a few additional FTAs that would help Chile gain access to some important markets. Bilateral deals, however, should be viewed as a complement to global liberalization, as the ultimate goal is to integrate Chile to the world as a whole.

In spite of these many challenges, the perspectives for Chile look quite promising at the end of the twentieth century and into the new millennium. Chile's structural economic reforms were mainly in place when democracy returned. The new democratic government had the sensible approach of providing policy continuity, while at the same time stressing urgent social matters. And the country surprised the world with one of the smoothest political transitions in memory from authoritarian rule to democracy. Credit for this goes not only to the government and the opposition, who were prime actors in the transition, but to the maturity of the Chilean people, the true force behind those actors.

BIBLIOGRAPHY

Calvo, G., L. Leiderman, and C. Reinhart. 1993. Capital inflows and real exchange rate appreciation in Latin America: The role of external factors. *IMF Staff Papers*, Vol. 40.

Castañeda, T. 1990. *Para combatir la pobreza: Política social y descentralización en Chile durante los 80*. Santiago: Centro de Estudios Públicos.

Coeymans, J. E., and F. Larraín. 1994. Efectos de un acuerdo de libre comercio entre Chile y Estados Unidos: Un enfoque de equilbrio general. *Cuadernos de Economica,* Universidad Católica de Chile (December).

Cortázar, R., and J. Marshall. 1980. Indice de precios al consumidor en Chile: 1970–78. *Colección Estudios CIEPLAN* (November).

Dornbusch, R. 1990. The new classical macroeconomics and stabilization policy. *American Economic Review* 80:143–47.

________. 1989. Real exchange rates and macroeconomics: A selective survey. *Scandinavian Journal of Economics* 2:401–32.

Dornbusch, R., and S. Edwards. 1991. *The macroeconomics of populism in Latin America*. Chicago: University of Chicago Press.

Edwards, S., and A. Cox-Edwards. 1987. *Monetarism and liberalization: The Chilean experiment*. Cambridge, MA: Ballinger.

Krugman, P. 1991. Is bilateralism bad? In *International trade and trade policy*, edited by E. Helpman and A. Razin. Cambridge: MIT Press.

Labán, R., and F. Larraín. 1993. The Chilean experience with capital mobility. In *The Chilean economy: Policy lessons and challenges*, edited by B. Bosworth, R. Dornbusch, and R. Labán. Washington: The Brookings Institution.

Labán, R., and F. Larraín. 1995. Continuity, change, and the political economy of transition in Chile. In *Reform, recovery and growth*, edited by R. Dornbusch and S. Edwards. Chicago: University of Chicago Press.

Labán, R., and H. C. Wolf. 1993. Large-scale privatization in transition economies. *American Economic Review* 83:1199–1210.

Larraín, F. 1991a. The economic challenges of democratic development. In *The struggle for democracy in Chile, 1982–1990*, edited by P. Drake and I. Jaksic. Lincoln: University of Nebraska Press.

________. 1991b. Public sector behavior in highly indebted country: The contrasting Chilean experience. In *The public sector and the Latin American crisis,* edited by F. Larraín and M. Selowsky. San Francisco: ICS Press.

Larraín, F., and P. Assael. 1992. Integración comercial selectiva: El caso de Chile. *Estudios Públicos* (46). Santiago: Centro de Estudios Públicos.

Larraín, F. and A. Velasco. 1990. Can swaps solve the debt crisis? Lessons from the Chilean experience. Princeton Studies in International Finance, no. 69. December. Princeton, NJ: Princeton University Press.

Larraín, F., and R. Vergara. 1993. Investment and macroeconomic adjustment: The case of East Asia. In *Striving for growth after adjustment: The role of capital formation*, edited by L. Servén and A. Solimano. Washington: World Bank.

Marfán, M. 1992. Reestimación del PGB potencial en Chile: Implicancias para el crecimiento. CIEPLAN: Corporación de Investigaciones Económicas para Latinoamérica. Mimeo.

Meller, P. 1992. The Chilean case. In *Latin American adjustment: How much has happened?* edited by J. Williamson. Washington: Institute for International Economics.

________. 1991. Adjustment and social costs in Chile during the 1980s. *World Development* 19 (11): 1545–61.

Pindyck, R. 1991. Irreversibility, uncertainty, and investment. *Journal of Economic Literature* 29 (3): 1110–48.

Sachs, J. 1990. Social conflict and populist policies in Latin America. In *Labour relations and economic performance*, edited by R. Brunetta and C. Dell'Aringa. London: Macmillan.

Torche, A. 1987. Distribuir el ingreso para satisfacer las necesidades básicas. In *Desarrollo económico en democracia*, edited by F. Larraín. Santiago, Chile: Ediciones Universidad Católica.

Reading 13

Economic Reform in Colombia

Miguel Urrutia
Central Bank of Colombia

As so often is the case, liberalization of Colombian trade, foreign exchange, and capital control liberalization do not fit the standard Latin American pattern. Colombian liberalization did not take place as a reaction to an economic or foreign exchange crisis, nor at the start of an administration, when its popularity would be at its highest. There was no great coherence or unanimity within the government in favor of liberalization. Nevertheless, the reforms, after an initial tentative start in the Barco administration, became coherent and radical in the first two years of the Gaviria administration (1990–94).

One of the distinguishing features of Colombian economic policy in the last two decades is its continuity and the lack of enthusiasm of policymakers and economists for economic experiments. The depth of the liberalizing reforms of 1989–91 is therefore surprising.

This paper is divided into three sections. The first shows the depth of the reforms, the second discusses the political and social basis for support of the reforms and for the pressures that made putting the reforms on the policy agenda necessary, and the third section draws conclusions about the likelihood that the economic liberalization will become permanent.

The Reforms

The most noticeable area of liberalization has been that of trade policy. Sebastian Edwards (1992) has an illustrative table on the economic opening in Latin America, presented here as table 1. The first column shows that tariffs plus paratariffs[1] in Colombia averaged 83 percent in 1985, the highest level of protection in the region. In 1992 these had been reduced to 6.7 percent, the second lowest in the region. Nontariff barriers went from 73.2 percent coverage, the highest in the region, to 1 percent. The range of the tariff rates also shrank dramatically.

[1] In Colombia the major paratariff was the opportunity cost of deposits frozen until an import payment could be authorized.

TABLE 1

Reduction of Barriers to Trade in Latin America, Selected Countries, 1985–92 (percentages)

	Tariff Protection (Tariffs Plus Paratariffs, Unweighted Averages)		Coverage of Nontariff Barriers (Unweighted Averages)		Range of Import Tariffs					
					1980s			Current		
Countries	1985	1991–92	1985–87	1991–92	Year	Minimum	Maximum	Year	Minimum	Maximum
Argentina	28.0	15.0	31.9	8.0	1987	0.0	55.0	1991	0.0	22.0
Bolivia	20.0	8.0	25.0	0.0	1985	0.0	20.0	1991	5.0	10.0
Brazil	80.0	21.1	35.3	10.0	1987	0.0	105.0	1992	0.0	65.0
Chile	36.0	11.0	10.1	0.0	1987	0.0	20.0	1992	11.0	11.0
Colombia	83.0	6.7	73.2	1.0	1986	0.0	200.0	1991	0.0	15.0
Costa Rica	92.0	16.0	0.8	0.0	1986	1.0	100.0	1992	5.0	20.0
Ecuador	50.0	18.0	59.3	n.a.	1986	0.0	290.0	1991	2.0	40.0
Guatemala	50.0	19.0	7.4	6.0	1986	1.0	100.0	1992	5.0	20.0
Mexico	34.0	4.0	12.7	20.0	1985	0.0	100.0	1992	0.0	20.0
Nicaragua	54.0	n.a.	27.8	n.a.	1986	1.0	100.0	1990	0.0	10.0
Paraguay	71.7	16.0	9.9	0.0	1984	0.0	44.0	1991	3.0	86.0
Peru	64.0	15.0	53.4	0.0	1987	0.0	120.0	1992	5.0	15.0
Uruguay	32.0	12.0	14.1	0.0	1986	10.0	45.0	1992	10.0	30.0
Venezuela	30.0	17.0	44.1	5.0	1987	0.0	135.0	1991	0.0	50.0

Source: Edwards (1992).

Another area of liberalization was foreign exchange transactions. Since 1967, Colombia had had foreign exchange controls that covered all foreign transactions. The sale of foreign exchange income from exports of goods and services was mandatory within a short period of the export being made and at an official exchange rate, and all purchases of foreign exchange had to be made and justified at the Colombian Central Bank. It was illegal for Colombians to have accounts or investments abroad, except when specifically approved, case by case, by the Planning Department. Foreign currency for travel abroad was limited to a fixed yearly amount, and all payments abroad had to be backed by an import license or service contract. By 1992, Colombians could freely buy foreign currencies for investment abroad, and there were no restrictions on foreign investment in Colombia.

The restrictive foreign investment legislation in place since 1967, and even more limiting legislation in existence since Colombia accepted Andean Group Foreign Investment Decision 24 in the early 1970s, was also reformed, and all foreign investment was authorized with almost no restrictions. In particular, Congress allowed foreigners to buy and invest in Colombian banks. All limits on profit remittances, royalty payments, and payments for know-how were also eliminated.

As a complement to the general trade liberalization, the Gaviria government also led an ambitious regional integration effort in the Andean Group. By 1992, free trade with zero tariffs was achieved with Venezuela and Ecuador. In addition to the direct benefits they expected this trade integration to bring, government officials believed that free trade with Venezuela would make it necessary to maintain a more general trade opening if Colombia wanted to avoid very serious economic distortions.

Liberalization of trade and foreign exchange transactions was accompanied by legislation to free the labor market. Complete job security after 10 years was abolished and replaced with a steeper severance pay schedule, and companies were given the alternative of hiring skilled and managerial workers with contracts that excluded fringe benefits. The expensive *cesantia*—a yearly bonus indexed to pay increases that could be withdrawn periodically without loss of indexing and be paid in full upon severance—was deindexed and made investible in private pension funds on a yearly basis. This last measure greatly decreased the cost to employees of changing jobs and to employers of having low turnover rates.

A financial reform law was also passed in 1990, and in 1989–90 many forced investments and interest rate ceilings in the financial sector were abolished or phased out.

As a complement to the liberalizing reforms, two revenue-enhancing tax reforms were carried out which, among other things, compensated for the decrease in customs taxes caused by trade liberalization.

Although Colombia had fewer public enterprises than other Latin American countries, during the Barco and Gaviria administrations some of the banks the government absorbed in the financial crisis of the early 1980s were reprivatized, and the state stake in the automobile manufacturing companies was sold, as well as other companies owned in whole or in part by the state industrial corporation (IFI). Legislation was passed privatizing the ports and the railroads, at the cost of paying workers in those enterprises generous severance settlements and creating endowed funds to guarantee their pensions.

A successful strike in 1992 on the part of telecommunications workers froze the privatization of public services in 1992, and this included state enterprises in water, electricity, and telephones. In addition, many of these enterprises belong to the municipalities, and it is not clear that local politicians are prepared to give up this source of clientelistic support.

Nevertheless, the private sector has been allowed to build new electricity generation capacity and cellular phone networks. Oil production will remain in the hands of joint ventures between foreign companies and the state oil company. In the Barco government, it was also decided that private foreign companies could exploit coal and other minerals without having a state company as a partner.

The constitutional reform of 1991, along with enabling legislation passed in 1992, has given the Colombian Central Bank complete independence from the government and authority over monetary and foreign exchange policy. The five permanent members of the bank's board are appointed by the president for four-year terms, but any one administration can change only two members. The minister of finance is the sixth member of the board, but he does not have a qualified vote or veto power. The president of the central bank is appointed by the board, also for four-year terms, with a maximum term of 12 years. The bank was made responsible for monetary, credit, and foreign exchange policy.

In addition, the constitutional reform of 1991 accelerated the decentralization of social services toward local governments, and in the last decade, after 100 years,[2] appointed mayors and governors have been replaced by elected officials.

Most of these reforms occurred during the last two years of the Barco government (1986–90) and the first two years of the Gaviria government, which started in August 1990. Eduardo Lora (1991a) gives a good description of the economic reforms carried out in 1989–90: trade liberalization, labor reform, exchange controls reform, the first tax reform, reform of the foreign investment regime, financial sector reform, and privatization of the ports and railroads. In 1991 and 1992 the tariff reductions were accelerated, exchange controls were further liberalized, the central bank was made independent, and the second tax reform was passed in Congress.

Few outside observers realize the depth of the reforms that took place in Colombia in these four years. In Colombia, there has also been no feeling of having lived through a major economic revolution probably because the reforms had become inevitable, and in some ways, legislation simply recognized the reality that economic actors were increasingly having to address.

The Politics of Trade Liberalization

For most of the postwar period, Congress has delegated to the executive the power to change tariffs and nontariff barriers. Therefore, the politics of trade and tariff policy have not involved Congress in a major way. This section, therefore, describes the capacity of the executive arm of the state to change a policy for which it is solely responsible. Congress only intervenes in the approval of international treaties that involve special trade aspects, but even then it gives the government wide powers to change tariffs within the parameters established in the treaty. Congress intervened in the process of ratification of the Andean Pact and the Foreign Investment Decision 24 of the Andean Pact in the early 1970s but has not intervened in many of the major changes made within the pact during the last two decades.

[2]The constitution of 1886 allowed for elected municipal and state assemblies, but with mayors and governors appointed by the elected president. Both houses of Congress were elected.

Although there was an aborted liberalization episode in 1966, we start the story of trade liberalization one decade later. In 1975, on the initiative of Rodrigo Botero, then minister of finance, meetings were held between the technocratic economic team in the cabinet[3] and President Alfonso Lopez. The decision to liberalize trade was taken. Despite the fact that the decision was made at the highest level, and with presidential support, almost no liberalization took place.

The announcement that some goods produced nationally were going to be put on the free import list generated very substantial opposition from the National Association of Industries, and in particular by the industrialists of Medellin, the traditional industrial city of Colombia, who were quite critical of the government after the 1974 tax reform. The opposition from industrialists was strong and unanimous, since most saw a protected national market as the source of growth. In addition, Antonio Urdinola was then head of the Foreign Trade Institute (INCOMEX), and he was a convinced interventionist. A brilliant economist who had pursued graduate studies at Harvard, he believed then and still believes now that industrial policy must be dealt with case by case. He therefore liberated imports of irrelevant items and maintained nontariff barriers when local industrialists complained of unfair competition or of potential displacement of local production by imports. By then, the opposition to the Lopez administration on the part of industrialists and the upper classes in general was substantial due to the effects of tax reform, which included confiscatory death duties and capital gains taxes without inflation adjustment. In that environment, Lopez allowed Urdinola to calm things down by not implementing the trade opening, a position that his pragmatic bosses, Ministers of Development Jorge Ramirez and Diego Moreno, found politically attractive.

Around 1980, Jaime Garcia Parra, as minister of finance, also announced a trade liberalization in the government of Julio Cesar Turbay. Opposition by the Colombian private sector was again substantial, and the bureaucracy of the Foreign Trade Institute and the minister of development (who was from Medellin and closely allied to the region's industrialists) again liberalized only what did not create undue competition for national producers. In addition, in the early 1980s the peso was clearly overvalued, and when international reserves started to decline as foreign credit dried up after the debt crisis, the enthusiasm for trade liberalization disappeared.

The liberalization policy of the early 1980s contained many mistakes common in the frustrated liberalization episodes in other countries. The currency was overvalued, and tariffs and nontariff barriers were decreased where they were highest: in consumer goods. The result was a rapid increase in the import of consumer durables, especially automobiles, and this makes it difficult to sustain liberalization, both due to the rapid drawing down of international reserves and to the difficulty of justifying a policy that diminishes investment in machinery and equipment and that seems to benefit primarily wealthy consumers. Add to this the Latin American debt crisis, and the return to controls was inevitable.

A return to import controls was part of the Betancur government's adjustment to the balance of payments crisis. In addition to the reintroduction of import controls, Minister of Finance Roberto Junguito accelerated the crawling devaluation to produce a substantial real devaluation and got Congress to pass a tax reform that brought down the fiscal deficit to

[3]This included Botero; Jorge Ramírez Ocampo, minister of development; and Miguel Urrutia, then director of the Planning Department.

TABLE 2

Colombia: Products on Free Import List and Average Tariffs, 1950–91 (percentages)

YEAR	LIBERALIZATION INDEX[a]	AVERAGE TARIFF	YEAR	LIBERALIZATION INDEX[a]	AVERAGE TARIFF
1950	65.00	17.02	1971	28.30	13.90
1951	75.00	25.01	1972	28.20	14.70
1952	80.00	19.42	1973	31.20	15.70
1953	85.00	21.01	1974	43.60	12.70
1954	90.00	21.75	1975	42.80	14.70
1955	85.00	23.76	1976	39.80	14.90
1956	77.84	21.07	1977	41.20	15.60
1957	70.91	16.67	1978	42.80	16.00
1958	57.76	18.27	1979	44.40	18.00
1959	61.02	18.47	1980	44.00	17.80
1960	59.91	17.78	1981	52.20	18.10
1961	60.61	16.43	1982	54.70	18.40
1962	52.65	15.51	1983	41.40	18.40
1963	37.62	13.68	1984	21.10	17.60
1964	37.30	12.70	1985	14.80	21.10
1965	15.12	15.83	1986	42.40	25.70
1966	56.36	22.74	1987	45.30	27.00
1967	3.78	16.05	1988	40.50	26.20
1968	17.00	14.40	1989	40.40	24.40
1969	17.20	15.00	1990	58.00	23.50
1970	19.00	16.00	1991	100.00	18.00

[a]Percentage of items on free import list.

Source: National Accounts-DANE.

manageable levels. The Junguito adjustment was successful in discouraging imports and promoting nontraditional exports, and it received the blessing of the International Monetary Fund (IMF) and the Federal Reserve, which in turn made possible the negotiation of "voluntary" loan packages from the international commercial banks and fast disbursing loans from the World Bank. The Colombian foreign exchange and debt crisis was thus solved in less than 18 months.

The index of liberalization in table 2, which measures the proportion of products on the free import list, shows the story of import licenses and import controls since 1967: the slight liberalization of 1974–75, the Garcia Parra liberalization of 1981–82, and the return to controls in 1984–85.

The IMF and World Bank's "certificate of good behavior," however, was conditioned on a move toward foreign trade liberalization. Colombia, therefore, negotiated with the World Bank a large, fast-disbursing trade adjustment loan, which included the commitment to liberalize trade. The policy, designed by Luis Jorge Garay, the adviser to the minister of finance and trade negotiator, turned out to be too clever. He put on the free import list a large portion of the items in the trade list but was careful not to liberalize imports of items that were produced locally. (Note in table 2 the increase in the index of trade liberalization in 1986.) The World Bank's conditions for disbursement of loans were therefore duly met, but when the World Bank staff realized what had happened, relations between that institution and the Colombian technocrats seriously deteriorated. The World Bank became very difficult with Colombia, despite the fact that it was the only major country in the region that was servicing its external debt. It was also the only country that was not even rhetorically supporting the conditionality of the emerging "Washington consensus." Since for political reasons President Belisario Betancur had publicly made it a point of honor not to sign a stand-by agreement with the IMF, this possibility was also closed to the Barco government, and for this reason the World Bank loans and reports to the commercial banks were crucial for Colombia's management of its foreign debt problem.

World Bank pressure for trade liberalization built up considerably as the Barco administration entered its second year, and obtaining commercial bank finance became harder and harder as the international debt crisis dragged on. In addition, some Colombian exports were running into protectionism in the United States, and US customs agents were harassing Colombian exporters in apparent retaliation against Colombian illegal drug exports. As a result of these problems, a trade discussion mechanism was set up with the Office of the US Trade Representative, and in those discussions additional pressure was brought to bear for trade liberalization in Colombia. In addition, the Barco government proposed trade preferences for Colombia as compensation for the human and economic costs the country was experiencing due to its war on the drug cartels, and the US government was surprisingly receptive to the idea, which later became the Andean Trade Initiative. These trade negotiations seemed to promise important benefits in the export area, but some measure of trade liberalization seemed to be the prerequisite.

By the late 1980s, exporters had become a very strong pressure group that included some industrialists (textiles, leather products, shoes, cement) but also the progressive members of the landed gentry who exported flowers and fruits and agribusinesses that exported bananas and the products of shrimp farms. In addition, there was a consensus among politicians and technocrats that the growth of nontraditional exports was a prerequisite for sustained economic growth. In the late '80s, even Cepalinos such as Antonio Urdinola had become convinced that, due to the pressure of international creditors and developed-country trade negotiators, Colombia could not handle its foreign debt and expand export markets without some liberalization of imports.

In addition, the slow growth of the economy during the 1980s had convinced many industrialists that the internal market was no longer a dynamic source of growth. Furthermore, they had realized that one cost of protection was the necessity to produce an excessively diverse range of products. If no textile imports were allowed, the large mills had to produce any sort of cloth demanded by clothing manufacturers. If they did not, the latter could effectively pressure the government to allow the import of products not produced locally, and there was no way of controlling contraband once the first textile licenses were given. The result was that a company such as Fabricato had to produce more than 3,000 types of cloth in the early 1980s, and these short production runs raised costs substantially. Around 1981, the management of the large textile companies in Medellin calculated that 30 percent of all textile consumption in the country was contraband.

Contraband has been an important activity in Colombia since the 18th century, but the illegal drug trade of the 1980s facilitated it, since contraband is the natural way to launder dollars. Merchandise paid for in cash in Miami or Colon is sold for pesos in Colombia. Because of contraband, the Colombian economy has always been to some extent open. Two anecdotes illustrate the contraband phenomenon (Urrutia 1982). By comparing household surveys and statistics on imports and production of color TV sets, I estimated that in 1982 at least 61 percent of all sets had been brought into the country illegally. Contraband of items with high value per kilo is understandable, but at one point there appeared to be contraband of construction steel from Venezuela, a product that can only be transported on the largest flatbed trucks. It was also found that in 1980, air travelers to the United States carried an average of 20 more kilos on the return trip. I estimated that this "quasi-legal" contraband may have been worth $500 million, compared with $1,627 million of declared nontraditional exports in that year. Traditional protection seemed to have lost much of its effectiveness.

For all these reasons, when the Barco government started to discuss trade liberalization, there was no unanimity at the National Association of Industrialists. Although its president and the Medellin chapter remained protectionist, the Bogotá and Cali chapters seemed to have a majority of members who were for economic liberalization in general and less state intervention. The latter were joined by industrialists who sold both in the local and foreign markets. Some local and transnational corporations also saw the possibility of improving profits by distributing imported products together with locally produced goods through their local sales networks.

The Barco government also decreased opposition to liberalization by setting up an infinitely complicated auction *cum* quota system for the import of products that had been on the prohibited imports list.[4] With the argument that nobody had any idea what the tariff equivalent of the nontariff barriers was, a system was developed in which import licenses would be awarded to the bidder willing to offer the highest tariff equivalent for goods previously on the forbidden or "difficult license" list. The system gave industrialists assurance that there would not be a flood of imports, and this disarmed some private and academic opposition to the new policy. Furthermore, Finance Minister Luis Fernando Alarcon accelerated the rate of devaluation via the crawling peg in 1989–90 to accompany the liberalization with a real devaluation (table 3).

The first auctions were complicated and took place with a significantly undervalued currency. There were few bidders that proposed higher tariffs than those on the books, and the pressure to import the auctioned items was often below the limited quotas established by the cautious trade bureaucracy. Given the limited bidding at the auctions and the evidence that there had been a lot of water in the tariffs and nontariff barriers, the new government of President Gaviria was able to eliminate the auctions and carry out a straightforward elimination of all import licenses and a gradual reduction of tariffs. This further policy step was encouraged by the fact that international reserves were growing rapidly (since the central bank was obliged to purchase all foreign exchange), and creating what appeared to be a dangerous increase in the monetary base.

During the presidential campaign, the team of economic advisers to candidate Gaviria had agreed that the new government should deepen trade liberalization, but it was to be a gradual process. This policy obtained the support of the economists on the interventionist

[4]The liberalization was scheduled to take five years. The complex auction system is described in Maria Mercedes de Martinez, *Memoria al Congreso Nacional: 1989–90.*

TABLE 3

Colombia: Selected Economic Indicators, 1970–92

Year	GNP in Millions of Dollars	Nonoil Exports as a Share of GNP	Nontraditional Exports as a Share of GNP	Real Exchange Rate Index (1986=100)	Percentage Change in Index	International Reserves in Months of Imports of Goods	International Reserves in Months of Imports of Goods and Services
1970	7,199	9.77	3.13	88.60		1.0	0.6
1971	7,821	8.61	3.31	88.52	–0.09	0.9	0.5
1972	8,672	10.36	4.47	84.20	–4.88	3.6	2.0
1973	10,287	11.46	5.50	84.94	0.88	5.6	3.2
1974	12,369	10.89	5.41	83.61	–1.57	3.0	1.9
1975	11,385	14.13	7.14	86.91	3.95	3.9	2.3
1976	12,269	17.50	6.84	79.96	–8.00	7.9	4.8
1977	14,646	17.67	6.75	75.25	–5.89	10.7	6.6
1978	17,452	17.76	6.25	75.00	–0.33	11.3	7.4
1979	19,736	17.21	6.20	70.63	–5.83	16.2	10.6
1980	24,450	17.16	6.82	73.06	3.44	14.8	10.0
1981	25,712	13.08	6.25	70.64	–3.31	14.0	9.1
1982	25,550	12.01	5.37	65.55	–7.21	10.8	6.9
1983	26,068	10.41	3.95	67.28	2.64	8.3	5.1
1984	27,503	11.56	4.00	71.88	6.84	5.4	3.1
1985	32,236	10.46	3.49	92.35	28.48	6.9	3.7
1986	34,943	13.49	3.90	100.00	8.28	12.6	6.1
1987	36,264	10.79	4.29	102.49	2.49	11.2	5.6
1988	38,307	11.37	4.85	102.61	0.12	10.4	5.7
1989	41,526	11.15	5.16	104.66	2.00	10.7	5.6
1990	47,106	10.89	5.65	117.46	12.23	11.0	5.9
1991	45,733	13.22	7.74	114.05	–2.90	17.3	8.9
1992(est.)	49,476	11.65	6.91	108.58	–4.80	17.0	9.5

Source: Banco de la Republica.

wing of the Liberal Party who were working in the campaign, such as Antonio Urdinola and Eduardo Sarmiento. Even Rudolf Hommes and Armando Montenegro, future ministers of finance and of planning, were not thinking of radical trade liberalization

In 1988, before the start of trade liberalization, 38.9 percent of tariff positions were on the different types of free import lists. At the end of the Barco government, 55.6 percent of tariff positions were on the free import list (either formally or informally, in cases where the granting of licenses was virtually automatic). The rest were subject to auctions and various degrees of strictness in the granting of import licenses. In November 1990 the new government of César Gaviria eliminated import licenses on 97 percent of tariff positions. Soon after, liberalization was extended to agricultural goods, but within a scheme of flexible tariffs that increaded protection in times of low international prices and decreased protection when these prices increased above a trend level.

At the same time, a gradual schedule of tariff reductions was established. The flat supplemental tariff of 16 percent on all goods was reduced to 13 percent in 1990 and was to decline to 8 percent in 1994. The differential tariffs, which had 14 levels and ranged from 0 to 100 percent, were reduced to 9 levels and would end up with only 4 levels in 1994. The average tariff, without the supplemental flat rate, was to decline from an average of 16.5 percent in 1990 to 7.0 percent in 1994. The largest reductions would occur in consumer goods, where the average tariff would decline from 47.6 percent in December 1990 to 22.2 percent in 1994.

This cautious reduction in tariffs, combined with the elimination of import licenses, again generated private-sector opposition, but it was not overwhelming. Imports were not growing, and international reserves continued to increase. The trade liberalization clearly was not affecting the demand of Colombian producers negatively.

The minister of finance and the governor of the central bank continued to allow the nominal exchange rate to rise faster than the rate of inflation throughout 1990 in preparation for the expected import surge generated by the elimination of import controls and tariffs. In December 1990, however, the consumer price index showed inflation to be above 30 percent per year, a threshold above which inflation could be considered out of control in Colombia (see table 4 for the historical record of inflation in Colombia). In January 1991, therefore, on the initiative of the minister of finance, the Monetary Board took radical action and established a 100 percent reserve requirement on the deposits of most financial institutions. The object was to curb the growth of credit and of the money supply.

Minister Hommes, in discussions with the author, has explained that he was aware that a reduction in credit would accelerate the inflow of foreign capital and that this would compensate in part for the decrease in the supply of money resulting from the control of bank reserves. At that point, however, he felt the increase of reserves would give credibility to and guarantee trade liberalization. At the time, however, no mention was made of the potential impact of the credit squeeze on international reserves, since all government pronouncements emphasized the need to control inflation and the money supply.

Monetary authorities seriously underestimated the amount and speed of capital flows. Despite an attempt to stem this flow by having the central bank buy the additional reserves via central bank certificates with 90–day maturity (a de facto revaluation and a way of postponing the monetary impact of the increases in international reserves), capital inflows continued, while imports decreased (table 5).

By the middle of the year, on his return from a trip to Ecuador, President Gaviria called the minister of finance and told him that, in his opinion, there was no alternative

TABLE 4

Colombia: Inflation, GNP, and Investment, 1950–92

Year	Annual Inflation Rate[a]	Real GNP (Millions of Constant 1975 Pesos)	Change in GNP (Percentage)	Private Investment (Millions of 1975 Pesos)[b]	Change in Private Investment (Percentage)	Public Investment (Millions of 1975 Pesos)	Change in Public Investment (Percentage)
1950	n.a.	118,655.7		22,568		1,669	
1951	n.a.	122,340.8	3.11	21,898	(2.97)	2,170	30.02
1952	n.a.	130,069.1	6.32	25,041	14.35	888	(59.08)
1953	n.a.	137,966.7	6.07	29,333	17.14	5,746	547.07
1954	n.a.	147,516.6	6.92	35,918	22.45	4,917	(14.43)
1955	n.a.	153,282.6	3.91	37,104	3.30	6,054	23.12
1956	7.82	159,498.4	4.06	34,310	(7.53)	6,644	9.75
1957	20.23	163,046.6	2.22	29,114	(15.14)	1,592	(76.04)
1958	8.10	167,063.4	2.46	27,248	(6.41)	1,946	22.24
1959	7.86	179,126.8	7.22	27,725	1.75	3,646	87.36
1960	7.22	186,779.7	4.27	32,867	18.55	4,082	11.96
1961	5.90	196,277.6	5.09	37,382	13.74	2,707	(33.68)
1962	6.41	206,901.8	5.41	34,181	(8.56)	6,059	123.83
1963	32.56	213,709.7	3.29	27,997	(18.09)	4,074	(32.76)
1964	8.92	226,887.7	6.17	37,985	35.68	3,673	(9.84)
1965	14.55	235,050.9	3.60	36,548	(3.78)	2,769	(24.61)
1966	12.98	247,358.8	5.24	30,144	(17.52)	4,881	76.27
1967	7.30	257,587.0	4.13	29,533	(2.03)	8,569	75.56
1968	6.55	272,873.4	5.93	33,305	12.77	10,048	17.26
1969	8.60	289,525.8	6.10	35,616	6.94	11,841	17.84
1970	6.78	307,497.0	6.21	37,730	5.94	15,471	30.66
1971	13.62	325,828.2	5.96	38,056	0.86	17,730	14.60

TABLE 4 (continued)

Year	Annual Inflation Rate[a]	Real GNP (Millions of Constant 1975 Pesos)	Change in GNP (Percentage)	Private Investment (Millions of 1975 Pesos)[b]	Change in Private Investment (Percentage)	Public Investment (Millions of 1975 Pesos)	Change in Public Investment (Percentage)
1972	14.01	350,812.2	7.67	34,515	(9.30)	20,172	13.77
1973	23.53	374,397.6	6.72	38,991	12.97	20,452	1.39
1974	26.04	395,908.1	5.75	46,185	18.45	18,419	(9.94)
1975	17.70	405,108.0	2.32	41,109	(10.99)	21,020	14.12
1976	25.68	424,261.5	4.73	44,909	9.24	13,130	(37.54)
1977	28.37	441,905.9	4.16	38,664	(13.91)	29,854	127.37
1978	18.77	479,335.8	8.47	49,589	28.26	25,334	(15.14)
1979	28.80	505,118.7	5.38	51,233	3.32	26,542	4.77
1980	25.96	525,765.0	4.09	51,267	0.07	36,754	38.47
1981	26.35	537,736.2	2.28	54,598	6.50	38,941	5.95
1982	24.03	542,836.6	0.95	51,684	(5.34)	44,623	14.59
1983	16.64	551,379.8	1.57	54,899	6.22	42,545	(4.66)
1984	18.28	569,854.9	3.35	49,226	(10.33)	49,430	16.18
1985	22.45	587,560.9	3.11	44,679	(9.24)	48,826	(1.22)
1986	20.95	621,780.8	5.82	52,184	16.80	48,466	(0.74)
1987	24.02	655,163.8	5.37	59,228	13.50	42,243	(12.84)
1988	28.12	681,791.0	4.06	66,440	12.18	44,321	4.92
1989	26.12	705,032.0	3.41	65,318	(1.69)	46,161	4.15
1990	32.37	734,250.0	4.14	67,372	3.14	42,570	(7.78)
1991	26.82	751,246.0	2.31	n.a.	n.a.	n.a.	n.a.
1992	25.13	776,037.1	3.30	n.a.	n.a.	n.a.	n.a.

n.a. = not available.

[a]Percentage variation in consumer price index.

[b]Public and private investment comes from national accounts.

TABLE 5
Colombia: Imports, 1970–92

YEAR	TOTAL IMPORTS (MILLIONS OF DOLLARS)	CHANGES IN IMPORTS (PERCENTAGE)	IMPORTS AS SHARE OF GNP (PERCENTAGE)
1970	796	n.a.	11.1
1971	892	12.06	11.4
1972	843	–5.49	9.7
1973	976	15.78	9.5
1974	1,502	53.89	12.1
1975	1,415	5.79	12.4
1976	1,654	16.89	13.5
1977	1,969	19.04	13.4
1978	2,552	29.61	14.6
1979	2,978	16.69	15.1
1980	4,283	43.82	17.5
1981	4,730	10.44	18.4
1982	5,358	13.28	21.0
1983	4,464	–16.69	17.1
1984	4,027	–9.79	14.6
1985	3,673	–8.79	11.4
1986	3,409	7.19	9.8
1987	3,793	11.26	10.5
1988	4,515	19.04	11.8
1989	4,558	0.95	11.0
1990	5,108	12.07	10.8
1991	4,548	–10.96	9.9
1992 (est.)	5,598	23.09	11.32

n.a. = not available.

Source: Banco de la Republica.

to accelerating the trade opening, given the need to control inflation. There were no more options. After a night of consultations, the economic team agreed to bring forward all the tariff reductions planned for 1991–94, despite the reluctance of Ernesto Samper, the minister of development and the politically most influential member of the cabinet (he controlled the largest number of Liberal Party members in Congress).

The public justification given was that without the acceleration nobody would import until all the announced tariff reductions had taken place. In addition to a sincere belief in the advantages of liberalization, the economic team was desperate to stop the increase in international reserves, which by then covered 17 months of imports (table 3). The belief in the need to promote nontraditional exports in Colombia was so widespread that floating the exchange rate and the revaluation this implied was unthinkable. In a sense, exporters had become the most legitimate pressure group in Colombia and therefore the most influential. The devaluation of 1984–85, plus the further devaluation of 1989–90 in preparation for trade liberalization, produced a current account surplus that required a deeper trade opening than originally envisioned, as revaluation or inflation were not considered acceptable options.

Rudolf Hommes described the administration's position to the author in the following terms: opening the economy put Colombia within the mainstream of economic thinking and international trends, and revaluing would have been shameful. It went against what officials had all been saying for years about the need to promote nontraditional exports.

One can also consider the hypothesis that although the president gave strictly economic arguments for his initiative, he might also have felt that, given the very comfortable level of international reserves, a once-and-for-all liberalization would be less costly politically than the possibility of a long, drawn-out debate about liberalization during the whole four years of the programmed tariff reductions. In a conversation with me, the president confirmed this hypothesis and added that he considered it politically unlikely that he would be able to execute the large tariff decreases scheduled for the last year of his administration.

Three additional comments on the politics of trade liberalization are in order. First, all four liberalization episodes were initiated in the Ministry of Finance and the Planning Department, at times in which the growth of international reserves was making money supply management difficult within the crawling peg regime. Unlike in other countries of Latin America, trade liberalization was only considered when there was no balance of payments crisis, and it was stimulated by a desire to control money supply and inflation without an export-destroying revaluation.

Second, in most episodes, there was no consensus on the policy among the economic team. In most of the cases, the Ministry of Finance and the Planning Department were checked by the Ministry of Development, which has been in charge of the trade bureaucracy and industrial policy. At the start of liberalization under President Barco, opposition came from German Montoya, the very influential chief of staff of the president and former industrialist from Medellin who later became a crucial advocate of the gradual and targeted liberalization finally approved in early 1990. It would appear that the start of successful liberalization did occur in Colombia on the one occasion in which the economic team was united behind the idea. The story of how this came about is of interest.

The first detailed studies of how to liberalize were carried out in the Ministry of Finance, and by early 1989, studies were being carried out at the Planning Department and the central bank on the macroeconomic effects of liberalization. When he found out about this, German Montoya called in the minister of finance and the head of planning to find out exactly what they proposed to do. Although an enemy of eliminating import controls, he was aware of the international pressures for liberalization. He therefore told them this was a very delicate issue, with serious political repercussions. He suggested that such a reform had to consider many ramifications, that the program would have to be very carefully crafted, and that an analysis should be carried out of why the previous liberalization attempts had failed. He then sounded out the other members of the economic team, including the head of the central bank and the minister of development. Although the minister of development was not deeply committed to defending such a reform, he favored it in principle. The president was then informed about the general ideas being studied, and the decision was taken to prepare a first proposal, which was then taken to the Council of Economic Policy, which was chaired by the president.

The minister of finance defended this proposal, but otherwise it was received coldly. German Montoya suggested that this was simply the initiation of a process, and the council decided that the issue should be studied further, although the president warned that the timing of the reform should be considered very carefully, given all the other political problems the government faced.

In the following weeks, the economic team continued to flesh out the proposal, in permanent contact with the chief of staff. By then, Maria Mercedes de Martinez had moved from head of the Planning Department to the Ministry of Development and made common cause with the minister of finance. For the first time in decades, the minister of development supported trade liberalization. Things came to a head after a call from the governor of the central bank to the chief of staff in which the former urged an immediate decision, given the favorable international reserve position and the apparent acceleration of the inflation rate. The governor insisted that the liberalization proposal, as it had been drafted, implied a gradual reform. A meeting was arranged for the following Saturday with the president, at which the ministers of development and finance, the head of the Planning Department, the governor of the central bank, and the chief of staff were present. At the meeting, the economic team took a common position, and it was agreed that the program of liberalization would be gradual and targeted. By then César Gaviria, the Liberal Party presidential candidate, had been consulted and had given his blessing, and German Montoya had sounded out executives from the textile and steel industry, particularly vulnerable sectors, and had not received very negative feedback. There was the feeling that reform was inevitable and that the political costs would not be major.

The liberalization program was then presented to the full Council of Economic Policy, where it was made clear that the agricultural sector would not be included. Very early on, the minister of finance had judged that the minister of agriculture was unlikely to support the reform, so he decided to exclude the agricultural sector from the program. The details of the Barco liberalization program can be found in Lora (1991b).

Over the issue of accelerating liberalization under President Gaviria, the economic team split in the traditional way. Finance and Planning were in favor of accelerating the process, and the minister of development opposed the policy. The president, however, was a convinced partisan, and he overruled his politically powerful minister of development, Ernesto Samper. In the case of Colombia in 1990, the hypothesis that opposition to trade liberalization can only be overcome by a unified front for it within the government seems to be valid.

Joan Nelson's idea that weakened opposition is critical in facilitating liberalization does not apply. The Conservative Party opposition was weakened, but it was in favor of liberalization. The protectionists that had to be defeated were what one could call the traditional ideological wing of the Liberal Party. This defeat was gradual. Criticism of protectionism and import substitution started in the Lopez wing of the party in the 1960s and became respectable in his presidency (1974–78). The generational change that took place when Gaviria became president—the first elected chief executive in his early 40s since the war—increased the influence of the new school of thinking in the government and within the Liberal Party.

Another interesting feature of the Colombian process is that it was started at the end of the Barco government, when support for liberalization was quite low. How could an unpopular government initiate a process that had been repeatedly blocked in the previous decade and a half? Clearly, the influence of private-sector groups in favor of protection had declined, and the new influential pressure groups, including exporters, were beginning to see that protectionism was incompatible with exports in a world more and more unwilling to allow Colombia to maintain trade policies no longer accepted anywhere else.

Traditional protectionist practices also seemed to be less effective, and the national market was no longer a dynamic source of growth.

Another reason, however, is that trade reform was not an important subject in a society in the middle of a violent war on drugs, a violent struggle with some guerrillas and peace negotiations with others, and a politically and legally complicated process of organizing the Constituent Assembly, which would reform in a major way a constitution in place for 100 years. In those circumstances, it was not wise for the private sector to mount major opposition against the government. Nevertheless, the hardest part of the discussion concerning trade liberalization did take place at the end of the Barco government, when the first tentative steps were taken. This made it easier for the Gaviria government to radically accelerate the process at the height of its popularity in its first year.

The acceleration of liberalization in 1991 also took place when the Congress was not meeting and the Constituent Assembly had decided that elections for a new Congress had to be held within the new rules established in the 1991 constitution. The first major debate of the new Congress, however, was organized by opposition groups to criticize the trade liberalization. The government and the minister of finance were much criticized by some of the more radical members of the opposition and by old-line interventionist Liberal Party congressmen. A commission was created to evaluate the economic and social costs of the *apertura*, or opening, but it came to nothing. By then the *apertura* was popular, and criticism of it appeared not to produce political dividends. Toward the end of 1991, polls were showing that the public liked the idea of opening up the economy.

It could be argued that in Colombia it was not difficult to decide at the highest administrative level that liberalization must take place. What was difficult was to get it implemented. The implementation took place at the beginning of the Gaviria government, when the bureaucracy could not easily oppose administration policy. In addition, Minister Hommes, who had seen how the bureaucracy had frustrated the Lopez liberalization when he was a young adviser at the Ministry of Finance, closely monitored the behavior of the Foreign Trade Institute. The elimination of all import licenses also did away with the possibility of the case-by-case approach so beloved of the INCOMEX bureaucracy. This was a fortunate strategic decision and shows the advantages of radical reform over any attempt at gradualism. The gradual dismantling of import controls gives the trade bureaucracy the power to frustrate a trade liberalization effort.[5]

THE ROLE OF TECHNOCRATS

Maria Mercedes de Martinez, then-head of the Planning Department, recounts that after a trip to Washington in early 1989, in which the World Bank had made clear that its future loan program with Colombia depended on the country's progress in trade liberalization, she asked the deputy governor of the central bank to study the impact of such a policy on the Colombian economy. He enthusiastically set some recently graduated PhDs at the bank to the task, and they soon produced good reasons for carrying out such a reform. The macro-

[5]There has been little evidence of open corruption at the Foreign Trade Institute (INCOMEX). Nevertheless, officials of the institute did become nationally known because of their posts and upon leaving became well-paid advisers to private industry or found attractive jobs with industrialists they met while working at the Institute.

economists at the Planning Department produced macroeconomic models showing that such a policy would accelerate growth, and the Ministry of Finance economists were also dedicated partisans of the idea. Among the young economists in government in the late 1980s, there were no structuralists or Cepalinos.

Due to low salaries in the Colombian government, there is a rapid turnover of highly qualified personnel. By 1989, there were no economists in government trained in CEPAL (Comisión Económica para América Latina) or who had studied development economics at the time in which planning and state-led growth were fashionable in academia. Most of these young PhDs had studied macroeconomics or monetary and fiscal economics with scholarships from the central bank, and free markets and free trade were the bias of the programs in the US universities where these people studied.

In the Colombian universities and think tanks, an older generation of economists still defended protectionism, but even there, a growing majority favored free trade. Even Salomon Kalmanovitz, the dean of radical economics, declared himself favorable to opening the economy in the late 1980s. There was therefore a growing consensus in the economics profession for an *apertura*. This was important, since in Colombia the private sector and the government listen to academic economists, who often have had previous policy experience.

Since the early 1970s, most ministers of finance and all heads of the Planning Department have been professional economists, and this has given Colombian economic policy a bias toward orthodoxy. In addition, President Virgilio Barco, an engineer with a degree from Massachusetts Institute of Technology, had been Colombian executive director at the World Bank and ambassador in Washington, and was well aware of the growing consensus at the international level on the advantages of market-based policies and free trade. President Gaviria was an economics graduate from Los Andes University, which had the best economics faculty in the country, and he was personally convinced of the necessity of liberalizing the economy. He encouraged the Barco economic team to start the liberalization process when he was a presidential candidate.

Without question, then, the liberalizing reforms were led by government officials who were professional economists and were convinced that such reforms would be necessary if the country were to resume rapid economic growth. This suggests that the political economy literature should take into consideration in policy analysis the scientific perspective of politicians and technocrats involved in policymaking.

Economists were particularly worried about slow productivity growth in Colombia in the 1980s. It appeared that the economy needed a major shake-up in order to start achieving greater productivity growth and efficiency. This was the official justification for trade liberalization (Departamento Nacional de Planeación 1990). Even José Antonio Ocampo, the best-known structuralist economist, declared in 1990 that trade liberalization was the Schumpeterian shock the economy needed, although he was also of the opinion that the liberalization should be gradual to allow industry to carry out its conversion.

The role of the young generation of economists in government was important, but the growing professional agreement on the need for liberalization, as reflected in the writings of economists in journals and newspapers, probably also influenced the political establishment and managers in the private sector. The influence of international economic opinion of the time and *The Economist* newspaper went in the same direction and helped to give respectability to the reforms the government proposed.

Rudolf Hommes also suggested to me that a major difference between the liberalization episodes of the 1970s and the 1990s was the changing nature of the executives in the private sector. In 1974, companies were in the hands of the men who had entered industry and the financial sector in the 1930s, usually from law faculties or local engineering schools. They had lived through the successful import substitution of the '40s and '50s and therefore found government protection natural. In 1990, private-sector enterprises were often in the hands of a new generation of economists, engineers, and MBAs with foreign postgraduate degrees. To them, the government economists' arguments were more familiar and fitted the ideas they had absorbed in their training.

The Politics of Exchange Control Liberalization

It is easier to understand why there was political support for dismantling exchange controls. The crawling-peg policy started in 1967 had kept the peso-dollar exchange rate at reasonable levels most of the time, and controls were not needed for rationing foreign exchange. Exchange controls increased the cost of trade transactions. They also harmed the middle and upper classes, who had to pay large transaction costs in order to diversify their portfolios without running into trouble with the Superintendency of Exchange Control. By the late 1970s, thousands of Colombians had foreign accounts, and many went to the parallel market to get dollars for travel abroad, for paying foreign services, or even for underinvoicing imports. (Since the mid-'70s, due in part to taxes and delays in the monetization of foreign exchange and to an adequate supply of foreign exchange in the parallel market, the official exchange rate has tended to be above the parallel rate, except at the time of the exchange crisis of 1983–85.)

It is hard to see who benefited from exchange controls. Policymakers often justified the regime as a means of diminishing the instability created by short-term capital flows. There was also a moral justification, in so far as it was believed these controls could keep away drug profits generated abroad and hinder capital flight. The former argument backfired when the Colombian and US press, and even the US embassy, started to claim that the central bank bought dollars from illegal drug dealers. This was inevitable since, according to the law, all foreign exchange, including remittances, had to be sold exclusively to the central bank.

The strongest argument for maintaining exchange controls, however, was the fact that Colombia had had only one balance of payments crisis since 1967, when those controls were introduced. Not too many people fully understood that you could maintain the crawling-peg mechanism and a realistic exchange rate, which were the real reasons for the stability in the foreign exchange front, without such a detailed exchange control system.

The Gaviria administration wanted to adopt legislation that would diminish the need for so many otherwise respectable citizens to enter into illegal activities and to allow some foreign exchange transactions to be carried out in a free exchange market. Since this was a major change in the existing regime, the matter had to be taken to Congress. The exchange control law (Decree 444 of 1967) gave the Monetary Board, dominated by the executive, wide powers to modify the exchange control legislation, but major changes in the general framework of the exchange regime had to be taken to Congress.

When the Congress opened after the Gaviria inauguration, the central bank had convinced the government to present legislation it had drafted that implied a less radical change. It emphasized making the regime more flexible by decentralizing foreign currency operations to financial intermediaries other than the central bank. When opposition congressmen presented an alternative reform, which involved complete elimination of exchange controls and a floating exchange rate, the minister of finance negotiated a law that closely resembled the scheme he and his colleagues had designed before the inauguration. By shifting the discussion on the exchange regime from the Monetary Board, where the governor of the central bank was very influential, to the Congress, the partisans of exchange controls were greatly weakened.

Once exchange controls were liberalized, the only opposition came from exporters, who thought tough controls would diminish the inflow of repatriated capital in 1991, both legitimate and drug-related, and this would diminish the pressure for revaluation. Since most exporters had illegal accounts and investments abroad, however, they did not pursue this line of reasoning too vigorously. Banks, on the other hand, were enthusiastically in favor of liberalization, since they now handled all foreign exchange transactions, previously the monopoly of the central bank, and their foreign currency departments started to account for an ever-higher proportion of profits.

In the case of exchange controls, the surprising thing is how long it took to dismantle them. There were only two groups interested in their maintenance: central bank officials who thought the controls made the management of monetary policy easier, and politicians identified with the 1967 exchange control legislation. The central bank, however, did not have a solid basis for support of exchange controls. Control of short-term capital flows is probably desirable but not easy, even with the complete array of exchange controls existing in Colombia after 1967. The resource costs of the controls were probably higher than the benefits provided in terms of effective control of short-term capital movements. These controls also created many enemies for the central bank, and the costs started to be viewed as outweighing the presumed benefits in the area of monetary policy.

Also, the old-guard interventionist Liberal Party politicians were outnumbered in Congress by a new generation, which easily had the majority to pass Exchange Reform Law 9 of 1991. This majority knew that legalizing private foreign currency accounts abroad was popular.

There was also no bureaucracy to defend the controls. The governor of the central bank wanted to move the controls out of the central bank and into the financial sector. Furthermore, the prosecuting arm of the government, the Superintendencia de Control de Cambios, was a weak agency. Prosecuting people for exchange control violations was not popular and had become dangerous as the illicit drug traffic increased. Few people wanted a job in the Superintendencia de Control de Cambios.

THE LABOR REFORM

Labor reform was also a reform waiting to happen. For over two decades, employers had been complaining about the legislation on job security. Fringe benefits and the *cesantia* bonus were becoming intolerable burdens for companies with an aging labor force.

In Colombia, labor legislation is the responsibility of Congress, and there has been a tradition of not diminishing previously legislated labor rights. Dismantling the legislation on job security was therefore considered very difficult.

In the 1980s, however, academic research showed that employers tended to fire workers before they obtained any rights to job security. It turned out that Colombia had passed from being a country with substantial job stability in the 1960s to having one of the highest labor turnover rates in the world. The job stability legislation appeared to have had an effect exactly opposite to that desired. This academic research was important in convincing many progressive congressmen that reforming this aspect of labor legislation was not a reactionary thing to do.

During its last session before the Constitutional Assembly, Congress wanted to demonstrate how enlightened, efficient, and courageous it could be in order to diminish the pressure for congressional reform at the Constituent Assembly. It therefore passed the government initiative on labor reform despite spirited opposition from the labor movement.

The political strength of the labor movement has historically been its capacity to threaten the government with politically disruptive strikes. This last tactic was not a realistic tool to use on the eve of the Constituent Assembly, when both the public and the government were concentrating on other political issues. Politically, labor has become weaker. There are about the same number of union members now as in 1967, but the union confederations are now completely dominated by Communists and have therefore little influence in the major parties and Congress, where there are only a handful of Communist or radical members. Furthermore, the unions have no funds to use in support of congressional elections.

The potential for disruption and violence from a general strike dissuades most governments and congresses from passing legislation strongly opposed by the unions. However, the special circumstances leading to the Constituent Assembly and the mood of reform of the first year of the Gaviria government, plus the argument that without labor market flexibility the trade liberalization could harm some industries and create unemployment, made the reform politically possible. In this area, the deep commitment of the president to reform was important. He had prepared the projects for reforming the labor legislation before taking office, and these were among the first that the congress received from the new government.

TAX REFORM

Tax reform in Colombia is the responsibility of Congress, although discussion of tax changes can only take place at the government's initiative. Tax reform projects are therefore always initiated by the executive branch.

All the literature on trade reform suggests that the liberalization process must start with a realistic or undervalued exchange rate and fiscal accounts in balance. Colombia followed the orthodox scenario. We saw that the real devaluations of 1984–85 and 1989–90 had made Colombian production quite competitive, and the Junguito adjustment of 1985 had reduced the fiscal deficit to 1 or 2 percent of GNP (table 6).

Trade liberalization, however, created a serious fiscal problem, since import taxes were as high as 25 percent of total central government revenues in 1989. Trade liberalization therefore could potentially have had disastrous fiscal effects.

In 1990 the Congress passed its first tax reform legislation, which enhanced fiscal revenues by increasing the value-added tax from 10 to 12 percent and increased the base of the tax. It also included rules governing a tax amnesty for the repatriation and declaration of capital held abroad, the rationalization of taxation of foreign investment, and tax incentives for the development of the capital market, such as the elimination of capital gains

TABLE 6

Colombia: Consolidated Government Fiscal Deficit as a Proportion of GNP

YEAR	NOT INCLUDING NATIONAL COFFEE FUND	TOTAL
1980	–2.64	–2.31
1981	–5.14	–5.50
1982	–6.16	–5.98
1983	–7.43	–7.44
1984	–5.51	–5.94
1985	–5.70	–4.38
1986	–2.68	–0.29
1987	–1.63	–1.94
1988	–2.40	–2.48
1989	–2.14	–2.29
1990	–0.31	–0.33
1991	0.66	0.16
1992 (est.)	0.35	–0.45

Source: Consejo Superior de Politica Fiscal: Programa Anual de Caja del Gobierno Nacional y Panorama del Sector Publico no Financiero 1992–1993 (Bogotá: Documento Asesores 030/92, Dic. 30, 1992).

on the sale of stocks through the stock market. This tax reform passed relatively easily in the activist congress of 1990 as part of the package of measures meant to open up the Colombian economy.

When the government implemented all the tariff reductions planned to take place in five years in 1991, it announced it would present to Congress a tax reform to compensate for the loss of revenue. Initially, most of the revenue to be generated was to be raised by increasing the rates of the value-added tax and increasing coverage of that tax by extending it to services. Some congressmen criticized the regressiveness of the VAT, and so the government agreed to raise those rates by less and increase income tax rates instead. Congress, against the government's wishes, also increased taxes on oil exports and did not decrease the dividend remittance tax for foreign companies. Clearly, foreign companies have little influence on congressmen.

The tax reform generated strong and vocal opposition from the private sector. The association of retailers went as far as to pay for radio and newspaper advertisements, as well as roadside billboards, against a tax increase. The only president of a business association who spoke for the reform was the president of the Association of Exporters. Some weeks before, President Gaviria had explained to him and the board of directors of the association that there were only two alternatives for the control of inflation: a tax reform that would eliminate the fiscal deficit or a revaluation. The opposition of the press to the reform was also very strong, and private lobbying against it was intense.

The president put all his political skills to work and met daily with groups of congressmen to convince them of the need for the tax reform. He was fortunate in having the support of Minister Hommes at Finance, who in addition to being technically very knowledgeable, turned out to be a very skilled negotiator with an easygoing personality that made him popular in Congress. The reform was in fact passed, with the help of Victor Renan Barco, a congressman who, with more than two decades of legislative experience, has become the leader in the Senate on most economic legislation by creating a complicated series of political alliances based on ideology. This time around, the government was unable to maintain discipline in the Liberal Party, and the income tax part of the reform was voted through by a combination of Liberal and M19 (the former guerrilla movement) congressmen, who were for an increase in the income tax on equity grounds. The increase in the VAT was voted by a coalition of liberals and the Andres Pastrana wing of the Conservative Party, which favored trade liberalization and the substitution of trade taxes by a VAT.

Throughout the debates, in the press and in upper-class circles there was widespread criticism of the president and his minister of finance for including in the budget funds for projects close to the heart of congressmen that needed persuasion and for appointing supporters of other congressmen to middle-level administrative positions. In the moralistic ambience of Colombia in 1991, the press acted as if these practices were not usual in most democracies, and these allegations of favors rendered were used as arguments against the reform and the government.

However, in Colombia, as opposed to other Latin American countries, Congress does pass tax reforms. The political class is not closely related to or influenced by the private sector, and so private-sector opposition to tax reforms is not effective. The business of congressmen is politics, and they do not like inflationary fiscal deficits because inflation is not popular with the electorate. I will not go more deeply into the politics of tax reform in Colombia because I have analyzed the subject in detail elsewhere (Urrutia 1989) using the tax reforms of the 1970s as case studies. The 1991 tax reform followed the same pattern and required a deep commitment on the part of the president and his minister of finance. The reform of 1991, as was the case in 1974, had a clear cost in terms of popularity for the president and his government. It is also significant that all of the revenue-generating tax reforms in the last two decades have been passed by technocratic ministers of finance who have no future political ambitions.

Conclusion

Apparently, the economic liberalization of 1989–92 will not be reversed. On 10 January 1993, a newspaper (*El Tiempo*) poll of 500 enterprises showed that there was no longer much opposition to trade liberalization. While 21 percent of industrialists considered the *apertura* to be negative, 60 percent thought it positive, and 19 percent were indifferent. Taking all economic sectors together, only 14 percent of respondents were against the trade liberalization. On 19 January 1993, the newsweekly *Semana* published a survey of 1,000 citizens in which 39.6 percent of respondents declared that the *apertura* was somewhat good for the country, and 16.1 percent declared it had been very good for the country (9.7 percent answered they did not know).

International reserves continue to grow and cover about 19 months of imports, so there is little danger of a balance of payments problem that would stimulate a new episode of import controls. In addition, at the end of 1992 it was confirmed that there was a very major oil field in the Llanos area, and this guarantees that there will be no balance of payments problems in the next decade. The challenge is, on the contrary, to avoid a Dutch Disease problem.

Consumers are also beginning to be aware of and enjoy the opening of the economy. The unpopular part, the tax reform, was passed and will not again be on the agenda for a few years. Programs for financial reform and central bank independence have now passed Congress, and the latter cannot be reversed without a difficult process of constitutional reform. Inflation has been decreasing for two years in a row, and there is no reason to think it cannot continue to decrease gradually until it reaches single-digit levels. The independent central bank, now responsible for exchange rate management, has declared that it will not allow a significant real revaluation, and most economists in the country, as well as policymakers, consider such a policy a prerequisite for economic growth. The avoidance of an overvaluation of the exchange rate will be a crucial ingredient for the survival of the recent trade and exchange liberalization.

In 1992 there was a budget surplus for most of the year, and the deficit was probably close to zero in December. There is, however, the danger that in the following years the deficit may increase. This must be closely watched in order to maintain the macroeconomic balance that will be necessary if economic liberalization is to persist. The reform agenda of the future must therefore give priority to making public services more efficient and to the targeting of public expenditure in favor of the poor in order to build a just and peaceful society.

With respect to the politics of the economic reforms of 1989–92 in Colombia, the first enabling circumstance was the mood for change that has existed in the society. The violence generated by the war on drugs and the guerrillas in the second half of the 1980s had led to a generalized feeling that major institutional changes were required. The murder of three presidential candidates, most of the Supreme Court, a minister of justice, and other high government officials and members of the judicial branch, as well as terrorist attacks in the cities and against economic infrastructure, were all circumstances that put into question some of the basic institutions of society. The governments of Presidents Barco and Gaviria therefore supported and finally were able to gain support for the calling of a Constituent Assembly. Originally, the objective was to change voting rules to give greater access to the political process to political minorities that felt excluded and to make the judicial system more efficient and operational. By 1991, however, the Constituent Assembly received a mandate to consider all of the institutional arrangements in society, and the government created venues at all levels for popular discussion of what reforms the Constituent Assembly should discuss.

The elections for the assembly produced a body with a political profile quite different from the traditional profile of the Congress. There were representatives of the small Indian population in the country, representatives of the growing Protestant sects, intellectuals, and the more ideological members of the traditional parties. In addition, 27 percent of the assemblymen belonged to M19, the party created by a former guerrilla movement. In this general mood for change, the economic reforms seemed tame, but there was also a greater willingness to experiment with reform than in the past.

The constitutional reform of 1991 strengthened the Congress in many ways but also reformed it. In general, the executive lost leverage over Congress, and this may have made the passing of the 1992 tax reform more difficult than in the past. On the other hand, the mood for change created by the calling of the Constituent Assembly facilitated economic reform.

With this background in mind, the following considerations about the sources of support for the reforms may be useful.

Trade Liberalization

- Trade liberalization became possible when, after two decades of consistent export promotion policies, exporters had become the most legitimate and influential pressure group in the country.
- The conversion of the majority of highly trained economists in the country, and particularly in the government, to economic liberalization was an important ingredient in the reform.
- In the first stage, the pressure of the World Bank and US trade negotiators forced consideration of the first steps toward trade liberalization. In 1990, on the other hand, the shift in the position of the World Bank, and its reluctance to support the trade liberalization scheme developed by the government with loan commitments that would facilitate trade liberalization, almost killed the program.
- The radicalization of trade liberalization occurred when substantial current account surpluses threatened a revaluation in the absence of trade liberalization.
- In all cases, except in 1989, the agencies in charge of industrial policy and trade opposed liberalization, and the reforms were pushed by the Ministry of Finance and the Planning Department, which are responsible for macroeconomic policies.
- The deep commitment to economic liberalization of a president who was also an economist was crucial for the implementation of the reforms.
- Technocratic ministers with no future political ambitions were crucial in the process of economic liberalization and the fiscal reforms it entailed.

Foreign Exchange Regime

- The effectiveness of the foreign-exchange control regime put in place in 1967 had decreased significantly. A great number of Colombians had illegal foreign exchange accounts, and many influential people and entrepreneurs found exchange controls costly and dangerous. A constituency against them had built up.
- Many economists in middle levels of the government and the central bank were doubtful about the usefulness of the controls.
- A shift in the discussion from the Monetary Board to Congress weakened the influence of the central bank's defenders of the policy. In Congress, the interventionist wing of the Liberal Party had been seriously weakened between 1967 and 1990.

Labor Reform

- There was growing evidence that the job security legislation was in fact decreasing job security.
- In the generalized crisis and violence of 1989–90, the labor unions could not frighten the government with the threat of a general strike, and the violence these usually generate. The major reforms being discussed in the country as the Constituent Assembly was being organized put labor opposition to the labor reform at the bottom of the agenda of the government and of the society.
- At the Constituent Assembly, labor representatives attempted a counterreform but were defeated.

TAX REFORM

- The tax reform was difficult to pass in 1992, but the Congress once again showed its independence from private-sector pressure groups.
- The fact that tax reform must be an initiative of the government and that in order to pass it the president has to commit himself totally to its defense identifies tax reform with the executive. The political cost of increasing taxes costs the executive much more popularity than it does individual congressmen. A deep commitment and identification of the executive with the reform therefore makes it possible in Congress.
- As has been mentioned, congressmen fear inflation, since it makes the traditional parties unpopular and favors new movements not identified with economic management. At the same time, congressmen favor public expenditures. This makes the desire for low fiscal deficits translate into suppo pfor tax increases.
- Public expenditure not financed by taxes (money creation) strengthens the political factions that control the executive and decreases the bargaining power of congressmen. This also makes for fiscal orthodoxy on the part of Congress.
- Technocratic ministers of finance with no future political ambitions have been responsible for all the major revenue-enhancing tax reforms of the last two decades.

REFERENCES

Departamento Nacional de Planeación. 1990. "Programa de Modernización de la Economía Colombiana." *Revista de Planeación y Desarrollo* 12, nos. 1 and 2 (Enero-Junio).

Edwards, Sebastian. 1992. "Trade Policy, Exchange Rates and Growth." Paper presented at Stabilization, Economic Reform and Growth Conference. Sponsored by National Bureau of Economic Research and Inter-American Development Bank, Washington, D.C. (17 December).

Lora, Eduardo, ed. 1991a. *Apertura y Modernización: Las reformas de los noventa.* Bogotá: Tercer Mundo-Fedesarrollo.

Lora y Catalina Crane, Eduardo. 1991b. "La Apertura y la Recuperación del Crecimiento Económico." In E. Lora, ed., *Apertura y Crecimiento: El reto de los noventa.* Bogotá: Tercer Mundo-Fedesarrollo.

Mercedes de Martinez, Maria. 1991. *Memoria al Congreso Nacional: 1989–90.* Bogotá: Banco de la República.

Urrutia, Miguel. 1982. "Una Política nueva para combatir el contrabando." *Coyuntura Económica* 12, no. 1 (Mayo).

Urrutia, Miguel. 1989. "The Politics of Fiscal Policy in Colombia." In M. Urrutia, S. Ichimura, and S. Yukawa, eds., *The Political Economy of Fiscal Policy*. Tokyo: The United Nations University.

PART 4

Economic Reform and Integration

READING 14

The Opening of Latin America

SEBASTIAN EDWARDS
University of California Los Angeles

After decades of protectionism, most of Latin America began to open up to the rest of the world in the late 1980s. This process is perhaps the most impressive of the reform programs, and it effectively ended more than four decades of import-substitution policies that encouraged what turned out to be a largely inefficient industrial sector.

The process leading to these trade reforms was not easy. In the mid-1980s, the protectionist view was still influential in many parts of Latin America. In fact, the debt crisis of 1982 provided a new impetus to the protectionist paradigm. Initially, many analysts interpreted the crisis as a failure of the world economic order and argued that the only way for Latin America to avoid a recurrence of this type of shock was to isolate itself further through selective protectionism and government intervention (Griffith-Jones and Sunkel 1986). This sentiment was compounded by the fact that a number of observers considered the liberalization reforms of the Southern Cone countries during the 1970s as a failure. This perspective is synthesized clearly by Lance Taylor 1991 (119, 141), who argues that "trade liberalization strategy is intellectually moribund" and that there are "no great benefits (plus some costs) in following open trade and capital market strategies. . . . Development strategies oriented internally may be a wise choice towards the century's end."

Immediately following the eruption of the debt crisis, increased protectionism was indeed the path that Latin American countries chose. Even Chile, the strongest supporter of free trade, tripled its import tariffs. This sudden and drastic increase in the degree of protectionism was dictated largely by necessity. Faced with the need to generate an almost instantaneous reversal in the resource transfer of more than $30 billion, in the short run countries had very little alternative but to compress imports by some means or other. An increase in tariffs and quantitative restrictions was not surprising.

In the mid-1980s, Latin America's external sector was the most distorted in the world. Central America had the highest degree of import protection—in terms of both tariff and nontariff barriers—among developing countries, with South America following closely behind (see table 1). However, by 1987–88, it became apparent that a fundamental change was needed in Latin America's development strategy.[1] In particular, policymakers realized that

[1]Starting in the 1970s, a handful of countries—Brazil, Colombia, and Mexico—followed a trade strategy that combined import protection with active (selective) export promotion. In fact, the National Bureau of Economic Research study on trade policy in developing countries classifies Brazil and Colombia as having reached stage four of reduced anti-export bias (see Krueger 1978). I am grateful to Jaime Ros for calling this point to my attention.

TABLE 1
Import Protection in the Developing World, 1985 (percentage)

REGION	TOTAL TARIFF PROTECTION[a]	COVERAGE OF NONTARIFF BARRIERS[b]
Latin America and the Caribbean		
South America	51	60
Central America	66	100
Caribbean	17	23
Africa		
North	39	85
Other	36	86
Asia		
West	5	11
Other	25	21

[a]Tariffs and paratariffs; weighted averages.

[b]Measures as a percentage of import lines covered by nontariff barriers; weighted averages.

Source: Erzan and others 1989.

the long-standing protectionist trade policy was at the heart of the region's problems. With the help of the multilateral institutions, more and more countries reduced their levels of protection during the late 1980s and early 1990s. The process of trade reform proceeded at an accelerating pace. Tariffs were drastically slashed, many countries completely eliminated import licenses and prohibitions, and several countries began negotiating free trade agreements with the United States. . . .

This paper documents and evaluates the process of trade reform in Latin America and the Caribbean. It begins by discussing the extent of trade reform in the region and analyzing some of the results of the reforms. The analysis concentrates on productivity and exports and deals with the experiences of several countries. This is followed by a discussion of attempts to revive regional integration agreements and of future prospects for free trade agreements with the United States.

Recent Trade Liberalization Reforms in Latin America and the Caribbean

The pioneer in the trade liberalization process, Chile unilaterally eliminated quantitative restrictions and reduced import tariffs to a uniform level of 10 percent between 1975 and 1979. After a brief interlude with higher tariffs (at the uniform level of 35 percent), Chile imposed a uniform tariff of 11 percent and eliminated licenses and other forms of quantitative controls. Uruguay implemented a reform in 1978 and, after a brief reversal, pushed forward once again in 1986. Bolivia and Mexico embarked on their reforms in 1985–86, followed by a series of countries in the late 1980s. The members of the Caribbean Community (CARICOM) intensified trade liberalization reforms in the late 1980s and early 1990s. As of 1994, several nations, including Brazil, are proceeding steadily with scheduled rounds of tariff reductions and the dismantling of quantitative restrictions. However, it is still unclear whether all these reforms will be sustained and become permanent features of the Latin American economies.

The Latin American and Caribbean trade reforms were characterized by four basic elements: (1) reduction of the coverage of nontariff barriers, including quotas and prohibitions; (2) reduction of the average level of import tariffs; (3) reduction of the degree of dispersion of the tariff structure; and (4) reduction or elimination of export taxes. These measures generally were supported, during the early years of the reforms, by exchange rate policies aimed at maintaining a competitive real exchange rate. This section documents the extent of the recent liberalization programs; it is followed by analysis of the effects of the reforms, specifically on the growth of productivity and expansion of exports (portions of this section draw on Edwards 1992a).

NONTARIFF BARRIERS

A fundamental component of the trade reform programs was the elimination, or at least the severe reduction, of the coverage of nontariff barriers. During the early and mid-1980s in some countries, such as Colombia and Peru, more than 50 percent of import positions were subject to licenses or outright prohibitions. In Mexico, the coverage of nontariff barriers reached almost 100 percent of import categories in 1984, as was the case in most nations of Central America that year.

Table 2, which contains data on protectionism in the period before reform (1985 or 1987, depending on availability) and in the recent period (1991–92), shows that almost every country dramatically reduced the coverage of nontariff barriers.[2] In fact, some eliminated nontariff barriers altogether. The process through which nontariff barriers were eased varied from country to country. In some cases, such as Honduras, they were initially replaced by (quasi) equivalent import tariffs and then slowly phased out. In other countries, like Chile, they were eliminated rapidly without a compensating hike in tariffs.

In spite of the progress experienced in the last few years, significant coverage of nontariff barriers remains in a number of countries. In most cases, these nontariff barriers correspond to agricultural products. In Mexico, approximately 60 percent of the agriculture sector's tariff positions were still subject to import licenses in late 1993. An important feature of the region's liberalization programs is that they proceeded much slower in agriculture than in industry, largely because the authorities desired to isolate agriculture from fluctuations in world prices and unfair trade practices by foreign countries.[3] However, an

[2]These are unweighted averages and thus are not comparable to those presented in table 1. There has been a long discussion in applied international trade theory on whether tariffs and nontariff barriers should be measured as weighted or unweighted averages. Both views have some merits and some limitations. An obvious problem of the weighted average approach (where the weights are the import shares) is that more restrictive distortions tend to have a very small weight. In the extreme case, prohibitive tariffs that effectively ban the importation of a particular item have no weight! Corden (1966) provides an early and still highly relevant discussion of these issues.

[3]The issue of protecting local producers from dumping is important in the design of the new liberalized trade regimes. The crucial problem is to enact legislation that is able to distinguish true cases of unfair trade practices from simple cases of increased foreign competition stemming from more efficient productive processes. At this time, the approval of a dynamic and flexible antidumping legislation should be high on the region's agenda for legal and institutional reform.

TABLE 2

Opening in Selected Countries of Latin America, 1985–92 (percentage)

Country	Average Protection of Tariffs and Paratariffs[a]		Average Coverage of Nontariff Barriers[a,b]		Range of Import Tariffs					
					1980s			Current		
	1985	1991–92	1985–87	1991–92	Year	Minimum	Maximum	Year	Minimum	Maximum
Early reformers										
Bolivia	20.0	8.0	25.0	0.0	1985	0.0	20.0	1991	5.0	10.0
Chile	36.0	11.0	10.1	0.0	1987	0.0	20.0	1992	11.0	11.0
Mexico	34.0	4.0	12.7	20.0	1985	0.0	100.0	1992	0.0	20.0
Second-phase reformers										
Costa Rica	92.0	16.0	0.8	0.0	1986	1.0	100.0	1992	5.0	20.0
Uruguay	32.0	12.0	14.1	0.0	1986	10.0	45.0	1992	10.0	30.0
Third-phase reformers										
Argentina	28.0	15.0	31.9	8.0	1987	0.0	55.0	1991	0.0	22.0
Brazil	80.0	21.1	35.3	10.0	1987	0.0	105.0	1992	0.0	65.0
Colombia	83.0	6.7	73.2	1.0	1986	0.0	200.0	1991	0.0	15.0
Guatemala	50.0	19.0	7.4	6.0	1986	1.0	100.0	1990	0.0	10.0
Nicaragua	54.0	—	27.8	—	1986	1.0	100.0	1990	0.0	10.0
Paraguay	71.7	16.0	9.9	0.0	1984	0.0	44.0	1991	5.0	86.0
Peru	64.0	15.0	53.4	0.0	1987	0.0	120.0	1992	5.0	15.0
Venezuela	30.0	17.0	44.1	5.0	1987	0.0	135.0	1991	0.0	50.0
Nonreformers										
Ecuador	50.0	18.0	59.3	—	1986	0.0	290.0	1991	2.0	40.0

— Not available.

[a]Unweighted.

[b]Data on nontariff barriers refer mostly to 1989 and, thus, are not necessarily comparable with those presented in table 1.

Sources: World Bank, several country-specific reports; UNCTAD 1987; Erzan and others 1989.

approach based on quantitative restrictions entails serious efficiency costs (Valdés 1992). Slowly, however, more and more countries are replacing quantitative restrictions with variable levies and are introducing a system for smoothing price fluctuations based on price bands.

TARIFF DISPERSION

The import-substitution development strategy pursued for decades in Latin America created highly dispersed protective structures. During the 1960s, Brazil, Colombia, and Uruguay had among the highest degrees of dispersion in effective protection in the world, while Chile had *the* highest rate of tariff dispersion in the world, with a standard deviation of 634 percent (Heitger 1987; World Bank, *World Development Report 1987*). Highly dispersed protective structures generate high welfare costs, because they increase uncertainty and negatively affect the investment process (Cardoso and Helwege 1991). These highly dispersed tariffs and nontariff barriers were the result of decades of lobbying by different sectors to obtain preferential treatment. As the relative power of the different lobbies changed, so did their tariff concessions and the protective landscape.

An important goal of the Latin American trade reforms was to reduce the degree of dispersion of import tariffs. Table 2 contains data on the range of tariffs for a group of countries for two points in time—mid-1980s (1985–87) and 1991–92—and clearly documents the fact that the reforms indeed diminished the range between minimum and maximum tariffs. In many cases, this meant *increasing* tariffs on goods that were originally exempt from import duties. In fact, in many countries, the minimum tariff was 0 percent in the mid-1980s. Generally, zero tariffs are applied to intermediate inputs used in the manufacturing process.[4] From a political economy perspective, the process of raising some tariffs, while maintaining a pro-liberalization rhetoric, was often difficult. Those sectors that traditionally benefited from the exemptions strongly opposed them as it became evident that their privileged situation was coming to an end.

An important question addressed by policymakers throughout the region is how much tariff dispersion should be reduced. Should the reforms implement a uniform tariff, or is some (small) degree of dispersion desirable? Although from a strict traditional welfare perspective, uniform tariffs are only advisable under very special cases, they have a strong administrative and political economy appeal. In particular, a system of uniform tariffs is very transparent, making it difficult for the authorities to grant special treatment to particular firms or sectors (Harberger 1990).

AVERAGE TARIFFS

Reducing the average degree of protection is, perhaps, the fundamental policy goal of trade liberalization reforms. Traditional policy manuals on the subject suggest that once the exchange rate has been devalued and quantitative restrictions have been reduced or eliminated, tariffs should be slashed in such a way that both their range and average are

---

[4]This system with very low (or no) tariffs on intermediate inputs and high tariffs on final goods generated very high rates of effective protection to domestic value added. The use of effective protection is misleading, because effective rates of protection cannot provide much information on the general equilibrium consequences of tariff changes (Dixit 1986). In spite of this, they are still useful, because they indicate the degree of inefficiency a country is willing to accept for a particular sector.

reduced.[5] Table 2 contains data on average total tariffs (tariffs plus paratariffs) in 1985 and 1991–92. As can be seen, tariffs were significantly reduced in almost every country. Even those nations that acted somewhat cautiously on the reform front, such as Ecuador, made significant cuts in import tariffs, allowing a more competitive environment and reducing the degree of anti-export bias of the trade regime.

Countries that embarked on trade liberalization after 1990 moved at a much faster speed than those nations that opened up earlier. There has, in fact, been a clear change in what is perceived to be *abrupt* and *rapid* removal of impediments to imports. What fifteen years ago were seen as brutally fast reforms are now considered to be mild and gradual liberalizations. When Chile initiated trade reform in 1975, most analysts thought that the announced tariff reduction from an average of 52 to 10 percent in four and a half years was an extremely aggressive move that would cause major dislocations, including large increases in unemployment. In the early 1990s, more and more countries began opening up their external sectors very rapidly. For instance, Colombia slashed (total) import tariffs 65 percent *in one year,* from 34 percent in 1990 to 12 percent in 1991. This fast approach to liberalization was also followed by Argentina, Nicaragua, and Peru. Peru eliminated quantitative restrictions in one bold move, slashing import tariffs from an average of 110 percent in 1990 to 15 percent in March 1992.

Exchange Rate Policy

In the vast majority of countries, the first step in the recent process of trade reform was the implementation of large (nominal) devaluations. In many cases, this measure unified the exchange rate market. Most countries implemented large adjustments of the exchange rate as early as 1982 in order to face the urgencies of the adjustment process. The purpose of these policies was to generate real exchange rate devaluations and, thus, reduce the degree of anti-export bias of incentive systems.

. . . Many countries adopted crawling peg regimes, characterized by periodic small devaluations of the nominal exchange rate, as a way to protect the real exchange rate from the effects of inflation.[6] Table 3 contains data on real exchange rates for a group of Latin American countries. Once again, an increase in the index represents a *depreciation* of the real exchange rate and thus an improvement in the degree of competitiveness. Between 1980 and 1987, almost every country in the sample experienced very large real depreciations. In many cases, however, these were partially reversed as a consequence of the inflow of large volumes of foreign capital after 1990 and the use of the exchange rate as the cornerstone of disinflation policies. Overall, however, in most countries the real exchange rate was depreciated significantly more by late 1991 than in 1981. This greatly encouraged exports, helping to revert decades of discriminatory policies.

---

[5]However, tariff is sometimes a misleading term, since many countries traditionally relied on both import duties (that is, tariffs proper) and import duty surcharges or paratariffs (see Harberger 1992 for a discussion of the actual mechanics for reducing uneven tariffs).

[6]Some countries, most notably Brazil, Chile, and Colombia, experimented with crawling pegs as early as the 1960s. However, only Colombia maintained a regime that avoided overvaluation of the real exchange rate.

TABLE 3

Bilateral Real Exchange Rate Relative to the U.S. Dollar in Selected Countries of Latin America and the Caribbean, 1980–93 (1985=100)

COUNTRY	1980	1983	1987	1992	1993[a]
Argentina	35.8	96.4	80.8	36.9	34.0
Bolivia	88.1	84.6	107.9	109.6	113.3
Brazil	70.7	88.7	78.0	51.7	45.7
Chile	55.3	75.3	94.8	75.1	75.2
Colombia	79.2	78.3	115.9	119.9	102.6
Costa Rica	65.8	103.0	94.9	88.2	82.9
Ecuador	105.6	104.5	153.3	165.7	153.9
El Salvador	172.6	133.9	121.0	103.7	—
Guatemala	124.9	120.5	162.0	149.5	—
Honduras	121.6	106.2	93.2	141.5	152.3
Jamaica	60.1	54.8	80.1	94.5	70.7
Mexico	83.3	119.8	123.9	68.7	63.8
Panama	102.0	100.7	98.8	107.8	106.5
Paraguay	74.4	60.7	111.4	113.0	—
Peru	77.3	80.6	46.2	21.7	23.6
Trinidad and Tobago	152.9	117.3	122.8	112.1	129.0
Uruguay	49.7	89.4	77.2	55.5	40.5
Venezuela	84.2	70.3	134.8	122.3	119.1

— Not available.

Note: Increases indicate currency depreciation against the dollar.

[a]Preliminary.

Source: Calculated using data from the database of the IMF's *International Financial Statistics,* various years.

EFFECTS OF TRADE LIBERALIZATION

The trade liberalization reforms implemented in Latin America had three objectives: (a) to reduce the anti-export bias of the old regime and, thus, to encourage exports; (b) to help increase the growth of total factor productivity through greater competition and enhanced efficiency; and (c) to increase consumer welfare by reducing the real prices of importable goods. In this section, the evolution of productivity and exports in the period after the reforms is analyzed in some detail.

TRADE LIBERALIZATION AND PRODUCTIVITY GROWTH

The relaxation of trade impediments had a fundamental impact on the region's economies. Suddenly, Latin America's industry, which to a large extent had developed and grown behind protective walls, was forced to compete. Many firms did not survive this shock and went bankrupt. Others, however, faced the challenge of lower protection by embarking on major restructuring and increasing their level of productivity.

The ability (and willingness) of firms to implement significant adjustment depends on two main factors: the degree of credibility of the reform and the level of distortions in the labor market. If entrepreneurs believe that the reform will not persist through time, they have no incentives to incur the costs of adjusting the product mix and of increasing the degree of productive efficiency. In fact, if the reform is perceived as temporary, the optimal behavior is not to adjust but rather to speculate through the accumulation of imported durable goods. This was, as Rodríguez (1982) documents, the case in Argentina during the failed Martínez de Hoz reforms (see Corbo, Condon, and de Melo 1985 for a detailed microeconomic account of the process of adjustment in a large group of Chilean manufacturing firms).

In their studies on the interaction between labor markets and structural reforms, Krueger (1980) and Michaely, Choksi, and Papageorgiou (1991) find that most successful trade reforms indeed result in major increases in labor productivity. In most cases where this happens, labor markets are characterized by some degree of flexibility. Countries with rigid and highly distorted labor markets—including countries with high costs of dismissal, limitations on temporary contracts, and rigid minimum wage legislation—generally exhibit modest improvements in labor productivity after the trade reform process.

Some of the early Latin American reformers experienced important improvements in the productivity of labor. Labor productivity in the manufacturing sector increased at an annual rate of 13.4 percent in Chile between 1978 and 1981 and at a very significant annual rate of almost 4 percent in Mexico between 1986 and 1991, more than double the 1.6 percent annual rate of growth in that country between 1960 and 1982 (Edwards and Edwards 1991; Elías 1992; Sánchez 1992).

Recent models of growth suggest that countries that are more open to the rest of the world exhibit a faster rate of technological improvement and productivity growth than countries that are isolated. From an empirical point of view, this means that countries that open up their external sectors and engage in trade liberalization reforms experience an increase in growth of total factor productivity. Empirical evidence supports the notion that, when other variables (such as human capital formation, government size, political volatility, and the development gap) are held constant, the degree of openness of the economy is positively associated with the rate of growth of productivity. What is particularly important is that this result appears to be robust to the proxy used to measure the orientation of trade policy.

Table 4 contains data on the change in aggregate growth of total factor productivity in the period following the implementation of trade liberalization reform in six Latin American countries.[7] As can be seen, Chile and Costa Rica, two of the early reformers, expe-

[7]The original data on growth of total factor productivity are from Martin's (1992) study on sources of growth in Latin America. The countries in table 4 initiated the reform before 1988. To compute a series on growth of total factor productivity, Martin analyzes the contributions of capital and labor and explicitly incorporates the role of changes in the degree of capital use. The countries considered in this study are Argentina, Bolivia, Chile, Colombia, Costa Rica, Dominican Republic, El Salvador, Guatemala, Honduras, Mexico, Nicaragua, Panama, Peru, Uruguay, and Venezuela. Harberger (1992) presents data on growth of total factor productivity before and after a series of historical trade reform episodes. He finds that, in the majority of the cases, productivity growth increased after the liberalization process.

TABLE 4

Changes in Growth of Total Factor Productivity in Selected Countries of Latin America, 1978–82 to 1987–91

COUNTRY	PERCENTAGE CHANGE FROM 1978–82 TO 1987–91
Argentina	1.91
Bolivia	0.11
Chile	4.96
Costa Rica	3.25
Mexico	–0.32
Uruguay	2.02

Note: For Chile, the pre-reform period is 1972–78.

Source: Martin 1992.

rienced very large increases in growth of total factor productivity in the period following reform. The results for Chile coincide with those obtained by Edwards (1985), who finds that in the late 1970s, after the trade reforms had been completed, growth of total factor productivity was approximately three times higher than the historical average (it may be argued, however, that the major increase in growth of total factor productivity was the result of the complete structural reform package implemented in that country). Although the outcome is less spectacular, Argentina and Uruguay still exhibited substantial improvements in productivity growth in the period following reform. Bolivia, in contrast, presented a flat profile of total factor productivity growth. Sturzenegger (1992) argues that the very slow improvement in the growth of Bolivian productivity was, to a large extent, the result of negative terms of trade shocks and, in particular, the collapse of the tin market. In a series of recent studies, Ocampo (1991a, 1991b) calculates growth in total factor productivity in Colombia and finds that the increase in protectionism in 1982–85 was accompanied by a decline in productivity growth.

Perhaps the most puzzling result in table 4 is the slight decline in aggregate total factor productivity growth in Mexico after the reforms. Martin (1992) shows that this finding is robust to alternative methods of measuring growth of total factor productivity, including different procedures for correcting for capacity use. Also, Harberger (1992) finds that the growth in total factor productivity in Mexico was slower in 1986–90 than in 1975–82.[8] However, the aggregate nature of the data in table 4 tends to obscure the actual sectoral response to trade reform in Mexico. According to endogenous growth models, faster productivity will be observed in those sectors where protectionism has been reduced and will not be observed in those still subject to trade barriers or other forms of regulation.

A distinctive characteristic of the Mexican reform is that, contrary to the Chilean case, it proceeded at an uneven pace. In particular, in 1993, most of the agriculture sector

[8]However, according to Harberger's data, growth of total factor productivity in 1986–90 exceeded the level of the years immediately after the crisis. The actual numbers calculated by Harberger are the following: 1950–60 = 3.8; 1960–75 = 3.9; 1975–82 = –2.5; 1982–86 = –2.8; 1986–90 = 0.8. An important difference between the Martin and Harberger computations is that Martin does not correct for different degrees of capacity use.

was still protected by relatively high tariffs and substantial nontariff barriers. Also, the existence of important distortions in the labor market probably dampened the effect of trade reform on productivity growth. Moreover, until 1992 the Mexican land tenure system was subject to a legal system—the *ejido* system—that, among other things, severely restricted the market for land and distorted economic incentives. Although most regulations on land ownership in the agricultural sector were legally eliminated in early 1992, these reforms have yet to have a practical impact because the titling process, where property rights are actually assigned, is still in its infancy. By late 1994, practically no *ejidos* had been converted into private landholdings (several observers argue that the titling process will, by itself, take between five and ten years). Also, during much of the period following the debt crisis, large fragments of the service sector in Mexico, including telecommunications and financial services, were under direct government control and subject to distortions.

Table 5 contains data on growth of total factor productivity in Mexico's manufacturing sector for 1940–89 (since these figures come from two different sources, they may not be fully comparable and, thus, should be interpreted with care). In the period following trade reform, the rate of productivity growth in the Mexican manufacturing sector exceeded that of every period after 1940 for which data are available. This suggests that, once the sectors actually subject to increased competition are considered, growth of Mexican productivity indeed improved after the trade reform. This proposition is supported by Weiss (1992), who uses regression analysis to investigate the impact of the trade reforms on productivity and cost margins. In a recent and detailed econometric study at a disaggregated level, Oks (1994) finds that trade reform has indeed had a positive impact on productivity growth in Mexico's manufacturing sector.

An important question in evaluating the effects of trade reform refers to the speed with which productivity growth will react to the new incentives. Will the response be rapid, or will a long period of time pass before the fruits of the reforms are visible? Existing data for Chile provide some support for the idea that growth of total factor productivity will react quite fast. For example, Edwards (1985) finds that by 1979—the year the trade reform reached its goal of a uniform 10 percent import tariff—aggregate growth of total factor productivity had already reached 5.4 percent, significantly higher than the historical level. Agacino, Rivas, and Román (1992) find that growth of total factor productivity averaged 3.9 percent a year during 1976–81, greatly exceeding the historical average of approximately

TABLE 5

Growth of Total Factor Productivity in Manufacturing in Mexico, Selected Years, 1940–89 (percentage)

PERIOD	GROWTH IN TOTAL FACTOR PRODUCTIVITY
1940–50	0.46
1950–60	0.53
1960–70	3.00
1970–80	—
1985–89	3.40

— Not available.

Sources: For 1940–80, Elías 1992; for 1985–89, Ibarra 1992.

1 percent, and varied significantly across industries. In some cases, average productivity growth exceeded the 10 percent annual mark—wood products and glass industries—while in others it was negative, such as in nonelectric machinery. Agacino, Rivas, and Román (1992) find that total factor productivity did not grow in Chile during the late 1980s. This result is consistent with the findings of Marfán and Bosworth (1994), who argue that after the reforms Chile experienced very moderate productivity growth. This result is puzzling and somewhat counterintuitive; according to the authors, it may be due to their treatment of cyclical changes in growth. Lefort and Solimano (1994) revisit the issue of productivity growth in Chile. After analyzing the evolution of six measures of growth of total factor productivity, they conclude that the reform process positively affected productivity in the 1976–81 period.

TRADE REFORMS AND EXPORTS

Important goals of the trade reforms were to reduce the traditional degree of anti-export bias of Latin American trade regimes and to generate a surge in exports. In fact, based on the East Asian model, more and more Latin American leaders have called for the transformation of the external sector into the region's engine of growth. The reduction of the traditional anti-export bias is expected to take place through three channels: a more competitive—that is, more devalued—real exchange rate, a reduction in the cost of imported capital goods and intermediate inputs used to produce exportables, and a direct shift in relative prices in favor of exports.[9]

The volume of international trade in Latin America, and, in particular, the volume of exports, increased significantly after the reforms were initiated.[10] For example, the volume of exports for the region as a whole grew at an annual rate of only 2.0 percent between 1970 and 1980, at a rate of 5.5 percent between 1980 and 1985, and at an annual average of 6.7 percent between 1986 and 1990. The real value of exports, however, evolved at a somewhat slower pace, because the terms of trade in every subgroup of countries deteriorated significantly during 1980–91 (see CEPAL 1992a). Although, strictly speaking, it is not possible to attribute this export surge fully to the reforms, ample country-specific evidence suggests that a more-open economy, and, in particular, a more depreciated real exchange rate, positively affected the growth of exports (Nogués and Gulati 1992). Some countries, especially Costa Rica, accompanied the reform process with the implementation of a battery of export-promotion schemes, including tax credits—through the Certificado de Abono Tributario—duty-free imports, and income tax exemptions. However, it has been argued that these systems are fiscally expensive and do not encourage exports effectively (see Nogués and Gulati 1992; Nogués 1990).

---

[9]Naturally, exports can grow as a result of other policies, including an activist and selective industrial policy aimed at picking winners. The extent to which this is an efficient channel continues to be controversial. The recent World Bank study on the East Asian miracle argues that these types of policies were *not* important. For critiques of that study, see Wade (1994) and Rodrik (1994).

[10]Trade liberalization aims at increasing a country's total volume of trade. Under textbook conditions, it is expected that, at the end of the reform, trade will be balanced. However, in a number of circumstances, including the need to pay the country's foreign debt, trade will not grow in a balanced way after reform. This was the case in the majority of the Latin American countries.

TABLE 6

Value of Exports of Goods and Nonfactor Services in Selected Countries of Latin America, 1970–93 (annual percentage rate of growth in constant prices)

COUNTRY	1970–80	1982–87	1987–92	1991–93[a]
Argentina	4.8	–0.1	6.6	1.8
Bolivia	0.6	0.6	8.1	–8.3
Brazil	9.9	9.7	5.5	7.5
Chile	10.2	6.5	10.9	3.9
Colombia	5.7	10.2	6.7	2.9
Costa Rica	5.9	5.7	10.9	12.2
Ecuador	14.0	3.3	9.1	2.6
Mexico	8.3	5.8	3.5	3.1
Paraguay	6.1	5.4	9.5	1.1
Peru	2.7	–4.5	0.8	1.6
Uruguay	7.2	4.2	7.1	–1.7
Venezuela	–7.3[b]	3.6	4.4	–7.0

[a]Preliminary.

[b]1974–80.

Source: Database of the International Economics Department, World Bank.

Table 6 presents detailed country-level data on the rate of growth of the total value of exports (in constant dollars) for four periods. Table 7 contains information on the evolution of the volume of exports throughout the period. Several facts emerge from these tables. First, while the growth in exports was rapid for the region as a whole, nontrivial variations occurred across countries; in some cases (such as Peru), the real value of exports declined. Second, the performance of exports (1982–87 and 1987–92) was not homogeneous. In the majority of the countries, exports performed significantly better during 1987–92 than in the previous five years, reflecting, among other things, the fact that it takes some time for exports to respond to greater incentives.

In Ecuador, the country whose trade reform has lagged the most, the volume of exports in recent years was below the 1970–80 historical average. In Bolivia and Chile, two of the early reformers, exports were very strong in 1987–91. The case of Chile is particularly interesting. Since most of its liberalization effort was undertaken prior to 1980, there are enough data points to allow a more detailed evaluation of export response to the new regime. Between 1975 and 1980, when tariffs were reduced to a uniform 10 percent and nontariff barriers were completely eliminated, the behavior of Chilean exports was spectacular, growing (in volume) at an average of 12 percent a year—many times higher than the historical average in 1960–70 of only 2.6 percent a year. What is particularly impressive is that most of the surge in exports took place in the nontraditional sector (CEPAL 1992a).

Chile's success in the last few years was closely related to a boom in agriculture, forestry, and fishing exports. During the 1960–70 period, Chile was basically a net importer of agricultural goods. Today, agricultural, as well as forestry and fishing, exports are becoming increasingly important in the Chilean economy. In 1970, Chile exported $33 million in agricultural, forestry, and fishing products; by 1991, this figure had jumped to

TABLE 7

Volume of Exports of Goods in Selected Countries of Latin America, Selected Years, 1970–93 (annual percentage rate of growth)

COUNTRY	1970–80	1982–87	1987–91	1991–93[a]
Argentina	2.1	0.8	12.8	–0.1
Bolivia	–1.7	–5.2	13.2	5.3
Brazil	8.2	8.0	1.5	11.2
Chile	7.4	7.6	7.4	10.5
Colombia	3.6	14.8	7.3	12.6
Costa Rica	3.8	6.2	7.5	15.4
Ecuador	14.6	6.8	8.2	6.7
Mexico	10.2	6.1	5.5	8.7
Paraguay	7.3	9.2	17.2	2.2
Peru	2.3	–1.0	1.3	5.2
Uruguay	5.4	–0.5	4.8	–0.6
Venezuela	–5.8	2.1	7.5	6.5

[a]Preliminary.

Source: CEPAL, *Statistical Yearbook for Latin America and the Caribbean,* various years.

$1.2 billion! Notice that this excludes manufactured goods based on the elaboration of the agriculture sector. There is little doubt that economic policy lies behind the stellar behavior of the Chilean agriculture and export sectors in the last few years. First, the liberalization of international trade substantially lowered the costs of imported inputs and capital goods for agriculture, making the sector more competitive. In fact, the liberalization of international trade ended a long trend of discrimination against agriculture. This contrasts with Mexico, where agriculture has not yet benefited from the recent liberalization measures, including the reform of the old *ejido* system. Second, the exchange rate policy pursued aggressively in Chile after 1985 provided clear incentives for the expansion of exports. However, the current trend toward appreciation of the real exchange rate represents a cloud in the future of the sector. A third fundamental policy-based explanation of Chile's agricultural success has to do with the pursuit of a stable macroeconomic policy, which allowed entrepreneurs to have confidence in the system and to plan their activities over the longer run. Many export-oriented agricultural activities require sizable investments that are only undertaken in an environment of stability and policy continuity. And fourth, the strict respect for property rights, and the emergence of a stable and legal framework, also had significant, positive effects on the evolution of Chilean agricultural exports.

As tables 6 and 7 show, Mexico exhibited a slower rate of growth of total exports in the period after reform than during 1970–80. This, however, is largely an illusion, because during the 1970s Mexico's oil production increased very rapidly—at more than 18 percent a year. When nontraditional exports are considered, the performance after the reform is remarkable, with an annual average rate of growth for 1985–91 exceeding 25 percent (see table 8; a large percentage of this growth, however, was in the *maquiladora,* or in-bond sector).

After two successive years of decline, the volume of exports increased rapidly in Brazil during 1992 to 14.9 percent. Although it is too early to determine the exact forces behind

TABLE 8

Nontraditional Exports as a Percentage of All Exports in Selected Countries of Latin America, 1980–91

COUNTRY	1980	1982	1985	1987	1991
Argentina	0.27	0.31	0.28	0.31	0.35
Bolivia	0.15	0.09	0.05	0.19	0.30
Brazil[a]	0.57	0.59	0.66	0.69	0.71
Chile	0.38	0.22	0.35	0.39	0.36[b]
Colombia	0.41	0.42	0.41	0.55	0.64[c]
Costa Rica	0.36	0.38	0.37	0.42	0.50
Ecuador[d]	0.24	0.09	0.12	0.14	0.12
Mexico	0.13	0.20	0.18	0.38	0.50
Paraguay	0.58	0.71	0.82	0.68	0.69
Peru	0.21	0.23	0.24	0.27	0.28
Uruguay	0.61	0.58	0.66	0.67	0.71
Venezuela	0.04	0.07	0.09	0.13	0.17

[a]Industrial products.

[b]1989 data; subsequent data are classified differently.

[c]1990 data.

[d]Manufactured products.

Source: CEPAL, *Economic Survey of Latin America*, several years.

this rapid growth, and whether it will be sustained, there is some indication that the highly depreciated real exchange rate and the reduction in the degree of protection increased the degree of international competitiveness of Brazil's exports (the reduction in internal demand could also have affected the recent rapid growth of exports). This interpretation is supported by Bonelli (1992), who finds that productivity growth in Brazil's manufacturing sector was positively affected by export orientation.

A stated objective of trade reforms was to increase the degree of diversification of exports. In the period following the trade reforms, the importance of nontraditional exports, including manufacturing exports, increased steadily in the early reformers—Bolivia, Chile, and Mexico (see table 9). Also, in the majority of the countries, the share of the ten most important export goods in total exports declined significantly (CEPAL 1991). . . .

REGIONAL TRADING BLOCS IN LATIN AMERICA

There is little doubt that, as we approach the twenty-first century, the world economy is moving toward the formation of a small number of trading blocs. Although the European Economic Community and NAFTA are the best known cases, several other trading blocs, with different degrees of cohesion, are rapidly emerging. Among these, the Association of Southeast Asian Nations (ASEAN), with its dynamic and aggressive members, is especially promising. This is particularly so if the often-feared formation of a Yen Zone in the

TABLE 9

Exports of Manufactured Goods as a Percentage of All Exports in Selected Countries of Latin America, 1970–91

COUNTRY	1970	1980	1982	1985	1987	1991
Argentina	0.14	0.23	0.24	0.21	0.31	0.28
Bolivia	0.03	0.02	0.03	0.01	0.03	0.05[a]
Brazil	0.15	0.37	0.38	0.44	0.50	0.55
Chile	0.04	0.09	0.07	0.11	0.09	0.11
Colombia	0.11	0.20	0.24	0.17	0.19	0.33
Costa Rica	0.19	0.28	0.25	0.22	0.24	0.25
Ecuador	0.02	0.03	0.03	0.01	0.02	0.02
Mexico	0.33	0.11	0.10	0.21	0.38	0.44[a]
Paraguay	0.08	0.04	0.09	0.06	0.10	0.11
Peru	0.01	0.17	0.16	0.13	0.17	0.19[a]
Uruguay	0.15	0.38	0.32	0.35	0.55	0.52
Venezuela	0.01	0.02	0.02	0.10	0.06	0.11[a]

[a]1990 data.

Source: CEPAL, *Statistical Yearbook for Latin America and the Caribbean*, several years.

Pacific, including Japan and the ASEAN countries, takes shape in the next few years (see Schott 1991 for a general discussion of the recent formation and prospects of trading blocs in the world economy).

In the last few years, however, some new important trading blocs have emerged in the Western Hemisphere and are attracting the attention of policy analysts. Among these, the Mercado Común del Sur (MERCOSUR) and the Andean Pact, which jointly group nine Latin American countries, are two of the most important and have a volume of international trade that is expected to approach $250 billion a year by 2000 (MERCOSUR groups Argentina, Brazil, Paraguay, and Uruguay; the Andean Pact groups Bolivia, Colombia, Ecuador, Peru, and Venezuela). What makes the new integrationist effort in Latin America particularly interesting is that it takes place within a context that strongly favors export expansion and the growth of international trade throughout most of the developing world.

In addition to the somewhat large multimember trade agreements, there is a proliferation of recent bilateral integration agreements (see table 10 for a brief summary of trade agreements negotiated after 1990). The majority of the Latin American countries have expressed keen interest in joining NAFTA and see the bilateral—or small multilateral, for that matter—agreements as an intermediate step. Table 11 contains data on the evolution of intraregional trade and table 12 on bilateral trade for selected countries. Several important facts emerge from these tables. First, after reaching a low in 1985, intraregional trade expanded greatly in the late 1980s and early 1990s. Contrary to popular belief, intraregional trade as a portion of total trade is still significantly below its 1975–80 level. Naturally, this means that there is significant room for expansion. In this context, intraregional trade in East Asia borders on 30 percent of total trade. In a recent study, Losada (1993) finds that, with reduced trade impediments, distance is the main determinant of bilateral trade,

TABLE 10

Regional Integration Agreements in the Americas after 1990

Agreement, Date, and Membership	Objective	Current Status	Status/Comment
Andean Trade Preference Act, 1991 Bolivia Colombia Ecuador Peru United States	Duty-free status for $324 million in imports from Andean countries to the United States	Operational	
Chile–Colombia Free Trade Agreement, 1993	Establishment of a free trade area	Operational as of January 1994	
Chile–Mexico Free Trade Agreement, 1991	Establishment of a free trade area by January 1996	Present maximum reciprocal tariff of 7.5 percent	Aggregate GDP, $241.2 billion; population, 94.9 million; intraregional trade, 0.1 percent of total foreign trade
Chile–Venezuela Free Trade Agreement, 1993	Establishment of a free trade area by 1999	Maximum tariff to imports from Chile to be 20 percent in 1994; Chile's tariff rate remains at 11 percent; tariffs scheduled to reach 0 percent in 1999	Aggregate GDP, $76.7 billion; population, 32.5 million; total foreign trade, $38.9 billion; intraregional trade, 1.4 percent of total foreign trade
Colombia–Venezuela Free Trade Agreement, 1992	Establishment of a free trade area by 1992	Common tariff agreed in 1992; conversations initiated with Mexico (Group of Three) to establish free trade area	Aggregate GDP, $91.3 billion; population, 52 million; total foreign trade, $34.7 billion; intraregional trade, 1.4 percent of total foreign trade

El Salvador–Guatemala Free Trade Agreement, 1991	Establishment of a free trade area	Entered into operation in October 1991	
North American Free Trade Agreement, 1992 Canada Mexico United States	Establishment of a free trade area by 2009; elimination of tariffs in five, ten, or fifteen years, depending on the product; exceptions to Canadian agricultural and Mexican petroleum products; contains precedent-setting rights and obligations regarding intellectual property rights, services, trade, and investment; U.S.–Canada dispute settlement system extended to Mexico	Agreement signed and ratified; in phase as of January 1, 1994	Aggregate GDP, $6,204.6 billion; population, 362.7 million; total foreign trade, $1,223.8 billion; intraregional trade, 18.8 percent of total foreign trade
Group of Three: Colombia–Mexico–Venezuela Free Trade Agreement, 1993	Economic cooperation; in April 1993, the three countries agreed to establish a free trade area by 1994	Energy sector agreements signed; negotiations under way; draft accord of November 1993 provides for an immediate 0 tariff for some items and a ten-year transition for others, except in automobiles and agricultural goods; Mexico will cut tariffs faster than Colombia and Venezuela; signing date of January 1994 postponed because of Chiapas rebellion; agreement ratified by new Venezuelan authorities in February 1994	Aggregate GDP, $305.8 billion; population, 138.2 million; total foreign trade, $94.4 billion; intraregional trade, 0.8 percent of total foreign trade

continued

TABLE 10 (continued)

AGREEMENT, DATE, AND BEMBERSHIP	OBJECTIVE	CURRENT STATUS	STATUS/COMMENT
Costa Rica–Mexico Free Trade Agreement, 1994	Establishment of a free trade area	Negotiations in progress; removal of all tariff and nontariff barriers between both countries; Mexican exports of goods that Costa Rica does not produce will enter duty-free beginning in 1995; tariffs on the remainder of Mexican exports to be reduced over five, ten, and fifteen years; most of Costa Rican exports will be allowed to enter Mexico duty-free in five years or less; rigid rule of origin requires goods to be made with inputs from the region	
Mexico–Central America Free Trade Agreement, 1992 Costa Rica El Salvador Guatemala Honduras Mexico Nicaragua	Establishment of a free trade area by December 1996	Safeguard regime, technical rules, and dispute-resolution agreements under negotiation; framework agreement for trade cooperation signed August 1992; Costa Rica engaged in bilateral negotiations with Mexico	Aggregate GDP, $240.3 billion; population, 112.4 million; total foreign trade, $72.4 billion; intraregional trade, 1.6 percent of total foreign trade
Venezuela–Central America Free Trade Agreement, 1992 Costa Rica Nicaragua El Salvador Panama Guatemala Venezuela Honduras	Provides for a nonreciprocal transition period in which unilateral tariff cuts will be made by Venezuela, with the eventual goal of a free trade agreement	Negotiations gained impetus after the Group of Three presidential summit in 1993 but have proceeded slowly since	

Nueva Ocotepeque Agreement, 1992 El Salvador Guatemala Honduras	Establishment of a free trade area by 1993; long-run objective is to create a customs union; includes recent complementary agreements signed among these countries	Not clear	Aggregate GDP, $17.1 billion; population, 19.7 million; total foreign trade, $7.3 billion; intraregional trade, 11.8 percent of total foreign trade
MERCOSUR, 1991 Argentina Brazil Paraguay Uruguay	Establishment of a common market by January 1995; commercial liberalization program, macroeconomic policy coordination, common tariff, sectoral agreements	Present tariff preferences, 68 percent; dispute-resolution agreement signed; products gradually removed from national lists of exclusion; common external tariff negotiations hung up on differences over capital goods and electronics; process of liberalization well under way, but attaining a customs union by 1995 doubtful	Aggregate GDP, $492.3 billion; population, 190 million; total foreign trade, $76.3 billion; intraregional trade, 8.6 percent of total foreign trade
CARICOM–Colombia Free Trade Agreement, 1991 Antigua and Barbuda The Bahamas Barbados Belize Colombia Dominica Grenada Jamaica Montserrat St. Kitts and Nevis St. Lucia St. Vincent and the Grenadines Trinidad and Tobago	Provides for a nonreciprocal transition period in which unilateral tariff cuts will be made by Colombia, with the eventual goal of a free trade agreement	Negotiations are proceeding slowly due to CARICOM's demands for unilateral tariff reductions	

continued

TABLE 10 (continued)

Agreement, Date, and Membership	Objective	Current Status	Status/Comment
CARICOM–Venezuela Free Trade Agreement, 1993 Antigua and Barbuda The Bahamas Barbados Belize Dominica Grenada Jamaica Montserrat St. Kitts and Nevis St. Lucia St. Vincent and the Grenadines Trinidad and Tobago Venezuela	Provides for duty-free imports from CARICOM into Venezuela to be phased in over a five-year period; after five years, negotiations are to begin to eliminate tariffs on Venezuelan exports to signatory countries	Negotiations are proceeding slowly due to CARICOM's demands for unilateral tariff deductions	
Colombia–Central America Free Trade Agreement, 1993 Colombia Honduras Costa Rica Nicaragua El Salvador Panama Guatemala Venezuela	Provides for a nonreciprocal transition period in which unilateral tariff cuts will be made by Colombia, with the eventual goal of a free trade agreement	Negotiations gained impetus after the Group of Three presidential summit of 1993 but have proceeded slowly since	

Source: Lustig 1994; World Bank.

TABLE 11

Intraregional Exports as a Percentage of Total Exports in Latin America and the Caribbean, 1970–93

COUNTRY	1970	1975	1980	1981	1982	1983	1984	1985	1986	1987	1988	1989	1990	1991	1992	1993[a]
Argentina	21.1	25.9	23.8	19.7	20.4	14.1	18.5	13.7	23.9	21.6	20.5	25.9	26.3	30.3	34.1	37.3
Bolivia	9.7	35.9	36.7	42.6	51.6	55.0	52.8	60.2	64.5	57.8	47.7	44.0	45.6	51.2	40.7	44.6
Brazil	11.8	15.7	18.1	19.3	15.6	10.4	11.5	9.7	12.4	12.4	12.1	12.1	11.6	16.7	22.6	22.9
Chile	12.2	23.7	24.3	21.9	19.4	12.1	15.0	14.5	17.0	17.0	12.8	12.1	12.5	14.4	17.1	18.5
Colombia	10.5	21.7	17.6	23.7	21.7	14.0	13.5	14.0	11.4	17.3	16.0	16.0	16.9	24.1	23.0	24.8
Costa Rica	23.9	29.3	35.0	35.7	29.3	30.6	26.6	23.2	17.6	16.6	17.1	17.8	16.5	18.1	19.8	16.5
Mexico	9.8	14.3	6.9	9.8	8.8	7.5	6.4	5.4	6.7	7.8	7.5	7.1	6.6	4.3	4.8	4.9
Peru	6.5	16.7	21.2	12.8	15.4	10.4	11.9	14.1	14.5	16.1	14.5	15.3	15.4	16.1	18.1	21.7
Uruguay	12.8	29.3	37.3	26.6	30.8	23.7	26.2	[illegible]7.8	39.2	30.3	27.4	36.8	39.0	40.4	41.9	45.7
Venezuela	33.5	33.2	37.4	36.6	21.4	20.9	19.2	8.3	20.0	23.9	21.6	21.5	22.8	20.1	27.2	30.3
All Latin America	17.6	21.0	22.2	21.1	17.5	14.0	13.7	2.6	14.1	14.9	14.3	15.4	16.0	16.1	18.6	19.0

[a]Through October.

Source: IMF, *Direction of Trade Statistics*.

TABLE 12

Intraregional Exports (Freight-on-Board Value) as a Percentage of Total Exports, 1980–93

Exporting and Importing Area or Country	1980	1981	1982	1983	1984	1985	1986	1987	1988	1989	1990	1991	1992	1993[a]
From Argentina to														
Brazil	9.5	6.5	7.4	4.6	5.9	5.9	10.2	8.5	6.7	11.8	11.5	12.4	13.7	30.4
Chile	2.7	2.1	2.2	2.4	1.8	1.3	2.0	2.3	2.8	3.7	3.7	4.1	4.7	6.7
Colombia	0.5	0.6	0.9	0.8	0.7	1.6	0.9	1.0	0.9	0.8	0.6	0.7	0.9	1.0
Peru	1.5	1.0	1.4	1.2	1.6	1.9	2.8	2.2	1.9	1.7	1.5	1.7	1.9	2.2
Venezuela	0.8	1.1	1.3	0.7	1.4	0.9	0.7	0.9	1.4	1.0	1.2	1.7	1.7	1.8
From Brazil to														
Argentina	5.4	3.8	3.2	3.0	3.2	2.1	3.0	3.2	2.9	2.2	2.1	4.7	8.5	9.2
Chile	2.2	2.7	1.4	1.0	1.0	0.9	1.1	1.4	1.6	2.1	1.5	2.1	2.6	2.8
Colombia	0.7	0.9	1.3	0.7	0.6	0.4	0.5	0.5	0.7	0.6	0.5	0.5	1.0	1.0
Peru	0.6	1.2	1.1	0.3	0.5	0.4	0.7	0.8	0.6	0.4	0.5	0.7	0.6	0.6
Venezuela	1.1	1.8	2.3	1.2	1.4	1.2	1.6	1.4	1.5	0.8	0.9	1.4	1.2	1.2
From Chile to														
Argentina	6.0	4.8	4.1	3.1	3.2	2.2	3.8	3.4	2.3	1.3	1.3	2.9	4.6	5.1
Brazil	9.6	7.3	8.3	4.3	6.2	5.4	6.9	6.8	4.7	6.4	5.7	5.0	4.5	5.2
Colombia	1.6	1.8	1.2	1.1	1.2	1.4	1.0	1.0	0.8	1.0	0.9	0.6	0.7	0.9
Peru	1.5	1.8	1.3	1.0	1.2	1.2	1.6	1.7	0.9	0.7	0.9	1.6	1.7	1.5
Venezuela	1.7	1.8	1.2	0.8	1.1	0.9	1.0	1.4	1.5	0.4	0.4	0.6	0.7	0.8
From Colombia to														
Argentina	1.7	1.7	1.2	1.4	1.7	1.0	1.3	0.8	1.0	0.6	0.4	0.5	1.0	1.3
Brazil	0.2	0.2	0.1	0.2	0.4	0.2	0.2	0.4	0.2	0.4	0.4	0.7	0.9	2.0

TABLE 12 (continued)

Chile	1.6	1.0	0.4	0.4	0.5	0.6	0.6	2.0	2.4	2.3	2.4	2.2	1.3	1.3
Peru	0.7	1.5	1.1	0.6	0.7	0.9	1.4	2.4	1.7	1.1	1.3	2.9	4.2	4.6
Venezuela	7.1	11.5	11.8	3.8	2.8	3.6	2.9	4.4	4.4	3.2	3.0	5.9	6.8	7.3
From Peru to														
Argentina	1.5	0.6	0.8	1.2	1.1	1.2	2.3	1.5	0.6	0.5	0.9	0.9	0.8	1.0
Brazil	3.2	1.5	2.2	2.0	1.5	1.8	2.9	4.2	3.0	4.5	3.9	3.1	4.7	0.0
Chile	1.2	1.8	1.2	1.5	1.6	1.7	2.0	1.2	1.5	1.9	1.7	1.3	1.2	1.2
Colombia	1.4	2.8	4.2	1.7	2.4	2.5	2.6	2.4	3.1	3.0	2.9	3.2	2.5	3.2
Venezuela	1.3	1.4	1.7	1.0	1.6	1.4	1.8	2.4	3.1	1.2	1.7	2.4	3.1	3.6
From Venezuela to														
Argentina	0.3	0.2	0.1	0.0	0.0	0.0	0.1	0.0	0.2	0.2	0.0	0.1	0.2	0.2
Brazil	3.5	4.7	5.3	3.7	3.2	1.8	0.8	1.4	1.5	2.0	1.9	1.8	2.8	2.9
Chile	1.3	1.7	1.4	1.4	1.4	1.7	1.4	1.3	1.4	1.2	1.0	0.8	0.8	0.3
Colombia	1.4	1.6	1.8	2.2	2.0	1.6	1.2	0.1	1.7	2.1	2.1	1.5	2.2	2.5
Peru	0.1	0.1	0.1	0.1	0.1	0.2	0.4	0.1	0.5	0.2	0.2	0.5	0.8	0.9
From the world to														
Argentina	0.6	0.5	0.3	0.3	0.3	0.2	0.3	0.3	0.2	0.2	0.1	0.3	0.4	0.4
Brazil	1.0	1.1	1.1	0.9	0.8	0.8	0.7	0.7	0.6	0.7	0.6	0.6	0.6	0.5
Chile	0.3	0.3	0.2	0.2	0.2	0.1	0.2	0.2	0.2	0.2	0.2	0.2	0.3	0.5
Colombia	0.3	0.3	0.3	0.3	0.2	0.2	0.2	0.2	0.2	0.2	0.2	0.1	0.2	0.2
Peru	0.2	0.2	0.2	0.1	0.1	0.1	0.1	0.1	0.1	0.1	0.1	0.1	0.1	0.1
Venezuela	0.6	0.6	0.7	0.3	0.4	0.4	0.4	0.4	0.4	0.2	0.2	0.3	0.3	0.2

[a]Through October 1993 except for the case of exports from Argentina to Brazil, which corresponds to May 1993.

Source: IMF, *Direction of Trade Statistics*.

TABLE 13

Amount and Percentage of Direct Foreign Investment Coming from within Latin America, 1987 and 1992

	1987[a]		1992[b]	
COUNTRY	AMOUNT (MILLIONS OF DOLLARS)	PERCENTAGE OF TOTAL	AMOUNT (MILLIONS OF DOLLARS)	PERCENTAGE OF TOTAL
Argentina	21.07	28.0	99.00	32.6
Bolivia	0.01	1.1	31.89	31.6
Brazil	< 0.00	< 0.0	84.78	7.9
Chile	30.82	5.7	73.71	7.5
Colombia	< 0.00	< 0.0	58.65	27.2
Ecuador	17.70	30.1	4.70	38.2
Paraguay	0.05	5.1	50.30	43.0
Peru	17.85	65.3	46.91	29.0
Uruguay	15.51	56.4	3.24	59.3
Venezuela	22.49	4.7	94.39	40.8

[a]Argentina, 1986; Paraguay, 1984.

[b]Argentina, 1989; Bolivia, 1990; Brazil, Ecuador, and Venezuela, 1991.

Source: CEPAL 1993.

which suggests that in a context of generalized liberalization, investment projects, especially in infrastructure, aimed at facilitating intraregional trade will have a particularly high (social) rate of return.

An interesting development during the early 1990s is that intraregional direct foreign investment—that is, investment going from one country to another country within the region—greatly increased (see table 13). This suggests that privatization generated forces toward a market-driven integration going well beyond what planners envisaged during the 1960s.

MERCOSUR

MERCOSUR is a trade agreement signed by Argentina, Brazil, Paraguay, and Uruguay in 1991.[11] Its main goal is to eliminate all tariffs for intraregional trade by December 1994 and to establish a common external tariff that would guide international trade between the member countries and the rest of the world. What is particularly interesting about MERCOSUR is that it groups the two largest countries in South America—Argentina and Brazil—with two of the smallest (Chile, which was invited to join but declined, is moving briskly toward integration with Argentina through the signature of bilateral agreements). The data contained in table 14 clearly highlight some of the differences among these coun-

[11]The legal document that sets the basis for MERCOSUR is the Asunción Treaty, which had its origins in an integration act signed between Argentina and Brazil in 1986. New acts were signed between these two countries in 1989 and 1990 (for details, see Nogués and Quintanilla 1992).

TABLE 14

Economic Indicators for Members of MERCOSUR and the Andean Pact, 1992

	MERCOSUR				ANDEAN PACT				
INDICATOR	ARGENTINA	BRAZIL	PARAGUAY	URUGUAY	BOLIVIA	COLOMBIA	ECUADOR	PERU	VENEZUELA
GDP, 1992 (millions of U.S. dollars)	154,400	406,500	6,500	11,400	5,300	46,200	12,400	26,300	61,100
GNP per capita, 1992 (U.S. dollars)[a]	4,160	2,940[b]	1,410	2,840	680	1,300	1,060	1,080	2,920
GDP growth, 1980–92 (annual average, percent)	0.6	1.2	2.7	0.7	0.7	3.4	2.4	–0.7	2.1
Share of manufacturing in GDP 1992 (percent)	22	22[b]	17	25	16[b]	20[b]	21[b]	—	16
Investment ratio, 1992 (percent)	17	19	24	13	16	18	20	16[b]	23
Merchandise exports, 1992 (millions of U.S. dollars)	12,000	36,200	920	1,700	600	7,300	3,000	3,500	14,000
Growth of exports, 1980–92[c] (annual average, percent)	3.5	7.1	7.2	4.2	3.4	5.7	5.0	–0.9[b]	2.0
Total external debt, 1992 (millions of U.S. dollars)	66,500	118,700	1,800	5,200	4,200	16,700	12,300	21,000	33,700
Inflation, 1980–92[d] (annual average, percent)	341	373	23	63	170	25	38	287	22

— Not available.

Note: All 1992 data are preliminary estimates.

[a]Calculated according to the method of the *World Bank Atlas*.

[b]1991 data.

[c]Exports of goods and nonfactor services, in constant prices.

[d]Growth in GDP deflator, compound rate.

Sources: World Bank, *World Development Report 1993*, "World Development Indicators"; database of the International Economics Department and country department staff estimates.

TABLE 15
Trade among Members of MERCOSUR, 1992

COUNTRY	PERCENTAGE OF TOTAL EXPORTS	AMOUNT (MILLIONS OF U.S. DOLLARS)
Argentina	17	2,100
Brazil	11	4,100
Paraguay	37	220
Uruguay	34	540

Source: Database of the IMF, *Direction of Trade Statistics*.

tries, including size, recent performance, and extent of international indebtedness. There is little doubt that the future of MERCOSUR will depend on the policies of Argentina and Brazil; Uruguay and Paraguay, as (much) smaller members, are likely to play a limited role in the political-diplomatic process that will determine the actual characteristics of the agreement. The big question is whether Brazil will be able to maintain its stabilization program on course and thereby reduce inflation to international levels in the near future. (Baldinelli 1991 discusses some of the most important macroeconomic policies in the MERCOSUR countries.)

The differences in strategy regarding the speed and depth of privatization and trade reform suggest that disagreements could easily erupt between Argentina and Brazil with regard to points closely related to MERCOSUR. In particular, many observers in Argentina are concerned that Brazil will insist on a relatively high common external tariff. The current structure of protection in the individual members of MERCOSUR shows that there may indeed be some room for disagreement. While Argentina recently embraced a significant free trade stance—slashing tariffs, considerably reducing nontariff barriers, and completely eliminating export taxes—Brazil is aiming at a higher and more variable tariff structure.

Table 15 contains data from 1992 on the level of intraregional trade for the MERCOSUR members. As can be seen, intraregional trade is more important for Argentina (with 17 percent) than for Brazil (11 percent; historically, Brazil's intraregional trade was significantly lower, on the order of 4 percent of total exports). It is, in fact, Argentina that is bound to lose more if MERCOSUR is aborted. From a political economy perspective, this means that in negotiations regarding policies toward third parties, Brazil may have an important edge. If this is the case, and MERCOSUR is implemented around high import tariffs—with a range of 0 to 40 percent, which corresponds to the Brazilian liberalization target—it is very unlikely that its members will experience a net gain over the long run. More specifically, if Argentina were to join a trade agreement with a Brazilian-level common external tariff, the result would probably be a diversion of trade that would more than offset any benefits derived from the creation of trade.

Table 16 presents the path that the elimination of tariffs is expected to take within MERCOSUR. Two main differences with respect to previous attempts at integration immediately stand out (on historical integrationist attempts in Latin America, see Edwards and Savastano 1988). First, there is a very high degree of automaticity in the integration process within MERCOSUR, and, second, the time frame allowed for integration is significantly shorter than those attempted previously. These features of the Asunción Treaty

TABLE 16
Percentage of Imports Subject to Free Trade in MERCOSUR, 1991–94

DATE	PERCENTAGE
1991	
June	47
December	54
1992	
June	61
December	68
1993	
June	75
December	82
1994	
June	89
December	100

Source: Asunción Treaty.

are a clear reflection that, even in an agreement dominated by a reluctant reformer such as Brazil, the rules governing opening up are aggressive and dynamic. An important, and as yet unresolved, question, however, is whether this ambitious, automatic intraregional liberalization program can be sustained in the presence of major macroeconomic imbalances in Brazil.

REVIVAL OF THE ANDEAN PACT

In November 1990, more than two decades after its initial launching, the Andean Pact was renewed by the presidents of Bolivia, Colombia, Ecuador, Peru, and Venezuela (Chile, an original signatory of the pact, declined to participate). The new agreement, which came to be known as the Acta de la Paz, established a number of ambitious targets, including (1) the implementation of a regional free trade zone by 1992, (2) an agreement on the level and structure of the common external tariff by December 1991, (3) the implementation of the common external tariff by December 1995, (4) the liberalization of maritime and air transportation, and (5) the facilitation of foreign investment and capital mobility within the Andean group (Nogués and Quintanilla 1992 provide a detailed account of the Acta de la Paz).

There is great heterogeneity among the countries in the pact (table 14). These differences refer both to economic structure as well as to macroeconomic policy. For instance, while Bolivia is moving steadily toward low inflation and price stability, Venezuela is facing a new macroeconomic and political crisis. Despite large increases during 1992 and 1993, the volume of intraregional trade remains somewhat limited (see table 17). This reflects both the similarity of factor endowments across these countries and the existence of significant impediments related both to administrative and commercial regulations as well as to an extremely poor system of land transportation. The relatively low level of current intraregional trade suggests, in fact, the possibility of a significant diversion of trade once the

TABLE 17
Trade among Andean Pact Countries, 1992

COUNTRY	PERCENTAGE OF ALL EXPORTS	AMOUNT (MILLIONS OF U.S. DOLLARS)
Bolivia	13	90
Colombia	13	920
Ecuador	3	90
Peru	8	270
Venezuela	3	510

Source: Database of the IMF, *Direction of Trade Statistics.*

customs union is launched. Whether this actually happens will depend largely on the level and structure of the common external tariff. This, in fact, is a highly controversial issue that is threatening the future of the pact.

As the discussion of the extent of the reforms showed, the Andean Pact nations have a significantly more homogeneous structure of protection than the MERCOSUR countries. In spite of this, there are still some important differences regarding the objectives of overall trade policy. While Bolivia and Peru pursued aggressive free trade reforms, Colombia and Venezuela maintained a more protectionist stance, arguing that higher tariffs are still necessary to encourage the formation of a strong industrial base. More recently, however, the Colombian government has been more inclined to accelerate its opening up and its integration with the rest of the world. The differences regarding commercial policies have already generated serious friction among the Acta de la Paz signatories, with Peru threatening to abandon the pact altogether if the common external tax is set at an "excessively protectionist" rate (the new political development in Peru, and especially the Fujimori "coup," added some uncertainty to the integrationist process).

In December 1991, and in accordance with the Acta de la Paz, a new agreement was signed by the Andean group's political authorities. The Act of Barahona established free trade zones among Bolivia, Colombia, and Venezuela starting on January 1, 1992. Ecuador and Peru were expected to join the free trade zone later. With respect to the common external tariff, the Act of Barahona established an extremely cumbersome mechanism, with exceptions across both countries and goods. More specifically, the common external tariff had four levels (0, 5, 10, and 15 percent), except for Bolivia, which only had levels of 5 and 10 percent. There were also exceptions for agricultural goods, automobiles, and noncompeting regional products; their tariff levels are still to be determined. From the beginning, this agreement on common external tariff had a serious problem, including the fact that rules of origin were not determined. For all practical purposes, the lowest tariffs (those of Bolivia) could become the effective common external tariff for the region as a whole.

In May 1992, only a few months after the common external tariff agreement, the future of the Andean Pact suffered a blow when Peru unilaterally suspended the preferential treatment granted to imports from within the pact. This action was part of a general Peruvian policy aimed at imposing a lower common external tariff. As a consequence, the governments of Colombia and Venezuela suspended negotiations with Peru. It is too early to say whether the Andean integrationist movement will continue to move forward or whether it will result in its (second) death. In fact, the border conflict between Peru and Ecuador has greatly increased the level of political-diplomatic tension in the region.

REVITALIZATION OF THE CENTRAL AMERICAN COMMON MARKET AND STRENGTHENING OF THE CARICOM

During the early and mid-1980s, and largely as a result of the international debt crisis, the Central American Common Market (CACM) began to break down. Most countries in the area responded to the debt crisis by imposing massive nontariff barriers, including multiple exchange rates. The most important consequence of this increase in protectionism was that the CACM's common external tariff ceased to be relevant as, de facto, members had different implicit tariffs for imports coming from outside the region. In 1986, the CACM received a fatal blow when the Central American payments clearing mechanism collapsed (partially as a result of Nicaragua's accumulation of very large debt; see Saborio and Michalopoulos 1992).

In July 1991, after several years of independently undertaking trade adjustment, the presidents of the Central American nations agreed to revitalize the CACM (the details of the agreement appear in the *Declaration of San Salvador,* July 17, 1991). Three important features of the renewed CACM are worth noting: first, the agreed common external tariff contemplated a range between 5 and 20 percent. This was significantly lower than the tariff structure of most Central American countries until recently and represented a clear move toward trade liberalization (see table 18). Second the newly revitalized CACM included two new countries: Panama, which never joined the original agreement, and Honduras which withdrew from it in 1969. And, third, members of the CACM actively used export-promotion schemes to diversify and increase exports. Although it is still too early to know how successful these schemes are, Saborio and Michalopoulos (1992) suggest that they are costly from a fiscal perspective, without expanding exports significantly over and above what could be obtained through more competitive real exchange rates. The renewed CACM is a far cry from the agreement originally enacted in the 1960s. Instead of promoting an inefficient and forced process of industrialization behind protective walls, the countries in the region are uniting forces as a way to compete internationally and expand exports rapidly.

The attempts at commercial integration among the very small and extremely open Caribbean economies date back to the mid-1960s. In 1965, Antigua, Barbados, and Guyana subscribed to the articles of a Caribbean Free Trade Association (CARIFTA). Three years later, in May 1968, eight other Caribbean countries (Dominica, Grenada, Jamaica,

TABLE 18

Tariff Structures in the Central American Common Market (percentage)

COUNTRY	PRE-REFORM AVERAGE TARIFFS[a]	AVERAGE LEGAL TARIFF, 1987	1991 RANGE	1993 RANGE	1995 RANGE
Costa Rica	52	26	10–50	5–30	5–20
El Salvador	48	23	5–35	5–25	5–20
Guatemala	50	25	5–37	5–20	5–20
Honduras	41	20	4–35	5–20	5–20
Nicaragua	54	21	5–20	5–20	5–20

[a]Ad valorem equivalent of average external tariff.

Source: Saborio and Michalopoulos 1992.

Montserrat, St. Kitts-Nevis-Anguilla, St. Lucia, St. Vincent and the Grenadines, and Trinidad and Tobago) ratified this agreement; the remaining Caribbean nation, Belize, joined the association in 1971 (this paragraph and the two that follow draw on Edwards and Savastano 1988).

The CARIFTA agreement immediately freed most of the trade among its member countries from import and export duties and from nontariff barriers. A five-year schedule for eliminating intraregional tariffs was designed for the few import-substituting products exempted from the regulation. However, the agreement did not consider any measure related to the imposition of a common external tariff. Intraregional trade increased significantly after the establishment of CARIFTA; between 1967 and 1973, the share of intraregional trade rose from approximately 8 to 11 percent.

The gains from this integration, however, were strongly biased in favor of the more industrial countries of the agreement, which accounted for more than 90 percent of the intraregional trade. Given this asymmetry in the distribution of benefits, the less industrial countries exerted pressure for broadening the scope of integration. In particular, they sought to establish mechanisms that would imply a more favorable treatment for them within the agreement. As a result, CARICOM was established in August 1973. Its objectives went further than commercial integration; they included harmonizing monetary and fiscal policies and creating planning agencies for agricultural and industrial development. Also, a common external tariff for imports from nonmember countries was established. Despite the almost immediate adoption of the common external tariff, the adverse external terms of trade caused by the oil shock of the 1970s prompted protectionist responses—in the form of restrictive import licensing—from Guyana and Jamaica. This action not only negatively affected the level of intraregional trade—the share in total trade dropped to 8 percent in 1975 and 7 percent in 1976—but also provoked antagonism and retaliatory responses from the other members of CARICOM. Although conciliatory measures were subsequently attempted, the share of intraregional trade remained around 7 percent, and the trade flows continued to be heavily concentrated among the four more industrial countries of the region.

In February 1991, the CARICOM heads of state decided to revive the association and to rationalize the trade regime. The most important step was to reduce the common external tariff band from 0–70 percent to 0–45 percent. In October 1992, a further step was taken when the common external tariff was reduced to a 5–20 percent range within a period of four to five years. Although the pace of reform was somewhat slower than that followed by some other recent reformers, this measure clearly put the CARICOM nations on the path of liberalization and outward orientation.

The North American Free Trade Agreement

As in most of Latin America, Mexico's trade policy was characterized for decades by a significant degree of protectionism and inward orientation. Starting in late 1985 and as a component of a major structural adjustment plan, Mexico embarked on an ambitious unilateral program of trade liberalization. Import tariffs were halved, and import licenses were reduced from 92 to 20 percent.

After almost a decade of intensive, and often confrontational, trade negotiations, the United States and Mexico agreed in November 1990 to move toward a free trade agreement. In February 1991, Canada, Mexico, and the United States began negotiating the North American Free Trade Agreement, and later that year the U.S. Congress approved the fast-track treatment of the agreement. On August 12, 1992, the three parties announced that a consensus had been reached on the exact nature of the proposed agreement.

Both the United States and Mexican negotiators had originally expected that the U.S. government would submit the agreement to Congress in the summer of 1992. However, U.S. presidential politics, plus deep disagreements regarding details of the agreement, delayed its submission until late 1993. The most important areas of contention between U.S. and Mexican negotiators referred to (1) defining the rules of origin for specific products, (2) establishing the rules for agricultural trade, (3) determining the treatment that would be given to automobiles, (4) workers' protection in Mexico, and (5) environmental rules in Mexico, especially on the border. Of these, perhaps the most important problem was defining rules of origin. After a grueling debate, and the hasty implementation of a number of side agreements, the U.S. Congress finally passed NAFTA in November 1993. The agreement established very different speeds of liberalization for different sectors. For example, according to the final text, in order for motor vehicles to be subject to free trade within NAFTA, their regional value added should initially be at least 50 percent. This figure, however, will increase slowly for a period of eight years, until it reaches 62.5 percent. Regarding the agriculture sector, the agreement proposes, for most items, the slow elimination of tariffs over a period of fifteen years.

Various authors predict that NAFTA will have a severely negative effect on Mexico's agricultural sector (ITAM 1994). In fact, the January 1994 uprising in Chiapas by the Zapatista Mayan Indians was, at least in part, the result of the perception that NAFTA would destroy traditional agriculture in that state. A recent study by Velez and Rubio (1994) indicates that production of most grains in Mexico—sorghum, wheat, barley, soybeans, beans, and maize—will suffer considerably by implementation of the free trade agreement. Grain production in Mexico is extremely inefficient and subject to a high degree of protection. To avoid the devastating impact that free trade could have on Mexican agriculture, NAFTA considered the implementation of high initial tariffs at a level that would replicate the protection granted by traditional licenses. These duties will be phased out gradually through time. For instance, NAFTA established an initial import tariff on barley of 128 percent, which will be eliminated gradually in ten years. Maize is, perhaps, the most dramatic case of inefficient production. Mexico's average yields are approximately 1.7 tons per hectare, barely one-fourth of average yields in the United States. NAFTA established a tariff quota for maize imports into Mexico. Initially, Mexico will be able to import 2.5 million tons of maize duty-free. During the first year of NAFTA, imports above that level will be subject to a 215 percent tariff, but it will be completely liberalized in fifteen years.

As Nogués and Quintanilla (1992) argue, the heavy media coverage received by NAFTA negotiations tended to overshadow the broader commitment made by the Mexican government toward freer trade. In fact, after becoming a member of the General Agreement on Tariffs and Trade (GATT) in 1986, Mexico consistently and systematically pursued freer trade policies. This was reflected in the reduction in trade impediments, in the signing of bilateral trade agreements with Chile (1991), and in the discussions to sign free trade agreements with Venezuela (1993), Colombia, and Central America. The recent negotiations to become a member of the Organization for Economic Cooperation and Development also underlie the importance of freer trade as a fundamental component of the national development strategy for the next decade. However, for this policy position to be translated into additional gains in productivity and welfare, it will be necessary to reduce tariffs and license coverage even further and to extend the reforms to all areas of the economy, especially agriculture.

The GATT and the Prospects for Global Trade Liberalization

There is little doubt that Latin America has embarked on one of the most substantial unilateral trade liberalization reforms in modern economic history. However, a serious concern among the region's political leaders is the lack of reciprocity from the industrial countries. While the Latin American nations greatly opened up their trade sector to foreign competition, most industrial nations continued to follow protectionist practices. In fact, as captured in table 19, the industrial countries traditionally imposed significant restrictions on Latin American exports. These trade impediments mostly took the form of nontariff barriers, including quotas, prohibitions, and licenses. The approval of the GATT's Uruguay Round package in December 1993 provides some hope that in the years to come multilateralism will produce a more-open system of world trade (see table 20 for a summary of the Uruguay Round's most important implications for Latin America).

Before 1947, when the first round of multilateral trade negotiations was held in Geneva, average tariff protection in industrial countries was above 100 percent (this discussion is based on Losada 1994). Fueled by the Smoot-Hawley Tariff Act of 1930, protectionist ideas grew during the 1930s, 1940s, and 1950s. After seven rounds of GATT-sponsored negotiations, average tariff protection had been reduced to 5 percent by 1993; however, most industrial countries continued to use an extensive array of nontariff barriers that effectively raised the degree of protection. By 1993, imports from developing countries into some industrial countries were, for all practical purposes, prohibited.

The liberalization of world trade contemplated in the Uruguay Round will be implemented gradually throughout a period of ten years. From an institutional point of view, one of the most important elements of the agreement is the creation of the World Trade Organization, which replaced the GATT in 1995. Negotiations about market access, which will largely determine the extent of the liberalization effort, were completed in mid-1995.

Table 19

Protection in OECD Countries against Latin American Exports, Mid-1980s (percentage)

Country	Import-Weighted Level of Nontariff Barriers
Argentina	63.0
Brazil	38.3
Chile	23.8
Mexico	8.4
Peru	12.8
Uruguay	23.2
Venezuela	3.2
Central America	17.1
Average for Latin America and the Caribbean	28.6

Source: Leamer 1990.

Some authors (Corden 1984, for example) predict that regional integration schemes will act as intermediate steps toward a more perfect multilateral system based on the GATT and the World Trade Organization. There are, however, some problems with this idea. The current structure of trading blocs is not cooperative across groups, so that the gains from more trade within a bloc have to be compared with the losses from less trade between blocs. Moreover, the United States is currently pushing a policy of reciprocity rather than free trade.

The Uruguay Round covers trade in agriculture and textiles and the regulation of services and investment. Overall, according to the agreement, industrial countries will have to reduce the average trade-weighted tariffs on exports from developing countries 34 percent in ten years (from 6 to 4 percent). Developing countries, in turn, will have to increase the coverage of duties bound and to remove export subsidies. In some cases, the reduction will be impressive; for instance, Brazil is committed to lowering import tariffs from a maximum of 105 percent to a ceiling of 35 percent. Trade-distorting investment measures, such as local content requirements, will be eliminated in five to seven years.

The streamlining of the protection of intellectual property is expected to help some developing countries that have started exporting knowledge-intensive goods, such as software and agricultural technology. However, the liberalization measures agreed to in December 1993 are rather timid in some areas, especially agriculture, and the timetable for implementation is too lengthy. Safeguard rules are expected to be softened and could be introduced in a discriminatory way and without compensation. Unfortunately, these antidumping measures could give rise to a new form of disguised protectionism.

The successful completion of the Uruguay Round is expected to provide both static and dynamic gains to the world economy. The developing countries will receive about one-third of these gains. Trade is expected to grow 12 percent in the next ten years, due exclusively to the Uruguay Round. Developing countries will not receive a significant share of the dynamic gains, however, since economies of scale and technological spillovers through greater innovation are likely to accrue to exporters of industrial goods.

TABLE 20

Main Results of the Uruguay Round for Latin America and the Caribbean

AREA	RESULTS
Market access	Overall cut of 33 percent in import tariffs on industrial products, reductions in peaks and escalation; tariffs reduced in five equal annual steps, starting when the World Trade Organization comes into effect; weighted average tariff down from 6.4 to 4.0 percent in industrial countries; share of duty-free imports from 20 to 43 percent in industrial countries; developing-country tariff bindings increased from 12 to 56 percent of imports
	Lower than average tariff cuts made in sensitive sectors, such as textiles, clothing, footwear, and transport equipment
	42 percent reduction in tariffs on tropical agricultural products and 57 percent on tropical industrial products in industrial countries; erosion of preference margins experienced by some developing countries
	34 percent cut in tariffs on natural resource-based products; larger than average gains for some metals and minerals, smaller gains for fish
	Developing countries with high per capita income required to phase out subsidies within eight years
Agriculture	Gradual liberalization process in this sector: over six years for industrial countries and ten years for developing countries; bindings on agricultural tariffs increased from 81 to 95 percent of imports (industrial countries) and from 23 to 90 percent (developing countries); virtual elimination of all nontariff barriers; minimum tariff cut of 15 percent on all tariff lines by industrial countries, with an average tariff reduction of 36 percent over six years from a 1986–88 base; restrictions against imports subject to a tariff commitment
	Export subsidies reduced 36 percent in value and 21 percent in volume over the implementation period; domestic support programs reduced 20 percent
	Special safeguard provisions enacted that permit the imposition of additional duties up to certain limits, triggered by both price and volume clauses

TABLE 20 (continued)

AREA	RESULTS
Textiles and clothing	Four-step phaseout of the Multi-Fibre Agreement over ten years; gradual integration of the sector into the World Trade Organization; expansion of outstanding quota restrictions; provisions to redistribute quotas in favor of quota-constrained and efficient exporters; developing-country exporters accounting for less than 3 percent of a country's imports of a product exempted from safeguard action if all developing-country members with less than a 3 percent share account for less than 9 percent overall
Intellectual property rights	National treatment and most-favored-nation clauses applied to all intellectual property rights; subsidies for research activities are declared nonactionable; minimum standards provided for copyrights, trademarks, industrial design, patents, and so forth Patent protection for twenty years in all areas of technology, including pharmaceuticals One year's delay in the implementation of trade-related intellectual property rights after the establishment of the World Trade Organization; the delay for developing and transitional economies extended to five years, except for the most-favored-nation and national treatment clauses
Services	Multilateral rules extended to a large segment of world trade (20 percent); general agreement on trade in services that establishes the nondiscrimination principle, including most of the GATT-type provisions Framework for establishing and maintaining liberalization commitments; continuing negotiations related to safeguards, subsidies, and government procurement; special appendixes that address specificity of sectors

Source: Author's elaboration from several GATT documents.

REFERENCES

Agacino, R., Gonzalo Rivas, and Enrique Román. 1992. "Apertura y eficiencia productiva: La experiencia chilena, 1975–1989." Working Paper 113. Inter-American Development Bank, Washington, D.C.

Agarwala, Ramgopal. 1983. *Price Distortions and Growth in Developing Countries.* World Bank Staff Working Paper 575. Washington, D.C.

Agenor, Pierre-Richard, and Mark P. Taylor. 1992. "Testing for Credibility Effects." *IMF Staff Papers* 39 (September): 545–71.

Aghevli, Bijan, James Boughton, Peter Montiel, Delano Villanueva, and Geoffrey Woglom. 1990. "The Role of National Saving in the World Economy: Recent Trends and Prospects." *IMF Occasional Paper No. 67.* Washington, D.C.

Aizenman, Joshua. 1990. "Trade Reforms, Credibility, and Development." Working Paper 3600. National Bureau of Economic Research, Cambridge, Mass.

Alesina, Alberto. 1988. "Macroeconomics and Politics." In Stanley Fischer, ed., *NBER Macroeconomics Annual.* Cambridge, Mass.: MIT Press.

Alesina, Alberto, and Allan Drazen. 1991. "Why Are Stabilizations Delayed?" *American Economic Review* 81 (5): 1170–88.

Alesina, Alberto, and Guido Tabellini. 1988. "Voting on the Budget Deficit." Working Paper 2759. National Bureau of Economic Research, Cambridge, Mass.

Alexander, Myrna, and Carlos Corti. 1993. "Privatization in Argentina." World Bank, Latin America and Caribbean Region, Washington, D.C.

Altimir, Oscar. 1982. *The Extent of Poverty in Latin America.* World Bank Staff Working Paper 522. Washington, D.C.

Altimir, Oscar, and Sebastian Piñera. 1979. "Análisis de descomposiciones de las desigualdades de ingreso en América Latina." In Oscar Muñoz, ed., *La desigualdad del ingreso en América Latina.* Buenos Aires: El Cid.

Arellano, José Pablo. 1982. *Modelo económico chileno: Trayectoria de una critica.* Santiago: Editorial Aconcagua.

Arellano, Rogelio. 1990. "On the Causes and Consequences of Real Exchange Rate Variability: A Comparative Analysis of the East Asian and Latin American Experiences." Ph.D. diss. University of California, Los Angeles, Department of Economics.

Aschauer, David Allan. 1989. "Does Public Capital Crowd out Private Capital?" *Journal of Monetary Economics* 24 (2): 171–88.

Aspe, Pedro. 1993. *Economic Transformation the Mexican Way.* Cambridge, Mass.: MIT Press.

Azariadis, Costas, and Allan Drazen. 1990. "Threshold Externalities in Economic Development." *Quarterly Journal of Economics* 105 (May): 501–26.

Balassa, Bela, and Associates. 1971. *The Structure of Protection in Developing Countries.* Baltimore, Md.: Johns Hopkins University Press.

________ . 1982. *Development Strategies in Semi-Industrial Economies.* Baltimore, Md.: Johns Hopkins University Press.

________ . 1985. "Exports, Policy Choices, and Economic Growth in Developing Countries after the 1973 Oil Shock." *Journal of Development Economics* 18 (2): 23–25.

________ . 1988. "Outward Orientation." In Hollis Chenery and T. N. Srinivasan, eds., *Handbook of Development Economics.* Amsterdam: North-Holland.

Baldinelli, Elvio. 1991. "Armonización de políticas fiscales, crediticias, y de promoción de exportaciones." *Instituto para la Integración de América Latina* 16 (May): 3–17.

Baliño, Tomás. 1991. "The Argentine Banking Crisis of 1980." In Tomás Baliño and Vasudevan Sundararajan, eds., *Banking Crisis: Cases and Issues.* Washington, D.C.: International Monetary Fund.

Banco Central de Chile. 1993. *Compendium of Rules on International Exchange.* Santiago.

———. Various years. *Boletín Mensual.* Santiago.

Bank of Mexico. 1995. *Exposición sobre politica monetaria: para el lapso de enero de 1995–31 de diciembre de 1995.* Mexico City.

Barro, Robert. 1974. "Are Government Bonds Net Wealth?" *Journal of Political Economy* 81 (December): 1095–1117.

________. 1991. "Economic Growth in a Cross-Section of Countries." *Quarterly Journal of Economics* 106 (May): [407]–43.

Barros, Ricardo. 1992. "Welfare, Inequality, Poverty, and Social Conditions in Brazil in the Last Three Decades." Paper presented at the conference Poverty and Inequality in Latin America, Brookings Institution, Washington, D.C., July.

Becker, Gary S. 1983. "A Theory of Competition among Pressure Groups for Political Influence." *Quarterly Journal of Economics* 98 (August): 371–400.

Beristain, Javier, and Ignacio Trigueros. 1990. "Mexico." In John Williamson, ed., *Latin American Adjustment: How Much Has Happened?* Washington, D.C.: Institute for International Economics.

Bhagwati, Jagdish. 1978. *Foreign Trade Regimes and Economic Development: Anatomy and Consequences of Exchange Control Regimes.* Cambridge, Mass.: National Bureau of Economic Research.

Bianchi, Andrés, Robert Devlin, and Joseph Ramos. 1987. "The Adjustment Process in Latin America, 1981–1986." Paper presented at the World Bank and International Monetary Fund Symposium on Growth-Oriented Adjustment Programs, Washington, D.C., February.

Bianchi, Andrés, and Takahashi Nohara, eds. 1988. *A Comparative Study on Economic Development between Asia and Latin America.* Tokyo: Institute of Developing Economies.

Binswanger, Hans P., Klaus Deininger, and Gershon Feder. 1993. "Agricultural Land Relations in the Developing World." *American Journal of Agricultural Economics* 75 (December): 1242–48.

Blanchard, Olivier, and Stanley Fischer. 1989. *Lectures on Macroeconomics.* Cambridge, Mass.: MIT Press.

Boeninger, Edgardo. 1992. "Governance and Development: Issues, Challenges, Opportunities, and Constraints." *Proceedings of the World Bank Annual Conference on Development Economics 1991.* Washington, D.C.: World Bank.

Bonelli, Regis. 1992. "Growth and Productivity in Brazilian Industries: Impacts of Trade Orientation. *Journal of Development Economics* 39 (1): 85–109.

Boskin, Michael. 1978. "Taxation, Savings, and the Rate of Interest." *Journal of Political Economy* 86 (supplement: S3–S27).

Bosworth, Barry. 1993. *Saving and Investment in the Open Economy.* Washington, D.C.: Brookings Institution.

Bruno, Michael. 1991. "High Inflation and the Nominal Anchors of an Open Economy." Princeton Essays in International Finance 183. International Finance Section, Department of Economics, Princeton University, Princeton, N.J.

Buffie, Edward, and Allen Sangines. 1988. "Economic Policy and Foreign Debt in Mexico." In Jeffrey Sachs, ed., *Developing Country Debt and Economic Performance.* Vol. 2: *Country Studies.* Chicago, Ill.: University of Chicago Press.

Bulow, Jeremy, and Kenneth Rogoff. 1988. "The Buyback Boondoggle." *Brookings Papers on Economic Activity* 2: 675–98.

Caballero, Ricardo, and Vittorio Corbo. 1989. "The Effect of Real Exchange Rate Uncertainty on Exports: Empirical Evidence." *World Bank Economic Review* 3 (May): 263–78.

Calvacati de Albuquerque, Marcos. 1992. "A situação social: O que diz o passado e o que promete o futuro." Instituto de Pesquisa Economica Aplicada, Brasília.

Calvo, Guillermo. 1978. "On the Time Consistency of Optimal Policy in a Monetary Economy." *Econometrica* 46 (November): 1411–28.

________. 1986. "Fractured Liberalism: Argentina under Martínez de Hoz." *Economic Development and Cultural Change* 34 (3): 511–33.

________. 1988. "Controlling Inflation: The Problem of Non-Indexed Debt." Working Paper 29. International Monetary Fund, Research Department, Washington, D.C.

________. 1989. "Controlling Inflation: The Problem of Non-Indexed Debt." In Sebastian Edwards and Felipe Larraín, eds., *Debt, Adjustment, and Recovery*. Oxford, Eng.: Basil Blackwell.

________. 1994. "Comments on Dornbusch and Werner." *Brookings Paper on Economic Activity*, No. 1.

Calvo, Guillermo, and Carlos A. Vegh Gramont, 1991. "Exchange Rate–Based Stabilization under Imperfect Credibility." Working Paper 77. International Monetary Fund, Washington, D.C.

Calvo, Guillermo, Leonardo Leiderman, and Carmen Reinhart. 1993. "Capital Inflows and Real Exchange Rate Appreciation in Latin America: The Role of External Factors." *IMF Staff Papers* 40 (March).

Canavese, Alfredo. 1991. "Hyperinflation and Convertibility-Based Stabilization in Argentina." Paper presented at the Conference on Stabilization and Growth, Instituto Torcuato Di Tella, Department of Economics, Buenos Aires, August.

Cárdenas, Mauricio, and Miguel Urrutia. 1992. "Macroeconomic Instability and Social Progress." Fedesarrollo, Bogotá, December.

Cardoso, Eliana A., and Rudiger Dornbusch. 1987. "Brazil's Tropical Plan." *American Economic Review* 77 (2): 288–92.

________. 1989. "Foreign Private Capital Flows." In Hollis Chenery and T. N. Srinivasan, eds., *Handbook of Development Economics*. Amsterdam: North-Holland.

Cardoso, Eliana A., and Ann Helwege. 1991. "Populism, Profligacy, and Redistribution." In Rudiger Dornbusch and Sebastian Edwards, eds., *The Macroeconomics of Populism in Latin America*. Chicago, Ill.: University of Chicago Press.

________. 1992. "Below the Line: Poverty in Latin America." *World Development* 20 (1): 19–37.

Cardoso, Eliana, Ricardo Barros, and Andre Urani. 1993. "Inflation and Unemployment as Determinants of Inequality in Brazil: The 1980s." In Rudiger Dornbusch and Sebastian Edwards, eds., *Stabilization, Economic Reform, and Growth Conference*. Cambridge, Mass.: National Bureau of Economic Research.

Cariaga, Juan. 1990. "Bolivia." In John Williamson, ed., *Latin American Adjustment: How Much Has Happened?* Washington, D.C.: Institute for International Economics.

Carroll, Chris, and Lawrence Summers. 1991. "Consumption Growth Parallels Income Growth." In D. Bernheim and J. Shoven, eds., *National Saving and Economic Performance*. Chicago, Ill.: University of Chicago Press and the National Bureau of Economic Research.

Carroll, Chris, and David N. Weil. 1993. "Savings and Growth: A Reinterpretation." Working Paper 4470. National Bureau of Economic Research, Cambridge, Mass.

Carroll, Lewis. 1872. *Through the Looking Glass: And What Alice Found There*. London: Macmillan.

Castañeda, Tarsicio. 1992. *Combating Poverty: Innovative Social Reforms in Chile during the 1980s*. San Francisco: Calif.: ICS Press.

Castro, Antonio, and Carlos Lessa. 1969. *Introducción a la economía: Un enfoque estructuralista*. Santiago: Editorial Universitaria.

Cavallo, Domingo. 1985. *Volver a crecer*. Buenos Aires: Editorial Sudamericana.

CEPAL (Comisión Económica para América Latina). 1985. "La pobreza en América Latina: Dimensiones y politicas." *Estudios e Informes de la CEPAL* 54. Santiago.

________. 1988. *Balance preliminar de la economía de América Latina y el Caribe*. Santiago.

________. 1989. *Políticas macroeconómicas y brecha externa: América Latina en los años ochenta*. Santiago.

________. 1991. *Statistical Yearbook of Latin America*. Santiago: Comisión Económica para América Latina y el Caribe.

________. 1992a. *Balance preliminar de la economía de América Latina y el Caribe*. Santiago.

________. 1992b. *Equidad y transformación productiva: Un enfoque integrado*. Santiago.

________. 1993. "Directorio sobre inversión extranjera en América Latina y el Caribe 1993: Marco legal e información estadística." Santiago.

________. Various years. *Economic Survey of Latin America*. Santiago.

________. Various years. *Statistical Yearbook for Latin America and the Caribbean*. Santiago.

Cheyre, Hernando. 1991. *La reforma previsional en Chile*. Santiago: CEPAL.

Cline, William. 1989. "From the Baker Plan to the Brady Plan." In Ishrat Husain and Ishac Diwan, eds., *Dealing with the Debt Crisis.* World Bank Symposium. Washington, D.C.

Cochrane, J. 1988. "How Big Is the Random Walk of GNP?" *Journal of Political Economy* 96 (October): 893–920.

Coes, Donald. 1991. "Brazil." In Michael Michaely, Armeane Choksi, and Demetris Papageorgiou, eds., *Liberalizing Foreign Trade.* New York: Basil Blackwell.

Corbo, Vittorio, Timothy Condon, and Jaime de Melo. 1985. "Productivity Growth, External Shocks, and Capital Inflows in Chile: A General Equilibrium Analysis." *Journal of Policy Modeling* 7 (3): 379-405.

Corbo, Vittorio, Jaime de Melo, and James Tybout. 1986. "What Went Wrong in the Southern Cone?" *Economic Development and Cultural Change* 34 (3): 607–40.

Corbo, Vittorio, and Klaus Schmidt-Hebbel. 1991. "Public Policies and Saving in Developing Countries." *Journal of Development Economics* 36 (1): 89–115.

Corden, Warner Max. 1966. "The Structure of a Tariff System and the Effective Protection Rate." *Journal of Political Economy* 74 (3).

________. 1972. "Monetary Integration." Essays in International Finance 93. Princeton University, Princeton, N.J., April.

________. 1984. "The Normative Theory of International Trade." In R. Jones and P. Kenen, eds., *Handbook of International Economics.* Vol. 1. Amsterdam: North-Holland.

________. 1991a. "Exchange Rate Policy in Developing Countries." In Jaime de Melo and A. Sapir, eds., *Trade Theory and Economic Reform.* Cambridge, Mass.: Basil Blackwell.

________. 1991b. "Macroeconomic Policy and Growth: Some Lessons of Experience." *Proceedings of the World Bank Annual Conference on Development Economics 1990.* Washington, D.C.: World Bank.

Cortázar, René. 1982. "Precios y remuneraciones." In *Modelo económico chileno: Trayectoria de una crítica.* Santiago: Editorial Aconcagua.

Cox-Edwards, Alejandra. 1984. "Three Essays on Labor Markets in Developing Countries." Ph.D. diss., University of Chicago, Department of Economics, Chicago, Ill.

________. 1992. "Economic Reforms and Labor Market Legislation in Latin America." California State University, Long Beach, Department of Economics.

Cuddington, John. 1986. "Capital Flight: Estimates, Issues, and Explanations." Princeton Studies in International Finance 58. Princeton University, Princeton, N.J.

Cukierman, Alex. 1992. *Central Bank Strategy, Credibility, and Independence.* Cambridge, Mass.: MIT Press.

Cukierman, Alex, Sebastian Edwards, and Guido Tabellini. 1992. "Seignorage and Political Instability." *American Economic Review* 82 (June): 537–55.

Cumby, Robert, and Richard Levich. 1987. "On the Definition and Magnitude of Recent Capital Flight." Working Paper 2275. National Bureau of Economic Research, Cambridge, Mass.

de Gregorio, José. 1992. "Economic Growth in Latin America." *Journal of Development Economics* 39 (1): [59]–84.

________. 1994. "Inflation, Growth, and Central Banks: Theory and Evidence." Paper presented at the Latin American Seminar on Economic Growth, sponsored by the World Bank and the Inter-American Development Bank, Bogotá, Colombia, June.

De Long, Bradford, and Lawrence Summers. 1991. "Equipment Investment and Economic Growth." *Quarterly Journal of Economics* 106 (May): [445]–502.

De Soto, Hernando. 1986. *El otro sendero.* Lima: Instituto Libertad y Democracia.

Devarajan, Shantayanan, and Dani Rodrik. 1992. "Do the Benefits of Fixed Exchange Rates Outweigh Their Costs? The CFA Zone in Africa." In Ian Goldin and Alan Winters, eds., *Open Economics: Structural Adjustment and Agriculture.* Cambridge, Eng.: Center for Economic Policy Research and Cambridge University Press.

Diamond, Peter, and Salvador Valdés-Prieto. 1994. "Social Security Reforms." In Barry Bosworth, Rudiger Dornbusch, and Raúl Labán, eds., *The Chilean Economy: Policy Lessons and Challenges.* Washington, D.C.: Brookings Institution.

Dias Carneiro, Dionisio. 1987. "El plan cruzado: Una temprana evaluación despues de diez meses." In José Antonio Ocampo, ed., *Planes antiinflacionarios recientes en la América Latina.* Special issue of *El Trimestre Económico* 54 (September).

Díaz-Alejandro, Carlos. 1970. *Essays on the Economic History of the Argentine Republic.* New Haven, Conn.: Yale University Press.

________. 1976. *Foreign Trade Regimes and Economic Development: Colombia.* New York: National Bureau of Economic Research.

________. 1981. "Southern Cone Stabilization Plans." In William Cline and Sidney Weintraub, eds., *Economic Stabilization in Developing Countries.* Washington, D.C.: Brookings Institution.

Diwan, Ishac, and Dani Rodrik. 1992. "External Debt, Adjustment, and Burden Sharing: A Unified Framework." Princeton Studies in International Finance 73. Princeton University, Princeton, N.J.

Dixit, Avinash. 1986. "Tax Policy in Open Economies." In Alan Auerbach and Martin Feldstein, eds., *Handbook of Public Economics.* Amsterdam: North-Holland.

Dornbusch, Rudiger. 1986. "Special Exchange Rates for Capital Account Transactions." *World Bank Economic Review* 1 (September): 3–33.

________. 1989a. "Los costos y beneficios de la integración económica regional: Una revisión." *Pensamiento Iberoamericano* 15 (January–June): 25–53.

________. 1989b. "Debt Problems and the World Macroeconomy." In Jeffrey Sachs, ed., *Developing Country Debt and the World Economy.* Chicago, Ill.: University of Chicago Press.

________. 1991a. "Credibility and Stabilization." *Quarterly Journal of Economics* 106 (August): 837–50.

________. 1991b. "Policies to Move from Stabilization to Growth." *Proceedings of the World Bank Annual Conference on Development Economics 1990.* Washington, D.C.: World Bank.

________. 1992. "Lessons from Experiences with High Inflation." *World Bank Economic Review* 6 (January): 13–31.

Dornbusch, Rudiger, and Sebastian Edwards. 1990. "Macroeconomic Populism." *Journal of Development Economics* 32 (2): 247–77.

Dornbusch, Rudiger, and Sebastian Edwards, eds. 1991. *Macroeconomic Populism in Latin America.* Chicago, Ill.: University of Chicago Press.

Dornbusch, Rudiger, and Stanley Fischer. 1993. "Moderate Inflation." *World Bank Economic Review* 7, 1 (January): 1–44.

Dornbusch, Rudiger, and Alejandro Werner. 1994. "Mexico: Stabilization, Reform and No Growth." *Brookings Papers on Economic Activity,* No. 1.

Easterly, William. 1993. "Explaining Miracles: Growth Regressions Meet the Gang of Four." Paper presented at the East Asian Seminar on Economics, National Bureau of Economic Research, San Francisco, Calif., June.

Edwards, Sebastian. 1984. "The Order of Liberalization of the External Sector in Developing Countries." Princeton Essays in International Finance 156. Princeton University, Princeton, N.J.

________. 1985. "Stabilization with Liberalization: An Evaluation of Ten Years of Chile's Experiment with Free Market Policies, 1973–1983." *Economic Development and Cultural Change* 32 (January): 223–54.

________. 1986a. "Country Risk, Foreign Borrowing, and the Social Discount Rate in an Open Developing Economy." *Journal of International Money and Finance* 5 (March, supplement: S79–S96).

________. 1986b. "Pricing of Bonds and Bank Loans in International Markets: An Empirical Analysis of Developing Countries' Foreign Borrowing." *European Economic Review* 30 (June): 565–89.

________. 1986c. "Stabilization with Liberalization: An Evaluation of Ten Years of Chile's Experience with Free Market Policies, 1973–1983." In Armeane Choksi and Demetris Papageorgiou, eds., *Economic Liberalization in Developing Countries.* Oxford, Eng.: Basil Blackwell.

________. 1988a. *Exchange Rate Misalignment in Developing Countries.* World Bank Occasional Paper 2, New Series. Baltimore, Md.: Johns Hopkins University Press.

________. 1988b. "Financial Deregulation and Segmented Capital Markets: The Case of Korea." *World Development* 16 (January): 185–94.

________ . 1989a. "The Debt Crisis and Macroeconomic Adjustment in Latin America." *Latin American Research Review* 24 (3): 172–86.

________ . 1989b. "Exchange Rate Misalignment in Developing Countries." *World Bank Research Observer* 4 (1): 3–21.

________ . 1989c. "The International Monetary Fund and the Developing Countries: A Critical Evaluation." *Carnegie-Rochester Conference Series on Public Policy* 31 (autumn): 7–68.

________. 1989d. *Real Exchange Rates, Devaluation, and Adjustment: Exchange Rate Policy in Developing Countries.* Cambridge, Mass.: MIT Press.

________ . 1991. "Capital Flows, Foreign Direct Investment, and Debt-Equity Swaps in Developing Countries." In Horst Siebert, ed., *Capital Flows in the World Economy.* Symposium 1990. Tübingen, Ger.: JBC Mohr.

________ . 1992a. "The Sequencing of Structural Adjustment and Stabilization." ICEG Occasional Paper 34. International Center for Economic Growth, San Francisco, Calif.

________ . 1992b. "Sequencing and Welfare: Labor Markets and Agriculture." In Ian Goldin and Alan Winters, eds., *Open Economies: Structural Adjustment and Agriculture.* Cambridge, Eng.: Center for Economic Policy Research and Cambridge University Press.

________ . 1992c. "Trade Orientations, Distortions, and Growth in Developing Countries." *Journal of Development Economics* 39 (July): 31–57.

________ . 1993a. "Exchange Rates, Inflation, and Disinflation: Latin American Experiences." Working Paper 4320. National Bureau of Economic Research, Cambridge, Mass.

________ . 1993b. "Exchange Rates as Nominal Anchors." *Weltwirtschaftliches Archiv* 129 (1): 1–32.

________ . 1993c. "Openness, Trade Liberalization, and Growth in Developing Countries." *Journal of Economic Literature* 31 (3).

________ . 1993d. "The Political Economy of Inflation and Stabilization in Developing Countries." Working Paper 4319. National Bureau of Economic Research, Cambridge, Mass.

________ . 1994a. "Trade Liberalization Reforms in Latin America: Recent Experiences, Policy Issues and Future Prospects." In Graham Bird and Ann Helwege, eds., *Latin America's Economic Future.* San Diego: Academic Press.

________ . 1994b. "Why Are Latin America's Savings Rates so Low?" Working Paper. Latin America and Caribbean Region, World Bank, Washington, D.C.

Edwards, Sebastian, and Alejandra Edwards. 1991. *Monetarism and Liberalization: The Chilean Experiment.* Chicago, Ill.: University of Chicago Press.

________ . 1992. "Markets and Democracy: Lessons from Chile." *The World Economy* 15 (March): 203–19.

Edwards, Sebastian, and Fernando Losada. 1994. "Fixed Exchange Rates, Inflation, and Macroeconomic Discipline." Working Paper 4661. National Bureau of Economic Research, Cambridge, Mass.

Edwards, Sebastian, and Miguel Savastano. 1988. "Latin America's Intra-Regional Trade: Evolution and Future Prospects." Working Paper 2738. National Bureau of Economic Research, Cambridge, Mass.

Edwards, Sebastian, and F. Sturzenegger. 1992. "Inflationary Inertia and Endogenous Indexation." Department of Economics, University of California, Los Angeles.

Edwards, Sebastian, and Guido Tabellini. 1991. "Explaining Fiscal Policies and Inflation in Developing Countries." *Journal of International Money and Finance* 10 (March, supplement: S16–S48).

Elías, Victor. 1992. *Sources of Growth: A Study of Seven Latin American Economies.* San Francisco, Calif.: ICS Press.

Erzan, Refik, Kiroaki Kuwahara, Saratino Marchese, and Rene Vossenar. 1989. "The Profile of Protection in Developing Countries." *UNCTAD Review* 1 (1): 1–22.

Fajnzylber, Fernando. 1990. *Unavoidable Industrial Restructuring in Latin America.* Durham, N.C.: Duke University Press.

Feder, Gershon. 1983. "On Exports and Economic Growth." *Journal of Development Economics* 12 (February–April): 59–73.

Feldstein, Martin. 1980. "International Differences in Social Security and Saving." *Journal of Public Economics* 14 (October): 225–44.

Fernández, Arturo. 1992. "Deregulation as a Source of Growth in Mexico." Working Paper. Instituto Tecnológico Autónomo de México, Tizapán, Mexico.

Ferretti, Martina. 1991. "Latin American Survey: Foreign Investment Regimes." *International Financial Law Review* 10 (July): 30–35.

Ffrench-Davis, Ricardo. 1973. *Políticas económicas en Chile, 1952–1970.* Santiago: Ediciones Nueva Universidad.

________. 1990. "Debt and Growth in Chile: Trends and Prospects." In David Felix, ed., *Debt and Transfiguration? Prospects for Latin America's Economic Revival.* New York: Sharpe.

Ffrench-Davis, Ricardo, and Thomas Griffin. 1967. *Teoría del comercio internacional.* Mexico City: Fondo de Cultura Económica.

Fischer, Stanley. 1985. *Indexing, Inflation, and Economic Policy.* Cambridge, Mass.: MIT Press.

________. 1988. "Recent Developments in Macroeconomics." *The Journal of the Royal Economic Society* 98 (June): 294–339.

Fishlow, Albert. 1985. "Revisiting the Great Debt Crisis of 1982." In Kwang Suk Kim and David Ruccio, eds., *Debt and Development in Latin America.* North Bend, Ind.: University of Notre Dame Press.

________. 1987. "The State of Latin American Economics." *In Economic and Social Progress in Latin America.* Washington, D.C.: Inter-American Development Bank.

________. 1989. "Lessons of the 1890s to the 1980s." In Guillermo Calvo, Ronald Findlay, Pentti Kouri, and Jorge Braga de Macedo, eds., *Debt, Stabilization, and Development: Essays in the Honor of Carlos Díaz-Alejandro.* Oxford, Eng.: Wider and Basil Blackwell.

________. 1990. "The Latin American State." *Journal of Economic Perspectives* 4 (summer): 61–74.

________. 1991. "Liberalization in Latin America." In Tariq Banuri, ed., *Economic Liberalization: No Panacea.* Oxford, Eng.: Oxford University Press.

Fiszbein, Ariel, and George Psacharopoulos. 1992. "Income Inequality Trends in Latin America in the Eighties: A Decomposition Analysis." Paper presented at the conference Poverty and Inequality in Latin America, Brookings Institution, Washington, D.C., July.

Flaño, Nicolás, and Francisco Ochoa. 1993. "The Chilean Path to Democratic Consolidation: Equitable Growth and Stability." Paper presented at the conference Chile: Model for Latin America, University of Wisconsin, Milwaukee, September.

Fleisig, Heywood. 1992. "Infrastructure and Economic Growth in Latin America." World Bank, Latin America and Caribbean Region, Washington, D.C.

Flood, Robert, and Peter Isard. 1988. "Monetary Policy Strategies." Research Dept., *International Monetary Fund Staff Papers* 36 (3).

Folkerts-Landau, D. 1985. "The Changing Role of International Bank Lending in Development Finance." *IMF Staff Papers* (June).

Fontaine, Arturo. 1992. "Sobre el pecado original de la transformación capitalista chilena." In Barry Levine, ed., *El desafío neoliberal: El fin del tercermundismo en América Latina.* Bogotá: Editorial Norma.

Fontaine, Juan. 1989. "The Chilean Economy in the Eighties: Adjustment and Recovery." In Sebastian Edwards and Felipe Larraín, eds., *Debt, Adjustment, and Recovery.* Oxford, Eng.: Basil Blackwell.

Foxley, Alejandro. 1982. "Resuelve el modelo económico los problemas de fondo?" In *Modelo económico chileno: Trayectoria de una crítica.* Santiago: Editorial Aconcagua.

________. 1983a. "Después del monetarismo." In Alejandro Foxley, René Cortázar, Patricio Meller, Andrés Solimano, José Pablo Arellano, Ricardo Ffrench-Davis, and Oscar Muñoz, eds., *Reconstrucción económica para la democracia.* Santiago: CIEPLAN.

________. 1983b. *Latin American Experiments in Neoconservative Economics.* Berkeley, Calif.: University of California Press.

Frenkel, Jacob, Michael Dooley, and Peter Wickham, eds. 1989. *Analytical Issues in Debt.* Washington, D.C.: International Monetary Fund.

Frenkel, Roberto, and José María Fanelli. 1987. "El Plan Austral: Un año y medio después." In José Antonio Ocampo, ed., *Planes antiinflacionarios recientes en la América Latina*. Special issue of *El Trimestre Económico* 54 (September).

Fry, Maxwell. 1988. *Money, Interest, and Banking in Economic Development*. Baltimore, Md.: Johns Hopkins University Press.

Fukuda, Shinichi. 1993. "The Conditional Convergence in East Asian Countries." Paper presented at the East Asian Seminar on Economics, National Bureau of Economic Research, San Francisco, Calif., June.

Furtado, Celso. 1969. *La economía latinoamericana desde la conquista ibérica hasta la revolución cubana*. Santiago: Editorial Universitaria.

Galal, Ahmed. 1993. "Regulation and Commitment in the Development of Telecommunications in Chile." World Bank Policy Research Working Paper Series 1278. Washington, D.C.

Galal, Ahmed, Raúl Saez, and Clemencia Torres. 1992. "Welfare Consequences of Selling Public Enterprises: Chile." In Ahmed Galal, Leroy Jones, Pankaj Tandon, and Ingo Vogelsang, *Welfare Consequences of Selling Public Enterprises: An Empirical Analysis*. New York: Oxford University Press, 1994.

Gallagher, David. 1992. "Chile: La revolución pendiente." In Barry Levine, ed., *El desafío neoliberal: El fin del tercermundismo en América Latina*. Bogotá: Grupo Editorial Norma.

Garcia Márquez, Gabriel. 1970. *One Hundred Years of Solitude*. New York: Harper & Row.

Gavito Mohar, Javier, Sergio Sánchez García, and Ignacio Trigueros Legarreta. 1992. "Los servicios financieros y el acuerdo de libre comercio: Bancos y casas de bolsa." In *México y el tratado trilateral de libre comercio*. Mexico City: ITAM and McGraw-Hill.

Gelb, Alan. 1989. "Financial Policies, Growth, and Efficiency." Policy Research Working Paper 202. World Bank, Washington, D.C.

Gersovitz, Mark. 1989. "Savings and Development." In Hollis Chenery and T. N. Srinivasan, eds., *Handbook of Development Economics*. Amsterdam: North-Holland.

Gil Díaz, Francisco. 1988. "Macroeconomic Policies, Crisis, and Growth in the Long Run: Mexico Country Study." World Bank, Latin America and Caribbean Region, Washington, D.C.

________ . 1992. "Mexico's Recent Economic Policy." Paper presented at the Latin American Economics Workshop, University of California, Los Angeles, Department of Economics, April.

Giovannini, Alberto. 1983. "The Interest Elasticity of Savings in Developing Countries: The Existing Evidence." *World Development* 11 (July): 601–7.

Glade, William. 1991. *Privatization of Public Enterprises in Latin America*. San Francisco, Calif.: ICS Press.

Glaessner, Thomas C. 1992. "Colombia: Securities Market Development." World Bank, Latin America and Caribbean Region, Washington, D.C.

Glaessner, Thomas C., and Ignacio Mas. 1991. "Incentive Structure and Resolution of Financial Institution Distress: Latin American Experience." LAC Technical Department Report 12. World Bank, Latin America and Caribbean Region, Washington, D.C.

Griffith-Jones, Stefany, and Osvaldo Sunkel. 1986. *Debt and Development Crises in Latin America: The End of an Illusion*. Oxford, Eng.: Oxford University Press.

Grosh, Margaret E. 1990. *Social Spending in Latin America: The Story of the 1980s*. World Bank Discussion Paper 106. Washington, D.C.

________ . 1992. "From Platitudes to Practice: Targeting Social Programs in Latin America." LAC Human Resource Division Report 10720. World Bank, Latin America and Caribbean Region, Washington, D.C.

________ . 1993. "Five Criteria for Choosing among Poverty Programs." Paper presented at the conference Confronting the Challenge of Poverty and Inequality in Latin America, Brookings Institution, Washington, D.C.

Grossman, Gene M., and Elhanan Helpman. 1990. "Comparative Advantage and Long-Run Growth." *American Economic Review* 80 (September): 796–815.

________ . 1991. *Innovation and Growth in the Global Economy*. Cambridge, Mass.: MIT Press.

Gutentag, Jack, and Richard Herring. 1985. *The Current Crisis of International Lending*. Washington, D.C.: Brookings Institution.

Gylfason, Thorvaldur. 1993. "Optimal Saving, Interest Rates, and Endogenous Growth." Seminar Paper 539. University of Stockholm.

Hachette, Dominique, and Rolf Luders. 1992. "Privatization in Argentina and Chile: Lessons from a Comparison." LAC Internal Discussion Paper 18. World Bank, Latin America and Caribbean Region, Washington, D.C.

Haggard, Stephan, and Robert Kaufman, eds. 1992. *The Politics of Economic Adjustment: International Constraints, Distributive Conflicts, and the State*. Princeton, N.J.: Princeton University Press.

Haggard, Stephan, and Steven Webb. 1993. "What Do We Know about the Political Economy of Economic Policy Reform?" *World Bank Research Observer* 8 (July): 143–68.

Hanson, James A. 1992. "Opening the Capital Account: A Survey of Issues and Results." Policy Research Working Paper 901. World Bank, Washington, D.C.

Hanson, James A., and Craig R. Neal. 1986. *Interest Rate Policies in Selected Developing Countries, 1970–1982*. World Bank Staff Working Paper 753. Washington, D.C.

Harberger, Arnold. 1959. "Using the Resources at Hand More Efficiently." *American Economic Review* 49 (May): 134–46.

________. 1971. "Three Basic Postulates of Applied Welfare Economics." *Journal of Economic Literature* 9 (September): 785–97.

________. 1972. "Investment in Men versus Investment in Machines: The Case of India." In Arnold Harberger, ed., *Project Evaluation: Collected Papers*. Chicago, Ill.: University of Chicago Press.

________. 1982. "The Chilean Economy in the 1970s: Crisis, Stabilization, Liberalization, Reform." In Karl Brunner and Allan Metzler, eds., *Economic Policy in a World of Change*. Carnegie-Rochester Conference Series on Public Policy 17. Amsterdam: North-Holland.

________. 1985a. "Lessons for Debtor-Country Managers and Policymakers." In Gordon Smith and John Cuddington, eds., *International Debt and the Developing Countries*. Washington, D.C.: World Bank.

________. 1985b. "Observations on the Chilean Economy, 1973–1983." *Economic Development and Cultural Change* 33 (April): 451–62.

________. 1990. "Toward a Uniform Tariff Structure." University of Chicago, Department of Economics, Chicago, Ill.

________. 1992. "The Sources of Economic Growth and Economic Liberalization, with Application to Mexico for the 1990s." University of California, Los Angeles, Department of Economics.

Hayashi, Fumio. 1986. "Why Is Japan's Saving Rate so Apparently High?" In *NBER Macroeconomics Annual 1986*. Cambridge, Mass.: MIT Press.

Heitger, Bernhard. 1987. "Import Protection and Export Performance: Their Impact on Economic Growth." *Weltwirtschaftliches Archiv* 132 (2).

Herrera, Alejandra. 1993. "The Privatization of Telecommunications Services: The Case of Argentina." *Columbia Journal of World Business* 28 (spring): 46–61 (reprint).

Hicks, Norman. 1992a. "The Role of the World Bank in the Latin American Reform Process." World Bank, Latin America and Caribbean Region, Washington, D.C.

________. 1992b. "Trends in Government Expenditures and Revenues in Latin America, 1975–1988." LAC Internal Discussion Paper. World Bank, Latin America and Caribbean Region, Washington, D.C.

Hill, Alice, and Manuel Abdala. 1993. "Regulation, Institutions, and Commitment: Privatization and Regulation in the Argentine Telecommunications Sector." World Bank, Policy Research Working Paper 1216. Washington, D.C.

Hirschman, Albert O. 1968. "The Political Economy of Import Substituting Industrialization in Latin America." *Quarterly Journal of Economics* 82 (February): 1–32.

________. 1987. "La economía política del desarrollo latinoamericano: Siete Ejercicios en Retrospectiva." *El Trimestre Económico* 54 (October–December): 769–804.

________. 1988. "How Keynes Was Spread from America." *Challenge* 31 (November): 4–7.

Ibarra, Luis. 1992. "Credibility of Trade Policy Reform: The Mexican Experience." Ph.D. diss., University of California, Los Angeles, Department of Economics.

IFC (International Finance Corporation). Various years. *Quarterly Review of Emerging Stock Markets.* Washington, D.C.

Iglesias, Enrique. 1990. "From Policy Consensus to Renewed Economic Growth." In John Williamson, ed., *Latin American Adjustment: How Much Has Happened?* Washington, D.C.: Institute for International Economics.

________. 1992. *Reflections on Economic Development: Toward a New Latin American Consensus.* Washington, D.C.: Inter-American Development Bank.

Iglesias, Enrique, and L. Emmerij, eds. 1991. *Restoring Financial Flows to Latin America.* Paris: Organization for Economic Cooperation and Development.

IMF (International Monetary Fund). Various years. *Annual Report (of the Board of Directors).* Washington, D.C.

________. Various years. *Annual Report on Exchange Rate Arrangements and Exchange Rate Restrictions.* Washington, D.C.

________. Various years. *Government Financial Statistics.* Washington, D.C.

________. Various years. *International Financial Statistics.* Washington, D.C.

________. Various years. *World Economic Outlook.* Washington, D.C.

Inter-American Dialogue. 1992. *Convergence and Community: The Americas in 1993.* Washington, D.C.

ITAM (Instituto Tecnológico Autónomo de México). 1992. *México y el tratado trilateral de libre comercio.* Mexico City: ITAM and McGraw-Hill.

________. 1994. *Lo negociado del tratado de libre comercio.* Mexico City: ITAM and McGraw-Hill.

Jappelli, Tulio, and Marco Pagano. 1994. "Saving, Growth, and Liquidity Constraints." *Quarterly Journal of Economics* 109 (February): 83–109.

Jaspersen, Frederick. 1992. "External Resource Flows to Latin America: Recent Developments and Prospects." Working Paper 116. Inter-American Development Bank, Washington, D.C.

Kamin, Steven. 1991. "Argentina's Experience with Parallel Exchange Markets: 1981–1990." International Finance Discussion Paper 407. Board of Governors of the Federal Reserve System, Washington, D.C., August.

Kessel, Georgina. 1992. "El sector petroquímico mexicano ante la integración del mercado norteamericano." In ITAM, *México y el tratado trilateral de libre comercio.* Mexico City: ITAM and McGraw-Hill.

Kiguel, Miguel Alberto. 1991. "Inflation in Argentina: Stop and Go since the Austral Plan." *World Development* 19 (8): 969–86.

Kiguel, Miguel Alberto, and Nissan Liviatan. 1992. "The Business Cycle Associated with Exchange Rate Stabilizations." *World Bank Economic Review* 6 (May): 279–305.

Kikeri, Sunita, John Nellis, and Mary Shirley. 1992. *Privatization: The Lessons of Experience.* Washington, D.C.: World Bank.

Kim, Kwang Suk. 1991. "Korea." In Michael Michaely, Armeane Choksi, and Demetris Papageorgiou, eds., *Liberalizing Foreign Trade.* New York: Basil Blackwell.

King, Robert, and Ross Levine. 1993a. "Finance and Growth: Schumpeter Might Be Right." *Quarterly Journal of Economics* 108 (August): 717–37.

________. 1993b. "Finance, Entrepreneurship, and Growth." Paper presented at the conference How Do National Policies Affect Long-Term Growth? World Bank, Washington, D.C., February.

Klaus, Václav. 1991. "A Perspective on Economic Transition in Czechoslovakia and Eastern Europe." Paper presented at the annual conference Development Economics 1990, World Bank, Washington, D.C.

Korean Development Institute. 1989. *Korea's Macroeconomic and Financial Policies.* KDI/11E Proceedings, Conference Series 89–3. Seoul.

Krueger, Ann. 1978. *Foreign Trade Regimes and Economic Development: Liberalization Attempts and Consequences.* Cambridge, Mass.: National Bureau of Economic Research.

________. 1980. "Trade Policy as an Input to Development." *American Economic Review* 70 (2).
________. 1981. *Trade and Employment in Developing Countries.* Chicago, Ill.: University of Chicago Press.
________. 1983. *Exchange Rate Determination.* Cambridge, Eng.: Cambridge University Press.
________. 1990. *Perspectives on Trade and Development.* Exeter, Eng.: Harvester Wheatsheaf.
________. 1993. "East Asian Experience and Endogenous Growth Theory." Paper presented at the East Asian Seminar on Economics, National Bureau of Economic Research, San Francisco, Calif., June.

Krugman, Paul R. 1979. "A Model of Balance of Payments Crises." *Journal of Money, Credit, and Banking* 11 (3): 311–25.

________. 1988. "Financing vs. Forgiving a Debt Overhang." Working Paper 2486. National Bureau of Economic Research, Cambridge, Mass.

Kydland, Finn, and Edward Prescott. 1977. "Rules Rather Than Discretion: The Inconsistency of Optimal Plans." *Journal of Political Economy* 85 (3): 473–92.

Kyle, J., and Jeffrey Sachs. 1984. "Developing Country Debt and the Market Value of Large Commercial Banks." Working Paper 1470. National Bureau of Economic Research, Cambridge, Mass.

Laffont, Jean-Jaques, and Jean Tirole. 1993. *A Theory of Incentives in Procurement and Regulation.* Cambridge, Mass.: MIT Press.

Lago, Ricardo. 1991. "The Illusion of Pursuing Redistribution through Macropolicy: Peru's Heterodox Experience, 1985–1990." In Rudiger Dornbusch and Sebastian Edwards, eds., *The Macroeconomics of Populism in Latin America.* Chicago, Ill.: University of Chicago Press.

Lal, Deepak. 1985. *The Real Aspects of Stabilization and Structural Adjustment Policies: An Extension of the Australian Adjustment Model.* World Bank Staff Working Paper 636. Washington, D.C.

Lamdany, Ruben. 1988. *Voluntary Debt-Reduction Operations: Bolivia, Mexico, and Beyond.* World Bank Discussion Paper 42. Washington, D.C.

Larraín, Felipe. 1988. "Debt Reduction and the Management of Chilean Debt." World Bank, Latin America and Caribbean Region, Washington, D.C.

Larraín, Felipe, and Patricio Meller. 1991. "The Socialist-Populist Chilean Experience: 1970–1973." In Rudiger Dornbusch and Sebastian Edwards, eds., *The Macroeconomics of Populism in Latin America.* Chicago, Ill.: University of Chicago Press.

Larraín, Felipe, and Andrés Velasco. 1990. "Can Swaps Solve the Debt Crisis? Lessons from the Chilean Experience." Princeton Studies in International Finance 69. Princeton University, Princeton, N.J.

Latin Finance. Various years. Miami, Fla.

Leamer, Edward. 1990. "Latin America as a Target of Trade Barriers Erected by the Major Developed Countries in 1983." *Journal of Development Economics* 32 (April): 337–68.

Leff, Nathaniel. 1968. *Economic Policy-making and Development in Brazil, 1947–1964.* New York: Wiley.

Lefort, Fernando, and Andrés Solimano. 1994. "Economic Growth after Market-Based Reform in Latin America: The Cases of Chile and Mexico." Working Paper. World Bank, Macroeconomics and Growth Division, Washington, D.C.

Leipziger, Danny, and Vinod Thomas. 1993. *The Lessons of East Asia: An Overview of Country Experience.* Washington, D.C.: World Bank.

Lewis, Arthur. 1955. *The Theory of Economic Growth.* London: Allen and Unwin.

Lin, Ching-Yuan. 1988. "East Asia and Latin America as Contrasting Models." *Economic Development and Cultural Change* 36 (S153–197, April).

Little, Ian, Tibor Scitovsky, and Maurice Scott. 1970. *Industry and Trade in Some Developing Countries.* Oxford, Eng.: Oxford University Press.

Losada, Fernando. 1993. "Partners, Neighbors, and Distant Cousins: Explaining Bilateral Trade Flows in Latin America." Working Paper. University of California, Los Angeles, Department of Economics.

________. 1994. "The Uruguay Round, GATT, and Regionalism." World Bank, Latin America and Caribbean Region, Washington, D.C.

Lucas, Robert E., Jr. 1988. "On the Mechanics of Economic Development." *Journal of Monetary Economics* 22 (July): 3–42.

_________. 1993. "Making a Miracle." *Econometrica* 61 (March): 251–72.

Luders, Rolf. 1991. "Massive Divestiture and Privatization: Lessons from Chile." *Contemporary Policy Issues* 9 (October): 1–19.

Luders, Rolf, and Beatriz Arbildua. 1968. "Una evaluación comparada de tres programas anti-inflacionarios en Chile: una década de historia monetaria 1956–1966." *Cuadernos de Economía* 5 (April): 25–105.

Lustig, Nora. 1994. *The Future of Trade Policy in Latin America.* Washington, D.C.: Brookings Institution.

Maddison, Angus. 1985. *Two Crises: Latin America and Asia, 1929–38 and 1973–83.* Paris: Organization for Economic Cooperation and Development.

Marfán, Manuel, and Barry Bosworth. 1994. "Savings, Investment, and Economic Growth." In Barry Bosworth, Rudiger Dornbusch, and Raul Labán, eds., *The Chilean Economy: Policy Lessons and Challenges.* Washington, D.C.: Brookings Institution.

Márquez, Gustavo. 1992. "Poverty and Social Policies in Venezuela." Paper presented at the conference Poverty and Inequality in Latin America, Brookings Institution, Washington, D.C., July.

Martin, Ricardo D. 1992. "Sources of Growth in Latin America." World Bank, Latin America and Caribbean Region, Washington, D.C.

McGreevey, William Paul. 1990. *Social Security in Latin America: Issues and Options for the World Bank.* World Bank Discussion Paper 110. Washington, D.C.

McKinnon, Ronald. 1973. *Money and Capital in Economic Development.* Washington, D.C.: Brookings Institution.

_________. 1982. "The Order of Economic Liberalization: Lessons from Chile and Argentina." *Carnegie-Rochester Conference Series on Public Policy* 17 (autumn).

_________. 1991. *The Order of Economic Liberalization: Financial Control in the Transition to a Market Economy.* Baltimore, Md.: Johns Hopkins University Press.

Meller, Patricio, Ernesto Livacich, and Patricio Arrau. 1984. "Una Revision del Milagro Economico Chileno 1975–1981." *Coleccion Estudios CIEPLAN,* Santiago, Chile, Vol. 15 (December): 5–109.

Mesa-Lago, Carmelo. 1991. *Social Security and Prospects for Equity in Latin America.* World Bank Discussion Paper 140. Washington, D.C.

Michaely, Michael. 1985. "Demand for Protection against Exports of Newly Industrializing Countries." *Journal of Policy Modeling* 7 (spring): 123–32.

Michaely, Michael, Armeane Choksi, and Demetris Papageorgiou, eds. 1991. *Liberalizing Foreign Trade.* New York: Basil Blackwell.

Mill, John Stuart. 1884. *Principles of Political Economy.* New York: Appleton and Co.

Mincer, Jacob. 1965. "Investment in Human Capital and Personal Income Distribution." *Journal of Political Economy* 66 (3).

Modigliani, Franco. 1980. "The Life Cycle Hypothesis of Savings Twenty Years Later." In Michael Parkin, ed., *Contemporary Issues in Economics.* Manchester, Eng.: Manchester University Press.

Molina, Sergio. 1982. "Poverty: Description and Analysis of Policies for Overcoming It." Comisión Económica para América Latina, Santiago. *CEPAL Review* 18 (December): 87–110.

Montes-Negret, Fernando. 1988. "Colombia's Financial Sector." World Bank, Latin America and Caribbean Region, Washington, D.C.

Morales, Juan Antonio. 1987. "Estabilización y nueva política económica en Bolivia." In José Antonio Ocampo, ed., *Planes antiinflacionarios recientes en la América Latina.* Special issue of *El Trimestre Económico* 54 (September).

Morgan Guaranty and Trust Company. 1987. "World Financial Markets." Morgan Guaranty International Economics Department, New York.

Morley, Samuel. 1992. "Macroconditions and Poverty in Latin America." Inter-American Development Bank, Washington, D.C.

Morris, Felipe, Mark Dorfman, José Pedro Ortiz, and María Claudia Franco. 1990. *Latin America's Banking Systems in the 1980s: A Cross-Country Comparison*. World Bank Discussion Paper 81, Washington, D.C.

Musgrove, Philip. 1991. "Feeding Latin America's Children: An Analytical Survey of Food Programs." LAC Technical Department, Regional Studies Program Report 11. World Bank, Latin America and Caribbean Region, Washington, D.C.

Nam, Chon-Hyun. 1993. "The Role of Trade and Exchange Rate Policy in Korea's Growth." Paper prepared for East Asian Seminar on Economics, National Bureau of Economic Research, San Francisco, Calif., June.

Newfarmer, Richard. 1992. "Argentina: Fiscal Assessment." World Bank, Latin America and Caribbean Region, Washington, D.C.

Newman, John, Steen Jorgensen, and Menno Pradhan. 1991. "How Did Workers Benefit from Bolivia's Emergency Social Fund." *World Bank Economic Review* 2 (5): 367–93.

Nogués, Julio. 1990. "The Experience of Latin America with Export Subsidies." *Weltwirtschaftliches Archiv* 126 (1): 97–115.

Nogués, Julio, and Sunil Gulati. 1992. "Economic Policies and Performance under Alternative Trade Regimes: Latin America during the 1980s." LAC Technical Department Report 16. World Bank, Latin America and Caribbean Region, Washington, D.C.

Nogués, Julio, and Rosalinda Quintanilla. 1992. "Latin America's Integration and the Multilateral Trading System." Paper presented at the conference New Dimensions in Regional Integration, World Bank and CEPR, Washington, D.C.

North, Douglass. 1989. "Institutions and Economic Growth: An Historical Introduction." *World Development* 17 (9): 1319–332.

________. 1990. *Institutions, Institutional Change, and Economic Performance*. Cambridge, Eng.: Cambridge University Press.

OAS (Organization of American States). 1992. *Statistical Bulletin*. Washington, D.C.

Ocampo, José Antonio. 1989. "Colombia and the Latin American Debt Crisis." In Sebastian Edwards and Felipe Larraín, eds., *Debt, Adjustment, and Recovery: Latin America's Prospects for Growth and Development*. Oxford, Eng.: Oxford University Press.

________. 1991a. "Determinants and Prospects for Medium-Term Growth in Colombia." Paper presented at the conference The Colombian Economy: Issues of Debt, Trade, and Development, Lehigh University, Department of Economics, Bethlehem, Penn., April.

________. 1991b. "Trade Policy and Industrialization in Colombia, 1967–1991." Paper presented at the conference Trade and Industrialization in LDCs, WIDER, Paris, September.

Ocampo, José Antonio, ed. 1987. *Planes antiinflacionarios recientes en la América Latina*. Special issue of *El Trimestre Económico* 54 (September).

Oks, Daniel. 1994. "Structural Reforms and Productivity Growth: Sectoral Analysis for Chile and Mexico." Paper presented at the Cross Fertilization Seminar Series, World Bank, Latin America and Caribbean Region, Washington, D.C.

Ortiz, Javier. 1993. "The Early History of Central Banking in Latin America: Legal Independence and Monetary Policies." Working Paper. University of California, Los Angeles, Department of Economics.

Oum, Baum. 1989. "Korea's Real Exchange Rate Policy in the 1980s: Evaluation and Prospects." In *Korea's Macroeconomic and Financial Policies*. Conference Series 89–3. Seoul: Korean Development Institute.

Paz, Pedro, and Osvaldo Sunkel. 1971. *El subdesarrollo latinoamericano y la teoría del desarrollo*. Madrid: Siglo Veintiuno de España.

Pérez-Campanero, Juan, and Alfredo Leone. 1991. "Liberalization and Financial Crisis in Uruguay, 1974–1987." In Tomás Baliño and Vasudevan Sundararajan, eds., *Banking Crisis: Causes and Issues*. Washington, D.C.: International Monetary Fund.

Persson, Torsten, and Guido Tabellini. 1990. *Macroeconomic Policy, Credibility, and Politics*. New York: Harwood Academic Publishers.

Philippe, Bernard. 1991. "The Chilean Electric Power Sector in the Last Decade: The Design and Implementation of New Policy." Universidad Católica de Chile, Department of Economics, Santiago.

Pinto, A., and Osvaldo Sunkel. 1966. "Latin American Economists in the United States." *Economic Development and Cultural Change* 15 (October): 79–86.

Prebisch, Raúl. 1947. *Introducción a Keynes.* Mexico City: Fondo de Cultura Económica.

________. 1950. "Commercial Policy in the Underdeveloped Countries." *American Economic Review* 40 (2).

________. 1984. "Five Stages in My Thinking on Development." In Dudley Seers, ed., *Pioneers in Development.* Oxford, Eng.: Oxford University Press.

Presidencia de la República del Perú. 1986. *Plan Nacional de Desarrollo.* Lima.

Psacharopoulos, George. 1992. "Poverty and Income Distribution in Latin America and the Caribbean." World Bank, Latin America and Caribbean Region, Washington, D.C.

________. 1993. "Human Resources in Latin America and the Caribbean: Priorities and Action." World Bank, Latin America and Caribbean Region, Washington, D.C.

Psacharopoulos, George, and Ariel Fiszbein. 1991. "A Cost-Benefit Analysis of Educational Investment in Venezuela, 1989." World Bank, Latin America and Caribbean Region, Washington, D.C.

Psacharopoulos, George, and Ying Ng. 1992. "Earnings and Education in Latin America: Assessing Priorities for Schooling Investments." Working Paper 1056. World Bank, Latin America and Caribbean Region, Washington, D.C.

Pyo, Hak. 1993. "A Time-Series Test on the Endogenous Growth Model with Human Capital." Paper presented at the East Asian Seminar on Economics, National Bureau of Economic Research, San Francisco, Calif., June.

Rabello de Castro, Paulo, and Mauricio Ronci. 1991. "Sixty Years of Populism in Brazil." In Rudiger Dornbusch and Sebastian Edwards, eds., *The Macroeconomics of Populism in Latin America.* Chicago, Ill.: University of Chicago Press.

Ramírez, G. G., and Francisco Rosende. 1992. "Responding to the Collapse: Chilean Banking Legislation after 1983." In Philip Brock, ed., *If Texas Were Chile: A Primer on Banking Reform.* San Francisco, Calif.: ICS Press.

Ramos, Joseph. 1986. *Neoconservative Economics in the Southern Cone of Latin America, 1973–1983.* Baltimore, Md.: Johns Hopkins University Press.

Rebelo, Sergio. 1991. "Long Run Policy Analysis and Long Run Growth." *Journal of Political Economy* 99 (June): 500–21.

Rodríguez, Carlos. 1982. "The Argentine Stabilization Plan of December 20th." *World Development* 10 (9): 801–11.

________. 1994. "Interest Rates in Latin America." Working Paper. World Bank, Latin America and Caribbean Region, Washington, D.C.

Rodrik, Dani. 1993. "Trade and Industrial Policy Reform in Developing Countries: A Review of Recent Theory and Evidence." Working Paper 4417. National Bureau of Economic Research, Cambridge, Mass.

________. 1994. "King Kong Meets Godzilla: The World Bank and the East Asian Miracle." Working Paper. Overseas Development Council, Washington, D.C.

Romer, Paul. 1986. "Increasing Returns and Long-Run Growth." *Journal of Political Economy* 94 (October): 1002–37.

________. 1989. "Capital Accumulation in the Theory of Long-Run Growth." In Robert Barro, ed., *Modern Business Cycle Theory.* Cambridge, Mass.: Harvard University Press.

Roubini, Nouriel, and Xavier Sala-i-Martin. 1992. "Financial Repression and Economic Growth." *Journal of Development Economics* 39 (July): 5–30.

Saborio, Sylvia, and Constantine Michalopoulos. 1992. "Central America at a Crossroads." Policy Research Working Paper 922. World Bank, Europe and Central Asia Country Department III, Washington, D.C.

Sachs, Jeffrey. 1981. "The Current Account and Macroeconomic Adjustment in the 1970s." *Brookings Papers on Economic Activity* 1: 201–68.

________ .1987. "Trade and Exchange Rate Policies in Trade-Oriented Adjustment Programs." In Vittorio Corbo, Morris Goldstein, and Mohsin Khan, eds., *Growth-Oriented Adjustment Programs.* Washington, D.C.: International Monetary Fund.

________ . 1988. "Conditionality, Debt Relief, and the Developing Country Debt Crisis." Working Paper 2644. National Bureau of Economic Research, Cambridge, Mass.

________ . 1989a. "The Debt Overhang of Developing Countries." In Guillermo Calvo, Ronald Findlay, Pentti Kouri, and Jorge Braga de Macedo, eds., *Debt, Stabilization, and Development: Essays in the Honor of Carlos Díaz-Alejandro.* Oxford, Eng.: Wider and Basil Blackwell.

________ , ed. 1989b. *Developing Country Debt and the World Economy.* Chicago, Ill.: University of Chicago Press.

________ . 1989c. "New Approaches to the Latin America Debt Crisis." Princeton Essays in International Finance 174. Princeton University, Princeton, N.J.

Sachs, Jeffrey, and D. Cohen. 1986. "Growth and External Debt under Risk of Potential Repudiation." *European Economic Review* 30 (3, June): 529–60.

Samuelson, Paul. 1954. "The Pure Theory of Public Expenditure." *Review of Economics and Statistics* 36 (November): 387–89.

Sánchez, Manuel. 1992. "Entorno macroeconómico frente al tratado de libre comercio." In *México y el tratado trilateral de libre comercio.* Mexico City: ITAM and McGraw-Hill.

Sargent, T. 1983. "Stopping Moderate Inflations: The Methods of Poincaré and Thatcher." In Rudiger Dornbusch and M. Simonsen, eds., *Inflation, Debt, and Indexation.* Cambridge, Mass.: MIT Press.

Schott, Jeffrey. 1991. "Trading Blocks and the World Trading System." *World Economy* 14 (March): 1–17.

Schultz, T. W. 1961. "Investment in Human Capital." *American Economic Review* 51 (March): 1–17.

________ . 1980. "Nobel Prize Address." *Journal of Political Economy* 88 (August): 639–51.

Seabright, Paul. 1993. "Infrastructure and Industrial Policy in South Asia: Achieving the Transition to a New Regulatory Environment." South Asia Seminar Series, University of Cambridge, Department of Economics, Cambridge, Eng.

Selowsky, Marcelo. 1969. "On the Measurement of Education's Contribution to Growth." *Quarterly Journal of Economics* 83 (August): 449–63.

———. 1992. "Latin America: Protecting Children's Nutrition during the Adjustment." *Bank's World* 11 (February): 9–11, Washington, D.C.: World Bank.

Selowsky, Marcelo, and Herman van der Tak. 1986. "The Debt Problem and Growth." *World Development* 14 (9): 1107–24.

Shaw, Edward. 1973. *Financial Deepening in Economic Development.* New York: Oxford University Press.

Sheahan, John. 1987. *Patterns of Development in Latin America: Poverty, Repression, and Economic Strategy.* Princeton, N.J.: Princeton University Press.

Shome, Parthasarathi. 1994. "Recent Tax Policy Trends and Issues in Latin America." Working Paper. Fiscal Affairs Department, International Monetary Fund, Washington, D.C.

Singer, Hans. 1950. "The Distribution of Gains between Investing and Borrowing Countries." *American Economic Review* 40 (2): 473–85.

Solís, Leopoldo. 1988. "Raúl Prebisch at ECLA: Years of Creative Intellectual Effort." Occasional Paper 10. International Center for Economic Growth, San Francisco, Calif.

Spiller, Pablo. 1992. "Institutions and Regulatory Commitment in Utilities Privatization." Working Paper 51. Institute for Policy Reform, Washington, D.C.

Spulber, Daniel F. 1989. *Regulation and Markets.* Cambridge, Mass.: MIT Press.

Stigler, George. 1971. "The Theory of Economic Regulation." *Bell Journal of Economics* 2 (spring): 3–21.

Stiglitz, Joseph E. 1994. "The Role of the State in Financial Markets." *Proceedings of the World Bank Annual Conference on Development Economics 1993.* Washington, D.C.

Stiglitz, Joseph, and Andrew Weiss. 1981. "Credit Rationing in Markets with Imperfect Information." *American Economic Review* 71 (3): 393–410.

Sturzenegger, Federico. 1992. "Bolivia: Stabilization and Growth." University of California, Los Angeles, Department of Economics.

Summers, Robert, and Alan Heston. 1988. "A New Set of International Comparisons of Real Product and Price Level Estimates for 130 Countries." *Review of Income and Wealth* 34 (March).

Sunkel, Osvaldo. 1960. "Inflation in Chile: An Unorthodox Approach." *International Economic Papers* 10 (August).

Tandon, Pankaj. 1992. "World Bank Conference on the Welfare Consequences of Selling Public Enterprises: Case Studies from Chile, Malaysia, Mexico, and the U.K." World Bank, Washington, D.C., June.

Taylor, Lance. 1989. "Gap Disequilibria: Inflation, Investment, Saving, and Foreign Exchange." Working Paper (International) 76. United Nations University, World Institute for Development Economics Research, New York.

________ . 1991. "Economic Openness: Problems to the Century's End." In Tariq Banuri, ed., *Economic Liberalization: No Panacea.* New York: Clarendon Press.

Thomas, Vinod. 1986. *Linking Macroeconomic and Agricultural Policies for Adjustment with Growth: The Colombian Experience.* Baltimore, Md.: Johns Hopkins University Press.

________ . 1988. "Issues in Adjustment Lending." Policy, Planning, and Research Working Paper 2. Country Economics Dept., World Bank, Washington, D.C.

Thorp, Rosemary. 1992. "Reappraisal of the Origins of Import-Substituting Industrialization, 1930–1950." *Journal of Latin American Studies* 24: 181–95 (supplement).

Tironi, Ernesto. 1989. *Es posible reducir la pobreza.* Centro de Estudios del Desarrollo, Santiago.

El Trimestre Económico. Various issues. Fondo de Cultura Económica, Mexico City.

Tybout, James. 1992. "Linking Trade and Productivity: New Research Directions." *World Bank Economic Review* 6 (2): 189–211.

Uchimura, Kazuko, and Hong Gao. 1993. "The Impact of Infrastructure on Economic Development." World Bank, Latin America and Caribbean Region, Washington, D.C.

UNCTAD (United Nations Conference on Trade and Development). 1987. *Handbook of Trade Control Measures of Developing Countries.* Geneva.

UNDP (United Nations Development Programme). 1992. *Human Development Report, 1992.* New York: Oxford University Press.

UNICEF (United Nations Children's Fund). Various years. *The State of the World's Children.* New York: Oxford University Press.

Valdés, Alberto. 1992. "The Performance of the Agricultural Sector in Latin America." World Bank, Latin America and Caribbean Region, Washington, D.C.

Valdés, Jorge. 1989. *La Escuela de Chicago: Operación Chile.* Buenos Aires: Editorial Universitaria de Buenos Aires.

van Wijnbergen, Sweder. 1990. "Mexico in Transition: Toward a New Role for the Public Sector." World Bank, Latin America and Caribbean Region, Washington, D.C.

Velasco, Andrés. 1992. "Políticas de estabilización y teoria de juegos." *Colección Estudios CIEPLAN* 21 (May).

Velez, F., and G. Rubio. 1994. "El impacto del tratado de libre comercio en el campo mexicano." In Instituto Tecnológico Autónomo de México, *Lo negociado del tratado de libre comercio.* Mexico: McGraw-Hill.

Vuskovic, Pedro. 1970. "Distribución del ingreso y opciones de desarrollo." *Cuadernos de la Realidad Nacional* 7 (September).

Wade, Robert. 1994. "Is the Miracle Study Right That Selective Industrial Policies in Northeast Asia Are Unimportant?" Working Paper. Overseas Development Council, Washington, D.C.

Walton, Gary, ed. 1985. *The National Economic Policies of Chile.* Greenwich, Conn.: JAI Press.

Weiss, John. 1992. "Trade Policy Reform and Performance in Manufacturing: Mexico, 1975–1988." *Journal of Development Studies* 29 (October): 1–23.

WHO (World Health Organization). Various years. *Global Nutritional Status: Anthropometric Indicators.* Geneva: World Health Organization, Nutritional Unit, Division of Family Health.

Williamson, John. 1991. "Advice on the Choice of an Exchange Rate Policy." In Emil-Maria Claasen, ed., *Exchange Rate Policies in Developing and Post-Socialist Countries.* San Francisco, Calif.: ICS Press.

Williamson, John, ed. 1981. *Exchange Rate Rules: The Theory, Performance, and Prospects of the Crawling Peg.* New York: St. Martin's Press.

———. 1990. *Latin American Adjustment: How Much Has Happened?* Washington, D.C.: Institute for International Economics.

Willig, Robert. 1994. "Public versus Regulated Private Enterprise." *Proceedings of the World Bank Annual Conference on Development Economics 1993.* Washington, D.C., May.

Wisecarver, Daniel. 1985. "Economic Regulation and Deregulation in Chile, 1973–1983." In Gary Walton, ed., *National Economic Policies of Chile.* Greenwich, Conn.: JAI Press.

Wolff, Lawrence, Ernesto Schiefelbein, and Jorge Valenzuela. 1993. "Improving the Quality of Primary Education in Latin America: Towards the 21st Century." Regional Studies Program Report 28. World Bank, Latin America and Caribbean Region, Washington, D.C.

World Bank. 1993a. *The East Asian Miracle: Economic Growth and Public Policy.* New York: Oxford University Press.

———. 1993b. "Human Resources in Latin America and the Caribbean: Priorities and Action." Human Resource Division, Latin America and Caribbean Region, Washington, D.C.

———. 1994. *Trends in Developing Economics 1994.* Washington, D.C.

———. Various years. *Financial Flows to Developing Countries.* Washington, D.C.

———. Various years. *Social Indicators of Development.* Washington, D.C.

———. Various years. *World Debt Tables.* Washington, D.C.

———. Various years. *World Development Report.* New York: Oxford University Press.

———. Various years. *World Tables.* Baltimore, Md.: Johns Hopkins University Press.

Yepes, Guillermo, Luis Gutierrez, and Peter Gyamfi. 1992. "Infrastructure Maintenance in Latin America: The Costs of Neglect and Options for Improvement." LAC Technical Report 17. World Bank, Latin America and Caribbean Region, Washington, D.C.

Zuleta, Luis Alberto, Lino Jaramillo, Carlos Eduardo Bollén, Ana María Gómez, Juan Pablo Trujillo, Nubia Angarita, Tránsito Porras, and Gustavo Ramírez. 1992. "Privatización en Colombia: Experiencia y perspectivas." Working Paper 120. Inter-American Development Bank, Washington, D.C.

READING 15

Opening a Medium-Size Economy: A Case of Regional Agreements—Argentina and MERCOSUR

ROBERTO LAVAGNA
Harvard University

This paper examines the role of regional agreements as instruments for both trade discrimination and the promotion of freer trade. If a free trade dynamic is a basic goal, then "closed" regional agreements are not valid instruments. Consequently, the proponents of freer trade must think not only about deepening regional agreements but also about permanently enlarging and interrelating them. Both the *sequence* of enlargement and the *timing* of each step will prove crucial. This paper offers recommendations regarding the timing and sequence of enlarging and merging regional agreements.

The example of Argentina and its relationship with the Mercado Común del Sur (MERCOSUR) and the North American Free Trade Agreement (NAFTA) provide a basis for the discussion of such issues. However, I believe that conclusions affecting the entire region can also be drawn. Given the oversupply of regional agreements, policy makers face the task of choosing which *sequence* to follow in pursuing these accords.

Section I of this paper discusses the scope of regional trade agreements. Section II explains the situation facing the Southern Cone countries, and Section III recalls the theoretical problems related to international trade and normative policies. Section IV presents a qualitative analysis of both static and dynamic effects of timing and sequence that Argentina and Brazil must consider in choosing between deepening MERCOSUR or switching to a large agreement with NAFTA.

I. The Scope of the Subject

Since World War II, one of the central issues facing individual countries has been the degree and characteristics of their relationship with other economies. This is basically a discussion about international trade. Debate over this aspect of applied political economy has existed in all countries but has been particularly intense in the underdeveloped ones. Fifty years ago, theories of international trade were based on assumptions that did not capture all real-world phenomena. As a consequence, these theories did not offer clear policy prescriptions but rather resulted in disarray. Today, economists still debate the subject of international trade but in quite different terms. More relaxed assumptions have helped bring economists closer both to free trade and its theoretical prescriptions and to a more subtle approach with fewer mechanical solutions.

The basic stages in the postwar debate over trade policy can be summarized chronologically:

- *Free trade versus no trade.* This stage corresponded to the period when the General Agreement on Tariffs and Trade (GATT) was created. During this stage of the debate, the United States sustained the goal of free trade, while in reality an extremely restricted and managed trade existed. In the underdeveloped countries, this stage corresponded to the initial period of import-substitution industrialization (ISI), which was essentially a sectoral position in favor of no trade.
- *No trade versus restricted trade.* In the 1950s and 1960s, theories and arguments more closely reflected the real-world situation and the scope of the debate narrowed. During this stage, the debate ranged between no trade (that was the actual position for agricultural products in the developed countries and for industrial goods in the underdeveloped ones) and restricted trade. Successive GATT rounds sought to create trade (or move away from no trade) while in practice accepting some forms of trade restrictions. Specifically, the GATT made exceptions for certain goods (agriculture, textiles, tropical products) and regional agreements.
- *Free trade versus restricted trade.* From the latter part of the 1970s and through the present, the options of free versus restricted trade have been debated. In reality, the Uruguay Round of GATT has brought actual practice closer to free trade. The inclusion of agriculture, textiles, and service, with a schedule for phasing out trade restrictions, has lessened the amount of restricted trade. Nevertheless, some degree of restricted trade is still maintained because Article XXIV exempts regional agreements. In effect, within this specific waiver (Article XXIV) is the choice between what we can call *less restricted* and *more restricted* trade. For underdeveloped countries, very large regional agreements, which may include countries in different stages of development, imply a position of unilateral openness and virtually complete free trade. For developed countries, such agreements offer the possibility of diverting trade in their favor from other developed countries. More exclusive and homogeneous regional agreements, on the other hand, offer more restricted trade, even though the term *restricted* is less rigid today than it was two decades ago.

II. The Terms of the Problem in the Southern Cone

Since 1986, Argentina has opened its economy in order to replace its previous industrial development model, which had been based on import substitution (1945–1975 and 1981–1983). In fact, in that year two decisions were made concurrently:[1]

[1]A third decision was taken in 1985 in the institutional field. To prepare for these changes, a new ministry (secretary of Industry and Foreign Trade) was created and charged with managing industry and foreign trade through the same strategy. Until that time, industry and foreign trade had been governed separately and at lower levels of government. That is, they were not part of the national cabinet. Technocrats and lobbyists were protectionist in the area of industry and moderate free traders in the area of foreign trade.

- The decision to eliminate import licenses (admission certificates to import), which had previously been distributed by the government.
- The decision to negotiate an agreement for integration with Brazil which sought from the beginning to eliminate tariffs for certain goods (0 percent tariff or 100 percent preference) and to partially reduce tariffs on a large number of other industrial products.[2]

From the end of World War II until 1986, many governments have used a deliberate model of a closed economy for the industrial sector. The only exception was the military government between 1977 and 1981, which represented a case of unilateral economic openness financed by short-term speculative capital.[3]

However, since 1980, and especially since the constitutional government came to power in 1983, the sectors supporting a closed economy were left outside the debate over the direction of the Argentine economy. Rather, the discussion has been framed by those who insist on "unilateral openness" and those who have argued in favor of "dynamic openness."[4] The policy chosen by Argentina in 1986 was, in fact, a mix of policies or what we now call "open regionalism," which meant a simultaneous decrease in import restrictions together with the negotiation of "preferential relationships" with Brazil.[5]

Policy makers were acutely aware that the strategy behind this move was to depart significantly from previous policy for two reasons: first, import licenses had represented infinite protection, and, second, trade between Argentina and Brazil had been very restricted.[6] Concerning this last point, it is possible to say that bilateral trade was particularly limited due to administrative practices in both countries which favored trade with other countries or a very low degree of information among producers and importers in both economies.[7] Following the first move to open the economy in 1986, across-the-board reductions in tariffs, the phasing out of nontariff barriers, and further integration with Brazil continued under all successive administrations.[8] Progress was made despite serious concern over the different external sector policies of each country.

With a mixed policy, the degree of each component is important. That degree depends partly on the exchange rate policy. In fact, since 1991 Argentina has been using the rate of exchange as an anchor for its stabilization policy and this has resulted in something similar to unilateral openness. However, the magnitude of the external deficit—5 percent of the gross domestic product in terms of purchasing power parity (GDP) (PPP) in the

---

[2]It will be acceptable for capital goods produced internally to be traded between the two countries with 100 percent preference.

[3]That experience ended with a large increase in the external debt, the crisis of 1982, and a very low rate of disposable net internal savings.

[4]The same debate occurred in Brazil in 1990, four years after decisions were made in Argentina.

[5]The World Bank considered the replacement of quantitative restrictions with tariffs (called "tarification") as the most difficult and optimal first step in moving to free trade.

[6]In the early 1980s, trade with Brazil accounted for less than 10 percent of Argentina's total exports.

[7]In 1987, Argentina held its first public exhibition of industrial products in Brazil, and it met with extreme success. The geography, of course, had not changed, but the perceptions about this geographic reality had changed with the agreements.

[8]This includes two presidencies in Argentina (Alfonsín and Menem) and four in Brazil (Sarney, Collor de Melo, Franco, and Cardoso).

current account—has pushed policy makers to increase tariff and nontariff barriers in Argentina. A "hidden" (statistical) tariff of 10 percent across the board was instituted in the latter part of 1992. For the first time since 1986, Argentina had reversed its tendency toward openness, as an indirect consequence of the real rate of exchange.

However, the external deficit and the frustration over failure to reach a quick agreement with NAFTA, or at least with the United States, created the necessary conditions within Argentina to continue the process of integration. In August 1994, Argentina gave final approval to a "flexible customs union" with Brazil, Uruguay, and Paraguay within the framework of MERCOSUR.[9] Thus, a kind of forced reequilibrium in the external strategy was attained.

In 1990 Brazil followed Argentina's example by creating a mixed policy of integration and reductions in trade restrictions.[10] The Collor government implemented a program for progressive reductions in tariff and nontariff barriers to trade. Until now, one difference between the two countries has been that Brazil has avoided any kind of unilateral openness as well as any kind of import-biased model.[11]

In summary, a growing external deficit forced the Argentine government to slow the process of unilateral openness, and a loss of competitiveness forced the Brazilian government to begin with a more flexible trade policy, thus following a similar path to that of Argentina. This convergence is the basis of the August 1994 agreement in which both countries, along with Uruguay and Paraguay, decided to adopt a flexible common external tariff and create the second largest customs union in the world.[12]

Although this convergence exists and an agreement was signed, the debate has not ended. Essentially, two positions still exist: some experts advise a change to an "indirect" system of unilateral openness to trade, whereas others support the idea that a "balanced," mixed

---

[9]The use of the word *flexible* is due to the type of agreement reached. There is a complete accord covering 85 percent of goods, and beginning January 1, 1995, a common external tariff was implemented. The average tariff is now 14 percent and the maximum is 20 percent. Also since January 1, 1995, each country has set different external tariffs—between 0 percent and 35 percent on the remaining 15 percent of goods, including capital goods, telecommunications, and computer goods. The chosen tariff, however, will have to converge "linearly and automatically" with the approved external tariff, which will be an average of 14 percent for capital goods and 16 percent for computer goods and telecommunications goods. The deadline for this linear convergence is January 1, 2001, for the first group of products and January 1, 2006, for the second. Because of this 15 percent, some use the term *partial* or *incomplete* to describe the customs union. I do not believe that this is correct, because since January 1995 each country no longer has the power to fix its external tariff. Only a common decision can change that. Moreover, the deadlines for convergence are fixed. That is why the term *flexible* seems to be a more appropriate description.

[10]The Sarney government had started reducing some nontariff barriers in 1988–1989, but the basic policy was still very restrictive.

[11]The new exchange rate policy (March 1995) confirms that point. It appears that the overvaluation of the national money will not be accepted.

[12]The original members, Argentina and Brazil, account for more than 95 percent of the regional GDP. Measured by purchasing power parity, the regional GDP is $850 billion and the total trade (imports plus exports) is around $100 billion.

system of unilateral openness and regional agreements (becoming progressively larger and larger) is still the best way to become a global trader.

"Indirect" in this case refers to the notion of a quickly reached agreement between NAFTA and MERCOSUR or even to the possibility of abandoning MERCOSUR and attempting to enter NAFTA or a free trade agreement with the United States. "Balanced" refers to strengthening and deepening MERCOSUR and later starting a negotiation between NAFTA and MERCOSUR that would enlarge the free trade area. The right time to do so would depend on internal developments within NAFTA and MERCOSUR.

From an economic perspective, only Canada seems now ready to negotiate an agreement with other countries. Mexico is opposed to any enlargement of NAFTA for it is trying to preserve the preferences it has obtained through it, and the United States is hesitant about expanding the agreement and uncertain about the type of approach (bilateral or multilateral) it would like to take. Doubts also exist in the United States about the consequences of enlarging a free trade area in America, especially because of the possibility of affecting its relationship with Southeast Asia.

The group of experts who support the indirect approach think that a speedy convergence will lead to an indirect convergence of regional agreements and the global system of free trade represented by the General Agreement on Tariffs and Trade/World Trade Organization (GATT/WTO) agreements. The people thinking in terms of what I call the balanced approach are stressing the importance of timing and the best sequence for the process of opening economies that are not yet fully developed. These alternatives are not unique to Latin America. In fact, the situation in Southeast Asia is quite similar. Malaysia is calling for regional agreements before launching the Trans-Pacific Asia Pacific Economic Cooperation (APEC) Plan. China, an enormous market in itself, is trying to postpone constraining obligations for at least 15 to 20 years.

Since the MERCOSUR has been confirmed and the enlargement of NAFTA postponed, some might ask why we should continue this discussion. The issue, however, is not closed. Although the enlargement of NAFTA has been postponed, the idea of expanding this agreement remains a valid one.[13] Two arguments suggest the continuing relevance of the debate between the indirect approach and the balanced approach:

- *A general interest in the subject.* With different processes of integration occurring at the same time, problems relating to timing and sequence in the pursuit of other agreements multiply.[14]
- In more concrete terms, MERCOSUR's case is relevant because a simple preelection statement by an American official (especially if it is made by the president himself) announcing a rapid negotiation to enlarge NAFTA would be enough to produce a serious change of priorities in the Southern Cone. Additionally, eventual disparities in rates of

[13]The postponement of NAFTA enlargement resulted from internal problems in Mexico, a difficult preelectoral period in the United States, and even the renewed problems in Canada over Quebec.

[14]The relatively new acceptance of the regional or subregional accords is now drawing attention to other related subjects, such as the preference between customs unions or free trade areas. See, for example, Krueger, *Free Trade Agreements vs. Customs Unions*. Stanford 1995 Working Papers.

exchange within the group could strengthen the position of those arguing against MERCOSUR.[15]

III. The Theoretical Backdrop

The controversy between nondiscriminatory systems and preferential systems for opening an economy could be applied to the analysis of the previous choices over the process of integration. "Nondiscrimination" means complete liberalization without import restrictions such as tariffs, quotas, or other nontariff barriers on imported goods irrespective of their origin.[16] "Preferential" means that special conditions could be extended only to goods imported from specific countries with whom some reciprocity agreement has been reached. Of course, if the preferential policy is applied to all goods in a relationship with another large economy that has high productivity, then the preferential agreement would be a proxy for a nondiscriminatory policy and the problem of timing and sequence would become irrelevant. This is, in fact, the indirect approach. By contrast, if the discriminatory approach is applied only to some products or even to all products in countries with relatively similar levels of productivity, then the debate over the timing and sequence for enlarging the preferential agreements becomes highly relevant. This is the situation for Argentina, Brazil, and the MERCOSUR.

The pervasive effects of protection are well known. Tariffs imply higher internal prices and the substitution of previously imported goods with locally produced goods.[17] The change in relative prices is favorable to import substitution and against exported goods and also produces a reallocation of capital, labor, natural resources, and entrepreneurial capacity in favor of import substitution. As a result, the total domestic supply can be a new combination of local and imported goods, or it may become purely local in origin. The latter implies that some goods become nontradable. On the demand side, protectionism will mean a reduction in exports, and it might even result in no exports at all. In terms of economic welfare, protectionism wastes resources, and consumers experience a reduced standard of living.[18]

---

[15]One month *after* the final accord of August 1994, the Argentine minister of economy proposed to reverse the common market agreements and to move to a free trade area in order to maintain liberty of action and at the same time introduce Chile into the group. That same month, an expert working as a professor in the Foreign Affairs Ministry published a paper arguing that a pact with NAFTA is more important than MERCOSUR.

[16]Nondiscrimination is equivalent to the principle of most favored nation (MFN), which forms the theoretical basis of the GATT agreement.

[17]Lerner and later Metzler, however, have demonstrated that under specific assumptions a tariff may lower the internal price of imported goods. These assumptions are related to the private sector's propensity to spend on imports and on the government's marginal propensity to spend tariff revenue on imports. See Metzler, "Tariff and Terms of Trade."

[18]Once more, it is necessary to point out that this is true regardless of income distribution only when we compare situations of free trade, nontrade, or restricted trade. When comparing two different levels of tariffs, or two different types of restricted trade, it is necessary to recall that the ranking of trade policies is affected by the type of income distribution chosen. See Bhagwati, "A Generalized Theory of the Effects of Tariffs on Terms of Trade."

Nevertheless, these prescriptions rely on very restrictive assumptions related to the model of perfect competition. Under that model, all countries accept free trade principles, and there are no access problems in markets. More broadly, there is no deviation between private and social cost due to economic externalities and there are no decreasing costs as output increases. However, in reality, deviations do exist and can be explained by, among other things, the process of "learning by doing," which is a central argument in the case of infant industries.[19]

The model also fails to consider two factors: rigidities in the internal mobility of factors (W. A. Lewis or E. E. Hagen) and dynamic effects (Myrdall, R. Nurkse, P. N. Rosenstein-Rodan, H. H. Singer, J. M. Fleming, and A. Hirschman). In fact, international trade theory was divorced from the problems studied by development theorists of the 1950s and 1960s. Even the empirical evidence from trade among developed countries is not compatible with the factor endowment theory. The growth of intraindustry trade did not correspond to the classical idea of comparative advantage.

In the real world, these types of "disturbances" require a new positive explanation about why trade occurs. At the same time, examined normatively, they leave room for cases in which discrimination could be beneficial. Some of these questions contain an "original sin," because they were part of the work on development theory and were not formally treated. They were finally introduced, directly and indirectly, under the "new theory" of international trade.[20]

According to this theory, competitive advantage resulting from a country's endowment of resources is one of the reasons for trade. Other important additional reasons for trade include static economies of scale reflecting increasing returns internal to the firm; dynamic economies of scale linked to the learning curve in which productivity is a function of past accumulative output; and economic externalities due to geographical concentrations, technological trajectories or interindustry spillovers, and even some cases of reciprocal dumping.

The correlative changes on the normative side are less neat. Policy prescriptions are always more elusive, especially if welfare considerations have to be made. As was the case for traditional theory, the assumptions of the new models make it difficult to come up with sure prescriptions, but some general points have been made:

- If learning and agglomeration effects matter, then history and economic trajectory also matter.
- If scales matter, then the size of the country and the size of the internal market also matter.
- If trajectory is important, then some events, natural or related to economic policy, could change permanently the pattern of production and trade.
- If scales and the internal development of technology (endogenous innovation) are important, then monopolies or oligopolies could play a useful social role.

The logical conclusion is that it is probable, but not always certain, that some kind of discrimination, such as using export subsidies and temporary tariffs, could change the specialization in favor of the protecting nation.

---

[19]Scitovsky, "Economic Theory and Western European Integration."

[20]P. Krugman, "Rethinking International Trade," MIT Press, 1990. P. Krugman, "Empirical Evidence on the New Trade Theories: The Current State of Play," *CERP,* 1993.

At this point, it helps to look at an actual situation in international trade. Let us consider, for example, the case of free trade specialization under "access restrictions." This is still the case for agricultural-primary goods and agricultural-manufactured goods in many countries. Because of access restrictions, specialization is impossible. Other alternatives must be explored considering that, because know-how and scales are important, some kind of active policy is required for the industrial sector. If an active policy is not pursued, then a reduction in the consumer's standard of living will result.[21]

The problem that policy makers face is predicting how much and for how long this discrimination will play a positive role. Despite the theoretical and practical problems, some operational rules can be established:

- Under all circumstances, a discriminatory approach is better than a closed economy, the latter representing a case of extreme import substitution.
- Under some circumstances of actual free trade, a discriminatory policy could be better than nondiscriminatory theoretical free trade.
- Tariffs are a better discriminatory instrument than quotas.[22]

The real problems considered in the previous section are precisely related to finding the best (Pareto optimum) discriminatory or preferential policy—that is, best at minimizing the waste of resources under the actual conditions of international markets and under dynamic analysis. The timing and sequence of liberalization and, by extension, integration, are also part of identifying the best policies.

IV. The Timing and Sequence

If the regional agreements are considered in the framework of "open regionalism" and as a way to arrive at general free trade, then concerns about timing occur over the duration of each stage of the progressive process of opening. Open regionalism means that regional discrimination is decided simultaneously with decreasing tariff and nontariff barriers for all nonmember countries. This is not a minor requisite. A regional agreement not only reduces the difference between internal and external prices but also modifies the terms of exchange.[23] Obtaining positive results requires a high demand elasticity for imports, a small difference between the prices of the new suppliers (members of the accord) and the previous ones, and relatively low tariffs vis-à-vis the rest of the world.

[21]The European Union used mobile tariffs (sliding scale), which in fact create conditions of totally closed markets.

[22]This is true even though R. McKinnon and K. C. Fung demonstrated that, with a flexible exchange rate system, quotas are better instruments for avoiding fluctuations in prices.

[23]The results for each member country could be different. In general, as Robert Mundel pointed out, the terms of exchange are modified in a similar way if member countries are rivals (noncomplementaries) in their trade. If they are complementaries, countries having a similar trade structure to the rest of the world will see their terms of exchange deteriorate.

The consensus over timing could be defined within the framework of the idea of the life cycle and applied to every regulatory policy—in this case, discriminatory trade. It will allow for the recognition of the fact that, at some point, the positive effects of discrimination are compensated by cost, thereby dooming any justification for a permanent departure from a nondiscriminatory system. That means that any discriminatory or preferential policy must be phased out sooner or later.

In the field of trade, one way of coping with this rule is to expand continuously the geographical scope of products under the umbrella of discriminatory policies. To enlarge a preferential system means spreading the preference up to the point at which a global preference becomes, in practice, no preference at all. Each expansion of preferences tends to dilute the preferences previously agreed upon. That is why preagreed and preannounced schedules between countries as part of regional arrangements became extremely useful instruments for both the private and the public sector. The European Union adopted this method after a period of stagnation, which was also employed by the MERCOSUR from the beginning.

Additionally, the sequence of the expansion program becomes a real problem. Because preferential policies were considered and practically accepted as an intermediate step to global free trade, these initiatives have flourished.[24] In fact, today an oversupply of integration schemes and proposals of how to link them exist.[25]

Which will be the criteria to fix a sequence having global trade as the final goal? Two rules seem quite clear:

- If, from the beginning, the sequence includes a mix of high-performing countries with low-medium or small performers, the effect would be similar to a nonpreferential policy and unilateral openness. This occurs for two reasons. On the one hand, static specialization will arise, thereby avoiding the effects of "learning by doing" and, in general, other dynamic effects. On the other hand, it is probable that access problems for primary goods will not be resolved if these goods are internally produced and considered to be socially important to the developed country.
- On this point, my analysis is opposed to Krueger's static analysis which, on the basis of factoral proportions (those of underdeveloped countries being skewed toward unskilled labor) concludes that "it is arguable that customs unions between developing countries are less likely to provide welfare gains than those between developed and developing."[26] My own conclusion requires some qualifications. Indeed, one exception might occur because of geographical continuity and the existence of political and social issues (e.g., illegal immigration) that draw specific compensatory policies in favor of the lower-performing country, as in the case of the United States and Mexico.

---

[24]The qualitative change in judgment was produced after the U.S.-Canada agreement in 1988.

[25]In the American case alone, we can now count MERCOSUR, NAFTA, the Andean Group, G3 (Mexico, Venezuela, and Colombia), G2 (Mexico and Chile), MERCOSUR-Chile, MERCOSUR Andean Group, and some minor pacts in the Caribbean and Central America. It is evident that this oversupply does not make the problem of sequence a theoretical one.

[26]Krueger, Anne. *Free Trade Agreements vs. Customs Unions*, Stanford, February 1995. Preliminary working papers.

- If the sequence gives preference to countries very far from the high-performing ones and from the bulk of international trade, the union will be similar to an import substitution policy, irrelevant in terms of decreasing the waste of resources and deteriorating the social welfare. If the agreement is between small countries, probably with relatively low tariffs, the agreement itself becomes less important.

The first rule prevents the Southern Cone countries from taking the initial step toward integrating with NAFTA and switching from MERCOSUR. The second limits the process of opening the economy only among the four MERCOSUR countries or enlarging it only to add small economies like Chile, Peru, or Bolivia. Applying the rule of limited timing and best sequence, future negotiations with NAFTA cannot be, and must not be, rejected.

IV.1 The Static Effects

The case of NAFTA-MERCOSUR deserves a more detailed analysis. We can begin with Viner's scheme of trade creation and trade diversion.[27] In the case of trade creation, a higher degree of division of labor and specialization can be found in the production of goods for which each member has a comparative advantage. Locally made products are substituted for imported goods, and consumers gain as a result of lower prices. Trade diversion occurs when, due to the preferential tariff, the member countries reduce what they actually purchase from best-performing third countries. In other words, a more efficient producer is replaced with a less efficient one.

At least in static terms, a preferential arrangement will increase economic welfare if the creation effect is greater than the diversion effect. That relationship depends on Viner's initial assumptions about constant returns and demand elasticity equaling zero in each member. Even in a static analysis, the MERCOSUR provides its members with a creation/diversion ratio greater than an agreement with NAFTA or the United States could provide. It is possible to demonstrate this argument by analyzing each of the two big MERCOSUR countries in relation to the major country in NAFTA. By using dummy variables with values between 0 (minimum) and 4 (maximum) to measure the potential effects of trade creation and diversion, we can apply that system to Pavitt's taxonomy for different kinds of goods.[28] (See Table 1.)

The diversion is quite small. In both cases, the countries are not producers (in general terms of the classification) of science-based goods. That means that no diversion is possible.[29] As for traditional goods (agriculture and energy goods), Argentina is an efficient producer.[30]

[27] J. Viner, "The Customs Union Issue."

[28] Pavitt, "Sectoral Patterns of Technological Change."

[29] In the case of capital goods, both countries demand goods that are not produced in the area (meaning no change in the patterns of trade) or they have agreed on some exceptions in the external tariff until the year 2001 or 2006 in order to minimize negative welfare effects.

[30] In the first case some diversion occurred (the sale of petroleum and wheat by Argentina to Brazil), but because these products are sold at international prices and Argentina is a price taker, there is no negative effect on Brazilian consumers because the diversion is produced under conditions established by the international market. In fact, some favorable effect could result from lower transportation costs that could, in part, compensate for the fiscal losses of the Brazilian government.

TABLE 1
Effects of MERCOSUR

	DIVERSION		CREATION	
GOODS BASED ON	ARGENTINA	BRAZIL	ARGENTINA	BRAZIL
	A	B	C	D
Science	0	0	3	3
Scale intensive	2	1	4	3
Specialized	2	2	3	4
Traditional	0	3	1	2

A: Goods that were formerly purchased abroad (by Argentina) and are now purchased from Brazil as a consequence of MERCOSUR.
B: Goods that Brazil previously purchased abroad and are now purchased from Argentina.
C: Goods that Argentina produced internally and are now purchased from Brazil (totally or partially).
D: Goods that Brazil produced internally and are now bought from Argentina (totally or partially).

For Brazil, some positive structural diversion will occur due to the replacement of subsidized products coming from the United States and the European Union with products from Argentina, at international market prices adjusted for transportation costs.

For Argentina, some diversion could occur in scale and specialized goods in which Brazil has a relatively competitive supply. This diversionary effect could also take place in Brazil, but it will be even less significant. A considerable substitution in favor of Argentina is less probable for scale goods; it is only probable for specialized goods.

By contrast, in both countries a strong possibility exists that trade will replace, totally or partially, local production. The nearly 20 percent annual growth in mutual trade since the beginning of the agreement in 1986 offers the best proof of this possibility.

Argentina will continue to replace proportionally most of its scale-based goods whereas Brazil will do so for specialized goods.[31] As far as traditional goods are concerned, Brazil will restrict part of its subsidized local production of some cereals, and Argentine consumers will experience an increase in the variety of tropical traditional goods that are normally unavailable in the local market. In science-based industries, some joint ventures (biotechnology, civil nuclear goods, software, pharmaceutical products) could produce considerable intraindustry trade.[32]

These results may be compared with the effects of an eventual accord with NAFTA by using the results of trade with the United States representing NAFTA. (See Table 2.)

---

[31]The effect of trade creation is very clear in the processed foods industry, the automotive industry (including car parts), the steel industry, and the petrochemical industry, among others.

[32]In the 1986 agreement, some provisions were made to undertake the joint development of all relevant science-based goods except computer hardware (which was omitted because of the total protection existing in Brazil at that time). These provisions included an investment fund; exchange of human resources; and joint ventures in software, biotechnology, civil aviation, telecommunications, nuclear and new materials, and capital goods. The provisions were abandoned in the 1990 treaty.

TABLE 2
Effects of NAFTA

	Diversion		Creation			
Goods Based On	Argentina	Brazil	Argentina	USA	Brazil	USA
	E	F	G	H	I	J
Science	4	4	4	0	4	0
Scale	4	4	4	0	2	3
Specialized	3	3	4	2	2	2
Traditional	0	0	0	0	3	0

E: Goods that Argentina purchased that will now be diverted to the United States.
F: Goods that Brazil purchased that will now be diverted to the United States.
G: Goods that Argentina produces internally that will be replaced by U.S. goods.
H: Goods that the United States produces internally that will be replaced by Argentinean goods.
I: Goods that Brazil produces internally that will be replaced by U.S. goods.
J: Goods that the United States produces internally that will be replaced by Brazilian goods.

In both cases, Brazil and Argentina experience substantial diversion effects in science-based goods, scale-based goods, and, to a lesser degree, specialized goods. Europe, Japan, and Southeast Asia will also be affected. Additionally, the local consumer will be affected by the replacement of former suppliers with less efficient ones.[33]

On the creation side, except in the traditional area, an agreement with the United States will have the effect of unilateral openness. Much internal production will be substituted, and except for some specialized goods, little possibility exists for expansion into the U.S. market. As for traditional goods, Argentina's production is similar and competitive to that of the United States. Moreover, primary production in the United States receives direct subsidies of more than $10 billion, and it would not be realistic to expect a change in this policy. In fact, the data from 1991 to 1994 in which Argentina produced a kind of unilateral openness support these trends, exhibiting a negative bias toward imports and a smaller impact on exports.

Concerning some scale goods and specialized goods, the fact that Argentina already has relatively low tariffs in the United States under the General System of Preferences allows for some expansion but at very low rates. Around 50 percent of the exports to the United States had no tariffs as a result of the preferences whereas the other 50 percent had low tariffs. The problems lie more on the supply side, and are caused by the effects of a weak industrial sector and a competitive primary goods sector, which are directly or indirectly discriminated against. Figure 1 clearly shows the different potential paths for development.

For Brazil, the situation is different, although only in relative terms. Local suppliers will be replaced in favor of U.S. suppliers of some science-based goods and in scale goods and specialized goods. In both cases, because Brazil is more competitive than Argentina, the

[33]That diversion is so evident and significant that the European Union proposed to the MERCOSUR (immediately after some enlargement in the NAFTA was announced) that they begin negotiations for creating a free trade area.

FIGURE 1
Type of Economy (x)

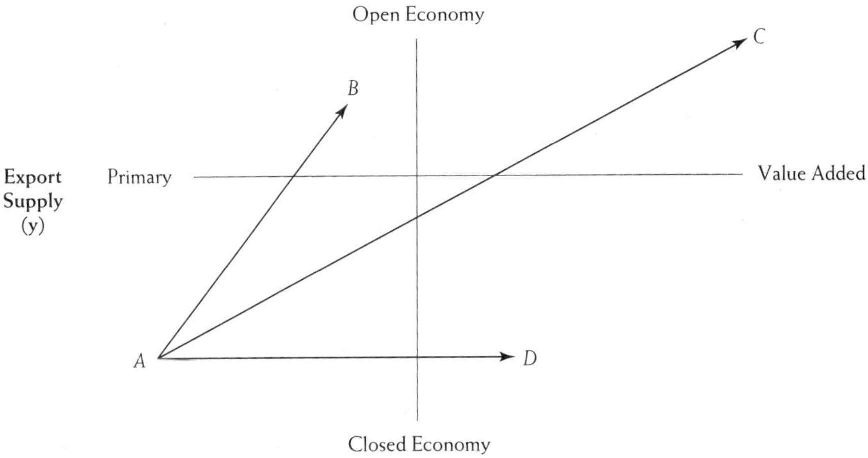

Note: *A* represents the initial point. *B* represents unilateral openness. *C* represents export-led growth. *D* corresponds to import-substituting industrialization.

trade deflection will be less intense.[34] Also local production in agricultural traditionals (subsidized) will be replaced with production from the United States (also subsidized), thus making it very difficult to undertake welfare calculations.

The impact of creation in favor of Brazil will be more significant than that for Argentina. With better access, Brazil could increase its exports of scale goods and some specialized goods to the United States. Nevertheless, the most important aspect of Brazil's trade strategy toward the United States is derived from its defensive strategy, which makes sense because of the possibility that its exports might be diverted in favor of Mexico and because of the growing differences of opinion between the United States and Brazil over new topics of concern such as labor and environmental policies.

Comparing all of these qualitative effects, it is clear that the ratio of creation/diversion is higher within the MERCOSUR than in an alternative arrangement involving NAFTA and the United States. This is true for both Argentina and Brazil.[35]

For tradable services, the effect of agreements with NAFTA would clearly divert commerce from other developed areas. In conclusion, MERCOSUR fulfills one of the general rules of trade unions better than NAFTA. The degree of competition with respect to protected industries is higher among MERCOSUR countries than between any Southern Cone

[34]Trade was diverted from Brazil to Mexico and some specific products (footwear and fruit juice) face trade restrictions in the United States that could be phased out.

[35]In fact, the ratio is an incremental coefficient because it results from the comparison of the actual situation in terms of trade with potential situations deriving from changes in the rules of discrimination.

country and NAFTA.[36] The greater the quantity of similar goods produced under conditions of protection (that means the more competitive they are), the greater the elements that are able to create trade. Considering the net increase in trade between Argentina and Brazil in the eight years from mid-1986 to mid-1994, it is possible to support this conclusion, which was one of Meade's criteria for estimating the existence of an increase in welfare.[37] At the same time, Kemp and Wan's criterion for the maintenance of trade with the rest of the world as a welfare condition is largely fulfilled.[38]

Moreover, considering only the creation side, it is possible to see that although this effect is relatively balanced between Argentina and Brazil, it is quite unbalanced between Brazil and the United States, and it is still less balanced between Argentina and the United States. For Argentina, the agreement with Brazil by itself implies a challenge because Brazil's economy is more than three times larger than Argentina's and the industrial density is greater.

IV.2 The Dynamic Effects

The other way to compare NAFTA and MERCOSUR as sequential alternatives for a Southern Cone country is to examine the dynamic factors that are not normally taken into account under the creation/diversion analysis. Earlier in this paper we discussed the theoretical reasons for including dynamic effects when analyzing trade. The same is true for the process of integration.

A final consideration of the limits of static analysis could be made by examining some estimates concerning the potential repercussions of both the Maastricht Treaty and the Uruguay Round/GATT Agreement. The Cecchini Report estimated that the impact of the changes introduced at Maastricht in 1992 would result in a one-time surge of 2.5 percent in the level of European GDP.[39] The GATT estimated the benefits of the Uruguay Round at around $250 billion, also a one-time change in the level of global GDP after eight years.[40] It is evident that this static analysis underestimates the effects of better allocation, more efficient use of factors, and economic externalities.

What kind of dynamic effects could be considered when thinking in terms of normative economics? Basically, four types of effects should be examined: the effects on investment, endogenous growth factors, innovation, and the structure of the market.

First, investment is linked to the internal rate of return that is itself related to the flow of net income. In a world where economies of scale do count, this flow is influenced by the size of the market. When the markets increase as a result of trade pacts, there is a boost in rentability, savings, and investment. A new equilibrium capital/labor ratio is reached in

[36]For a quantitative analysis, see Erzan and Yeats, "U.S.-Latin America Free Trade Areas"; also, Bianchi and Robbio, "Tratado de Libre Comercio Desvio de Comercio en Perjuicio de Argentina y Brasil."

[37]Meade, "The Theory of Customs Unions."

[38]Kemp and Wan, "An Elementary Proposition Concerning the Formation of Customs Unions."

[39]Cecchini, *Europa 1992: Una Apuesta al Futuro.*

[40]These figures seem very modest, especially compared with the losses in global GDP due to the last recession in the developed world, which was not less than the same amount ($250 billion) for *each* point below the average of growth in the past decade.

the medium term. The static effect of a better allocation of resources has a dynamic consequence for a new path of stable growth.

Second, if the economies of scale at an aggregate level are introduced as a factor in the model of growth based on endogenous forces, the marginal productivity of capital will not decrease even if the capital/labor (K/L) ratio increases.

Third, trade pacts will affect innovation, whose level is related to the cost of research and development. A bigger market will provide a reduction in the fixed costs of research, encourage a flow of technical knowledge, and lessen costs through standardization. Additionally, part of the innovation process is achieved though imitation, specifically in the developing countries, and a better flow of information and less particular technical regulations increase imitation and the rate of innovation. This "catching up" could decrease the rate of benefits in the developed countries as a result of a reduction in their monopolistic power, thus giving some rationality to policies aimed at restricting transfers of technology.

The change in the structure of markets is the fourth important effect. Following integration, markets become more competitive because of the dilution of rent-seeker groups, the practice of more stable economic policies (or at least more modern regulatory policies), and the creation of better-functioning institutions.[41]

What role do these elements play when we compare the dynamic effects of switching from MERCOSUR to an agreement between Argentina and NAFTA or the United States? At first glance, considering the size of the market and technology, it may seem evident that Brazil/MERCOSUR cannot compete with NAFTA/United States. But this is, again, a static analysis based on the actual availability of capital, technology, and entrepreneurial capacity in the United States. The arguments promoted by pundits who support an accord with NAFTA or the United States include the following: a bigger market, more technological capacity, the possibility of larger investment flows, and more institutional impact to "anchor" internal economic reform. They also point out that Brazil/MERCOSUR will face problems such as the difficulty of coordinating economic policies; the different visions of entrepreneurs within each country and the varied nature of their relationship with government officials; and, surprisingly, the possibility that Brazil might be more attractive to foreign investors than Argentina.[42]

A closer examination, however, reveals a different answer to the previous question, based on both theoretical and practical elements. Because the dynamic effects are, in the medium term, related to the capacity of the integrated market to attract investments and to adapt technology, a specialization in primary or low value-added products is not the best way to attract fixed investments, technology, and modern entrepreneurial capacity. That type of integration is precisely what could happen to Argentina, and to a lesser extent Brazil, under a sudden agreement with a very high-performing country. Under some circumstances, the

---

[41]Argentina could be a good example of this because since 1989 the general structure of tariffs was changed five times and not always in the same direction. There were decreases, increases, homogenization, differentiation, and many ad hoc changes. In terms of productivity and new investment, the cost of these discretionary policies is enormous.

[42]With the United States, no coordination would be necessary because "going with the tendency" would be enough.

economic integration could reduce the incentives to invest and to innovate in at least one of the countries.[43]

It is possible for a small country to face a decrease in rentability and investments in sectors that promote innovations. That will reduce the effect of spillovers in the economy and produce additional losses in productivity. A relatively advanced human capital will move from the innovative sectors to the more traditional ones because the lower level of wages fosters specialization in low-tech goods.[44] Even an eventual entry into the international markets with "mature" goods could be difficult if the exporting function contains, as I believe, "sunk" costs.[45] Of course, if we include the subsidization of agriculture and some careful restrictions in the transfer of technology by the more advanced country, the negative final effect is even more pronounced.

Competition implies lower input/output ratios and the reallocation of resources, but it could also mean the better use of available resources under existing uses. The argument for internal economic efficiency is connected to the same conclusions.[46]

All these dynamic effects could be diverted by an agreement (prior to the right time) with a high-productivity arrangement like NAFTA or its largest member, the United States. This is even more evident in the absence of any geographical or political reasons, such as those existing in the case of Mexico, to include compensatory policies in the agreement (principle of differentiation) that favor the less developed country.

A process of integration that tends toward sectoral specialization (interindustry trade) tends to attract less capital than a strategy of intraindustry trade. Specifically, this is the case when Argentina is a producer of primary and industrial primary goods that are not complementary with NAFTA/United States.[47]

Being identified as a very specialized global trader is less attractive to fixed investment than being identified as a country with a large but deep intraindustry specialization.

Movements of factors of production can serve as an alternative to trade discrimination, if the conditions are good for investing in relatively large markets with a stable economy, private enterprise, and a progressive but firm insertion into the global economy.

A regional agreement between relatively similar economies— having at the same time a considerable scale, a medium level of development, and human resources, and undertaking the decision to be a global trader—is more likely to attract investment and to reap dynamic advantages. Given a convenient scale, important changes could result from ideas about "learning by doing," external economies of agglomeration, spillover effects, the tendency to increase exports over the base of a solid internal market, and even the effects related to endogenous innovation.

---

[43]Grossman and Helpman, *Innovation and Growth in the Global Economy.*

[44]Rodrik, "Do Low Income Countries Have a High-Wage Option?"

[45]Roberts and Tybout, "An Empirical Model of Sunk Cost and the Decision to Export."

[46]Scitovsky, "Economic Theory and Western Integration"; Johnson, "The Economic Gains from Freer Trade with Europe."

[47]Since the 1980s, Chile, which has an economy 20 percent the size of Argentina's and a population one-third its size, has followed a very narrow specialization and is now cleverly trying to make progress in other industrial sectors. The previous model reached its limits, and today there are problems in the current account and a modest rate of decrease in the poverty level.

TABLE 3
Integration/Dynamic Effects

ELEMENT	WITH UNITED STATES/NAFTA	WITH BRAZIL/MERCOSUR
Sectoral specialization	4	2
Intratrade	1	4
Investments	2	4
Endogenous factors	1	4
Innovation/imitation	2	4
Spillovers	2	4
Institutional factors	2	4
"Anchor" factors	4	2

Finally, although the United States is the biggest anchor factor in terms of a private-oriented, free economy, MERCOSUR is more important in terms of institutional factors because it is not a free trade area (FTA) but rather a customs union.[48] That means that every country gives up a substantial part of its economic sovereignty (i.e., setting external tariffs) to the group. The difference is not a minor one. In order to avoid deflection in trade, an FTA requires rules of origin. These usually very complex and costly requirements become anti-trade instruments and are strongly influenced by powerful groups lobbying for protection.

An FTA does not create more trade than a customs union and is generally much more diverting. Dynamically, the customs union has a greater potential to affect the production/trade relationship because it creates additional possibilities in terms of joint industrial restructuring, the development of new sectors, and intraregional spillovers. All these effects are more difficult under FTA conditions due to the degree of liberty that each economy preserves and the bureaucratic limits (i.e., rules of origin) that are imposed.[49]

Using dummy variables as we previously did to exhibit the arguments, in my opinion it is possible to write what we see in Table 3.

The last valid question is this: In the next five or six years, what could change in the previous arguments to make NAFTA/United States the next step in the sequence after Brazil/MERCOSUR? Three justifications are possible. The first, which I previously gave, is that every discriminatory policy has decreasing returns. Some of the advantages which now favor MERCOSUR will be less evident in a few years. It is even possible that new rent seekers might develop. Second, the difference in foreseeable growth between the MERCOSUR countries and the United States may be around three points per year which, in six years, means around 20 percent of relative growth. It may be even greater if the transition period that normally follows these accords is added. Finally, and more important, there is a qualitative factor: the know-how embodied in the openness of the economy and in executing an agreement concerning discriminatory policies.

[48]Globalization itself ensures the "anchor" in favor of a private-oriented and free economy.

[49]Comparing the experiences of the European Community and the European Free Trade Area (EFTA) provides a real and dynamic example of the differences between a customs union and a free trade area in promoting growth and trade.

Within MERCOSUR, after a long period of preparation (1986–1994), including some regressions (1989–1990), entrepreneurs, labor, and governments are now looking at a moment for structural change. The GDP could differ in two ways. It could be 20 percent larger in relative terms (provided that a new financial crisis in the emergent markets is avoided), and it could be very different structurally, having greater progress not only in scale sectors and specialized sectors (with those products related to primary inputs being particularly important) but also in the science-based and service sectors.

Because history is a relevant factor and the present productivity depends on the past trajectory, after no more than five or six years of deep, regional effort, the conditions for negotiating a larger agreement with NAFTA/United States will have a very different history behind them.[50] This can clearly be a case of hysteresis. Of course, this will be true provided that macroeconomic policies remain consistent, structural reforms (i.e., privatization and deregulation) continue, the private sector remains the engine, and social disequilibrium is managed within a framework of medium-term solutions. On the other hand, NAFTA itself needs some internal time.[51]

The result of such a sequence could be more interesting and result in more free trade. A speedy negotiation with a wrong sequence would produce a system known as "hub and spoke," which contains plenty of "hidden" discrimination, rules of origin, and so forth. The "best" sequence would be one that gives countries the maximum opportunity to develop dynamic advantages during a short period. In that way, they can respect the time rule and phase out discrimination.

MERCOSUR, whose core is composed by Argentina and Brazil, provides a sequence that respects this previous rule. These core economies avoid both extremes: the deterrence of dynamic effects that could emerge from a quick integration with countries having much higher productivity, and the prevention of the best allocation of resources due to an association with or within countries having very low productivity or lacking some minimal economies of scale.

V. Conclusion

Conditions for less restricted trade have developed in the last few years under a formula of regionalism plus multilateralism. Regional agreements, starting with the Argentina-Brazil agreement in 1986 and the United States-Canada agreement in 1988, occurred simultaneously with the launch of the Uruguay Round of the GATT. More recently new initiatives or enlargements have been applied to the earlier agreements. This process poses new

[50]It is impossible to ignore that the European Union has proposed the creation of a free trade area and a requisite is that the MERCOSUR be completed and confirmed. That is different from a hesitant U.S. strategy that sometimes believes in bilateral agreements and other times believes in large and blurred continental agreements. Also, some interest is now appearing in Japan. In a recent work, Kotaro insisted that Japan needs its own strategy toward Latin America, which should have a bilateral approach that could serve as an "alternative to the U.S." Moreover, he argued that "it seems naive to imagine that Japan would follow the U.S. Free Trade Area Agreement strategy." See Kotaro, "Political Options for Japan."

[51]For an analysis of the U.S. interest in Brazil and Argentina, see Dornbusch, "The Case for Bilateralism."

questions including, first of all, problems of identification. Many believe that regionalism has been possible only because countries have decided to liberalize their economies. They cite the failure of regional schemes, particularly in Latin America during the period of import-substituting industrialization. Others, with whom I agree, believe that liberalization is only possible because these regional agreements supply a methodology for opening economies without making countries face unbearable social and economic costs due to a sudden restructuring of production.

In the first case regionalism is the result, whereas in the second case it is the explanatory variable. If we agree with the first thesis, it is possible to say that in some way regionalism could be a waste of time and resources or even a dangerous instrument for stopping free trade. Following the second thesis, however, open regionalism is actually an instrument for free trade. In positive economics, the new theories of international trade explain patterns of trade and production on the basis of historical trajectories, economies of scale, and economic externalities; the latter ranges from "learning by doing" to spillovers, including agglomeration effects. On the normative side, new theories of international trade provide enough room to sustain a positive instrumental role for regionalism without forgetting that welfare considerations are always difficult to make without an explicit social welfare function.

Applying the life cycle theory and the law of decreasing returns to every discriminatory or regulatory policy poses the problem of timing for these regional agreements and calls for a progressive movement, a dynamic, in favor of freer trade. The enlargement of these regional accords is, under existing trade restrictions and access problems, the best way to reach the goal of freer trade.

The oversupply of regional proposals and the fact that some of these proposals overlap add the issue of determining the best sequence for forming accords and expanding them. Avoiding two extremes—either joining countries with very high productivity to those with medium or less-developed productivities, or uniting those with very low rates of productivity or economic scale—could serve as a practical rule for the best allocation of resources. A qualification is needed for cases in which a highly productive country has strategic reasons to sustain an agreement with a developing country through compensatory policies (NAFTA/Mexico).

Using these criteria to evaluate Argentina's situation suggests that strengthening and deepening the accord with Brazil/MERCOSUR is valuable, both in terms of the static analysis of trade creation and trade diversion and in its dynamic effects. A subsequent, not remote, agreement between NAFTA and MERCOSUR will secure a move toward freer trade.

BIBLIOGRAPHY

Bhagwati, J. "A Generalized Theory of the Effects of Tariffs on Terms of Trade." In *Oxford Economic Papers,* edited by H. G. Johnson, (October 1961).

Bianchi, E., and J. Robbio. "Tratado de Libre Comercio Desvio de Comercio en Perjuicio de Argentina y Brasil." *CEI* (1993).

Cecchini, Paolo, ed. *Europa 1992: Una Apuesta al Futuro.* Alianza, Madrid:, 1992.

Corden, Map. "The Revival of Protectionism in Developed Countries." In *Protectionism and World Welfare,* edited by Salvatore. Cambridge: Cambridge University Press, 1993.

Dornbusch, R. "The Case for Bilateralism." In *Protectionism and World Welfare,* edited by Salvatore. Cambridge: Cambridge University Press, 1993.

———. *The Cost and Benefits of Regional Economic Integration.* Cambridge, MA: MIT Press, 1987.

Erzan, R., and A. Yeats. *U.S.-Latin American Free Trade Areas: Some Empirical Evidence.* (1992).

Grossman, G. M., and E. Helpman. *Innovation and Growth in the Global Economy.* Cambridge, MA: MIT Press, 1991.

Johnson, H. G. "The Economic Gains from Freer Trade with Europe." *Three Banks Review* (September 1958).

Kemp, M., and H. Wan. "An Elementary Proposition Concerning the Formation of Customs Unions." (1976).

Kotaro, Horisaka. "Political Options for Japan: Considering the U.S. New Strategic Regional Doctrine." *IDCJ*, (1994).

Krueger, Anne. *Free Trade Agreements vs. Customs Unions.* Stanford, CA: Stanford University Press, 1995.

Krugman, Paul. "Empirical Evidence on the New Trade Theories: The Current State of Play." *CERP,* (1993).

________. *Rethinking International Trade.* Cambridge, MA: MIT Press, 1990.

Lavagna, Roberto. "Cambios en la Estructura Productiva Inducidos por el MERCOSUR." *IDEAS,* (1992).

Meade, James E. "The Theory of Customs Unions" (1995).

Metzler, L. "Tariff and Terms of Trade, and the Distribution of National Income." *Journal of Political Economy* (February 1949).

Motta Veiga, P. "Relaciones comercialies Estados Unidos-MERCOSUR: El Caso Brasil." Flacso, (1994).

Pavitt, K. "Sectoral Patterns of Technological Change: Toward a Taxonomy and Theory." *Research Policy* (1984).

Roberts, M., and J. Tybout. "An Empirical Model of Sunk Cost and the Decision to Export." *CESPRI* Milan, 1993.

Rodrik, D. "Do Low Income Countries Have a High-Wage Option?" *CEPR,* (1994).

Scitovsky, T. "Economic Theory and Western European Integration." (1958).

Viner, J. "The Customs Union Issue." Carnegie Endowment, 1950.

READING 16

The Andean Group's Integration Strategy*

MIGUEL RODRÍGUEZ-MENDOZA
Organization of American States

INTRODUCTION

"Bolivia wants to be like Doña Flor, it would like to be married to both the Andean Group and MERCOSUR," Bolivian President Sanchez de Lozada told his Latin American colleagues in an attempt to explain his country's economic integration strategy. Doña Flor, the protagonist of one of Jorge Amado's most successful novels, is a young widow who marries a mature and kind man, but is unable to forget her highly sensual former husband. Despite her happy marriage, she would really like to live simultaneously with her two, somehow complementary husbands.

Notwithstanding its long-term membership in the Andean Group, Bolivia has contemplated becoming the fifth member of MERCOSUR ever since it was established five years ago. In this, Bolivia's intentions are not much different from those of other Andean countries, not only with regard to MERCOSUR but also with respect to trade and integration agreements with other Latin American countries.

In fact, President Sanchez de Lozada's comments on his country's approach to integration could apply to all the Andean countries. Like Bolivia, they are formally married to the Andean Group. At the same time all are trying to strengthen their links with other Latin American countries. This combination of formal commitment to the Andean Group and flirtation with the other Latin American countries illustrates the development of the new integration movement in Latin America. Subregional groups are not ends in themselves. Instead, they are seen as "paths" toward larger integration efforts at both the Latin American and hemispheric level.

*This paper has been prepared for the Economic Integration Project of the Inter-American Dialogue. The views expressed in the paper are those of the author and do not represent those of the Organization of American States (OAS). The author would like to acknowledge the expert assistance of Ms. Isabel Hagbrink, who provided research assistance in the preparation of this paper.

There are sound economic reasons for such an approach. Despite their recent progress, none of the Latin American subregional integration groupings in themselves account for the bulk of trade conducted by their member countries. This has led the countries to enter into new arrangements to ensure that their products have access to a greater variety of markets. To a certain extent, the Andean countries are simply practicing what the United Nations Economic Commission on Latin America and the Caribbean (ECLAC) has defined as "open regionalism." Countries can simultaneously participate in different trade and integration arrangements as long as this participation is driven by trade liberalization among the member countries and with the rest of the world.

However, a coherent approach to open regionalism is not easy to achieve. The recent experience of the Andean Group illustrates the challenge Latin American and Caribbean countries face in both strengthening their own subregional integration mechanisms and moving in the direction of regional and hemispheric trade liberalization. The evolution of the Andean Group is also a good example of the difficulties countries in the region encounter when trying to implement mechanisms such as a common tariff schedule or when moving from trade integration to a higher stage of economic policy coordination. Furthermore, the experience of the Andean Group shows how the liberal trade policies adopted by most countries of the region in the 1980s have influenced the old Latin American integration mechanisms.

The Andean Group is one of Latin America's most successful integration arrangements. Its accomplishments in the present decade include the establishment of a free trade area among four of its five member countries, the implementation of a common external tariff (CET) for most of its tariff schedule, and the adoption of common sectoral policies in a number of areas such as foreign investment, intellectual property rights and air transportation. The success of the Andean Group can also be measured by its impact on the member countries' reciprocal trade. In the last five years, exports among the Andean countries have increased at an average annual rate of 27 percent, a result that is all the more impressive when compared with the meager 5 percent increase in Andean exports to the rest of the world.

In spite of these accomplishments, the Andean Group faces tremendous difficulties which may prevent it from strengthening its integration efforts. Some of these difficulties are policy related; for example, differences in economic policies may limit the ability of individual countries to fully implement some of the Group's decisions. Other difficulties are linked to the inability of the Andean Group to develop a common approach toward Latin American and hemispheric integration, an issue that has weakened the stand of the Andean Group as a customs union. Moreover, the armed confrontation between Peru and Ecuador in early 1995 has had consequences for the integration process that have not yet been fully evaluated.

Some of these issues will be examined in greater detail in the sections that follow. The first section reviews the current status and the main institutions of the Andean Group. It is followed by an analysis of intra-subregional trade. Then, the third section addresses some of the difficulties the Andean countries currently face and their impact on the Andean integration process, while the final section offers some considerations regarding the Group's position in the movement toward wider Latin American and hemispheric integration.

THE ACCOMPLISHMENTS

During the 1990s, the Andean Group changed dramatically. Its achievements in the last five years involving subregional trade and the adoption of trade-related disciplines far outweigh the shortcomings of the previous two decades during which the import-substitution policies left little room for reciprocal trade liberalization and hampered any successful integration arrangement.

The Andean Group is one of the oldest Latin American integration arrangements. It was established in 1969 with the signing of the Cartagena Agreement by Bolivia, Colombia, Chile, Ecuador and Peru. Venezuela joined the Andean Group in 1973, and Chile withdrew in 1976. The main objective of the Andean Group was, and remains, the promotion of the balanced and equitable development of its member countries through greater economic integration between the members. To this end, the Andean countries agreed to implement the following mechanisms over a ten-year period: a program for the liberalization of their reciprocal trade, a common external tariff, and the gradual harmonization of economic and social policies. In other words, the Andean countries decided to move toward a customs union.[1]

In order to achieve these goals the Andean countries established a strong institutional framework. The Commission, a policy-making body made up of plenipotentiaries from each member country, was given legislative powers to allow its decisions to be directly enforced in all member countries. The Board is the technical secretariat of the Andean Group, and has the capacity to develop and formulate policy proposals to the Commission on all issues relevant to the Andean integration process. The Andean Court of Justice provides both countries and citizens alike with a judicial framework to protect their interests. Finally, a development fund, the Andean Development Corporation, was established to finance projects that would strengthen the integration process. Some of these mechanisms have supranational powers comparable to those of the European Community which served as a model for the Andean institutional framework.[2]

In spite of its clearly defined goals and its strong institutional framework, the Andean Group did not achieve much progress during its first two decades. Reciprocal trade increased in the 1970s, but rapidly decreased in the decade that followed. Andean trade and the entire integration effort nearly collapsed during the "lost decade" of the 1980s. The "new" Andean Group, as member countries now like to call it, is a product of the new policy environment in Latin American countries. Since the mid-1980s most Latin American and Caribbean countries have modified their economic policies and development strategies. Trade liberalization has replaced the protectionist barriers that were previously

[1]The Andean Group also initially intended to undertake an ambitious development program at the subregional level, "the joint industrial program," but this was soon abandoned.

[2]At the recent meeting of the Andean Presidents, a new protocol was approved that introduces significant institutional changes in the functioning of the Andean Group. The Presidents and Foreign Ministers are granted specific powers to provide guidance to the Andean integration process, and the composition of the *Junta del Acuerdo de Cartegena* (JUNAC) was modified. These proposals still have to be approved by the Parliament of each member country. For further details, see *Protocolo Modificatorio del Acuerdo de Integración Subregional Andino*, Trujillo, March 10, 1996.

considered a precondition for industrialization. Open trade regimes and greater transparency have become the cornerstones of a new outward-oriented development strategy in which access to international markets is a top priority.

All the Andean countries liberalized their trade regimes in the 1980s and early 1990s. Bolivia took the lead in 1985 by embracing a trade policy based on a simplified tariff structure in the form of a flat rate of 10 percent for most tariff items and complete elimination of non-tariff barriers. Next followed Colombia and Venezuela. Each implemented a trade liberalization strategy by which tariffs were reduced to a few tariff levels and non-tariff measures eliminated. Ecuador followed a similar path in 1992. In the case of Peru, the economy opened up and its trade regime changed in the fashion of the other Andean countries. With regard to its tariff structure, it followed the Bolivian (and Chilean) model rather than that of the other Andean countries, something which later became an important source of friction within the Andean Group.

Unilateral trade liberalization in the Andean countries translated rapidly into a collective approach to integration. In 1989, the Andean presidents started to meet regularly to review progress in the Group and to set guidelines for its revival and reorientation. In a rapid succession of meetings, the Presidents decided to adopt a new strategic design for the Andean Group (Galápagos, December 1989), to expand and intensify their countries' commitments to the integration process (La Paz, Bolivia, November 1990), and finally, in Cartagena, Colombia (December 1991), to establish a free trade area among the five Andean countries and to adopt a four-level Common External Tariff (CET). The only exception was Bolivia which was allowed to keep its flat tariff rate. These agreements were included in the Act of Barahona, which also set up guidelines for the coordination of the Andean countries' economic policies and their negotiations of trade arrangements, either individually or in concert with other Latin American and Caribbean countries.

As a result of these developments, the Andean Group's integration efforts were rapidly reactivated. The main achievements in the last few years include the complete liberalization of trade among most Andean countries, the definition and implementation of a common external tariff and the adoption of common policies in a number of areas.

The Andean Free Trade Area

The Andean free trade area came into effect in early 1993. Since then trade between Bolivia, Colombia, Ecuador and Venezuela has been completely liberalized, in that both tariff and non-tariff measures have been eliminated. Reaching that point was not an easy task. The Act of Barahona had established the preconditions for a free trade area among the Andean countries, which should have taken effect by early 1992. This schedule proved to be too optimistic. Peru and Ecuador conditioned their participation in the free trade area on a previous understanding of the meaning of the presidents' agreement regarding the CET levels. Although both countries took a revisionist approach, their respective positions differed.

Ecuador wanted a higher degree of flexibility in the implementation of the CET and a postponement of its commitments due to its forthcoming general election. Peru's difficulties were of a more fundamental nature. Although the economic reform program implemented in 1991 by the new president, Alberto Fujimori, government had succeeded in reducing the hyperinflation of the previous years, inflation still exceeded 400 percent. Growth was stagnant, the trade deficit continued growing and the exchange rate was vastly overvalued. To participate in a free trade area under these conditions was certainly risky.

The differences between the trade policy adopted by Peru and that of countries like Colombia and Venezuela were more difficult to resolve. As described above, Peru implemented a flat rate for most of its tariff schedule.[3] This ran counter to the CET agreed upon by the Andean presidents, which resembled more the planned tariff schedules of Colombia and Venezuela and was structured around four different tariff levels (5, 10, 15 and 20 percent), with exceptions for a few items.

Peru's insistence on a revision of the CET as a condition for its participation in the Andean free trade area, and Ecuador's lack of enthusiasm for the Act of Barahona as a whole, led Colombia and Venezuela to move ahead independently of the other Andean countries. In February 1992, the two countries adopted the proposed CET as their respective national tariff schedules. They succeeded in dismantling all tariff and non-tariff barriers to their reciprocal trade, hence starting a bilateral free trade area that soon became one of the greatest success stories of the new Latin American economic integration movement. Since then, bilateral transactions between these two countries have experienced a fivefold increase.

The advent of a new government in Ecuador in August 1992 set the stage for a new round of discussions among the Andean countries. Through a series of agreements reached by the Commission of the Cartagena Agreement, it was decided that Bolivia would join the free trade area by September 1992, and Ecuador by January 1993. As for Peru, it was granted a temporary waiver regarding its obligations to the free trade area and the CET.[4] Bilateral trade negotiations were held between Peru and the other Andean countries in order to keep trade flows from deteriorating. In fact, the bilateral agreements that were reached allowed for the continuation of the large portion of duty-free trade between Peru and the other Andean countries.

Thus by early 1993, the Andean Group free trade area was fully implemented by Bolivia, Colombia, Ecuador and Venezuela. Trade among these four countries was completely liberalized through the elimination of all tariff and non-tariff restrictions. It continues to be so to this day, despite the difficulties created by the adoption of exchange and price controls in Venezuela following the 1994 inauguration of President Rafael Caldera. Peru reached a new agreement with the other Andean countries in December 1995 to expand the bilateral arrangements that they had previously negotiated.[5]

THE COMMON EXTERNAL TARIFF

Implementation of the Andean Common External Tariff has moved to be a more difficult and lengthy process. As already indicated, in 1992 Colombia and Venezuela implemented a CET along the lines established by the Act of Barahona. However, not until November 1994 was a formal decision taken regarding the inclusion of Ecuador. The Commission of the Cartagena Agreement passed Decision 370, which settled all the pending issues regarding the structure and content of the Andean Group's Common External Tariff. In March 1995, after years of discussion, the CET was finally implemented by Colombia, Ecuador and Venezuela.

---

[3]Peru adopted a two-level approach, with most items at a rate of 15 percent and the remaining few at 25 percent.

[4]See Decision 321 (1992) of the Commission of the Cartagena Agreement.

[5]See Decision 387 (1995) of the Commission of the Cartagena Agreement.

FIGURE 1
Andean Group: Common External Tariff

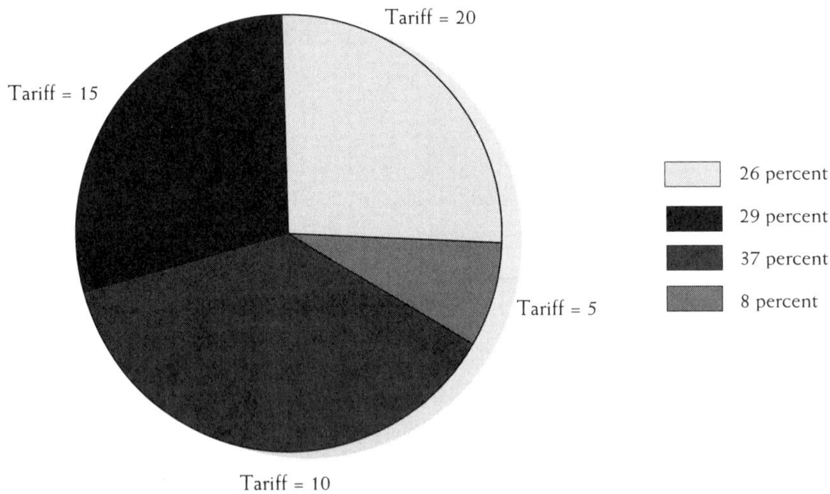

Source: Junta del Acuerdo de Cartagena.

Decision 370 established a four-level CET for most tariff items based on the degree of processing of products, with a tariff rate of 5 percent applied to raw materials and industrial inputs, 10 and 15 percent to intermediate products, and 20 percent on final consumption goods. In addition to these four levels, Decision 370 envisaged differential treatment for certain health and educational products whose tariff level is zero, and for assembled and unassembled automobiles which have maximum tariff rates of 40 and 5 percent, respectively.

There are country-related and product-related exceptions to the Andean CET. Bolivia was authorized by the Act of Barahona to maintain its flat national tariff schedule. Peru, for all practical purposes, has received a treatment similar to that of Bolivia. As already mentioned, Decisions 353 and 377 allow Peru to maintain its current tariff structure of 15 percent for a majority of products and 25 percent for certain exceptions. Consequently, the CET applies to only three out of five of the Andean countries: Colombia, Ecuador and Venezuela.

Furthermore, Colombia and Venezuela each have the right to exclude 230 items from the CET, while Ecuador is allowed to exempt 400 items. These exceptions are to be eliminated over a period of four years, with each country reducing 50 of its exempted products annually. The remaining exempted items will be eliminated the fourth year. It is expected that by early 1999 the Andean CET will be fully implemented by the three countries that have agreed to it.

The structure of the Andean Common External Tariff is presented in Figure 1. It covers 6650 tariff items of which 513 items (8 percent) are subject to the minimum tariff of 5 percent; 2542 items (37 percent) require a 10 percent tariff; 1899 items (26 percent) apply a 15 percent tariff; and 1696 items (29 percent) are subject to the maximum tariff of 20 percent. The CET simple average is 13.6 percent.

POLICY HARMONIZATION

Together with the Andean movement towards free trade and a common tariff structure, there has been considerable progress in the area of harmonization of economic and social policies which has been a major goal of the Andean Group from the outset. In the Andean context, policy harmonization is understood as the adoption of common regulations in areas considered instrumental in achieving the Andean Group's integration objectives. This approach was facilitated by giving law-making capabilities to the Commission.

In the Andean Group's early years, the Commission was active in establishing the Group's legal framework for industrial policy and the treatment of foreign investment. Common rules on transfer of technology and the protection of industrial patents and trademarks were also among the areas regulated by the Andean countries. In all these cases, the import-oriented strategies formerly implemented by the Andean countries left their mark.

To a certain extent, in recent years the policy harmonization has been directed toward undoing or updating the measures adopted during the previous period. For example, new regulations were set regarding foreign investment and the protection of intellectual property rights. This, together with a set of common policies for transportation, can be considered among the major achievements of the "new" Andean Group.

In the field of foreign investment, Decision 24, well-known for its negative effects on foreign investors, was reversed in 1991 by Decision 291 which liberalized the Andean regimes for foreign investment. The new regulations were oriented toward promoting foreign investment by granting national treatment and eliminating most restrictions on capital and profit remittances. Decision 291 also eliminated the concept of reserved sectors, which had restricted investment in certain economic sectors to citizens of Andean countries exclusively.

In 1993, the Commission adopted Decisions 344 and 351 by which the Andean Group established a new common regime for the protection of intellectual property rights. The regulations included in Decision 344 granted patent rights to pharmaceutical products that had previously been excluded, extended the duration of patents, and expanded the protection granted by trademarks. Decision 351 deals with copyrights and includes among its main achievements the protection of software and other computer-related programs.

A concerted effort toward liberalization also took place in the area of transportation. As the Andean free trade area entered into force, the member countries adopted new regulations allowing the free movement of passenger and commercial vehicles throughout the countries' territories.[6] The reserved cargo restrictions were abolished for maritime transportation between the Andean countries, and on a reciprocal basis, between Andean and other countries.[7] Most importantly, in 1992 the Andean Group adopted an "open skies" policy that had a positive impact on air transportation between the Andean countries. It led to a considerable increase in the frequency of flights and a reduction in airfares.[8]

---

[6]See Decisions 257, 289, 358 and 359 of the Commission of the Cartagena Agreement.

[7]See Decisions 285 and 314 of the Commission of the Cartagena Agreement.

[8]The Board of the Cartagena Agreement has estimated that as a result of the "open skies" policy the number of weekly flights linking Andean cities reached the unprecedented number of 425 in 1994. The Commission's Decisions 297 and 320 regarding the liberalization of air transportation were adopted in 1991 and 1992, respectively.

The adoption of common policies and regulations in the above mentioned areas has contributed to strengthening the Andean Group and has demonstrated the Group's determination to move ahead even in difficult areas such as the protection of intellectual property rights. However, little progress has been made in the coordination of macroeconomic policies, such as exchange rate policies. This may be due to the difficulties the Andean Group is facing with regard to the CET and the free trade area, its two most important integration mechanisms, as well as differences in economic policies among some of the Andean countries, discussed later in this paper.

The Boom in Intra-Subregional Trade

The trade record of the "new" Andean Group is very impressive. The steady liberalization process initiated in the late 1980s has had a highly positive effect on intra-subregional trade. While trade among the Andean countries experienced a drastic decline through most of the 1980s, it has boomed in the 1990s. In 1990, when the liberalization measures of the previous year were felt, intra-subregional exports amounted to $1.3 billion. Since then, exports among the Andean countries have increased at an annual rate of 27 percent, reaching the unprecedented level of $3.4 billion in 1994 (Table 1).

As can be seen by Table 1, Venezuela was the largest intra-subregional exporter in 1994, followed by Colombia. These two countries accounted for 73.3 percent of total exports among the Andean countries, while Ecuador and Peru contributed 11 and nine percent, respectively. Bolivia is the smallest exporter to the Andean market. Despite these differences in relative exports, Table 1 also shows that all the Andean countries have increased their exports to the region over the last six years. This, in turn, has led to a considerable increase in the importance of the Andean market as a destination for the Andean countries' non-oil exports (Table 2).

Except for Peru, the Andean market has grown in importance for all the Andean countries. The case of Venezuela is particularly impressive, as can be seen in Table 2. While only

TABLE 1

Andean Group: Evolution of Intra-Subregional Exports, 1990–1994 (U.S. $ millions)

	1990	1991	1992	1993	1994	1995*
Bolivia	59.9	82.3	99.5	119.9	195.9	199
Colombia	372.7	778.4	1,014.3	1,138.6	1,109.8	1,805
Ecuador	188.5	203.7	178.1	294.8	385.6	364
Peru	214.0	269.4	269.6	269.0	310.1	412
Venezuela	493.6	478.7	665.8	1,045.3	1,426.3	1,847
Andean Countries	**1,328.9**	**1,812.6**	**2,227.5**	**2,867.8**	**3,427.9**	**4,627**

*Projection by JUNAC.

Source: JUNAC, Sistema Subregional de Información Estadistica.

TABLE 2
Relative Importance of the Andean Market (%)*

	1990	1991	1992	1993	1994
Bolivia	8.6	13.4	15.5	18.4	20.9
Colombia	7.2	12.3	16.3	18.8	15.4
Ecuador	4.1	3.7	6.0	10.8	11.7
Peru	7.0	8.5	8.2	8.5	7.3
Venezuela	10.9	12.9	19.7	26.5	30.9
All Andean Countries	7.9	10.6	13.8	17.6	16.8

*Non-oil exports.
Source: JUNAC, Sistema Subregional de Información Estadistica, 1996.

TABLE 3
Andean Group: Total Exports/Non-Oil Exports (1990–1994) (U.S. $ millions and %)

	1990	1991	1992	1993	1994
Total Andean	1,328.9	1,812.6	2,227.5	2,867.8	3,427.9
Non-oil Andean	1,075.0	1,504.7	1,966.4	2,655.9	3,171.6
Percentage	80.8	83.0	88.2	92.6	92.5
Total World	31,407.1	29,494.7	28,562.7	29,740.0	34,252.3
Non-oil World	13,464.4	14,120.3	14,204.4	15,079.0	18,845.5
Percentage	**42.8**	**47.9**	**49.7**	**50.7**	**55.0**

Source: JUNAC, Sistema Subregional de Información Estadistica.

11 percent of Venezuelan non-oil exports went to Andean countries in 1990, the percentage grew to 31 percent in 1994, a three-fold increase. Ecuador also nearly tripled the percentage of its exports to the Andean market, while Bolivia and Colombia doubled theirs. For the Andean Group as a whole, the importance of the Andean market for non-oil exports of member countries rose from 8 percent in 1990 to nearly 17 percent in 1994.

The growing importance of the Andean market for most Group members has introduced some important changes in the ranking of their trading partners. In 1993, Venezuela became Colombia's second most important trading partner. A year later, Colombia displaced the United States as Venezuela's most important trading partner for its non-oil exports.

Interestingly, the composition of intra-Andean trade varies from the composition of its trade with the rest of the world. As Table 3 shows, the increase in intra-subregional exports over the last few years consisted mainly of growth in non-oil exports, which increased their share of total intra-Andean exports from 80.8 percent in 1990 to 92.5 percent in 1994. This situation contrasts with the stabilization of non-oil exports as a share of total Andean exports to the world at approximately 50 percent.

The Andean market plays an important role in developing the Andean exporters' ability to compete in international markets. According to the Inter-American Development Bank,

TABLE 4

Andean Countries: Average Annual Increase in Non-Oil Imports (1990–1994)

	ANDEAN GROUP	WORLD
Bolivia	36.1%	13.8%
Colombia	36.8%	21.2%
Ecuador	51.6%	14.5%
Peru	41.5%	22.8%
Venezuela	30.0%	5.3%
Andean Group	33.4%	12.5%

Source: JUNAC, Sistema Subregional de Información Estadistica, 1995.

approximately 73 percent of intra-Andean exports are manufactured goods, which have increased and become more diversified in recent years. Of the Andean countries, Colombia has been the most successful in diversificating manufactured exports.[9]

It is debated whether the increase in intra-subregional trade in a trading group such as the Andean Group can be attributed to the unilateral trade liberalization efforts by the individual countries, or to the concerted opening of the Andean market to reciprocal trade through the Andean free trade area. The data in Table 4 show that the Andean Group's non-oil imports from member countries have grown faster than imports from the rest of the world, which can be seen as an indication of the importance of the Andean Group's integration efforts in fostering intra-subregional trade.

Between 1990 and 1994, the Andean countries' imports from all sources increased at an average annual rate of 12.5 percent while the growth rate of imports from the subregion was 33.4 percent. This trend also holds true for the individual member countries. In 1990–94, Venezuela's non-oil imports from the Andean countries increased at an average annual rate of 30.6 percent while the corresponding growth rate for imports originating in the rest of the world was 5.3 percent. In Colombia, the growth rates were 36.8 and 21.2 percent, respectively. Imports by Bolivia, Ecuador and Peru showed a similar pattern (Table 4).

There is no doubt that the Andean Group movement toward greater integration among member countries, in particular through the dismantling of all tariff and non-tariff barriers to reciprocal trade, has had a very positive effect on intra-Andean trade flows.

Apart from trade liberalization, trade flows are influenced by a number of factors including the real exchange rate, the level of economic activity and the geographic proximity of the trading partners. Still, the remarkable increase in trade among the Andean countries in recent years seems to be directly related to their concerted efforts to reactivate the integration process. These efforts gained credibility among private sector exporters as it became evident that countries were committed to dismantling trade barriers. New trade and investment opportunities created by opening the economies led to closer links between businessmen from the different countries, thereby strengthening the integration process.

[9]Banco Interamericano de Desarrollo, *Grupo Andino, Documento de Programación Regional,* Division de Integración, Comercio y Asuntos Hemisféricos, mimeo, June 1995.

If further evidence were needed of the positive relationship between integration efforts and increasing trade, Peru offers the example of a country whose limited participation in the Andean countries' movement towards freer trade has prevented it from increasing the trade links with its Andean partners. Peru's trade performance is poor when compared with the other Andean countries, both individually and as a bloc. As can be seen in Tables 1 and 2, during 1990–1994 Peruvian exports to Andean nations grew at a slower pace than that shown by other Andean countries. In addition, the importance of the Andean market for Peruvian exporters has remained constant throughout the booming '90s.

OLD ISSUES AND NEW DIFFICULTIES

While the Andean Group has proven successful in terms of progress by member countries regarding freer trade among themselves and the adoption of a common approach in a number of policy areas, it confronts tremendous difficulties in advancing its integration process. There are differences among member countries concerning the CET and free trade area, as well as political strains. Diplomatic relations between Peru and Venezuela cooled off after President Fujimori temporarily closed the Peruvian Congress in 1992. In 1995 there was an armed confrontation between Ecuador and Peru. These incidents prevented the Andean Presidents from meeting as frequently as when they were directly involved in the Andean Group decision making process in the late 1980s and early 1990s.[10]

The Andean Group has not yet consolidated itself as a customs union. The CET has been implemented solely by Colombia, Ecuador and Venezuela, with a number of temporary exceptions allowed in each case. Bolivia and Peru have kept their national tariff schedules. This dual approach with regard to the CET cannot be sustained indefinitely. It lessens the credibility of the Andean Group and prevents it from acting in concert vis-à-vis other trading groups and nations. Eventually, the Andean Group will have to decide on either (a) getting all member countries to accept the disciplines associated with the CET, or (b) abandoning the idea of a fully functioning customs union altogether.

The establishment of a customs union requires a higher degree of discipline by member countries than the creation of a free trade area. In a customs union, the adoption of a common external tariff signals the intention of participating countries to develop a common trade policy. Moreover, the adoption of a common trade policy is generally considered a first step toward greater coordination of macroeconomic policies. In free trade areas, no such coordination is contemplated and individual countries retain the ability to decide their trade policy with other countries.

The Andean Group cannot be half customs union and half free trade area. The failure to recognize this in the past has led to a certain "Balkanization" within the Group. It has caused individual countries to conclude bilateral free trade agreements with other Latin American and Caribbean countries, diluting the impact of the Andean Group as a collective undertaking. For example, Colombia and Venezuela jointly negotiated the Group of Three Agreement with Mexico; each separately negotiated a trade agreement with Chile and with the CARICOM countries; yet Bolivia concluded similar agreements with Mexico

[10]After the meeting of the Andean Presidents in December 1991, they did not meet again until September 1995.

and Chile. These divergent strategies will persist until a political definition is formulated that sets out the Andean Group's identity. In other words, the Andean Group needs to achieve greater internal cohesion if it is to move forward in its integration process.

Given the recent evolution of the Andean Group and its economic policies, the goal of establishing a customs union consisting of all members seems to have vanished. As already stated, Bolivia is not expected to implement the CET as formulated by the Andean Presidents in 1991. The Commission's decisions on Peru's participation in the Andean free trade area have recognized the country's intention to keep its own tariff schedule.[11] In addition, the trade policies of Peru and Bolivia seem so well established that their governments would not consider adjusting them to the tariff structure of the Andean CET. By the same token, it does not seem feasible that Colombia, Ecuador and Venezuela would alter their trade policies in the direction of a flat rate, as used by Bolivia and Peru. While a flat rate would create a different CET, it would still establish the Andean Group as a customs union.[12]

The Andean Group may have to define itself as a free trade area, and to postpone or abandon altogether the objective of establishing a customs union among its five member countries. Still, even to function as a free trade area, the Andean Group needs to ensure Peru's full participation in the Andean trade arrangements. So far, Peru has regulated its trade relations with the Andean Group countries through bilateral agreements. These agreements have allowed for duty-free trade to take place for a large portion of Peru's exports to, and imports from, other Andean countries. In addition, Peru has eliminated all trade restrictions for those products which, according to the CET, would have tariff levels of 5 and 10 percent. It has also agreed to lift restrictions under certain conditions for a number of items with tariff levels of 15 and 20 percent.[13]

Were Peru to participate fully in the Andean free trade area, the Andean Group would be the first trading group in the hemisphere to have completely liberalized their mutual trade.[14] It remains to be seen whether Colombia, Ecuador and Venezuela, who have fought hard to turn the Andean Group into a customs union, are willing to accept this outcome. The CET which they have set up is the result of more than three years of intense discussions. However, for the time being, they may not have another choice.

As a free trade area, the Andean Group would not only experience a drastic change in its ultimate objectives, but also an increase in its internal cohesion and a more consistent

[11]See Article 1 of Decision 353 (April 1994), Article 6 of Decision 377 (June 1995) and Article 2 of Decision 387 (December 1995).

[12]It should be pointed out that the Andean Presidents' decision on the common external tariff provided that, a year after its implementation, it would have three instead of four levels: 5, 10 and 15 percent. This portion of the Andean Presidents' decision was all but forgotten in the ensuing discussion, but may form the basis of a future decision on the Andean CET if member countries were to move in that direction.

[13]This applies to products that Peru does not produce domestically, but are produced in any of the other Andean Group member countries. Peru's pace for the elimination of trade restrictions was established by Decisions 353 and 377 of the Commission of the Cartagena Agreement.

[14]Other groups, like MERCOSUR and NAFTA, are making progress in that direction, but still have a long way to go. MERCOSUR's exceptions to its free trade area are expected to be eliminated by the year 2000, whereas NAFTA's process of lifting exceptions will not be completed until the year 2005, with a number of products still subject to trade restrictions until the year 2010.

strategy in its relations with other countries. By reducing internal differences, the Group could play a crucial role in the overall Latin American integration process.

The time has come for the Andean presidents to be directly involved again in the subregional integration process. Much of what the Andean Group has achieved during the last five years is a direct result of decisions taken at the presidential level at the beginning of the decade. To lead the Andean Group out of its present difficulties, political guidance would be helpful. In addition, leadership from the Andean presidents is necessary to strengthen the role of the Andean Group in the Latin American and hemispheric integration process.

REGIONAL REALITIES AND HEMISPHERIC CHALLENGES

Ever since its creation, the Andean Group has been defined as a transitional arrangement leading to the formation of a Latin American common market, the main objective of the Montevideo Treaty of 1960.[15] To this day, the Andean Group continues to view itself in this way. Either individually or as a bloc, the Andean Group countries are among the most active participants in the recent trend of "open regionalism" that has swept through the region.

Initially, the Andean Group had envisaged it would first consolidate its own integration efforts and then forge closer links with the main beneficiaries of trade gains associated with LAFTA; Brazil, Mexico and Argentina. However, the initial targets of the Andean Group regarding integration—subregional free trade, adoption of a common external tariff—could not be met. Some objectives of regional integration were postponed, while others were abandoned. Consequently, building closer links with other Latin American countries was delayed.

During the "lost decade" of the 1980s there was little talk about free trade agreements. Trade relations among Latin American countries were restricted to the reciprocal negotiation of tariff preferences prescribed by the Montevideo Treaty of 1980, and these were limited in coverage of products and/or level of preferences.[16] Latin American economic integration again emerged as an important issue in the early 1990s, when existing trade arrangements like the Andean Group and the Central American Common Market (CACM) were reactivated, and new groups such as MERCOSUR were established.

---

[15]The Montevideo Treaty of 1960 established the Latin American Free Trade Association (LAFTA) made up of all South American countries plus Mexico. Dissatisfied with their countries' participation in the new trade environment, the Andean governments negotiated a separate agreement in 1969, the Cartagena Agreement. This arrangement continued to be formally linked to LAFTA until a new Treaty of Montevideo was negotiated in 1980, transforming LAFTA into the Latin American Integration Association (ALADI).

[16]The Montevideo Treaty of 1980 is a looser agreement than its predecessor. It contains no specific schedule for the achievement of its goals. Instead, it provides a framework for its member countries to conclude bilateral or multilateral preferential trade agreements—"partial scope agreements"—that may, somehow, "converge" into a region-wide trade agreement. The Andean countries have concluded partial scope agreements with all ALADI members, as well as with most Central American and Caribbean countries.

Trade liberalization policies adopted in the Andean Group first appeared on the subregional level, and subsequently evolved to the regional level. New bilateral as well as multilateral free trade agreements, which have entered into force between most Latin American countries, may lead to the complete liberalization of intra-regional trade in the next few years. Similarly, the discussions on the establishment of the Free Trade Area of the Americas (FTAA), as envisaged in the Declaration and Plan of Action adopted at the Summit of the Americas in December 1994, may count the Andean Group members among its most active participants. Although the path toward an FTAA is still undecided, the Andean countries could well play an important role in the negotiations for hemispheric integration.

Latin American Realities

The Andean countries are among the most active practitioners of "open regionalism." In 1992, the Commission adopted Decision 322, which set up the parameters for trade negotiations between Andean and other Latin American and Caribbean countries. This Decision encourages Andean countries to negotiate trade agreements with other countries in the region, individually or in concert.[17] Since then, a number of free trade agreements involving the Andean countries have been concluded.

In 1992, Venezuela and Chile signed a free trade agreement eliminating all tariff and non-tariff restrictions to most of their reciprocal trade by early 1999. A similar agreement was concluded between Colombia and Chile in 1993. In 1994, Colombia and Venezuela reached an accord with Mexico, known as the Group of Three Agreement, which provides for free trade among the three countries by the year 2005. It also presents a common framework for investments by the participating countries and for the protection of intellectual property rights. Furthermore, it adopted a NAFTA-like system concerning rules of origin and included certain commitments regarding government procurement.

Colombia and Venezuela have also concluded separate trade agreements with the CARICOM countries. These agreements provide for unilateral liberalization of the Colombian and Venezuelan markets for a substantial portion of CARICOM exports. It is envisaged that five years after the implementation of the agreements, some degree of reciprocity will be offered by the CARICOM countries. In addition, Colombia and Venezuela have committed to negotiate jointly a free trade agreement with the Central American countries. Bolivia has secured comprehensive bilateral agreements with Chile and Mexico. Presently, Chile is negotiating trade liberalization separately with both Ecuador and Peru.

These are not small achievements. Once tariffs and non-tariff measures are phased out as anticipated in the agreements, free trade among the participating countries will become a reality. This should be achieved around the year 2000 or shortly thereafter. Still, it will not involve all the Andean countries since the existing agreements have been negotiated by only a few of them. Notable absences are Ecuador and Peru. A critical issue which the Andean Group faces is to ensure that these two countries are not left behind as the others move toward greater integration with other Latin American and Caribbean countries. The Andean Group should start thinking about how to "multilateralize" the agreements at

[17]To a certain extent, Decision 322 represents a waiver of the more stringent requirements of Article 68 of the Cartagena Agreement, which required trade agreements negotiated by Andean countries with third countries to be authorized first by the Commission.

the subregional level. This is a difficult task, but one that the Andean Group may find easier to accomplish once the internal cohesion of the Group is assured.

The greatest challenge to the Andean Group strategy of developing closer links with its Latin American and Caribbean partners would come from MERCOSUR. All Andean countries favor a trade agreement with MERCOSUR, and vice versa. For some, this has become a national priority. For example, Bolivia regards itself as a political and economic bridge between MERCOSUR and the Andean Group, and has repeatedly expressed its intention to become MERCOSUR's fifth member.[18] Brazil sees an agreement between the two organizations as a step forward in its effort to establish a free trade area throughout South America, a SAFTA. To this end, Brazil and Venezuela have recently signed a bilateral agreement aimed at strengthening relations between the two groups.

For the Andean Group, a prospective trade agreement with MERCOSUR is crucial on two levels. First, it would test the Andean Group's commitment to act as one in implementing its Latin American strategy. There are signals that this may actually be occurring. Recently, the Andean countries decided on a two-track strategy vis-à-vis MERCOSUR: while the disciplines included in an agreement would be negotiated jointly by the Andean countries, trade liberalization measures would be settled individually.[19] Second, an agreement with the MERCOSUR countries would represent a major step forward in the Andean Group's commitment to open regionalism. It would demonstrate that Andean countries are prepared to conclude free trade agreements with larger and more developed countries, such as Brazil and Argentina, thereby paving the way for freer trade among all countries in the region.[20]

In fact, a free trade agreement between the Andean Group and MERCOSUR would be a major contribution not only to the Latin American integration movement, but also to hemispheric trade liberalization. This will certainly depend on the nature of such an agreement and its commitment to trade liberalization. If the Andean Group's trade arrangements with other countries in the region serve as any guide, one would expect the Andean Group and

[18]The legal impediments to this may disappear shortly. Article 20 of the Treaty of Asunción, which established the MERCOSUR, prohibited its expansion for a period of five years from its signing. It remains to be seen whether Bolivia can simultaneously be a member of the Andean Group and MERCOSUR, two emerging customs unions, each with a different common external tariff. Of course, it is always possible that Bolivia is granted the same treatment by MERCOSUR that it receives from the Andean Group, and be allowed to keep its current national schedule. Then MERCOSUR may encounter the same problems that the Andean Group is facing today.

[19]This is not very different from what Colombia and Venezuela did when negotiating the Group of Three Agreement with Mexico. The schedule for the phase-out of trade restrictions between Mexico and Colombia and Mexico and Venezuela was the result of separate bilateral negotiations, whereas the agreement itself was negotiated by the three countries. The NAFTA agreement also contains different schedules for the phasing out of trade restrictions between Mexico and the United States and Mexico and Canada.

[20]It should not be forgotten that the uneven distribution of benefits among the LAFTA countries caused the Andean countries to move out of LAFTA to form their own integration scheme. Countries like Brazil and Argentina were running large trade surpluses vis-à-vis the Andean countries, which was considered unfair. The fact that the Andean Group now is prepared to conclude a free trade agreement with these two countries goes a long way in describing how the new integration efforts undertaken by the Latin American countries differ from previous experiences.

MERCOSUR to agree to gradually eliminate all trade restrictions, phasing in a free trade agreement over a number of years and perhaps allowing a limited number of exceptions.[21]

The Hemispheric Challenge

The Andean countries face the additional challenge of devising a common approach to hemispheric trade liberalization. Greater cohesion would facilitate the participation of the Andean countries in the FTAA, as well as in the negotiations leading to its establishment. Whatever path the countries choose regarding the FTAA—a country-by-country accession to NAFTA, a merging of the various subregional arrangements, or a framework agreement on a WTO-plus basis—the Andean countries will be better off if they solve their internal difficulties and develop a common approach to this larger challenge.

There are sound economic reasons behind the Andean countries' commitment to hemispheric trade liberalization. Despite the growing importance of the Andean market, the United States remains by far the single most important trading partner of each Andean country.[22] As can be seen in Figure 2, more than 40 percent of total Andean exports went to the United States in 1993. The corresponding figure for the European Union is 15 percent, while only 9 percent of exports went to other Andean Group countries.

By the same token, the Andean Group is an important trading partner for the United States. The Andean countries imported U.S. $14.4 billion worth of oil and non-oil products from the U.S. in 1994. This total trade is comparable to the volume of imports from the U.S. by MERCOSUR, and far surpasses trade between the U.S. and the Central American and Caribbean countries.[23]

A free trade agreement would offer advantages to both the United States and the Andean Group. The Andean nations would benefit from a more secure access to their most important market and from the investments that may result from hemispheric trade liberalization. For its part, the United States may find in the Andean countries a group of reliable partners with satisfactory economic performances. With the exception of Venezuela, which experienced negative growth rates in 1993 and 1994, the Andean countries increased their GDP by more than four percent in 1994. Inflation is decreasing or has remained stable—again, except in Venezuela—and all countries have maintained or even reinforced their commitments to liberal trade policies.

Still, a free trade agreement between such asymmetrical partners—the mid-sized economies of the Andean Group and the overwhelmingly large and developed economy of the United States—will not be easy to negotiate, whatever path is chosen. This also applies to the other Latin American and Caribbean countries. The challenge ahead is to organize the Free Trade Area of the Americas in such a way that all countries party to the

---

[21]The Andean countries seem to have decided to prepare a joint list of exceptions to an eventual agreement with MERCOSUR. This is unfortunate as it may lead to more rather than fewer exceptions to the agreement, since such a list of exceptions would include the products considered sensitive by *all* member countries.

[22]This is not the case when non-oil exports are excluded, as discussed in the section above dealing with the evolution of the Andean countries trade flows.

[23]VanGrasstek, Craig, *The U.S. Perception of Trade in the Americas*, mimeo, 1995.

FIGURE 2

Andean Countries' Main Trading Partners: Oil and Non-Oil Exports from Andean Group (1993)

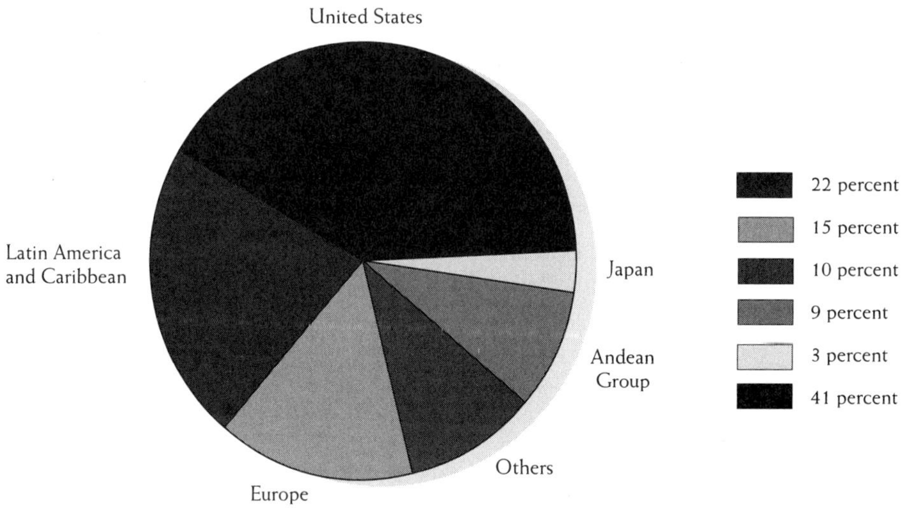

Source: IMF, *Direction of Trade Statistics Yearbook,* 1994.

agreement recognize its advantages, and not only its risks. The FTAA should be a sum plus, not a zero-sum game.

CONCLUSION

The transformation of the Andean Group in the 1990s has been remarkable. It emerged from the "lost decade" of the 1980s as an entity on the brink of collapse, but reformed itself and succeeded in meeting its initial, and until then continuously postponed, integration goals in a scant number of years. At the core of this transformation lie the economic reforms, particularly the trade liberalization measures, implemented by the Andean countries since the mid-1980s.

The creation of the Andean free trade area is a major achievement. All trade flows between Bolivia, Colombia, Ecuador and Venezuela are now completely freed of tariff and non-tariff restrictions, with no exemptions. A large proportion of Peru's exports to, and imports from, the other Andean countries has also been liberalized through bilateral trade agreements. Another important accomplishment has been policy harmonization seen in the Andean Group's adoption of new common rules in foreign investment and intellectual property rights.

With regard to the creation of a Common External Tariff, the Andean Group has been less successful. Only three of its five member countries have implemented the CET, insisting on a number of exceptions. This makes it difficult, if not impossible, to develop a common trade policy vis-à-vis third countries. Herein lies one of the most important challenges facing the Andean Group. In order to move forward in the integration process at the Latin American and hemispheric levels, as the Andean countries wish, the Andean Group needs to bring about greater internal cohesion.

Internal cohesion could be achieved in a number of ways: by convincing Peru and Bolivia to accept the present CET, which is highly unlikely given their tariff schedules; by modifying the CET, which Colombia, Ecuador and Venezuela would find difficult to accept; or by abandoning altogether the objective of establishing a customs union and creating instead a free trade area among the five Andean countries. Were Peru to join an Andean Group free trade area, the member countries could preserve their bilateral arrangements with other countries, without the restrictions that would be imposed upon them by a common trade policy.

Still, a free trade area is a lesser form of integration since its aims are related almost exclusively to the promotion of trade liberalization among the participating countries. In this sense, the "conversion" of the Andean Group into a free trade area would imply forsaking some of its stated goals, such as promoting the "harmonious and balanced" development of the member countries and the adoption of common approaches in policy areas vital for the Andean integration process. This would be difficult to accept by all the Andean countries. Indeed, the recent reforms approved by the Andean presidents seem to indicate movement in the opposite direction, since they involve a significant institutional restructuring, while leaving the objectives of the Andean Group unchanged.

It is not without irony that the Andean Group has to face these "existential" questions at a time when its economic performance is at its best. Trade among the Andean countries has reached previously unimaginable heights. In the first five years of this decade, the Andean countries traded more among themselves than during the 20 years that followed the establishment of the Andean Group in 1969. Intra-subregional investment flows are growing, and the liberalization measures undertaken by the Andean Group are encouraging business to look to the Andean market for new trade and investment opportunities.

Under these circumstances, one would expect the Andean Group to strengthen its political aims, and to put aside differences in national economic policies to facilitate the development of a collective approach to integration, within the Andean Group itself and with other countries in the region and in the hemisphere. But, this has not occurred. For the foreseeable future, promoting stronger units and further liberalization of trade within the Group may be blocked or postponed as the attention of most Andean countries shifts away from the integration process, towards their own internal difficulties.

Appendix

APPENDIX

Electronic Research on Economic Reform in Latin America

KATE RANDALL HALEY
University of Massachusetts, Dartmouth

Although electronic research using the Internet is uppermost in the minds of most researchers today, multiple online services that are extremely valuable are available, and many tried and true print sources still meet a variety of needs. This overview of resources focuses, first, on online or other electronic reference materials and, second, on print sources that can typically be found in academic or large public libraries.

The Internet is many researchers' first starting point for very current, full-text information on a variety of topics. This overview presupposes that the user has access to a World Wide Web browser such as Netscape Navigator and is familiar with at least one of many World Wide Web search engines such as Infoseek, Lycos, or the Yahoo subject index. Using any of these engines to search for information on economic reform in Latin America ought to point the user toward five central resources. Although this is not intended to be a broad discussion of Internet search engines, it is good for the researcher to be aware of the differences.

Subject engines like Yahoo require the user to begin within broad categories, such as Regions—Latin America—Economics, whereas engines such as Infoseek or Lycos can do word searching within Web pages for terms such as "economics" or "economic reform" and "Latin America" or "Argentina." In many cases, the Boolean "and" is the default, and phrases such as "economic reform" must be indicated as such or the search will be conducted for "economic" and "reform" anywhere within the document, potentially lessening the relevance of the search. Also important is the choice of country or region; "Latin America" will retrieve regional documents that may also include individual country information, whereas specific country searches ("Venezuela" and "economic reform") should be performed if the researcher desires data about the individual country, or if regional efforts are not successful. In addition, not every engine searches every Web page or document, so frequently the researcher must check multiple engines to make sure that he or she has not missed something that might be helpful. However, because no "whole wide world" index exists as yet, it is better not to become obsessive. Users will find that increased familiarity with the Web and various search engines will give them a greater degree of satisfaction with the results.

If specific data are required, it may prove wiser to search (or have searched) online databases that charge the user fees to ensure the timeliness, accuracy, and clear source of origin of the data. Although the sources mentioned here appear to be reliable, it is important that researchers maintain an awareness of these concerns when using the World Wide Web, as it is not standardized or regulated in the fashion of online databases, those offered through Knight-Ridder, for example.

World Wide Web Sources

The Inter-American Development Bank, at **http://ww2.iadb.org**, is a good jumping-off point. This web site has, in particular, an entire page on "Economic and Social Progress in Latin America" at **http://ww2.iadb.org/ipes/ipese.htm**. In addition, it provides access to other detailed information categorized by individual country or by related institutions such as Latin World, at **http://www.latinworld.com**, as well as to newspapers and journals available in full text. The listings for related institutions are excellent, and many of the hot-linked web pages provide different, in-depth information as well. Many of these resources are available simultaneously in English, Spanish, and Portuguese, whereas some are non-English only.

The Latin American Trade and Information Network, at **http://www.latinet.com**, is a more company-specific web site, focusing on individual country resource materials as well as having a regional focus. The other excellent regional focus web site is the World Bank, at **http://www.worldbank.org**. The World Bank is an essential source of financial and economic statistics on Latin America.

Last but not least is the Latin American Information Network at the University of Texas, with both World Wide Web and gopher access at **http://lanic.utexas.edu** or **gopher://lanic.utexas. edu**. This comprehensive resource includes general information, Latin American Studies pointers, economic and social data from USAID, regional indicators, economic data, investment information, trade, and more. Individual countries (Argentina, Brazil, Chile, Colombia, Cuba, Ecuador, Mexico, Peru, and Venezuela) also have extensive files available, from news articles to economic data.

It can only be assumed that these sources will improve, that new web sites will emerge, and that change is constant on the Internet. Using search engines wisely is key. The following is a quick list of WWW resources.

http://ww2.iadb.org	Inter-American Development Bank
http://www.latinworld.com	Latin World
http://www.latinet.com	Latin American Trade and Information Network
http://www.worldbank.org	World Bank
http://lanic.utexas.edu	Latin American Information Network, University of Texas
http://www.stat-usa.gov	Stat-USA (U.S. government)
http://www.natlaw.com	National Law Center for Inter-American Free Trade

Online, CD-ROM, and Print Sources

Country information, usually industrial and economic statistics, is often the first step to understanding regional economies. Many print sources will be very useful in providing background information on Latin American countries. The following sources are standard in most academic libraries, large public libraries (or those with a business branch), and special (corporate) libraries where the company is already involved in or wishes to become involved in doing business abroad.

- *Countries of the World*
- *CIA World Factbook*
- *Statesman's Year-book*
- *South America, Central America,* and the *Caribbean Yearbook*
- *OECD* (Organization for Economic Cooperation and Development) *Economy Surveys* (by country)

Always consult the information professional of a particular library to determine local resources.

The U.S. government is literally a gold mine of information with statistics and text from the U.S. Department of Commerce available on CD-ROM, in print, on the Internet, and by telephone. Because telephone numbers change nearly as often as Internet addresses, it is best to begin with the main Department of Commerce telephone number, 202-482-2000, and proceed to contact directly the country desk officers and the industry desk officers for each country and line of business and to discover access to general import/export statistics.

The Department of Commerce has published some excellent CD-ROM resources. They include the **National Trade Data Bank (NTDB)** and the **Foreign Traders' Index**. The first comprises two CD disks, with full text of publications such as the *CIA World Factbook,* trade agreements such as NAFTA, current country marketing and economic reports, and import/export statistics by country and by commodity using international harmonized codes. It contains many other useful documents geared toward doing business abroad, including current telephone numbers of country and industry desk officers and other points of contact. The second disk includes the *Foreign Trader's Index,* containing listings of individuals and organizations wishing to do business with the United States as distributors, agents, partners, and so forth. Another recent CD-ROM is the **U.S. Dept. of Commerce Imports/ Exports by Commodity**, which includes the following:

- recent month statistics by commodity and by country port of entry
- year-to-date statistics also by commodity and by country port of entry
- historical annual statistics back to 1989

Only the government depository library receives a complimentary copy of the NTDB CD-ROM. One can subscribe to the NTDB on CD-ROM or elect to access the NTDB and several other data sources via the World Wide Web Stat-USA site, at **http://www.stat-usa.gov**.

Many information providers repackage some Department of Commerce data, such as the **AT&T Export Hotline**. This free fax service lists various sectors of country and industry marketing reports and offers customized industry analyses, trade information, Department of Commerce trade opportunity leads, and an *Export Hotline Directory* listing 7,500 different companies from more than 80 countries. Dial 1-800-USA-XPORT to register.

Though not always standard in most libraries, the extremely useful Economist Intelligence Unit produces **Country Reports, Country Profiles, Global Forecasting Service, Global Outlook, World Outlook, World Commodity Outlook**, and **World Commodity Forecasts** in addition to numerous other industry-specific publications directed toward an international market. These publications are available in print, on CD-ROM, and online through Knight-Ridder's DIALOG and Data-Star services, as well.

Other notable publishers of country and industry analyses include the twice-annual **Walden Country Reports,** a series of 60-page reports on 100 countries, focusing more on major industries and companies than on the macroeconomic data given in **EIU Country Profiles**. Formerly published by Reuters, they are now available through LEXIS/NEXIS.

OECD Economic Surveys are published on each member country alternating every two years. These surveys review the most important recent economic developments and include numerous statistics.

WorldTrade Executive, Inc., of Concord, Massachusetts, publishes a variety of print materials on Latin America and NAFTA, including **Latin American Law and Business Report, U.S.-Mexico Trade Report, NAFTA Law Reporter,** and the **NAFTA Handbook**.

The International Monetary Fund and the World Bank also produce some country-level analyses in print and on disk. The World Bank publishes statistics such as **World Debt Tables, World Development Indicators**, and so forth on diskette, and the International Monetary Fund publishes a CD-ROM containing **International Financial Statistics** for more than 100 countries with annual entries beginning in 1948. These new technological developments are relatively expensive and may not be found in all libraries. Print sources are still more widely available in most cases.

The National Law Center for Inter-American Free Trade publishes a weekly bulletin and online service focusing on Mexican and Latin American legal and regulatory information. One can view a sample library at no cost by accessing **Inter-Am** on the World Wide Web at **http://www.natlaw.com**. The center is a nonprofit research and educational corporation located in Tucson, Arizona.

Many directories offer specific country or international listings of companies located in Latin America. Most libraries own the general international sources such as **Dun's Principal International Businesses** or the **International Directory of Corporate Affiliations**, and many may have access on CD-ROM or through online vendors to **Worldscope Profiles** or **D&B International Market Identifiers**. Recently, Dun & Bradstreet introduced two CD-ROM products specifically related to Latin America. **Latin America 25,000: Handbook of Major Companies in the Region** and a separate CD-ROM listing information on 185,000 Mexican firms are now available.

When it comes to providing current market conditions, up-to-date economic data, or real-time newspaper articles and stock market information, online electronic databases are essential. Most offer direct access to market research reports, either in full text or abstracts, and to market analyses through a variety of international publications. International news, company directories, and industry information as well are available from the major online vendors such as **Knight-Ridder's DIALOG** and **Data-Star, Corporate Profound, Dow Jones News/Retrieval, LEXIS/NEXIS, Extel,** and many others.

For example, DIALOG has two broad categories that search several databases at one time: Latin American Business News or LATINNEWS and Latin American Company Information or LATINCO. Economist Intelligence Unit Latin American Business Intelligence is also available here. Within these broad categories, however, it is most useful to search specifically by country or country groups, such as Mexico, Brazil, Argentina, and Venezuela, or by smaller regional areas such as the Southern Cone. Because Latin America has no "single market," most successful searches will be performed on a country-by-country basis. At present, current news is the most thorough and most readily represented by most online vendors, particularly DIALOG, LEXIS/NEXIS, and Dow Jones News/Retrieval. Many bibliographies list the variety of databases included; refer to **Business Information Sources** and **International Business Information: How to Find It, How to Use It** (see Works Cited).

For those researchers who would like to search for information produced within Latin America, Mexico is currently the primary source of online data. Many Latin American countries, Mexico included, do not yet have the telephone/modem infrastructure in place required to support the large online databases found in the United States, but many CD-ROM databases do exist. Growth in the CD-ROM market is much more rapid than is online access. The primary provider of gateway service in Mexico is SECOBI, the Information Bank Consulting Service, offering access to services outside Mexico, such as DIALOG, as well as to services produced within Mexico, such as BIDESRE, the source of state and regional data on social conditions and regional development. Two firms offering access to Mexican financial data include Telerate Financial Information Services (the Mexican representative of the Dow Jones subsidiary, Telerate) and Reuters. The information is relayed via satellite linkup to Mexico from New York. This information is readily available in North America through Dow Jones News/Retrieval, DIALOG, and other vendors.

These sources are not generally free to researchers unless subsidized by libraries or corporate information centers; fees for searching individual databases vary. Frequently libraries offer what are known as "fee-based services," which allow researchers access to the databases for charges that include the direct access costs as well as the information professional's searching time.

Using the many electronic resources wisely and cost-effectively is the researcher's greatest challenge. Even though Internet access is free for some, most sources of information are not acquired without some expenditure of time or money, and frequently both are required. Knowing where to start is often the most critical step. Frequently, information professionals can assist in the process of identification, in addition to adding value and analysis to the information accessed. Academic business librarians; information brokers or fee-for-service providers within college, university, or public libraries; and "cybrarians" who navigate the Internet make up the networks of people who can be as valuable as the data.

Works Cited

Braun, Carl. "Latin American Business and Economic Information on the Internet." *SLA Business and Finance Division Bulletin,* no. 99 (spring 1995): 23–27. Excellent overview of the wide variety of resources available through LANIC, the Latin American Information Network at the University of Texas, Austin.

Daniells, Lorna. *Business Information Sources,* 3rd ed. Berkeley, CA: University of California Press, 1993. Long considered the bible of business information.

Lau, Jesus. "A Selection of Mexican Business Reference Sources." June 1994. Conference presentation of local resources generally available in large university libraries in Mexico.

Levison, Andrew. "Latin America Online. Best Databases for News, Business, and Current Affairs." *Database* (December 1993): 14–28. Concise and thorough analysis of online resources at that time.

Levison, Andrew, and Heberto Reynel Iglesias. "The Online Industry in Mexico." *Online* (May 1993): 116–19. Very useful overview of Mexican online services and users.

Pagell, Ruth, and Michael Halperin. *International Business: How to Find It, How to Use It.* Phoenix, AZ: The Oryx Press, 1994. Exceptional general resource, with specific chapters devoted to industrial and economic statistics and international transactions, in addition to company and marketing information.

"Where to Locate Latin American Directories." *The Information Advisor* 7, no. 11 (November 1995): 4–5. Very thorough compilation of print directories of Brazilian, Mexican, and Venezuelan companies specifically, and of general Latin American directories.

CREDITS

Reading 1: Victor Bulmer-Thomas, *The Economic History of Latin America since Independence.* Reprinted with the permission of Cambridge University Press.

Reading 3: This chapter was originally published in *Reflections on Economic Development* by Enrique Iglesias. Washington, D.C.: Inter-American Development Bank, 1992. Reprinted with permission.

Reading 7: John Williamson, Senior Fellow, "Latin America Reform: A View from Washington," pp. 1–13, August 4, 1994. Used with permission of the Institute for International Economics. Copyright 1994 by the Institute for International Economics, Washington, D.C. All rights reserved.

Reading 8: Paul Krugman, "Dutch Tulips and Emerging Markets," from *Foreign Affairs* (July/August 1995) Vol. 74 No. 4, pp. 28–44. Reprinted by permission of *Foreign Affairs,* July/August 1995. Copyright 1995 by the Council on Foreign Relations, Inc.

Reading 13: Miguel Urrutia, "The Political Economy of Policy Reform: Columbia," pp. 285–315, January 1994, edited by John Williamson. Used with permission of the Institute for International Economics. Copyright 1994 by the Institute for International Economics, Washington, D.C. All rights reserved.

Reading 14: From *Crisis and Economic Reform in Latin America: From Despair to Hope* by Sebastian Edwards. Copyright 1995. Used by permission of Oxford University Press, Inc.

Index

A

Access restrictions, free trade specialization and, 304
Acción Democrática, 102
Act of Barahona, 321
Acuna, Carlos H., 48
Adjustment, 66. *See also* Trade liberalization
  in Chile, 196–199
  debt crisis and, 60
  and economic growth, 48
  neostructuralists on, 51
  as stimulus for transformation, 67
Afonso, José Roberto, 176
Agacino, R., 254, 255
Agency for International Development (AID), 109
Agriculture, 9
  in Bolivia, 165–166
  exports and, 257
  factor productivity growth and, 253–254
  industrialization and, 75
  integration and, 65
  land-tenure system and, 13–14, 254, 257
  Uruguay Round and, 278–279
AID. *See* Agency for International Development (AID)
Airlines, Andean Group's "open skies" policy and, 323
ALADI (Latin American Integration Association), 329n
Alfonsín administration, in Argentina, 132
Alianza Popular Revolucionaria Americana (APRA), 100
Alliance for Progress, 65, 76
Altimer, Oscar, 51
Amazon Basin, 10
Amsden, Alice H., 49
Andean Group
  accomplishments of, 319–324
  Andean Free Trade Area and, 320–321
  Common External Tariff of, 321–322
  Decision 24 of, 219, 323
  Decision 291 and, 323
  Decision 344, 323
  Decision 351, 323
  difficulties in integration process, 327–329
  economic and social policy harmonization within, 323–324
  institutional framework of, 319
  integration strategy of, 317–334
  intra-subregional trade and, 324–327
  main trading partners of, 333
  regional and hemispheric challenges to, 329–333
"Andean Group's Integration Strategy, The" (Rodríguez-Mendoza), 317
Andean Pact, 220, 259, 271–272
  economic indicators for, 269
  trade among countries of, 272
Andean Trade Initiative, 223
Andean Trade Preference Act (1991), 260
Anti-inflationary program, in Brazil, 174–176
Antipoverty programs, 51
APEC (Asia Pacific Economic Cooperation) Plan, 301
APRA. *See* Alianza Popular Revolucionaria Americana (APRA)
Arbenz regime, 100
Argentina, 66
  Austral Plan in, 52, 80, 128
  balance of, 130
  banking crisis in, 140
  Bolivian trade and, 150, 151
  Brazil and, 299, 300
  Cavallo Plan in, 173
  convertibility plan in, 125, 128–134, 139–141, 143–144
  demise of autarkic capitalism in, 90
  Falkland/Malvinas islands dispute with UK, 3n
  growth and price stability in, 125–144
  growth performance and aggregate coefficients of investment in, 137
  inflation in, 119–120, 125, 126–128
  international monetarism and, 80
  MERCOSUR, NAFTA, and, 297, 302–315
  monetary liabilities and international reserves of, 130
  Peronists in, 100
  recovery after Tequila effect, 141–143
  regional income to, 75
  remonetization of economy in, 135–136
  restoring growth and price stability in, 125–144
  structural reforms in, 131–134
Argentine Plan Austral. *See* Austral Plan (Argentina)
Arndt, H. W., 44n
Arthur, Brian, 77
ASEAN (Association of Southeast Asian Nations), 258–259
Asia
  capital flows to, 119
  as model, 122
Asian tigers, 119
Asia Pacific Economic Cooperation Plan. *See* APEC (Asia Pacific Economic Cooperation) Plan
Aspe, Pedro, 103n
Assael, P., 211n
Asuncíon Treaty, 268n
Asymmetric integration, 76

Atkins, G. Pope, 104n
Austral Plan (Argentina), 52, 80, 127
Autarkic capitalism, inadequacy of, 89–90
Aylwin, Patricio, 193, 201–202, 204, 213n

B

Baer, Werner, 44n, 45n
Balance of payments, 50, 75
  in Chile, 209
Balassa, B., 14n, 47
Bankruptcies, in Brazil, 191
Banks and banking
  in Argentina, 129, 134, 140
  bank runs in Brazil, 191
  in Brazil, 182–184
  in Chile, 198–199, 205
  in Colombia, 220
  as creditors, 60–61
Banzer, Hugo, 146, 147, 154
Barber, William J., 47n
Barbier, E. B., 10n
Barco administration, in Colombia, 217, 219, 220, 224, 231
Barriers to trade, 17n, 245–246
  in Argentina, 300
  in Brazil, 184
  in Colombia, 216, 217
  nontariff barriers, 247–249
Barro, Robert, 161
Bastos, Maria Ines, 45n
Bath, C. Richard, 45n
Bauer, P. T., 47
Belize, 4
  Guatemala border and, 3n
Berlin, Isaiah, 105n
Betancur, Belisario, 221, 223
Bhagwati, Jagdish, 47, 77, 302n
Biachi, Andrés, 103n
Bilateral free trade agreements, within Andean Group, 327–328
Bilateral trade, 259–268
Bitar, Sergio, 49n
Black market, Bolivian exchange rate and, 150
Bolivia. *See also* Andean Group
  collapse of tin prices and, 150–151
  democracy in, 146
  economic growth rate of, 161
  export collapse and, 150–151
  exports of, 256
  factor productivity growth in, 253
  financial sector recovery in, 156–157
  foreign debt reduction by, 155
  future growth in, 159–167
  GDP in, 162–164
  growth in (1989–1993), 154–157
  health and education in, 166–167
  hyperinflation in, 145
  income in, 13
  inflation in, 148
  investment needs in, 162–164
  limitations of economic adjustment (1985–1992), 158–159
  MERCOSUR and, 317
  natural gas trade crisis and, 150–151
  New Economic Policy (NEP) in, 147, 149–154
  nontraditional exports of, 155–156
  poverty in, 158, 159
  public and private exports of, 157
  public sector in, 157
  response to inflation in, 80
  rural productivity and social services in, 165–167
  savings and investment in, 158, 162–165
  social conditions in, 159, 160
  stabilization in, 152–154
  terms of trade, 151
  trade collapse and, 150–151
  trade liberalization by, 246
"Bolivia 1985–1992: Reforms, Results, and Challenges" (Larrain and Sachs), 145–168
Bonelli, Regis, 258
Border disputes, 3n
Bosch, Juan, 202
Bosworth, Barry, 255
Boundaries
  border disputes and, 3n
  stability of, 3
Bourgeois revolutions, impact of, 88
Brady plan, 82
Brasília, 7n
Brazil, 66
  Argentina and, 299, 300
  assessment of Plano Real program, 185–190
  bank runs in, 191
  critical day in, 179–185
  Cruzado Plan in, 52, 80
  debt in, 79
  economic liberalization in, 90, 170–172
  economy in 1995, 190–192
  education in, 110
  elections in, 84
  exports of, 258
  GDP in, 183
  growth of, 78
  hyperinflation in, 169–192
  import substitution policies in, 75
  interest rates in, 182
  Japanese people and language in, 4
  Mexican currency crisis and, 185
  movement from hyperinflation to anti-inflationary program, 174–176
  NAFTA-MERCOSUR and, 307–314
  Plano Real and, 109, 111, 169–192
  real in, 169
  response to inflation in, 80
  trade deficit in, 184
  trade liberalization by, 246
  urbanization in, 7n
  URV in, 175, 177
Bresser Pereira, Luiz Carlos, 104n, 110
Britain. *See* Great Britain
Brundenius, C., 13n
Bruno, Michael, 48

Bubbles, era of deflated expectations and, 112–122
Bulmer-Thomas, Victor, "Latin American Economic Development: An Overview," 3–18
Bunge & Born program, 128

C

CACM (Central American Common Market), 273
Cairns Group, Argentina and, 132
Calvo, G., 138n
Campero, Fernando, 145n
Canada. *See* NAFTA (North American Free Trade Agreement)
Candia, Gaby, 145n
Capital, and labor, 252n
Capital flows, 70, 76. *See also* Developing countries
  in Brazil, 191
  in Chile, 205–207
  in Colombia, 226
  to developing countries, 119–121
  disappointing real growth and, 120
  export-led growth and, 16
Capital formation, neostructuralists on, 51
Capital goods, ISI and, 45
Capitalism. *See also* Economic liberalization
  "third way" and, 99–100
Cardoso, Eliana, 76, 249
Cardoso, Fernando Henrique, 14n, 84, 111, 172, 175–176, 184
Carey, John M., 95n
Caribbean Free Trade Association. *See* CARIFTA (Caribbean Free Trade Association)
Caribbean region, 202
  expenditures on agricultural research in, 166
  nationalism and economic reform in, 97–105
CARICOM (Caribbean Community), 246–247, 274
  Andean Group and, 327, 330
CARICOM-Colombia Free Trade Agreement (1991), 263–264
CARIFTA (Caribbean Free Trade Association), 273–274
Carr, R., 4n
Cartagena Agreement, 321, 323n
Carvalho, Luiz Gonzaga de, 176
Castañeda, T., 201n
Cavallo, Domingo, 84, 103n
Cavallo Plan (Argentina), 173
CD-ROM research sources, 339
Cecchini Report, 310
"Center" (advanced countries), 14
Central America. *See also* specific countries
  republics of, 4
Central American Common Market. *See* CACM (Central American Common Market)
Central Bank
  in Argentina, 129, 134, 140
  in Brazil, 180, 182, 183
  in Chile, 205, 206–207
  in Colombia, 220
Centrally planned economies, inefficiencies in, 45–46
Certificado de Abono Tributario, 255
CET. *See* Common External Tariff (CET)
Chenery, Hollis, 78
Chiapas uprising, 275
"Chicago School," 47n
Chile, 82, 102, 110
  advances in, 84
  Chicago School economists and, 47n
  demise of autarkic capitalism in, 90
  depression in (1982–1989), 196–199
  economic policies in, 193–216
  exports of, 15, 256–257
  factor productivity growth in, 252–253
  fiscal policy in, 207–208
  future of economy in, 213–215
  GDP of, 197–198
  growth performance and aggregate coefficients of investment in, 137
  income distribution and poverty in, 199–201
  and integration into world economy, 211–213
  international monetarism and, 80
  labor reform in, 211
  macroeconomic indicators in, 195
  macroeconomic policy in, 201–209
  macroeconomic quarterly data for (1989–1994), 206
  under military government, 193–201
  monetary policy making with mobile capital in, 205–207
  neoliberal restructuring in, 52
  regional income to, 75
  savings and investment in, 208
  social demands in, 202–205
  specialization in, 312n
  stabilization, privatization, and liberalization in, 194
  tax reform in, 209–210
  trade liberalization by, 246
  trade of, 197
Chile-Colombia Free Trade Agreement (1993), 260
Chile-Mexico Free Trade Agreement (1991), 260
Chile-Venezuela Free Trade Agreement (1992), 260
Chile-Venezuela Free Trade Agreement (1993), 260
Chinese people, in Latin America, 4
Choksi, Armeane, 252
Christian Democrats, in Chile, 102
Cities and towns
  population growth and, 5–6
  size of, 7
Civil society, institutional change and, 94–96
Class structure, 66
Clinton, Bill
  economic strategy of, 113n
  Washington Consensus and, 106, 107–109
Closed countries, 115. *See also* Protectionism
Clothing, Uruguay Round and, 279
Coca paste, Bolivia and, 151
Coeymans, J. E., 213
Coffee industry, 9
Cohen, Isaac, 104n
  "New Latin American and Caribbean Nationalism and Economic Reform, The," 97–105
Cold war, 99

Collier, David, 101n
Collor, Fernando, 82, 170–171, 174
Collor Plan, 172, 174
Colombia, 110. *See also* Andean Group
constitutional and political reform in, 220
economic indicators in, 225
economic reform in, 217–241
foreign exchange control policy in, 234–235
foreign exchange regime in, 240
imports in, 229
inflation, GNP, investment, and, 227–228
labor reform in, 235–236, 240
labor strike in, 219–220
politics of exchange control liberalization in, 234–235
politics of trade liberalization in, 220–232
private sector in, 220
products on free import list and average tariffs, 222
tax reform in, 236–238, 241
technocrats in, 232–234
trade liberation in, 217–219, 240
Venezuela border and, 3n
Colombia-Central America Free Trade Agreement (1993), 264
Colonialism
economic development and, 14
as shared experience, 3
Colosio, Luis Donaldo, 121
COMIBOL (Bolivia), 80, 150, 151, 153, 157
Commodity exports, 9–10
Commodity lottery, 15, 16
Common External Tariff (CET), 320
Andean Group and, 321–322, 327, 333–334
in Argentina, 132
Commons, John, 53
Communism, collapse of, 88
Comparative advantage, 45
Competition, trade and, 312
Competitive advantage, 303
from resource endowment, 303
Concensus, economic liberalization and, 93
Concertacion government, in Chile, 207
Condon, Timothy, 252
Consensus, 60–62, 63. *See also* Washington Consensus
economic, in Latin America, 71–73
on role of state, 74
Washington, 60–61
Constitutional reform, 93
in Brazil, 171
in Colombia, 220
Consumer price index, in Brazil, 180–181
Consumption, in Argentina, 136–138
Consumption reducing measures, neostructuralists on, 51
Contraband, in Colombia, 223–224
Convertibility plan (Argentina), 125, 128–134, 143–144
during Mexican currency crisis (Tequila effect), 139–141
outcomes of, 134–139
Copyrights, 323. *See also* Intellectual property rights
Corbo, Vittorio, 252
Corden, Warner Max, 277
Corporate taxation, in Chile, 209
Cortázar, R., 195n
Costa Rica, factor productivity growth in, 252
Costa Rica-Mexico Free Trade Agreement (1994), 162
Covert operations, by U.S. against Arbenz regime, 100
Cox-Edwards, A., 194n
Crawling peg regimes, 250
Credit, deficit and, 81
Credit countries, 60–61
Creditor banks, 60
Cruzado Plan (Brazil), 52, 80, 172, 183
Cuba, 4
Culture, Latin American, 4–5
Currency crisis
implications of, 113
in Mexico, 139–141
Customs union
Andean Group and, 318, 327–328
free trade area and, 313, 327
MERCOSUR and, 213n, 300

D

Dahrendorf, Ralf, 102n
Darwinian capitalism, 93
Debt, 76
of Bolivia, 155
Brady plan and, 82
foreign, 10
reduction of, 118
reduction programs, 68
as stimulus for transformation, 67–69
Debt crisis, 48, 60, 87–88
structural reform and, 62–63
in Third World (1980s), 117–118
Debt service, 79
Decision 24, 219, 323
Decision 291, 323
Decision 332, 330
Decision 344, 323
Decision 351, 323
Defensive nationalism, 97, 98–99
demise of, 101–102
limits of, 100–101
primacy of economics and, 103–105
Deficit
in Brazil, 186, 191
credit and, 81
domestic finance of, 79
fiscal adjustment programs and, 68
redesigning government and, 82
stagflation and, 78–82
De Franco, M., 159n
De Melo, Jaime, 252
Democracy
in Bolivia, 146
in Chile, 201–209
economic liberalization and, 90–91

effects of, 95
movement toward, 87
return to Latin America, 68
Democratic Labor Party (Brazil), 102
Demographic indicators, 8
Demonstration effects, 88
Dependency theory, 14, 42n
Depreciation, of exchange rate, 250
Depression. *See also* Great Depression
in Chile, 196–199
of 1980s, 76–77, 102
Deregulation, 63, 82, 90
in Argentina, 132–133
of markets, 70
De Soto, Hernando, 14n, 78, 106n
Developed countries
vs. developing regions, 4, 5
economic growth of, 63–64
Developing countries
capital flows to, 119–121
customs unions between, 305
deflated expectations in, 121–122
vs. developed regions, 4, 5
import protection in, 246
speculation in, 116–117
Development. *See also* Economic development
comparative indicators for Latin America, 5
Development crisis, 76
Development economics, 46, 75–78
Development theory, 61
Diakosavvas, Dimistris, 45n
Díaz-Alejandro, Carlos, 43
Direct foreign investment, from within Latin America, 268
Discrimination, in trade, 303
Disequilibrium, 75
Disindexation
for fighting inflation without recession, 189–190
stabilization and, 187–188
Diversification, of exports, 258
Diversity, commodities and, 15
Dixit, Avinash, 249n
Dobb, Maurice, 43
Dollarization, Plano Real and, 173–174
Domestic market, size of, 16
Domestic savings. *See* Savings (domestic)
Dominican Republic, 4
Dornbusch, Rudiger, 83n, 117n, 203, 204n
Dosi, Giovanni, 53n
Dosman, Edgard, 99n
Drugs
exports of, 10
trade in Colombia, 223–224, 232
Dumping, protection from, 247n
Dynamic effects, of trade, 310–314
Dynamic macroeconomic analysis, 46

E

East Asia, capital flows and, 119
East-West contradiction, 99
EC. *See* European Community (EC)
Echavarria, José Medina, 64
Echeverría, R., 159n
ECLA (Economic Commission for Latin America), 43, 44, 45, 74, 99
ECLAC (Economic Commission for Latin America and the Caribbean), 43n, 105
on open regionalism, 318
Economic development, 4–18, 69
consensus and, 71–73
government and, 82–84
Economic development theories, 12–15. *See also* Commodity lottery; Economic-policy environment; Export-led growth; Import-substitution-industrialization (ISI)
dependency theory, 14, 42n
land-tenure system and, 13–14
Marxist, 42n
neoliberalism, 14–15, 45–49
neoliberal vs. neostructural views and, 52–53
neostructuralism, 49–52
new classical economics and, 45
racial, 12–13
structuralism, 42–45
"Economic Development Theory and Policy in Latin America: The Second World War to the Present" (James), 42–53
Economic growth, 70, 76
in Argentina, 142
in Bolivia, 154–157, 159–167
capital flows and, 119–120
in Chile, 196, 214–215
in Colombia, 223, 233
and inflation (Argentina), 126
limitations of Bolivian, 158–159
underdeveloped vs. advanced countries, 63–64
Economic indicators, 5
for members of MERCOSUR and Andean Pact, 269
Economic integration, 72
structuralists and, 64–65
Economic liberalization. *See also* Open economy
in Brazil, 170–172
in Chile, 194
contradictory logics of, 90–91
external environment of, 87–88
institutional change and, 92–93
new consensus and, 93
structural inhibitors to, 91–92
Economic performance, deterioration in, 79–80
Economic policies. *See also* New Economic Policy (NEP)
in Andean Group, 323–324
in Chile, 199–201
Washington Consensus and, 106–107, 112–114
Economic-policy environment, 15, 17
Economic reform. *See also* Economic liberalization; Reforms
in Chile, 209–213
in Colombia, 217–241
"Economic Reform in Colombia" (Urrutia), 217–241
Economics
development, 75–78

Economics *(cont'd)*
economic development as subdiscipline of, 46
primacy of, 103–105
Economic Solidarity Pact. *See* Pact for Stability and Growth
Economies of scale, 77, 303, 311
Economists, of post-World War II era, 43
Economy
in Argentina, 125
in Chile, 193–216
openness in, 68–70, 87
outward focus of, 67
Ecuador. *See also* Andean Group
exports of, 256
Peru border and, 3n
Education
in Bolivia, 166–167
in Brazil, 110
completion of primary, 110
Edwards, Alejandra, 252
Edwards, Sebastian, 49n, 83n, 115, 194n, 217, 247, 252, 253, 270, 274
"Opening of Latin America," 245–296
Efficiency, 47
privatization and, 81
Ejido system, 254, 257
Electronic research, on economic reform in Latin America, 337–341
Elías, Victor, 252
Elites, economic liberalization and, 92
El Salvador-Guatemala Free Trade Agreement (1991), 261
Emergency Social Fund (ESF), 153–154
Employment, in Chile, 196
Enos, John, 43
Enterprise for the Americas, Bolivian debt and, 155
Environment
external, 87–88
industrialization and, 9
natural resources and, 10
Erzan, Refik, 246n, 310n
Escude, Carlos, 90n
Europe. *See also* European Community (EC); European Union (EU)
economic development of Latin America and, 14
European Community (EC), 72
European Union (EU)
MERCOSUR and, 308n
mobile tariffs of, 304n
Evans, Peter, 74
Exchange control policy, in Colombia, 234–235
Exchange rate, 75
bilateral real exchange rate relative to U.S. dollar, 251
in Bolivia, 149–150
in Brazil, 184
of Chile, 197, 198–199
in Colombia, 226
dollarization of, in Brazil, 173–174
in Mexico, 119, 120
trade liberalization and, 115–116
Exchange rate policy, 250, 251
Argentine convertibility plan and, 129
flexible, 304
Export-led growth, 15–17
capital and, 16
labor and, 16
state and, 16
Exports, 9–10, 78–79. *See also* Trade entries
Andean intra-subregional, 324–327
Bolivian, 150–151, 156, 157
of Brazil, 184
of Chile, 197
Colombia and, 223
commodity as proportion of total, 9
debt crisis and, 87–88
diversification of, 258
exchange rates and, 75
foreign debts and, 10
growth of, 77, 103
intraregional, 265, 266–267
of manufactured goods, 259
neostructuralists on, 51
nontraditional, in Bolivia, 155–156
trade reforms and, 255–258
value of goods and nonfactor services, 256
volume of goods, 257
External economies, 77
External environment, economic liberalization and, 87–88
Externalities, market failures and, 75

F

Factor productivity, 252–253
Fade-away policies, 50
Fajardo Villela de Andrade, Manoel Jorge, 169n
Faletto, E., 14n
FDI. *See* Foreign Direct Investment (FDI)
Feder, G., 14n
Feinberg, Richard, 106n
Felix, David, 87n
Ffrench-Davis, Ricardo, 49n
Finance, as goal, 81
Financial markets, 66
rewards for reform from, 118–119
speculative bubbles and, 116–117
Financial reform, in Colombia, 219
Financial sector
Bolivian recovery and, 156–157
reform in Argentina, 133–134
Fiscal adjustment programs, 68
Fiscal policy
Argentine convertibility plan and, 129–131
in Chile, 207–208
Fischer, Stanley, 108
Fishlow, Albert, 76, 77
"Latin American State, The," 74–86
Fleming, J. M., 303
Flexible customs unions, of Argentina with Brazil, Uruguay, and Paraguay, 300
Foreign capital, 47
from Great Britain, 10
from United States, 10

Foreign credit, of Chile, 196
Foreign debt, in Chile, 196
Foreign Direct Investment (FDI), 110
Foreign exchange. *See also* Exchange rate
  in Chile, 207
  in Colombia, 219
  neoliberalist disagreements over, 49
Foreign investment
  in Colombia, 219
  Decision 24 and, 323
  Decision 291 and, 323
  from within Latin America, 268
Foreign loans, 10
Foreign policy, U.S., Soviet Union, and, 100
Foreign relations, 72
Foreign resources, structuralists on, 64
Foreign trade, 66
  growth rate of value, in Argentina, 139
  increasing openness to, 68–70
Foreign Trade Institute. *See* INCOMEX (Foreign Trade Institute)
Forests, 10
Four Asian tigers, 119
Foxley, Alejandro, 44
France, economic development and, 14
Franco, Itamar, 172, 174–175, 178–179
Frank, A. G., 13n
Free market economy, in Chile, 202
Free trade
  Colombia and, 219
  in developing countries, 118
  protection and, 114
  virtues of, 111
Free trade agreements (FTAs), Chile and, 212–213
Free trade area, 104
  Andean, 320–321
  Andean Group and, 327–328
  customs union and, 313, 327
Free Trade Area of the Americas. *See* FTAA (Free Trade Area of the Americas)
Frei Ruiz-Tagle, Eduardo, 193
Friedman, Milton, 47n
"From Adjustment Policies to Structural Reforms" (Iqlesias), 59–73
"From the Military to Democracy: Two Decades of Chilean Economic Policies" (Larrain and Laban), 193–216
FSE. *See* Fundo Social de Emergência (FSE)
FTAA (Free Trade Area of the Americas), 330
FTAs. *See* Free trade agreements (FTAs)
Fujimori, Alberto, 320
Fundo Social de Emergência (FSE), in Brazil, 176
Fung, K. C., 304n
Furtado, Celso, 44n, 64

G

Garcia Meza, Luis, 146
Gardels, Nathan, 105n
Garten, Jeffrey, 113n
GATT (General Agreement on Tariffs and Trade), 98, 275, 298, 310
  Chile and, 213
GATT/WTO agreements, 301
Gaviria administration, in Colombia, 217, 219, 220, 226–227, 231, 234, 237
GDP. *See* Gross domestic product (GDP)
Gellner, Ernest, 94n
General Agreement on Tariffs and Trade. *See* GATT (General Agreement on Tariffs and Trade)
General System of Preferences, 308
Gerchunoff, Pablo, 52n
Gini coefficient, in Chile, 199
Gleijeses, Piero, 100n
Global complementario tax, 209n
Global economy
  involvement in, 69
  neoliberal thought and, 47
Global issues, Andean Group and, 329–333
Global trade liberalization, 276–277
Global warming, 10
GNP. *See* Gross national product (GNP)
Godoy, R., 159n
Gold standard, 80
González, Erman, 128
Goodman, D., 10n
Goods
  value of exports of, 256
  volume of exports of, 257
Government
  expenditures by, 50, 75
  export-led growth and, 16
  interventions by, 47, 77, 78
  Latin American, 74–86
  neostructuralists on, 52
  popular election and, 84
  and private sector, 50
  redefined role of, 77
  redesigning Latin American developmental state and, 82–84
  removal from economic affairs, 113
  reorganization of, 69–70
  role of, 65, 67, 74–86, 75
  society and, 89
  tax revenues of, 75
Grabel, Ilene, 53n
Grain production, in Mexico, 275
Great Britain
  economic development and, 14
  Falkland/Malvinas islands dispute and, 3n
  investment by, 10
Great Depression, of 1930s, 98
Greenhouse effect, 10
Griffin, K., 13n
Griffith, K., 43n
Griffith-Jones, Stefany, 245
Grofman, Bernard, 95n
Gross domestic product (GDP), 5, 100–101
  in Argentina, 125, 139, 142
  in Bolivia, 153, 155, 162–164
  in Brazil, 176, 183
  in Chile, 195–196, 197–198

Gross domestic product (GDP) *(cont'd)*
exports and, 16
protectionism and, 114
sectoral contribution to (1990), 11
Grossman, G. M., 312n
Gross national product (GNP), 5, 11–12
in Colombia, 227–228
per head, 13
Group of Three: Colombia-Mexico-Venezuela Free Trade Agreement (1993), 261, 327
Growth policies, 61–62
trade liberalization and, 251–255
Guano, 15n
Guatemala
Arbenz regime in, 100
Belize border and, 3n
Gulati, Sunil, 255
Gurevich, Beatriz, 90n
Gurrieri, A., 44n
Guyana, Venezuela border and, 3n

H

Habeler, Gottfried, 47
Hagbrink, Isabel, 317n
Hagen, E. E., 303
Haggard, Stephan, 90n, 117n
Haiti, 4
income in, 13
Hall, A., 10n
Hall, John A., 94–95n
Hall, Peter A., 98
Harberger, Arnold, 47, 249, 252n, 253n
Health services
in Bolivia, 166–167
in Chile, 200–201
in Costa Rica, 166–167
Heitger, Bernhard, 249
Helpman, E., 312n
Helwege, Ann, 249
Hemispheric liberalization, Andean Group and, 332–333
Higgins, Benjamin, 43
Hirschman, Albert, 43, 46, 50, 98, 99n, 102n, 303
Hodara, Joseph, 44n
Hopkins, A. G., 14n
"Hothouse" economic environment, 44
Household income. *See* Income
Housing, health, and education expenditures, 44
Hughes, H., 73n
Human Development Report, on education in Brazil, 110
Hurrell, A., 10n
Hyperinflation, 68. *See also* Inflation
in Argentina, 128, 135
in Bolivia, 145, 147, 150
in Brazil, 169–192

I

Ibarra, David, 104n
ICOR. *See* Incremental capital output ratio (ICOR)
ICP-FIPE, in Brazil, 180–181
IFI (state industrial corporation), in Colombia, 219
Iglesias, Enrique, 99n
Illegal drugs. *See* Drugs
ILO. *See* International Labour Organization (ILO)
IMACEC. *See* Indicator of economic activity (IMACEC)
IMF. *See* International Monetary Fund (IMF)
Imperfect information, 75
Imperial Preferences and Reciprocal Trade Agreements, 98
Import controls, in Colombia, 221–223
Import protection, with active (selective) export promotion, 245n
Imports, 65, 75. *See also* Export-led growth; Exports; Trade entries
in Argentina, 138
barriers to, 10
in Brazil, 184
in Chile, 197
in Colombia, 229
curtailment of, 203
increase in Andean Group, 326
protectionism and, 245–246
resource reallocation and, 65
Import substitution, 98
obsolescence of model, 66
policies, 75–76
Import-substitution-industrialization (ISI), 17, 44–45
stagnation from, 89
Income. *See also* Income Distribution
allocation of regional, 75
in Chile, 205
classification by, 5
neostructuralists on, 50–51
Income distribution, 11–12, 66, 67
in Brazil, 110
in Chile, 199–201
Income tax, in Chile, 209
INCOMEX (Foreign Trade Institute), 221, 232
Incremental capital output ratio (ICOR), in Bolivia, 162–163
Independence, of Latin American countries, 4
Indexation, 172. *See also* Disindexation
in Brazil, 174
URV and, 178–179
Indicator of economic activity (IMACEC), in Chile, 205
Indicators. *See* Demographic indicators; Development; Economic indicators; Indicator of economic activity (IMACEC)
Industrialization, 9
in Brazil and Mexico, 75
and bureaucratic authoritarianism, 101n
ISI and, 44
poverty and, 75
society and, 89
Industrialized countries. *See also* Developed countries
consensus with, 73
Industrial policy, 88
Industry, trade creation and, 307n

Inertialism, 188
  in Brazil, 172–173
Infant mortality, in Bolivia, 159
Inflation, 45, 67, 79
  abatement of, 70
  in Argentina, 125
  in Bolivia, 80, 146–147, 148
  in Brazil, 110
  in Colombia, 226, 227–228
  critical day in Brazil and, 179–185
  and fiscal deficit (Argentina), 127
  Hirschman on, 50
  market economies and, 115
  neostructuralists on, 50
  reduction in Argentina, 134–136
  response to, 80
  stabilization and, 68
Informal sector, labor market and, 6
Information, imperfect, 75
Information sources
  online, CD-ROM, and print, 338–341
  World Wide Web and, 338
Infrastructure, investments in, 10
Institutional change
  economic liberalization and, 92–93
  political design of, 94–96
Institutions, colonial, 13, 14
Integrated world economy, 59
Integration. *See also* Regional integration
  Andean Group and, 317–334
  of Chilean trade, 212–213
Intellectual property rights
  Andean Group and, 323
  protection of, 277
  Uruguay Round and, 279
Inter-American Development Bank, 76, 78, 108–109, 325–326
Interest rate control, 114
Interest rates
  in Argentina, 242
  in Brazil, 182, 186
  in Chile, 198, 214
International Center for the Settlement of Investment Disputes (ICSID), 133
International demonstration effects, 88
International Labour Organization (ILO), 46n
International monetarism, 80–81
International Monetary Fund (IMF), 60, 110
  Colombia and, 222
  new classical economists and, 46, 48
International trade. *See* Trade
Internet, research via, 337–341
Intervention
  governmental, 47
  by State, 70
Intraregional exports, 265, 266–267
Intra-subregional trade, within Andean Group, 324–327
Investment
  Bolivian, 145, 158, 162–164
  Chilean, 208
  Colombian, 219, 227
  direct foreign, 268
  as speculative bubble, 116–117
Invisible hand, 77
Iqlesias, Enrique, "From Adjustment Policies to Structural Reforms," 59–73
ISI. *See* Import-substitution-industrialization (ISI)

J

James, Dilmus D., 45n
  "Economic Development Theory and Policy in Latin America: The Second World War to the Present," 42–53
Japanese people and language, in Brazil, 4
JUNAC (Junta del Acuerdo de Cartegena), 319n

K

Kahler, Miles, 87n
Kaufman, Robert R., 88n, 90n
Kay, Cristobal, 44n, 45n
Kemp, M., 310n
Keynes, John Maynard, 98, 99n
Keynesian economics, 98
Keynesian policies, 42–43, 45
Kiguel, Miguel A., 138n
  "Restoring Growth and Price Stability in Argentina: Do Policies Make Miracles?", 125–144
Killick, Tony, 46n
Kréyol language, 4
Krueger, Anne, 14n, 47, 77, 115, 252, 301n, 305
Krugman, Paul, 213, 303n
  "1995 and Beyond: The Era of Deflated Expectations . . .," 112–122
Kuznets, Simon, 202

L

Labán, Raul, 202n, 205n
  "From the Military to Democracy: Two Decades of Chilean Economic Policies," 193–216
Labor
  Brazilian wages policies and, 177–178
  capital and, 252n
  in Chile, 203–204, 210–211
  commodity specialization and, 15
  export-led growth and, 16
  organization of, 66
  reform in Colombia, 235–236, 240
Labor market, 6
  and structural reforms, 252
Labor strikes. *See* Strikes
Labor unions
  in Brazil, 178
  in Chile, 211
Lafeber, W., 4n
LAFTA (Latin American Free Trade Association), 74, 329n
  Andean Group and, 331n

Laissez-faire, 77
Lal, Deepak, 46, 47n, 48, 74
Land. *See also* Agriculture
  distribution of, 11
  reform, 44
Landholding system, 66
Land-tenure system, 13–14, 254, 257
Languages
  Japanese, 4
  kréyol as, 4
  Spanish and Portuguese as, 4
Larrain, Felipe, 69n, 147n, 154n, 194n, 200n, 205n, 211n, 213
  "Bolivia 1985–1992: Reforms, Results, and Challenges," 145–168
  "From the Military to Democracy: Two Decades of Chilean Economic Policies," 193–216
Latin America
  Andean Group and open regionalism in, 330–332
  countries in, 4
  culture of, 4–5
  as developing region, 4
  development indicators for, 5
  economic consensus in, 71–73
  economic growth of, 59–60
  in 1826, 6 (map)
  expenditures on agricultural research in, 166
  income classification of republics in, 5
  independence of countries in, 4
  language and peoples of, 4
  living standards in, 4–5
  needs of individual countries in, 72
  in 1930s, 98
  in 1990, 7 (map)
  opening of, 245–296
  Puerto Rico and, 4
  regional trading blocs in, 258–279
  stability of boundaries within, 3
  transformation of, 67–70
  use of term, 3
"Latin American Economic Development: An Overview" (Bulmer-Thomas), 3–18
Latin American Free Trade Association. *See* LAFTA (Latin American Free Trade Association)
Latin American Integration Association. *See* ALADI (Latin American Integration Association)
"Latin American Reform: A View from Washington" (Williamson), 106–111
"Latin American State, The" (Fishlow), 74–86
Latin languages, 3
Lavagna, Roberto, "Opening a Medium-Size Economy: A Case of Regional Agreements-Argentina and MERCOSUR," 297–316
LDCs. *See* Less-developed countries (LDCs)
Lefort, Fernando, 255
Legal reform, 93
Leijonhufvud, Axel, 173
Lerner, 302n
Less-developed countries (LDCs), urban and rural populations in, 9–10
Lewis, Arthur, 43
Lewis, W. Arthur, 43, 303
Liberalization, 87. *See also* Economic liberalization; Trade liberalization
LIBOR. *See* London Inter-bank Offered Rate (LIBOR)
Life cycle theory, regional agreements and, 313
Life expectancy, in Bolivia, 159
Lijphart, Arend, 90n, 95n
Linz, Juan J., 95n, 96n
Lipset, Seymour M., 102
Little, Ian, 14n, 47, 76n
Liviatan, 138n
Loans. *See* Banks and banking; International Monetary Fund (IMF); World Bank
London Inter-bank Offered Rate (LIBOR), Chile and, 196
Lopes, Francisco, 173
Lopez, Alfonso, 221
Lora, Eduardo, 220, 231
Losada, Fernando, 259
Low-income republics, 5
Lucas, Robert, 46n
Lula da Silva, 176

M

Maastricht Treaty, 310
Macroeconomic equilibrium, economic development and, 83
Macroeconomic point of view, 64
Macroeconomic policy
  in Chile, 197
  in Chile (1990–1994), 201–209
Mainwaring, Scott, 95n
Majoritarian systems, proportional representation and, 95–96
Malaysia, 4n
Manley, Michael, 102
Manufactured goods, exports of, 9, 43, 259
Manufacturing, 10
  in Mexico, 254
Maquiladora sector, 257
Maravall, Jose M., 90n
Marfán, Manuel, 205n, 255
Market(s). *See also* Financial markets
  deregulation of, 70
  failures of, 75
  imperfections of, 75
  international opportunities and, 78
  resource allocation and, 509
  rules of, 66
  in underdeveloped countries, 64
Market access, Uruguay Round and, 278
Market concentration, 66
Market-driven economic models, neoliberalism and, 45–46
Market economies. *See* Trade liberalizations
Market-friendly policies, 108
Marshall, J., 195n
Martin, Ricardo D., 252n, 253
Martínez de Hoz reforms, 252
Marxist development theory, 42n

McKinnon, R., 304n
Meade, James E., 310n
Means of production, control of, 66
Meier, Gerald M., 43, 46, 49n
Meller, P., 194n, 200n
Mellor, Patricio, 49n
Menem administration (Argentina), 82, 128
Mercedes de Martinez, Maria, 224n, 231
MERCOSUR (Mercado Común del Sur), 84, 213n, 259, 263, 268–271
  Andean Group and, 328n, 331, 332n
  Argentina and, 132, 297, 302–315
  economic indicators for, 269
  effects of, 307
  NAFTA and, 306–314, 328n
  trade among members of, 270
Metzler, L., 302
Mexico, 4, 110. *See also* NAFTA (North American Free Trade Agreement); Partido Revolucionario Institucional (PRI)
  capital imports and, 85
  currency crisis in, 113, 125, 139–141, 185
  debt in, 79
  export rate of, 257
  factor productivity growth in, 253–254
  government in, 82
  grain production in, 275
  growth of, 78
  import substitution policies in, 75
  inflation in, 119
  nontariff barriers in, 247
  peso crisis in, 52
  response to inflation in, 80
  slowdown in, 120–121
  trade liberalization by, 118, 246
Mexico-Central America Free Trade Agreement (1992), 262
Mexico City, 7
Meyer, Arno, 169n
Michaely, Michael, 252
Michalopoulos, Constantine, 273
Microeconomic level, structuralism and, 65
Middle-income republics, 5
Migration
  population growth and, 6
  rural-urban, 9
Military
  in Brazil and Argentina, 66
  and economy in Chile, 193–201
  legacy in Chile, 201
Mining, 9
Minsky, Hyman, 53
MNCs. *See* Multinational companies (MNCs)
Monetarism, 45n, 47n, 80–81
Monetary adjustment. *See also* Adjustment
  debt crisis and, 60
Monetary policy
  Argentine convertibility plan and, 129
  in Brazil, 172, 186
  in Chile, 205–207
Monetary reform, in Brazil, 172, 173, 180
Monetization, in Argentina, 135–136
Money, in Brazil, 173
Money multiplier, in Brazil, 182–183
Monopoly power, protection and, 114
Montevideo Treaty (1960), 329n
Montoya, German, 230–231
Movement Toward Socialism, 102
Multilateral system, 98
  Andean Group and, 330–331
  regional integration and, 277
Multinational companies (MNCs), industrial growth and, 10
Mundel, R., 304
Myint, Hla, 43
Myrdal, Gunnar, 43
Myrdall, R., 303

N

NAFTA (North American Free Trade Agreement), 84, 104, 213, 259, 261, 274–275
  Andean Group and, 331n
  Argentina and, 297, 302–315
  effects of, 308
  MERCOSUR and, 306–314
Narcotics. *See* Drugs
Nationalism
  defensive, 97, 98–99, 100–102, 103–105
  new form of, 97–105
  roots of new, 102–103
Natural gas, trade crisis and, 150
"Natural" rate of unemployment, 45
Natural resources, 9–11
Nelson, Joan, 88n, 231
Neoclassical economists, 45
  thinking on underdeveloped economies, 64
  view of, 66
Neoconservative, 45n
Neoliberalism, 14–15, 45–49
  disagreements within, 48
  vs. neostructuralism, 52–53
  Washington Consensus and, 110–111
Neomonetarism, 45n
Neo-Schumpeterian economists, 53
Neostructuralism, 49–52, 66
  vs. neoliberalism, 52–53
NEP. *See* New Economic Policy (NEP)
New classical economics, 45–46. *See also* Neoliberalism
New Economic Policy (NEP), in Bolivia, 147, 149–154
Newland, Robert A., 95n
"New Latin American and Caribbean Nationalism and Economic Reform, The" (Cohen), 97–105
New nationalism, roots of, 103
NGOs. *See* Nongovernmental organizations (NGOs)
"1995 and Beyond: The Era of Deflated Expectations . . ." (Krugman), 112–122
Nino, Carlos S., 95n

Nogués, Julio J., 255, 268n
"Restoring Growth and Price Stability in Argentina: Do Policies Make Miracles?", 125–144
Nondiscriminatory systems, preferential systems and, 302–304
Nonfactor services, value of exports of, 256
Nongovernmental organizations (NGOs), in Bolivia, 154
Nontariff barriers (NTBs), 247–249
in Argentina, 132
in Colombia, 217
North American Free Trade Agreement. *See* NAFTA (North American Free Trade Agreement)
North-South confrontation, 98
NTBs. *See* Nontariff barriers (NTBs)
Nueva Ocotepeque Agreement (1992), 263
Nurkse, P. N., 303
Nurkse, Ragnar, 43

O

Ocampo, José Antonio, 233, 253
OECD. *See* Organization for Economic Cooperation and Development (OECD)
Oil crises, 10, 60
Oil shock, 76
Olivera, Julio, 79n
Online information sources, 338–339
Open economy, 302. *See also* Economic liberalization
foreign trade and, 68–70
growth and, 115
in Latin America, 245–296
movement toward, 87
"Opening a Medium-Size Economy: A Case of Regional Agreements-Argentina and MERCOSUR" (Lavagna), 297–316
"Opening of Latin America" (Edwards), 245–296
Open-market economy, 95
Open regionalism, 304, 318
Andean Group and, 330–332
"Open skies" policy, of Andean Group, 323
Organization for Economic Cooperation and Development (OECD), 5n, 76, 275, 276
Orthodox development theories, 14–15
ISI implementation and, 45
Output. *See also* Agriculture; Manufactured goods; Manufacturing
in Argentina, 136
in Chile, 207
Ownership, changes in, 81

P

Pact for Stability and Growth, 52n
Panama, 4
Papageorgiou, Demetris, 252
Parallel money, in Brazil, 173
Pareto efficiency argument, 75, 77, 304
Partido Revolucionario Institucional (PRI), 100, 102
Patents, 323. *See also* Intellectual property rights
Path dependence, 77
Paus, 52
Pavitt, K., 306n
Paz Estenssoro, Victor, 146, 147, 149, 154
Pazos, Filepe, 49n
Paz Zamora, Jaime, 145n, 154, 155, 157, 158
Pereira, Luis C., 90n
Perez-Diaz, Victor M., 95n
"Periphery" (Latin America), 14, 44
Peronists, 102
in Argentina, 100
Peru, 82. *See also* Andean Group
Alianza Popular Revolucionaria Americana (APRA) in, 100
Andean free trade area and, 320, 321
debt servicing by, 154
Ecuador border and, 3n
Peso crisis (Mexico), 52
Pindyck, R., 203
Pinochet, 82
Planned economies, 45
Plano Cruzado (Brazil). *See* Cruzado Plan
Plano Real, 109, 111, 169–192
assessment of program, 185–190
doctrinal issues related to, 172–174
"'Plano Real': The End of Hyperinflation in Brazil" (Ramalho), 169–192
Polarization, social, 90–91
Policy reform, 109–110
Washington Consensus and, 63n
Political conditions, in Bolivia, 161–162
Political consensus, 62
"Political Dynamics of Economic Reform in Latin America" (Waisman), 87–96
Political factors
economic liberalization and, 88
and exchange control liberalization in Colombia, 234–235
in institutional change, 94–96
and trade liberalization in Colombia, 220–232
Political liberalization. *See* Democracy; Economic liberalization
Political parties
in Brazil, 170
in Mexico, 100, 102
Political reform, in Colombia, 220
Political system, 66
Pollock, David, 99n
Pollution, 10
Popular election, 84
Population, racial development theories and, 13
Population growth
slowdown of, 8
urbanization and, 5–7
Populism, 83
Portuguese empire, Latin America and, 3
Portuguese language, 4
Post-Keynesians, 53
Poverty
in Bolivia, 158, 159

in Chile, 193, 199–201, 205
income distribution and, 67
industrialization and, 75
in Latin America, 4
neostructuralists on, 50–51
Prebisch, Raúl, 43, 44, 45, 64, 74, 75, 99
Preferential systems, nondiscriminatory systems and, 302–304
PRI. *See* Partido Revolucionario Institucional (PRI)
Price controls, 50
Price freezes, in Brazil, 170, 171, 172–173
Price level, 50
Price stabilization, Plano Real in Brazil and, 188–189
Price system, 64
Primacy (principal city growth), 7
Primary education. *See* Education
Private sector, state and, 50
Privatization, 90
in Argentina, 133
in Brazil, 172
in Chile, 194
efficiency and, 81
Productive structure, 66
Productivity
in Bolivia, 159
Bolivian rural, 165–167
trade liberalization and growth of, 251–255
Proportional representation, majoritarian systems and, 95–96
Prosperity, economic impact of, 59
Protected economic environment, 44
Protectionism, 98, 114–115, 270, 302. *See also* Barriers to trade; Nontariff barriers (NTBs); Trade liberalization
average tariffs and, 249–250
in Colombia, 232
dispersed, 249
opening after, 245
Przeworski, Adam, 90n
Public development programs, 44
"Public interest view," of government, 75
Public sector, Bolivian, 157
Puerto Rico, 4
Putnam, Robert D., 95n

Q

Quintanilla, Rosalinda, 268n

R

Racial theories, of economic development, 13
Rain forests, 10
Ramalho, Valdir, "'Plano Real': The End of Hyperinflation in Brazil" (Ramalho), 169–192
Ramirez, Miguel D., 50
Ramos, Joseph R., 48n, 51
R&D. *See* Research and development (R&D)
Rational expectations theory, 46
inflation and, 80
Reeve, Andrew, 95n
Reforms. *See also* Economic liberalization; Political liberalization
in Bolivia, 145–168
economic, 62, 97–105
economic liberalization and, 92–93
financial structural, 76
of Latin American policy, 109–110
payoff to, 114–116
quality of, 71
rewards for, from financial markets, 118–119
structural, 62–63
trade opening and, 245–296
U.S. view on, 106–111
Regional economies, differences among, 71–72
Regional growth, 76
Regional integration, 72
Andean Group and, 317–334
of developing countries, 44
Regionalism, growth of, 84
Regional trading blocs. *See also* Trade agreements
Andean Pact as, 271–272
Argentina and MERCOSUR relationship and, 297–316
CACM as, 273
CARICOM as, 274
CARIFTA as, 273–274
GATT, global trade liberalization, and, 276–277
integration agreements in Americas after 1990 and, 260–264
intraregional exports as percentage of total exports and, 265–267
in Latin America, 258–279
MERCOSUR as, 84, 132, 210n, 268–271
NAFTA as, 274–275
Uruguay Round and, 278–279
Representation, proportional, 95
Republics, of Latin America, 4
Requena, Juan Carlos, 145n
Research, electronic, 337–341
Research and development (R&D), agricultural, 165–166
Resource allocation, 47
market mechanism and, 50
Resources. *See also* Natural resources; Resource allocation
reallocation to import sector, 65
transfer of, 66–67
"Restoring Growth and Price Stability in Argentina: Do Policies Make Miracles?" (Kiguel and Nogués), 125–144
Revolutions
autarkic capitalism and, 90
weakening of, 88
Rienner, Lynne, 88n
Rio de Janeiro, 7n
Rivas, Gonzalo, 254, 255
Roberts, M., 312n
Robinson, Eugene, 104n
Robinson, S., 78
Rodríguez, Carlos, 252
Rodriguez, Octavio, 44n

Rodríguez-Mendoza, Miguel, "Andean Group's Integration Strategy, The," 317
Rodrik, Dani, 117, 118, 255n
Román, Enrique, 254, 255
Roosevelt, Theodore, 4
Ros, Jaime, 245n
Rosales, Osvaldo, 49n
Rosenstein-Rodan, H. H., 43, 303
Rostow, Walter, 43
Rubio, G., 275
Rueschmeyer, D., 74
Rural areas
  populations of, 8–9
  productivity in Bolivia, 165–166

S

Saborio, Sylvia, 273
Sachs, Jeffrey, 83n, 147n, 154n
  "Bolivia 1985–1992: Reforms, Results, and Challenges," 145–168
SAFCO. *See* State Administration and Financial Control (SAFCO, Bolivia)
Salazar-Xirinachs, Jose Manuel, 52
Salinas, 82
Sánchez, Manuel, 252
Sánchez de Losada, Gonzalo, 145n, 146, 147, 165, 317
São Paolo, 7
Sarney, José, 170
Savage capitalism, 93
Savastano, Miguel, 270, 274
Savings (domestic), 85
  in Bolivia, 145, 158, 162, 164–165
  in Brazil, 178
  in Chile, 208
Scale economies, 47
Scale goods, 308
Scandizzo, Pasqual L., 45n
Schott, Jeffrey, 259
Schultz, Theodore W., 47
Scitovsky, T., 14n, 76n, 303n, 312n
Scope economies, 47
Scott, M., 14n, 76
Security. *See* Defensive nationalism
Selowski, M., 69n, 72
Services, Uruguay Round and, 279
Sharpe, M. E., 87n
Shleifer, Andre, 77
Shugart, Matthew S., 95n
Siles Suazo, Hernan, 146–147
Silva, Patricio, 47n
Simonsen, Mario, 173
Sims-Granger causality criterion, 77
Singer, H. H., 43, 99n, 303
Skocpol, T., 74
Slavery, as labor, 16
Smith, William C., 48
Smoot-Hawley Tariff Act, 276
Social conditions, in Bolivia, 160
Social democratic parties, 102
Socialism, "third way" and, 99–100
Social policies, in Andean Group, 323
Social problems, 70, 72. *See also* specific problems
Social reforms, in Chile, 209–213
Social Security, in Chile, 198
Social services, in Bolivia, 165–167
Society. *See also* Social conditions; Social problems
  in Bolivia, 159
  in Chile, 202–205
  impact of economic transformation on, 94–96
  international demonstration effects and, 88
Solimano, Andrés, 255
South America, republics of, 4
Southern Cone countries, 48
  autarkic capitalism in, 89
  trade liberalization efforts by, 245
  trade problems in, 298–302
South Korea, 4n
Soviet Union, United States and, 100
Spanish empire, Latin America and, 3
Spanish language, 4
Specialization
  commodity, 15–16
  free trade, under access restrictions, 304
Specialized goods, 308
Speculative bubbles, 116–117
Stability, 50
  in Bolivia, 154–155
Stabilization, 66, 67, 68
  in Argentina, 127, 134
  in Bolivia, 152–154
  in Brazil, 191
  in Chile, 194
  disindexation and, 187–188
  and economic growth, 48
  neostructuralists on, 51
  Plano Real in Brazil as, 169
  recession and, 81
  successful, 80
Stagflation, 45
  deficit and, 78–82
Stallings, Barbara, 88n
Standards of living, 4
State. *See* Government
State Administration and Financial Control (SAFCO, Bolivia), 157
Static analysis, 305, 306–310
Stern, Nicholas, 47n
Stewart, Frances, 48, 51
Stiglitz, Joseph, 77
Streeten, P., 73n
Strikes, in Colombia, 219–220
Structuralism, 42–45, 64–67. *See also* Neostructuralism
  attacks on, 65–66
  and limitations of Latin American development, 66
Structural reforms, 62–63. *See also* Adjustment; specific countries
  Argentine convertibility plan and, 131–134
  labor markets and, 252
Sturzenegger, F., 253
Sugar industry, 9
Summer Plan, in Brazil, 170

Summit of the Americas, 330
Sunkel, Osvaldo, 49, 49n, 51, 53, 66n, 245
Supply-side deficiencies, 45
Supply-side shocks, 45
Supreme Decree 21060. *See* New Economic Policy (NEP)
Surplus, capital, 16
Syrquin, M., 78

T

Tablita, in Argentina, 129, 134–135
Taiwan, 4n
Tanzi, Vito, 79n
Tanzi-Olivera effect, 79
Tariff dispersion, 249
Tariffs, 10. *See also* Common External Tariff (CET); Regional trading blocs; Trade policy
  in Argentina, 132
  average, 249–250
  in Brazil, 184
  in Colombia, 217, 220, 226
  regional agreements and, 304
Taxation
  in Chile, 203–204, 209–210
  government expenditures and tax, 75
  inflation and, 79
  reform in Colombia, 236–238, 241
Tax credits, export promotion and, 255
Tax revenues, 75
Taylor, Lance, 245
Technical learning linkages, 17
Technocrats, in Colombia, 232–234
Technology, advanced, 66
Tequila effect, 125. *See also* Mexico, currency crisis in
Textiles, Uruguay Round and, 279
"Third way" between capitalism and socialism, 97, 99–100
  demise of, 101–102
Third World
  investing in, 116–117
  organizations sensitive to, 46n
Thompson, A., 14n
Thorp, Rosemary, 43
Thorstensen, Vera, 104n
Tin, trade collapse and, 150
Tinbergen, Jan, 43
Todaro, Michael P., 43, 46n
Torche, A., 201
Toronto terms, Bolivia's foreign debt and, 155
Torres, Juan Carlos, 52n
Torres Caicedo, José María, 3
Toye, John, 46n
Trade. *See also* Drugs; Economic liberalization; Free trade; Southern Cone countries
  among Andean Pact countries, 272
  balanced growth of, 255n
  barriers to (*See* Barriers to trade)
  Bolivian, 155–156
  Brazilian deficit in, 184
  breakdown of multilateral system, 98
  Chilean, 196
  collapse of (1985), 150–151
  Colombian, 222
  dynamic effects of, 310–314
  intra-subregional, 324–327
  liberalization of, 67, 82, 88, 92, 103
  among members of MERCOSUR, 270
  "new theory" of, 303
  opening of (*See* Open economy; Trade liberalization)
  in postwar years, 298
  protection and, 114
  of raw commodity exporting countries, 43, 45
  static effects of, 306–310
Trade agreements. *See also* Regional trading blocs; specific agreements
  Argentina and MERCOSUR relationship, 297–316
  open regionalism and, 304
  regional integration in Americas after 1990, 260–264
  timing and, 304–306
Trade liberalization, 110, 114–115, 245–296
  in Andean countries, 318, 320, 330
  Andean Group and hemispheric, 332–333
  Andean intra-subregional trade and, 326
  in Argentina, 132
  average tariffs and, 249–250
  in Brazil, 189
  in Chile, 211–213
  in Colombia, 217, 220–232, 240
  exchange rate policy and, 250, 251
  global, 276–277
  in Mexico, 118
  nontariff barriers and, 247–249
  opening in selected countries, 248
  productivity growth and, 251–255
  recent reforms in Latin America and Caribbean, 246–251
  tariff dispersion and, 249
  trade reforms, exports, and, 255–258
Trademarks, 323. *See also* Intellectual property rights
Trade pacts, 311
Trade policy
  in Argentina, 132
  of Colombia, 231–232
Trade reforms, and exports, 255–258
Trading blocs, regional Latin American, 258–279
Treaty of Miami (1994), 84
Tropical rain forests. *See* Rain forests
Trujillo, 319n
Turbay, Julio Cesar, 221
Tybout, J., 312n

U

UNCTAD. *See* United Nations Conference on Trade and Development (UNCTAD)
Underdeveloped countries, economic growth of, 63–64
Unemployment
  in Argentina, 142

Unemployment *(cont'd)*
  in Chile, 199, 200, 203, 207
  "natural" rate of, 45
UNIDO. *See* United Nations Industrial Development Organization (UNIDO)
Unions. *See* Labor unions
United Kingdom. *See* Great Britain
United Nations
  ECLAC and, 44n
  Economic Commission for Latin America (ECLA) and, 43, 44, 99
United Nations Conference on Trade and Development (UNCTAD), 44, 46n, 99
United Nations Industrial Development Organization (UNIDO), 46n
United States. *See also* NAFTA (North American Free Trade Agreement)
  Colombian trade and, 223
  covert operations of, 100
  as creditor country, 60–61
  economic development and, 14
  relationship with, 72
  Soviet Union and, 100
  view of Latin American reform, 106–111
  Washington Consensus and, 106–109
Urbanization, 5–7
  principal city growth (primacy) and, 7
Urquidi, Victor, 64
Urrutia, Miguel, 224
  "Economic Reform in Colombia," 217–241
Uruguay
  rural population of, 9
  trade liberalization by, 246
Uruguay Round, 276, 277, 310
  Argentina and, 132
  Chile and, 213
  results for Latin American and Caribbean, 278–279
URV (unidade real de valor) (Brazil), 175, 177
  disindexation and, 187
  indexation and, 178–179
  as unit of account, 179–180

V

Valdes, Juan Gabriel, 47n
Valdéz, Alberto, 249
Valenzuela, Arthuro, 95n
Value added tax (VAT)
  in Chile, 209, 210
  in Colombia, 238
Van Grasstek, Craig, 332n
Vargas Llosa, 82
VAT. *See* Value added tax (VAT)
Veblen, Thorstein, 53
Végh, Carlos, 138n
Velez, F., 275
Venezuela, 102, 110. *See also* Andean Group
  border disputes of, 3n
Venezuela-Central America Free Trade Agreement (1992), 262
Viner, J., 306n

W

Wade, Robert, 69n, 255n
Wage labor, 16
Wage policies, 44
  of Plano Real, 177, 187–188
Wages, in Chile, 196, 199, 204, 212
Waisman, Carlos H., 89n, 90n, 95n
  "Political Dynamics of Economic Reform in Latin America," 87–96
Wan, H., 310n
Ware, Alan, 95n
Washington Consensus, 60–61, 63
  deflated expectations and, 112
  economic performance of countries adopting, 120–121
  limitations of, 113–114
  neoliberalism and, 110–111
  present endorsement of, 107–109
  Williamson on, 106–109
Webb, Steven B., 117n
Weiss, John, 254
Wesson, Robert G, 88n
Westphal, 78
Williamson, John, 61n, 62, 63n, 106n, 113–114
  "Latin American Reform: A View from Washington," 106–111
Williamson, Oliver, 53
Wionczek, Miguel S., 88n
Wolf, H. C., 202n
Workers. *See also* Labor; Labor unions
  in Chile, 211
  in Colombia, 235–236
World Bank, 60, 109
  Colombia and, 222, 223
  Fischer and, 108
  new classical economists and, 46, 48
  on "public interest" view, 75
World economy, Latin America in, 15
World Trade Organization. *See* WTO (World Trade Organization)
World Wide Web
  electronic research and, 337–341
  research sources on, 338
WTO (World Trade Organization), 276
  GATT and, 301

Y

Yacimientos Petrolíferos Fiscales de Bolivia (YPFB), 157
Yeats, A., 310n
Yen Zone, 258–259

Z

Zapatista Mayan Indians, uprising by, 275
Zimbalist, A., 13n
Zuleta, Luis Alberto, 49n